Complete Edition

Computers
in your Future
2004

Bryan Pfaffenberger

Bill Daley

Contributions by Ken Royal

PEARSON
Prentice
Hall

D0074171

Upper Saddle River, New Jersey

Library of Congress Cataloging-in-Publication Data

Pfaffenberger, Bryan, 1949-
  Computers in your future 2004. Complete edition / Bryan Pfaffenberger, William Daley.
    p. cm.
  ISBN 0-13-140450-4
  1. Computers. I. Daley, William, 1953- II. Title.

QA76.5P39826 2003
004--dc21   2002192970

Publisher and Vice President: Natalie E. Anderson
Executive Acquisitions Editor: Jodi McPherson
Senior Project Manager, Editorial: Mike Ruel
Assistant Editor: Melissa Edwards
Editorial Assistants: Jodi Bolognese & Jasmine Slowik
Development Editor: Shannon Leuma
Special Features Author: Ken Royal
Senior Media Project Manager: Cathi Profitko
Senior Marketing Manager: Shannon Turkovich
Manager, Production: Gail Steier de Acevedo
Senior Project Manager, Production: April Montana
Associate Director, Manufacturing: Vincent Scelta
Manufacturing Buyer: Natacha St. Hill Moore
Manager Print Production: Christy Mahon
Design Manager: Maria Lange
Art Director: Pat Smythe
Interior Design: Quorum Creative Services
Cover Design: Quorum Creative Services
Composition: Quorum Creative Services
Full Service Management: Pre-Press Company Inc.
Photo Research: Shirley Webster
Printer/Binder: R.R. Donnelly and Sons Company/Willard
Cover Printer: Phoenix Color

Credits and acknowledgments borrowed from other sources and reproduced, with permission, in this textbook appear on page C.1.

Microsoft Excel, Solver, and Windows are registered trademarks of Microsoft Corporation in the U.S.A. and other countries. Screen shots and icons reprinted with permission from the Microsoft Corporation. This book is not sponsored or endorsed by or affiliated with Microsoft Corporation.

Selected screen shots supplied courtesy of Prentice-Hall, Inc.

10 9 8 7 6 5 4 3 2
ISBN 0-13-140450-4

ACKNOWLEDGMENTS

We are grateful for the assistance of the following reviewers of the fifth edition:

Judith F. Bennett, Sam Houston State University

Judy Clark, Northwest Missouri State University

Mark DuBois, Illinois Central College

Gina M. Dunatov, DeVry College

Alan D. Evans, Montgomery County Community College

Michelle M. Hansen, Davenport University

Shelly Hawkins, Western Washington University

Cheryl Jordan, San Juan College

Bhushan Kapoor, California State University at Fullerton

Emilio A. Laca, University of California at Davis

We are grateful for the assistance of the following reviewers of the fourth edition:

Beverly Amer, Northern Arizona University

Dennis Anderson, Pace University

Bob Bretz, Western Kentucky University

Joseph DeLibero, Arizona State University

Mark DuBois, Illinois Central College

Said Fares, Valdosta State University

Nancy Grant, Community College of Allegheny County

Carolyn Hardy, Northwest Missouri State University

Michelle Hulett, Southwest Missouri State University

Emilio Laca, University of California at Davis

Kuber Maharjan, Purdue University

Karen Norwood, McLennan Community College

Anthony J. Nowakowski, Buffalo State College

Chuck Riden, Arizona State University

John Ross, Fox Valley Technical College

Ray Smith, Salt Lake City Community College

Steve Smith, El Paso Community College

Lynn Wermers, North Shore Community College

Linda Woolard, Southern Illinois University

I'd like to recognize Jodi McPherson, Executive Acquisitions Editor, for believing in me and for her unabashed support of my work. Special thanks go to Shannon Leuma, Development Editor, for her expert advice and her keen eye for detail. She pushed me very hard at times, and the book reflects her dedication to excellence. April Montana, Senior Project Manager, once again saw the book through the complex production process with the coolness and calmness that comes only from a consummate professional. I sincerely appreciate the artistic flair with which Debbie Iverson of Quorum Creative Services composed the text, photos, and artwork seen in this book. Jennifer Carley and the dedicated workers at Pre-Press provided the best copyediting and proofreading an author could hope for. Their attention to detail has helped ensure that you are reading the cleanest textbook on the market today. Shirley Webster, Photo Researcher, worked long and hard hours in researching the photos. She was a joy to work with and provided photos that accurately depict the topics in the text. I'd also like to acknowledge Caleigh McPherson for her timely delivery during the project. Her arrival was much anticipated, and it is with great pleasure that I welcome her to the team. Finally, I would like to express my deepest appreciation to everyone in my Prentice Hall family. Quality comes from caring, and Prentice Hall is a company full of people who care.

—Bill Daley

PREFACE

About This Edition

You've made suggestions, and we've listened.

- ✓ You want the new edition of *Computers in your Future* to be more current and streamlined than the fifth edition—but without forcing changes in the way you're teaching the course.

- ✓ You want choices in how much coverage is included in the book.

- ✓ You want a concepts book with great learning tools that hold your students' interest and reinforce critical material—but without causing them to lose focus.

- ✓ You want a text-specific, interactive Web site that enhances your students' learning ability—as long as they are lead intuitively to key information that is concise, intelligent, and clearly laid out.

- ✓ You want a Web site with additional resources and practice exercises that are valuable for your students.

Now available as an annual edition, *Computers in your Future 2004* brings an improved design, updated coverage, updated end-of-chapter materials, and a revised accompanying Web site. This text is ready for the challenge of teaching even your most diversified class—without sacrificing quality, integrity, or choice. *Computers in your Future 2004* comes in three versions—Brief, Introductory, or Complete—to meet the needs of your classroom.

The 2004 edition offers you the flexibility and currency that were hallmarks of the previous edition, plus a range of significant improvements:

- As was the case in the previous edition, *Computers in your Future 2004* is available in three options to better suit your teaching needs. Our **Brief** version contains Chapters 1–9, our **Introductory** version contains Chapters 1–12, and, for the full breadth of coverage, our **Complete** version offers Chapters 1–16.

- Electronic commerce Web case videos, E-COMMERCE IN ACTION, are available on the book's companion Web site. In our six videos, students follow PFSWeb, Inc., a company based in Plano, Texas, that helps e-commerce companies keep up with the online buying and selling marketplace. Each video is designed to introduce students to electronic commerce strategies and issues, including privacy, security, and ethics.

- New and improved SPOTLIGHT "minichapters" highlight innovative thinking in various subject areas. This edition's Spotlights include in-depth looks at file management, buying and upgrading a computer system, Microsoft Office XP, multimedia and virtual reality, Information Age ethics, and emerging technologies.

- New and improved IMPACTS boxes offer chapter-by-chapter insights into the societal implications of computing. Students are introduced to thought-provoking ideas to stimulate class discussion or team debates on all aspects of the impact technology is having on life today.

- New and improved CURRENTS boxes examine issues in computing as well as cutting-edge computer technology. Topics range from robots to national security issues to stopping spam. Like IMPACTS, CURRENTS boxes offer you and your students a chance to explore and discuss a topic relevant to technology today.

- All chapters have been significantly UPDATED, a necessity in the fast-paced world of computers. In addition, a number of chapters have been REORDERED to better suit your teaching needs.

- The 2004 edition continues to emphasize computer FLUENCY. It's one thing to be computer literate, but it's quite another to be computer fluent. Computer-literate people are skilled computer and Internet users; computer-fluent people are able to navigate the digital world easily. Their knowledge of the underlying concepts and principles of computers and the Internet gives them tremendous advantage.

For the Instructor

Instructor Resources

The new and improved Prentice Hall Instructor's Resource CD-ROM includes the tools you expect from a Prentice Hall Computer Concepts text, such as:

- The Instructor's Manual in Word and PDF formats
- Solutions to all questions and exercises from the book and Web site
- Multiple, customizable PowerPoint slide presentations for each chapter
- A Windows-based test manager and the associated test bank in Word format with over 1,500 questions
- Computer concepts animation videos
- PFSWeb, Inc. Videos and Case Studies
- An image library of all of the figures from the text

…and the brand new **Present IT software** with a user-friendly, browser-based interface, organized by chapter, with search and sort functions and prebuilt PowerPoint slides. The Present IT software also gives you the ability to build a presentation from scratch incorporating any of the Instructor's Resources, and includes browse and preview functions. This software allows you to present directly from the CD or collect and save your custom presentations to disk for later use in the classroom or to upload to your online course.

My Companion Website   www.prenhall.com/ciyf2004

This text is accompanied by My Companion Website at **www.prenhall.com/ciyf2004**. Features of this site include the ability to customize your home page with technology updates, Internet exercises, e-commerce case videos, an interactive study guide, downloadable supplements, and much more. My Companion Website also offers the option to answer end-of-chapter materials online.

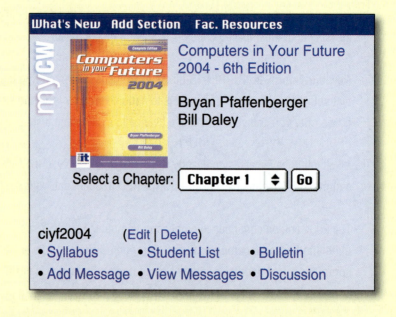

Tools for Online Learning

TRAIN & ASSESS IT   www.prenhall.com/phit

The Prentice Hall Information Technology (PHIT) team understands that every day you're asked to do something extraordinary—teach rapidly changing computer concepts topics to students of varying experience levels. That is why we offer Concepts Topics in our multiplatform training and assessment program: Train & Assess IT.

Train & Assess IT is a performance-based training and assessment software package housing Computer Concepts, Microsoft Office XP, and Office 2000 training and assessment material. Designed by Educators for Educators, Train & Assess IT is a proven leader in the training and assessment of students around the world. Class tested for more than two years, Train & Assess IT provides you with tools for accurate grading, premade tests and quizzes, the ability to customize a learning path for each student, and the opportunity to train and test your students anytime, anyplace. For a demo of this exciting, time-saving product, please visit **www.prenhall.com/phit** and select "IT Solutions."

Use Train & Assess IT for homework, to level the playing field of students' computer experience, for extra credit, when a student misses class, or for anything that suits the needs of you and your students.

Online Courseware for Blackboard, WebCT, and CourseCompass

Now you have the freedom to personalize your own online course materials!

Prentice Hall provides the content and support you need to create and manage your own online course in WebCT, Blackboard, or Prentice Hall's own CourseCompass. Content includes lecture material, interactive exercises, individual and team research projects, and additional testing questions.

CourseCompass   www.coursecompass.com

CourseCompass is a dynamic, interactive online course-management tool powered exclusively for Pearson Education by Blackboard. This exciting product allows you to teach market-leading Pearson Education content in an easy-to-use, customizable format.

Blackboard   www.prenhall.com/blackboard

Prentice Hall's abundant online content, combined with Blackboard's popular tools and interface, result in robust Web-based courses that are easy to implement, manage, and use—taking your courses to new heights in student interaction and learning.

WebCT   www.prenhall.com/webct

Course-management tools within WebCT include page tracking, progress tracking, class and student management, a grade book, communication tools, a calendar, reporting tools, and more. GOLD LEVEL CUSTOMER SUPPORT, available exclusively to adopters of Prentice Hall textbooks, is provided free of charge upon adoption and provides you with priority assistance, training discounts, and dedicated technical support.

EXPLORE IT   www.prenhall.com/PHIT

Prentice Hall offers computer-based training just for computer literacy. Designed to cover some of the most difficult concepts as well as some current topical areas, EXPLORE IT is a Web- and CD-ROM-based product designed to complement any course. Available for free with any Prentice Hall title, our coverage includes Troubleshooting, Programming Logic, Mouse and Keyboard Basics, Databases, Building a Web Page, Hardware, Software, Operating Systems, Building a Network, and more!

For the Student

Welcome to *Computers in your Future 2004!* The following pages are designed to help you get the most out of the material in this book and to make your learning process rewarding. We call your attention to areas that may help you as you read through the book.

SPOTLIGHT

sections highlight important ideas about computer-related topics, and provide in-depth useful information to take your learning to the next level.

IMPACTS boxes in each chapter illustrate thought-provoking cultural, ethical, and societal implications of computing you may face.

EMERGING TECHNOLOGIES

How "Human" Can Robots Become?

Robots have come a long way since the term was first used to describe man-made laborers in a 1921 play by Czech author Karel Capek. Once found only in scientific labs, today robots paint cars for auto manufacturers, help surgeons conduct surgery, and make trips to outer space.

Robots are entering our homes, too. Can't have a pet in your dorm room? How about AIBO, the dog-like "Entertainment Robot" from Sony (see Figure 1.4a)? According to Sony, AIBO has the "five instincts of love, curiosity, movement, hunger, and sleep" as well as the "emotions of happiness, sadness, anger, surprise, fear, and dislike." How can you tell what AIBO is "feeling"? According to the Japanese company, AIBO conveys its "feelings" through melodies, body language, and lights in its eyes and on its tail. You can even train AIBO to do tricks. Best of all, AIBO doesn't need to be house-trained!

Even more human-like is the Japanese-made PaPeRo (short for **Pa**rtner-type **Pe**rsonal **Ro**bot) (see Figure 1.4b). PaPeRo's colorful, rounded canister shape may not look huggable at first, but when treated with kindness, it's irresistible. PaPeRo can welcome you home after a long day, and when you're away, it wanders around looking for human companionship. If it doesn't find any, it takes a nap. PaPeRo even has the ability to recognize voice patterns; if these patterns are unfriendly, it runs away.

While AIBO and PaPeRo are human-like toys, robots are taking the place of humans in industry in many ways. In 2001, IBM conducted an experiment in which robots participated in simulated trading of commodities such as pork bellies and gold. By using specially designed algorithms, the robots performed the same tasks as human commodity brokers—and made seven percent more money than their human counterparts! Can you imagine a future in which robots make economic decisions? It would certainly give the stock exchange floor a new look. (And speaking of which, are robots capable of insider trading?)

Researchers are also working on a robot that changes its shape to accomplish a specific task. The shape-changing robot has moving pieces similar to a Rubik's cube, and a computer uses an algorithm to move about the various pieces. Such shape-changing robots will one day walk, crawl, carry tools, and fit into tight spaces humans can't.

Lockstep logic is wonderful for a machine, but humans rely on intuitive and often illogical decisions. Will robots ever act nonrationally? A team of researchers at MIT is working on a "sociable humanoid robot" able to learn from and interact with humans. Called Kismet, the big-eyed robot uses algorithms based on what we know about child development to react in a human way. According to MIT's research team, Kismet can perceive a variety of social cues from its "parent" through its eyes and ears, and can then deliver feedback through its facial expression, posture, and "voice." So will robots ever act illogically? With humans as surrogate parents, anything is possible.

Figure 1.4
(a) AIBO and (b) PaPeRo are popular home robots.

high speeds. To check your document's spelling, a word processing program uses a simple but reasonably effective algorithm. Here's how it works: The program begins by constructing a list of all the words in your document. Then it compares these words, one by one, with a huge list of correctly spelled words. (If you tried to do this manually, it would take many hours.) If you've used a word that isn't in the dictionary, the program puts the word into a list of suspect words.

Output The result of the processing operation is a list of apparent misspellings. The word "apparent" is important here because the program doesn't actually know whether the word is misspelled. It is able to tell only that these words aren't in its massive, built-in dictionary. But many correctly spelled words, such as proper nouns (the names of people and places), aren't likely to be found in the computer's dictionary. For this reason, the program won't make any changes without asking you to confirm them.

EMERGING TECHNOLOGIES

Wearables: The Fashion of Technology

It's a new day and you're trying to decide what to wear. Yesterday you wore your video glasses, but today you want to make more of a statement. How about a green- or rose-tinted Internet-enabled monocle? That would go perfectly with the ring controlling your computer. Or maybe you should wear your computerized suspenders. Your cell-phone vest needs a cleaning, so it looks like it'll be a backpack day.

All dressed, you head down the street in your "wearables." As you walk to the library, you e-mail a friend on your wrist pad, asking her to meet you for lunch later. At the library, the network automatically recognizes you from your ring. You search your pocket for your stylus, find it, and point to a library computer screen. The computer acknowledges you, and viewing through your monocle, you access your documents, open one, and begin jotting down notes by waving your pen in the air. Leaving the library, you call three of your friends. You visually chat together through your monocle and earpiece until your next class. You are seamlessly network-connected throughout your day through your wearable fashions.

Sound intriguing but unbelievable? While not all of this is possible just yet, some of it is. Take the Xybernaut company's "Poma," which combines a head-mounted display with a portable, lightweight CPU and an optical pointing device. Selling for about $1500, Poma gives you wearable computer access to the Internet, e-mail, Word files, and games. It's also compatible with wearable keyboards and other input devices.

In fact, Xybernaut wearable computers may one day be used by astronauts in space (see Figure 3.42). They were already selected to be used in field tests for a research project dedicated to exploring the planet Mars. It is hoped that the equipment will enable the one-day Mars explorers to learn how to use hands-free computing in their work. The wearable computers may also someday be used to enable two-way video- and audio-conferencing from Mars to the Earth.

Most wearable technologies to date have been incorporated into headsets and glasses, backpacks and fanny packs, rings and wristbands, and multipocketed pants. Recently, however, Santa Fe Science and Technologies created a commercial fiber that is similar to nylon but conducts electricity. Called "Smart Thread," this fiber can be woven into clothing like traditional threads, but it gives clothing computer-like abilities. The possibilities of Smart Thread are limitless. No more heavy packs for soldiers, who will instead be able to wear lightweight computers. Emergency search and rescue teams may one day wear computers that could seamlessly connect them to a command center. Smart Thread could also be woven into a child's clothing to act as a tracking device. The list goes on and on.

Products using Smart Thread are still two or three years away, but soon you may be wearing your computer, cell phone, music device, and other technologies as if they were a sweater, avoiding those unflattering bulges. Get ready for wearables with style!

Figure 3.42
Xybernaut equipment is helping would-be Mars explorers learn to use hands-free computing technology.

CURRENTS boxes in each chapter examine cutting-edge issues in computing and computer technology.

Page excerpt 2.4

COMPUTERS IN YOUR FUTURE 2004: CHAPTER 2

ATX form factor
The form factor of today's standard personal computer case. The previous design, called the AT case, didn't handle ventilation very well. It drew air in from anywhere and expelled it by means of a fan mounted on the case's back cover. The result? Dust, dirt, and grime were drawn into the case, coating the components with a layer of greasy fuzz, which insulated them from the cooling fan. The ATX case solves this problem. It reverses the fan and adds a filter—which means that clean air is drawn into the case. If you're using a personal computer with an ATX case, be sure to keep the cover tightly sealed so the fan can do its work.

Techtalk

mounting internal components, protects these components from physical damage, and keeps them cool. A good case also provides room for system upgrades, such as additional disk drives.

System units come in a variety of styles. In some desktop computing systems, the system unit is a separate metal or plastic box that's designed to sit on top of a desk. Ideally, the case should have a small **footprint** (the amount of room taken up by the case on the desk). However, a small case may not have enough room for add-on components. One solution to this problem is the **tower case**, a large system unit case that is designed to sit on the floor next to a desk. Smaller versions of tower cases are called **minitower cases**.

Notebook computers and personal digital assistants (PDAs) are called **all-in-one computers** because the system unit contains all of the computer's components, including input components (such as a keyboard or pen interface) and the display. Some desktop computers, such as Apple's iMac, contain the display within the system unit (see Figure 2.3).

System units also vary in what is called their **form factor**. A form factor is a

specification for how internal components, such as the motherboard, are mounted in the system unit. Early desktop computers used the **AT form factor**, a system unit case design that was introduced with IBM's Personal Computer AT (short for Advanced Technology) in 1984. More recent desktop systems use **ATX form factor** cases. Developed by Intel, the ATX form factor provides better accessibility to system components, better cooling, more full-sized expansion slots, and a more convenient layout for system upgrades.

The following sections explore the system unit of a typical desktop computer, beginning with the most important component: the computer's motherboard.

INSIDE THE SYSTEM UNIT

Most computer users don't need to open their system unit: they receive their computer in a ready-to-use package. However, if you ever do need to open your system unit, for example, to install more memory, bear in mind that the computer's components are sensitive to static electricity. If you touch certain components while you're charged with static electricity, you could destroy them. Always disconnect the power cord before removing your computer's case, and discharge static electricity by touching something that's well grounded, such as a water faucet. If it's one of those dry days when you're getting shocked every time you touch a doorknob, don't work on your computer's internal components.

If you do open your system unit, you'll see the following components (see Figure 2.4):

- **Motherboard** The **motherboard** is a large **printed circuit board** (**PCB**), a flat piece of plastic or fiberglass that contains thousands of electrical circuits that are etched into the board's surface. They connect numerous plug-in receptacles, which accommodate the computer's most important components (such as the microprocessor). The motherboard contains the computer's **central processing unit** (**CPU**). You'll learn more about the CPU later in this chapter; for now remember that the

Figure 2.3 a&b
(a) The Apple iMac's system unit sits on the desktop and also contains the computer's display. (b) The Macintosh G4 uses a tower case that sits on the floor next to the desk.

TECHTALK margin notes define commonly used computer jargon.

DESTINATIONS margin notes direct you to related Web sites where you can explore chapter topics in more depth.

Page excerpt 2.2

COMPUTERS IN YOUR FUTURE 2004: CHAPTER 2

Describing Hardware Performance

Destinations
For a great Web guide to personal computer hardware, see "PC Guide" at **www.pcguide.com**. Author Charles Kozierok presents a free, detailed survey of PC system components, including special sections on system care, system enhancement, and troubleshooting. If you're looking to upgrade your system or understand what a particular component does, this site is a great place to start.

Before we launch into our discussion of the system unit and its components, it's important that you understand a few things about hardware performance. As you learned in the last chapter, computers perform four basic functions: inputting data, processing this data, displaying the results using output devices, and storing the results for subsequent use. Computer hardware, and especially the system unit, is involved in all of these functions. When we talk about hardware *performance*, we're referring to how much data the computer can store and how fast it can process this data. To understand the capabilities of computer hardware, you need to learn some of the terminology that's used to describe how much data computers can transfer or store.

BITS AND BYTES

A basic distinction differentiates bits from bytes:

- A **bit** (short for **binary digit**) is the basic unit of information in a computer. A bit is either a 1 or a 0, the only two options available in the computer's binary numbering system. Bits are the

point of reference for measuring the **data transfer rate** (the number of bits transmitted per second) of communication devices, such as modems. You can think of a bit as being similar to a light switch: it has only two possible states, and is always in one or the other. If you have one light switch, you have the possibility that the switch is on or that it is off. If you have two light switches, then you have four possibilities: both switches are on, both switches are off, the first switch is on and the second switch is off, or the first switch is off and the second switch is on. Three switches allow for eight possibilities, and so on—up to eight switches, which results in 256 possible combinations.

- A **byte** consists of eight bits. Since it takes eight bits (on/off switches) to make a byte, and eight bits result in 256 possible on/off combinations, you'll see the number 256 appearing behind the scenes in many computer functions and applications. A single byte usually represents one character of data, such as the essential numbers (0–9), the basic letters of the alphabet in English and European languages, and the most common punctuation symbols. For this reason, you can use the byte as a baseline for understanding just how much information a computer is storing. For example, a typical college essay contains 250 words per page, and each word contains (on average) 5.5 characters. So the page contains

Terms that Describe Units of Data

Term Equivalent	Abbreviation	Approximate Amount	Exact Amount	Text	
Kilobyte	KB or K	1 thousand bytes	1,024 bytes		(one page)
Megabyte	MB or M	1 million bytes	1,048,576 bytes		(1,000 pages)
Gigabyte	GB or G	1 billion bytes	1,043,741,824 bytes		(1,000 books)
Terabyte	TB or T	1 trillion bytes	1,099,511,627,776 bytes		(1 million books)

Figure 2.1

END-OF-CHAPTER MATERIAL

includes updated multiple choice, matching, fill-in, and short answer questions as well as Web research projects so you can prepare for tests.

EXPLORE IT LABS present you with
an interactive look into the world of computer concepts.
These labs bring challenging topics in computer concepts to life and assess your knowledge via a Quiz section, which can be e-mailed, saved to disk, or printed.

TABLE OF CONTENTS
At a Glance

Chapter 1

Becoming Fluent with Computers

What You'll Learn . . .

When you have finished reading this chapter, you will be able to:

1. Explain the importance of computer fluency.

2. Define the word *computer* and name the four basic operations in the information processing cycle.

3. Give an example of the information processing cycle in action.

4. Explain why responsible computer usage always involves ethical considerations.

5. Provide examples of hardware devices that handle input, processing, output, and storage tasks.

6. Explain the difference between system software and application software.

7. List the most popular Internet services.

Spotlight   1.A

File Management

Chapter 2

Inside the System Unit

What You'll Learn . . .

When you have finished reading this chapter, you will be able to:

1. Define the terminology that's used to describe how much data computers can transfer or store.

2. List the components found inside the system unit and explain their use.

3. List the components found on the computer's motherboard and explain the role they play in the functioning of the computer's systems.

4. Discuss (in general terms) how a computer's central processing unit (CPU) processes data.

5. Explain the characteristics that determine a microprocessor's performance.

6. List the various types of memory found in a computer system and explain the purpose of each.

7. Describe the various physical connectors on the exterior of the system unit and explain their use.

8. Differentiate between analog and digital methods of representing data and explain the advantages and disadvantages of each.

Chapter 3

Input and Output: Data In, Information Out

What You'll Learn . . .

When you have finished reading this chapter, you will be able to:

1. List the four types of input and explain the purpose of each.

2. List the characteristics of a computer keyboard.

3. Explain the purpose of the special keys on the computer's keyboard.

4. List the most frequently used pointing devices and explain why users sometimes prefer alternatives to the mouse.

5. Describe the benefits and drawbacks of speech recognition as an alternative to keyboard use.

6. List devices that are used to get sound, video, and images into the computer.

7. Identify the two major types of output and give examples of each.

8. Explain how the characteristics of a computer's video adapter determine the overall quality of the image displayed on the monitor.

9. List the various types of monitors, and indicate the advantages and disadvantages of each.

10. Identify the two major types of printers, and indicate the advantages and disadvantages of each.

Chapter 4

Storing Data: Electronic Filing Cabinets

What You'll Learn . . .

When you have finished reading this chapter, you will be able to:

1. Distinguish between memory and storage.

2. Discuss how storage media are categorized.

3. List two ways to measure a storage device's performance.

4. Explain how data is stored.

5. Explain the uses of removable disks.

6. List the performance characteristics of hard drives.

7. List and compare the various optical storage media available for personal computers.

8. Identify the types of new storage technologies, such as FMD-ROM discs, solid state storage devices, and enterprise storage systems.

Spotlight   **4.A**

Buying and Upgrading Your Computer System

Chapter 5

System Software: The Operating Environment

What You'll Learn . . .

When you have finished reading this chapter, you will be able to:

1. List the two major components of a computer's operating system software.

2. Explain why a computer isn't useful without an operating system.

3. List the five major functions of an operating system.

4. Explain what happens when you turn on a computer.

5. List the three major types of user interfaces.

6. Discuss the strengths and weaknesses of the most popular operating systems.

7. List the six system utilities that are considered essential.

8. Discuss data backup procedures.

Chapter 6

Application Software: Tools for Productivity

What You'll Learn . . .

When you have finished reading this chapter, you will be able to:

1. Differentiate between horizontal and vertical applications.

2. List the most popular types of horizontal applications.

3. Differentiate between commercial software, shareware, freeware, and public domain software.

4. Explain the concept of software versions.

5. Discuss the advantages and disadvantages of standalone programs, integrated programs, and suites.

6. Describe the essential concepts and skills of using application software, including installing applications, launching applications, understanding and using application windows, getting on-screen help, using menus and toolbars, and working with documents.

7. Discuss the advantages of Web integration.

Spotlight   6.A

Microsoft® Office

Chapter 7

Networks: Communicating and Sharing Resources

What You'll Learn . . .

When you have finished reading this chapter, you will be able to:

1. List the three main types of computer networks.

2. Discuss the ways that connecting computers increases the value of an organization's information technology investment.

3. Explain the importance of protocols in a computer network.

4. Contrast circuit switching and packet switching networks and explain their respective strengths and weaknesses.

5. Distinguish between peer-to-peer and client/server LANs.

6. Name the most widely used LAN protocol and discuss its benefits.

7. Identify three business applications of WANs.

Chapter 8

The Internet: The Network of Networks

What You'll Learn . . .

When you have finished reading this chapter, you will be able to:

1. Define the Internet and discuss why it's so popular.

2. Differentiate the Internet from online services and the Web.

3. Explain the difference between client and server software.

4. List the most popular Internet services and explain what they do.

5. Define the elements of Internet addresses, including domain names.

6. Discuss the use of Internet-based networks within large organizations.

7. List the initiatives underway to improve the Internet's performance.

Chapter 9

The World Wide Web and Electronic Commerce

What You'll Learn . . .

When you have finished reading this chapter, you will be able to:

1. Explain the concept of hypertext.

2. Contrast Web browsers and Web servers.

3. Explain the parts of a URL.

4. Name the browser navigation buttons and their functions.

5. Contrast Web subject guides and search engines.

6. Explain how search operators can improve Web search results.

7. Evaluate the reliability of information on a Web page.

8. Define business-to-business e-commerce and explain why it's moving to the Internet.

9. List the fastest growing public e-commerce applications and explain why customers like them.

Spotlight 9.A

Multimedia & Virtual Reality

Chapter 10

Telecommunications: Exchanging Data via the Telephone System

What You'll Learn . . .

When you have finished reading this chapter, you will be able to:

1. Explain the limitations of the public switched telephone network (PSTN) for sending and receiving computer data.

2. Discuss how modems transform digital computer signals into the analog tones suited for the telephone system.

3. Define *bandwidth* and discuss the bandwidth needs of typical users.

4. List two digital telephony standards that can bring digital connections into homes and offices using existing wiring.

5. Provide examples of how convergence is blurring the boundaries among popular communication devices, including phones, computers, and TVs.

6. Discuss the prospects for telephony through the Internet.

Chapter 11

Computer Crime and Security

What You'll Learn . . .

When you have finished reading this chapter, you will be able to:

1. Explain how attackers and intruders can gain entry to computer systems and harm or destroy data.

2. List ways you can help system administrators keep a computer system safe from unauthorized access and computer viruses.

3. Identify the stereotypes of people who are most likely to attack or harm computer systems, and explain their motives.

4. List the types of losses caused by computer system intrusions and attacks.

5. List and explain the tools and techniques used to defend computer systems against intruders and attackers.

Chapter 12

Privacy and Encryption

What You'll Learn . . .

When you have finished reading this chapter, you will be able to:

1. Explain the threat to privacy posed by the sale of sensitive personal information on the Internet.

2. Define anonymity and discuss how it can be abused.

3. Describe how technological developments are eroding privacy and anonymity.

4. Explain the reasons why many employers feel that they need to monitor their employees' computer usage.

5. State why U.S. security officials believe public key encryption poses a threat to U.S. security, both foreign and domestic.

6. Describe the U.S. government's proposed key recovery plan, and explain why it threatens the growth of Internet commerce.

Spotlight — 12.A

Ethics: Standards of Information Age Conduct

Chapter 13

Databases and Information Systems

What You'll Learn . . .

When you have finished reading this chapter, you will be able to:

1. Recognize the potential uses of a database program.

2. Describe the basic components of a database.

3. Describe the basic capabilities of a good database program.

4. Distinguish between flat file and relational database programs and explain the advantages and disadvantages of each.

5. List the three basic characteristics of a computerized information system.

6. List the four functions of managers.

7. Identify the characteristics of valuable information.

8. Describe the major types of computerized information systems used in today's organizations.

9. Describe how the retail sector is taking advantage of computer databases to increase sales and gain a competitive edge.

Chapter 14

Systems Analysis and Design

What You'll Learn . . .

When you have finished reading this chapter, you will be able to:

1. Explain what systems analysts do.

2. Discuss the reasons for the widespread use of the systems development life cycle (SDLC).

3. List the SDLC's five phases.

4. Describe the classic mistakes of failed information systems development projects.

5. Discuss the activities in each of the SDLC's five phases.

Chapter 15

Programming Languages and Program Development

What You'll Learn . . .

When you have finished reading this chapter, you will be able to:

1. Explain what a programming language is.

2. Contrast machine language and assembly language.

3. Discuss the benefits of a high-level programming language.

4. List the measures taken to improve third-generation languages.

5. Identify the shortcomings of early languages and explain how object-oriented languages attempt to remedy these shortcomings.

6. List several popular programming languages and explain their advantages and disadvantages.

7. List the six phases of the program development life cycle (PDLC) and explain why the PDLC is needed.

8. Explain why top-down programming makes programs easier to debug and maintain.

9. List the three basic types of control structures.

10. Differentiate between syntax errors and logic errors in programs.

Chapter 16

Careers and Certification

What You'll Learn . . .

When you have finished reading this chapter, you will be able to:

1. Describe the traditional information technology (IT) career paths.

2. Compare and contrast computer science (CS), systems engineering, and computer information science (CIS) curricula in colleges and universities.

3. Describe two settings in which most IT workers find employment.

4. List at least three typical job titles in information systems (IS) departments and vendor companies.

5. Identify the business skills IS managers want in new IT workers.

6. List the technical skills currently in high demand.

7. Discuss the positive and negative aspects of certification.

Spotlight **16.A**

Artificial Intelligence and Other Emerging Technologies

Computers
in your Future
2004

Becoming Fluent with Computers

CHAPTER **1**

What You'll Learn...

When you have finished reading this chapter, you will be able to:

1. Explain the importance of computer fluency.

2. Define the word *computer* and name the four basic operations in the information processing cycle.

3. Give an example of the information processing cycle in action.

4. Explain why responsible computer usage always involves ethical considerations.

5. Provide examples of hardware devices that handle input, processing, output, and storage tasks.

6. Explain the difference between system software and application software.

7. List the most popular Internet services.

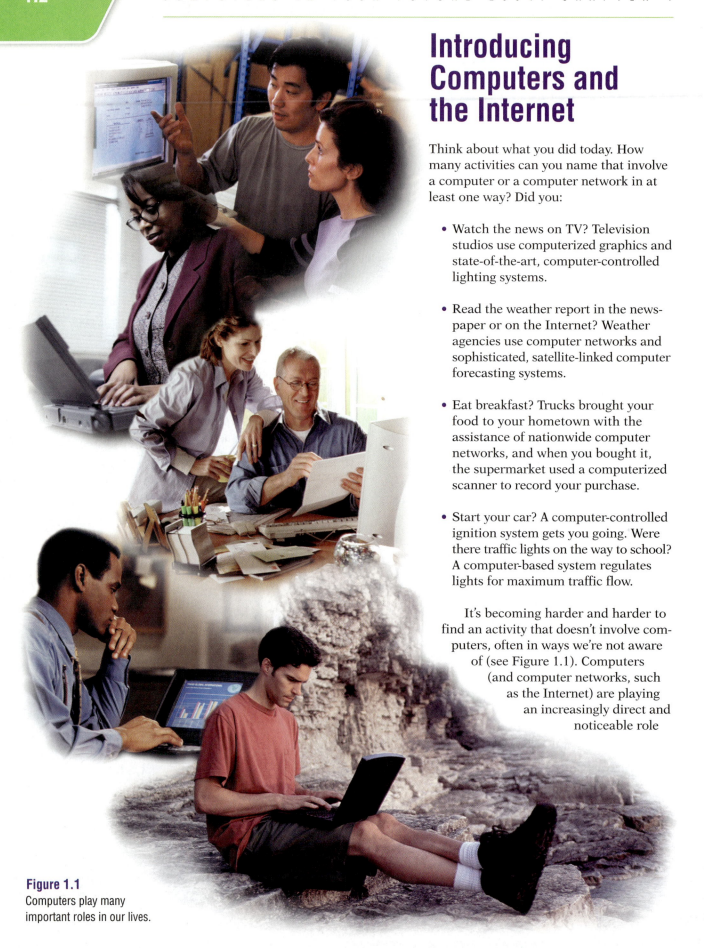

Introducing Computers and the Internet

Think about what you did today. How many activities can you name that involve a computer or a computer network in at least one way? Did you:

- Watch the news on TV? Television studios use computerized graphics and state-of-the-art, computer-controlled lighting systems.

- Read the weather report in the newspaper or on the Internet? Weather agencies use computer networks and sophisticated, satellite-linked computer forecasting systems.

- Eat breakfast? Trucks brought your food to your hometown with the assistance of nationwide computer networks, and when you bought it, the supermarket used a computerized scanner to record your purchase.

- Start your car? A computer-controlled ignition system gets you going. Were there traffic lights on the way to school? A computer-based system regulates lights for maximum traffic flow.

It's becoming harder and harder to find an activity that doesn't involve computers, often in ways we're not aware of (see Figure 1.1). Computers (and computer networks, such as the Internet) are playing an increasingly direct and noticeable role

Figure 1.1
Computers play many important roles in our lives.

in our personal lives, as well. At home, computers help us pay bills, determine account balances, and even buy movie tickets. And if you're like millions of people in the United States, you use e-mail and instant messaging to stay in touch with your friends and family members. At work, computer and Internet skills are needed for success in almost every occupational area. Studies consistently show that workers with computer and Internet skills tend to make more money and have more satisfying careers than do workers who don't have such skills (see Figure 1.2).

Clearly, you'd be wise to learn all you can about computers and the Internet. But what should you learn? Educators agree that skills are important. You should know how to use a computer, the Internet, and popular programs such as Microsoft Word or Excel. But skills alone aren't enough. To be a fully functional member of today's computerized society, you also should learn the fundamental concepts that underlie computer and Internet technology, such as the distinction between hardware and software. Once you understand these concepts, you'll be better able to apply computer technology wisely and creatively, judge the likely impact of computer

innovations, and sort through the difficult ethical and moral challenges that computers place before us.

The Need for Computer Fluency

The term **computer fluency** describes the ease with which people are able to navigate the digital world successfully. Computer-fluent people are **computer literate**, meaning they're skilled computer and Internet users. Their knowledge of the underlying concepts and principles of computers and the Internet gives them a tremendous advantage. The more they work with computer technology, the deeper and richer their understanding grows. Instead of being threatened by new technologies, they're quietly confident in their abilities. As their confidence and knowledge grow, they become more and more adept in their use of computers.

As we mentioned earlier, if you want to become fluent with computers and the Internet, you'll need to learn skills in addition to concepts. In particular, you should

Figure 1.2
Workers with computer and Internet skills tend to make more money and have more satisfying careers than do workers who do not have such skills.

learn how to use a desktop or notebook computer, an operating system such as Microsoft Windows XP, and the software applications included in office suite packages such as Microsoft Office XP. You should also develop essential Internet skills, including how to find information on the Web and how to use e-mail. Of course, computer technology changes rapidly. The skills you learn now may be outdated in a few years, and you may need to learn new skills based on improved technologies. Just 15 years ago, the Internet was all but unknown to the general public. Very few people used e-mail—and, consequently, very few people had to worry about infecting their computers with a computer virus when they opened e-mail attachments. Today, the Internet and e-mail are household words. More than 60 percent of U.S. households have Internet connections—a fact that, a decade ago, was almost unimaginable. Computer viruses and Web sites have become common topics of conversation among the young and old alike.

Computer-fluent people worry about viruses, but their conceptual knowledge enables them to gauge their true level of risk—and to avoid them. A computer-fluent person knows that computer viruses are contained only in *executable files*, which contain some sort of program or set of instructions that the computer can carry out (or execute). Such files usually have a give-away extension (the part of the filename that comes after the period), such as exe, js, or bat. Computer-fluent people never open e-mail attachments unless they know the source of the e-mail and they are positive that the attached file is virus-free. But they don't worry about opening nonexecutable data files, such as text files, because they know such files cannot contain computer viruses.

Computer and Internet concepts such as these are not difficult to learn. In many respects, learning them is like learning a foreign language. When you learn a foreign language, you can't escape the need to learn new vocabulary. Similarly, as you read this book, you'll come across hundreds of terms, many of which may be new to you. As you learn them, your understanding of computer and Internet technology will grow. Before long, you'll find that you've started down the path of computer fluency.

Destinations

To learn more about computer fluency, see "Being Fluent with Information Technology," an influential report authored by the U.S. National Research Council, at **www.nap.edu/ catalog/6482.html**.

What Is a Computer, Anyway?

Learning computer and Internet concepts is partly about learning new terms, as the previous section concluded. So let's start with the most basic term of all: *computer*.

UNDERSTANDING THE COMPUTER: BASIC DEFINITIONS

A **computer** is a machine that, under a program's direction and control, performs four basic operations: input, processing, output, and storage (see Figure 1.3). A **program** is a list of instructions that tells the computer how to perform these four operations in order to accomplish a task.

Input

In the first operation, called **input**, the computer accepts data that has been represented in a way the computer can use. Here, the term **data** refers to unorganized raw materials, which can be made up of words, numbers, images, or sounds (or a combination of these). Computer input can include the words of Sylvia Plath, graphic images of Impressionist paintings, and video clips of Tiger Woods's golf swing. The computer's ability to work with all types of media is the first major reason for its remarkable penetration into almost every occupational area and nearly two-thirds of U.S. households.

Processing

In the second operation, called **processing**, the computer performs arithmetic or comparison (logical) operations on the represented data.

These operations are really very simple. In fact, much of what a processor does boils down to adding two numbers or comparing them to see which is larger. What makes computers so amazing is that they can perform these simple operations at very high speeds. The most brilliant human mathematicians can perform only a few dozen of these operations per second, whereas an inexpensive computer can perform hundreds of millions—even billions—of them in a second. The computer's speed gives it amazing capabilities. For example, a transcontinental computer network used for research purposes is capable of moving the equivalent of all the information stored in the Library of Congress from Washington to San Francisco in just a few minutes.

If computers capable of processing data at such impressive speeds did not already exist, we would have to invent them. According to one recent estimate, humans will create more information in the next three years than they have in all the previous centuries of our existence on this planet. In fact, people are generating so much information today that they often experience **information overload**, the feelings of anxiety and incapacity experienced when people are presented with more information than they can reasonably handle.

Not only do they generate huge amounts of information, computers are exceptionally reliable, too. Even the least expensive personal computers perform several million operations per second, and can do so for years without making an error caused by the computer's physical components. (Almost all "computer errors" are actually caused by flaws in computer programs or mistakes in the data people supply to computers.) As you'll learn in this book, the major challenge facing computing is the fact that computer hardware—the physical components of the computer—is more technologically advanced than the software, the instructions that tell the computers what to do.

Output

In the third operation, called **output**, the computer shows the results of the processing operation in a way that people can understand. The processed data become

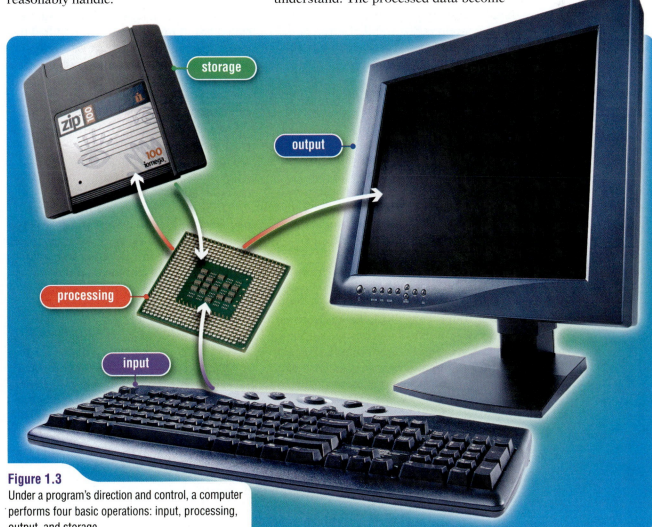

Figure 1.3
Under a program's direction and control, a computer performs four basic operations: input, processing, output, and storage.

information. This term refers to data that have been simplified and organized in a way that people can use. You may see the output on a monitor or a printer—or, if the computer is processing sounds, you may hear the results on the computer's speakers. Experimental computer systems may point the way to a future in which computers will engage additional senses, including our sense of touch and even our sense of smell.

Storage

In the fourth operation, called **storage**, the computer saves the results so that they can be used again later. Computers can store enormous amounts of information. Even an inexpensive desktop computer can store and provide quick access to a 32-volume encyclopedia, the entire collected works of Shakespeare, a world atlas, an unabridged dictionary, and much more.

Together, these four operations are called the **information processing cycle**. Input, processing, output, storage—that's what computers do. And that's true no matter what kind of data the computer is working with.

HOW COMPUTERS "THINK"

Computers can transform data into information. But they can't ride bicycles or write poems about the moonlight—unless, that is, somebody figures out how to write a program that mimics these complex human activities by means of simple, repetitive processing actions organized into an algorithm.

The term **algorithm** refers to the overall, step-by-step procedure used to solve a problem. Recipes contain algorithms for cooking dishes. Long division is an algorithm for dividing numbers that are too big to divide in your head. These examples suggest the important point about algorithms: by detailing the exact step-by-step procedure to follow, they enable people—and machines—to solve problems without requiring a lot of intelligence or skill.

Some computer scientists believe that there are algorithms out there for doing just about anything—including writing good poems about the moonlight—but they just haven't been created yet. For example, experts once thought that decades would

pass before computers could transcribe human speech accurately. Thanks to the creation of powerful new algorithms, speech recognition is now a reality. In fact, you can equip a personal computer to transcribe your speech with an accuracy of 95 percent or more—which is better than most people's typing accuracy.

What all this means is simple: Don't put your money down on a statement such as "A computer could never compose music like Mozart's or Beethoven's." All it takes is for someone to come up with the necessary algorithm.

THE INFORMATION PROCESSING CYCLE IN ACTION: BATCH VS. INTERACTIVE PROCESSING

In the early days of computing, the computer's four basic operations—input, processing, output, and storage—had to be conducted in a rigid, lockstep sequence, called **batch processing**. You first had to make an appointment to use the computer, as there were few computers available back then. You then fed data into the computer, the computer processed the data, and out came the results. If the results proved that there was something wrong with the program, you had to wait until your next appointment to run the program all over again. Needless to say, using a computer in those days was very frustrating.

Today's computers use **interactive processing**, in which you initiate several information processing cycles in a single session. If something goes wrong, you see the problem right away, and you can launch a new information processing cycle to get better results.

Here's an example that shows how interactive processing works:

Input You've just finished writing a research paper for one of your classes. You think it's probably riddled with misspellings, so you run your word processing program's spell-checking utility on it. In this example, your entire document is the input.

Processing A spell-checking utility makes use of the computer's ability to perform very simple operations at very

EMERGING TECHNOLOGIES

How "Human" Can Robots Become?

Robots have come a long way since the term was first used to describe man-made laborers in a 1921 play by Czech author Karel Capek. Once found only in scientific labs, today robots paint cars for auto manufacturers, help surgeons conduct surgery, and make trips to outer space.

Robots are entering our homes, too. Can't have a pet in your dorm room? How about AIBO, the dog-like "Entertainment Robot" from Sony (see Figure 1.4a)? According to Sony, AIBO has "the five instincts of love, curiosity, movement, hunger, and sleep" as well as the "emotions of happiness, sadness, anger, surprise, fear, and dislike." How can you tell what AIBO is "feeling"? According to the Japanese company, AIBO conveys its "feelings" through melodies, body language, and lights in its eyes and on its tail. You can even train AIBO to do tricks. Best of all, AIBO doesn't need to be house-trained!

Even more human-like is the Japanese-made PaPeRo (short for **Pa**rtner-type **Pe**rsonal **Ro**bot) (see Figure 1.4b). PaPeRo's colorful, rounded canister shape may not look huggable at first, but when treated with kindness, it's irresistible. PaPeRo can welcome you home after a long day, and when you're away, it wanders around looking for human companionship. If it doesn't find any, it takes a nap. PaPeRo even has the ability to recognize voice patterns; if these patterns are unfriendly, it runs away.

While AIBO and PaPeRo are human-like toys, robots are taking the place of humans in industry in many ways. In 2001, IBM conducted an experiment in which robots participated in simulated trading of commodities such as pork bellies and gold. By using specially designed algorithms, the robots performed the same tasks as human commodity brokers—and made seven percent more money than their human counterparts! Can you imagine a future in which robots make economic decisions? It would certainly give the stock exchange floor a new look. (And speaking of which, are robots capable of insider trading?)

Researchers are also working on a robot that changes its shape to accomplish a specific task. The shape-changing robot has moving pieces similar to a Rubik's cube, and a computer uses an algorithm to move about the various pieces. Such shape-changing robots will one day walk, crawl, carry tools, and fit into tight spaces humans can't.

Figure 1.4
(a) AIBO and (b) PaPeRo are popular home robots.

Lockstep logic is wonderful for a machine, but humans rely on intuitive and often illogical decisions. Will robots ever act nonrationally? A team of researchers at MIT is working on a "sociable humanoid robot" able to learn from and interact with humans. Called Kismet, the big-eyed robot uses algorithms based on what we know about child development to react in a human way. According to MIT's research team, Kismet can perceive a variety of social cues from its "parent" through its eyes and ears, and can then deliver feedback through its facial expression, posture, and "voice." So will robots ever act illogically? With humans as surrogate parents, anything is possible.

IMPACTS

high speeds. To check your document's spelling, a word processing program uses a simple but reasonably effective algorithm. Here's how it works: The program begins by constructing a list of all the words in your document. Then it compares these words, one by one, with a huge list of correctly spelled words. (If you tried to do this manually, it would take many hours.) If you've used a word that isn't in the dictionary, the program puts the word into a list of suspect words.

Output The result of the processing operation is a list of apparent misspellings. The word "apparent" is important here because the program doesn't actually know whether the word is misspelled. It is able to tell only that these words aren't in its massive, built-in dictionary. But many correctly spelled words, such as proper nouns (the names of people and places), aren't likely to be found in the computer's dictionary. For this reason, the program won't make any changes without asking you to confirm them.

Be aware that the computer isn't really "checking spelling" when it performs this operation. The computer can't check your spelling because it doesn't possess the intelligence to do so. All it can do is tell you which of the words you've used aren't in the dictionary. Ultimately, only you can decide whether a given word is misspelled.

Storage Once you've corrected the spelling in your document, you save the revised document to disk.

In sum, computers transform some kind of raw material (here, a document full of misspellings) into a more polished product (a document that is free of misspellings). They do so by performing very simple operations over and over, at very high speeds.

WHAT'S TO BE LEARNED?

Earlier, you learned that computer-fluent people are more adept with computers and better able to adapt to rapid change than are people who don't understand the basic concepts and principles of computing. So here's the test: if that's true, what's to be learned from our definition of "computing"? Actually, just about everything you'll learn in the rest of this book flows from this definition, but here are three points that you should keep in mind.

Don't Let Hardware Scare You
Many people feel threatened by computers because they fear that computers are too intelligent. But computers have no intelligence at all. The processing operations they do are almost ridiculously simple. The average insect is a genius compared with a computer.

As you learned earlier, the computer's saving grace is that it performs these simple operations quickly and reliably. So there is nothing scary about computer hardware. Without a program to tell it what to do, the computer is no more frightening—or useful—than a lump of clay.

What's disturbing about computers isn't the computers themselves but what people might do with them—which leads to the next point.

Take Ethics Seriously
Responsible computing requires that you understand the limitations and risks of using the computer, as well as the potential that computer misuse could subject others to harm. Every day there are stories in the news of people misusing computerized data. Names and e-mail addresses are distributed freely without permission or regard for privacy. Viruses are launched against unsuspecting victims. Credit card information is stolen and fraudulently used. Computerized dialing machines call thousands of households an hour with unwanted solicitations. The list of grievances goes on and on.

Recognize the Risks of Using Flawed Software
Computer hardware is amazingly reliable, as you've just learned. But software is another matter.

All programs contain errors, and here's why: computers can perform only a limited series of simple actions, which makes constructing a computer program that accomplishes something meaningful similar to trying to build a house out of toothpicks. Many programs contain millions of lines of programming code (see Figure 1.5). In general, each line of a program tells the computer to perform an action, such as adding two numbers or comparing them.

With so many lines of code, errors inevitably occur—and they are impossible to eradicate completely. On average,

To Do Interesting Things, Programs Need to Be Big, and They're Getting Bigger

Program	Lines of Programming Code
ATM Machine	90,000
Air Traffic Control	900,000
Microsoft Windows 98	18 million
Microsoft Windows 2000	27 million
Microsoft Office XP	35 million (estimated)
Internal Revenue Service (IRS)	100 million (all programs)

Figure 1.5

EMERGING TECHNOLOGIES

Nanotechnology: Atoms Shaping the Future

In the early days of computing, room-sized noisy machines spindled and punched cards to perform their calculations. Today, computers are smaller than the palm of your hand and can accomplish a wide array of tasks. But what will computers be like in the future?

What would you say if you were told that various products would one day be able to manufacture themselves, or that computers would work billions of times faster than they do now? How about that there would be an end to famine and disease? And what if it were possible for extinct animals and plants to live again? What about distant planets, now uninhabitable, being made to look earth-like? All of these things and more may one day be possible with nanotechnology.

Merriam-Webster's defines **nanotechnology** as "the art of manipulating materials on an atomic or molecular scale especially to build microscopic devices (as robots)." Nanotechnology is based on a unit of measure called a **nanometer**, which is a billionth of a meter. The atoms and molecules used to perform certain tasks in nanotechnology, or **nanorobots**, will one day be able to perform an array of tasks. And because of their size, they'll be able to do things we never before thought possible.

The tie between medical and corporate research in nanotechnology is already strong. In fact, breakthroughs in nanomedicine and uses for medical nanorobots will most likely come first. For instance, medical nanorobots may one day be able to destroy fatty deposits in the bloodstream or be used to organize cells to restore artery walls, thereby preventing heart attacks. Nanorobots may also one day help improve our immune system by disabling or getting rid of viruses within our bodies. Cancer research may also use nanorobots to one day deliver drugs to specific areas of the body.

Meanwhile, NASA recently funded research to create nanoparticles and nanocapsules. While this research will be invaluable medically, NASA is interested in using the technology in space travel and long-term space habitation as well. NASA is concerned about the effect of radiation on its astronauts. They believe that nanomedicine could be the answer for radiation protection, self-diagnosis of disease in space, and delivery of medication during long space missions, among other things. Nanotechnology may also be able to alter the properties of known materials, making them lighter and stronger for lengthy space flights.

Nanotechnology sounds complex, and it is, but its possibilities and implications are truly endless. In fact, nanotechnology has been called the most important technological breakthrough since steam power. Looking for a new career? With corporate and medical research and development on parallel "nanopaths," they may create a high demand for nanotechnicians in your lifetime.

CURRENTS

commercial programs contain between 14 and 17 errors for every thousand lines of code. The best software, such as the avionics software for NASA's space shuttle, contains only about one error for every thousand lines of code, but achieving such a low error rate with traditional methods is very expensive. And the more lines of code you add, the more complex the program becomes—and the harder it is to eradicate the errors.

The fact that every computer program contains errors means that all computer use entails a certain level of risk. A bug might occur when you least expect it and cause your computer to freeze up. You may be forced to restart your computer, losing your unsaved work.

The foregoing explains why it's not a good idea to put off writing a paper until the night before your assignment is due.

Picture yourself at four in the morning, just putting the finishing touches on a brilliant English paper, and zap! A bug rears its head, and your computer goes into the electronic equivalent of catatonia. Did you save your work to the disk drive? If not, you've lost everything. If this hasn't happened to you already, rest assured, it will. (Tip: Always use your word processing program's Autosave feature, which saves your work at a specified interval—say, every five minutes—so that you'll lose, at the most, only five minutes of work.)

Bugs in a word processing program aren't usually life threatening, but computers are increasingly being used in mission-critical and safety-critical systems. Mission-critical systems are essential to an organization's viability, such as a company's computerized cash register system. If the

Techtalk

bug

An error or defect in software or hardware that causes a program to malfunction. The term derives from an incident in the very early days of computing when pioneer programmer Grace Hopper witnessed a moth fly into the computer she was manipulating, causing her program to crash.

system goes down, the organization can't function—and the result is often a very expensive fiasco (see Figure 1.6). A safety-critical system is one on which human lives depend, such as an air traffic control system or a computerized signaling system used for high-speed commuter trains. When these systems fail, human lives are at stake (see Figure 1.7). Don't worry too much about getting on a plane or train, though, because safety-critical systems are designed to much higher quality standards. In addition, safety-critical systems have backup systems that kick in if the main computer goes down.

Bitten by the Bug: Famous Software Fiascoes

A computer in Paris charged 41,000 parking ticket offenders with a series of much more serious crimes, including prostitution, drug dealing, extortion, and murder.

A bug in a British bank's payment order system mistakenly transferred $2 billion to the bank's customers within the space of one hour.

Due to a software glitch, a Japanese bank overhauled certain investments, leading to a loss of $83 million.

In Los Angeles County, pension fund managers used a bug-ridden model to forecast the fund's performance. As a result, they put too little money into the fund, leading to a $1.2 billion shortfall.

A department store chain's new computer cash register system failed the day after Thanksgiving, the busiest shopping day in the United States each year. The firm lost 20 percent of its normal holiday revenues.

A software glitch caused the *Mars Polar Lander* to switch off its braking engines too early, leading to the loss of the $139 million spacecraft and further delays in our understanding of our nearest planetary neighbor.

Figure 1.6

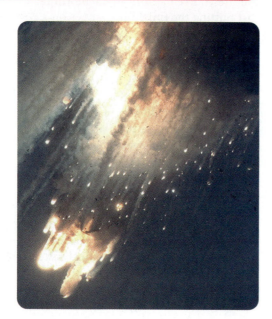

Figure 1.7
A software error caused the European Space Agency's $3 billion *Ariane* missile to spiral out of control.

COMPUTER SYSTEMS

You'll often hear the term *computer system*, which is normally shortened to *system* (as in "Sorry, our system is down"). This term is more inclusive than *computer*. A **computer system** is a collection of related components that have all been designed to work together smoothly (see Figure 1.8). It includes both the computer's hardware (its physical components) and its software (the programs that run on it).

Introducing Hardware: The Computer's Physical Components

As you'll agree after looking at a computer retail company's catalog, computer systems have many parts—keyboards, monitors, speakers, and so on. These parts are known as the computer's **hardware**. In this section, you'll see how the various physical components of the computer system are designed to implement the four stages of the information processing cycle: input, processing, output, and storage. Let's start with input.

INPUT: GETTING DATA INTO THE COMPUTER

Input devices enable you to enter data into the computer for processing. In interactive processing, input devices are also used to give commands to the computer and to respond to the computer's messages. A **command** is a type of input through which you tell the program what to do. In response, most programs usually provide some sort of **confirmation**, a message that indicates that the command was carried out. If the command fails, you'll see an **error message**. The best error messages explain what went wrong and suggest strategies for overcoming the error, but not all programs are this helpful.

a **Keyboard:** The most common means of getting data into the computer as well as controlling computer operations

b **Monitor:** The display that shows the results of computer operations

c **Mouse:** A pointing device that moves an on-screen pointer, enabling the user to select items and choose options

d **System unit:** Contains the computers system's processing and storage components

e **Floppy disk drive:** Accepts magnetically coated 3.5" disks, which allow the computer to read data from other computers or to write data for backup or exchange

f **CD- and/or DVD-ROM Read & Write drive:** Accepts CD-ROM/RW and DVD-ROM/RW discs that can store large amounts of data. Most software publishers provide their programs on these types of discs. RW discs allow the user to write data for backup or exchange.

g **Microphone:** Accepts voice input that can be translated into text or used to control the computer

h **Speakers:** Play the computer's audio output

i **External modem:** Communicates with other computers and the Internet through the telephone system. Today most modems are contained within the system unit.

j **Network interface card:** Enables the computer to communicate with other computers in a local area network

k **Printer:** Produces output on paper or transparencies

Figure 1.8
Components of a Typical Computer System

Figure 1.9 a&b

(a) The keyboard is the most widely used input device. (b) A mouse can be used to input lines, shapes, colors, and textures, among other things.

Destinations

One of the most promising uses of the computer lies in online education, the use of the Internet as a teaching medium. Try it yourself—and learn more about PCs—at free-ed.net's "Introduction to PCs," a free online course located at **www.free-ed.net/ fr02/lfc/021200/101**

By far the most widely used input device is the **keyboard**, which enables you to input characters (see Figure 1.9a). A **character** is one of a standard set (called a **character set**) of letters, numbers, and punctuation marks. Computer keyboards also include special keys that enable you to give commands to programs. For example, the keyboard's **arrow keys** are used to move the cursor around on the screen. The **cursor**, also called the **insertion point**, shows where text will appear when you start typing.

Most computers are also equipped with a type of **pointing device**, such as a **mouse** (see Figure 1.9b), that enables the user to move an on-screen **pointer**, which usually looks like an arrow. By moving the pointer to certain areas on-screen and clicking one of the mouse's buttons, you can issue commands. Some programs transform the mouse into an input device. For example, when you're running a painting or drawing program, you can use a mouse to input lines, shapes, colors, and textures, among other things.

Computers are often equipped with **microphones**. In a computer equipped with **speech-recognition software**, which transcribes spoken words into on-screen text, you can enter spoken data as if you were typing. You can also control the computer by giving spoken commands.

Many additional devices, such as scanners and digital cameras, provide alternative ways of getting data into the computer. You'll learn about these devices in Chapter 3.

PROCESSING: TRANSFORMING DATA INTO INFORMATION

The computer's processing circuitry, called the **central processing unit** (**CPU**), is located within the system's case. This case, called the **system unit**, contains many additional components as well, including storage devices and connectors for input and output devices.

Most of today's computers use a miniaturized CPU called a **microprocessor** (or just **processor** for short). A microprocessor is a complex electronic circuit fabricated on a wafer, or **chip**, of silicon (see Figure 1.10a). The achievement of microprocessor technology is responsible, in large part, for the computer revolution. Although just postage stamp–sized flakes of silicon, today's microprocessors offer CPU circuitry for a few hundred dollars that's far more advanced than computers of 20 years ago—computers that cost millions of dollars then. Microprocessor technology enables manufacturers to create millions of copies of this complex circuitry easily and quickly.

The microprocessor is one of several chips on the computer's main circuit board, also known as the **motherboard** (see Figure 1.10b). Among the other chips are those that provide the computer's **memory**. The CPU needs to interact with multiple input/output requests at the same time. That's the job performed by the computer's memory. Memory chips store program instructions (the tools) and data

Figure 1.10 a&b
(a) The microprocessor is one of several chips on the computer's (b) motherboard.

(the parts) so that the CPU can access them quickly.

A typical computer includes several different types of memory, but the most important of these is **random access memory** (**RAM**). The computer's RAM stores the programs and data you're working with. To work with programs successfully, you'll need to make sure that your computer has enough RAM. The capacity of RAM is measured in **megabytes** (**MB**). A megabyte is roughly one million characters. That sounds like a lot, but most of today's programs require 16 to 32 MB of RAM—and that's a bare-bones minimum.

Also found on the motherboard are **expansion slots**. An expansion slot is a receptacle that's designed to accept a plug-in **expansion card** (also called an *expansion board*, *adapter board*, or *adapter*). (This is one of several areas you'll run into where the terminology isn't very well standardized.) Expansion cards are used to connect the computer with various peripherals. A **peripheral** is an input or output device that's housed outside the system unit, such as a monitor or printer. Some peripherals connect to built-in connectors on the back of the computer's case.

OUTPUT: DISPLAYING THE INFORMATION

Output devices show the results of processing operations. **Monitors** show the results of processing operations on a screen. Most monitors are **cathode ray tube** (**CRT**)

devices (see Figure 1.11a). Also used in televisions, CRTs form an image by projecting a tightly focused light beam on a matrix of light-sensitive materials. Although the best computer monitors can produce a brilliant, detailed, and colorful display, CRTs are heavy. They consume a great deal of electrical power and produce heat as an unwanted byproduct. Increasingly popular as an alternative to CRTs on the desktop are **LCD displays** (also called **flat-panel displays**), which use low-power, liquid crystal diodes (LCDs) to generate the display (see Figure 1.11b).

Figure 1.11 a&b
(a) Cathode ray tubes and (b) LCD displays are common output devices.

1.12 a&b
(a) Inkjet printers
and (b) laser printers.

Speakers enable you to hear the results of sound processing, including music and synthesized speech. They also reproduce the signals that programs provide to confirm that commands have been executed successfully or to alert the user that an error has occurred.

Printers generate output on paper. Printers fall into two general categories, **impact printers** and **nonimpact printers**. An impact printer forms an image on paper by physically striking an ink-saturated ribbon, whereas nonimpact printers use various other technologies to transfer the image to the page. Most printers in use with today's computer systems are nonimpact printers, including **inkjet printers** (see Figure 1.12a) and **laser printers** (see Figure 1.12b). Inkjet printers form an image by spraying tiny droplets of ink on the page, whereas laser printers use a laser beam to transfer patterns to a rotating drum. The drum then uses a heat process to fuse tiny particles (called toner) to the page in a way that duplicates the laser-generated patterns.

STORAGE: HOLDING PROGRAMS AND DATA FOR FUTURE USE

In the best of all possible worlds, computers would be equipped with enormous amounts of RAM, and storage devices wouldn't be needed. Perhaps this day will come, but it isn't here yet. RAM is very fast, but it's also very expensive. Most computers are equipped with enough RAM to hold programs and data while the computer works with them, but no more. There must be additional space to keep programs and data that aren't in use at the moment. What's more, RAM is **volatile**. This means that the memory's contents disappear if the power is switched off.

   Storage devices are used to hold all of the programs and data that the computer system uses. Typically, storage devices are much slower than RAM, but they also have much more storage capacity. There are lots of different types of **storage media**, a term that is used collectively to describe all types of storage devices. (The term *media* is plural; the singular form is *medium*.) The two basic types are **magnetic storage media**, which store data on disks or tape encoded with magnetically sensitive material, and **optical storage media**, which store data in the form of microscopic pits that are etched into the surface of a disc. Storage devices are also distinguished by whether they can "record" data or just "play" it. In computing, the process of recording data is called **writing**, while the playback process is called **reading**. A device that can read and write is called a **read/write device**, while a device that can read (but not write) is called a **read-only device**.

   Most computers are equipped with both types of storage media. Magnetic storage media include the **hard disk drive** and the **floppy disk drive**. Both are read/write devices.

   The computer's hard disk provides the lion's share of storage. Most hard disks are nonremovable media. They typically include two or more disks that are enclosed within a permanently sealed case, which is mounted inside the system unit. Major advances in magnetic media technology are leading to ever-increasing hard disk capacities. Many new computers come equipped with hard disks capable

Figure 1.13 a&b
(a) A Zip disk can store up to 750 MB of data. (b) DVD-ROM discs can store as much as 4.7 GB of data.

of storing 20 to 60 gigabytes of programs and data. A **gigabyte** (**GB**) is roughly equivalent to one billion characters.

Floppy disk drives are designed to work with **floppy disks**, which are a removable medium you've probably used many times. Because they are a removable medium, floppy disks provide a convenient way to move data from one computer to another. However, standard floppy disks are woefully short on storage space, with most having room for only 1.44 MB of data. Because of this, many computers are equipped with **Zip drives**, which are designed to work with **Zip disks**. A Zip disk can store up to 750 MB of data (see Figure 1.13a).

Because software publishers typically use optical media to distribute their products, almost all computers are equipped with a **CD-ROM drive**. A CD-ROM drive is a read-only, optical storage medium. The drive reads the data encoded on a CD-ROM by using a laser to detect tiny pits etched into the CD-ROM's plastic surface. A CD-ROM closely resembles an audio CD except that it contains computer-readable data rather than sound. Most CD-ROM drives can also read audio CDs.

Increasingly, computers are equipped with **DVD-ROM drives**. DVD-ROM drives are designed to work with DVD-ROM discs, which can store much more information than a CD-ROM (see Figure 1.13b).

COMMUNICATIONS DEVICES

Much of what computers do involves moving data around within the computer at very high speeds. This same capability can be used to move data between computers as well. To move data between computers,

communications devices are necessary. Communications devices enable computers to connect to **computer networks**. A computer network links two or more computers by means of some type of connection, called a **network medium**. Network media can be both physical (using wires) and nonphysical (using airwaves).

Many computers are equipped with a **modem**, which enables the computer to access other computers and the Internet by means of a telephone line. Other computers use a **network interface card** (**NIC**) to hook up to a **local area network** (**LAN**). A LAN is a group of computers located within a limited geographic area (a building or several buildings situated next to each other). The computers are typically connected by special high-speed cables.

TYPES OF COMPUTERS

Computers come in all sizes, from large to small. It's convenient to divide them into two categories: computers for individuals (see Figure 1.14) and computers for organizations (see Figure 1.15).

Computers for Individuals

A **personal computer** is designed to meet an individual's computing needs. Also called **microcomputers**, personal computers have steadily dropped in price, even as they have become more powerful and more useful. The two most commonly used types of personal computers are Apple Computer's Macintosh systems and the more numerous **IBM-compatible personal computers**, also called PCs, made by many manufacturers. These machines are called "IBM-compatible" because the first such computer was made by IBM.

Desktop computers are personal computers designed for an individual's use. They run programs designed to help individuals accomplish their work more productively. They're also used to gain access to the resources of computer networks such as the Internet.

Notebook computers are small enough to fit in a briefcase. Many of them are as powerful as desktop computers and include nearly all of a personal computer's components, such as stereo sound, a CD-ROM drive, and a modem. **Laptop computers** are like notebook computers except that they are a bit too large to fit into a briefcase. Fewer laptops are being sold now that the smaller notebooks have become so powerful.

Subnotebooks are notebook computers that omit some components (such as a CD-ROM drive) to cut down on weight and size. A significant advantage is that some of them weigh less than three pounds. One disadvantage is that users must often carry along external disk drives with their attendant wiring.

Personal digital assistants (**PDAs**), sometimes called **handheld computers**, pack much of a notebook's power into a much lighter package. Most include built-in software for appointments, scheduling, and e-mail, and **pen computers** accept handwritten input.

Network computers (**NCs**) provide much of a personal computer's functionality but at a lower price. Because they get their software from a computer network, they don't need disk drives. In the consumer market, NCs such as WebTV enable consumers to use their televisions to connect to the Internet.

Professional workstations provide powerful tools for engineers, architects, circuit designers, financial analysts, and other professionals who need exceptionally powerful processing and output capabilities. They're the most expensive type of computers made for individuals.

microcomputer or PC

handheld computer

laptop

workstation

Figure 1.14
Computers for Individuals.

Computers for Organizations

Servers are computers that are not designed to be used directly. They make programs and data available for people hooked up to a computer network. To use servers, employees run desktop programs called **clients**, which know how to contact the server and obtain the needed information. This use of desktop clients and centralized servers is called **client/server computing**. It plays an important role in today's businesses. Servers range in cost from $5,000 to $150,000.

Minicomputers are multiuser systems that can handle the computing needs of a smaller corporation or organization. They enable dozens, hundreds, or even thousands of people to use them simultaneously by means of remote terminals or personal computers. Minicomputers range in cost from $10,000 to several hundred thousand dollars.

Mainframes are huge multiuser systems designed to handle gigantic processing jobs in large corporations or government agencies, such as handling an airline's reservations. Some mainframes are designed to be used by hundreds of thousands of people. People connect with mainframes using **terminals** (remote keyboard and display units) as well as personal computers. Mainframes are usually stored in special, secure rooms that have a controlled climate. They generally cost several hundred thousand to several million dollars.

Supercomputers are ultrafast computers designed to process huge amounts of scientific data and then display the underlying patterns that have been discovered. In 2000, IBM announced that it had built a supercomputer capable of executing 12 trillion calculations per second. Known as the ASCI White, the supercomputer covers an area the size of two basketball courts and is used by the Department of Energy. In March of 2002, Japan's NEC Corporation announced it had created an even faster supercomputer. The system, known as "the Earth Simulator," takes up the space of four tennis courts and is said to be five times faster than the ASCI White. Such supercomputers can cost hundreds of millions of dollars.

Figure 1.15
Computers for Organizations

Introducing Software: Telling the Computer What to Do

In a computer system, **software** includes all the programs that give the computer's hardware its step-by-step marching orders. Without software to tell it what to do, the computer is completely useless.

CREATING SOFTWARE

Trained experts called **programmers** create computer programs by writing instructions in a **programming language**, a special-purpose language that enables them to describe step-by-step processes. Most programming languages are designed to make things easy for the human programmers rather than the computer. Before a program can be used, the **source code**—the program instructions as they are actually written by the programmer—must be translated into **object code**, which the computer can read. Most object code is created by programs called **compilers**, which read the source code and generate the object code as output. In software, a **module** is a part of a program. Programs are composed of one or more independently developed modules that are not combined until the program is compiled.

USING SOFTWARE

Most computer programs are not a single entity; instead, they consist of hundreds or even thousands of distinct units, called **files**, that must be properly installed on the computer's hard disk. A file is a basic unit of storage in a computer system. Every file has a name and is stored along with a variety of attributes. An **attribute** is a setting that provides information such as the file's date of creation, its size, and the date it was last modified. Because most programs consist of many files, they are

sometimes called packages. A **package** is a set of program files, as well as associated data and configuration files, that are all designed to work together.

In order to use a compiled program, you must transfer the program to the computer's memory. This process, called **loading**, enables the program to **execute** (carry out the instructions that it contains).

TYPES OF SOFTWARE

You can divide programs into two categories: system software and application software. **System software** includes all the programs that help the computer function properly. **Application software** consists of all the programs you can use to perform a task such as writing a research paper or browsing the Web.

SYSTEM SOFTWARE

System software falls into two general categories: the operating system and system utilities.

Operating System (OS)

The most important type of system software is the computer's **operating system** (**OS**). The operating system is designed to work with a specific type of hardware, such as a PC or a Macintosh. Its most important role lies in coordinating the various functions of the computer's hardware. The operating system also provides support for running application software. Before you can use your computer, the operating system must be loaded into memory, which usually takes a minute or two.

Most operating systems come with a built-in **user interface**. The user interface provides the means by which users and programs communicate with each other.

Early computers offered only a primitive user interface, called a **command-line interface**. In this type of interface, users must interact with the computer by typing instructions at the keyboard, one line at a time. To ensure they are giving the command correctly, users must follow complicated rules, called **syntax**, that specify just how the command must be typed.

Figure 1.16
Windows XP provides a graphical user interface.

Computers would not have become a mass-market item without the development of the **graphical user interface** (**GUI**, pronounced "gooey"). In a GUI, users interact with the computer by choosing items from menus and using a pointing device to click on pictures, called **icons**, which represent various computer resources and commands (see Figure 1.16).

System Utilities

System software also includes a variety of **utility programs**, which are used to keep the computer system running smoothly. An example of a utility program is an **antivirus program**, which checks your system for computer viruses. As you probably know, a **computer virus** is rogue programming code, devised by a prankster, that attaches itself to the programs in your computer. If you give an "infected" program to other people and they run the program on their computers, the virus will spread.

APPLICATION SOFTWARE

Application software (also called applications) includes all the programs that enable you to apply your computer in a useful way.

Custom vs. Packaged Software

In the world of application software, a basic distinction is made between **custom software** and **packaged software** (also called **off-the-shelf software** or **shrink-wrapped software**).

As the name implies, custom software is developed by programmers to meet the specific needs of an organization, such as a company or a university. Custom software is expensive, but sometimes an organization's needs are so specialized that no alternative exists. An example of a custom software package is the grade tracking program used by your college's registrar's office.

Packaged software, in contrast, is aimed at a mass market that includes home as well as business users. Although packaged software can be customized, it is designed to be immediately useful in a wide variety of contexts. An example of packaged software is the presentations software program your professor may use to create class presentations. The payoff comes with the price: packaged software is much cheaper than custom software.

Office Applications

Office applications are the best-selling packaged software products. Whether sold individually or in an **office suite** (a package containing multiple programs; see Figure 1.17), they typically include the following:

- **Word processing programs** enable you to create, edit, and print your written work. They also offer commands that enable you to format your documents so that they have an attractive appearance. Although some people still prefer to use other writing tools, word processing programs are the most often used office suite software.

- **Spreadsheet programs** present users with a grid of rows and columns, the computer equivalent of an accountant's worksheet. By embedding formulas within the cells, you can create "live" worksheets in which changing one of the values forces the entire spreadsheet to be recalculated. Spreadsheets are indispensable tools for anyone who works with numbers.

- **Presentation graphics** programs enable you to create transparencies, slides, and handouts for oral presentations.

- **Database programs** give you the tools necessary to store data in an organized form, as well as to retrieve this data in such a way that it can be meaningfully summarized and displayed.

Figure 1. 17

Microsoft Office XP is a popular office suite containing a word processing program, a database program, a spreadsheet program, and a presentation graphics program.

The Internet

As you probably know, the **Internet** is "the" global network of networks. Currently, the Internet links hundreds of millions of users worldwide, providing them with a pool of shared resources (see Figure 1.18). According to growth rate estimates published in the respected journals *Science* and *Nature*, several billion pages of information are currently available on the Internet—and roughly four to five million more are added *each day*. According to the Internet Society, a professional organization devoted to advancing Internet technology, the Internet is on track to exceed the size of the global telephone network by 2006.

Most users connect to the Internet by means of a dial-up connection, which requires a modem and a telephone line. The connection is provided by an **Internet service provider** (**ISP**). Some ISPs are local mom-and-pop operations, whereas others are national or even international in scope.

To use the Internet, you take advantage of **Internet services**. An Internet service is a set of standards and software that make a specific type of resource available to Internet users, such as Web pages, files, or e-mail. Two types of software are required: client software and server software. Client software enables users to request a specific resource from the server. Server software accepts these requests and sends the resource to the client.

The following are the most popular Internet services:

Figure 1. 18
The Internet spans the entire globe.

- **E-mail** (short for electronic mail) enables Internet users to send and receive messages via the network (see Figure 1.19). Transmission isn't instantaneous, but it rarely exceeds five minutes. E-mail is fast becoming indispensable for individuals as well as businesses, and it is well on its way to replacing the postal system as the medium of choice for interpersonal written communication. To use e-mail, you need an e-mail address and an e-mail account. These are usually provided by your Internet service provider.

- The **World Wide Web** (**Web** or **WWW**) enables Internet users to access billions of **Web sites** worldwide. To use the Web, you need a client called a **Web browser**. Web browsers provide tools for accessing Web sites, searching the Web, and bookmarking your favorite pages. (Note that the Web is not the same thing as the Internet. The Web is the subset of sites that uses the Internet as its transportation system.)

- **Instant messaging systems**, such as Microsoft's Windows Messenger, let you know when a friend or business

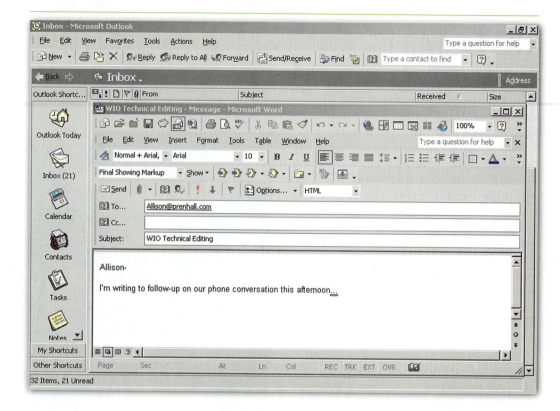

Figure 1.19
E-mail is an extremely popular form of interpersonal written communication.

associate is online (connected to the Internet). You can then contact this person and exchange near real-time messages (see Figure 1.20).

- **Electronic commerce (e-commerce)** involves all kinds of traditional business transactions, including buying, selling, renting, borrowing, and lending. Much e-commerce occurs in what you've

Figure 1. 20
Instant messaging is a popular way for Internet users to exchange near real-time messages.

heard referred to as the **dot-com** world, the universe of Internet sites with the suffix *com* appended to their names. Web-based retail sites, called **e-tailers**, sell books, CDs, clothes, and much more. Most successful among e-tailers are **click-and-brick** e-commerce sites, which offer the convenience of solving customer service issues and returns at a local conventional store. The bulk of e-commerce involves **business-to-business (B2B)** exchanges, which link corporations with suppliers, research labs, and industrial customers. E-commerce isn't about to replace older methods of buying and selling, but e-commerce is still growing, and some e-commerce sites, such as auctioning giant eBay, are highly profitable.

- **Peer-to-peer (P2P)** data exchange networks enable Internet users to make computer resources (including videos, images, and music files) available to other users.

- **File Transfer Protocol (FTP)** enables Internet users to exchange files via the Internet. Web browsers can act as FTP clients.

HOME | Takeaway Points | Key Terms and Concepts | Matching | Multiple Choice | Fill-In | Short Answer | Exercises/Projects | Web Research | **CHAPTER REVIEW**

TAKEAWAY POINTS

- Computer fluency refers to the ease with which people are able to navigate the digital world successfully. Computer-literate people are able to adapt to new computer technologies with ease and grasp the risks as well as the benefits of these new technologies.

- A computer is a machine that, under a program's direction and control, performs the following four operations: input, processing, output, and storage. These four operations are called the information processing cycle.

- In batch processing, the four basic computer operations are performed in a rigid sequence: input, processing, output, and storage. In interactive processing, the user can initiate and repeat information processing cycles without beginning a new session for each one.

- Spell-checking a word processing document exemplifies the information processing cycle. The input consists of the original document, which contains spelling mistakes. In processing, the computer detects and flags possible spelling errors by checking every word in the document against a massive spelling dictionary. Output consists of a list of words that the spell-checker doesn't find in its library. User interaction is required to confirm whether the apparent misspelling needs to be corrected. The user saves the corrected document to storage for future use.

- A computer system is a collection of related components that have been designed to work together. It includes both the computer's hardware (its physical components) and its software (the programs that run on it).

- In a typical desktop personal computer, a keyboard and a mouse provide input capabilities, while the processing is done by the microprocessor (CPU) and RAM (random access memory). You see the results (output) on a monitor, and you typically use a hard disk for long-term storage.

- System software refers to the programs that help the computer function properly, such as the operating system and system utilities. Application programs enable users to perform useful tasks.

- The Internet is "the" network of networks. The more the Internet grows, the richer its resources become.

- Popular Internet services include e-mail, the Web, instant messaging systems, e-commerce, peer-to-peer data exchange networks, and FTP file transfer.

1
2
3
4
5
6
7
8
9
10
11
12
13
14
15
16

Go to **www.prenhall.com/ciyf2004** to review this chapter, answer the questions, and complete the exercises and Web research questions.

KEY TERMS AND CONCEPTS

algorithm
antivirus program
application software
arrow keys
attribute
batch processing
business-to-business (B2B)
cathode ray tube (CRT)
CD-ROM drive
central processing unit (CPU)
character
character set
chip
click-and-brick
clients
client/server computing
command
command-line interface
communications device
compiler
computer
computer fluency
computer literate
computer network
computer system
computer virus
confirmation
cursor
custom software
data
database program
desktop computer
dot-com
DVD-ROM drive
e-commerce (electronic commerce)
e-mail (electronic mail)
error message
e-tailer
execute
expansion card
expansion slot
file
File Transfer Protocol (FTP)
flat-panel display
floppy disk
floppy disk drive
gigabyte (GB)
graphical user interface (GUI)
handheld computer

hard disk drive
hardware
IBM-compatible personal computer
icon
impact printer
information
information overload
information processing cycle
inkjet printer
input
input device
insertion point
instant messaging system
interactive processing
Internet
Internet service provider (ISP)
Internet services
keyboard
laser printer
laptop computer
LCD display
loading
local area network (LAN)
magnetic storage media
mainframe
megabytes (MB)
memory
microcomputer
microphone
microprocessor
minicomputer
modem
module
monitor
motherboard
mouse
network interface card (NIC)
network computer (NC)
network medium
nonimpact printer
notebook computer
object code
off-the-shelf software
office application
office suite
operating system (OS)
optical storage media
output
output device

package
packaged software
peer-to-peer (P2P) data exchange network
pen computer
peripheral
personal computer
personal digital assistant (PDA)
pointer
pointing device
printer
presentation graphics program
processing
processor
professional workstation
program
programmer
programming language
random access memory (RAM)
reading
read-only device
read/write device
server
software
source code
speakers
speech recognition software
spreadsheet program
storage
storage device
storage media
subnotebook
supercomputer
syntax
system software
system unit
terminal
user interface
utility program
volatile
Web browser
Web site
word processing program
World Wide Web (Web or WWW)
writing
Zip disk
Zip drive

HOME | Takeaway Points | Key Terms and Concepts | **Matching** | Multiple Choice | Fill-In | Short Answer | Exercises/ Projects | Web Research | CHAPTER REVIEW

MATCHING

Match each key term in the left column with the most accurate definition in the right column.

_____ 1. program

_____ 2. processing

_____ 3. hardware

_____ 4. software

_____ 5. modem

_____ 6. server

_____ 7. operating system

_____ 8. electronic mail

_____ 9. antivirus

_____ 10. file

_____ 11. bug

_____ 12. mouse

_____ 13. NIC

_____ 14. cyberphobia

_____ 15. mainframe

a. the most important type of system software

b. a utility software application

c. an error or defect in an electrical or electronic system

d. a software application that enables Internet users to send and receive messages

e. an exaggerated fear of computers

f. a list of instructions that describes how to perform input, processing, output, and storage operations to accomplish a task

g. includes all the programs that give the computer its instructions

h. the computer's physical components

i. connects a computer to a local area network

j. a pointing device that moves an on-screen pointer

k. a computer that is used by large companies or government agencies

l. the operation that describes the computer performing arithmetic or comparison operations

m. enables a computer to access other computers and the Internet via a telephone line

n. makes programs and data available for people connected to a computer network

o. the basic unit of storage in a computer system

CHAPTER REVIEW: 1 2 3 4 5 6 7 8 9 10 11 12 13 14 15 16

MULTIPLE CHOICE

Circle the correct choice for each of the following.

1. What are the four basic operations performed by a computer?
   a. Processing, communication, storage, data creation
   b. Input, processing, output, storage
   c. Input, output, storage, communication
   d. Input, printing, storage, retrieval

2. Which of the following is a common input device?
   a. Keyboard
   b. Printer
   c. Disk drive
   d. Monitor

3. Which of the following is not a type of output device?
   a. Monitor
   b. Speakers
   c. Printer
   d. Mouse

4. Which of the following is not a type of storage?
   a. Floppy drive
   b. DVD-ROM
   c. Microphone
   d. Zip disk

5. When referring to memory, what does the acronym RAM mean?
   a. Read and manipulate
   b. Random access memory
   c. Refreshable auxiliary memory
   d. Read alone memory

6. Which of the following is an example of the earliest computer?
   a. Supercomputer
   b. Mainframe computer
   c. Minicomputer
   d. Personal computer

7. What does the acronym PDA stand for?
   a. Personal data aid
   b. Professional digital attachment
   c. Personal digital assistant
   d. Programmable data acquisition

8. Which of the following is not considered application software?
   a. Operating system software
   b. Project management software
   c. Word processing software
   d. Presentation graphics software

9. This application is not typically included in an office suite.
   a. Word processor
   b. Spreadsheet
   c. Database
   d. Antivirus

10. Which of the following characterizes local area networks?
    a. Often use high-speed fiber-optic cables and satellites
    b. Create point-to-point connections between widely separated computers
    c. A network capable of spanning the globe
    d. Limited in geographic scope, creating a community of computers

COMPUTERS IN YOUR FUTURE 2004

1.27

HOME | Takeaway Points | Key Terms and Concepts | Matching | Multiple Choice | Fill-In | Short Answer | Exercises/ Projects | Web Research | CHAPTER REVIEW

FILL-IN

In the blanks provided, write the correct answer for each of the following.

1. A _____ allows users to interact with the computer by choosing items from menus or clicking on icons.

2. An _____ refers to the overall, step-by-step procedure used to solve a problem.

3. _____ are also known as flat-panel displays.

4. Trained experts who create computer programs are called _____.

5. Professional _____ are tools for professionals who need powerful processing and output capabilities.

6. Before a program can be used, a _____ must translate the source code into object code.

7. A type of notebook computer that is actually smaller that a notebook computer is called a _____.

8. The two basic types of storage media are _____ and _____.

9. The _____ is the computer's main circuit board.

10. _____ software enables users to exchange files via the Internet.

11. The bulk of e-commerce involves _____, which links corporations with suppliers, research labs, and industrial customers.

12. _____ software transcribes spoken words into on-screen text, or allows a user to control a computer by giving spoken commands.

13. A _____ is rogue programming code that can attach itself to programs on a computer.

14. Program instructions as they are actually written by a programmer must be translated into _____, which the computer can read.

15. Most users connect to the Internet using an _____.

SHORT ANSWER

1. Define computer fluency. Why is it important to be computer-fluent?

2. What is the difference between hardware and software?

3. What is the difference between system software and application software? Provide an example of each.

4. Explain the difference between packaged software and custom software. Which type of software would a typical individual user buy? Give an example of such a purchase.

5. Describe your experiences with the Internet. Specifically, identify the browser and e-mail software applications that you have used. Have you used other Internet-related software? If you have, describe these applications.

6. Select a course that you are taking this semester. List two course activities that could require the use of a computer, and identify two different software applications that would be needed to complete these activities.

Chapter review numbers: 1 2 3 4 5 6 7 8 9 10 11 12 13 14 15 16

CHAPTER REVIEW | Takeaway Points | Key Terms and Concepts | Matching | Multiple Choice | Fill-In | Short Answer | Exercises/ Projects | Web Research | HOME

1 2 3 4 5 6 7 8 9 10 11 12 13 14 15 16

EXERCISES/PROJECTS

1. What type of network do you use in your lab at school? How are the computers connected? What effect does the network have on the work you do at school? Can you connect to the campus network from off-campus?

2. Institutions usually provide on-campus Internet connections. Contact your institution's computing services and see if they provide off-campus Internet connections. If they do provide this connectivity, do students pay an extra fee for this service, or is it funded from general student fees? If your school does not provide off-campus Internet access, how do you connect to the Internet, and what are the monthly fees?

3. For various reasons, most individuals use either a desktop or, if they want or need more portability, a laptop computer. Use the Internet or contact a local vendor and compare the prices for comparably equipped desktop and laptop computers. Based on your needs and finances, explain which computer you would buy, and give reasons to support your purchase. Why or why would you not consider purchasing a subnotebook or handheld computer in place of a desktop or laptop?

4. Have you ever made a copy of software that you've bought for yourself? Did you ever give a copy of it away? Although purchasers are permitted to make a backup copy of software that they have purchased, they are not allowed to make additional copies and distribute them to others. What are your feelings about software piracy, that is, making illegal copies of software? Originally, software applications were installed from a series of floppy disks. However, since most software is now supplied on CD-ROMs, copies must be created using a "CD burner." Do you own or have access to one of these burners?

5. Contact a faculty member in the department of your current or intended major and determine what software applications are needed by professionals in this discipline. List these applications, and explain how they are used.

COMPUTERS IN YOUR FUTURE 2004

1.29

HOME | Takeaway Points | Key Terms and Concepts | Matching | Multiple Choice | Fill-In | Short Answer | Exercises/ Projects | Web Research | CHAPTER REVIEW

WEB RESEARCH

1. The speed at which the Internet is growing is phenomenal, and the number of users can only be estimated. To compare the growth of the Internet with that of other media, visit the Computer Almanac site at **www-2.cs.cmu.edu/afs/cs.cmu.edu/user/bam/www/numbers.html**. This site is an online treasury of statistical information about computers. How many years did it take radio to have 50 million listeners? How many years did it take television to achieve 50 million viewers? How many years did it take the Web to reach 50 million U.S. users? (This is a lengthy Web site, so use your browser's *find on page* feature, and search for "50 million.")

2. Major software companies frequently release new versions of their popular software packages. At the time you read this book, Microsoft should have just released or be near release of its new Office product. To see if this software is worth its several hundred–dollar price tag, visit Microsoft's comparison site at **http://microsoft.com/office/evaluation/indepth/compare.asp** and identify a new feature in each of the following areas:

   - Productivity and Efficiency
   - Access to Information
   - Reliability, Data Recovery, and Security
   - Collaborative Document Review
   - Collaborating with Others: Integration with SharePoint Team Services
   - Connecting and Coordinating with Others

   Which two of the new features are most important to you? Explain why you would or would not purchase or upgrade this product.

3. Easter eggs are special, fun screens or information that software developers put into commercial versions of software. Many different programs include Easter eggs. You can find out about some existing Easter eggs at The Easter Egg Archive at **www.eeggs.com**. How difficult is it to display Easter eggs in some programs? Using the information from the Web site, can you locate any Easter eggs in the programs on your computer? Which Easter eggs surprised you the most?

4. Compared with the other types of computers, supercomputers are very small in number. Some major universities (such as the University of Tokyo), specialized governmental organizations (such as NASA), and businesses (such as Verizon) use these extremely fast and expensive computers. Visit the list of the world's most powerful computing sites to see some other types of organizations, agencies, and companies that have supercomputers. Begin your search at: **www.top500.org**.

   - What is the minimum processing speed needed to be included in this list?
   - What are the type and speed of the supercomputer that is used by George Lucas's Industrial Light and Magic (ILM) company to make movie special effects?
   - What are the types of supercomputers that CitiBank uses to maintain its many accounts?
   - What are the types and speeds of supercomputers that AOL uses to maintain its vast databases?
   - What are the types and speeds of supercomputers that the FBI uses to maintain its enormous number of records?

5. Using media such as radio, television, newspapers, and, of course, the Internet, people are able to obtain information about current events. The Internet Public Library maintains a worldwide list of newspapers at **www.ipl.org**. This site allows international students attending schools in the United States to read (in their native languages) about events that are happening in their countries. This site also allows U.S. students to read (in English) about global political, financial, or cultural events from the perspective of other nations. Can you think of other reasons why someone would read "foreign" newspapers?

   Find the headline or lead story from the following newspapers:

   - The *Cape Argus*, published in Cape Town, South Africa
   - The *Viet Nam News*, published in Hanoi, Vietnam
   - The *Buenos Aires Herald*, published in Buenos Aires, Argentina
   - The *Moscow Times*, published in Moscow, Russia
   - The *Kuwait Times*, published in Kuwait City, Kuwait

CHAPTER REVIEW 1 2 3 4 5 6 7 8 9 10 11 12 13 14 15 16

Spotlight

FILE MANAGEMENT

Learning to manage your computer files is an essential step in becoming computer-fluent. Fortunately, you only have to learn two main things: the big picture of file management (what files, folders, and paths are), and the specific practice of actually managing your files.

For most people, managing files is an intuitive task and is simple once they learn the basics. You can think of managing files as being similar to managing the way you store food and utensils in your kitchen, or files and folders in a file cabinet (see Figure 1A). We've always categorized and organized items for storage, and the principles are the same when managing files in a computer.

Let's start our exploration of file management by taking a look at the big picture.

The Big Picture: Files, Folders, and Paths

You've probably worked with computers enough to know that a **file** is simply a storage device for digital data. Files store such things as Microsoft Word documents, MP3 music, photo images, Excel spreadsheets, applications, and a variety of other digital compilations.

Files are usually organized in **folders**. Folders help you to organize groups of files that have something in common. For example, if you had a folder called "Classes," you could store all the drafts of your college essays. Many folders have **subfolders**—or folders within folders—that allow you to organize your files even further. For example, in your Classes folder, you may have two subfolders: one for your class called Expository Writing 101 and one for your class called Biology 201.

All files and folders you create on your computer must reside on a storage device, called a **drive**. Storage devices are called drives because they have motors that "drive" the movement of the media that store your data. The primary storage devices on desktop computers are the **hard disk**, a **CD-RW**, **floppy disks**, and **Zip disks**. If you

Figure 1A
Your computer's digital storage organization is like that of a filing cabinet.

have such a CD read-write drive, you can store your files by burning them to the CD in the drive.

On PCs, storage devices are designated by **drive letters**. The floppy disk is almost always referred to as Drive A and is usually indicated by a following colon and backslash character: A:\. The hard disk is generally referred to as Drive C (C:\). Other drives such as an external Zip drive might be labeled Drive D (D:\). (On the Mac, the drives are not labeled with letters. You'll see them as icons appearing on your screen.)

In order for your computer to access a particular file, it needs to know the **path** it should take to get to the file. A typical path might look like this:

C:\Classes\Expository Writing 101\Homework #1\Summer_essay_draft1.doc

In this case, the C:\ in the path indicates that the file is located on the C drive. The **primary folder**, "Classes," contains, as the name indicates, things that have to do with classes. The folder named "Expository Writing 101" is one of the **secondary folders** (or subfolders) in the Classes folder. You have multiple homework assignments to complete in your writing class. The folder named

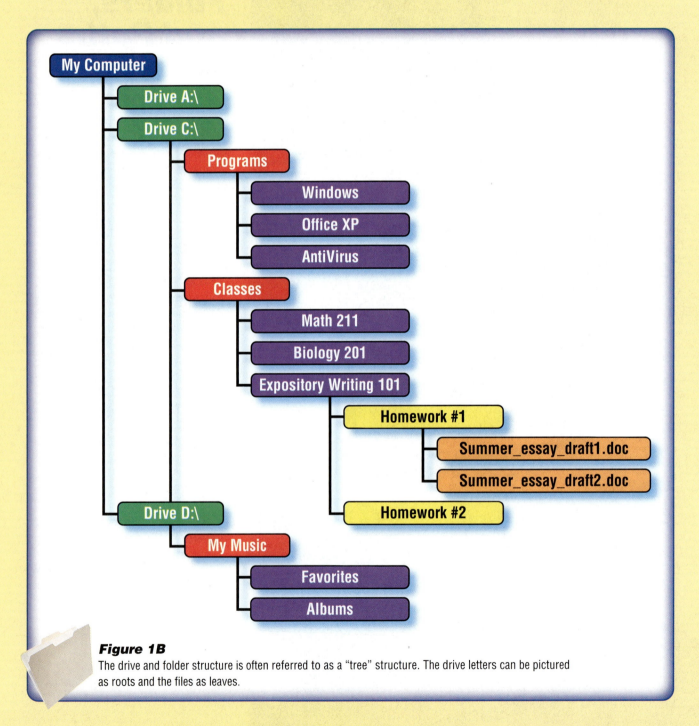

Figure 1B
The drive and folder structure is often referred to as a "tree" structure. The drive letters can be pictured as roots and the files as leaves.

"Homework #1" is a **tertiary folder**. The file at the end of the path (Summer_essay_draft1.doc) is your attempt at completing your first homework assignment. The .doc extension on the file indicates that it is in the Microsoft Word format. (We'll discuss folder structures and file extensions in greater depth shortly.)

Figure 1B illustrates what a hierarchical drive, folder, and file structure might look like.

FILE NAMING CONVENTIONS

As is obvious from our discussion so far, in order to save a file, you need to know where you're going to store it—in other words, in which storage device and in which folder. In addition, each file needs a specific **filename**. The filename is the name that the storage device uses to identify the file uniquely, so the name must differ from all other filenames used within the same folder.

Every filename has two parts, which are separated by a period (sometimes called a dot). The first part, the part you're most familiar with, is called, simply, the **name**. The second part is called the **extension**. In a file called Summer_essay_draft1.doc, Summer_essay_draft1 is the name and .doc is the extension; together they make up the filename.

Typically, extensions are used to identify the type of data that the file contains (or the **format** it is stored in), and sometimes the application that created the file. In Microsoft Windows, many applications automatically assign an extension to a file when you save it for the first time. For example, Microsoft Word automatically assigns the .doc extension. Workbooks created in Microsoft Excel use the .xls extension. **Program files** (also called **application files**) usually use the .exe

Commonly Used Extensions

Extension	File Type
.exe	Program or Application
.doc	Microsoft Word
.xls	Microsoft Excel
.ppt	Microsoft PowerPoint
.mbd	Microsoft Access
.pdf	Adobe
.txt	SimpleText
.htm or .html	Web pages
.rtf	Files in Rich Text Format
.jpeg or .jpg	Picture or image format

Figure 1C

extension, which stands for "executable." The term **executable** is used because when you use an application, you execute, or run, the file.

Figure 1C lists the most commonly used extensions and their file types. Note that in Mac OS, extensions are not needed because Macintosh files include a code representing the name of the application that created the file. However, it's generally recommended that Mac users add a three-letter extension to their filenames so that they can more easily exchange them with PC users.

Even Web addresses use file naming conventions. The ubiquitous term *dot-com* was created because the extension *com* is used to designate commercial Web sites. Other Web site types are .edu for higher education, .au for Australia, .uk for the United Kingdom, .net for noncommercial groups, .gov for governmental agencies, and .org for not-for-profit organizations. In 2002, several new extensions were created, including .biz for businesses; .info for portals, libraries, and information services; and .us for the United States.

In the early days of DOS and Windows 3.1, filenames were limited to eight characters for the name and three characters for the extension. Today, you can use up to 250 characters in a filename in Microsoft Windows, and you're also allowed to use spaces. Filenames in Microsoft Windows cannot include any of the following characters: forward slash (/), backslash (\), greater than sign (>), less than sign (<), asterisk (*), question mark (?), quotation mark ("), pipe symbol (|), colon (:), or semicolon (;). In Mac OS, you can use up to 31 characters in a filename, including spaces and all characters except a colon.

Now that you understand the basics of paths, folders, and file naming conventions, let's turn our attention to the business of managing files.

Managing Files

Files can be managed in two ways: with a file management utility such as My Computer, and from within the programs that create them. In the following sections, we'll explore both methods.

Figure 1D

The default view in the My Computer program is divided into two panes: the left pane shows system tasks and links to other places; the right pane shows the various files and drives you can choose from.

Figure 1E

When you click the Folders button on the Standard Buttons toolbar in My Computer, you'll see the file management view.

FILE MANAGEMENT UTILITIES

The primary file management utility for PCs is the My Computer program. The My Computer icon is usually available on your desktop as well as on the right panel on the Start menu.

My Computer opens by default to the familiar Windows title bar, menu bar, and a toolbar (see Figure 1D). The window is split into two panes. The **left pane** displays links to system tasks, such as viewing system information, adding and removing programs, and changing a setting. The left pane also links to places other than the physical system you're working on, such as My Network Places, My Documents, Shared Documents, and the Control Panel.

In the default view, the left pane is dynamic; that is, if you click items in the **right pane**, the left pane gives you choices that are specific to the particular folder or drive you've clicked. You can use this view to manage folders and files. Simply double-click the drive name in the right pane, and the left pane will change to show you the tasks you can accomplish, such as creating, managing, and deleting folders and files.

To use My Computer in strictly file management mode, click the Folders button on the Standard Buttons toolbar. In file management view, the left pane shows the names of the drives and folders, and the right pane shows the folders and files within the folders (see Figure 1E). To open drives or folders, simply click the icons in the left pane. To open folders and files, double-click the icons in the right pane.

You can view the contents of the right pane in several ways. The different views are accessible from the View menu or from the View button on the Standard toolbar. The thumbnail view is particularly helpful if you're searching through pictures and photographs because it allows you to preview a thumbnail-sized copy of the images you

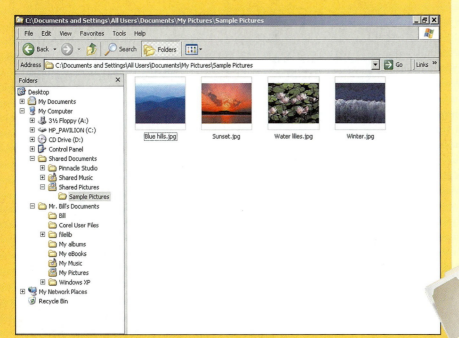

have in the folder before you open them (see Figure 1F). The list view simply lists the names of the files, whereas the details view offers you information regarding file size, file type, and the date the file was last modified (see Figure 1G).

Creating Folders

In order to manage your files effectively, you'll need to create a **folder structure**—an organized set of folders within which to save your

Figure 1F
The thumbnail view is especially handy for previewing images.

Figure 1G
The details view allows you to see the file size, file type, and the date the file was last modified.

files. The process of creating a folder structure is both simple and easy, and is accomplished in just two steps:

Step 1. Decide which physical storage location, such as a floppy disk, hard disk, CD-R or CD-RW disc, you want to create your folder on. Click the device letter or designator in the left pane of your file management utility.

Step 2. Establish the primary or **top-level folder**. Choose the File, New, Folder menu sequence to place a new folder at the root of the storage device or in a selected folder. In other words, if you have selected the C:\ drive, the new folder will be placed at the top level. See Figure 1H for an example of a new folder that has been created at the root of the C:\ drive.

If, however, you have selected a top level or deeper folder as your beginning point, then the new folder will be placed within it (see Figure 1I).

You can repeat this process as many times as is necessary to create your desired folder structure. For example, if you're taking three classes, you might want to create three separate subfolders with the appropriate class names under a top-level folder called Classes. That way, you'll know exactly where to save files each time you create them and you'll avoid having a cluttered and disorganized desktop.

Of course, creating a well-organized folder structure requires that you add, rename, and move folders as your needs change. For example, if you add a class to your schedule, you'll want to create a new subfolder in your top-level Classes folder. Likewise, next semester you may want to rename your Classes folder "Classes-Fall Semester 2004," or move the folder altogether.

Transferring Folders and Files

Once you've created a folder structure that fits your needs, you're ready to create new files or

Figure 1H
This top-level folder on the hard disk has been created at the root of the C:\ drive.

Figure 1I
This new folder (a tertiary folder) is located three levels deep on the hard disk.

transfer already existing files and folders. We'll cover creating new files in the next section. For now let's look at transferring files and folders among drives and directories, an important skill involved in basic file management.

There are two basic ways to transfer your files and folders: you can move them or you can copy them. You move items that you simply wish to relocate, whereas you copy items that you wish to keep in more than one folder or on alternative storage devices.

The easiest way to accomplish these tasks is simply to right-drag the folders and files you want to move or copy to the new location. When you release the right mouse button, a context-sensitive menu appears, allowing you to choose the result of your right-drag (see Figure 1J). The choices on this menu are to move, copy, create a shortcut, or cancel the action.

- **Moving** is similar to cutting and pasting; the file or folder is moved from its original location to a new location.

- **Copying** creates a duplicate folder(s) or file(s) at the new location and leaves the existing folder(s) or file(s) as is.

- **Creating a shortcut** leaves the original in place and creates a pointer that will take you to the folder or file you've created the shortcut to. This action is handy for placing shortcuts on the desktop to your favorite programs or to files that you often access.

If you **left-drag** a folder or file *within the same drive*, the folder or file is automatically moved to the new location on the drive. When left-dragging *between drives*, the default action is to create a copy of the folder or file in the new location.

Right-clicking a file or folder invokes a context-sensitive menu

that allows you to choose among many common tasks, such as copying, deleting, renaming, and creating shortcuts (see

Figure 1K). You may also use the File menu or toolbars to accomplish these and other file management tasks.

Figure 1J
The right-drag context-sensitive menu allows you to move, copy, create a shortcut, or cancel the action.

Figure 1K
The right-click custom menu allows you to choose from many common tasks.

Figure 1L

When you use the Open dialog box in Microsoft Word, it displays only the files in a folder that have the .doc extension.

Figure 1M

The Save As dialog box allows you to designate the drive or folder you want to save your file in, as well as the filename you want the file to have.

PROGRAM-ENABLED FILE MANAGEMENT

As we mentioned earlier, in Microsoft Windows, all software applications use program-specific filename extensions. The advantage of using a default file extension is that both you and your computer will easily be able to associate the file with the program with which it was created. By using appropriate extensions, you can double-click a file in a file management utility and the computer will launch the appropriate application.

In addition, with file extensions, when you use the File, Open command sequence from within an application, the Open dialog window displays only those files that have the appropriate filename extension. For example, as you can see in Figure 1L, the Open dialog box in Microsoft Word displays all files in a folder that have the .doc extension.

Save or Save As?

The biggest decision you'll make when using application programs to manage files is whether to use the **Save** or **Save As** command when you save files. When you choose the Save command under the File menu, the program takes what you've created or modified in memory and writes over or replaces the file that is stored on disk. Note that the *initial* File, Save menu sequence always invokes the Save As dialog box because the drive, path, and filename must be designated the first time a file is saved.

Thus, the Save command doesn't allow you to designate a different drive, folder, or filename; it simply replaces what is stored on disk with the contents of memory. The Save As command, however, does allow you to change one or all of these parameters (see Figure 1M). You might also use the Save As command to save an additional copy of your finished work on a floppy disk or in an alternate folder as a backup, just in case something happens to your original work. It's often advisable to save intermediate copies of your work, thus allowing you to go back to a previous version should something go wrong with a subsequent version.

Other Management Tasks

Most software applications allow you to perform file management tasks such as deleting, renaming, copying, and creating shortcuts to files. Right-clicking a file in either the Save As or Open dialog box invokes file management commands (see Figure 1N). You may also use software applications to create folders.

Computer Management

Computers, like any other piece of equipment or machinery, need to be managed. This section covers basic computer management practices and principles.

SOFTWARE MANAGEMENT

The number one rule in effectively and safely managing your computer is to purchase your own copy of every program, or to be sure that any shareware or freeware is from a reliable source and is virus-free. This is the best practice for several reasons:

• It respects the right of the manufacturer to receive compensation for its work.

• It provides you with programs in their full and unadulterated form.

Figure 1N
Right-clicking a file in either the Save As or Open dialog box invokes file management commands.

Figure 1O
Always use the Add or Remove Programs feature in your computer's Control Panel when you're removing a program.

ANTIVIRUS PROTECTION

Unfortunately, it is the case today that we must protect our computers from **viruses**. We are all vulnerable to those misfortunate individuals who unleash these worthless and destructive programs on us. Fortunately, there are **antivirus programs** that help catch viruses before they infect our computers, such as Norton AntiVirus and McAfee Virus Scan Online (see Figure 1P).

There are two things you should remember about antivirus programs:

- They need to be updated regularly.

- They need to be used every time you put a new file or program on your computer.

- It's the only legal way to own programs and software.

- It's your moral and ethical responsibility.

In addition, when you own an original and legitimate copy of a program, you're entitled to certain warranties and guarantees. You often qualify for technical assistance, upgrades, or other forms of support, and you can expect that the manufacturer will stand behind its product should there be a bug or defect.

Once you've purchased software, read the directions before and during installation. Know where the program is being installed, how to access it, and whether shortcuts have been created on the desktop. Shortcuts will usually use the company logo for an icon and will have a title that is the name of the program. If you don't want these shortcuts on your desktop, delete them by right-clicking them and choosing delete. This doesn't affect the program in any way; remember, a shortcut is just a pointer to a program or file. The program will still be available via the Start, Programs menu sequence.

The proper way to remove a program from your computer is to choose the **Add or Remove Programs** icon located on the Control Panel, which is listed on the Start menu (see Figure 1O). Choose the program that you wish to uninstall from the list of installed programs. Be advised: simply deleting the program icon from the Start menu doesn't remove the program. Neither does deleting the program files from within a file management utility. This is because most programs create library files and ancillary files in various directories; these files won't be removed if you delete the program icon or delete the program file from within the file management utility. The operating system may not run efficiently if you don't remove program files correctly, so always use the uninstall utility to remove unwanted programs.

Figure 1P
Antivirus software is an essential add-on to today's computers.

Figure 1Q
Visit Snopes.com for information on urban legends, folklore, and hoaxes.

Files can get onto your computer in only a few ways. You can create the file yourself, you can receive the file as an e-mail attachment, or you can load the file from a floppy disk, CD or DVD drive, or from a network connection. If you take the time to scan all files that come to your computer from an external source, you'll be well on your way to a virus-free computing experience.

Should your computer become infected with a virus, run your antivirus program to try to eradicate the virus before it causes any more damage. You may need to reinstall or run fix-and-repair on programs that have been infected or affected.

A particularly insidious pseudo-virus that has been making the rounds for several years now works like this: You receive an e-mail, usually from a friend, with a dire warning about a new virus that will "wipe out your hard drive." The letter goes on to say that "fortunately for you" there is a way to eradicate the virus by following a few steps. If you follow these steps, you end up deleting a file that your system needs either to run at all or at least to run efficiently. So, the result is that, by following the directions, you actually cause harm to your own system. You see, there is no virus to begin with—the "virus" is the fact that we all trust and follow directions, and in doing so cause damage to our own systems. Insidious at best!

For information about computer hoaxes such as this, visit **www.snopes.com** (see Figure 1.Q). You can also find good information at **www.urbanlegends.about.com**.

A Few Last Reminders...

Don't be intimidated by file or computer management. Computers are tremendously complex and powerful devices, but the principles of managing the computer are simple. Always begin at the beginning. If something doesn't work, go back to when it did, or install it again. Read the manuals. Follow the directions carefully. Make backup copies of your work. Create folder structures and name files so that you can find them easily. And, if all else fails, don't be afraid to ask for help.

Inside the System Unit

What You'll Learn . . .

When you have finished reading this chapter, you will be able to:

1. Define the terminology that's used to describe how much data computers can transfer or store.

2. List the components found inside the system unit and explain their use.

3. List the components found on the computer's motherboard and explain the role they play in the functioning of the computer's systems.

4. Discuss (in general terms) how a computer's central processing unit (CPU) processes data.

5. Explain the characteristics that determine a microprocessor's performance.

6. List the various types of memory found in a computer system and explain the purpose of each.

7. Describe the various physical connectors on the exterior of the system unit and explain their use.

8. Differentiate between analog and digital methods of representing data and explain the advantages and disadvantages of each.

Describing Hardware Performance

Destinations

For a great Web guide to personal computer hardware, see "PC Guide" at **www.pcguide.com**. Author Charles Kozierok presents a free, detailed survey of PC system components, including special sections on system care, system enhancement, and troubleshooting. If you're looking to upgrade your system or understand what a particular component does, this site is a great place to start.

Before we launch into our discussion of the system unit and its components, it's important that you understand a few things about hardware performance. As you learned in the last chapter, computers perform four basic functions: inputting data, processing this data, displaying the results using output devices, and storing the results for subsequent use. Computer hardware, and especially the system unit, is involved in all of these functions. When we talk about hardware *performance*, we're referring to how much data the computer can store and how fast it can process this data. To understand the capabilities of computer hardware, you need to learn some of the terminology that's used to describe how much data computers can transfer or store.

BITS AND BYTES

A basic distinction differentiates bits from bytes:

- A **bit** (short for **binary digit**) is the basic unit of information in a computer. A bit is either a 1 or a 0, the only two options available in the computer's binary numbering system. Bits are the

point of reference for measuring the **data transfer rate** (the number of bits transmitted per second) of communication devices, such as modems. You can think of a bit as being similar to a light switch: it has only two possible states, and is always in one or the other. If you have one light switch, you have the possibility that the switch is on or that it is off. If you have two light switches, then you have four possibilities: both switches are on, both switches are off, the first switch is on and the second switch is off, or the first switch is off and the second switch is on. Three switches allow for eight possibilities, and so on—up to eight switches, which results in 256 possible combinations.

- A **byte** consists of eight bits. Since it takes eight bits (on/off switches) to make a byte, and eight bits result in 256 possible on/off combinations, you'll see the number 256 appearing behind the scenes in many computer functions and applications. A single byte usually represents one character of data, such as the essential numbers (0–9), the basic letters of the alphabet in English and European languages, and the most common punctuation symbols. For this reason, you can use the byte as a baseline for understanding just how much information a computer is storing. For example, a typical college essay contains 250 words per page, and each word contains (on average) 5.5 characters. So the page contains

Terms that Describe Units of Data

Term Equivalent	Abbreviation	Approximate Amount	Exact Amount	Text	
Kilobyte	KB or K	1 thousand bytes	1,024 bytes		(one page)
Megabyte	MB or M	1 million bytes	1,048,576 bytes		(1,000 pages)
Gigabyte	GB or G	1 billion bytes	1,043,741,824 bytes		(1,000 books)
Terabyte	TB or T	1 trillion bytes	1,099,511,627,776 bytes		(1 million books)

Figure 2.1

about 1,375 characters. In other words, you need about 1,375 bytes of storage for one page of a college paper.

MILLIONS, BILLIONS, AND MORE

As you've just learned, bits (1s and 0s) are commonly used for measuring the data transfer rates of computer communication devices such as modems, whereas bytes are commonly used to measure data storage. But computers fling millions of bits around, and they can store millions of bytes of data. For this reason, terms such as **kilobyte**, **megabyte**, **gigabyte**, and **terabyte** are used to describe larger units of data. Figure 2.1 fully defines these terms and shows how much data each is approximately equivalent to. Because computer data is stored using binary numbers (which we'll discuss later in the chapter), a kilobyte is not exactly one thousand bytes, nor is a megabyte exactly one million bytes. However, the exact amount is close enough that you can think in these rounded, approximate terms (one thousand, one million, or one billion) for most purposes.

To describe rapid data transfer rates, terms such as **kilobits per second** (**Kbps**), **megabits per second** (**Mbps**), and **gigabits per second** (**Gbps**) are used. These rates correspond (roughly) to one thousand, one million, and one billion bits per second. Remember that these terms refer to *bits* per second, not *bytes* per second. A modem that can transfer 53 Kbps (about 53,000 bits per second) is transferring only about 8,000 bytes per second, or about five pages of text.

Introducing the System Unit

Now that you understand bits, bytes, and other important hardware performance terminology, we can take a close look at the system unit, where these terms will come into play. The **system unit** is a box-like case that houses the computer's main hardware components (see Figure 2.2). The system unit is more than just a case, however; it provides a sturdy frame for

Figure 2.2 a–d
Every kind of computer has a system unit:
(a) Apple eMac
(b) desktop (c) laptop
(d) handheld.

Techtalk

ATX form factor
The form factor of today's standard personal computer case. The previous design, called the AT case, didn't handle ventilation very well. It drew air in from anywhere and expelled it by means of a fan mounted on the case's back cover. The result? Dust, dirt, and grime were drawn into the case, coating the components with a layer of greasy fuzz, which insulated them from the cooling fan. The ATX case solves this problem. It reverses the fan and adds a filter—which means that clean air is drawn into the case. If you're using a personal computer with an ATX case, be sure to keep the cover tightly sealed so the fan can do its work.

mounting internal components, protects these components from physical damage, and keeps them cool. A good case also provides room for system upgrades, such as additional disk drives.

System units come in a variety of styles. In some desktop computing systems, the system unit is a separate metal or plastic box that's designed to sit on top of a desk. Ideally, the case should have a small **footprint** (the amount of room taken up by the case on the desk). However, a small case may not have enough room for add-on components. One solution to this problem is the **tower case**, a large system unit case that is designed to sit on the floor next to a desk. Smaller versions of tower cases are called **minitower cases**.

Notebook computers and personal digital assistants (PDAs) are called **all-in-one computers** because the system unit contains all of the computer's components, including input components (such as a keyboard or pen interface) and the display. Some desktop computers, such as Apple's iMac, contain the display within the system unit (see Figure 2.3).

System units also vary in what is called their **form factor**. A form factor is a

specification for how internal components, such as the motherboard, are mounted in the system unit. Early desktop computers used the **AT form factor**, a system unit case design that was introduced with IBM's Personal Computer AT (short for Advanced Technology) in 1984. More recent desktop systems use **ATX form factor** cases. Developed by Intel, the ATX form factor provides better accessibility to system components, better cooling, more full-sized expansion slots, and a more convenient layout for system upgrades.

The following sections explore the system unit of a typical desktop computer, beginning with the most important component: the computer's motherboard.

INSIDE THE SYSTEM UNIT

Most computer users don't need to open their system unit: they receive their computer in a ready-to-use package. However, if you ever do need to open your system unit, for example, to install more memory, bear in mind that the computer's components are sensitive to static electricity. If you touch certain components while you're charged with static electricity, you could destroy them. Always disconnect the power cord before removing your computer's case, and discharge static electricity by touching something that's well grounded, such as a water faucet. If it's one of those dry days when you're getting shocked every time you touch a doorknob, don't work on your computer's internal components.

If you do open your system unit, you'll see the following components (see Figure 2.4):

- **Motherboard** The **motherboard** is a large **printed circuit board** (**PCB**), a flat piece of plastic or fiberglass that contains thousands of electrical circuits that are etched into the board's surface. They connect numerous plug-in receptacles, which accommodate the computer's most important components (such as the microprocessor). The motherboard contains the computer's **central processing unit** (**CPU**). You'll learn more about the CPU later in the chapter; for now remember that the

Figure 2.3 a&b
(a) The Apple iMac's system unit sits on the desktop and also contains the computer's display. (b) The Macintosh G4 uses a tower case that sits on the floor next to the desk.

CPU *is* the computer in the strict sense of the term; all other components (such as disk drives, monitors, and printers) are peripheral to, or outside of, the CPU.

- **Power supply** A computer's **power supply** transforms the alternating current (AC) available from standard wall outlets into the direct current (DC) needed for the computer's operation. It also steps the voltage down to the low voltage required by the motherboard. Power supplies are rated according to their peak output in watts. A 250-watt power supply is adequate for most desktop systems, but 300 watts provides a margin of safety if you plan to add many additional components.

- **Cooling fan** The computer's components can be damaged if heat accumulates within the system unit. **Cooling fans** are therefore used to keep the system unit cool. Often, the fan is part of the power supply, although some high-powered systems include auxiliary fans to provide additional cooling.

- **Speaker** The computer's internal **speaker** isn't designed for high-fidelity reproduction. It's useful only for the beeps you hear when the computer encounters an error. To produce good sound from a PC, you need to upgrade the system with sound components (including a sound card and speakers), although Macintoshes come with built-in stereo sound.

- **Drive bays** **Drive bays** are designed to accommodate the computer's disk drives, such as the hard disk drive, floppy disk drive, and CD-ROM or DVD-ROM drive. **Internal drive bays** are used for hard disks, in which the disk is permanently contained within the drive's case. Therefore, they do not enable outside access. **External drive bays** mount drives so that they are accessible from the outside (a necessity if you need to insert and remove disks from the drive). External drive bays vary by size. Some bays are designed to accommodate 5.25-inch drives (for CD-ROMs and DVD-ROMs), whereas others are designed for 3.5-inch drives (for floppy and Zip disks).

power supply

motherboard

internal drive bays

cooling fan

external drive bays

speaker

expansion cards

Figure 2.4
Inside the system unit, you'll find the motherboard, power supply, cooling fan, speaker, internal drive bays, external drive bays, and various expansion cards (such as the sound card and network interchange card).

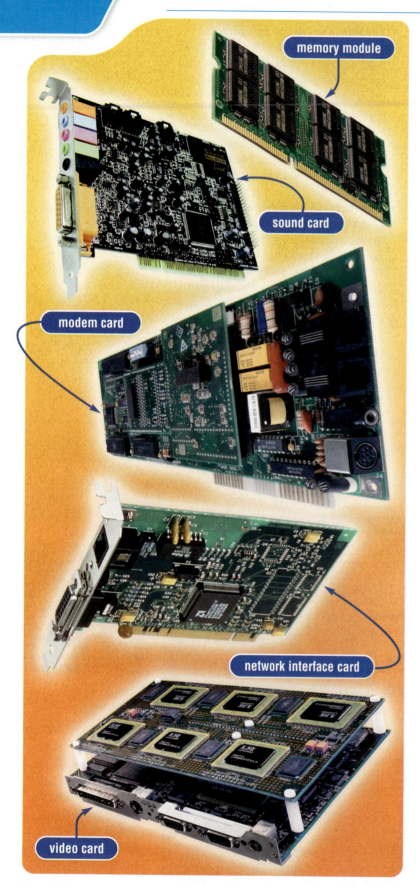

memory module

sound card

modem card

network interface card

video card

Figure 2.5
Expansion cards allow you to add enhancements to your system.

- **Expansion Cards** The system unit also contains slots that will accept additional circuit boards, or **expansion cards**. Examples of expansion cards are memory modules, sound cards, modem cards, network interface cards, and video cards (see Figure 2.5).

What's on the Motherboard?

As you've just learned, the motherboard provides both the physical and electrical settings for the computer's most important components (see Figure 2.6). Most of the components on the motherboard are **integrated circuits**. An integrated circuit (IC), also called a **chip**, can carry electrical current and contains millions of **transistors**. A transistor is an electronic switch (or **gate**) that controls the flow of electrical signals to the circuit. Much of what a computer does boils down to using such electronic switches to route data in different ways, according to the software's instructions.

Housed in black plastic boxes, most chips are packaged so that their pins fit into specially designed receptacles on the motherboard's surface. Many types of chip packages exist. Common are **dual inline packages** (**DIPs**), which are affixed to the motherboard by means of two parallel rows of downward-facing pins. More complex chips may use a **pin grid array** (**PGA**), in which a complex pattern of downward-facing pins is designed to fit into a compatible receptacle. Because PGA pins are prone to bending if the chip is inserted incorrectly, some PGA-packaged chips use a **zero-insertion force** (**ZIF**) socket in which the pins are not engaged until the chip is properly positioned and a lever is pushed down to its closed position. **Single-edge contact** (**SEC**) packages are designed to be pressed into a slot; the connectors are aligned along one of the package's edges (see Figure 2.7). Some chips may be soldered directly to the motherboard.

Let's look at some of the most important components you'll see on the motherboard: the system clock, the central processing unit (or microprocessor), memory, the chipset, and input/output (I/O) buses.

THE SYSTEM CLOCK

Within the computer, events happen at a pace controlled by a tiny electronic "drummer" on the motherboard called the **system clock**. This component is an electronic circuit that generates pulses at a rapid rate, measured in billions of cycles per second (GHz). Almost any computer you purchase today will have a clock speed of more than 1 GHz. A hertz is an electrical cycle per second. So, a 2-GHz processor is capable of processing two billion cycles in one second. (As a frame of reference, can you figure out how many seconds there are in the average human life span? The answer may surprise you!)

A given processor's clock rate is called its **clock speed**, and a single beat of the clock is called a **clock tick**. Note that the system clock doesn't have anything to do with keeping the time and date (in most computers, there's another circuit that handles this job); the system clock synchronizes the computer's internal activities.

THE CENTRAL PROCESSING UNIT: THE MICROPROCESSOR

The **central processing unit (CPU)** interprets the instructions given to it by software and carries out these instructions by processing data and controlling the rest of the computer's components. The CPU is a **microprocessor**, an integrated circuit chip that is capable of processing electronic signals. No other single element of a computer determines its overall performance as much as the CPU.

Because the computer's microprocessor is so important, let's spend some time looking at it in detail before moving on to the remaining components of the motherboard. Although microprocessors are complex devices, the underlying ideas are easy to understand. Any computer-literate person should understand these ideas because they help to explain what computers can (and cannot) do. In addition, you need to know enough about microprocessors to understand the capabilities and limitations

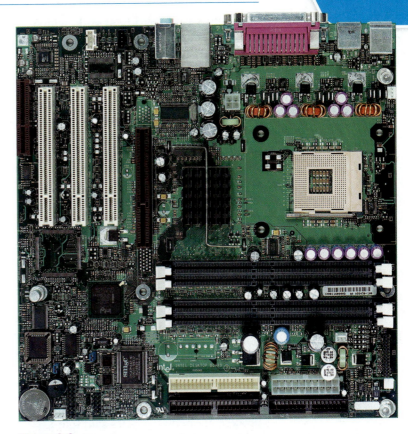

Figure 2.6
A Typical PC Motherboard

Figure 2.7
This single-edge contact (SEC) package fits into a specially designed slot on the motherboard's surface.

of a given computer system when you considering buying one.

Processor Slots and Sockets

An integrated circuit (IC) of fabulous complexity, a microprocessor is designed to plug into a motherboard in much the same way that other ICs do. However, motherboard designers have created special slots and sockets to accommodate microprocessors. Part of the reason is simply that microprocessors are larger and have more pins than do most other chips. In addition, microprocessors generate so much heat that they could destroy themselves or other system components. The microprocessor is generally covered by a **heat sink**, which drains heat away from the chip. To accomplish this, the heat sink may contain a small auxiliary cooling fan. The latest, high-end microprocessors include their own built-in refrigeration systems, which are needed to keep these speedy processors cool.

The Instruction Set

Every processor can perform a fixed set of operations, such as retrieving a character from the computer's memory or comparing two numbers to see which is larger. Each of these operations has its own unique number, called an **instruction**. A processor's list of instructions is called an **instruction set**. Different processors have different instruction sets. Because each processor has a unique instruction set, programs devised for one computer type won't run on another. For example, a program written for the Apple Macintosh will not run on an IBM PC. A program that can run on a given computer is said to be **compatible** with that computer's processor. Alternatively, it's said that a given program is a **native application** for a given processor design.

Microprocessor manufacturers must carefully consider compatibility when introducing new models. In particular, manufacturers must decide whether to make the new chip **downwardly compatible** with previous models. A downwardly compatible chip can run the programs

designed to run with earlier chips. To introduce a microprocessor that is not downwardly compatible with previous models is risky, as people may buy a computer that cannot run the programs they already own.

The Control Unit and the Arithmetic-Logic Unit

CPUs contain two subcomponents: the control unit and the arithmetic-logic unit (ALU). The **control unit** coordinates and controls all the other parts of the computer system. Under the direction of a program, the control unit manages four basic operations (see Figure 2.8):

- **Fetch** Retrieves the next program instruction from the computer's memory.

- **Decode** Determines what the program is telling the computer to do.

- **Execute** Performs the requested instruction, such as adding two numbers or deciding which one of them is larger.

- **Write-back** Writes the results to an internal register (a temporary storage location) or to memory.

This four-step process is called a **machine cycle**, or a **processing cycle**, and consists of two phases: the **instruction**

Figure 2.8
The control unit manages four basic operations: fetch, decode, execute, and write-back.

cycle (fetch and decode) and the **execution cycle** (execute and write-back). Today's microprocessors can go through this entire four-step process billions of times per second. Typically, a machine cycle requires more than one tick of the system clock. Some instructions take many clock ticks to execute.

The **arithmetic-logic unit** (**ALU**), as its name implies, can perform arithmetic or logical operations. **Arithmetic operations** include the usual grade-school calculations, including addition, subtraction, multiplication, and division. **Logical operations** involve comparing two data items to see which one is larger or smaller.

Registers

Some operations require the control unit to store data temporarily. **Registers** are temporary storage locations in the microprocessor that are designed for this purpose. For example, one type of register stores the location from which data was retrieved from memory. Registers also store results of intermediate calculations.

Microprocessor Performance: Data Bus Width and Word Size

What determines a given microprocessor's performance? The first element is its data bus width, which is measured in bits (8, 16, 32, or 64). The **data bus**, a highway of parallel wires, connects the internal components of the microprocessor. The bus is a pathway for the electronic impulses that form bytes. The more lanes this highway has, the faster data can travel.

The width of a CPU's data bus partly determines the maximum number of bits the CPU can process at once (its **word size**). Data bus width also affects the CPU's overall speed, because a CPU with a 32-bit data bus can shuffle data around twice as fast as a CPU with a 16-bit data bus. But other factors play a role in determining a CPU's word size, such as the width of internal registers. The terms *8-bit CPU*, *16-bit CPU*, *32-bit CPU*, and *64-bit CPU* are used to sum up the maximum number of bits a given CPU can handle at a time.

A CPU's word size is important because it determines which operating systems the CPU can use. An Intel 8088 is limited to 8-bit operating systems, which—like CPUs with 8-bit word lengths—can work

Word Length Requirements of Popular Operating Systems for Intel Processors	
Operating System	**Required Word Length**
CP/M	8
MS-DOS	8
Windows 3.1	16
Windows 95/98/NT/2000/XP	32
Linux	32
64-bit Linux	64

Figure 2.9

with only eight bits at a time. Figure 2.9 lists the word length requirements of past, current, and future operating systems.

Today's personal computer market is dominated by 32-bit CPUs and 32-bit operating systems. However, 64-bit CPUs and 64-bit operating systems are currently in use in high-end, high-capacity server systems. Intel's 64-bit Itanium processor, introduced in late 2000, brings 64-bit computing to the personal computer market for the first time. Recently, 64-bit versions of the popular Linux and Microsoft Windows operating systems have also been released.

Microprocessor Performance: Operations per Cycle

The number of operations per clock tick (one pulse of the system clock) also affects microprocessor performance. You might think that a CPU can't perform more than one instruction per clock tick, but thanks to new technologies, that's not true. Any CPU that can execute more than one instruction per clock cycle is referred to as **superscalar**, and its design is called a **superscalar architecture**. Today's fastest CPUs, such as the Pentium 4, use superscalar architectures. One of the design tricks that makes superscalar architectures possible is called **pipelining**, a processing technique that feeds a new instruction into the CPU at every step of the processing cycle so that four or more instructions are worked on simultaneously (see Figure 2.10).

Destinations

To learn more about the 64-bit versions of the Linux and Microsoft Windows operating systems, visit **www.itworld.com/Comp/2388/IDG020107redhat/** and **www.microsoft.com/windowsxp/64bit/overview.asp**.

Figure 2.10
Pipelining

Pipelining resembles an auto assembly line in which more than one car is being worked on at once. Before the first instruction is finished, the next one is started. But what if the CPU needs the results of a completed instruction to process the next one? This problem is called **data dependency**. It can cause a pipeline stall, in which the assembly line is held up until the results are known. To cope with this problem, advanced CPUs use a technique called **speculative execution** in which the processor executes and temporarily stores the next instruction in case it proves useful. CPUs also use a technique called **branch prediction**, in which the processor tries to predict what will likely happen (with a surprisingly high degree of accuracy).

Microprocessor Performance: Parallel Processing

Another way to improve CPU performance doesn't involve making CPUs faster. It involves using more than one of them at the same time. A **parallel processing** computer has many processors running simultaneously, in parallel (see Figure 2.11).

Figure 2.11
Parallel processing computers have multiple processors that run simultaneously.

CISC and RISC

Another aspect of microprocessor design that you should be aware of is the distinction between CISC and RISC.

CISC stands for **complex instruction set computer**. A CISC chip, such as the Motorola 68040, includes many special-purpose circuits that carry out instructions at high speeds. CISC chips, however, are complex and expensive to produce, and they run hot because they consume a lot of current.

RISC stands for **reduced instruction set computer**. A RISC chip offers a bare-bones instruction set. For this reason, RISC chips are less complex, less expensive to produce, and more efficient in power usage. The drawback of the RISC design is that the computer must combine or repeat operations to complete many processing operations. RISC chips also place extra demands on programmers, who must consider how to get complex results by combining simple instructions. But careful tests show that this design results in faster processing than the CISC chips.

Even so, the distinction between CISC and RISC is becoming less meaningful. The earliest CISC processors included what were then advanced design features, such as superscalar architecture, pipelining, and branch prediction. But RISC processors now include these, and their performance has improved. In the meantime, RISC manufacturers are finding that they must include some CISC design components to ensure compatibility. Today, the leading CISC processor (Motorola PowerPC) and RISC processor (Intel Pentium 4) are virtually indistinguishable in terms of instruction set size.

Popular Microprocessors

The most commonly used microprocessors are those in IBM PC compatibles and Macintoshes. The chips powering most PCs are made by Intel Corporation, although Advanced Micro Devices (AMD), Cyrix Corporation, and other firms make Intel-compatible chips. Figure 2.12 shows how popular personal computer microprocessors have improved since the days of the first PC. In 2001, Intel released a version of the Pentium 4 microprocessor running at a clock speed of 2 GHz, the

The Continuing Evolution of Intel Microprocessors

Year	Chip	Bus Width	Clock Speed	Transistors
1971	4004	4 bits	740 KHz	2,300
1974	8080	8 bits	2 MHz	6,000
1979	8088	8 bits	Up to 8 MHz	29,000
1982	80286	16 bits	Up to 12 MHz	134,000
1985	80386	32 bits	Up to 33 MHz	275,000
1989	Intel 486	32 bits	Up to 100 MHz	1.6 million
1993	Pentium (original)	32 bits	Up to 200 MHz	3.3 million
1995	Pentium Pro	32 bits	200 MHz and higher	5.5 million
1997	Pentium MMX	32 bits	233 MHz and higher	4.5 million
1998	Pentium II	32 bits	233 MHz and higher	7.5 million
1998	Xeon	32 bits	400 MHz and higher	7.5 million
1998	Celeron	32 bits	400 MHz and higher	7.5–19 million
1999	Duron	32 bits	600 MHz and higher	18 million
1999	Pentium III	32 bits	450 MHz and higher	9.5–28.1 million
2000	Pentium 4	32 bits	1.4 GHz and higher	34 million
2000	Itanium	64 bits	800 MHz and higher	25 million

Figure 2.12

first commercially available chip to attain that speed (see Figure 2.13).

The IBM PC, introduced in 1981, used the Intel 8088, an 8-bit processor running initially at 4.77 MHz. A major limitation of this processor was its maximum memory size of 1 MB. Another major limitation was that programs could directly access the computer's memory. If you tried to run more than one program at a time, one of the programs might overwrite the other one's portion of memory, causing a crash.

To deal with this problem, in 1982, Intel introduced the 80286, which had two modes. The first mode, called **real mode**, emulated the 8088. The second mode, called **protected mode**, introduced

Figure 2.13

The Pentium 4

Figure 2.14
The Pentium MMX

Figure 2.15
The Pentium III

Figure 2.16
Advanced Micro Devices (AMD) beat Intel to the market with the first 1-GHz processor in 1999.

two major technical improvements. In protected mode, programs could use up to a gigabyte of RAM. Also, the processor gave programs a certain section of memory and prevented other programs from using the same section. This allocation reduced the number of system failures when users tried to run more than one program. The 80286 was followed in 1985 by the 80386, also called the 386, Intel's first 32-bit microprocessor.

The IBM PC's operating system, MS-DOS, runs in real mode and can't take advantage of the benefits of protected mode. The reason for the popularity of Microsoft Windows lies in its capability to switch the 80386 and later processors into protected mode, enabling users to make full use of more than 640 KB of memory and providing protection for **multitasking**, in which the processor runs more than one program at once by switching among them.

By the time the 80486 came along in 1989, several manufacturers had created clones of Intel processors, and a court ruled that Intel could not protect the 80386 nomenclature. So the 80486 came to be called the Intel 486. In 1993, Intel released the first Pentium microprocessors, which used a 64-bit data bus. Pentium is derived from the Latin word for *five*. (This chip would have been called the 80586 if Intel had stuck with the old numbering system.) The Pentium chip was followed in 1995 by the Pentium Pro, an advanced Pentium design intended for use in servers and engineering workstations. In 1997, the Pentium MMX was introduced, containing a new set of 57 multimedia instructions. These instructions enabled Pentium MMX–based systems to run games and multimedia applications more quickly (see Figure 2.14).

The year 1998 saw the first of a series of Pentium II processors, which incorporated the Pentium Pro's advanced design as well as MMX graphics and the games circuitry of earlier chips. A low-priced version of the Pentium II, called Celeron, reduced costs by cutting down on the amount of secondary cache. An advanced version of the Pentium II, the Xeon, was designed for professional applications. In 1999, Intel released the Pentium III (shown in Figure 2.15), an upgraded version of the Pentium II with clock speeds of up to 1,000 MHz (1 gigahertz). However, Intel's main competitor, Advanced Micro Devices (AMD), beat Intel to the 1-GHz mark with the company's Athlon processor (see Figure 2.16).

Providing the CPU for Macintoshes over the years are chips made by Motorola Corporation. They fall into two processor families: the 68000 series (68000 to 68040) and the PowerPC family. PowerPC microprocessors are RISC chips that run earlier Macintosh software by emulating the earlier processor's characteristics. Figure 2.17 shows how these processors have improved since the first ones appeared in 1979. Note that Apple Computer gives its own name to the PowerPC chips: Motorola's 750 is the same thing as Apple's G3, while Motorola's 7400 becomes the G4 in Apple's marketing.

Benchmarks

As the previous discussion suggests, two 200-MHz processors made by different manufacturers may turn out to perform very differently, depending on variations in bus width and architecture. To provide some basis for comparison, **benchmarks** have been developed. A benchmark is a test that puts a processor through a series of operations to provide a basis for comparison. The idea sounds good, but a variety of benchmarks are available, and some do a better job than others of measuring the real-world conditions that a processor is likely to encounter. Another problem is that benchmarks don't test

only the CPU, but may react to other system components.

Although benchmark tests provide information about processor performance, they may fail to describe a computer system's overall performance accurately. Real-world benchmark tests measure a system's overall performance in running complex applications.

MEMORY

Now that you understand the basics of microprocessors, we can move on to another important motherboard component: the computer's memory. **Memory** is a general term used for any device that enables the computer to retain information. As you'll see in this section, the computer's motherboard contains several different types of memory, each optimized for its intended use.

Memory chips are typically packaged in two different types of modules, **single inline memory modules** (**SIMMs**) and **dual inline memory modules** (**DIMMs**). SIMMs pack memory chips into modules with 30- or 72-pin connectors. Some SIMMs have connectors on both edges, but they are the same. SIMMs are available in 1-MB, 4-MB, 16-MB, and 32-MB versions. DIMMs have 168-pin connectors, which are different on each edge of the package. DIMMs are newer and are available in larger sizes (8 MB, 16 MB, 32 MB, and 64 MB), reflecting the heftier memory demands of today's computers.

Techtalk

overclock

To configure a computer system so that it runs a processor faster than it is designed to run. Some processors can run faster than the manufacturer's rated clock speed. However, overclocking can make your system unstable. At the extreme, it could destroy the processor, leaving your computer useless.

Destinations

For the latest info on the hottest and fastest processors, take a look at the aptly named "Chip Geek" at **www.ugeek.com/ procspec/procmain.htm**. You'll find the latest news on new, super-fast processors, including performance comparisons, reviews, and tips on putting together the ultimate high-speed system.

For help on comparing microprocessor performance, take a look at the "Processor Buyer's Guide" at **www.buybuddy.com**. You'll find up-to-date information on the latest processors, as well as tips on how to compare them meaningfully.

The Continuing Evolution of Motorola Microprocessors

Year	Chip	Bus Width	Clock Speed	Transistors
1979	68000	16 bits	8 MHz	68,000
1984	68020	32 bits	Up to 40 MHz	272,000
1988	68040	64 bits	Up to 120 MHz	2.8 million
1994	PowerPC 603	64 bits	Up to 160 MHz	1.6 million
1995	PowerPC 603e	64 bits	Up to 300 MHz	2.6 million
1995	PowerPC 604e	64 bits	Up to 300 MHz	3.6 million
1998	PowerPC 750 (G3)	64 bits	200 MHz and higher	6.35 million
2000	PowerPC 7400 (G4)	64 bits	400 MHz and higher	10.5 million

Figure 2.17

Techtalk

PC 100 SDRAM

A type of SDRAM that is capable of keeping up with the latest and fastest motherboards, which have bus speeds of 100 MHz.

Destinations

To learn more about RAM, see Kingston Technology's "Ultimate Memory Guide," at **www.kingston.com/tools/umg/default.asp**, which thoroughly explains how memory works, what memory technologies are available, and how to select the best RAM chips for your computer system.

Volatile vs. Nonvolatile Memory

Every computer has several types of memory. They fall into two categories: **volatile memory** and **nonvolatile memory**. In volatile memory, the memory's contents are erased when the computer's power is switched off. This is obviously a disadvantage. However, volatile memory technologies provide much higher data transfer rates. Nonvolatile memory, in contrast, retains information even when the power is switched off.

RAM (Random Access Memory)

The large memory modules housed on the computer's motherboard contain the computer's **random access memory** (**RAM**). A volatile memory technology, RAM stores information temporarily so that it's directly and speedily available to the microprocessor. This information includes software as well as the data to be processed by the software. RAM is designed for fast operation because the processor acts directly on the information stored in RAM.

Why is it called *random access* memory? The term *random access* doesn't imply that the memory stores data randomly. A better term would be each memory location has an address, just like a post office box. Using this address, called a **memory address**, the processor can store and retrieve data by going directly to a single location in memory (see Figure 2.18).

Of the various types of RAM available, today's computers use a type of RAM called **dynamic RAM** (also called **DRAM**). DRAM (pronounced "dee-RAM") must be energized constantly or it loses its contents.

Figure 2.18
Random access memory stores data in specific, addressed locations for easy access and retrieval.

Most computers made recently contain a faster, improved type of DRAM called **synchronous DRAM** (also called **SDRAM**). SDRAM's operations are very fast because they are synchronized to the pulses of the computer's system clock. The newest and fastest PCs contain **Rambus DRAM** or **DDR SDRAM** memory chips. Rambus DRAM uses a narrow but very fast bus to connect to the microprocessor, which enables Rambus DRAM chips to send and receive data within one clock cycle. **Double data rate** (**DDR**) **SDRAM**, also called DDR SDRAM, is a type of SDRAM that can both send and receive data within a single clock cycle.

How much RAM does a computer need? In general, the more memory, the better. For today's Microsoft Windows, Linux, and Macintosh operating systems, 128 MB of RAM is a practical working minimum, but the computer will not run well with so little memory. Oftentimes these operating systems use **virtual memory** in addition to RAM. Through virtual memory, the computer can use the hard disk as an extension of RAM. It does this when RAM gets full (which can easily happen if you run two or more programs at once). Disk drives are much slower than RAM so when virtual memory kicks in, the computer slows down to a frustratingly slow pace. To avoid using virtual memory, you're better off with 256 MB of RAM, and increasingly, systems are sold with 512 MB of RAM.

ROM (Read-Only Memory)

If everything in RAM is erased when the power is turned off, how does the computer start again? The answer is **read-only memory** (**ROM**). The instructions to start the computer are stored in read-only memory chips, which are nonvolatile. (They don't lose their contents when the power is switched off.) To allow ROM upgrades, most computers use **flash memory**, also called **flash BIOS**. The use of flash memory enables the ROM to be upgraded. If the computer manufacturer finds an error in the ROM code, the customer can obtain an upgrade disk or can use the Internet to access a downloadable file that writes the revised code to the flash memory circuit.

In PCs, ROM is used to store the computer's **basic input/output system**

(**BIOS**). When you start your PC (also called **booting** your computer), BIOS executes a **boot sequence**. In the boot sequence, the BIOS conducts various **power-on self-tests** (**POSTs**), including conducting memory tests, configuring and starting the video circuitry, configuring the system's hardware, and locating the disk drive containing the **boot sector**. The boot sector contains the computer's **operating system** (**OS**), which you'll recall is the software that controls the computer's basic functions. Similar software performs the same functions on Macintosh systems.

PCs enable knowledgeable users to access a **setup program** during the boot sequence. Typically, you start the setup program by pressing the Delete key or the F8 key, although some computers use different keys for this purpose. The setup program enables you to configure your system settings, including the type and number of disk drives attached to the system, the number of physical connectors available for serial ports, and the location of the disk drive containing the boot sector. You should not attempt to change any of these settings; if you choose the wrong setting, your computer may not work.

CMOS

The settings in the BIOS setup program are stored in a special type of memory referred to as the **complementary metal-oxide semiconductor** (**CMOS**). CMOS is a special type of memory used to store essential startup configuration options, such as the amount of memory that has been installed in the computer. CMOS chips also track the time and date. Unlike ROM, CMOS is volatile. Even though CMOS uses very little battery power, and should last years, a common cause of system errors in older computers is a failed battery. If you see a dead battery warning when you start the computer, or if your system suddenly loses the correct time and date, take your computer to a technician. On Macintoshes, this type of memory is called **parameter RAM**.

Cache Memory

RAM is fast, but it isn't fast enough to support the processing speeds of today's superfast microprocessors, such as the Motorola G3 or Pentium 4. To enable these microprocessors to function at maximum speed, computer designers use **cache memory**. (The term *cache* is pronounced "cash.") Cache memory is much faster than RAM, but it's also more expensive. Although generally no larger than 512 KB, cache memory greatly improves the computer system's overall performance. The processor can use the cache to store frequently accessed program instructions and data.

Two types of cache memory are available. The first type, called **primary cache**, or level 1 (L1) cache, is included in the microprocessor chip. The second type, called **secondary cache**, or level 2 (L2) cache, is included on a separate printed circuit board. To improve secondary cache performance, the latest microprocessors are provided in plastic modules that contain a special type of secondary cache, called **backside cache**. Keeping the secondary cache as close as possible to the processor improves performance (see Figure 2.19).

Figure 2.19

Primary cache is included in the microprocessor chip. Secondary cache is included on a separate printed circuit board. Keeping the secondary cache as close as possible to the processor improves performance.

CURRENTS

EMERGING TECHNOLOGIES

Dreams of Homework Machines? Computers in Your Pocket

Now, don't deny that you have dreamed of owning a machine of some sort that could do your homework and class assignments for you. You may have even written about a "homework machine" in elementary school. Well, keep dreaming—such machines are not here yet. But personal digital assistants, or PDAs—those small, handheld computing devices—come pretty close.

PDAs have been used successfully in the corporate world for years and have more recently entered the realm of everyday student life—and for good reason. PDAs can fit in your pocket, remind you when and where a class or meeting is taking place, and keep those little gems you think up and don't want to forget from vanishing into thin air. With PDAs, you can take notes in class and, with special software, even give yourself pop quizzes throughout the day. They can also connect you with the Internet, where you can access your library's online catalog and other useful sites.

Today, many colleges and universities are requiring that their students own a computer. As most students know, real estate on a classroom desk is limited, so having a small computer is important. With notebook-sized desks, laptops leave little room for other student needs, such as textbooks. That's where PDAs come in handy.

With PDAs, you can leave your laptop at home and still carry a great deal of computing power in a small system unit. Inexpensive accessories like folding, detachable keyboards enable you to take notes easily in class. And once you've finished using your PDA, you can download the information you've stored on it to your traditional computer. Desktops and laptops now offer docking bays for PDAs along with the traditional USB, FireWire, or other port hookups for transferring data. In addition, infrared data beaming between PDA devices allows for easy wireless exchange of information (and, of course, games).

If you're considering buying a PDA, you'll have a wide range of choices, from Palm to Sony, monochrome or color screen, battery or rechargeable. Priced anywhere between $99 and $599 and up, depending on which options you choose, PDAs combine small size, low price, and portability. What PDA is right for you? Obviously, the higher-end PDAs, such as the Zaurus SL 5550 (see Figure 2.20), have more functions, including MP3 players, color screens, high resolution, super-fast processors, and wireless connectivity. But even the cheaper PDAs pack a lot of computing punch into a small container.

PDAs are not all about hardware, of course. Specially designed software can turn your PDA into a true technical marvel. Most software for PDAs is reasonably priced, and some can be downloaded as shareware from the Internet. (For information on software that is specially targeted toward students, visit **www.palmgear.com** and search under the keywords *students* and *school*.)

No, they're not homework machines just yet, but PDAs are more than just paperless storage islands for information. They're great homework tools.

Figure 2.20
The Zaurus SL 5550 has a standard keyboard hidden under a sliding cover.

THE CHIPSET AND INPUT/OUTPUT (I/O) BUSES

Another important motherboard component is the **chipset**. The chipset is a collection of chips that are designed to work together (that's why they're called a "set"). They provide the switching circuitry that the microprocessor needs in order to move data to and from the rest of the computer. One of the jobs handled by the chipset involves linking the microprocessor to the computer's input/output (I/O) buses. **Input/output** (**I/O**) **buses** extend the computer's internal data pathways beyond the boundaries of the microprocessor so that the microprocessor can communicate with input and output devices. Typically, an I/O bus contains **expansion slots**, which are designed to accommodate expansion cards (also called expansion boards, adapter cards, or adapters). An expansion card is a printed circuit board that's designed to fit into an expansion bus's receptacles.

Today's PCs and Macs use the **Personal Computer Interface (PCI) bus**, which supports the **Plug and Play (PnP)** system. With PnP, the computer detects a new card and configures the system automatically. Many motherboards still contain an **Industry Standard Architecture (ISA) bus** and make one or two ISA slots available. The **Accelerated Graphics Port (AGP)** is a bus designed for video buses. **Input/output (I/O) buses** extend adapters.

What's on the Outside of the Box?

You'll find the following on the outside of a typical desktop computer's system unit: the power switch; connectors for plugging in keyboards, mice, monitors, and more; and a front panel with various buttons and lights. The following sections examine these system unit components.

THE POWER SWITCH

Usually, the **power switch** is located in the rear of the computer so you can't hit it by accident. Computers don't handle power losses well. For example, a power outage caused by a service interruption could scramble the data on your hard drive. You should always shut off your computer by following an orderly shutdown procedure. In Microsoft Windows, for example, you click Start and choose Shut Down. In the Macintosh operating system (Mac OS), you click Special and choose Shut Down.

CONNECTORS AND PORTS

A **connector** is a physical receptacle that is designed for a specific type of plug that fits into the connector (and is sometimes secured by thumbscrews). Connectors are found inside the system case on the back of expansion cards, the plug-in adapters that are pressed into the computer's expansion slots on the motherboard. Connectors on the outside of the case enable you to connect peripheral devices,

such as a printer, keyboard, or mouse (see Figure 2.21). These connectors are designed to work with plugs that can be securely fastened to the connector. Usually, this is done by means of screws that are mounted on the plug. Connectors are described as being **male connectors** (which have external pins) or **female connectors** (which have receptacles for external pins).

In general, you shouldn't connect anything to a computer while it's running. Some of the newer peripheral connection technologies, such as USB, allow **hot swapping** (connection and disconnection while the computer is running), but it's best to play it safe. If you plug in or unplug most connectors while the computer is running, you'll probably cause the computer to crash and lose any unsaved work in the computer's memory. To make sure that a cable doesn't come loose accidentally, make sure the plug is securely fastened to the connector.

Figure 2.21

The connectors on the outside of a system unit enable you to connect peripherals such as a printer, a keyboard, or a mouse.

Figure 2.22 summarizes the connectors you may find on the computer's case. Most of these connectors are on the back of the case, but sometimes you'll find one or more of them on the front.

People often call these connectors *ports*, but this usage is not necessarily accurate. A **port** is an electronically defined pathway, called an **interface**, for getting information into and out of the computer. In order to function, a port must be linked to a specific receptacle. This is done by the computer system's start-up and configuration software. In the following, the term *port* is used as if it were synonymous with connector, in line with everyday usage, but it's important to keep the distinction in mind. Let's now look at the types of ports found on the exterior of a typical computer system's case.

Serial Ports

A **serial port** creates an interface in which data flows in a series of pulses, one after another (see Figure 2.23). Because serial ports do not transmit data rapidly, they are used for devices that don't require fast data transfer rates. One device that uses a serial port is a modem.

On IBM-compatible PCs, there are four serial ports: COM1, COM2, COM3, and COM4. However, a PC may have only one or two physical connectors for serial devices. In addition, some expansion boards contain serial ports that connect directly to the computer's internal wiring.

As you can see from this discussion, it's important to remember that a connector isn't the same thing as a port. The connector is the physical device—the plug-in—while the port is the interface—the matching of input and output flows. A port almost always uses a connector, but a connector isn't always a port. For example, a USB port uses a USB connector, but a telephone jack is just a connector—not a port.

Serial ports conform to one of two international standards. The **RS-232 standard** is commonly used on PCs. The faster **RS-422 standard** is used on Macintoshes. On the exterior of a PC's case, male 9-pin (DB-9) connectors provide access to serial ports, although older PCs may use 25-pin (DB-25) male connectors. Macs provide serial port access by means of a round, 8-pin (DIN-8) female connector.

Parallel Ports

A **parallel port** has eight wires. The difference between a serial port and a parallel port is similar to the difference between a one-lane road and a freeway. Unlike a serial port, which can transfer only one bit of information at a time, parallel ports can transfer 8 bits of information simultaneously (see Figure 2.24). As you may have

Connector	Use
DB-25, 25-pin female	parallel port for printer
DB-25, 25-pin male	serial port for printers, modems, or scanners
DIN, 6-pin female	mouse or keyboard
DB-15, 15-pin female	VGA video (monitor)
RJ-11	phone line
RJ-45	local area network (LAN)
Stereo mini-plug female	microphone, speakers, or headphones
USB	port for many devices on PCs and Macintoshes

Figure 2.22

Most of these connectors are on the back of the computer's case, but some of them may be in front.

Data flows in a series of pulses, one after another

100110010001

DB-9 Female Connector

DB-9 Male Connector

Figure 2.23
Serial ports are used for devices that do not require fast data transfer rates.

8 bits of data are simultaneously transferred

00110011

DB-25 Female Connector

DB-25 Male Connector

Figure 2.24
Faster than serial ports, parallel ports can transfer 8 bits of data simultaneously and are used for printers, which require high-speed connections.

already concluded, parallel ports are much faster than serial ports. They are used for printers, which require high-speed connections. Parallel ports are sometimes called **Centronics ports** (or **Centronics interfaces**) after the printer company named Centronics that first defined the parallel interface.

On PCs, access to the parallel port is provided by means of a 25-pin (DB-25) female connector. Older PCs use Amphenol connectors, which have distinctive wire clamps on either end of the plug. Macs use a 6-pin (mini-DIN) connector for this purpose.

The newest parallel ports, called **enhanced parallel ports** (**EPPs**) and **extended capabilities ports** (**ECPs**), offer higher speeds than traditional parallel ports. In addition, they enable two-way communication between the printer and computer. If the printer encounters an error, it can send back a detailed message explaining what went wrong and how to fix it.

SCSI Ports

Short for **small computer system interface**, **SCSI** (pronounced "scuzzy") is a type of parallel interface that is found increasingly on PCs. Unlike a standard Centronics parallel port, a SCSI port enables users to connect up to eight SCSI-compatible

devices, such as printers, scanners, and digital cameras, in a daisy-chain series. The most recent SCSI standard, called SCSI-2, can transfer data at very fast rates.

External connectors for SCSI peripherals vary. Some SCSI adapters have 50- or 68-pin connectors with a click-in locking mechanism for the plug, while others use a standard 50-pin (D50) connector.

Some high-end systems use a SCSI-2 connection, made internally, to hook up the computer's hard disk. (A high-end system is a computer priced higher than systems with a typical configuration.) These hard disks offer the best performance.

Universal Serial Bus (USB) Ports

Like a SCSI port, a **universal serial bus** (**USB**) **port** can connect more than one device at a time—up to 127 of them. The mouse on most new computer systems uses a USB port. As you learned earlier, USB allows you to connect and disconnect devices without shutting down your computer (hot swapping). This is convenient when you're using devices that you often want to disconnect, such as a digital camera.

An additional advantage of USB is its built-in Plug and Play (PnP) support. With PnP, the computer automatically detects the brand, model, and characteristics of

Destinations

To learn more about PC interfaces, including serial and parallel ports, see "Beyond Logic" at **www.beyondlogic.com**. If you're having trouble getting a serial or parallel device to work, check out this page, which offers helpful tips and troubleshooting strategies.

the device when you plug it in, and configures the system accordingly.

1394 Port (FireWire)

Closely resembling the USB design, the **FireWire port** offers a high-speed connection for dozens of peripheral devices (up to 63 of them). On non-Apple systems, this port is called a **1394 port** after the international standard (IEEE 1394) that defines this port. Like USB, FireWire enables hot swapping and PnP. However, it is more expensive than USB and is used only for certain high-speed peripherals, such as digital video cameras, that need greater throughput (data transfer capacity) than USB provides.

IrDA Port

Some keyboards, mice, and printers are designed to communicate using an **IrDA port**. (IrDA is an abbreviation of the Infrared Data Association, which created the IrDA standard.) IrDA ports use infrared signals. This method is also used by television remote controls. No physical connection is required, but the transmitter must be in the direct line of sight with the receiver, a transparent panel mounted on the computer's surface.

Monitor Connector

Most computers use a **video adapter** (also called a **video card**) to generate the output that is displayed on the computer's screen. On the back of the adapter, you'll find a standard **VGA connector**, a 15-pin male connector that is designed to work with standard monitor cables.

Some computers have the video circuitry built into the motherboard. This type of video circuitry is called **on-board video**. On such systems, the video connector is found on the back of the case.

Additional Ports and Connectors

You may find the following additional ports and connectors on the exterior of a computer's case or one of the computer's expansion cards:

- **Telephone connector** Provided with modems, this connector (called RJ-11) is a standard modular telephone jack that will work with an ordinary telephone cord.

- **Network connector** Provided with networking adapters, this connector (called RJ-45) looks like a standard telephone jack, but it's bigger.

- **PC card slots** On notebook computers, one or more PC card slots are provided for plugging in PC cards. A **PC card** is a credit card-sized adapter that provides notebook users with the ability to use modems, networking, and additional functions. Like USB devices, PC cards can be inserted or removed while the computer is running. This device is a port.

- **Sound card connectors** PCs equipped with a **sound card** (an adapter that provides stereo sound and sound synthesis), as well as Macs with built-in sound, offer two or more sound connectors. These connectors, also called jacks, accept the same stereo miniplug used by portable CD players. Most sound cards provide four connectors: Mic (microphone input), Line In (accepts output from other audio devices), Line Out (sends output to other audio devices), and Speaker (sends output to external speakers).

- **Game card** Game cards provide a connector for high-speed access to the CPU and RAM for graphics-intensive interaction. These devices are ports.

- **TV/sound capture board connectors** If your computer is equipped with TV and video capabilities, you'll see additional connectors that look like those found on a television monitor. These include a connector for a coaxial cable, which can be connected to a video camera or cable TV system.

THE FRONT PANEL

On the front panel of most computers, you'll find a **reset switch** (which enables you to restart your computer in the event of a failure), a **drive activity light** (a light that tells when your hard disk is accessing data), and a **power-on light** (a light that tells you whether the power is on). You may also find a keylock that enables you

Techtalk

PCMCIA
Short for Personal Computer Memory Card International Association, PCMCIA refers to the input/output (I/O) bus design that this organization invented. Developed for notebook computers, PCMCIA provides one or more slots for credit card–sized adapters, such as modems and networking cards. Originally, these cards were called PCMCIA cards—but just try pronouncing that phrase! Today, PCMCIA cards are simply called PC cards.

to prevent others from operating the machine. Do not press the reset switch unless you are certain that your computer is no longer operating. If you have any unsaved work, you will lose it.

How Computers Represent Data

To understand computer hardware, you need to understand the basic concepts of digital computing—and that means you need to know the essentials of how computers represent data.

Why is this topic important? As you've already learned, computers are devices that accept input, process that input according to a program's instructions, generate output showing the results of the processing, and store the output for future use. In order for a computer to work with data, the data must be represented inside the computer. Computers can't do anything without represented data to work with. In the next section, you'll learn that the technique used to represent data within the computer—by means of digits—explains a great deal about both the strengths and the limitations of modern computers.

DIGITAL VS. ANALOG REPRESENTATION

Digital computers represent data by means of an easily identified symbol of some kind (called a digit), one that can't be confused with any other. Digits can be represented in only two possible ways: a high-power circuit and a low-power circuit. The computer's components can tell the difference between them with an infinitesimal chance of error. To be sure, people are always talking about computer "glitches," such as the $1 million gas bill that was delivered to a very surprised customer. But such errors are almost always attributable to mistakes in the underlying programming or data input, not the computer's hardware.

Not all computers use digital representation. **Analog computers** use a continuously variable scale, like the mercury in a thermometer, to measure an ongoing process. Analog computers are used in scientific labs and commercial devices, such as computerized gas pumps that are automatically linked to point-of-sale terminals.

A good way to sum up this discussion is to say the following: digital computers count, whereas analog computers measure. The human brain can do both, albeit more slowly, but it can perform additional operations that today's computers can only emulate, and very imperfectly. One such capability is pattern recognition, the ability that enables you to pick a friend's face out of a crowd, or to tell the difference between an apology sincerely delivered and one that sounds contrived. Computers can be programmed to emulate this and other capabilities of human intelligence, but progress in this area (called *artificial intelligence*) has been slow.

NUMBERING SYSTEMS

Every numbering system has a **base** (also called a **radix**). For example, the decimal numbers you use every day have a base of 10. Different numbering systems use other bases. For example, we keep track of time using a numbering system with a base of 60.

What's the difference between numbering systems with varying bases? The answer lies in what happens when you count up to the maximum number that the numbering system allows. In base 10 numbers (decimals), you can count from 0 to 9, and then you have to carry over to the next column (tens). In base 60 numbers, you can count from 0 to 59 (minutes), and then you have to carry over to the next column (hours). In other words, these numbering systems are *positional*. When you look at the decimal number 840, for example, you know what the numbers mean from their position (8 = 800, 4 = 40, and 0 = 0). A number's position is called its **place value**.

REPRESENTING NUMBERS

Because computers represent information using only two possible states, they're ideally suited to work with **binary numbers**. With binary numbers, you must carry over to the next column when you reach the equivalent of decimal 2. Although binary numbers are difficult for people to read and use, they are perfectly suited to the two-state world of computer circuits. In binary numbers, 0 refers to a low-power (off) circuit, and 1 refers to a high-power (on) circuit. As you learned at the beginning of the chapter, when used to represent a computer circuit in this way, a binary number is called a binary digit, or bit for short. A bit is the smallest unit of information that a computer can work with (see Figure 2.25).

In decimal numbers, each place value is a power of ten (10, 100, 1,000, and so on). In binary numbers, each place value is a power of two (2, 4, 8, 16, and so on).

Binary numbers are difficult to work with because so many digits are required to

represent even a small number. (In binary, for example, the decimal number 14 is represented as 1110.) Also, it's tedious to translate binary numbers into their decimal equivalents. For these reasons, programmers like to translate binary numbers into **hexadecimal numbers** (called **hex** for short), a numbering system with a base of 16. These numbers use the symbols 0 through 9 and A through F to make a total of 16 symbols. It's easy to translate binary numbers into the much more readable hexadecimal ones. For example, a commonly used code for the letter K, 01001011, quickly translates to 4B (see Figure 2.26).

REPRESENTING VERY LARGE AND VERY SMALL NUMBERS

Although character codes are useful for representing textual data and whole numbers (0 through 9), they are not useful for numbers that have fractional points, such as 1.25. To represent and process numbers with fractions, as well as extremely large numbers, computers use **floating-point notation**. The term *floating-point* suggests how this notation system works: no fixed number of digits are before or after the decimal point, so the computer can work with very large, as well as very small, numbers. Floating-point notation requires special processing circuitry, which is generally provided by the **floating-point unit** (**FPU**). Almost a standard in the circuitry of today's microprocessors, the FPU on older computers was sometimes a separate chip, the **math coprocessor**.

REPRESENTING CHARACTERS: CHARACTER CODE

Computers would be impossible to use if they just spat out binary numbers at us. Fortunately, thanks to character code, they don't. **Character code** translates between the numerical world of the computer, and the letters, numbers, and symbols we're accustomed to using.

ASCII and EBCDIC
The most widely used character code is the **American Standard Code for Information Interchange** (**ASCII**, pronounced "ask-ee",

Figure 2.25
A binary number is called a binary digit, or bit for short. A bit is the smallest unit of information with which a computer can work.

Binary digit	0	1
Bit	○	●
Status	On	Off

Counting with Binary, Decimal, and Hexadecimal Numbers

Decimal Number	Binary Number	Hexadecimal Number
0	0	0
1	1	1
2	10	2
3	11	3
4	100	4
5	101	5
6	110	6
7	111	7
8	1000	8
9	1001	9
10	1010	A
11	1011	B
12	1100	C
13	1101	D
14	1110	E
15	1111	F

Figure 2.26

which is used on minicomputers, personal computers, and computers designed to make information available on the Internet. IBM mainframe computers and some other systems use a different code, called **Extended Binary Coded Decimal Interchange Code** (**EBCDIC**), pronounced "ebb-see-dic").

Originally, ASCII and EBCDIC used a total of 7 bits to represent **characters** (letters, numbers, and punctuation marks). Seven bits allows the computer to encode a total of 128 characters, which is enough for the numbers 0–9, uppercase and lower-case letters A–Z, and a few punctuation symbols. This 128-bit code is suitable, how-ever, only for English language-speaking users. Looking for a wider market for their personal computers, both IBM and Apple expanded the amount of space reserved for the character code to 8 bits, equivalent to 1 byte (see Figure 2.27). However, these **extended character sets** (characters added to the standard 7-bit set) are not standardized; the Macintosh and PC ver-sions differ. This explains why you may encounter some character representation errors if you try to open a Macintosh document on an IBM PC. (There's less of a problem going the other way because the Macintosh comes with translation software that automatically translates IBM PC characters.) You may see errors if the document contains special characters such as foreign language characters or special punctuation marks.

Unicode

Although ASCII and EBCDIC contain some foreign language symbols, both are clearly insufficient in a global computer market. **Unicode** solves this problem for most languages by expanding the number of available bits to 16. Because 16 bits is enough to code more than 65,000 charac-ters, Unicode can represent many, if not most, of the world's languages. At this writing, nearly 40,000 characters have been encoded. Some languages are not repre-sented because more research is needed to determine how best to encode their scripts. Examples of as-yet-unsupported languages are Cherokee, Mongolian, and Sinhala (the most widely spoken language on the island nation Sri Lanka).

ASCII and EBCDIC Character Codes

Character	ASCII Representation	EBCDIC Representation
0	00110000	11110000
1	00110001	11110001
2	00110010	11110010
3	00110011	11110011
4	00110100	11110100
5	00110101	11110101
6	00110110	11110110
7	00110111	11110111
8	00111000	11111000
9	00111001	11111001
A	01000001	11000001
B	01000010	11000010
C	01000011	11000011
D	01000100	11000100
E	01000101	11000101
F	01000110	11000110
G	01000111	11000111
H	01001000	11001000
I	01001001	11001001
J	01001010	11010001
K	01001011	11010010
L	01001100	11010011
M	01001101	11010100
N	01001110	11010101
O	01001111	11010110
P	01010000	11010111
Q	01010001	11011000
R	01010010	11011001
S	01010011	11100010
T	01010100	11100011
U	01010101	11100100
V	01010101	11100101
W	01010101	11100110
X	01011001	11100111
Y	01011001	11101000
Z	01011010	111010011

Figure 2.27

TECHNOLOGICAL PIONEERS

IMPACTS

Bill Gates, Make Way for Admiral Grace: The First Lady of Technology

If you were asked to list the names of people who had the greatest influence on the advancement of computing technology, who would you name? Would you name a naval officer or a woman born in 1906? Not many of us would, but we should. Admiral Grace Murray Hopper was a pioneer computer scientist who made technology her life, an unusual choice for a woman of her day (see Figure 2.28).

Grace Murray Hopper graduated with a BA in mathematics from Vassar in 1928 and continued her studies at Yale, where she earned an MA (in 1930) and a Ph.D. (in 1934) in mathematics. In 1931, she began teaching math at Vassar. Because Hopper came from a military background, she resigned in 1943 from Vassar to join the Navy WAVES (Women Accepted for Voluntary Emergency Service). In 1944, she became a lieutenant, reporting to Harvard University's Bureau of Ordnance Computation Project. She joined a small research team, learning to program the electromechanical Mark I computing machine.

Hopper is probably best known for her invention of the *compiler*, a program that translates English instructions into computer language. This system, which later became COBOL (short for Common Business-Oriented Language) is extremely important because it made it possible for computers to respond to words rather than numbers. Without her work, the average computing public might still look at computers as something used only by mathematicians.

Hopper was also the coiner of the term *computer bug*. While working for the Navy on a project using a Mark II computer, she noted that the computer wasn't working properly. She began to troubleshoot the error, back-tracking it to a relay on the computer. To her surprise, trapped in the relay was a moth! To honor the day the first computer "bug" occurred, Hopper taped the moth into her daily logbook. (You'll find Hopper's logbook and the moth neatly taped to it in a display at the Smithsonian.)

Admiral Hopper wasn't shy either. When asked about her work and discoveries in technology, she always had something to say. During her life, she was constantly in demand as a speaker, and her quotes are as alive today as when she first said them. For example, she never listened to anyone telling her that something couldn't be done. "They told me that computers could only do math," she is quoted as saying. With her feisty personality, that was plenty of incentive for her to prove the nay-sayers wrong. When commenting on technology bringing change to people's lives, she had this to say: "Humans are allergic to change. They love to say, 'We've always done it this way.' I try to fight that. That's why I have a clock on my wall that runs counterclockwise." The following quote is a favorite of many who appreciate Hopper: "It's always easier to ask for forgiveness than to get permission."

Admiral Grace Hopper is at the top of the list of technology's heroes. Her counterclockwise, can-do attitude led to many important computer science contributions. When she died on January 1, 1992, the world of computing lost a true pioneer.

Figure 2.28
Grace Murray Hopper was a true computer science pioneer.

Parity

No matter which coding system is used to represent characters in the computer's memory, the code must be stored correctly in order to avoid errors. To check each character, computers are designed to add an additional bit to each character code. This extra bit, called a **parity bit**, is generated by an automatic operation that adds all the bits in the character's code. It records a 0 or a 1 to make the total number of bits odd (**odd parity**) or even (**even parity**). If one of the bits in the code has been changed due to a storage error, the computer generates a **parity error**. Some systems stop processing data if a parity error occurs because the error may indicate a component failure that could scramble all the data. Most personal computers, however, are configured so that **parity checking** (the procedure followed to check for parity errors) is turned off. Although parity errors are rare, they do sometimes occur. But they rarely cause problems serious enough to warrant shutting down the computer, which could cause users to lose hours of work.

HOME | **Takeaway Points** | Key Terms and Concepts | Matching | Multiple Choice | Fill-In | Short Answer | Exercises/Projects | Web Research | **CHAPTER REVIEW**

TAKEAWAY POINTS

- The basic unit of information in a computer is the bit, a single-digit binary number (either 1 or 0). An 8-bit sequence of numbers, called a byte, is sufficient to represent the basic letters, numbers, and punctuation marks in most European languages. For this reason, the term byte is synonymous with the term character (a letter or number).

- Larger units of data are described by the terms kilobyte (K or KB, approximately one thousand bytes), megabyte (M or MB, approximately one million bytes), gigabyte (G or GB, approximately one billion bytes), and terabyte (T or TB, approximately one trillion bytes). Data transfer rates are measured in bits per second (bps). Common terms to describe data transfer rates include Kbps (approximately one thousand bits per second), Mbps (approximately one million bits per second), and Gbps (approximately one billion bits per second).

- The computer's motherboard contains numerous receptacles for a variety of chips, including the system clock (which generates pulses to synchronize the computer's activities), the microprocessor (the CPU), memory modules, and the chipset (chips that help the processor move data around). Also provided are slots that give expansion cards access to the computer's input/output (I/O) bus.

- A computer's central processing unit (CPU) contains two components, called the control unit and the arithmetic-logic unit (ALU). The control unit follows a program's instructions and manages four basic operations: fetch (get the next program instruction from memory), decode (figure out what to do), execute (issue commands that carry out the requested action), and write-back (record the results of the operation in memory). Each four-step cycle is called a machine cycle. The arithmetic-logic unit can perform arithmetic or logical operations. Arithmetic operations include the usual grade-school calculations, including addition, subtraction, multiplication, and division. Logical operations involve comparing two data items to see which one is larger or smaller.

- Factors that affect a microprocessor's performance include the data bus width (how many bits it can process at once), and the number of operations the chip can execute per clock cycle.

- A computer's memory includes several different components, each of which uses a memory technology appropriate to its purpose. The computer's main memory, random access memory (RAM), uses high-speed but volatile dynamic RAM chips, which require power in order to operate correctly. Read-only memory (ROM) uses a type of nonvolatile memory, called flash memory, that can be altered should an upgrade be required. The computer's configuration settings are stored in CMOS, a volatile memory that is powered by its own, on-board battery. Included within the microprocessor is a small amount of primary cache memory, which operates at very high speeds and keeps frequently accessed data available to the processor. Processor performance is greatly enhanced through the use of secondary cache memory, which is usually provided on a separate set of chips kept in close proximity to the microprocessor.

- To use a computer system, you need to know how to hook up the computer's external components to the connectors on the outside of the case. Almost all computers have serial ports (for mice, external modems, and some printers), parallel ports (mainly for printers), and a video port. Some computers also have a SCSI port (for SCSI devices such as scanners), a USB port (for USB peripherals, including USB digital cameras and USB printers), a 1394 (FireWire) port (for FireWire peripherals such as digital video cameras), an IrDA port (for infrared keyboards and mice), input and output jacks for microphones and speakers, a telephone connector, or a network connector.

- Analog computers measure, whereas digital computers count. Analog computers provide a quick, rough-and-ready measurement of a fluctuating quantity. Digital computers can perform calculations and move data with a very low probability of error.

1 **2** 3 4 5 6 7 8 9 10 11 12 13 14 15 16

CHAPTER REVIEW

Takeaway Points | Key Terms and Concepts | Matching | Multiple Choice | Fill-In | Short Answer | Exercises/ Projects | Web Research | HOME

1 2 3 4 5 6 7 8 9 10 11 12 13 14 15 16

KEY TERMS AND CONCEPTS

1394 port
Accelerated Graphics
    Port (AGP)
all-in-one computer
American Standard Code for
    Information Interchange
    (ASCII)
analog computer
arithmetic-logic unit (ALU)
arithmetic operation
AT form factor
ATX form factor
backside cache
base (radix)
basic input/output
    system (BIOS)
benchmarks
binary digit
binary number
bit
boot sector
boot sequence
booting
branch prediction
byte
cache memory
central processing unit (CPU)
Centronics port
    (Centronics interface)
character code
character
chip
chipset
clock speed
clock tick
compatible
complementary metal-oxide
    semiconductor (CMOS)
complex instruction set
    computer (CISC)
connector
control unit
cooling fan
data bus
data dependency
data transfer rate
decode
digital computer
double data rate SDRAM
    (DDR SDRAM)
downwardly compatible
drive activity light
drive bay
dual inline memory module
    (DIMM)
dual inline package (DIP)
dynamic RAM (DRAM)

enhanced parallel port (EPP)
even parity
execute
execution cycle
expansion card
expansion slot
Extended Binary Coded Decimal
    Interchange Code (EBCDIC)
extended capabilities port (ECP)
extended character set
external drive bay
female connector
fetch
FireWire port
flash memory (flash BIOS)
floating-point notation
floating-point unit (FPU)
footprint
form factor
gate
gigabits per second (Gbps)
gigabyte
heat sink
hexadecimal number (hex)
hot swapping
Industry Standard
    Architecture (ISA) bus
input/output (I/O) bus
instruction
instruction cycle
instruction set
interface
integrated circuit (IC)
internal drive bay
IrDA port
kilobits per second (Kbps)
kilobyte
logical operation
machine cycle
    (processing cycle)
male connector
math coprocessor
megabits per second (Mbps)
megabyte
memory
memory address
microprocessor
minitower case
motherboard
multitasking
native application
nonvolatile memory
odd parity
on-board video
operating system (OS)
parallel port
parallel processing

parameter RAM
parity bit
parity checking
parity error
PC card
Pentium MMX
Personal Computer Interface
    (PCI) bus
pin grid array (PGA)
pipelining
place value
Plug and Play (PnP)
port
power-on light
power-on self-test (POST)
power supply
power switch
primary cache
printed circuit board (PCB)
protected mode
Rambus DRAM
random access memory (RAM)
read-only memory (ROM)
real mode
reduced instruction set
    computer (RISC)
registers
reset switch
RS-232 standard
RS-422 standard
secondary cache
serial port
setup program
single-edge contact (SEC)
single inline memory module
    (SIMM)
small computer system
    interface (SCSI)
sound card
speculative execution
superscalar
superscalar architecture
synchronous DRAM (SDRAM)
system clock
system unit
terabyte
tower case
transistor
Unicode
universal serial bus (USB) port
VGA connector
video adapter (video card)
virtual memory
volatile memory
word size
write-back
zero insertion force (ZIF)

Go to www.prenhall.com/ciyf2004 to review this chapter, answer the questions, and complete the exercises and Web research questions.

HOME | Takeaway Points | Key Terms and Concepts | **Matching** | Multiple Choice | Fill-In | Short Answer | Exercises/ Projects | Web Research | **CHAPTER REVIEW**

MATCHING

Match each key term in the left column with the most accurate definition in the right column.

_____ 1. parallel port

_____ 2. expansion card

_____ 3. POST

_____ 4. character code

_____ 5. byte

_____ 6. parallel processing

_____ 7. Motorola

_____ 8. USB port

_____ 9. pipelining

_____ 10. register

_____ 11. parity bit

_____ 12. fetch

_____ 13. instruction set

_____ 14. cache memory

_____ 15. RJ-11

a. describes a computer that has many processors running at the same time

b. eight bits

c. connector used to connect a telephone line to a computer

d. additional memory that is used to improve the computer system's overall performance

e. retrieve the next program instruction from memory

f. a processing technique that feeds new instructions into the CPU at every step of the processing cycle

g. a port used for peripherals such as printers that require a high-speed connection

h. high-speed temporary storage location in the CPU

i. an extra bit that is used for error checking

j. a processor's list of instructions

k. a printed circuit board designed to fit into an expansion bus's receptacles that allows additional components to be connected to a computer

l. checks the memory, configures and starts the video circuitry, configures the system's hardware, and locates the boot sector

m. a code that translates between the numerical words of the computer and the letters, numbers, and symbols that we are accustomed to using

n. the company that manufacturers the processors for Macintosh computers

o. a port that can connect more than one device at a time

Chapter Review: 1 2 3 4 5 6 7 8 9 10 11 12 13 14 15 16

CHAPTER REVIEW | Takeaway Points | Key Terms and Concepts | Matching | Multiple Choice | Fill-In | Short Answer | Exercises/Projects | Web Research | HOME

MULTIPLE CHOICE

Circle the correct choice for each of the following.

1. This is not typically located outside the system unit.
   a. Port
   b. Power switch
   c. Console
   d. Motherboard

2. A CPU that will run the same software that ran on older CPUs is said to be what?
   a. Software compatible
   b. Outmoded
   c. Upwardly compatible
   d. Downwardly compatible

3. How many bytes are in a kilobyte?
   a. 100
   b. 1,000
   c. 1,100
   d. 1,500

4. What does SCSI mean?
   a. Standard Computer System Interface
   b. Small Computer System Interface
   c. Serial Computer System Interface
   d. Sequential Computer System Interface

5. Which of the following is not a variation of the Intel Pentium CPU?
   a. PowerPC
   b. Pentium II
   c. Xeon
   d. Celeron

6. This is not a type of memory.
   a. RAM
   b. ALU
   c. Cache
   d. ROM

7. What does ALU mean?
   a. Arithmetic-logic unit
   b. Advanced logic unit
   c. Asynchronous laser unit
   d. Accelerated level utilization

8. Although current processing speeds are approaching 2 GHz (2,000 MHz), the first IBM PC had a processor that operated at this speed.
   a. 1 MHz
   b. 2.5 MHz
   c. 4.77 MHz
   d. 8 MHz

9. This is the name given to an electronic circuit that carries data from one computer component to another.
   a. Trace
   b. Data lead
   c. Bus
   d. Chip

10. What is the ASCII code for the letter A?
    a. 01010101
    b. 10101010
    c. 11000001
    d. 01000001

COMPUTERS IN YOUR FUTURE 2004

2.29

HOME | Takeaway Points | Key Terms and Concepts | Matching | Multiple Choice | Fill-In | Short Answer | Exercises/ Projects | Web Research | CHAPTER REVIEW

FILL-IN

In the blanks provided, write the correct answer for each of the following.

1. A _____ is a physical receptacle designed for a specific type of plug.

2. _____ is another name for the IEEE-1394 port that is used for high-speed video input.

3. With _____, the computer automatically detects the brand, model, and characteristics of a device when you install it and configures the system accordingly.

4. _____ allows external components to be plugged and unplugged while the computer is running.

5. _____ means that a processor can run more than one program at the same time.

6. The most widely used character code is _____.

7. An _____ can emulate thousands or millions of transistors.

8. _____ is the number of bits a CPU can process at once.

9. The _____ contains almost all of a computer's central processing unit on a single chip.

10. A _____ is an electronically defined pathway for getting information into and out of a computer.

11. The _____ enables a computer to perform mathematical operations more quickly.

12. Programmers use the _____ numbering system, which is based on 16.

13. A test that puts a processor through a series of operations to provide a basis for comparison is called a _____.

14. The _____ is an input/output bus that is designed to connect devices to notebook computers.

15. The _____ is an electronic circuit that generates rapid pulses.

SHORT ANSWER

1. Describe the components of a computer system, including those that can be found inside and outside of the system unit.

2. Explain the difference between RAM and ROM. Why are both types of memory used in a computer?

3. What are buses used for? What types of buses are in a computer system?

4. What elements affect the performance of a computer system?

5. What is the difference between a serial port and a parallel port? Why are keyboards connected to the serial port? (Note: some keyboards, as well as mice, are connected to USB ports.)

6. What advantage does Unicode have over the ASCII and EBCDIC codes?

7. Explain why a megabyte is not exactly 1,000,000 bytes.

Chapter navigation: 1 2 3 4 5 6 7 8 9 10 11 12 13 14 15 16

CHAPTER REVIEW | Takeaway Points | Key Terms and Concepts | Matching | Multiple Choice | Fill-In | Short Answer | Exercises/ Projects | Web Research | HOME

1 2 3 4 5 6 7 8 9 10 11 12 13 14 15 16

EXERCISES/PROJECTS

1. You have read about a variety of input/ output ports, so now let's look at an actual computer to see which ones are installed. Using your own computer or a campus one, determine the number and types of ports that are available, and specifically identify the external devices that are connected to each port.

2. All computers, regardless of their size or manufacturer, follow the same four steps in the machine, or processing, cycle. Identify and explain the purpose of each of these steps. Most of the newer processors use pipelining. Explain how pipelining enhances the overall processing speed. Give a non-computer example of pipelining (that is, an activity that you have personally performed that requires multiple steps to complete and in which you can begin the next step before the current one is completed).

3. Many vehicle owners take active steps to protect their investments. They follow manufacturers' maintenance schedules, obtain insurance against damage or loss, and even install antitheft devices. Let's see how individuals and institutions protect their computer investments. If you own a computer, especially a laptop, what measures do you take to protect it from theft while on campus or when traveling? Is your computer covered by homeowner's or renter's insurance? If it is covered, what, if any, is the amount of the deductible? How does your school ensure that public computers and computer components are not stolen? Are there any special security provisions in place for computer laboratories? How are faculty and staff office computers protected? Check with your campus security and find out if any computers have been stolen in the past month. Do you feel that the laboratory and office computers and components are adequately protected from theft?

4. Although conventional computer memory (RAM) has increased in size and speed, most new computer systems use cache memory. What is the purpose of cache memory? Explain the difference between level 1 (L1) and level 2 (L2) cache. Although it was not discussed in the textbook, there is a third level of cache memory called L3. See what information you can find about this additional level of cache.

5. Besides the size and speed improvements in processors, there have been corresponding improvements to the system buses. However, the bus improvements have not been as dramatic as those for processors. The size of data buses on the first generation of personal computers was 8 bits, and they operated at a speed of 2 or 4 MHz. Find the current size and speed for the high-end Intel Pentium 4 and Motorola PowerPC data buses. How do the bus speeds compare with the processor speeds? This disparity is one of the reasons for cache memory.

COMPUTERS IN YOUR FUTURE 2004

PH it shaping generation IT

2.31

HOME | Takeaway Points | Key Terms and Concepts | Matching | Multiple Choice | Fill-In | Short Answer | Exercises/ Projects | Web Research | CHAPTER REVIEW

WEB RESEARCH

1. Since technology changes rapidly, some of the information printed in a textbook is no longer up to date. Currently, the fastest Intel processor for a personal computer is the Pentium 4 with a clock speed of more than 2 GHz, and the fastest Motorola processor is the G4 with a clock speed of more than 1 GHz. Visit Intel at **www.intel.com/home/ desktop/pentium4** and Apple at **www.apple.com/ owermac/processor.html** to find their fastest processors. Which would you purchase? (Remember that processor speed alone does not determine which computer is faster.)

2. Unlike today's computers, in which memory chips are located on the motherboard, memory for the first microcomputers (circa 1978) was located on separate expansion cards, and 4 KB (not 4 MB) cost $295! Warm up your calculator, and divide the cost by the number of bytes to determine the cost per byte of storage. Visit **www.cnet.com** and find the current price for 256 MB of RAM. Once again divide the cost by the number of bytes, and determine the cost per byte. Using 1978 prices, how much would 256 MB of RAM cost today?

3. Let's examine how peripheral devices can be connected to a computer. Most versions of serial and parallel devices, such as keyboards and printers, are being replaced by USB versions. To find out why, visit **www.macspeedzone.com**. State three advantages of using the USB connection rather than serial or parallel ones. Name two additional devices that can be connected via the USB.

   The IEEE-1394 (FireWire) port is one of the newest and fastest input/output ports, and it can be used to connect video devices, such as camcorders, directly to a computer. To find additional information on this interface, visit **www.firewire-1394.com**. FireWire is Apple's terminology for the IEEE-1394 specification. What name does Sony use to identify this high-speed interface? Besides video devices, name two other devices that use the FireWire interface.

   What are the current transfer rates for the serial, USB, and IEEE-1394 interfaces? Do you have any present or possible future needs that would require the use of USB or FireWire interfaces?

4. Due to the high cost of a new car, many people buy used ones. Have you considered purchasing a used or refurbished computer? Just as with automobiles, you can purchase a computer from a company or from an individual. What are some advantages and disadvantages of purchasing a used or refurbished car from a company or individual? Visit the refurbished laptop site, **http://buycsn.com**, and select a specific laptop computer. Identify the computer, its specifications, and cost.

   Have you ever bought or sold an item using an online auction? If you have, what did you buy or sell? Visit eBay at **www.ebay.com** and see if you can find the same or a very similar computer for sale. (Note: companies, as well as individuals, use auctions to sell merchandise.) Compare the purchase prices of a refurbished computer and a used one from a company or individual. Which, if either, would you purchase and why?

5. We do not all speak the same language, nor do we write using the same alphabet. Since the Internet is creating global communities, we need to be able to display the letters (characters) used in other languages. We also need computers and software that "understand" these codes. As discussed in this chapter, this is possible using the Unicode character code. To answer the following questions, you will have to visit the Unicode home page at **www.unicode.org/ unicode/standard/standard.html**.

   - What is the current version of Unicode?
   - Name two computer manufacturers who have adopted Unicode.
   - Name two software applications that use Unicode.
   - Which character set is used for English?
   - What native Canadian people's alphabet is represented in Unicode?

   If you wish to see some of the actual characters that have been implemented using the Unicode character code, go to **www.unicode.org/charts** and select a language.

Input and Output: Data In, Information Out

CHAPTER 3

What You'll Learn. . .

When you have finished reading this chapter, you will be able to:

1. List the four types of input and explain the purpose of each.

2. List the characteristics of a computer keyboard.

3. Explain the purpose of the special keys on the computer's keyboard.

4. List the most frequently used pointing devices and explain why users sometimes prefer alternatives to the mouse.

5. Describe the benefits and drawbacks of speech recognition as an alternative to keyboard use.

6. List devices that are used to get sound, video, and images into the computer.

7. Identify the two major types of output and give examples of each.

8. Explain how the characteristics of a computer's video adapter determine the overall quality of the image displayed on the monitor.

9. List the various types of monitors, and indicate the advantages and disadvantages of each.

10. Identify the two major types of printers, and indicate the advantages and disadvantages of each.

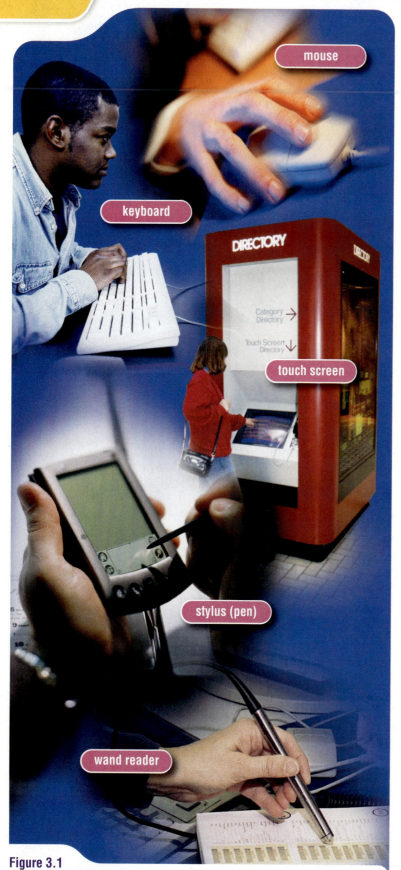

mouse

keyboard

touch screen

DIRECTORY

Category Directory →
Touch Screen Directory ↓

stylus (pen)

wand reader

Figure 3.1
Input devices enable you to get data, programs, commands, and responses into the computer's memory.

The heart of the computer is the CPU, but that's not the part of the computer that users experience. When you're using the computer, your attention is focused on the input and output devices you're using—typically, a keyboard, a mouse, and a monitor. Input devices enable you to transform information into a digital representation that the computer can process. They can be compared to human senses in that they enable the computer to see, hear, and even detect odors. Output devices transform processed digital information into forms that make sense to humans. They put our senses into contact with processed data, engaging our eyes, our ears, and even our sense of touch. This chapter explores the world of both input and output devices.

Understanding Input: Getting Data into the computer

Input refers to any data or instructions that you enter into the computer's memory. There are four main types of input:

Data The term **data** refers to unorganized (or relatively unorganized) words, numbers, images, or sounds that the computer can transform into something more useful. Data is different from **information**, which is data that is organized and meaningful.

Software programs **Software programs** give the computer specific instructions of what to do. Storage devices function as input devices when they are used to transfer software programs from storage media to the computer's memory. If you're sitting down at your computer to write a college paper, you'll begin by launching your word processing application. This causes your computer to transfer the word processing program from your computer's hard disk to its memory.

Commands A **command** tells the software program what to do. For example, if you're writing a paper, you may want to copy and paste a line of text from one place to another. To carry out this copying and pasting, you use the appropriate word processing commands. In other words, you use commands to tell the computer how to process the data that you have typed into the computer.

Responses Sometimes programs ask you to decide what to do. For example, if you quit your word processing application without saving your work, you will be asked whether you want to abandon the file or save it on a disk. In this way, the computer requires your input (a **user response**) for the process to continue.

Input Devices: Giving Commands

Input devices are hardware components that enable you to get data, programs, commands, and responses into the computer's memory (see Figure 3.1). The following sections explore various input devices, beginning with the most common ones:

Figure 3.2
The Keyboard

keyboards and pointing devices (such as mice and trackballs). Next, you'll learn about additional input devices you may encounter.

Keyboards

Unfortunately for those of us who hate to type, the **keyboard** is still the best way to get data into the computer (see Figure 3.2).

How do keyboards work? When you press one of the keys, the keyboard sends a digital impulse to the computer. Generally, this impulse travels through a cable (usually a USB cable) that is connected to the computer's keyboard connector. When the computer receives the impulse from the keyboard, it displays a character on-screen. A **character** is a letter, number, punctuation

QWERTY
These are the keys that identify the most common keyboard layout

function keys
These keys have different functions, depending on the program being used

num lock
Switch the keypad between a number entry and cursor movement

status indicators
These light up to inform you whether a toggle key's function is on or off

escape
Generally used to cancel or interrupt an operation

tab
Enables you to indent text

caps lock
Switches the keyboard between all-caps and normal modes

Alt and Ctrl
Pressed together with other keys gives commands to the program in use

shift
Allows you to enter a capital letter or punctuation mark

arrow keys
These move the cursor around the screen

numeric keypad
Designed for users to enter numbers quickly

Figure 3.3
Most computers use the standard QWERTY keyboard layout. This enhanced QWERTY keyboard also includes a number of special keys and a numeric keypad.

Destinations

For a list of keyboard shortcuts for many Microsoft products, see Microsoft's "Keyboard Assistance" at **www.microsoft.com/ enable/products/ keyboard/ keyboardsearch.asp**.

mark, or symbol (such as $ or #). The character appears at the on-screen location of the **cursor**, which shows where text will appear when you type. The cursor (also called the **insertion point**) may be a blinking vertical line, a blinking underscore, or a highlighted box.

USING A KEYBOARD

All keyboards include keys that allow you to type in letters, punctuation marks, and numbers, as well as an assortment of other special keys, such as Shift and Tab. Most keyboards use the **QWERTY keyboard**

layout, which is named after the first six letters at the upper left of the letter area (see Figure 3.3). Desktop PCs typically come equipped with an **enhanced keyboard**, which has 101 keys, including a number of special keys that nonenhanced keyboards don't have (see Figure 3.4). (The Macintosh equivalent, called the **extended keyboard**, has almost the exact same key layout.) Most notebook and laptop computers have fewer keys; however, you can hold down special keys that enable you to duplicate the functions of the additional keys on the enhanced keyboard.

Let's look at some of the special keys on the keyboard.

Cursor-Movement Keys

As you've learned, the cursor (insertion point) shows where your text will appear when you start typing. If you don't want to type where the cursor is located, you can use **cursor-movement keys** (also called **arrow keys**) to move the cursor around. Although programs implement the Home and End keys in different ways, they can also be used to move the cursor. (And of course, you can always use your mouse to move the cursor.)

Toggle Keys

A **toggle key** is a key named after a type of electrical switch that has only two positions: on and off. The **Caps Lock** key functions as a toggle key. It switches the caps lock mode on and off. When the caps lock mode is engaged, you do not have to press the Shift key to enter capital letters. To turn the caps lock mode off, just press the Caps Lock key again. The **Num Lock** key on the **numeric keypad** (located on the right-hand side of most enhanced keyboards) is also a toggle key. This key has two modes: a number-entry mode and a cursor-movement mode.

How do you know whether the toggle key is on or off without typing? The keyboard uses **status indicators** to show whether a toggle key's function is turned on or off. If the function is on, the indicator lights up.

Function Keys and Escape

Above the letters and numbers on the keyboard, you'll find **function keys** (labeled F1 through F10 or F15). Programs can give these keys different functions,

Special Keys on the PC Enhanced Keyboard

Key Name	Typical Function
Alt	In combination with another key, enters a command (example: Alt + X).
Backspace	Deletes the character to the left of the cursor.
Caps Lock	Toggles caps lock mode on or off.
Ctrl	In combination with another key, enters a command (example: Ctrl + C).
Delete	Deletes the character to the right of the cursor.
Down arrow	Moves the cursor down.
End	Moves the cursor to the end of the current line.
Esc	Cancels the current operation or closes a dialog box.
F1	Displays on-screen help.
Home	Moves the cursor to the beginning of the current line.
Insert	Toggles between insert and overwrite mode, if these modes are available in the program you're using.
Left arrow	Moves the cursor left.
Num Lock	Toggles the numeric keypad's num lock mode, in which the keypad enters numbers.
Page Down	Moves down one screenful or one page.
Page Up	Moves up one screenful or one page.
Pause/Break	Suspends a program. (This key is not used by most applications.)
Popup menu key	Displays the popup menu for the current context (Windows only).
Print Screen	Captures the screen image to a graphics file, or prints the current screen on the printer.
Right arrow	Moves the cursor right.
Up arrow	Moves the cursor up.
Windows key	Displays the Start menu in Microsoft Windows.

Figure 3.4

although F1 is almost always used to provide help to the user.

Near the function keys, you'll also notice a key called **Esc**, which is short for Escape. The Esc key's function also depends on which program you're using, but it's generally used to interrupt or cancel an operation.

Modifier Keys

Some keys have no effect unless you hold them down and press a second key. They are called **modifier keys** because they modify the meaning of the next key you press. You'll use modifier keys in **keyboard shortcuts**, which, as the name implies, provide a keyboard shortcut to menu commands.

On PCs, the modifier keys you use are called Alt and Ctrl. On Macintoshes, the modifier keys are called Ctrl, Command (indicated with the ⌘ symbol), and Option.

See Figure 3.5 for a list of standard keyboard shortcuts. Although these shortcuts aren't actually standardized by any independent standards body, they are widely used in Windows, Macintosh, and Linux applications.

Windows Keys

On keyboards specially designed for use with Microsoft Windows, you'll find two additional keys. The key with a window icon opens the Windows Start menu. The one with a box containing an arrow does the same thing as clicking the right mouse button.

Entering International Characters

If you're studying a foreign language, you may need to type letters that include **diacritical marks**, such as accent marks, tildes, and umlauts, that are not found in English. To enter diacritical marks, you use **dead keys**, a type of keyboard shortcut that adds a diacritical mark to the next letter you type. First you press and release the dead key. You won't see a character until you press one of the letters on the keyboard, which then appears with the appropriate diacritical mark. Figure 3.6 lists the keys you must type to get international characters on Macintosh and Windows systems. Note that if you're using a Macintosh, you don't use dead keys for some international letters. Instead, you use a combination of other keys, as shown in Figure 3.6.

USING ALTERNATIVE KEYBOARDS

Although most desktop computers come equipped with a keyboard that is connected by means of a keyboard cable, some computers are equipped with an infrared port

Standard Keyboard Shortcuts

PC Shortcut	Mac Shortcut	Purpose
Ctrl + A	⌘ + A	Selects all available items
Ctrl + B	⌘ + B	Bolds all selected items
Ctrl + C	⌘ + C	Copies text to the clipboard
Ctrl + F	⌘ + F	Finds text
Ctrl + I	⌘ + I	Italicizes selected text
Ctrl + J	⌘ + J	Justifies text
Ctrl + N	⌘ + N	Creates a new document
Ctrl + O	⌘ + O	Opens an existing document
Ctrl + P	⌘ + P	Prints an existing document
Ctrl + Q	⌘ + Q	Quits the application
Ctrl + S	⌘ + S	Saves the existing document
Ctrl + U	⌘ + U	Underlines the selected items
Ctrl + V	⌘ + V	Pastes the contents of the clipboard
Ctrl + X	⌘ + X	Cuts selected items

Figure 3.5

Inserting International Characters

Mac OS Keys to Press	Microsoft Windows Keys to Press	Example of Result
Option + ` (acute accent)	Ctrl + ` (acute accent) + any vowel	à
Option + e	Ctrl + ' (apostrophe) + any vowel	á
Option + ^ (caret)	Ctrl + Shift + ^ (caret) + any vowel	â
Option + n	Ctrl + Shift + ~ (tilde) + a, n, o, A, N, O	ñ
Option + u	Ctrl + Shift + : (colon) + any vowel	ä
Option + a or A	Ctrl + Shift + @ + a or A	å, Å
Option + ' (apostrophe)	Ctrl + Shift + & + a or A	æ, Æ
Option + q or Q	Ctrl + Shift + & + o or O	œ, Œ
Option + s	Ctrl + Shift + & + s	ß
Option + c or C	Ctrl + , (comma) + c or C	ç, Ç
Option + d	Ctrl + ' (apostrophe) + d	∂
Option + o or O	Ctrl + /, + o or O	ø, Ø

Figure 3.6

Figure 3.7
Portable keyboards are popular among handheld users because they allow users to type information quickly and easily.

that enables them to use a **wireless keyboard** (also called a **cordless keyboard**). These keyboards use infrared or radio waves to send signals to the computer.

Also popular among handheld computer users are **portable keyboards**, which allow you to connect a small folding keyboard to your handheld and type as you would using a normal computer (see Figure 3.7).

HEALTH RISKS OF KEYBOARD USE

Be aware that prolonged keyboard use can cause **cumulative trauma disorder**, also called **repetitive strain injury**, and **carpal tunnel syndrome**. In this type of injury, repeated motions cause damage to sensitive nerve tissue. Sometimes these injuries are so serious that they require surgery. To help prevent these problems, **ergonomic keyboards** are available. Ergonomic keyboards such as the Microsoft Natural Keyboard keep your wrists straight,

Figure 3.8
Ergonomic keyboards like this one can help prevent cumulative trauma disorder.

Pointer Name	Purpose
Normal Select	Selects an item on-screen.
Help Select	Shows help for this item.
Working	Informs you that the computer is busy.
Text Select	Moves the cursor to the pointer's location within text, or selects text by dragging.
Precision Select	Allows for exact on-screen selection.
Unavailable	Informs you that this item is not available now.
Vertical Resize	Resizes vertically as you drag the mouse.
Horizontal Resize	Resizes horizontally as you drag the mouse.
Diagonal Resize	Resizes diagonally as you drag the mouse.
Move	Moves the whole item when you drag the mouse.
Link Select	Moves to this item.

Figure 3.9
Common Pointers (Microsoft Windows)

clicking

Move the pointer to an item, and click the left button.

dragging

Click on something that you see on-screen, and hold down the left button. Then move the mouse to "drag" the item across the screen.

double-clicking

Point to something and click the button twice, in rapid succession.

Action	Procedure
Point	Move the mouse across the flat surface until the tip of the selection pointer (the arrow) rests on the desired item.
Click	Press and release the mouse button (Macintosh) or the left mouse button (PC).
Double-click	In quick succession, press and release the mouse button (Macintosh) or the left mouse button (PC) two times. If the double-click action doesn't work, try again, but do it faster.
Right-click	Press and hold the mouse button (Macintosh) or the right mouse button (PC).
Drag	Move the pointer to an item. On a Macintosh, hold down the mouse button. On a PC, hold down the left mouse button. Then drag the item to its new location, and release the button.
Right-drag	On a PC, move the pointer to an item, hold down the right mouse button, then drag the item to its new location. A custom menu will appear that offers choices such as Copy item here and Move item here, among others.

Figure 3.10
Pointing, Clicking, and Dragging Using a Mouse

reducing (but not eliminating) your chance of an injury (see Figure 3.8).

Pointing Devices

A **pointing device** gives you control over the movements of the on-screen pointer. The **pointer** is an on-screen symbol that signifies the type of command, input, or response you can give (see Figure 3.9). Pointing devices such as a mouse also enable you to initiate actions, such as clicking, double-clicking, selecting, and dragging (see Figure 3.10). By means of these actions, you can give commands and responses to whatever program the computer is

Figure 3.11
Common Pointing Devices

a) mouse   b) trackball

c) pointing stick   d) touchpad

e) joystick   f) touch screen

g) stylus

running. Pointing devices can also be used to provide input. For example, pointing devices can be used in graphics programs to draw and paint on-screen, as if you were using a pencil or brush.

THE MOUSE

The most widely used pointing device is the **mouse**, which is standard equipment on today's computer systems (see Figure 3.11a). As you probably know, a mouse is a palm-sized pointing device that is designed to move about on a clean, flat surface called a **mousepad**. As you move the mouse, the mouse's movements are mirrored by the on-screen pointer. To initiate actions, use the mouse buttons. On the Macintosh, the mouse has just one button. On the PC, the mouse typically has two buttons. Linux systems may be equipped with a three-button mouse. Some applications use a middle mouse button for certain purposes. If you're using a Linux system equipped with a two-button mouse, you may be able to emulate the middle button's action by pressing both buttons at the same time.

Types of Mice
Mice connect to computers in different ways. **PS/2 mice** connect to the computer's PS/2 port by means of a cable and a PS/2-compatible connector. Today, mice that connect via USB (universal serial bus) are increasingly popular. Less commonly used, but still available, are **serial mice**, which connect to a disused serial port. **Cordless mice** (also called **wireless mice**) use invisible infrared signals to connect to the computer's infrared (IrDA) port. Although cordless mice eliminate the clutter caused by the mouse's cord, the infrared transmitter must be in a direct line of sight with the receiving port on the computer's case.

Mice use two different technologies to generate and transmit positional information. **Mechanical mice** use a rotating ball to generate information about the mouse's position. One drawback is that the ball can get dirty, which interferes with the mouse's ability to determine its position. **Optical mice** use a low-power laser to determine the mouse's position. However, some optical mice require a special mousepad that uses

a grid to determine the mouse's location. Some mice combine the two technologies by using a laser to monitor the mechanical ball's movements.

Developed by Microsoft, the **wheel mouse** includes a rotating wheel that can be used to scroll text vertically within a document or Web page (see Figure 3.12).

Health Risks of Mouse Usage
Like keyboards, mice are associated with cumulative trauma disorders. If you're unable to use a mouse due to cumulative trauma disorder or because you're physically challenged, you may be able to use a **foot mouse**. A foot mouse uses two interchangeable foot pedals to control the pointer. One pedal enables the user to control the pointer's location, while the second is used as a clicking device.

MOUSE ALTERNATIVES

Although the mouse is by far the most popular pointing device, some people prefer alternatives such as trackballs, pointing sticks, or touchpads. These alternatives are especially attractive when desktop space is limited—or nonexistent, as in most of the places where people use notebook computers. For special purposes, such as playing games or using a computer that is made available for use by the public, additional input devices are available, including joysticks, touch screens, styluses, and light pens.

Destinations

For more information on foot mice and other hands-free pointing devices, visit the "NoHands Mouse" Web site at **www.footmouse.com**.

Figure 3.12
A Wheel Mouse

1. Wheel button allows for faster scrolling without your needing to use on-screen scroll bars.

2. Customizable buttons allow you to use the buttons to perform different comands for different programs.

3. An optical sensor enables you to use the mouse without a mousepad.

Trackballs

Trackballs are basically mice flipped on their backs (see Figure 3.11b). Instead of moving the mouse, you move the stationary ball directly. Trackballs usually come with one or more buttons that work in the same way as mouse buttons. Though not as popular as the traditional mouse, trackballs are handy when you have a small desk space, as they remain stationary.

Pointing Sticks

A **pointing stick** is a small, stubby pointing device that protrudes from the computer's keyboard (see Figure 3.11c). Because pointing sticks are pressure-sensitive devices, you use them by pushing them in various directions with your finger. Developed by IBM for its notebook computers, pointing sticks are now available for desktop computer keyboards as well.

Touchpads

Many notebook computers use a **touchpad** (also called a **trackpad**) for a pointing

Figure 3.13
Some desktop computer keyboards include touchpads.

device (see Figure 3.11d). Touchpads are pressure-sensitive devices that respond to your finger's movement over the pad's surface. Although you'll most often find touchpads on notebooks and laptops, you can purchase desktop computer keyboards that are equipped with built-in touchpads (see Figure 3.13).

Joysticks

A **joystick** is an input device with a large vertical lever that can be moved in any direction (see Figure 3.11e). Although joysticks can be used as pointing devices, they're most often used to control the motion of an on-screen object in a computer game. A variety of buttons (called triggers) are available for initiating actions, such as firing weapons. In industry and manufacturing, joysticks are used to control robots. Flight simulators and other training simulators also use joysticks to simulate vehicle controls.

Touch Screens

A **touch screen** uses a pressure-sensitive panel to detect where users have tapped the display screen with their fingertip (see Figure 3.11f). Touch screens are easy to use. In addition, they're more reliable than keyboards and pointing devices—and virtually impossible to steal. All these characteristics make touch screens an excellent choice for publicly accessible computers, such as those placed in kiosks. A **kiosk** is a booth that provides a computer service of some type, such as an automated teller machine (ATM) (see Figure 3.14). Though most frequently seen in banks, kiosks are used for many purposes, such as providing information to tourists and at airport e-ticket terminals.

Styluses

Styluses, which look like ordinary pens except that their tips are dry and semiblunt (see Figure 3.11g), are commonly found on personal digital assistants (PDAs). Styluses are also often used in computer-aided design (CAD) applications and other graphics applications with a **graphics tablet**, a digitizing tablet consisting of a grid on which users design such things as cars, buildings, medical devices, and robots.

To use a stylus with a PDA, you touch the stylus's tip to the PDA's screen to

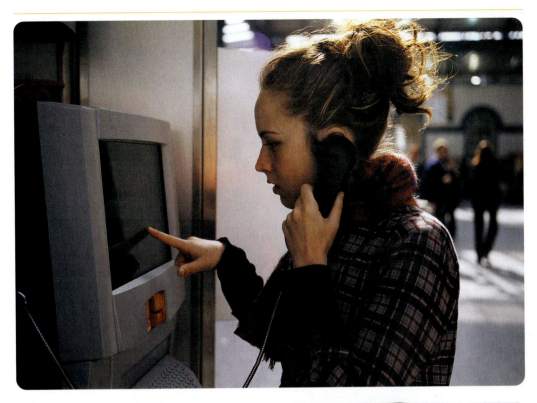

Figure 3.14
Kiosks use touch screens to provide information and services to the public.

choose icons. Most PDAs are equipped with handwriting recognition capabilities, which enable them to detect handwritten characters and transform these characters into text. However, to get the PDA to understand the letters you are writing, you may need to write them in a special way (see Figure 3.15).

Most experts believe that handwriting recognition will become one of the more popular methods of getting information into a computer, but people will continue to use keyboards. The main reason? People with good typing skills can enter information much more quickly with a keyboard. The term **pen computing** refers collectively to the branch of computing that involves PDAs, pens, and handwriting recognition.

Figure 3.15
To enter characters into a PDA, you often need to write them in a special way.

Light Pens

Although touch screens are easy to use, human fingers are much bigger than an on-screen pointer. As a result, software designers must provide fewer options and larger, on-screen buttons. These characteristics of touch screens make them best suited to simple, special-purpose programs. For more detailed work, light pens can be used. **Light pens** contain a light source that triggers the touch screen's detection mechanism (see Figure 3.16).

Figure 3.16
Light pens provide a way to get input into a touch screen system.

Other Ways to Get Data into the Computer

You can equip personal computers so that they can handle many different forms of input, including voice input, sound input, digital input, scanned input, and fax input.

VOICE INPUT: SPEECH RECOGNITION

Many experts believe that computing will not come into its own until computers learn to understand and respond to human speech. Thanks to recent advances in **speech recognition**, that day may be close at hand (see Figure 3.17). Also called **voice recognition**, speech recognition is a type of input in which the computer recognizes spoken words. Depending on the context, the words may be interpreted as part of a command (such as "Open Microsoft Word") or as data input. If the words are interpreted as data, they appear within a document as if you had typed them at the keyboard. Speech recognition requires special software as well as a microphone.

Although far from perfect, today's speech recognition software is much better than its predecessors. In the past, speech

recognition systems used **discrete speech recognition**. In discrete speech recognition systems, you had to speak each word separately, as in this example: "Please. Record. This. Sentence." If you didn't pause between words, the software would make a mistake. Today's **continuous speech recognition** software enables users to speak without pausing between words.

SOUND INPUT: SOUND CARDS

Computers equipped with **sound cards** can accept sound input from a microphone. In PCs, a sound card is an expansion board designed to record and play back **sound files**. (Sound is built into Macintosh computers.) Sound files contain digitized sound data, which is saved in one of several standardized sound formats. These formats specify how sounds should be digitally represented, and generally include some type of **data compression** that reduces the size of the file. Examples of popular sound file formats are the Windows WAV format (the standard Microsoft Windows stereo sound file format), AU sounds (a low-quality, monaural sound format often encountered on the Internet), and **Moving Pictures Experts Group** (**MPEG**) audio formats (called MP2 and MP3). The MPEG formats reduce file size significantly without sacrificing audio quality. A new digital format, called Ogg Vorbis, is an even faster format than MP3. Ogg files are also about 20 percent smaller than MP3 files, so you can fit more of them onto your hard disk or MP3 player.

DIGITAL INPUT: DIGITAL CAMERAS, DIGITAL VIDEO, AND VIDEOCONFERENCING

Digital cameras are among the hottest products on the consumer market (see Figures 3.18 and 3.19). This section extends past the topic of pure input and explores the bright frontier of personal digital photography.

Like traditional cameras, digital cameras have a lens, a shutter, and an optical viewfinder. What sets digital cameras apart is their inner workings—specifically, how

Figure 3.17
Speech recognition technology enables users to use spoken words to command the computer and enter textual data.

the image is saved. In digital cameras, the captured image's light falls on a **charge-coupled device** (**CCD**), a photosensitive computer chip that transforms light patterns into **pixels** (individual dots). (CCDs are also used in scanners and fax machines, which we'll discuss later in the chapter.)

A CCD consists of a grid containing light-sensitive elements. Each element converts the incoming light into a voltage that is proportional to the light's brightness. The digital camera's picture quality is determined by how many elements the CCD has. Each CCD element corresponds to one pixel, or dot, on a computer display or printout. The more elements, the sharper the picture. A one-megapixel digital camera has a CCD consisting of at least one million elements; such a camera can produce a reasonably sharp snapshot-sized image. With at least two million elements, two-megapixel cameras can take higher-resolution pictures; you can expect to get near-photographic quality prints at sizes of up to 5 by 7 inches with such a camera. Three-megapixel and four-megapixel cameras can produce images that can print at sizes of 8 by 10 inches or even 11 by 14 inches, but they're expensive.

Since digital cameras have no film, the shots you take need to be stored in the

Figure 3.18
Among the hottest products on the consumer market, digital cameras have a lens, a shutter, and an optical viewfinder.

camera until you can transfer them to a computer for long-term storage or printing. The two most popular methods of storing images in the camera are called **CompactFlash** and **SmartMedia**. Both use flash memory technologies to store from 4 MB to 1 GB of image data. About 12 MB of flash memory is the equivalent of a standard, 12-exposure film roll. However, most cameras enable you to select from a variety of resolutions, so the number of shots you get will vary depending on the resolution you choose. If you need more

Destinations

For reviews, comparisons, and price information for digital cameras, see the "Digital Camera Buyer's Guide," at **www.digital-camerastore.com**.

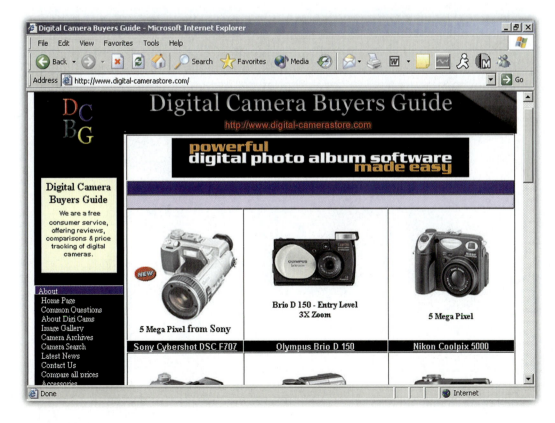

Figure 3.19
The World Wide Web is a great source of support for digital photo storage, sharing, creative ideas, and help.

"film," you need only carry more flash memory cards. Many digital cameras enable you to preview the shots you've taken on a small LCD screen, so you can create more room on the flash memory cards by erasing pictures that you don't like.

A variety of methods are available for printing the images you take with a digital camera. In most cases, you'll need to download the images to a computer for printing. Some cameras are designed to connect to a computer by means of a serial or USB cable. Others can transfer data by means of an infrared port. If you're using a digital camera that stores images on flash memory cards, you can obtain a PC card that contains a flash memory card reader. This type of PC card enables the computer to read the images from the flash memory card as if it were a disk drive. Also available are standalone flash memory readers, which serve the same purpose. Once you've transferred the images to the computer for safekeeping and printing, you can erase the flash memory card and reuse it, as if you had purchased a fresh roll of film.

Once transferred to the computer, the images can be enhanced, edited, cropped, or sized by a **photo-editing program**. The same program can be used to print the images on a color printer. (Some specially designed printers, called **photo printers**, have flash memory card readers that enable you to bypass the computer completely.)

How good are digital cameras? If you're hoping to create publication-quality prints, you'd be wise to stick to traditional cameras that use chemically processed film. With the exception of a few very expensive, high-end digital cameras, most digital cameras are the equivalent of the point-and-shoot 35mm cameras that dominate the traditional (film-based) camera market: they take pictures that are good enough for family photo albums, Web publishing, and business uses (such as a real estate agent's snapshots of homes for sale), but not for professional photography. A color printer or photo printer can make prints from a digital camera's images that closely resemble the snapshots you used to get from the drugstore, but only if you choose the highest print resolution and use glossy photo paper. Getting good printout results takes time—most consumer-oriented printers will require several minutes to print an image at the printer's highest possible resolution—and it costs money, too. The best photo printing papers cost as much as $1 per sheet.

Figure 3.20
Web-based photo communities, such as PhotoWorks.com, enable you to upload your pictures and make them available to your friends and family at no charge.

But printing is only one of the distribution options that are open to you when you use a digital camera—and that's exactly why so many people love digital photography. In addition to printing snapshots for the family album, you can copy the images to CD-R discs, send them to friends and family via e-mail, and even display them on the Internet. Several Web-based **photo communities** enable users to upload their pictures and make them available to friends and family at no charge (see Figure 3.20).

Point-and-shoot digital cameras are designed so that anyone can take good pictures. Their features typically include automatic focus, automatic exposure, built-in automatic electronic flash with red eye reduction, and optical zoom lenses with digital enhancement. Some point-and-shoot cameras come with a built-in LCD viewfinder, enabling you to preview the shot to make sure it comes out right.

Single-lens reflex (SLR) digital cameras are much more expensive than point-and-shoot cameras, but they offer the features that professional photographers demand, such as interchangeable lenses, through-the-lens image previewing, and the ability to override the automatic focus and exposure settings.

Digital Video

Digital cameras are revolutionizing still photography, and all the indications are that **digital video** technologies are poised to do the same for full-motion images—animations, videos, and movies.

In the past, most full-motion images were captured and stored by means of analog techniques. In order to input analog video to the computer, a **video capture board** (also called a **video capture card**) is required. A video capture board transforms an analog video into its digital counterpart. Because a digital video file for even a short video requires a great deal of storage space, most video capture boards are equipped to perform on-the-fly data compression using one of several **codecs** (compression/decompression standards). Popular codecs include MPEG (an acronym for Moving Picture Experts Group), Apple's QuickTime, and Microsoft's AVI (an acronym for Audio Video Interleave).

Video capture boards enable computers to display and process full-motion video, a "movie" that gives the illusion of smooth, continuous action. Like actual movies, digitized video actually consists of a series of still photographs, called **frames**, that are flashed on-screen at a rapid rate. A frame-flashing speed, called the **frame rate**, indicates how successfully a given video can create the illusion of smooth, unbroken movement. A rate of at least 24 frames per second (fps) is needed to produce an illusion of smooth, continuous action.

What can you "capture" with a video capture board? You can use just about any video source, including TV broadcasts, taped video, or live video from video cameras.

Increasingly popular are **digital video cameras**, which use digital rather than analog technologies to store recorded video images. Like digital cameras, digital video cameras can connect to a computer; often, this is done by means of a USB port. Because the signal produced by a digital video camera conforms to the computer's digital method of representing data, no video capture board is necessary. Most digital video cameras can take still images as well as movies.

Videoconferencing

Videoconferencing refers to the use of digital video technology to simulate face-to-face meetings (see Figure 3.21). In a videoconference, two or more people can see and communicate with each other, even though they are not physically present in the same room. Participants are filmed "live," so that all the participants can see the people with whom they're talking.

A **whiteboard**, generally shown as a separate area of the videoconferencing screen, enables participants to create a shared workspace. Participants can write or draw in this space as if they were using a physical whiteboard in a meeting.

Videoconferencing requires powerful and sophisticated computer systems and video technologies; it also requires a fast, high-capacity computer network. For this reason, most videoconferences are implemented on high-speed corporate networks rather than the Internet, which does not currently have sufficient bandwidth (data-carrying capacity) for high-quality video-conferencing. However, many Internet

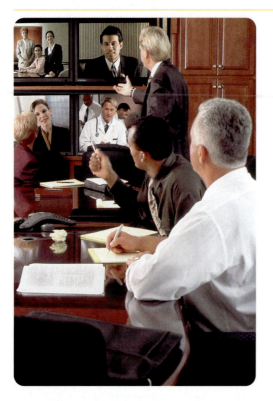

Figure 3.21
In a videoconference, two or more people can see and communicate with each other, even though they are not physically present in the same room.

computer monitor. When participants are all using Web cams and Internet-based videoconferencing software such as Microsoft's NetMeeting, they can implement a low-resolution version of corporate videoconferencing by means of Internet connections. The images are small, jerky, and liable to delays. Still, thousands of Internet users employ Web cams and programs such as NetMeeting to stay in touch with friends and family.

Sometimes an individual, company, or organization places a Web cam in a public location, such as a street corner, a railway station, or a museum (see Figure 3.22). Often, the camera is set up to take a "snapshot" of the scene every 15 minutes or so. The image is then displayed on a Web page. Some sites offer **streaming cams**, also called **live cams**, which provide more frequently updated images.

SCANNED INPUT

users enjoy engaging in low-resolution videoconferencing by means of Web cams. A **Web cam** is an inexpensive, low-resolution analog or digital video camera that is designed to sit on top of the

Scanners use charge-coupled devices (CCDs) to digitize an image formed by a lens. Scanners are designed to copy anything that's printed on a sheet of paper, including artwork, handwriting, printed

Figure 3.22
Earthcam.com provides a large number of links to Webcams that are positioned throughout the world.

Figure 3.23 a&b
(a) Flatbed scanners work on a single piece of paper at a time. (b) Handheld scanners are used most often to scan text into a microcomputer.

documents, or typed documents. **Flatbed scanners** work on a single sheet of paper at a time (see Figure 3.23a). **Sheetfed scanners** draw in the sheets to be copied by means of a roller mechanism. **Handheld scanners** can be used to copy smaller originals, such as photographs (see Figure 3.23b).

Scanners have varying **optical resolutions**, depending on the number of distinct light-sensitive elements packed into the scanner's CCD. Scanners may use image enhancement techniques to simulate higher resolutions. Scanners also vary in **bit depth**, the number of bits used to represent each dot (pixel). A 24-bit scanner can capture up to 16.7 million colors.

Most scanners come with **optical character recognition** (**OCR**) software that automatically decodes imaged text into a text file. This technology has improved to the point that most printed or typed documents can be scanned into text files, eliminating the need to retype such documents to get them into the computer.

Figure 3.24
A fax machine transmits documents via the telephone system.

line and the fax software is running, the computer can receive incoming faxes. The incoming document is displayed on-screen, and it can be printed or saved.

Input Devices in Business, Industry, and Science

The realms of business, industry, and science use a number of specialized input devices, including image processing systems, scanning systems, bar code readers, biofeedback devices, and chemical detectors.

IMAGE PROCESSING SYSTEMS, SCANNING SYSTEMS, AND BAR CODE READERS

Source data automation is the process of capturing data at its source, eliminating the need to file paper documents or to

FAX INPUT

Facsimile machines (**fax machines**) transmit scanned images of documents via the telephone system (see Figure 3.24). Fax machines do not require the use of a computer. However, you can set up a computer to simulate a fax machine. To do so, you'll need **fax software**, which enables the computer to send and receive faxes. You'll also need a fax modem. A **fax modem** is a communications device that enables a computer to send and receive faxes via the telephone system. When the fax modem is connected to a telephone record the data by keying it manually. The result is lower costs and fewer errors. For example, many businesses use **image processing systems** to file incoming paper documents electronically. The documents are scanned, and the images are stored on the computer, where it's easier and faster to retrieve them. Railroads, for example, use scanners to record and track the location of hundreds of thousands of freight cars.

The banking industry developed one of the earliest scanning systems in the 1950s for processing checks. The **magnetic-ink character recognition (MICR) system** is used throughout the banking industry. The bank, branch, account number, and check number are encoded on the check before it is sent to the customer. After the customer has used the check and it comes back to the bank, all that needs to be entered manually is the amount. MICR has not been adopted by other industries because the character set has only fourteen symbols.

Of all the scanning devices used in business, you're probably most familiar with **bar code readers**. Many retail and grocery stores use some form of bar code

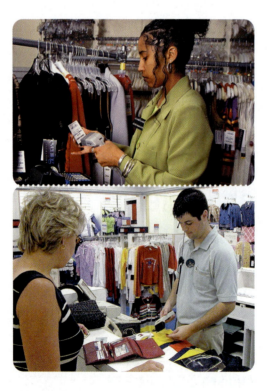

Figure 3.25
Many retail stores use a bar code reader to determine what's being sold and to retrieve the item's price from a computer system.

reader to determine the item being sold and to retrieve the item's price from a computer system (see Figure 3.25). The code reader may be a handheld unit or be embedded in a countertop. The bar code reader reads the **universal product code (UPC)**, a pattern of bars printed on merchandise. The UPC has gained wide acceptance since its introduction in the 1970s. Initially, workers resisted the use of the code because the system was used to check their accuracy and speed. Today, bar codes are used to update inventory and ensure correct pricing. Federal Express uses a unique bar code to identify and track each package. Federal Express employees can usually tell a customer within minutes the location of any package.

If you've taken a college exam, you're probably already familiar with **Mark Sense Character Recognition systems**. Every time you take a test with a "fill in the bubble" Scantron® form and use a #2 lead pencil, you're creating input suitable for an **optical mark reader (OMR)**. A #2 lead pencil works best because of the number of magnetic particles in that weight of lead. The OMR senses the magnetized marks, enabling the reader to determine which responses are marked. OMR is helpful to researchers who need to tabulate responses to large surveys. Almost any type of survey or questionnaire can be designed for OMR devices.

BIOLOGICAL FEEDBACK DEVICES

Biological feedback devices translate eye movements, body movements, and even brain waves into computer input. **Eye-gaze response systems** (also called **vision technology**) enable quadriplegics to control a computer by moving their eyes around the screen. A special camera tracks eye movements and moves the cursor in response.

Three-dimensional **virtual reality** programs use helmets and sensor-equipped gloves to enable users to "move" through a simulated "world." The helmet contains two miniature television screens that display the world in what appears to be three dimensions (see Figure 3.26). If you turn your head, your view of the world moves accordingly. Using a **data glove**, users can touch and manipulate simulated "objects."

CHEMICAL DETECTORS

What about the computer's sense of smell? The human nose can detect remarkably minute traces of chemicals in the air. And, increasingly, so can computers. If you've visited an airport recently, you may already have been "sniffed" by a computer input device designed to detect minute traces of explosives. Some patrons are asked to step into a special booth, where air jets dislodge chemicals adhering to a person's clothes and hands. The air is then sucked through a chemical sensor that can identify many types of explosives. A computer screen displays the results of the test, and instructs the operator if explosives are detected.

Figure 3.26
Where are "you" when you experience virtual reality?

EMERGING TECHNOLOGIES

Input for All

According to Bill Gates, the Internet and speech recognition are the way of the future. Almost everyone has used the Internet and knows what it has to offer. You may also have experimented with speech recognition software, which allows you to control your computer using voice commands. IBM's Via Voice and Dragon's Naturally Speaking are just two of the computer-dictating software products that have been around for some time. And if you have Microsoft's new XP operating system, its software allows you to use speech recognition with any document. Office XP comes with two modes of operation: dictation, which allows you to dictate letters and e-mail messages, and voice command, which allows you to access menus and commands, by speaking into a microphone.

To use speech-recognition software, you first have to "train" the software to understand how you speak and how to translate this speech into typed words. You do this by dictating a number of prepared passages into the computer through a microphone so that the software can "learn" how you speak—your accent, enunciation, and pronunciation. The more you train the software, the better it becomes at correctly recognizing your words. If the computer doesn't know which word you have spoken (say if it hears "to" but isn't sure if it's "to," "too," or "two," it will figure out which word is correct based on the context in which it is found.

Although many people use speech-recognition as a simple dictation device, speech recognition software not only improves productivity, relieving many tired and overused hands, but also provides an alternative input option for people who can't use a keyboard.

Meanwhile, Microsoft researchers are working on what they refer to as "vision technology," computer programs that allow computers to "see" and in turn respond to a user's physical presence, his or her gestures, and even certain facial expressions. Of course, it's not just Microsoft working on this technology. Research labs around the world are looking into ways in which machines can interact with people without them having to use standard input devices such as a keyboard. In fact, vision technology is part of a larger category of research (called perceptual user interfaces at Microsoft) that focuses not just on vision technology, but also on speech recognition, gesture recognition, and machines that "learn."

Gesture recognition research using hand movements has an obvious benefit when it is used with American Sign Language. It will also one day play a large role in making entertainment applications, including games, more, well, entertaining. It is also hoped that perceptual user interfaces will one day help physically challenged computer users control their computers by means of facial expressions and eye gazes. Already on the market, VisualMouse translates a user's head motions into mouse movements, allowing users to control a mouse without using their hands.

It's hard to tell when perceptual interfaces will hit computer store shelves. But one thing is clear: someday it will be possible for everyone to use their face, eyes, and mouth to interact with electronic devices. You may one day turn lights on and off with your voice. You may move a mouse with a blink of your eye or a turn of your head. And one day your whole body may be used to produce computer effects. Thanks to speech and gesture recognition and other innovative technologies, there will one day be computer input possibilities for us all.

IMPACTS

Understanding Output: Making Data Meaningful

Output refers to the results of the computer's processing operations, which transform unorganized (or disorganized) data into useful information. The four kinds of output are text, graphics, video, and audio (see Figure 3.27):

- **Text output** consists of characters (letters, numbers, punctuation marks, and symbols) that are organized in some meaningful way. Examples include a sorted list of names and addresses or a document that's been formatted for attractive printing.

- **Graphics output** consists of visual images, including charts and pictures. The images may appear on a monitor or be printed in permanent form on paper.

- **Video output** consists of a series of still images that are played back at a fast enough frame rate to give the illusion of continuous motion. (Frame rate refers to the number of images displayed per second.)

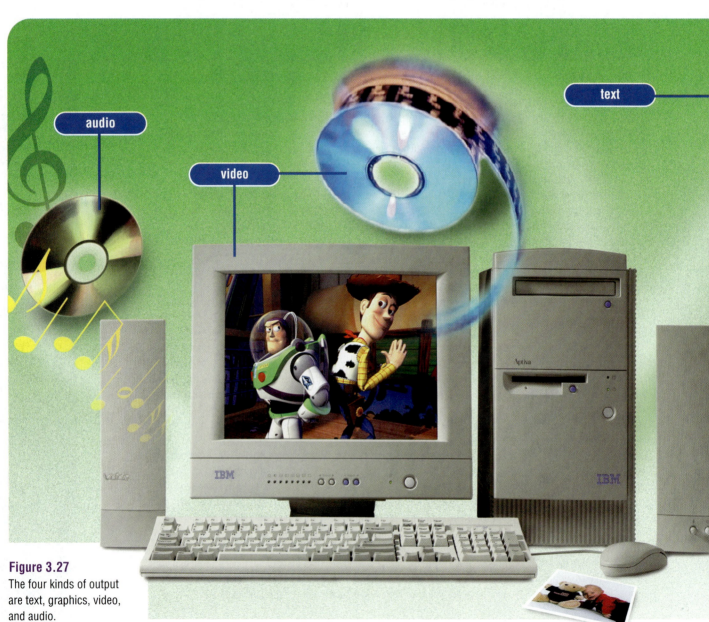

Figure 3.27
The four kinds of output are text, graphics, video, and audio.

- **Audio output** consists of sound, music, or synthesized speech.

Subsequent sections examine printers, sound systems, and cutting-edge output systems that engage our sense of touch.

Output Devices: Engaging Our Senses

Output devices enable people to see, hear, and even feel the results of processing operations. The most widely used output devices are visual display systems (monitors) and printers. We'll begin this section by looking at visual display systems.

graphics

Visual Display Systems

The computer's **visual display system** is its most important output system. Two components are required to generate the visual display: the video adapter and the monitor.

VIDEO ADAPTERS

The image displayed on a monitor is generated by a **video adapter** (also called a **display adapter**, **video card**, or **graphics card**), an expansion board that plugs into one of the computer's expansion slots. (On some computers, the video adapter circuitry is built into the motherboard.) The video adapter determines the overall quality of the image that the monitor displays. Video adapters contain their own processing circuitry as well as their own memory, which is called **video RAM** (**VRAM**). Because video adapters have their own memory and processors, they free the computer's main memory (RAM) and processor (CPU) for other tasks. Adapters with fast processors are called **video accelerators** because they can speed up the image's display. Most video adapters are designed to work with analog monitors. For this reason, they include a **RAMDAC** chip. RAMDAC is an abbreviation for Random Access Digital to Analog Converter. This chip converts the video card's digital output to the analog output required by most monitors. However, some monitors (including the LCD or flat-panel monitors we'll discuss later in this chapter) require the video adapter to produce digital output. The **Digital Display Working Group** (**DDWG**) is an industry association working to define digital video output. The standard they have created, called **Digital Video Interface** (**DVI**), provides connections for LCD and other flat-panel devices.

Numerous types of memory are used for VRAM; the most expensive (and most capable) video adapters are likely to use the same, super-fast RAM technologies found in a high-end computer's main memory, such as DDR SDRAM. However, no matter which type of RAM technology the adapter uses, the amount of VRAM determines the maximum resolution that can be displayed. The term **resolution** generally refers to an image's sharpness. Video adapters conform to standard resolutions that are expressed by the number of dots (pixels) that can be displayed horizontally, followed by an "x" and the number of lines that can be displayed vertically (for example, 1024 x 768). These standards have been developed by standards organizations such as the Video Electronics Standards Association (VESA), as well as by computer and video card manufacturers. Figure 3.28 lists common PC resolutions that are defined by industry-wide standards.

For color graphics displays, the lowest-resolution standard is the **video graphics adapter** (**VGA**) standard (640 x 480). Most of today's computers default to **Super VGA** resolution (1024 x 768).

Also requiring memory is the information needed to display color. The term **color depth** refers to the number of colors that can be displayed at one time. To display a maximum of 16 colors, only 4 bits of data are required for each screen pixel. Eight bits of color information are required to display 256 colors. To display 16.7 million colors, the adapter's memory must store 24 bits of information for each displayed pixel (see Figure 3.29).

How do resolution and color depth relate to each other when it comes to a given video adapter's performance? With 2 MB of installed VRAM, an adapter can display 16.7 million colors only at lower resolutions (such as 800 x 600). To display 16.7 million colors at higher resolutions, more memory is needed. Some video adapters can be upgraded with additional VRAM.

Another important measurement of video adapter quality is the refresh rate generated at a given resolution. **Refresh rate** refers to the frequency with which the screen image is updated, and it's measured in hertz (Hz), or cycles per second. Below 60 Hz, most people notice an annoying, eye-straining flicker. Very few people notice flicker when the refresh rate exceeds 72 Hz.

Most of the video adapters available for today's computers can display three-dimensional (3D) as well as two-dimensional (2D) images. A **3D graphics adapter** can display images that provide the illusion of depth as well as height and width. However, 3D-intensive applications, such as computer-aided design (CAD) and 3D games, require much more memory and processing power than 2D applications, such as word processing or other office suite applications.

Multidisplay Video Adapters

Today's operating systems, including Microsoft Windows 2000, Microsoft Windows XP, and the latest versions of Linux, can work with more than one monitor at a time. To work with two monitors, a computer must be equipped with two video adapters or a **multidisplay video adapter**. A multidisplay video adapter enables users to hook up two monitors without having to purchase a second video adapter.

MONITORS

As you have gathered, **monitors** (also called **displays**) display the video adapter's

Common PC Resolutions
640 x 480
800 x 600
1024 x 768
1280 x 1024

Figure 3.28

Common Color Depths	
Color Depth	Number of Colors
VGA (4 bits)	16
256-Color Mode (8 bits)	256
High Color (16 bits)	65,536
True Color (24 bits)	16,777,216

Figure 3.29

output. The on-screen display enables you to see how applications are processing your data, but it's important to remember that the screen display isn't a permanent record. To drive home this point, screen output is sometimes called **soft copy**, as opposed to **hard copy** (printed output). To make permanent copies of your work, you need to save it to a storage device or print it.

Monitors are categorized by the technology used to generate their images, the colors they display, their screen size, and additional performance characteristics.

Types of Monitors

Monitors that look like television screens use the TV's **cathode-ray tube** (**CRT**) technology, in which the image is formed by an electron "gun" shooting a stream of electrons at the screen's phosphorescent surface. The large monitors that you see connected to desktop computers are cathode-ray tube (CRT) monitors (see Figure 3.30). Although the term CRT is sometimes used to mean "monitor," it's properly used to refer only to the "picture tube" that generates the display. In a color monitor, three guns corresponding to the three primary colors (red, green, and blue) are combined in varying intensities to produce on-screen colors (see Figure 3.31). CRT monitors are inexpensive compared with other types of monitors, but they consume more energy and take up more room on the desk.

Figure 3.31
Monitors use cathode-ray tube (CRT) technology. Everything you see on the screen is a combination of red, green, and blue pixels.

The thinner monitors used on notebook and some desktop computers are known as **LCD monitors** (also called **LCD displays** and **flat-panel displays**). Compared with CRT-based monitors, LCD monitors consume less electricity and take up much less room. These features make LCD monitors ideal for portable computers, including notebook computers, personal digital assistants (PDAs), **Web-enabled devices** such as digital cellular telephones that have the ability to connect to the Internet, and **e-book readers**. An e-book reader is a book-sized device that displays an **e-book**, a book that has been digitized and distributed by means of a digital storage medium (such as flash memory or a CD-ROM disc) (see Figure 3.32).

Some believe that flat-panel displays will replace CRTs for desktop systems, but several problems remain to be solved, including expense (large LCD displays are still more expensive than CRTs, but their prices are coming down as a result of mass production). At their best, LCD monitors have many advantages, including elimination of screen flicker (an annoying CRT problem that can cause eye strain).

LCD monitors use **liquid crystal display** (**LCD**) technology. LCD displays sandwich cells containing tiny crystals between two transparent surfaces. An image is formed by varying the electrical current supplied to each crystal. The least expensive LCDs are called **passive-matrix LCDs** (also called **dual scans**). Passive-matrix

Figure 3.30
Desktop computers use cathode-ray tube technology.

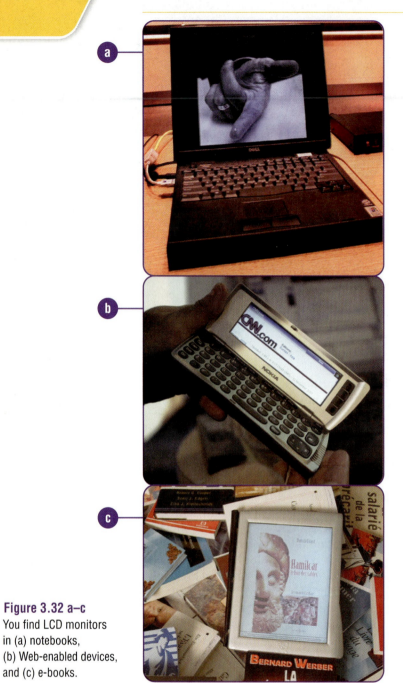

Figure 3.32 a–c
You find LCD monitors in (a) notebooks, (b) Web-enabled devices, and (c) e-books.

LCDs may generate image flaws, such as an unwanted shadow next to a column of color, and they are too slow for full-motion video. **Active-matrix LCDs** (also called **thin film transistors**) use transistors to control the color of each on-screen pixel. Speed and color quality improves, but active-matrix displays are more expensive. Other flat-panel display technologies include **gas plasma displays** and **field emission displays** (**FEDs**). An intriguing new technology, FED displays look like LCDs, except a tiny CRT produces each on-screen pixel.

Screen Size

Monitors are also categorized by their size. For CRTs, the quoted size is the size of the CRT's front surface measured diagonally. But some of this surface is hidden and unavailable for display purposes. For this reason, it's important to distinguish between the monitor's quoted size and the **viewable area**, the area available for viewing. Figure 3.33 shows typical relationships between quoted size and viewable area. Vendors now provide both sizes, thanks to a consumer lawsuit.

How big should your monitor be? Increasingly, 17-inch monitors are considered standard. For desktop publishing and other applications where full-page displays are needed, 21-inch monitors are preferred. An alternative to a 21-inch display is a type of 17-inch display that can rotate to a vertical position and display a full page.

Resolution

Although the monitor's resolution is determined by the video adapter's output, every monitor has a maximum resolution that it can't go beyond, even if the video adapter can do so. As we mentioned earlier in the chapter, *resolution* refers to the sharpness of the images displayed by a monitor. Like video adapter manufacturers, monitor manufacturers usually state screen resolution by specifying the number of pixels that the screen can display, followed by an "x," and then the number of vertical lines that the monitor can display. Examples of maximum monitor resolutions are 1024 x 768 and 1600 x 1200. Most monitors are downwardly compatible with lower-resolution video adapters, which means they can display the output generated by these adapters even if the adapter is not capable of generating the monitor's maximum resolution.

Quoted Monitor Size and Actual Viewable Area

Monitor Size	Viewable Area
21 inches	20 inches
19 inches	17 inches
17 inches	16 inches
15 inches	14 inches

Figure 3.33

First pass
Second pass

Interlaced monitors
Refresh every other line on each pass of the cathode gun, but this results in screen flicker

Noninterlaced monitors
Update the entire screen on each pass

Figure 3.34
Interlaced vs Noninterlaced Monitors

Dot Pitch

Monitor quality is also affected by **dot pitch**, a term that refers to the distance between each physical dot on the screen. A dot pitch of .28mm or lower is considered good.

Refresh Rate

Monitors vary in the maximum refresh rate they can accept. Some monitors are designed to run at a fixed refresh rate, but most monitors in use today are **multiscan monitors**. These monitors automatically adjust their refresh rate to the video adapter's output. If the monitor cannot display output at a refresh rate of 72 Hz or higher, you may experience eye fatigue.

In addition, older **interlaced monitors** cut costs by refreshing every other line on each pass of the cathode gun, but this resulted in screen flicker. Most of today's monitors are **noninterlaced monitors**, which update the entire screen on each pass (see Figure 3.34).

Televisions as Monitors

Although it's possible to use a television to display computer output, most TVs display images with such low resolution that the resulting image is not useful. To connect a computer to a TV, a device called an **NTSC converter** is needed. NTSC is an acronym for **National Television Standards Committee**, the organization that defines the display standards for broadcast television in the United States.

The use of TVs for computer output is certain to become more common once **High Definition Television** (**HDTV**) comes into widespread use. HDTV is the name given to several standards for digital television displays. Although all HDTV standards support higher resolution than today's NTSC standard, HDTV has been slow to develop, owing to the higher cost of HDTV devices and lack of international agreement concerning HDTV standards. One HDTV standard supports resolutions of up to 1920 x 1080.

Digital television enables manufacturers to include **interactive TV** features, which enable users to engage in two-way communication with a digital television set. Interactive TV features enable broadcasters and cable TV providers to implement features such as user-selectable movies, weather broadcasts selected by ZIP code, and news on selected topics.

Printers

Printers produce permanent versions (what we referred to earlier as *hard copy*) of the output that's visible on the computer's display screen. Two basic technologies dominate the world of computer printers: impact printers and nonimpact printers.

IMPACT PRINTERS

When part of the printer presses the paper to form a character, the printer is considered

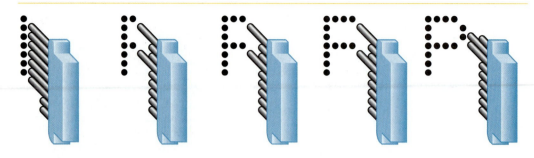

Figure 3.35
Dot-matrix printers use a matrix of pins to create images in a dot pattern.

an **impact printer**. Impact printers can produce carbon copies and are noisy, although covers are available to muffle the noise. These printers can produce a page, a line, or a character at a time. Large computers use **line printers** that can crank out hard copy at a rate of 3,000 lines per minute. Print quality is low, but these printers are mainly used for printing backup copies of large amounts of data. **Letter-quality printers**, which closely resemble office typewriters (except that they are controlled by the computer), are still used in some law offices.

Dot-matrix printers (see Figure 3.35), which were once the most popular type of printer used with personal computers, are decreasing in use. If you use a magnifying glass to look at a report created with a dot-matrix printer, you can see the small dots forming each character. The least expensive

dot-matrix printers print using a matrix of nine pins and produce poor quality printouts. Better dot-matrix printers use a 24-pin print head and can produce near–letter-quality printouts (printouts that look almost as good as printed text). Quality may still be poor, however, if the ribbon needs replacing, which is often the case for dot-matrix printers located in college computer labs.

NONIMPACT PRINTERS

Nonimpact printers are the most widely used printers for personal computers today. Nonimpact printers are much quieter than impact printers and can produce both text and graphics. Some of the most popular nonimpact printers are inkjet printers and laser printers (see Figure 3.36).

Inkjet printers (also called **bubble-jet printers**) are the least expensive (and most popular) nonimpact printers. Like dot-matrix printers, inkjet printers work by forming an image that is composed of tiny dots, but the dots are much smaller and more numerous. The result is a printout that's difficult to distinguish from the fully formed characters printed by laser printers. Inkjet printers can also print in color, which makes them popular choices for home users. Earlier inkjets had problems with smudging, but new ink formulations have all but eliminated this problem. Although inkjet printers are inexpensive and produce excellent output, they are slow, and per-page costs may exceed the costs of running a laser printer due to the generally high cost of ink cartridges.

Laser printers work like copy machines. Under the printer's computerized control, a laser beam creates electrical charges on a rotating print drum. These charges attract toner, which is transferred to the paper and fused to its

Figure 3.36 a&b
Nonimpact printers can produce both text and graphics and are quiet. The most popular non-impact printers are (a) inkjet printers and (b) laser printers.

surface by a heat process. In contrast to inkjets, laser printers print faster; some can crank out 60 or more pages per minute. Although they are more expensive initially than inkjet printers, laser printers generally have lower per-page costs.

Laser printers come in a variety of sizes. Generally, the larger and faster the printer, the more expensive it is. Small, **personal laser printers** are available for individual use, whereas corporate networks tend to use high-volume **network laser printers** to take care of their printing needs. Large laser printers are also used on mainframes and minicomputers where high-quality graphic output is required. **Color laser printers** are available, but they're expensive. Laser printer quality is judged by the number of dots per inch (dpi) that the printer can produce. The least expensive laser printers can generate 300 dpi, which is adequate for text (but not for graphics). The best laser printers can produce 1200 dpi or more.

The best color printers are **thermal transfer printers**. These printers use a heat process to transfer colored dyes or inks to the paper's surface. Because the colors run together, thermal transfer printers do a much better job of printing photographs and artwork than do other computer printers. The best results, however, require expensive glossy paper. The best thermal transfer printers are called **dye sublimation printers** (see Figure 3.37). These printers are slow and expensive, but they produce results that are difficult to distinguish from high-quality color photographs. Less expensive are **snapshot printers**, which are thermal transfer printers designed to print the output of digital cameras at a maximum size of 4 by 6 inches.

PLOTTERS

A **plotter**, like a printer, produces hard-copy output. Most form an image by physically moving a pen over a sheet of paper. A continuous-curve plotter is used to draw maps from stored data (see Figure 3.38). Computer-generated maps can be retrieved and plotted or used to show changes over time. Plotters are generally more expensive than printers, ranging from about $1,000 to $75,000 (or even more).

Figure 3.37
Thermal transfer printers are highly specialized devices.

Figure 3.38
Plotters are ideal for engineering, drafting, and many other applications that require intricate graphics.

Audio Output: Sound Cards and Speakers

Sound cards were introduced earlier as input devices. In this section, we'll look at the other side of the coin: sound cards as output devices.

Sound cards and speakers, the two accessories needed to listen to computer-generated sound, are increasingly found on new computer systems. Such sounds include various system beeps and warnings, the output of recorded sound files, and even synthesized speech. In **speech synthesis**, a program "reads" a text file out loud. Speech synthesis enables people who are blind or have low vision to access huge amounts of text-based material that would otherwise be inaccessible to them.

Like audio compact disc players, sound cards can play the contents of digitized recordings, such as music recorded in the Windows WAV or MPEG sound file formats. Some do this job better than others. Quality enters into the picture most noticeably when the sound card reproduces files containing **Musical Instrument Digital Interface** (**MIDI**) information. MIDI files are text files that tell a **synthesizer** when and how to play individual musical notes. (A synthesizer produces music by generating musical tones.) The least expensive sound cards use **FM synthesis**, an older technique that produces a sound associated with cheap electronic keyboards or the music accompanying old computer games. Better sound cards use **wavetable synthesis**, in which the sound card generates sounds using ROM-based recordings of actual musical instruments. The latest sound cards include surround-sound effects.

Alternative Output Devices

This section explores common output devices that you might add to your system.

DATA PROJECTORS

Data projectors take a computer's video output and project this output onto a screen, so that an audience can see it. Some data projectors are relatively inexpensive, portable devices, while others are more expensive devices that are built into an auditorium's audio-visual system.

For presentations to small audiences, **LCD projectors** are increasingly popular. An LCD projector enables a speaker to project the computer's screen display on a screen similar to the one used with a slide projector (see Figure 3.39). Some units have their own built-in projectors; others are designed for use with an overhead projector.

Digital light processing (**DLP**) **projectors** employ millions of microscopic mirrors embedded in a microchip to produce a bright, sharp image. Each mirror corresponds to a pixel and switches on and off to generate the image. Computer-controlled light beams reflect the image through a lens, which projects the image to a screen. This image is visible even in a brightly lit room, and it is sharp enough to be used with very large screens, such as those found at rock concerts and large auditoriums.

HEADSETS

A **headset** (also called **head-mounted display**) is a wearable output device that includes twin LCD panels. When used with special applications that generate stereo output, headsets can create the illusion that an individual is walking through a three-dimensional, simulated environment (see Figure 3.40). The **Cave Automated Virtual Environment** (**CAVE**)

Figure 3.39 a&b
(a) LCD projectors can enhance presentations.
(b) Such projectors come in various sizes and styles.

enables virtual reality explorers to dispense with the headsets in favor of 3D glasses. In the CAVE environment, the walls, ceiling, and floor display projected three-dimensional images. More than 50 CAVEs exist, enabling researchers to study topics as diverse as the human heart and the next generation of sports cars.

FAX AND MULTIFUNCTION DEVICE OUTPUT

As you learned earlier in this chapter, computers equipped with a fax modem and fax software can receive incoming faxes. They can also send faxes as output. To send a fax with the computer, save your document using a special format that is compatible with the fax program. The fax program can then send this document through the telephone system to a distant fax machine. It is not necessary to print the document locally in order to send it as a fax.

If the document you want to fax is available only in hard copy, computer faxing is not as convenient. You must first scan the document before you can fax it via the computer.

Multifunction devices combine inkjet or laser printers with a scanner, a fax machine, and a copier, enabling home office users to obtain all these devices without spending a great deal of money (see Figure 3.41).

TACTILE DISPLAYS

You've seen how output devices engage our eyes and ears. What about our sense of touch? If researchers in a new field called **haptics** have their way, you'll be able to feel computer output as well as see and hear it. (The term *haptics* refers to the sense of touch.) Haptics researchers are developing a variety of technologies, including **tactile displays** that stimulate the skin to generate a sensation of contact. Stimulation techniques include vibration, pressure, and temperature changes. When used in virtual reality environments, these technologies enhance the sense of "being there" and physically interacting with displayed virtual objects.

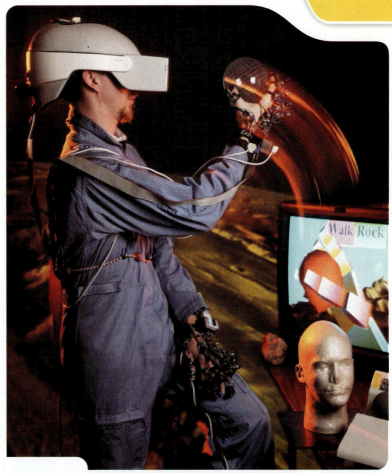

Figure 3.40
Headsets are essential to many virtual reality experiences.

Figure 3.41
Multifunction devices combine inkjet or laser printers with a scanner, a fax machine, and a copier.

CURRENTS

EMERGING TECHNOLOGIES

Wearables: The Fashion of Technology

It's a new day and you're trying to decide what to wear. Yesterday you wore your video glasses, but today you want to make more of a statement. How about a green- or rose-tinted Internet-enabled monocle? That would go perfectly with the ring controlling your computer. Or maybe you should wear your computerized suspenders. Your cell-phone vest needs a cleaning, so it looks like it'll be a backpack day.

All dressed, you head down the street in your "wearables." As you walk to the library, you e-mail a friend on your wrist pad, asking her to meet you for lunch later. At the library, the network automatically recognizes you from your ring. You search your pocket for your stylus, find it, and point to a library computer screen. The computer acknowledges you, and viewing through your monocle, you access your documents, open one, and begin jotting down notes by waving your pen in the air. Leaving the library, you call three of your friends. You visually chat together through your monocle and earpiece until your next class. You are seamlessly network-connected throughout your day through your wearable fashions.

Sound intriguing but unbelievable? While not all of this is possible just yet, some of it is. Take the Xybernaut company's "Poma," which combines a head-mounted display with a portable, lightweight CPU and an optical pointing device. Selling for about $1500, Poma gives you wearable computer access to the Internet, e-mail, Word files, and games. It's also compatible with wearable keyboards and other input devices.

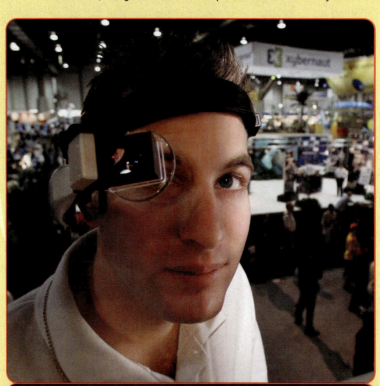

Figure 3.42
Xybernaut equipment is helping would-be Mars explorers learn to use hands-free computing technology.

In fact, Xybernaut wearable computers may one day be used by astronauts in space (see Figure 3.42). They were already selected to be used in field tests for a research project dedicated to exploring the planet Mars. It is hoped that the equipment will enable the one-day Mars explorers to learn how to use hands-free computing in their work. The wearable computers may also someday be used to enable two-way video- and audio-conferencing from Mars to the Earth.

Most wearable technologies to date have been incorporated into headsets and glasses, backpacks and fanny packs, rings and wrist-bands, and multipocketed pants. Recently, however, Santa Fe Science and Technologies created a commercial fiber that is similar to nylon but conducts electricity. Called "Smart Thread," this fiber can be woven into clothing like traditional threads, but it gives clothing computer-like abilities. The possibilities of Smart Thread are limitless. No more heavy packs for soldiers, who will instead be able to wear lightweight computers. Emergency search and rescue teams may one day wear computers that could seamlessly connect them to a command center. Smart Thread could also be woven into a child's clothing to act as a tracking device. The list goes on and on.

Products using Smart Thread are still two or three years away, but soon you may be wearing your computer, cell phone, music device, and other technologies as if they were a sweater, avoiding those unflattering bulges. Get ready for wearables with style!

HOME	Takeaway Points	Key Terms and Concepts	Matching	Multiple Choice	Fill-In	Short Answer	Exercises/ Projects	Web Research	CHAPTER REVIEW

TAKEAWAY POINTS

- Input refers to the software, data, or user-supplied information that is entered into the computer's memory. The four types of input are unorganized data that needs to be processed, software transferred from storage devices, commands that tell programs what to do, and user responses to a program's messages.

- The computer keyboard's special keys include cursor movement keys (arrow keys and additional keys such as Home and End), the numeric keypad (for entering numerical data), toggle keys (for switching keyboard modes on and off, such as Num Lock and Caps Lock), function keys (defined for different purposes by application programs), modifier keys such as Ctrl and Alt (for use with keyboard shortcuts), and special keys for use with Microsoft Windows.

- The most popular pointing devices are mice, trackballs, and touchpads. The latter two are preferred when space is limited.

- Mouse types include mice that connect in different ways (USB mice, serial mice, and cordless mice) and those that use one of two available technologies (optical and mechanical).

- Speech recognition software and a microphone enable users to dictate words to a computer. The words may be commands, or data to be entered as text in a document. Although speech recognition benefits users who cannot or should not type, the software still makes errors.

- To get sound, video, and images into the computer, you can use the microphone input of a sound card, a video capture board, a digital camera, a scanner, or a fax modem.

- Printers produce permanent versions of the output that's visible on the computer's display screen. Two basic technologies dominate the world of computer printers: impact printers and nonimpact printers.

- Among factors determining a computer's video output quality are the amount of VRAM on the video card and the adapter's refresh rate.

- CRT monitors are inexpensive compared with other types of monitors, but they consume more energy and take up more room on the desk. LCD or flat-panel displays are more expensive, but they take up much less room and are easier on the eyes.

- A monitor's quality is determined by its screen size (the larger, the better), its dot pitch (a dot pitch of .28mm or lower is good), the use of interlacing (noninterlaced monitors are better), and its ability to work with adapters that have a high refresh rate (72 Hz or higher).

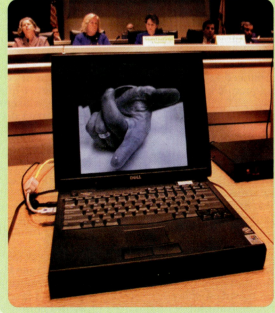

CHAPTER REVIEW

| Takeaway Points | Key Terms and Concepts | Matching | Multiple Choice | Fill-In | Short Answer | Exercises/ Projects | Web Research |

HOME

KEY TERMS AND CONCEPTS

3D graphics adapter
active-matrix LCD (thin film transistor)
bar code reader
biological feedback device
bit depth
Caps Lock
carpal tunnel syndrome
cathode-ray tube (CRT)
Cave Automated Virtual Environment (CAVE)
character
charge-coupled device (CCD)
codecs
color depth
color laser printer
command
CompactFlash
continuous speech recognition
cordless mouse (wireless mouse)
cumulative trauma disorder (repetitive strain injury)
cursor (insertion point)
cursor-movement keys (arrow keys)
data
data compression
data projector
dead key
diacritical marks
digital camera
Digital Display Working Group (DDWG)
digital light processing (DLP) projector
digital video
digital video camera
Digital Video Interface (DVI)
discrete speech recognition
dot-matrix printer
dot pitch
dye sublimation printer
e-book
e-book reader
enhanced keyboard
ergonomic keyboard
Esc
extended keyboard
eye-gaze response system (vision technology)
facsimile machine (fax machine)
fax modem
fax software
field emission display (FED)
flatbed scanner
FM synthesis
foot mouse
frame rate
frame
function keys
gas plasma display
graphics output

graphics tablet
handheld scanner
haptics
hard copy
headset (head-mounted display)
High Definition Television (HDTV)
image processing system
impact printer
information
inkjet printer (bubble-jet printer)
input
input device
interactive TV
interlaced monitor
joystick
keyboard
keyboard shortcuts
kiosk
laser printer
letter-quality printer
light pen
line printer
liquid crystal display (LCD)
LCD monitor (LCD display or flat-panel display)
LCD projector
magnetic-ink character recognition (MICR) system
Mark Sense Character Recognition system
mechanical mouse
modifier keys
monitor (display)
mouse
mousepad
Moving Pictures Experts Group (MPEG)
multidisplay video adapter
multifunction device
multiscan monitor
Musical Instrument Digital Interface (MIDI)
National Television Standards Committee (NTSC)
near–letter-quality printout
network laser printer
nonimpact printer
noninterlaced monitor
NTSC converter
Num Lock
numeric keypad
optical character recognition (OCR)
optical mark reader (OMR)
optical mouse
optical resolution
output
output device
passive matrix LCD (dual scan)
pen computing
personal laser printer
photo community

photo editing program
photo printer
pixel
plotter
point-and-shoot digital camera
pointer
pointing device
pointing stick
portable keyboard
printer
PS/2 mouse
QWERTY keyboard
RAMDAC
refresh rate
resolution
response
scanner
serial mouse
sheetfed scanner
single-lens reflex (SLR) digital camera
SmartMedia
snapshot printer
soft copy
software program
sound card
sound file
source data automation
speech recognition (voice recognition)
speech synthesis
status indicators
streaming cam (live cam)
stylus
Super VGA
synthesizer
tactile display
text output
thermal transfer printer
toggle key
touchpad (trackpad)
touch screen
trackball
universal product code (UPC)
user response
video accelerator
video adapter (display adapter, video card, graphics card)
video capture board (video capture card)
videoconferencing
video graphics adapter (VGA)
video output
video RAM (VRAM)
viewable area
visual display system
virtual reality
wavetable synthesis
Web cam
Web-enabled device
whiteboard
wheel mouse
wireless keyboard (cordless keyboard)

HOME | Takeaway Points | Key Terms and Concepts | **Matching** | Multiple Choice | Fill-In | Short Answer | Exercises/ Projects | Web Research | **CHAPTER REVIEW**

MATCHING

Match each key term in the left column with the most accurate definition in the right column.

_____ 1. input device
_____ 2. toggle key
_____ 3. Super VGA
_____ 4. speech recognition
_____ 5. Video Graphics Adapter (VGA)
_____ 6. data compression
_____ 7. digital light processing (DLP)
_____ 8. dye sublimation printers
_____ 9. Universal Product Code (UPC)
_____ 10. haptics
_____ 11. pen computing
_____ 12. refresh rate
_____ 13. optical mark reader (OMR)
_____ 14. plotter
_____ 15. sound card

a. an expansion board that can record and play sound files

b. reduces the size of a file

c. a pattern of bars printed on merchandise

d. a key that has two positions, on and off

e. a device that senses pencil marks on surveys or questionnaires

f. a hardware component that enables you to get programs, data, commands, and responses into the computer's memory

g. a field of study that involves the sense of touch

h. an output device that draws images on paper using pens

i. a type of input in which the computer recognizes spoken words

j. the branch of computing that involves PDAs and handwriting recognition

k. the frequency with which a screen image is updated

l. a resolution that is displayed in 1024 X 768 pixels

m. a resolution that is displayed in 640 X 480 pixels

n. printers that produce images that are similar to high-quality color photographs

o. projectors that use millions of microscopic mirrors to project an image

1 2 3 4 5 6 7 8 9 10 11 12 13 14 15 16

MULTIPLE CHOICE

Circle the correct choice for each of the following.

1. Which of the following is a popular input device?
   a. Synthesizer
   b. Monitor
   c. Plotter
   d. Mouse

2. Prolonged keyboard use can result in which of the following?
   a. Cumulative trauma disorder
   b. Malfunction of the mouse and other input devices
   c. A keyboard that becomes inoperable over time
   d. Dead keys

3. Which of the following devices uses handwriting recognition software?
   a. Touchpad
   b. Trackpoint
   c. Personal digital assistant (PDA)
   d. Touch screen

4. Which of the following expansion boards accepts analog or digital video signals and transforms them into digital data?
   a. Accelerator
   b. Sound card
   c. Web cam
   d. Video capture board

5. What kind of software accompanies most scanners and automatically decodes imaged text into a text file?
   a. Optical character recognition (OCR)
   b. Source data automation
   c. Image processing software
   d. Fax software

6. Which of the following does not generally apply to monitors?
   a. Monitors that look like TV screens use cathode-ray tube (CRT) technology.
   b. Monitors display "soft," or temporary, copy.
   c. Most monitors are wearable output devices that include twin LCD panels.
   d. Monitor quality is strongly affected by dot pitch.

7. Which output device can be used to print carbon copies?
   a. Dot-matrix printer
   b. Laser printer
   c. Plotter
   d. Inkjet printer

8. Which of the following printers is considered the best color printer?
   a. Laser printer
   b. Thermal transfer printer
   c. Line printer
   d. Color laser printer

9. Magnetic-ink character recognition (MICR) systems used by the banking industry contain how many characters?
   a. 10
   b. 14
   c. 26
   d. 101

10. When used with digital cameras and scanners, CCD represents what?
    a. Color coded display
    b. Charge-coupled device
    c. Common color display
    d. Comprehensive capture device

HOME	Takeaway Points	Key Terms and Concepts	Matching	Multiple Choice	Fill-In	Short Answer	Exercises/ Projects	Web Research	CHAPTER REVIEW

FILL-IN

In the blanks provided, write the correct answer for each of the following.

1. _____ marks include accent marks, tildes, and umlauts.

2. A _____ uses a transparent pressure-sensitive panel to detect where users have tapped the display screen with their fingers.

3. A _____ uses a lens to capture an image, but stores it in digital form rather than recording the image on film.

4. By using _____, a program can read a text file out loud.

5. Video adapters contain their own memory, which is called _____.

6. _____ is the distance between each physical dot on a monitor.

7. _____ printers produce output that resembles office typewriters.

8. The thinner monitors used on notebook and other small computers are known as _____ displays.

9. Most of today's monitors are _____ monitors, which update the entire screen on each pass.

10. _____ synthesis is used by sound cards to generate actual musical instrument sounds.

11. _____ devices combine an inkjet or laser printer with a scanner, a fax machine, and a copier.

12. Using a _____, users can touch and manipulate objects in a virtual reality environment.

13. A _____ is a pointing device that is commonly used to control the motion of on-screen objects in computer games.

14. _____ are mice flipped on their backs.

15. _____ and _____ are the two most frequently used keyboard layouts.

Chapter Review tabs: 1 2 3 4 5 6 7 8 9 10 11 12 13 14 15 16

SHORT ANSWER

1. If you have used a laptop computer, which of the various pointing devices—trackball, touchpad, or pointing stick—have you used? Which input device do you prefer to use? Explain why. Explain why you would or would not consider using an external mouse.

2. What are the advantages and disadvantages of modern speech recognition technology? Is a five percent error rate acceptable to you? Explain why or why not.

3. List three types of scanners. Describe how a computer scans a document. Which of these types have you personally used?

4. Many instructors use blackboards, whiteboards, or overhead projectors to display course material. In addition to these, do any of your instructors use data projectors to complement the presentation of their lectures or labs? If they do use them, are they LCD or DLP projectors? What types of software do they use? What are your feelings about using this technology to deliver classroom instruction?

5. What are the pros and cons of inkjet printers vs. laser printers?

EXERCISES/PROJECTS

1. Multifunction devices are devices that provide functionality beyond that of a simple printer. Identify the additional functions that these machines provide. Check newspaper advertisements, or call or visit a local vendor and compare the purchase price of a multifunction device with the cost of the devices needed to perform each function separately. What are the advantages and disadvantages of a multifunction device? Explain why you would or would not purchase a multifunction device.

2. According to a recent Associated Press article, the National Safety Council estimates that there will be 500 million obsolete computers by the year 2007. Because of the phosphor and lead used in CRTs, California and Massachusetts now prohibit dumping CRTs with household waste, placing them in landfills, or incinerating them. How do you think CRT monitors are disposed of in these states? One way of eliminating CRT monitors is to replace them with flat-panel LCDs. Check newspaper advertisements, or call or visit a local vendor and compare the purchase prices of CRTs with the cost of LCDs with the same display sizes—14/15, 17, 19, and 21/22 inches. Based on cost and convenience, explain why you would or would not upgrade to a flat-panel monitor or purchase one with a new computer.

3. Until the release of the first Macintosh computer in 1984, a mouse was just a rodent that ate cheese. With the advent of cordless technology, users of mice (and keyboards) are no longer tethered to their computers. Explain how cordless mice and keyboards work. Check newspaper advertisements, or call or visit a local vendor and compare the purchase prices of conventional mice and keyboards with the cost of cordless ones. A cordless mouse and an optical mouse are not the same. What is the difference between these two types of mice? Based on cost and convenience, explain why you would or would not upgrade to a cordless mouse or keyboard or purchase one with a new computer.

4. In order to provide equal opportunities to all citizens, the Americans with Disabilities Act (ADA) was passed on July 26, 1990. Consequently, as part of this act, your institution must provide computer access to persons with disabilities. Contact your school's computing services or visit some campus computer facilities to determine what types of special software and input or output devices have been installed or modified to specifically accommodate users with sight, hearing, and motor impairments. Explain how these devices are used to enter or display data.

5. Many instructors prefer that students submit assignments in hard copy form. Visit your school or department computer facilities to determine what types of printers are available for student use. Do students have access to dot-matrix, inkjet, or laser printers? Which, if any, of the printers are capable of color output? Are printing services free? If not, what are the printing costs? If you have a personal computer, which type of printer do you have? Explain why you prefer to use your own or your school's printers.

Some instructors no longer require hard copies of assignments. If any of your instructors accept soft copy assignments, describe the nature of these assignments and how you submit them to your instructors.

WEB RESEARCH

1. Question 4 in the Exercises/Projects section of this chapter examines how your school provides computer access for persons with disabilities. For this Web exercise, you will use the Internet to find additional information on supportive computer technology. To answer the following questions, visit the University of Wisconsin-Madison's Trace Center site at **http://trace.wisc.edu**. Besides the special hardware and software that is already used by your school, find one additional software application or hardware device that can be used for persons with each of the three disabilities—visual, audio, and motor. Describe the nature of the product and how it helps users with these disabilities to be able to use a computer.

2. Since most new computers now include a CD-ROM drive, a good set of speakers, and perhaps even a subwoofer, users are able to play their music CDs and enjoy high-quality music while working on their computers. When others are present, users have the option of connecting a headset to their computers. With the advent of MP3 files, users can now download these files, save them on a hard drive, and play high-quality music directly on their computers. Have you ever downloaded and played MP3 files? Why do you think that MP3 files are not saved on floppy disks? Unlike CDs, which are portable and can be used in any CD player, MP3 files reside on the computer's hard drive. Imagine carrying a desktop or even a laptop with you to listen to music! As you may know, this is not necessary. To learn about MP3 files, software, and portable players, visit the MP3 site at **www.mp3.com**. Although illegal MP3 copies of copyrighted music are available, why would an artist choose to place free copies of his or her work on the Internet? Explore the software link, determine which application you might purchase, and explain why. Explore the hardware link, choose which MP3 player you might purchase, and explain why.

3. Tired of entering input with a keyboard? One of the new features of Microsoft Office XP is speech recognition. Go to Microsoft's speech recognition site at **www.microsoft.com/ office/evaluation/indepth/speech.asp** to learn about this novel method of entering input. Speech recognition will help users with which three actions? According to this Web page, which users will and will not benefit from this technology? Why did Microsoft design a bimodal approach to their speech recognition? That is, why can users not enter dictation and commands simultaneously? How do users switch between dictation and command modes? Speech recognition is not perfect. Shown below are the results of reading the first two sentences of this question after one, two, and three voice recognition training sessions respectively.

   "Tired of intrigue with a keyboard? When of the new features of Microsoft Office Bixby is speech recognition."

   "Tired and train input with a keyboard? One of the new features of Microsoft Office Bixby is speech recognition."

   "Tired of entering input with a keyboard? One of the new features of Microsoft Office Bixby is speech recognition."

   In addition to voice recognition training, list at least two Microsoft suggestions to minimize speech recognition errors.

   Although most computer systems include a sound card and speakers, a microphone may not be supplied. If you have a computer, was a microphone included in the purchase price? What are the names and costs of the microphone and headset combinations that are suggested by Microsoft to be used with Office XP?

   Explain why you would or would not consider using speech recognition as a method of entering input.

Storing Data: Electronic Filing Cabinets

CHAPTER **4**

What You'll Learn . . .

When you have finished reading this chapter, you will be able to:

1. Distinguish between memory and storage.

2. Discuss how storage media are categorized.

3. List two ways to measure a storage device's performance.

4. Explain how data is stored.

5. Explain the uses of removable disks.

6. List the performance characteristics of hard drives.

7. List and compare the various optical storage media available for personal computers.

8. Identify the types of new storage technologies, such as FMD-ROM discs, solid state storage devices, and enterprise storage systems.

Techtalk

storage media
In a computer system, the devices that can store software and data, even when the computer is turned off. Media is plural; the singular is medium.

Storage (also called **mass storage** and **auxiliary storage**) refers collectively to all the various media on which a computer system can store software and data. Storage devices provide nonvolatile (permanent) storage for programs and data (see Figure 4.1). In this chapter, you'll learn why storage is necessary. You'll also take a look at the storage devices you're likely to find on today's personal computers and on computers at work.

Memory vs. Storage

To understand the distinction between memory and storage, think of the last time you worked at your desk. In your file drawer, you store all your personal items and papers, such as your checking account statements. The file drawer is good for long-term storage. When you decide to work on one or more of these items, you take it out of storage and put it on your desk. The desktop is a good place to keep the items you're working with; they're close at hand and available for use right away.

Computers work the same way. Storage devices are like file drawers in that they hold programs and data. In fact, programs and data are stored in units called **files**. In turn, the files are stored in digital envelopes

called **directories** or **folders**. When you want to work with the contents of a file, the computer transfers the file to the computer's **memory**, a temporary workplace.

WHY IS STORAGE NECESSARY?

Why don't computers just use memory to hold all those files? Here are some reasons:

- Storage retains data when the current is switched off. The computer's random access memory (RAM) is **volatile**. This means that when you switch off the computer's power, all the information in RAM is irretrievably lost. Storage devices are **nonvolatile**. They do not lose data when the power goes off. Without some way to store data and software permanently, a computer system would be much less useful.

- Storage is cheaper than memory. RAM is designed to operate very quickly so that it can keep up with the computer's CPU. For this reason, RAM is expensive—much more expensive than storage (see Figure 4.2). Most computers are equipped with just enough RAM to accommodate all the programs a user wants to run at once. RAM doesn't have enough room to store a whole library of software.

Figure 4.1
Storage Devices

hard disk · RAID device · DVD-ROM disc · tape backup unit

- Storage devices do not transfer data as rapidly as memory, but they're much less expensive. A computer system's storage devices typically hold much more data and software than the computer's memory does. Today, you can buy a storage device capable of storing four gigabytes (GB) of software and data for about the same amount you'll pay for 256 megabytes (MB) of RAM. (See Figure 4.3 for a reminder concerning the meaning of these and other essential ways of measuring a storage device's capacity.)

- Storage devices play an essential role in system startup operations. When you start your computer, the BIOS (Basic Input/Output System) reads essential programs into the computer's RAM, including one that begins loading essential system software from the computer's hard disk.

- Storage devices also play an input role when you start an application. The computer's operating system transfers the software from the computer's hard disk to the computer's memory, where it's available for use. If you use the application to work on a document that you previously stored on disk, the storage system functions as an input device again as it reads your document from the disk.

- Storage devices are needed for output, too. When you've finished working, you use the computer's storage system as an output device in an operation called **saving**. When you save your document, the computer transfers your work from the computer's memory to a read/write storage device, such as a hard or floppy disk. If you forget to save your work, it

Memory vs. Storage

	Device	Access Speed	Cost per MB
MEMORY	Cache Memory	Fastest	Highest
	RAM	Fast	High
STORAGE	Hard Disk	Medium	Medium
	CD-ROM Disc	Slow	Low
	Backup Tape	Very Slow	Lowest

Figure 4.2

Measuring Storage

Term	Abbreviation	Bytes (approximate)
kilobyte	K or KB	one thousand
megabyte	M or MB	one million
gigabyte	G or GB	one billion
terabyte	T or TB	one trillion
petabyte	P or PB	one quadrillion

Figure 4.3

PC card · **zip disk** · **mobile storage device**

Destinations

Looking for the latest news and information concerning storage media? SearchStorage.com at **http://searchstorage .techtarget.com** offers a wealth of information about storage technologies, including product reviews, background information, storage-related software, online discussions, and troubleshooting tips.

will be lost when you switch off the computer's power. Remember, the computer's RAM is volatile!

• Storage devices are increasing in capacity to the point that they can hold an entire library's worth of information. Organizations are increasingly turning to computer storage systems to store all of their information, not just computer software and data. The reason? Storing information on paper is just too expensive. Hard disks can store the same information for about $10 per gigabyte that would cost $10,000 to store on paper.

For all these reasons, demand for increased storage capacity is soaring. According to one estimate, the need for digital storage is increasing 60 percent each year, and the pace shows no signs of slowing down.

Storage Devices

Storage devices are categorized in various ways, including the type of operations they can perform (read or read/write), the method

used to access the information they contain (sequential or random access), the technology they use (magnetic, optical, or a combination of these), and where they're located in the storage hierarchy. Capacity and speed are also important factors with storage devices. The following sections explain these points.

READ/WRITE MEDIA VS. READ-ONLY MEDIA

Most storage devices are **read/write media**. They enable the computer to perform writing (output) operations as well as reading (input) operations.

Some storage devices are **read-only media**, which means they cannot perform writing operations. For example, CD-ROM drives are read-only devices; CD-R and CD-RW drives are read/write media.

SEQUENTIAL VS. RANDOM ACCESS STORAGE

Storage devices are categorized according to the way they get to the requested data. In a **sequential storage device**, such as a tape backup unit, the computer has to go through a fixed sequence of stored items to get to the one that's needed. (This is like a cassette tape, which forces you to fast forward or rewind to get to the song you want.) Sequential storage devices are slow but inexpensive (see Figure 4.4a).

A **random access storage device** can go directly to the requested data without having to go through a sequence. For example, a disk drive is a storage device that has a read/write head capable of moving across the surface of the disk. By moving across the disk, the read/write head can get to the requested data's location quickly. Random access storage devices are faster but more expensive (see Figure 4.4b) than sequential storage devices.

STORAGE TECHNOLOGIES: MAGNETIC AND OPTICAL

Two storage technologies are in widespread use: magnetic storage and optical storage. Most storage devices use one or the other; occasionally, they are combined.

Figure 4.4 a&b
(a) A tape backup unit is a sequential storage device; the computer has to go through a fixed sequence of stored items to get to the one that's needed. (b) A disk drive is a random access storage device; the computer can access the requested data without having to go through a sequence.

Magnetic storage media use disks or tapes that are coated with tiny magnetically sensitive materials. In all magnetic storage devices, the basic principle is the same: an electromagnet, called a **read/write head**, records information by transforming electrical impulses into a varying magnetic field. As the magnetic materials pass beneath the read/write head, this varying field forces the particles to rearrange themselves in a meaningful pattern. This operation is called **writing**. In **reading**, the read/write head senses the recorded pattern and transforms this pattern into electrical impulses.

The two most common types of magnetic media are **magnetic tapes**, which are sequential storage devices, and **magnetic disks**, which are random access devices. Popular magnetic disk devices include floppy disks, Zip disks, and hard disks, all of which we'll look at later in the chapter.

Just how much computer data can be stored on magnetic media? Scientists still aren't sure. In laboratories, storage densities of 35 gigabits per square inch have been achieved.

Optical storage media use tightly focused laser beams to read microscopic patterns of data encoded on the surface of plastic discs (see Figure 4.5). Tiny, microscopic indentations, called **pits**, absorb the laser's light in certain areas. The drive's light-sensing device receives no light from these areas, so it sends a signal to the computer corresponding to a 0 in the computer's binary numbering system. Flat, reflective areas, called **land**, bounce the light back to a light-sensing device, which sends a signal equivalent to a 1.

CD-ROM discs and CD-ROM drives are read-only media. However, several types of optical read/write media are available, including one time–recordable CD-ROM (CD-R) discs, rewritable CD-ROM (CD-RW), and DVD-ROM discs.

How much data can an optical medium store? Scientists believe that the physics of light limit optical media to a maximum of five gigabits of storage per square inch. However, new optical technologies break this barrier by using discs with more than one layer. We'll talk about this and other storage media later in the chapter.

Figure 4.5

In optical media, a tightly focused laser beam reads data encoded on the disc's surface. Some optical devices can write data as well as read it.

Some storage devices combine the two basic technologies. **Magneto-optical (MO) drives** combine the two basic storage technologies. In the coming years, MO discs no larger than today's CD-ROMs will contain up to 100 GB of storage.

THE STORAGE HIERARCHY

Storage devices fit into one of three locations in the **storage hierarchy**. Consisting of three levels, the storage hierarchy differentiates storage devices according to the availability of the data they contain. The three levels are as follows:

Online storage Also called **primary storage**, this is the most important component of the storage hierarchy. It consists of the storage devices that are actively available to the computer system and do not require any action on the part of the user. The computer's hard disk is a personal computer's online storage system (see Figure 4.6a).

Techtalk

disk or disc?
If the subject is magnetic media, the correct spelling is disk. However, some people prefer to use disc for optical media.

Figure 4.6 a&b
(a) A hard disk is an example of an online storage system. (b) Floppy disks and optical discs are near-online storage devices.

Near-online storage Also called **secondary storage**, this portion of the storage hierarchy consists of storage that isn't directly available. However, it can be made available easily by some simple action on the user's part, such as inserting a disk. Examples of near-online storage devices for personal computers are floppy disks and CD-ROMs (see Figure 4.6b).

Offline storage Also called **tertiary storage** or **archival storage**, this portion of the storage hierarchy consists of storage that is not readily available. Offline storage devices, such as magnetic tapes, are used for infrequently accessed data that needs to be kept for archival purposes. Some personal computers are equipped with tape drives, which can be used for archival storage.

CAPACITY OF STORAGE DEVICES

A storage device's capacity is measured in bytes (a unit of data composed of 8 bits). Capacities range from the floppy disk's 1.44 MB to huge, room-filling arrays of storage devices capable of storing a dozen or more terabytes of data. To provide this much storage with print-based media, you'd need to cut down several million trees.

People have varying storage needs. PC and Macintosh users often want to store items such as their e-mail, word processing documents, graphics, and music files. A 2 GB or 4 GB disk may be needed to hold these items plus software. A scientist working

with laboratory data may need 50 GB of storage, while a huge corporation may need several terabytes of storage to hold all the information it works with. Most personal computers sold today are equipped with 20 GB hard disks at a bare minimum.

SPEED OF STORAGE DEVICES (ACCESS TIME)

A storage device's most important performance characteristic—the speed with which it retrieves desired data—is measured by its **access time**, the amount of time it takes for the device to begin reading the data. For disk drives, the access time includes the **seek time**, the time it takes the read/write head to locate the data before reading begins.

The speed of storage devices varies considerably, but all storage devices are significantly slower than RAM (see Figure 4.7). RAM's speed is measured in **nanoseconds** (billionths of a second, abbreviated **ns**); a storage device's speed is measured in **milliseconds** (thousandths of a second, abbreviated **ms**).

Access Time: Memory vs. Storage	
Device	**Typical Access Time**
Static RAM (SRAM)	5–15 nanoseconds
Dynamic RAM (DRAM)	50–70 nanoseconds
Solid state disk (SSD)	0.1 millisecond
Hard disk drive	6–12 milliseconds
CD-ROM drive	80–800 milliseconds

Figure 4.7

One type of storage device offers the speed of memory with the high capacity of a hard disk. A **solid state disk** (**SSD**) is designed to trick the computer into thinking that it is an ordinary hard disk. However, it contains dynamic RAM or flash memory chips. Onboard batteries make sure the data remains secure when the power is switched off. SSDs can store up to 8 GB of data. SSD drives are much more expensive than hard disks, but they're also faster.

Disks and Disk Drives: Floppies, Superdisks, and Zip Disks

A **disk** (also called a **diskette**) is a portable storage medium that provides personal computer users with convenient, near-online storage. Disks are designed to work with **disk drives**, which allow the computer to read the disks. Disk drives come in internal versions (mounted in one of the system unit's drive bays) as well as external versions, which can be used with laptops, for example.

Disks are housed in a variety of cases, but all contain a circular plastic disk coated with a magnetically sensitive film, the same material that's on a cassette tape. The disk that has been around the longest is the **floppy disk**. Introduced by IBM in the 1970s, floppy disks were originally packaged in 8-inch flexible, or "floppy," packages. Even though most of today's floppy disks are packaged in 3.5-inch hard plastic cases, the term "floppy" is still used.

Almost all floppy disks you see being used today are of the **high density** (**HD**) type, giving them more storage capacity than their predecessors—up to 1.2 MB for Macintosh disks and up to 1.44 MB for PC disks. However, as computer programs (and users' data files) have grown significantly in size, floppies are becoming less useful. For this reason, several companies offer alternatives that have much higher storage capacities. These higher-capacity disk drives fall into two categories: those that are downwardly compatible with floppy disks and those that are not. (As you'll recall, when a device is downwardly compatible, it can work with previous versions of the technology.)

Two downwardly compatible disk drive technologies are available. Developed by Imation, **SuperDisk** is a storage device that uses 120-MB SuperDisks that are just a little bit thicker than a floppy. Although Imation no longer produces these drives, it has a new product on the market, a 240-MB SuperDisk. (Note that 120-MB disks are still available and can be read by the new 240-MB drives.) In addition, Sony's **High FD** (**HiFD**) drive uses 200-MB floppy disks. All these drives can read standard, 3.5-inch floppies. However, none of them has gained widespread acceptance.

More widely accepted is Iomega's **Zip disk**, which is not downwardly compatible with floppy disks. Zip disks are capable of storing up to 750 MB of data (see Figure 4.8).

PROTECTING YOUR DATA ON DISKS

Disks are **portable media**, which means that you can remove a disk from one computer and insert it into another. Accordingly, disks are designed to keep your data safe.

Figure 4.8
Zip disks offer an easy-to-use personal storage solution designed to make it easier for consumers to move, protect, share, and back up information on their computers.

A sliding metal **shutter** protects the disk from fingerprints, dust, and dirt. Still, the metal shutter can't protect your disks entirely. The following are a few things you should consider when using disks:

- Don't touch the surface of the disk. Fingerprints can contaminate the disk and cause errors.

write protected

notch open means you cannot write on the disk

not write protected

notch closed means you can write on the disk

Figure 4.9
To set the write-protect tab on a 3.5-inch floppy disk, move the tab to the locked position.

Figure 4.10 a&b
(a) A Floppy Disk Drive and (b) An External Floppy Disk Drive

- Don't expose disks to magnetic fields. Because data is magnetically encoded on the disks, direct exposure may cause loss of data.

- To avoid contamination, don't eat or drink around disks.

- To avoid condensation, keep disks away from humidity.

- Don't expose disks to excessive temperatures.

In addition, floppy disks contain a **write-protect tab** (also called a **write-protect notch**) that you can open to protect data from being overwritten or deleted (see Figure 4.9). The write-protect tab enables you to turn any floppy disk into a read-only disk. If you store an important document on a floppy disk, be sure to set the write-protect tab so that you don't erase the document accidentally. If you have difficulty writing data to a floppy disk, make sure the write-protect tab is set to read/write.

DISK DRIVES

As we mentioned earlier, all disks are used with disk drives. In desktop computer systems, a disk drive is installed in one of the system unit's drive bays. In laptops, the drive is also sometimes provided by means of an external unit that plugs into the system's case (see Figure 4.10). In PCs running Microsoft Windows, the first floppy disk drive is called Drive A (this drive is called fd0 in PCs running Linux). The second drive, if there is one, is called Drive B (Windows) or fd1 (Linux). Macintoshes usually have just one floppy drive, if any (Apple computers, including iMacs, now dispense with floppy drives entirely). Like floppy drives, **Zip drives** come in both internal and external versions.

HOW DISK DRIVES WORK

You've probably used a floppy disk or a Zip disk many times before. To do so, you simply insert it into the drive. With 3.5-inch disks, you can insert the disk in only one way: the sliding metal shutter must face the drive door (see Figure 4.11). When the computer needs to read data from the disk, the **head actuator** moves the read/write head over the surface of the disk to the area that contains the desired data. When the read/write head is in the correct position, it begins reading the data into the computer's memory.

How does the read/write head know where to look for data? To answer this question, you need to know a little about how stored data is organized on a disk. Like an old-style vinyl LP, disks contain circular bands called **tracks**. Each track is divided into pie-shaped wedges called **sectors**. Two or more sectors combine to form a **cluster** (see Figure 4.12).

To keep track of just where specific files are located, the computer's operating system records a table of information on the disk. This table contains the name of each file and the file's exact location on the disk. On Microsoft Windows systems, this table is called the **file allocation table** or **FAT** (see Figure 4.13).

Sometimes disks develop a defect that prevents the computer from reading or writing data to one or more sectors of the disk. These damaged areas are called **bad sectors**. If you see an on-screen message indicating that a disk has a bad sector, try to copy the data off the disk, if possible. Don't use it to store new data.

To store data as compactly as possible, the file might be stored in a **fragmented**

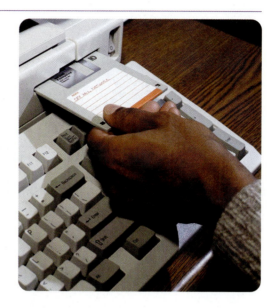

Figure 4.11
You can insert a 3.5-inch disk in only one way. Make sure the sliding metal shutter faces the drive door.

form, which means that it is split up into pieces and stored in whatever disk sectors happen to be available. Although it's disconcerting to think that a valuable document might be split up and stored here and there on the disk, it's actually quite safe. However, repeated write operations may result in excessive fragmentation. As the percentage of fragmented files reaches 10 percent, the drive's access time declines in a noticeable way. It declines because the read/write head must travel back and forth across the disk's surface to retrieve the various parts of a file.

Sectors
Each track is divided into pie-shaped wedges called sectors.

Cluster
Two or more sectors combine to form clusters.

Tracks
Data is recorded in concentric circular bands called tracks.

Figure 4.12
Disks contain circular bands called tracks, which are divided into sectors. Two or more sectors combine to form a cluster.

Filename	Track	Sector
letterz.WP	2	3
sales.WKS	14	2
memo.DOC	10	6
DPT.CHT	**deleted**	
logo.ART	18	2
forecast.WKS	13	6
agenda.DOC	21	4

DPT.CHT

file allocation table (FAT)

Figure 4.13
The FAT keeps vital records that show exactly where a given file is stored.

To remove a disk from a PC disk drive, press the eject button. When the read/write head is reading or writing data, the drive illuminates the **activity light**. Do not remove the disk while this light is on. On a Macintosh, you'll need to drag the disk icon to the Trash. (Alternatively, select the disk drive icon, click Special on the menu bar, and choose Eject.)

FORMATTING: PREPARING DISKS FOR USE

Before a magnetic disk can be used for storage, it must be prepared using a process called **formatting**. In the formatting process, the disk drive's read/write head lays down the magnetic patterns of tracks and sectors on the disk's surface. This pattern enables the disk drive to store data in an organized manner. This process is necessary because different types of computers store data in different ways. For this reason, a PC cannot read Macintosh disks unless the PC is running special software. However, most Macintoshes are equipped with software that enables them to read PC disks.

You can format floppy disks yourself using the formatting utility supplied with the computer's operating system. However, you probably won't need to do so because most floppy disks sold today are **preformatted**, which means that they're already ready to be used with the Windows or Macintosh formats. (If you're

buying disks, make sure you purchase the correct format for your computer.)

Be aware that formatting destroys all the data that's been recorded on a disk. You should never format a disk that contains valuable data. In addition, you should never format the computer's hard disk unless you've just purchased a new hard disk and are following the installation instructions.

Hard Disks

On almost all computers, the **hard disk** is by far the most important online storage medium (see Figure 4.14). A hard disk is a high-capacity, high-speed storage device that usually consists of several fixed, rapidly

Figure 4.14
A hard disk is an example of an online storage device.

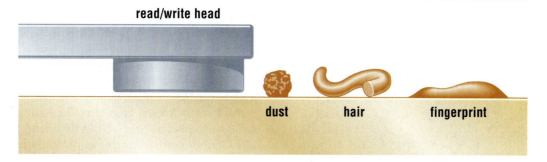

read/write head

dust   hair   fingerprint

Figure 4.15
The read/write head "floats" just above the disk, at a distance 300 times smaller than the width of a human hair. If the read/write head encounters an obstacle, such as dust or a smoke particle, it bounces on the disk surface and can cause serious damage.

rotating disks called **platters**. Most hard disks are **fixed disks**, which use platters that are sealed within the mechanism's case.

WHY ARE HARD DISKS NEEDED?

In the early days of personal computing, hard disks were optional. Programs were small enough to fit on floppy disks, and users rarely created files that exceeded a floppy disk's capacity. But those days are gone. Today's computer systems require a hard disk, one with at least several gigabytes of storage.

Why does an ordinary PC or Macintosh user need so much storage? Today's operating systems (such as Microsoft Windows or Mac OS) may require as much as 1.5 GB of storage or more. Applications can easily eat up another 750 MB of disk space. To leave room for data, you'll need roughly twice the amount taken up by software. According to this guideline, 2 GB is a working minimum—and you'd be wise to double this figure to provide room for additional software. As computer users ruefully observe, there is no such thing as enough storage space. As you keep on adding more software and data, you'll soon exhaust the available space.

HOW HARD DISKS WORK

A hard disk works like a floppy disk or Zip disk. Magnetic read/write heads move across the surface of a disk coated with magnetically sensitive material. But that's

where the resemblance ends. A hard disk contains two or more vertically stacked platters, each with two read/write heads (one for each side of the disk). The disk spins much faster than a floppy disk. The platters spin so rapidly that the read/write head floats on a thin cushion of air, at a distance 300 times smaller than the width of a human hair.

To protect the platter's surface, hard disks are enclosed in a sealed container. If the read/write head encounters an obstacle, such as a dust or smoke particle, the head bounces on the disk surface and can cause serious damage (see Figure 4.15). Hard disks can absorb minor jostling without suffering damage, but a major jolt—such as one caused by dropping the computer while the drive is running—could cause a **head crash** to occur. Head crashes are one of the causes of bad sectors—areas of the disk that have become damaged and can no longer hold data reliably.

Like floppy disks, hard disks must be formatted before use. The formatting process creates tracks and sectors, like those of a floppy disk. Because most hard disks have two or more platters, it is possible to define an additional storage area called a **cylinder**. A cylinder is a location made up of the same track location on all the platters (see Figure 4.16). If the platters contain 1,200 tracks, the hard disk will have 1,200 cylinders. In a six-platter drive in which data is recorded on both platter surfaces, each cylinder contains 12 tracks.

Hard disks can be divided into **partitions**. A partition is a section of a disk set aside as if it were a physically separate disk. Sometimes partitions are used to track

cylinder

Figure 4.16
All the tracks of the same number on a hard disk's platters are grouped as a cylinder.

enable computers to work with more than one operating system. For example, Linux users often create one partition for Linux and another for Microsoft Windows. In this way, they can work with programs developed for either operating system.

FACTORS AFFECTING HARD DISK PERFORMANCE

A hard disk's performance is determined by two factors: positioning performance and transfer performance.

Positioning performance refers to how quickly the drive can position the read/write head so that it can begin transferring data. This aspect of a drive's performance is measured by the drive's seek time, which, as you learned earlier, is the amount of time required to move the read/write head to the required

position. Constant advances in head actuator technology are continually driving seek times down.

Transfer performance refers to the drive's ability to transfer data from the drive as quickly as possible. To improve transfer performance, engineers use ever-increasing spindle speeds. **Spindle speed** refers to the speed, measured in revolutions per minute (rpm), at which the platters rotate. Many hard disks spin at a spindle speed of 7,200 rpm, and high-end drives operate at speeds as high as 15,000 rpm. Higher spindle speeds reduce the time that is wasted after the read/write head moves to the correct track. The read/write head must wait until the spinning disk brings the desired data around to the head's location. The amount of time wasted in this way is called **latency**. In a slow drive (3,600 rpm), latency can be as high as 17 milliseconds. In a fast drive (10,000 rpm), latency typically averages only three milliseconds.

HARD DISK INTERFACES

To communicate with the CPU, hard disks require a **hard disk controller**. A hard disk controller is an electronic circuit board that provides an interface between the CPU and the hard disk's electronics. The controller may be located on the computer's motherboard, on an expansion card, or within the hard disk.

The most widely used interface for PCs is called **Integrated Drive Electronics (IDE)**, also called **ATA** (short for **AT attachment**) or **IDE/ATA**. IDE drives incorporate the controller within the drive unit. The original IDE/ATA specification has been updated several times, generally by drive manufacturers, who have used a profusion of names to describe the newer standards. The current standard IDE/ATA interface for **entry-level drives** (drives found on the least expensive computers) is called **Fast IDE**, **Fast ATA**, or **ATA-2**. This type of interface enables you to connect up to four IDE-compatible drives, including CD-ROM drives, to the motherboard, and transfers data at a rate of 16 megabits per second (Mbps). A newer version of the IDE/ATA standard, called **Ultra DMA/66** or **ATA-5**, transfers data at speeds of up to 66 MHz. The latest version of this standard, called **Ultra DMA/100,** enables data transfer rates of up to 100 MHz, but these drives require a special cable. Most IDE/ATA drives are downwardly compatible with earlier standards, so they'll work with motherboards that don't support the latest standards.

A feature that used to be standard on Macintoshes and that is available for PCs is the **Small Computer System Interface** (**SCSI**). SCSI has many advantages. Up to seven SCSI-compatible devices, including hard disks, scanners, CD-ROM drives, and other peripherals, can be "daisy-chained" to a single SCSI connector. In addition, the newest SCSI standard, called **Ultra3 SCSI** or **Ultra160 SCSI**, supports data transfer rates of up to 160 Mbps, more than twice as fast as Ultra DMA/66. However, the fastest SCSI hard disk controllers are expensive and add considerably to the cost of the computer's storage system. The fastest SCSI controllers and drives are found only in high-end systems, which are the most expensive systems in a manufacturer's product line.

DISK CACHES: IMPROVING A HARD DISK'S PERFORMANCE

To improve hard disk performance, most computers have a type of cache memory called **disk cache** (see Figure 4.17). A disk cache is a type of RAM (random access memory) that is used to store the program instructions and data you are working with. When the CPU needs to get information from the drive, it looks in the disk cache first. If it doesn't find the information it needs, it retrieves the information from the hard disk. Because RAM chips are much faster than the disk, the use of a disk cache dramatically improves hard disk performance. On Macintosh computers, the disk cache is part of the computer's main memory (RAM). On PCs, the disk cache is part of the hard disk.

RAID DEVICES: PROTECTING AGAINST HARD DRIVE FAILURE

A device that groups two or more hard disks that contain exactly the same data is

Figure 4.17

Disk cache, a type of RAM, dramatically improves hard disk performance. When the CPU needs to get information from the drive, it looks in the disk cache first.

Figure 4.18
RAID devices help protect against hard drive catastrophes.

Destinations

For an excellent Web-based tutorial on varieties of RAID, see Advanced Computer & Network Corporation's "RAID Technology" at **www.acnc.com/raid.html**.

called **RAID**, which is short for **redundant array of independent disks** (see Figure 4.18). The key word in this phrase is redundant, which means "extra copy." No matter how many disks a RAID device contains, the computer "thinks" it's dealing with just one drive. Should one of the drives fail, there's no interruption of service. All the drives contain an exact copy of all the data, so one of the other drives kicks in and delivers the requested data. RAID devices offer a high degree of **fault tolerance**; that is, they keep working even if one or more components fail. For this reason, RAID devices are widely used wherever a service interruption could prove costly, hazardous, or inconvenient to customers. Most of the major Web sites use RAID devices to ensure the constant availability

Figure 4.19
Iomega's Zip drive can store up to 750 MB of data in removable cartridges.

of their Web pages. Most personal computer users don't need RAID devices as long as they back up their data regularly.

REMOVABLE HARD DISKS

Most hard disks are fixed disks, a type of hard disk that is nonremovable. **Removable hard disks** enclose the platters within a cartridge, which can be inserted into the drive and removed, much like a Zip disk. Removable hard disks are a near-online storage medium. A computer system equipped with dozens of removable cartridges will have a near-online storage system that is many times larger than the hard disk's capacity.

Although removable hard disks aren't as fast and can't store as much data as one-piece hard disks, they are convenient additions to a personal computer system. Removable hard disks are very useful for **data archiving** (keeping long-term copies of important files) and **data backup** (performing regular backup operations that ensure full system recovery after a total system failure). The cartridges can be exchanged with other computer users, as long as they have the same type of drive. Removable hard drives have security benefits, too. If you are working with sensitive data, you can remove the cartridge at the end of a working session and keep it under lock and key. An example of a removable drive is Iomega's popular **Zip drive**, which can store up to 750 MB (see Figure 4.19). Because fixed disks are faster than removable disks, most users prefer to rely on fixed disks as their main storage medium.

INTERNET HARD DRIVES

An **Internet hard drive** is storage space on a server that is accessible from the Internet. The management of this storage is usually conducted as a business enterprise in which a computer user subscribes to the storage service and agrees to rent a block of storage space for a specific period of time. You might store files there that you wish to share with family and friends. Instead of sending attachments with your e-mail you might simply post the files to your storage device and then allow them to be viewed or retrieved by others. You might create backup copies of critical files or of all the data on your hard disk.

The key advantage of this remote storage is the ability to access data from multiple locations at any time. You're able to access your files from any device that can access the Internet, so anything you store on the site is available to you at any time. Some disadvantages are that your data may not be secure, the storage device might corrupt or lose your data, and the company may go out of business.

Magnetic Tape

Magnetic tape was once the most commonly used storage medium. You've probably seen film clips of 1960s-era "electronic brains," with big banks of whirling reel-to-reel tapes. The earliest personal computers came with cassette tape drives. Although tapes store data sequentially, making access times slow, they're still useful for storing very large amounts of data that don't need to be accessed frequently.

Quarter-inch cartridge (QIC) tape drives work with cartridges that can store up to 10 GB of data, enough to back up most personal computer hard disks with just one cartridge (see Figure 4.20). Although QIC tape drives have the lowest data transfer rates among today's tape backup technologies, they're inexpensive.

Digital audio tape (DAT) drives offer better data transfer rates and higher storage capacity. The most popular DAT format is called **DDS (digital data storage)**, which stores up to 40 GB on a cartridge. **Digital linear tape (DLT)** drives are more expensive than QIC or DAT drives, but they transfer data much more rapidly and offer cartridge capacities of up to 100 GB. The latest tape drive technology, **advanced intelligent tape (AIT)**, offers cartridge capacities of up to 100 GB.

CD-ROM Discs and Drives

The most popular and least expensive type of optical disc standard is **CD-ROM** (see Figure 4.21), short for **compact disc–read-only memory**. As the ROM part of the name indicates, this near-online storage medium is strictly read-only; CD-ROM drives cannot write data to optical discs.

Because most software is distributed by means of CD-ROM discs, CD-ROM drives are standard and necessary equipment for today's personal computers. CD-ROM discs are capable of storing up to 650 MB of data, the equivalent of more than 400 floppy disks. These discs provide the ideal medium for distributing operating systems, large applications, office suites, and multimedia products involving thousands of large graphics or audio files.

Figure 4.20
Quarter-inch cartridge (QIC) tape drives work with cartridges that can store up to 10 GB of data.

Figure 4.21
The CD-ROM is the most popular and least expensive optical disc. CD-ROM drives come standard on today's personal computers.

As is the case with disks, it's important that you handle CD-ROM discs carefully. The following are a few things to remember about caring for CDs:

- Do not expose discs to excessive heat or sunlight.

- Do not touch the underside of discs. Hold them by their edges.

- Do not write on the label side of discs with a hard instrument, such as a ballpoint pen.

- Do not eat, drink, or smoke near discs.

- To avoid contamination, do not stack discs.

- Store discs in **jewel boxes** (plastic protective cases) when they are not being used.

CD-ROM disc drives vary in speed, which is measured in the unit's **data transfer rate** (the number of bits transferred per second). The original CD-ROM format transferred data at a maximum rate of only 150,000 bits per second, a very slow speed in comparison to hard disks (or even floppy disks). Faster CD-ROM drives improve the transfer rates by spinning the disc faster. The speed of such drives is claimed to be a multiple of the original 150,000 bits per second standard; a 2X (double-speed) drive, for example, can transfer data at 300,000 bits per second. The latest drives can transfer as much as 7.8 million bits per second (Mbps).

Most CD-ROM drives can play audio CDs. However, you may not hear the sound unless the drive's audio output is connected to the computer's sound card. You'll also need a program that can control the drive and play the tracks you want to hear.

Most CD-ROM drives can also work with Kodak **PhotoCDs**. Developed by photography giant Kodak, this format makes use of **multisession CDs**. Unlike **single-session CDs**, the type of CD used to distribute software, PhotoCDs can accept more than one "burn" (recording session). When you have your film developed, you can get a PhotoCD that contains digitized images of the prints. The next time you shoot a roll, you can take the same PhotoCD back and have more prints added.

Some CD-ROM drives can accommodate more than one disc. **CD-ROM jukeboxes**, containing as many as 256 CD-ROM drives, make large amounts of software or data available to network users (see Figure 4.22).

The future of CD-ROM drives and discs is already marked. In the home entertainment market, the DVD player has decimated the market for CD players. As the technology develops and DVD drives become less and less expensive, the use of CD-ROM drives will decline. In fact, the day will come in the not so distant future when we'll use DVD-read/write drives in the same manner that we once used the ubiquitous floppy disk drive.

Figure 4.22
CD-ROM jukeboxes provide storage for massive amounts of data.

CD-R and CD-RW Discs and Recorders

Read/write CD technologies, called CD-R and CD-RW, are now common. Declining

COMPUTING IMPLICATIONS

Decaying Data

Many people believe that computers are a great boon to society because once information is stored on the computer, paper records are no longer necessary. After all, once data has been digitized, it's available forever, right? Well, not necessarily. Researchers say that the data you store in your computer may not be as safe as you think. As we rush further and further into the computer age, much of the world's data is either decaying or becoming obsolete.

How can data decay? Any data is only as reliable as the medium on which it is stored. Perhaps the least reliable storage medium is the RAM in your computer system. When the power goes off, anything stored in memory is lost forever. Diskettes run a close second in lack of reliability. Many "old school" computer users have war stories of data that was corrupted or lost because it was on a floppy disk that became damaged or accidentally erased.

Diskettes aren't the only physical medium that suffers from reliability problems. Much of the world's data is stored on some sort of magnetic tape. Despite the fact that these tapes hold quite a bit of information, they're also very susceptible to environmental influences. Tapes can physically break down from exposure to air, heat, and humidity. As they deteriorate, the information stored on them becomes unrecoverable.

Problems with data recovery from deteriorating media have led to the loss of quite a bit of priceless data. For instance, some researchers believe that up to 20 percent of the data generated during NASA's 1976 Viking mission to Mars is no longer accessible due to deteriorated tapes. Computerized data archives at other government agencies and at large corporations are experiencing similar problems.

The data decay problem even reaches to relatively new storage devices. For instance, CD-ROM drives were once heralded as a permanent storage medium. Findings by different laboratories have shown that CD-ROMs can deteriorate in as few as five years, depending on how they're stored.

Decay is not the only problem. A bigger problem with stored data is outright obsolescence. If you've been using computers for any length of time, you know that programs and equipment change rapidly. Every year or so a new version of an old software program is brought to market. Frequently, the program changes the way it stores information on disk. Over time, some older programs are no longer available on computer systems. In addition, new computer systems are brought into an organization to replace older systems, and the new systems don't use the same technology as the old. The upshot is that if the programs or equipment used to create data are gone, and the data files have not been updated or transferred to a new format, the data becomes essentially worthless.

With more and more of the world's data being either converted to digital formats or created that way in the first place, the longevity of the data is bound to become a bigger and bigger issue. Government, business, and educators are going to have to test their data periodically and review their storage methods to make sure that their information is still accessible. The problem (and subsequent solutions) may lead to a new category of computer career for those specializing in data storage and recovery.

prices have placed these devices within the budget of many computer owners. For this reason, CD-R and CD-RW discs are a popular, cost-effective alternative medium for archival and storage purposes.

CD-R drives can read standard CD-ROM discs and write data to **CD-R discs**, which have a coating of temperature-sensitive dye that is easily recognized by its greenish-gold color. When the laser hits this dye, it changes the color and alters the dye's reflective properties. Although the writing technique differs from that used to create CD-ROM discs,

standard CD-ROM drives can read the data from CD-R discs.

CD-R is a "write-once" technology. After you've saved data to the disc, you can't erase it or write over it. An advantage of CD-R discs is that they aren't expensive; in quantities of 20 or more, they're often available for less than $1 per disc.

CD-RW drives provide full read/write capabilities using erasable **CD-RW discs**, which are more expensive than CD-R discs. CD-RW drives can also write to less expensive CD-R discs, giving users the best of both worlds.

DVD-ROM Discs and Drives

As we mentioned earlier, the newest optical disc format, **digital video disc (DVD)**, also called digital versatile disk, is capable of storing an entire digitized movie. DVD discs are designed to work with **DVD-ROM drives** and **DVD players**, and are very popular with movie-watching consumers.

DVD-ROM discs can store up to 17 GB of data, and DVD-ROM drives can transfer data at high speeds (up to 12 Mbps; comparable to the data transfer rates of hard drives). In addition, DVD-ROM drives are downwardly compatible with CD-ROM. This means that DVD-ROM drives can read CD-ROM discs as well as DVD-ROM discs (see Figure 4.23).

DVD-R discs operate the same way as CD-R discs; you write to them once and read from them many times. **DVD+RW** discs allow you to write, erase, and read from the disc many times. A relatively new read/write version, called **DVD-RAM** (digital video disc-RAM), enables computer users to burn DVD-ROM discs containing up to nearly 5 GB of data. Like most new technologies including DVD-ROM, a profusion of incompatible formats has made consumers reluctant to embrace DVD-RAM, but it is expected to take off once clear standards emerge.

Figure 4.23
DVD-ROM drives read CD-ROM discs as well as DVD-ROM discs.

Other Optical Storage Technologies

Although other optical storage technologies exist, they have not proven popular, due to a lack of standards. As a result, discs must be read by the same brand and type of drive that created them. Similar to CD-R, **write once**, **read many** (**WORM**) systems use recordable 12-inch optical discs that can store up to 15 GB. Also used for large-scale data archiving are **magneto-optical (MO) discs**, erasable discs that combine the magnetic principles used on tape and disk with new optical technology.

Storage Horizons

In response to the explosive demand for more storage capacity, designers are creating storage devices that store more data and retrieve this data more quickly. Exemplifying these trends are FMD-ROM discs, solid state storage devices, and enterprise storage systems.

FMD-ROM

A single optical disk, scientists believe, can store no more than about 5 gigabits per square inch. But why not create transparent disks with more than one layer? Here's the idea: each layer contains data, but the layer is transparent enough to allow a laser beam to shine through. The laser beam focuses on only one layer at a time. If this sounds futuristic, take a look at a DVD-ROM disc. It contains two layers—which is why DVD-ROMs store so much more data than their single-layer predecessor, the CD-ROM.

Why not create more than two layers? In research laboratories, efforts to create more than two layers failed because the layers created too much reflected light, which caused errors in reading the data. However, a potential new technology called **FMD-ROM** (short for **fluorescent multilayer disc–read-only memory**) would solve this problem. In an FMD-ROM drive, each layer is coated with a fluorescent substance. When the laser beam strikes this layer, the light that is bounced back is also fluorescent. This type of light can pass undisturbed through the disc's many layers, so the errors are eliminated. Research indicates that FMD-ROM discs of up to 100 layers are possible. While no larger than today's CD-ROM, such discs could each contain up to one terabyte of data.

The first efforts to bring this technology to market stalled in 2002, but the idea is sound and there will surely be others who will try. A trillion bytes on a single disk—imagine the possibilities!

SOLID STATE STORAGE DEVICES

A **solid state storage device** consists of nonvolatile memory chips, which retain the data stored in them even if the chips are disconnected from their current source. The term *solid state* suggests that these devices have no moving parts; they consist only of semiconductors. Although solid state memory chips are more expensive than the volatile RAM chips used to provide most computers with random access memory, prices for these chips have declined to the point that they can be used to increase the amount of storage available to a computer or computerized device. Solid state storage devices have a number of important advantages over mechanical storage devices such as disk drives: they are small, lightweight, highly reliable, and portable. Among the solid state storage devices in common use are PC cards, flash memory cards, and smart cards.

PC Cards

A **PC card** (also called a **PCMCIA card**) is a credit card–sized computer accessory typically used with notebook computers (see Figure 4.24). PC cards are designed to fit into PC card slots, which are included with most notebooks. PC cards can provide a variety of functions. For example, some PC cards are modems, others are network adapters, and still others provide additional memory or storage capacity.

Three types of PC cards are available. **Type I PC cards** are 3.3mm thick and are used to provide notebook computers with nonvolatile flash memory. (Flash memory cards use nonvolatile memory technologies we'll talk about in the next section.) **Type II PC cards** are 5mm thick and are used to provide notebook computers with network adapters, modems, SCSI support, access to external disk drives, and support for many additional types of peripherals. **Type III PC cards**, 10.5mm thick, can accommodate a highly miniaturized hard disk.

When used as storage devices, PC cards are most commonly used to transfer data from one PC card slot–equipped computer to another. For example, a notebook computer user can store documents created on a business trip on a solid state memory card and then transfer these documents to a desktop computer (as long as it is equipped with a PC card reader).

PC cards are standardized by the Personal Computer Memory Card International Association (PCMCIA), a consortium of industry vendors. As a result, a notebook computer equipped with a PC card slot can use PC cards from any PC card vendor.

Flash Memory Cards
Increasingly popular among digital camera users are **flash memory cards**, which use nonvolatile flash memory chips (see Figure 4.25). Flash memory cards are wafer-thin, highly portable solid state

Figure 4.24
PC cards are about the size of a credit card and fit into PC card slots, which are included with most notebooks.

Figure 4.25
Flash memory cards are thin, portable solid state storage systems.

storage systems that are capable of storing as much as 1 GB of data. Flash memory cards are also used with digital cellular phones, portable MP3 music players, digital video cameras, and other portable digital devices. However, in order to use a flash memory card with one of these devices, the device must have a compatible **flash memory reader** (a slot or compartment into which the flash memory card is inserted.) Although flash memory cards are small, portable, and capable of storing many megabytes of data, they are not well standardized. Several competing flash memory standards exist. For users, the lack of standards is inconvenient. A device (such as a digital camera) that works with one type of flash memory card will not work with the others.

SmartMedia flash memory cards are among the smallest solid state storage systems available, but their small size and relative simplicity places limits on their storage capacity (up to 128 MB). Increasingly popular are **CompactFlash** cards. CompactFlash cards are thicker than SmartMedia cards, enabling CompactFlash cards to contain more memory. CompactFlash cards can store up to 1 GB of data. Recently introduced is Sony's

Memory Stick, a chewing gum–sized flash memory card, currently available in capacities of up to 128 MB. Memory Stick readers are found mainly in Sony-made devices, although a few other manufacturers are beginning to use Sony's technology.

Flash memory cards can be used with notebook and desktop computers as well as portable digital devices such as digital cameras. Flash memory card readers can be connected to a computer by means of a PC card or a standalone reader that connects to the computer by means of a USB cable.

Smart Cards

A **smart card** is a credit card–sized device that combines flash memory with a tiny microprocessor, enabling the card to process as well as store information (see Figure 4.26). Smart cards have many applications, including replacing credit cards. Tomorrow's credit cards will utilize smart card technology to provide far more convenience, functionality, and safety than today's credit cards can provide. One smart card will replace the collection of credit cards, club cards, store cards, and travel mileage cards that the average consumer carries around today. By inserting the card into a compatible reader, users will be able to access their account information by means of a secure Internet connection. Because smart cards use encryption and other measures for security, they'll be all but impossible to misuse if they're stolen.

Many applications for smart cards already exist, and more are on the way. Where a computer network contains highly confidential data, smart cards can be used to provide network users with a highly secure means of verifying their identity; unlike a typed user name and password, the identifying information on the smart card cannot be easily stolen or duplicated. **Digital cash systems**, in widespread use in Europe and Asia, enable users to purchase a prepaid amount of electronically stored money, which can be used to pay the small amounts required for parking, bridge tolls, transport fares, museum entrance fees, and similar charges. In general, the United States lags behind Europe and Asia in smart card usage, but this is beginning to change.

Some smart card advocates believe that smart cards will eventually replace ordinary cash altogether. However, the ability to carry out anonymous, difficult-to-detect transactions would disappear along with the cash; most of the digital cash systems currently envisioned in the United States would leave an electronic "trail" linked to the individual using the card. Law enforcement agencies would welcome this development because it would sharply reduce a wide variety of illegal transactions that are currently carried out in cash. Tax collection agencies are also eager to see cash disappear. Currently, a significant amount of income is not reported to tax agencies because it's received in cash. With a smart card-based digital cash system, individuals could no longer receive income without leaving a trail behind.

Some believe that digital cash systems pose a significant danger to basic freedoms. A world in which every cash transaction, no matter how minute, is traced is one in which every person's purchases—no matter how tiny—can be assembled and scrutinized. In short order, an investigator could put together a list of the magazines and newspapers you purchase and read, where and when you paid bridge tolls and subway fares, and what you had for lunch. A

Figure 4.26
Smart cards combine flash memory with a tiny microprocessor.

government leaning toward tyranny could use this information to identify and neutralize its political opponents—or for even more nefarious purposes. In Nazi Germany, for example, government officials used the telephone records of persons known to be Jewish in order to locate and apprehend Jews in hiding.

ENTERPRISE STORAGE SYSTEMS

According to a recent estimate, the amount of information a large corporation must store doubles each year. What's more, employees, managers, executives, and customers increasingly expect this information to be readily available when and where it's needed—and to be kept safe from prying eyes if it's confidential. At the same time, corporations are becoming more dependent on computer systems for storing and retrieving vital information. If a storage system fails, it must be possible to bring backup systems online in short order. Not surprisingly, corporate demand for fast, secure, and reliable storage systems is skyrocketing.

To cope with their information storage needs, corporations develop **enterprise storage systems** that typically consist of several of the storage technologies discussed in this chapter. An enterprise storage system may make use of servers connected to hard disks, massive RAID systems, **tape libraries** (high-capacity tape systems; see Figure 4.27), optical disc libraries, and tape backup systems.

SAFETY AND SECURITY

IMPACTS

September 11: Business the Day After

September 11, 2001, was a day of extraordinary human tragedy for America. Terrorists not only took many lives, they also tried to knock the United States off its economical feet. As the country attempted to recover, Americans realized that the way to prove to terrorists that they weren't going to succeed in quashing the American spirit was to get back to business as quickly as possible. Of course, victims and their families were everyone's top priority, but showing the world that business would continue to function was important, too.

One company hit especially hard was bond house and financial services firm Cantor Fitzgerald, along with its sister companies eSpeed and TradeSpark, which operated from the top floors of One World Trade Center, employing about 1,000 people. Of these, more than 650 perished in the WTC disaster, including half of its senior leadership staff. However, because of the dedication of its surviving employees, as well as its redundant and concurrent backup computing centers in Rochelle, New Jersey, and London, England, Cantor Fitzgerald was miraculously up and running just two days after the attack.

September 11 forced companies not just in New York City but across the United States to take a closer look at their backup capabilities—not just *whether* they had a backup system, but also *where* it was located. In fact, many of the companies at the Trade Towers did have backup systems on September 11, but many of these companies relied on systems at the other Tower or at another nearby building in the area affected by the attack. The WTC disaster changed all that. The idea governing backup systems today is not just to ensure redundancy of data, but to ensure that backup data is stored in geographically dispersed places. Most important, these facilities must be located far from major cities, which are seen as potential terrorist targets. Thus, in the aftermath of September 11, many companies are moving their backup centers to suburban areas with independent utility and transportation systems. The New York Stock Exchange, for example, is planning on creating a backup trading floor in Westchester, New York, to ensure trading can continue in case of an emergency.

Some redundancy centers are used solely in case of an emergency and serve only as storage facilities, complete with their own electrical generators and telecommunications grids. Others are fully functioning business facilities that act as satellite offices while they also duplicate all company data. Because such "mirroring" of data needs to be performed in an organized fashion, professional backup and security companies have experienced an increased demand for their services in the wake of September 11. Meanwhile, some building companies are now advertising themselves as specialists in constructing backup buildings.

Back at Ground Zero, cleanup is complete and the rebuilding goes on. Companies once located in the WTC are now located across New York and its surroundings. Whether these companies will ever return to downtown Manhattan is uncertain. What is certain is that the business landscape has changed, and backup computing systems are now a necessity.

New technologies are being developed to meet the unique needs of large organizations. With storage technologies such as

Figure 4.27
Tape libraries are high-capacity tape systems that are often found in enterprise storage systems.

those we've discussed in this chapter, users must be able to locate and gain access to the server that contains the appropriate storage. If the server is not available, the storage isn't available either. One solution to this problem is called a **storage area network** (**SAN**). A storage area network links high-capacity storage devices to all of the organization's servers. In this way, any of the storage devices are accessible from any of the servers. Storage area networks often make use of **network attached storage** (**NAS**) devices. These high-performance devices provide shared data to clients and other servers on a local area network. Storage capacities range from 120 GB to as much as 6.7 TB (terabytes).

HOME | Takeaway Points | Key Terms and Concepts | Matching | Multiple Choice | Fill-In | Short Answer | Exercises/Projects | Web Research | CHAPTER REVIEW

TAKEAWAY POINTS

- Memory uses costly, high-speed components to make software and data available for the CPU's use. Memory needs to have enough capacity to hold the software and data that are currently in use. RAM is volatile and doesn't retain information when the computer is switched off. In contrast, storage is slower and less costly, but it offers far greater capacity. Storage devices are nonvolatile; they retain information even when the power is switched off. Storage devices play important input and output roles, too. When you start your computer or launch an application, storage devices function as input devices as they transfer information into memory. When you've created documents with your application, storage devices play an important output role by saving and storing your work.

- Storage media are categorized by the type of operations they can perform (read-only or read/write), the type of data access they provide (sequential or random access), the type of technology they use (magnetic or optical), and their location in the storage hierarchy (online, near-online, or offline). A storage device's performance is measured in terms of its capacity (in bytes), as well as its access speed, the time that elapses before the device begins transferring the requested data.

- Disks store data in circular bands called tracks. Each track is divided into pie-shaped wedges called sectors. The sectors are combined into clusters, which provide the basic unit for data storage. To access data on the drive, the drive's actuator moves the read/write head to the track that contains the desired data.

- Hard disks store data in much the same way floppies do, except the hard disk contains multiple platters. Because hard disks offer so much storage space, it is sometimes convenient to divide them into sections, called partitions, which appear to the operating system as if they were separate disks.

- A hard disk's performance is measured by its positioning performance (how quickly the drive can position the read/write head to begin transferring data) and its transfer performance (how quickly the drive sends the information once the head has reached the correct position). Positioning performance is expressed by the drive's seek time, whereas transfer performance is affected by the drive's spindle speed.

- The two leading hard disk interfaces are descended from the original IDE and SCSI specifications. IDE drives are cheaper and more widely available. SCSI drives are faster and offer greater storage capacity, but they require an expensive interface card.

- CD-ROM discs and drives are standard equipment in today's computer systems, largely because most software is now distributed on CD-ROM discs. CD-ROM is a read-only technology. CD-R drives can record once on inexpensive CD-R discs; CD-RW drives can write repeatedly to erasable CD-RW discs, which are more expensive. Read-only DVD-ROM discs offer much more storage capacity. A read/write version, DVD-RAM, has been slow to catch on due to standardization squabbles.

- Solid state storage technologies, such as PC card–based flash memory, flash memory cards, and smart cards offer several attractive advantages, including small size, high capacity, and light weight. They are used in notebook computers, digital cameras, portable digital music players, and other portable devices.

- To cope with their information storage needs, corporations develop enterprise storage systems that may make use of servers connected to hard disks, massive RAID systems, tape libraries, optical disc libraries, and tape backup systems.

1 2 3 **4** 5 6 7 8 9 10 11 12 13 14 15 16

CHAPTER REVIEW | Takeaway Points | Key Terms and Concepts | Matching | Multiple Choice | Fill-In | Short Answer | Exercises/ Projects | Web Research | HOME

KEY TERMS AND CONCEPTS

access time
activity light
advanced intelligent tape
   (AIT)
ATA (AT attachment)
bad sector
CD-R disc
CD-R drive
CD-RW disc
CD-RW drive
CD-ROM (compact
   disc–read-only memory)
CD-ROM jukebox
cluster
CompactFlash
cylinder
data archiving
data backup
data transfer rate
digital audio tape (DAT)
digital cash system
digital data storage (DDS)
digital linear tape (DLT)
digital video disc (DVD)
directory
disk (diskette)
disk cache
disk drive
DVD player
DVD-R
DVD-RAM
DVD-ROM disc
DVD-ROM drive
DVD+RW
enterprise storage system
entry-level drive
Fast IDE (Fast ATA or ATA-2)
fault tolerance
file allocation table (FAT)
file
fixed disk
flash memory card
flash memory reader
floppy disk
FMD-ROM
   (fluorescent multilayer
   disc–read-only memory)

folder
formatting
fragmented
hard disk
hard disk controller
head actuator
head crash
high-density (HD)
High FD (HiFD)
IDE/ATA
Integrated Drive Electronics
   (IDE)
Internet hard disk
Jaz drive
jewel box
land
latency
magnetic disk
magnetic tape
magnetic storage media
magneto-optical (MO) disc
magneto-optical (MO) drive
memory
Memory Stick
milliseconds (ms)
multisession CD
nanoseconds (ns)
near-online storage
   (secondary storage)
network attached storage (NAS)
nonvolatile
offline storage (tertiary storage
   or archival storage)
online storage
   (primary storage)
optical storage media
partition
PC card (PCMCIA card)
PhotoCD
pits
platters
portable media
positioning performance
preformatted
quarter-inch cartridge (QIC)
RAID (redundant array
   of independent disks)

random access
   storage device
reading
read-only media
read/write head
read/write media
removable hard disk
saving
sector
seek time
sequential storage device
shutter
single-session CD
Small Computer System
   Interface (SCSI)
smart card
SmartMedia
solid state disk (SSD)
solid state storage device
spindle speed
storage (mass storage
   or auxiliary storage)
storage area network
   (SAN)
storage device
storage hierarchy
SuperDisk
tape library
track
transfer performance
Type I PC card
Type II PC card
Type III PC card
Ultra3 SCSI
   (Ultra160 SCSI)
Ultra DMA/66 (ATA-5)
Ultra DMA/100
volatile
write once, read many
   (WORM)
write-protect tab
   (write-protect notch)
writing
Zip disk
Zip drive

COMPUTERS IN YOUR FUTURE 2004

4.25

HOME | Takeaway Points | Key Terms and Concepts | **Matching** | Multiple Choice | Fill-In | Short Answer | Exercises/Projects | Web Research | **CHAPTER REVIEW**

MATCHING

Match each key term in the left column with the most accurate definition in the right column.

_____ 1. near-online storage
_____ 2. latency
_____ 3. fault tolerance
_____ 4. sequential storage
_____ 5. optical storage
_____ 6. saving
_____ 7. MO
_____ 8. seek time
_____ 9. read-only
_____ 10. diskette
_____ 11. slack space
_____ 12. head crash
_____ 13. RAID
_____ 14. sector
_____ 15. track

a. using a computer's output device as a storage device

b. characterized by a computer going through a fixed sequence of stored items to locate the one that is needed

c. a device that groups two or more hard disks that contain exactly the same data

d. storage devices that combine both magnetic and optical technologies

e. unable to perform writing operations

f. storage that is not directly available

g. space wasted on a disk because the cluster size is too large

h. the time that the read/write head must wait until the data has spun around underneath it

i. physical contact between the read/write head and a hard disk

j. a circular band on a disk

k. an area on a disk that is a pie-shaped wedge

l. the ability of a storage device to provide data even if one or more of its components fail

m. the time it takes the read/write head to locate data before reading or writing begins

n. a floppy disk

o. media that use tightly focused laser beams to read microscopic patterns of data encoded on a disc's surface

Chapter review numbers: 1–16

CHAPTER REVIEW

| Takeaway Points | Key Terms and Concepts | Matching | Multiple Choice | Fill-In | Short Answer | Exercises/ Projects | Web Research | HOME |

MULTIPLE CHOICE

Circle the correct choice for each of the following.

1. This storage device does not use magnetic-sensitive materials for recording information.
   a. CD-ROM drive
   b. Tape drive
   c. Hard disk drive
   d. Floppy disk drive

2. Storage hierarchy consists of which of the following three levels?
   a. Offline storage, random access storage, online storage
   b. Online storage, near-online storage, optical storage
   c. Online storage, offline storage, read/write storage
   d. Online storage, near-online storage, offline storage

3. Which of the following is not a random access storage medium?
   a. Tape
   b. CD-ROM
   c. Hard disk
   d. Floppy disk

4. Which of the following enables you to turn any floppy disk into a read-only disk?
   a. Head actuator
   b. Write-protect tab
   c. Sector
   d. Read/write head

5. This technology allows CDs to be rewritten.
   a. CD-RAM
   b. CD-ROM
   c. CD-RW
   d. CD-R

6. Removable hard disks are what kind of storage medium?
   a. Online storage
   b. Offline storage
   c. Near-online storage
   d. Sequential storage

7. What does FAT mean?
   a. Floppy Advanced Transfer
   b. Fixed All-purpose Tape
   c. Fast access time
   d. File allocation table

8. This type of storage device retains its information, even when the power is switched off.
   a. Sequential
   b. Nonvolatile
   c. Solid state
   d. Volatile

9. How much data can a DVD-ROM store?
   a. 650 megabytes
   b. 1.44 megabytes
   c. 17 gigabytes
   d. 1 terabyte

10. Why is FMD-ROM a promising technology?
    a. It provides fast access to data.
    b. It allows multiple layers on which to store data.
    c. It creates network connections to CD-ROM jukeboxes.
    d. It stores redundant data on different DVD-ROMs.

Go to **www.prenhall.com/ciyf2004** to review this chapter, answer the questions, and complete the exercises and Web research questions.

HOME | Takeaway Points | Key Terms and Concepts | Matching | Multiple Choice | Fill-In | Short Answer | Exercises/ Projects | Web Research | CHAPTER REVIEW

1 2 3 4 5 6 7 8 9 10 11 12 13 14 15 16

FILL-IN

In the blanks provided, write the correct answer for each of the following.

1. A tape backup unit is one example of an _____ storage device.

2. Floppy disks are an example of _____ media, which means you can remove a floppy disk from one computer and insert it into another.

3. CD-ROM disc drives vary in speed, which is measured in the unit's _____ rate.

4. Access times for memory are measured in _____, while access times for storage devices are measured in _____.

5. Damaged areas on a disk are called _____.

6. _____ prepares a disk for use.

7. When data is _____, it is split into pieces and stored in whatever sectors happen to be available.

8. A _____ is a location made up of the same track location on all the platters of a hard drive.

9. _____ is the most widely used hard drive interface for PCs.

10. The digital envelopes that are used to store files are called _____ on PCs and _____ on Macintoshes.

11. Several fixed, rapidly rotating disks are called _____.

12. A _____ links high-capacity storage devices to all of an organization's servers.

13. The _____ moves the read/write head over the surface of the disk.

14. _____ is the operation of rearranging magnetic particles into a meaningful pattern.

15. _____ is memory that is used to improve hard disk performance.

SHORT ANSWER

1. What is the difference between memory and storage?

2. What is the difference between a sequential storage device and a random access storage device? Give an example of each.

3. What is the purpose of partitions, clusters, and sectors in a disk drive?

4. What factors affect disk drive performance?

5. What makes a Zip drive a convenient peripheral for a computer system? Have you ever had a file that was too big to save on a floppy disk? Describe the nature of the file and how you saved and transported it.

EXERCISES/PROJECTS

1. The ability to store data for long periods of time is extremely important. For example, how long would you want your school transcripts stored? Discuss the inability of computers to store data permanently. Describe the two major hindrances of computers storing and accessing data "forever," and give an example of each. Is paper a good storage medium? Why or why not?

2. Visit two different local retail merchants to determine how they save backup copies of their important personal computer files. Which media—tape, disk, network, etc.—do they use? How often do they make backups? Where do they keep their backup copies? What is the problem with keeping original and backup files in the same location (store)?

3. Some automotive repair garages no longer keep a collection of individual car "shop manuals" to help mechanics diagnose and complete repairs. Several companies now market complete manual sets for all major models on multiple CD-ROMs or DVD-ROMs. Visit two automobile repair shops to see if they are using this technology. In addition to diagnostic and repair procedures, what other types of information are on these discs? What is the cost of a set of these CDs or DVDs?

4. When hard drives first became available, their storage capacities were around 5 MB, and at the time this seemed like an enormous amount of storage. Since many applications and certain data files now use several megabytes of storage, current personal computers come with hard drives that are measured in gigabytes. Select any brand of personal computer and determine the hard drive capacity for the least and most expensive computer models. Do you think that you would ever fill the hard drive on even the least expensive model?

   If necessary, use the Internet to find the storage requirements for the following popular applications:

   • Any version of Microsoft Office®
   • Adobe Photoshop®
   • Netscape Navigator®

   Certain data files also require large amounts of storage. What types of files do you think would require several megabytes of storage?

5. When answering one of the questions in Chapter 2, you discovered that the amount of memory in computers has greatly increased, while its cost has greatly decreased. Similarly, the amount of hard disk storage has increased while its cost has decreased. The 5 MB hard drives mentioned in the preceding exercise once cost about $2,500! Once again, warm up your calculator and divide the cost by the number of bytes to determine the cost per byte of storage. Check a newspaper or visit a local retailer to find the size and price of a hard drive upgrade. Once again, divide the cost by the number of bytes and determine the cost per byte. Using the early 5 MB drive price, how much would the upgraded hard drive cost?

   In addition to higher storage capacities, what other improvements do you think have been made to hard drives?

HOME | Takeaway Points | Key Terms and Concepts | Matching | Multiple Choice | Fill-In | Short Answer | Exercises/ Projects | Web Research | CHAPTER REVIEW

1 2 3 4 5 6 7 8 9 10 11 12 13 14 15 16

WEB RESEARCH

1. The first CD-ROM drives had a transfer rate of 150 Kbps, which is referred to as single speed (1x). Compared with a hard drive, this transfer rate was relatively slow; consequently, 2x (300 Kbps) CD-ROM drives were quickly developed. How fast is the CD-ROM in your computer or a campus computer? Visit CNET's CD-ROM site at **www.cnet.com**, and find the speed and cost of the fastest CD-ROM drives that are being marketed. Would you consider upgrading to a faster CD-ROM? Why or why not?

2. Although Iomega was not the first company to market removable hard disks, they have been the most successful. Visit Iomega's Web site at **http://iomega.com/na/landing.jsp** to learn more about their products. What is the storage capacity of their Zip disks? What are two of the ways of connecting a Zip drive to a computer? Write a short paragraph about your findings. Be sure to include your thoughts on how the use of a removable storage device might or might not fit into your computing practices.

   One of the challengers to Zip drives has been the SuperDisk. Although not as popular as Zip drives, the technology costs approximately the same. To learn more about these removable hard disks, visit **www.imation.com**. What is the range of capacities of a SuperDisk? What feature makes them particularly competitive with Zip disks?

   Explain why you would or would not purchase either a Zip drive or a SuperDisk drive.

3. Since a DVD-ROM can store up to 14 times the amount of information that a CD-ROM can hold, DVD-ROM drives have replaced CD-ROM drives on some new computers. Visit CNET's DVD site at **www.cnet.com** and find the best price for the fastest DVD-ROM drive. (Hint: click re-sort by price.) In addition to video information, what other types of information could be stored on a DVD-ROM? Would you purchase a new computer with a DVD-ROM drive or upgrade your present CD-ROM drive to a DVD-ROM one? Explain why you would or would not get a DVD-ROM drive.

4. One method for increasing your storage capacity is to use Internet storage (sometimes called online storage). Have you ever considered using this option? Visit the WebWizards site at **www.webwizards.net/useful/wbfs.htm** to learn more about Internet storage sites. Which two major Internet service providers also offer Internet storage? List at least one advantage and one disadvantage of using Internet storage. In addition to storage, what other services do these sites provide? Some sites provide free storage, while others charge a fee. Select a free one, and describe the following:

   - the registration process
   - the amount of free storage space
   - additional services that are provided

   Would you consider using the selected site? Explain why or why not.

5. Besides the high cost of recordable and rewritable DVD media, the lack of a standard format has prevented the rapid acceptance that was seen with CD-R and CD-RW. This is reminiscent of the competition between the VHS and Betamax videotape formats, with VHS winning that battle. A similar incompatibility has prevented computer users from purchasing rewriteable DVD "burners," and we'll just have to wait to see which of the competing DVD formats will prevail. Visit the *PC Technology Guide's* DVD site at **www.pctechguide.com** to learn more about these formats. Perhaps some of the formats found at this Web site will no longer exist by the time you answer these questions!

   To find prices for media and burners, visit the DealTime site at **www.dealtime.com**. What is the name of the recordable format? Find the cost of a blank disc, and find a model and price for a burner.

Buying and Upgrading Your Computer System

Many college students already own a computer. At a typical state university, as many as 80 percent of students own a computer and make full use of high-speed network connections available in their dorm rooms. Increasing numbers of colleges are even expecting students to purchase a computer upon entering the university.

Owning a computer is the best way to ensure computer literacy, because when you own a computer, you have the opportunity to manage it. And employers are demanding higher levels of computer literacy than ever before. According to a recent study, more than 83 percent of surveyed employers described computer literacy as "important" or "very important" in a hiring decision. Particularly attractive to employers were the following skills: word processing (96 percent), e-mail (93 percent), spreadsheet analysis (86 percent), database entry and editing (83 percent), use of presentation software (75 percent), and Internet searching (63 percent). If you're in the market for a new computer, you'd be wise to buy a system that can run all this software, and then to try to use as much of it as you can while you're still in school.

Get Started the Right Way ✔

There's a right way and a wrong way to select a computer. The right way involves understanding the terminology and relative value of the components that make up a computer system. You then determine your software needs and choose the computer that runs this software in the most robust way. What's the wrong way? Buying strictly based on price, being influenced by sales hype, and buying a system you know nothing about.

For these reasons, this section begins by introducing you to the hardware-first approach. Then we'll move on to system configurations and software.

Choose the Right Hardware ✔

Computer systems are made up of many components. The following are the components you need to understand in order to make a good decision about which computer you should buy:

- ✗ processors
- ✗ memory
- ✗ hard disks
- ✗ internal drives
- ✗ video cards and monitors
- ✗ network cards
- ✗ modems
- ✗ sound cards and speakers
- ✗ keyboards and mice
- ✗ an uninterruptible power supply

This section will introduce you to these components. Keep in mind as you read that one of the best ways to prepare yourself for buying a computer is to peruse newspaper and magazine ads listing computer systems for sale. Another great source is the Internet. To research particular computer manufacturers (such as Apple, Dell, IBM, Gateway, and so on) simply type the computer manufacturer's name in the address bar of your Internet browser and add the .com extension. Several good comparison sites are also out there, such as CNET, MySimon, Yahoo, AOL, and PCWorld. On these sites you can perform side-by-side comparisons of different systems.

Let's start our discussion of hardware components by looking at the processor.

PROCESSORS

Of all the choices you make when you buy a computer, the microprocessor is the most important. Strictly speaking, the microprocessor (called a processor or CPU for short) *is* the computer, which is why it's the most important component in terms of shaping the system's overall performance. In general, the higher the processor's **clock speed**, the faster the computer (see Figure 4A).

4A
Computer systems are named after their processors and clock speed.

As you research processors, keep in mind that you'll pay a premium if you buy the newest and fastest processor available. One school of thought is to buy the second- or middle-fastest processor on the market. This way you'll be getting plenty of speed without paying a penalty for being the first to have the most. In addition, processors are so powerful today that it's not always necessary to have the fastest. You need enough processing power to handle the work or play you intend to accomplish. If you're a heavy game user you may need lots of processing power, but if you use your computer to surf the net, play audio files, and communicate using e-mail and instant messaging programs, the middle-speed processor on the market will suit you just fine.

MEMORY

The next item to consider when buying a computer is the amount of memory you need. Two important issues are how much random access memory (RAM) you need and whether your system is equipped with cache memory. You really can't have too much memory, so buy as much memory as you can afford and that matches your processor and motherboard.

RAM

Windows XP and Mac OS X theoretically require only 64 MB of RAM, but neither system functions very well with so little. When you try to run two or more programs, there's no more room in memory, so the operating system has to store portions of a program on your hard disk. The result is sluggish performance. You should strongly consider purchasing at least 128 MB of RAM; 256 MB would be even better. Several different types of RAM exist. Currently, the fastest is called synchronous DRAM (SDRAM). For PCs with Pentium IV processors, you need SDRAM capable of running at a speed of 100 MHz. This type of RAM is often called PC100 SDRAM.

Secondary Cache

Cache memory is memory that is built into the processor. As you research the memory built into computer systems, keep in mind that systems with cache memory tend to be faster than systems without. (Refer to Chapter 4 for an in-depth discussion of secondary cache memory.)

HARD DISKS

A common mistake made by first-time buyers is to underestimate the amount of disk storage they'll need. Today, 10 GB (gigabytes) sounds like a lot, but you won't believe how quickly you'll fill it up. A good rule of thumb is to use no more than 25 percent of your hard disk space for the operating system and applications. Because Windows XP and Microsoft Office consume up to 2 GB of disk space, a 10 GB drive should be a minimum. The good news is that most entry-level systems sold today come with a 20 GB hard disk, and it's relatively inexpensive to move up to 40 or 60 GB.

Among computer systems that have the same processor, hard disk speed makes the biggest contribution to overall system speed. Suppose you're looking at two Pentium IV systems with 1.5 GHz processors. The less expensive one might use a slow hard drive, which can slow the system down so much that it isn't much faster than a well-designed 1 GHz system. In particular, pay attention to rotation speed; drives that spin at 5,400 RPM are bottom-of-the-line products. The better drives spin at 7,200 or 10,000 RPM. (See Chapter 2 for a complete discussion of hard disk speed.)

INTERNAL DRIVES

To install new software, most of which is distributed on CD-ROM discs, you'll want a CD-ROM drive. You can get CD-ROM drives with speeds up to 70x (70 times the original CD-ROM standard of 150 Kbps). If you're splurging, consider a DVD drive instead of a CD-ROM; you'll be able to read DVD discs, which can store more data than CD-ROM discs (up to 4.7 GB). DVD drives can read ordinary CD-ROM discs, too (see Figure 4B). It's also a good idea to buy a system that has the ability to write to CDs.

Increasingly popular are internal Zip drives for backup and supplemental storage. You can add a Zip drive (with up to 750 MB removable disks) for about $100. Another option is Sony's HiFD, a removable storage drive that uses cartridges that hold 200 MB and more. HiFD drives have an advantage over Zip drives: they're downwardly compatible with 3.5-inch floppy disks. However, users are increasingly choosing Zip disks over floppies, so you should make your decision based on how large you expect your files to be and whether other computer systems you work with use floppies or Zip disks.

Figure 4B
DVD discs can store more data than CD-ROM discs, and a DVD drive also will read ordinary CD-ROM discs.

VIDEO CARDS AND MONITORS

The computer's **video card** determines the quality and resolution of the display you see on your monitor. The current standard display for a Windows PC is a **Super Video Graphics Array** (**SVGA**) monitor with a resolution of either 1024 x 768 or 1280 x 1024. High-end video cards can display resolutions of 1600 x 1200. The higher the resolution, the more memory is required. To display 1600 x 1200 resolution with a color palette of 16.7 million colors, for example, you need to equip your video card with 8 MB of **video RAM** (**VRAM**), memory that's set aside for video processing purposes.

Advanced systems offer a special bus design that directly connects the video circuits with the microprocessor, increasing performance speed considerably. In Windows PCs, the best systems currently offer an **Accelerated Graphics Port** (**AGP**), which transfers video data much more quickly than the standard PCI interface.

If you plan to run Microsoft Windows, look for a system that has a **graphics accelerator** built into the video card. This accessory can double or triple the performance of Windows.

Figure 4C (1&2)
(1) A 17-inch monitor is considered to be the industry standard.
(2) Flat-screen monitors are becoming increasingly popular.

On Macintosh systems, watch out for undersized video memory. If the Macintosh you're planning to buy has 512 KB of VRAM, you'd be wise to have more installed when you buy your system.

Monitors are available in different sizes. You can purchase anything from a 14-inch to a 21-inch monitor, but large monitors are expensive. Increasingly, a 17-inch monitor is considered the industry standard (see Figure 4C). If you plan to get into desktop publishing or CAD, you may want to upgrade to a 21-inch monitor. Keep in mind that for cathode-ray tube (CRT displays), the quoted size of the monitor is the size of the CRT's front surface measured diagonally. But some of this surface is hidden and unavailable for display purposes. For this reason, it's important to distinguish between the monitor's quoted size and the viewable area. Recently, flat-screen monitors have gained in popularity, although they're more expensive than traditional CRTs.

The monitor's **dot pitch** (also called **aperture grill**) is also important. This is a physical characteristic that determines the smallest dot the screen can display. Don't buy a monitor with a dot pitch larger than .28mm—the smaller, the better.

NETWORK CARDS

If you're planning to connect your computer to the campus network, you need a **network interface card** (**NIC**). Check with your college's computer center to find out what kind of network card you need. Most colleges run 10 Mbps (10baseT) Ethernets, but a few require you to get a 100 Mbps (100baseT) network card.

On Macintoshes, support for Ethernet networks is built in, but you need a **transceiver**, a device that handles the electrical connection between the cable and the Mac's Ethernet port. On Windows PCs, you need an Ethernet card, which includes the transceiver (see Figure 4D).

Look for a card that plugs into your computer's **Peripheral Computer Interconnect** (**PCI**) bus. **Bus** is the term that describes the pathways that are used to move data from one area of the system to another.

Figure 4D
An ethernet card is a network interface card designed to work with Ethernet local area networks (LANs).

MODEMS

If you plan to log on to the campus network by means of a telephone connection, you need a modem. Many computers now come with a modem built in to the system, so buying an external modem is unnecessary. Today's officially sanctioned standard modem is the 56 Kbps V.90 protocol. Avoid inexpensive modems that use the X.2 or K56flex protocols, which were marketed before the V.90 protocol's publication. Although many service providers continue to support X.2 and K56flex, this support is being phased out now that the V.90 protocol has been approved. Check with your campus computer center to find out which modem protocols they support.

SOUND CARDS AND SPEAKERS

To take full advantage of the Internet's multimedia capabilities, you need a sound card and speakers.

On Macs, the sound is built in; you need external speakers, though, to hear sounds in stereo. On Windows PCs, you'll need to equip your system with a sound card. Look for a sound card that offers **wavetable synthesis**, which uses stored samples of real musical instrument sounds, as well as a PCI interface, which reduces demands on your processor. For the richest sound, equip your system with a subwoofer, which reproduces bass notes more realistically.

Be aware that many computers come with cheap speakers, especially the lowest-priced systems. If sound matters a lot to you—and it does to many college students—consider upgrading to a higher-quality, name-brand speaker system.

KEYBOARDS AND MICE

Most computers come with standard keyboards. If you use your computer keyboard a lot and you're worried about repetitive stress injury (RSI), consider upgrading to an ergonomic keyboard, such as the Microsoft Natural Keyboard.

Most systems also come with a basic mouse, but you can ask for an upgrade. With Windows PCs, there's good reason to do so, thanks to the improved mouse support built into Windows XP. Any mouse that supports Microsoft's IntelliMouse standard includes a wheel that enables you to scroll through documents with ease. Wheel mice also include programmable buttons that allow you to tailor your mouse usage to the software application you're using (see Figure 4E).

In order to choose a decent keyboard and mouse, go to a local store that sells computers and type a paragraph or two on several keyboards and use as many mice as you can find. The button placement and action can be quite different from model to model. You'll be using these input devices a lot, so be sure to make an informed decision.

Figure 4E
The wheel mouse includes a scrolling wheel and programmable buttons.

UNINTERRUPTIBLE POWER SUPPLY (UPS)

"I'm sorry I don't have my paper. I finished it, and then a power outage wiped out my work." Many professors don't accept this excuse, which means using a computer for college work can be risky. Considering the comparatively low price of today's **uninterruptible power supply (UPS)**—you can get one for less than $200—it's wise to consider buying one for your campus computer. That's especially true if you experience frequent power outages where you live or work. A UPS allows you enough time to save your work and shut down your computer properly until the power comes back up. Be sure that the UPS you purchase has surge protection. Almost all do, but you want to be a savvy consumer.

Notebook or Desktop? ✔

Once you understand the hardware components to consider when buying a computer, it's important to think about whether you want your machine to be portable or not (see Figure 4F). Notebook or laptop computers rival desktop machines in terms of power these days. The best of them are truly awesome machines, with big (over 14-inch) displays and fast processors.

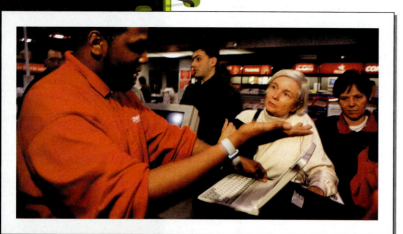

The advantages of having a notebook are many. They're obviously portable, allowing you to take them to class in your backpack or a specially designed carrying case (see Figure 4G). Once in class, you can easily fit a notebook on your desk and take notes on it. As you're probably well aware, campus housing or shared rental units often limit the amount of space for a desk, which makes notebooks even more appealing.

On the downside, notebook computers cost more than comparable desktop models. You should also consider that notebooks are easy to lose or steal, and if your notebook is missing, it could be a catastrophe. More than 250,000 notebook computers are stolen each year, mostly at airports and hotels, but thieves are targeting college campuses now. Miniaturization has its costs!

Figure 4F

Notebook computers are convenient but more expensive than comparable desktop models. Deciding whether to buy a notebook or a desktop computer is often one of the hardest decisions college students make when considering which computer system to buy.

So, the decision most often hinges upon convenience vs. expense. Ask around. You might want to pay a visit to your professor to ask his or her advice. In addition, your family, friends, and coworkers may be able to tell you what they have used and preferred. Notebooks have come a long way, but the desktop computer is still the most popular model on the market.

Figure 4G

Notebook computers allow you to take your work with you wherever you go. Special carrying cases are recommended, as they protect your computer better than backpacks do.

Mac or PC? ✔

No doubt you're aware that there are two main platforms of computer systems: Windows (PC) and Macintosh (see Figure 4H). As you'll find if you ask around, some users prefer the Mac, and other users prefer Windows. Each thinks their platform is the best, and rarely do they cross platforms. How do you know which system is best for you?

Here's the truth. *Today's top-of-the-line Macintoshes and PCs are virtually indistinguishable in terms of features and performance.* What's more, excellent software for all the important applications you'll need—word processing, e-mail, spreadsheets, database software, presentation graphics, and Web browsers—is available for both platforms. Macs used to be easier to set up and use, but that's no longer true, thanks to improvements in Microsoft Windows.

So is it a toss-up? Not quite. Some minor differences between Macs and PCs can become major issues for some people. Compatibility within an organization is critical. If your professor or place of work uses PCs, you might have fewer conversion troubles if you also have a PC (although Macs do read most PC files, and conversion software is available). Sometimes the type of computer doesn't make a difference, but oftentimes, compatibility issues can cause real headaches.

Figure 4H (1 & 2)
(1) Macs have a strong niche market in artistic fields, such as publishing, music, graphics, illustration, and Web site design. (2) PCs figure prominently on the desktops of engineers and businesspeople.

Career interests enter into the Mac-versus-PC picture, too. In general, Macs have a strong niche market in artistic fields, such as publishing, music, graphics, illustration, and Web site design. PCs figure prominently on the desktops of engineers and businesspeople. The classic stereotype is that the successful artist has a Mac, but her accountant uses a PC. Watch out for these stereotypes, though. You might think that scientists would go for PCs, but that's not necessarily the case. In the "wet" sciences (chemistry and biology), Macs have many adherents—and for good reason. These sciences involve visual representation, an area in which Macs excel.

If you're on a budget, consider the cost angle, too. On average, Macs and Mac peripherals and software are somewhat more expensive than comparable PC equipment, although the price gap has narrowed recently. Another point in favor of the PC is Linux. Although a version of Linux is available for the Mac, the PC version is where you'll find all the action. As you'll learn in Chapter 5, you can run Linux on the same hard drive as Windows or MacOS, giving you the best of both worlds.

What truly distinguishes Macs from PCs is software availability. Far more programs are available for Windows PCs than for Macintoshes, due to economics. Only about one Macintosh is sold for every 20 Windows PCs. Many software companies that formerly focused on the Macintosh are de-emphasizing Mac software and bringing out Windows products. Other publishers are dropping Mac products altogether. For example, Autodesk, publishers of the top-selling CAD program, AutoCAD, dropped its sluggish-selling Mac version to focus on its Windows products. This fact alone pretty much rules out the Mac if you're interested in architecture or engineering. Even software publishers that continue to support the Mac typically bring out the Mac versions later and don't include as many features.

Does software availability make a difference? If you're planning to use your computer only for basic applications, such as word processing, e-mail, Web browsing, and spreadsheets, the Mac-versus-PC issue simply isn't important. But look down the road. What if you declare a major a couple of years from now, only to find that your professors want you to use special-purpose programs designed to run on some other computer? This point doesn't rule out a Macintosh, especially if you're going into an arts-related field. But it does illustrate that you'll have to reinvest in learning a new system should you change platforms down the road.

Thus, as you decide whether to buy a PC or a Mac, it's important that you anticipate your future software needs. Find out which programs students in your major field of study are using, and which programs are used by graduates working in the career you're planning to pursue.

To find this out, visit the department and ask around. Find the computer lab where upper-division students hang out, watch what they're doing, and ask their advice. It might turn out that one of your major's required courses uses analytical software that runs only on a PC capable of crunching numbers at high speed, or uses a design program that runs only on a Mac loaded with memory.

To find out what type of computer is preferred by people working in your chosen career, interview appropriate professionals. If someone in your family works in that career, you already have one person to talk to. From there, you can get additional leads.

Keep in mind that any computer on the market will handle your basic needs of word processing, e-mail, Web browsing, and basic number crunching. If you can learn what specialized programs you might have the need for, you'll be one step ahead in making sure that the system you pur-chase can not only run the software, but run it without straining resources.

Get the Right Printer ✔

Printers fall into four basic categories: color inkjet printers, monochrome laser printers, color laser printers, and multifunction devices that include faxing and scanning as well as printing. For college use, cost considerations will probably rule out color laser and multifunction devices, so you'll most likely want to choose between color inkjet and monochrome laser printers.

Of course, if you need a color printer, you'll probably want to go with the color inkjet printer. But if color is not an issue, which printer is best depends for the most part on your budget. Although monochrome laser printers are more expensive than color inkjet printers, laser printers are cheaper to use in the long run because laser toner cartridges, priced on a cost-per-page basis, are cheaper than inkjet cartridges.

Speed matters, too. The slowest laser printers are faster than the fastest inkjet printers, and the slowest inkjet printers operate at a glacial pace. High-end laser printers can print as many 60 ppm (pages per minute). Still, the best inkjet printers churn out black-and-white pages at a peppy pace—as many as 18 ppm. If you go the inkjet route, look for a printer that can print at least 8 ppm.

Printing technology has come a long way in the past 10 years. Stay with a major brand name and you'll be served well. It's always a good idea to purchase an extra print cartridge and to stash it away with 30 or 40 sheets of paper. This way, Murphy's Law won't catch you at 2 in the morning trying to finish an assignment without ink or paper—never a fun thing to have happen!

Shop Wisely ✔

As you get ready to buy a computer, it's important that you shop wisely. Should you buy a top-of-the-line model or a bargain-bin special? Are mail-order companies safe? What about refurbished or used computers? Let's take a look at some of these issues.

TOP-OF-THE-LINE VS. BARGAIN BIN SPECIAL

Should you buy a top-of-the-line system, or try to save some money by getting a slower, older model? A good argument for getting the best system you can afford is that you don't want it to become obsolete before you graduate. In your senior year, do you want to spend time upgrading your hard drive when you should be focusing on your studies? In addition, every time you open the computer's cover and change something, you risk damaging one of the internal components.

The most important consideration here is the type of software you're planning to run. If you'll be using your computer for basic applications such as word processing, you don't need the most powerful computer available, so a bargain-bin special may be okay (although still exercise caution when making such a purchase). But what if you decide to declare a major in mechanical engineering? You might want to run a CAD package, and CAD programs demand a fast system with lots of memory. The same goes for any graphics-intensive software, such as illustration programs, and for advanced financial modeling programs.

LOCAL STORES VS. MAIL-ORDER/ONLINE COMPANIES

Whether you're looking for a Windows PC or a Macintosh, you need to consider whether you want to purchase your system locally or from a mail-order or online company. If you buy locally, you can resolve problems quickly by going back to the store (see Figure 4I). With a system ordered over the telephone or online, you have to call the company's technical support line.

But don't rule out ordering through the mail or online, though. Look for companies that have been in business a long time—and particularly those that offer a no-questions-asked return policy for the first 30 days. Without such a policy, you could get stuck with a "lemon" system that even the manufacturer won't be able to repair. Be aware that the lowest price isn't always the best deal—particularly if the item isn't in stock and will take weeks to reach you. Don't forget about shipping and handling charges, too, which could add considerably to the price of a system purchased online or through the mail.

Also, make sure you're not comparing arti-chokes and oranges. Some quoted prices include accessories such as modems and monitors; others do not. To establish a level playing field for comparison, use the Shopping Comparison Worksheet

Figure 4I

If you buy a computer locally, you can resolve problems quickly by going back to the store.

in Figure 4J. For the system's actual price, get a quote that includes all the accessories you want, such as a modem, a monitor, and a UPS.

BUYING USED OR REFURBISHED

What about buying a used system? It's risky. If you're buying from an individual, chances are the system is priced too high. People just can't believe how quickly computers lose value. They think their systems are worth a lot more than they actually are. Try this for yourself: find some used computer ads in your local newspaper and then find out how much it would cost to buy the same system new, right now, if it's still on the market. Chances are the new system is cheaper than the used one, or not much more expensive.

There are always reputable businesses that refurbish and upgrade systems for resale. National chains such as MacWarehouse have standards that help to ensure that their systems are "good as new" when you make a purchase. As is always the case though, be sure to check out the storefront and stay away from establishments that don't look or feel right. And make sure that your refurbished machine comes with a warranty.

NAME-BRAND VS. GENERIC WINDOWS PCS

The name-brand PC manufacturers, such as Compaq, Dell, and Gateway, offer high-quality systems at competitive prices. You can buy some of these systems from retail or mail-order stores, but some are available only by contacting the vendor directly.

For your money, you get a system that's been extensively checked out before it's shipped as well as a good warranty. If you're buying extended warranty protection that includes on-site service, make sure the on-site service is really available where you live; you may find out that the service is available only in major metropolitan areas. Make sure you get 24-hour technical support; you'll need it if something goes wrong at 2 in the morning, the night before a paper is due. (Computers seem to break down at the worst times.)

One disadvantage of name-brand systems is in their use of proprietary components. If something breaks down, you have only one repair option: go back to the manufacturer. And after the warranty has expired, you may find that you'll pay a premium price for parts and repairs. Fortunately, this is becoming less and less of an issue. Almost all name-brand computers run well right out of the box, and in-service failure rates are declining.

What about generic Windows PCs? In most cities, you'll find local computer stores that assemble their own systems using off-the-shelf components. These systems are often just as fast (and just as reliable) as the name-brand systems just discussed because they use the same components. You save because you don't pay for the name-brand company's marketing and distribution costs.

What you may not get from such stores is adequate technical support, and the warranty may not mean much if the company goes bankrupt. (Many do; the industry's profit margin is razor-thin.)

Still, it is often economically and psychologically comforting to do business with a local vendor. Just be sure to pay attention to the location and ambiance of the store. You can often learn a lot by observing the business operating environment.

4.K

Shopping Comparison Worksheet

VENDOR _____ Date _____
 Brand Name _____
 Model _____
 Real Price _____ (including selected components)

PROCESSOR
 Brand _____
 Model _____
 Speed _____ MHz

RAM
 Type _____
 Amount_____ MB

HARD DRIVE
 Capacity _____ GB   Seek time _____ ns
 Speed _____ rpm   Interface _____

MONITOR
 Size _____ x _____ pixels   Dot pitch _____ mm

VIDEO CARD
 Memory _____ MB   Max. resolution _____ x _____ pixels
 Accelerated? .... ☐ yes ☐ no

FLOPPY/ZIP DRIVE(S)
 Capacity _____ KB   Number _____

REMOVABLE DRIVE
 Type _____
 Location ....☐ internal ☐ external

CD-ROM DRIVE
 Speed _____

CD BURNER
 Included? .... ☐ yes ☐ no

DVD-ROM DRIVE
 Included? .... ☐ yes ☐ no

SPEAKERS
 Included? .... ☐ yes ☐ no   Upgraded? .... ☐ yes ☐ no

SUBWOOFER
 Included? .... ☐ yes ☐ no

SOUND CARD
 Included? .... ☐ yes ☐ no

NETWORK CARD
 Included? .... ☐ yes ☐ no   Speed (10/100) _____

MODEM
 Included? .... ☐ yes ☐ no   Protocol _____

KEYBOARD
 Upgraded? .... ☐ yes ☐ no   Model _____

MOUSE
 Included? .... ☐ yes ☐ no   Upgraded? _____

UPS
 Included? .... ☐ yes ☐ no

SOFTWARE
 _____
 _____
 _____

WARRANTY _____
Service location _____
Typical service turnaround time _____

Caring for Your Computer System ✔

After your computer is running smoothly, chances are it will run flawlessly for years if you follow a few precautions:

✘ Equip your system with a **surge protector** to protect all system components from power surges caused by lightning or other power irregularities (see Figure 4K).

✘ Consider purchasing an uninterruptible power supply (UPS). These devices help to ensure that your system is protected should the power go down.

✘ Don't plug your dorm refrigerator into the same outlet as the one the computer's using. This is a big one: a refrigerator can cause fluctuations in power, and consistent power supply is critical to the performance and longevity of your computer. Manage it well.

✘ Make sure there's sufficient air circulation around the components. Don't block air intake grills.

✘ If you connect or disconnect any cables, make sure you switch off the power first.

✘ Make sure the cables aren't stretched or mashed by furniture.

✘ Avoid eating or drinking near your computer. Crumbs can gum up your keyboard. Spilled liquids (even small amounts) can ruin the keyboard, or an entire system.

✘ Don't switch off the power without following the proper shut-down procedure.

✘ To keep your hard disk running smoothly, run a disk defragmentation program regularly. This program ensures that related data is stored as a unit, thus increasing retrieval speed. In Windows, the defragmenting program is usually found under the Accessories menu choice on the Start, Programs menu.

✘ Get a virus checker and run it frequently. Don't install and run any software someone gives you on a disk until you run a virus check on the disk and its contents. If someone gives you a document file on a disk, be sure to check for macro viruses.

Figure 4K
Surge protectors help prevent costly damage to delicate circuitry and components.

Be sure to keep your computer clean, too:

✗ Clean your computer and printer with a damp, soft, lint-free cloth.

✗ To clean your monitor, spray some window cleaner on a soft, lint-free cloth—*not* directly on the monitor—and then wipe the surface clean.

✗ If your mouse gets gummed up, twist off the ring on the bottom of the mouse, remove the ball, and clean the ball with warm, soapy water. Rinse and dry it thoroughly with a clean, lint-free cloth. Clean the rollers with a cotton swab, and remove any lint that may have accumulated.

✗ To clean your keyboard, disconnect it from the system unit and gently shake out any dust or crumbs. You can also use cans of compressed air to clear dust or crumbs from underneath keys. Also on the market are specially designed vacuums for keyboards. Never use a regular vacuum cleaner on your keyboard, as the suction is too strong and may damage the keys.

Upgrading Your System ✔

Many computer owners improve their system's performance and utility by adding new hardware to their systems, such as modems, sound cards, and additional memory. This section discusses the two most common hardware upgrades: adding expansion boards and memory.

Before you decide to upgrade your computer yourself, be aware that doing so may violate your computer's warranty. Read the warranty to find out. You may need to take your computer to an authorized service center to get an upgrade without violating the warranty. Also, while it can be relatively simple to install new components, it's also true that doing so can be fraught with peril. If you aren't absolutely certain of what you're doing—don't!

REMOVING THE COVER

To upgrade your system, begin by unplugging the power cord and removing all the cables attached to the back of the unit. Make a note of which cable went where so you can correctly plug the cables back in later. With most systems, you can remove the cover by removing the screws on the back of the case. If you don't know how to remove the cover, consult your computer manual. Keep the screws in a cup or bowl so they'll be handy when you reassemble the computer.

ADDING EXPANSION BOARDS

To add an expansion board to your system, identify the correct type of expansion slot (ISA, PCI, or AGP) and unscrew the metal insert that blocks the slot's access hole. Save the screw, but discard the insert. Gently but firmly press the board into the slot. Don't try to force it, though, and stop pressing if the motherboard flexes. If the motherboard flexes, it is not properly supported, and you should take your computer to the dealer to have it inspected. When you've pressed the new expansion board fully into place, screw it down using the screw you removed from the metal insert. Before replacing the cover, carefully check to make sure the board is fully inserted.

UPGRADING MEMORY

Many users find that their systems perform faster when they add more memory. With additional memory, it's less likely that the operating system will need to use virtual memory, which slows the computer down. In order to upgrade your computer's memory, you'll find it helpful to learn a few terms and concepts.

Older computers use memory chips supplied on 72-pin **single inline memory modules** (**SIMMs**); most newer computers use 168-pin **dual inline memory modules** (**DIMMs**). SIMMs and DIMMs are printed circuit boards (with affixed memory chips) that are designed to snap into specially designed sockets on the computer's motherboard. Most motherboards have either four SIMM sockets or two to three DIMM sockets (see Figure 4L). SIMMs must be installed in pairs, which limits their flexibility.

SIMMs and DIMMS are available in various capacities, ranging from 8 MB to 128 MB each. You need to consult your computer's manual to determine whether your computer uses SIMMs or DIMMs, and where you can add them. For example, suppose your computer has two 8 MB SIMMs in the first two sockets, leaving two sockets empty. Because you must install SIMMs in pairs, you can add two 8 MB SIMMs (for a total of 32 MB of memory—the original 16 plus the additional 16), two 16 MB SIMMs (for a total of 48 MB of memory—16 + 32), or two 32 MB SIMMs

Figure 4L
Memory modules are affixed to slots on the motherboard.

(for a total of 80 MB of memory—16 + 64). You may be able to add even more memory, but some motherboards place a limit on the amount of memory you can install. You don't need to install DIMMs in pairs, so they're easier to work with.

Consult your computer's manual to determine which type of memory technology your computer uses. Older computers use the slowest of these technologies, **fast-page mode (FPM) DRAM**, which is available only in SIMMs. Newer computers use the faster **extended data out (EDO) DRAM**, which is available in both SIMMs and DIMMs. Still newer computers use the fastest available memory technology, called **synchronous dynamic RAM (SDRAM)**, which is available only in DIMMs.

You also need to consider the memory chips' speed. FPM and EDO DRAM chips are rated in **nanoseconds (ns)**, billionths of a second. The smaller the number, the faster the chip. Pentiums require 60ns chips, while older systems can work with 70ns or 80ns chips. For SDRAM chips, the speed is rated in **megahertz (MHz)** (millions of cycles per second), and this speed must match the speed of the motherboard's data bus (66 MHz, 100 MHz, or 133 MHz).

When you purchase memory modules, a knowledgeable salesperson might help you determine which type of module you need and how much memory you can install. But it's more and more the case that the salesperson won't know any more about installing memory than you do. This is further reinforcement for the case of buying locally if you think that you'll need or want to upgrade your system during its life span.

Before you install memory modules, you also need to be aware that memory chips are easily destroyed by static electricity. Do not attempt to install memory chips without wearing a **grounding strap**, a wrist-attached device that grounds your body so that you can't zap the chips. Remember: Don't try to force the memory modules into their receptacles; they're supposed to snap in gently. If they won't go in, you don't have the module aligned correctly, or you may have the wrong type of module.

REPLACING THE COVER

When you have checked your work and you're satisfied that the new hardware is correctly installed, replace the cover and screw it down firmly. Replace the cables and then restart your system. If you added Plug and Play devices, you'll see on-screen instructions that help you configure your computer to use your new hardware.

Summary ✔

To be a savvy consumer, you need to become familiar with the terminology and significant components of the system you're buying. Among other components, the processor, memory, hard disk, and monitor will determine both the comfort and quality of your computing experience. Other things you need to consider are whether you want a desktop or a notebook, a PC or a Mac, and what storage devices, printer, and peripherals you'll need. Research is fairly painless and very powerful. The Internet makes side-by-side comparison easy. Use as many resources as you can, and then remember that no matter how happy or unhappy you are with the result, you'll most likely be doing it all again within three years.

System Software: The Operating Environment

What You'll Learn . . .

When you have finished reading this chapter, you will be able to:

1. List the two major components of a computer's operating system software.

2. Explain why a computer isn't useful without an operating system.

3. List the five major functions of an operating system.

4. Explain what happens when you turn on a computer.

5. List the three major types of user interfaces.

6. Discuss the strengths and weaknesses of the most popular operating systems.

7. List the six system utilities that are considered essential.

8. Discuss data backup procedures.

Without software—the set of instructions that tells the computer what to do—a computer is just an expensive collection of wires and components. Chances are you've already worked with one type of software, application software. Application software helps you accomplish a task, such as writing a college essay or balancing your checkbook. The second major type of software is **system software**. If you've used a computer, then you've used system software. This kind of software includes all the programs that are needed to enable a computer and its peripheral devices to function smoothly. Although some system software works "behind the scenes," some of it requires your guidance and control.

System software has two major components: (1) the operating system and (2) system utilities such as backup programs. Learning how to use an operating system and its system utilities is the first step you need to take toward mastery of any computer system. In this chapter, you'll learn what operating systems do, look at the most popular operating systems, and learn

which utilities you should use to ensure that your computing experience is safe and enjoyable.

The Operating System (OS): The Computer's Traffic Cop

Imagine the traffic in a downtown New York City intersection at rush hour, and you'll have a good idea of what it's like inside a computer. Electrons are whizzing around at incredible speeds transported this way and that by the **operating system (OS)**, the electronic equivalent of a harried traffic cop. Impatient peripherals and programs are honking electronic "horns," trying to get the cop's attention. As if the scene weren't chaotic enough, the "mayor" (the user) wants to come through right

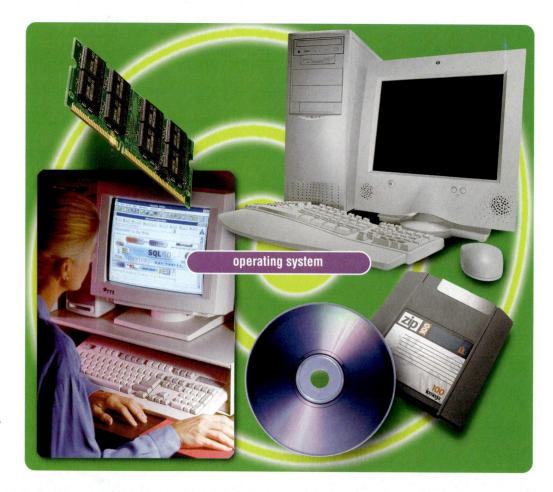

operating system

Figure 5.1
An operating system works at the intersection of application software, the user, and the computer's hardware. It manages programs, parcels out memory to applications, deals with internal messages from input and output devices, and provides a means of communicating with the user.

now. Keeping traffic running smoothly is the computer's operating system—just like a traffic cop, standing at the intersection of the computer's hardware, application programs, and the user.

An operating system is essentially a set of programs that perform certain basic functions. The operating system starts the computer, manages programs, parcels out memory, deals with input and output devices, and provides a means of interacting with the user (see Figure 5.1). The operating system is most often found on a hard disk, although on some small handheld computers you'll find the operating system on a ROM chip.

Because operating systems, sometimes called **operating platforms**, work closely with the computer's hardware and with application programs, all of these components must be designed to work together harmoniously. The major operating systems include UNIX, MS-DOS, Mac OS, Microsoft Windows, and Linux. We'll discuss all of these systems later in the chapter. For now, you just need to know that application programs are designed to work with a specific operating system. For example, Macintosh programs can run only on the Mac OS and will not run on Microsoft Windows. Likewise, PC programs can run only on the Windows operating system. (It is true, though, that some Windows programs will run on Macintoshes that are running a program that emulates Windows, but performance often suffers.)

STARTING THE COMPUTER

When you start or restart a computer, it reloads the operating system into the computer's memory. This process is called **booting**, after the notion that the computer "pulls itself up by its bootstraps." In a **cold boot**, you start the computer after the power has been switched off. In a **warm boot** (also called a **warm start**), you restart a computer that is already on. Warm boots are often necessary after installing new software or after an application crashes. In PCs, you can initiate a warm boot by pressing Ctrl + Alt + Del (hold down the Ctrl and Alt keys, and press Del) or by pressing the Reset button

that is usually located on the front of the system unit.

In both types of booting, the computer copies the essential portions of the operating system, called the **kernel** or the **supervisor program**, into the computer's memory, where they remain during the entire operating session. The kernel is called **memory resident** because it "resides" in memory at all times. Because the kernel is memory resident, it must be kept as small as possible. Less frequently used portions of the operating system, called **nonresident**, are copied from the disk as needed.

A cold or warm boot is a step-by-step process. The following sections discuss the steps followed by the computer after you initiate a cold or warm boot.

Step 1: The BIOS Screen and Setup Program

When you first turn on or reset a PC, you may briefly see the **BIOS screen**, a text-only screen that provides information about the BIOS software encoded in the computer's ROM. As its name suggests, BIOS equips the computer with the software needed to accept keyboard input and display information on-screen.

While the BIOS information is visible, you can access the computer's **setup program** by pressing a special key, such as Del or F8. (You'll see an on-screen message indicating which key to press to access the setup program.) The setup program includes many settings that control the computer's hardware. You should *not* alter or change *any* of these settings unless you are instructed to do so by technical support personnel.

Step 2: The Power-On Self-Test (POST)

After the BIOS loads, it executes a series of tests to make sure that the computer and associated peripherals are operating correctly. Collectively, these tests are known as the **power-on self-test** (**POST**). Among the components tested are the computer's main memory (random access memory, or RAM), the keyboard and mouse, disk drives, and the hard disk. If the computer encounters an error, you'll hear a beep and see an on-screen error message. Often, you can correct such problems by making sure components such as keyboards are plugged in securely.

.

Should any of the power-on self-tests fail, you may see an error message, and the computer will stop. Some failures are so serious that the computer cannot display a message; instead, it sounds a certain number of beeps. To help the technician repair the computer, write down any messages you see and try to remember how many beeps you heard.

Step 3: Loading the OS

Once the power-on self-test is successfully completed, the BIOS initiates a search for the operating system. When it finds the operating system, it **loads** the operating system's kernel into the computer's memory. (To load a program means to transfer it from a storage device to memory.) At this point, the operating system takes control of the computer.

Options (or settings) in the setup program determine where BIOS looks for the operating system. (These settings are set by default but can be modified by the user.) The settings are stored in a type of nonvolatile memory called **CMOS (complementary metal-oxide semiconductor)**. CMOS is a special type of memory used to store essential startup configuration options, such as the amount of memory that has been installed in the computer. On most PCs, BIOS first looks for the operating system on the computer's hard disk. On newer PCs, it's possible to load an operating system from a CD-ROM. The BIOS can also be set up to look for the operating system on a disk drive.

If your computer fails to start normally, you may be able to get it running by choosing the setup program option that loads from Drive A and inserting an **emergency disk** (also called a **boot disk**) in the disk drive. The emergency disk loads a reduced version of the operating system that can be used for troubleshooting purposes. An emergency disk sometimes

Figure 5.2
The Control Panel is accessed directly from the Start menu.

.

comes with a new computer but often-times is something that you need to create yourself. Consult the documentation that came with your computer, or choose Help from the My Computer program to learn about this process.

Step 4: Configuring the System

Once the operating system's kernel has been loaded, it checks the system's configuration to determine which drivers and other utility programs are needed. A **driver** is a utility program that is needed to make a peripheral device function correctly.

In Microsoft Windows, configuration information is stored in the **registry**, which is a database containing information about installed peripherals and software. The registry also contains information about your system configuration choices, such as background graphics and mouse settings.

Operating systems equipped with **Plug and Play** (**PnP**) capabilities can automatically detect new PnP-compatible peripherals that you may have installed while the power was switched off. Peripheral devices equipped with PnP features identify themselves to the operating system. If the driver required to operate the device is already present on the system, it will be installed and loaded automatically. If not, you may be prompted to insert a disk containing the needed driver.

Step 5: Loading System Utilities

Once the operating system has detected and configured all of the system's hardware, it loads **system utilities** such as speaker volume control, antivirus software, and a PC card unplugging utility. If these utilities offer configuration choices, these choices are made available to you. In Microsoft Windows, you can view the available choices by right-clicking one of the small icons located on the right side of the Windows taskbar (see Figure 5.2). You can access additional configuration choices in the Control Panel.

Step 6: Authenticating Users

When the operating system finishes loading, you may see a dialog box asking you to type a user name and password. This process is called **authentication** (or **login**). In authentication, you verify that you are indeed the person who is authorized to use the computer. If the computer is connected to a network, the authentication you provide enables you to access network resources.

Consumer-oriented operating systems such as Microsoft Windows and Mac OS do not demand that you supply a user name and password to use the computer. However, you can set up **profiles** on these systems. Associated with a user name and, optionally, a password, a profile is a record of a specific user's preferences for the desktop theme, icons, and menu styles. If you set up a profile for yourself, you'll see your preferences on-screen after you log in. You can also allow other users to create and log on to their profiles, and they'll see their preferences without disturbing yours.

On multiuser computer systems, you must have an **account** on the computer. Your account consists of your user name, your password, and your storage space, called a **home directory**. The account is created by the computer's **system administrator**, the person who's responsible for the computer. To access your account, you must supply your user name and password.

If you're given a user name and password that enable you to access network resources at your school, it's very important that you safeguard this information. Don't write it down where others could read it, and never give your password to others. If you do, somebody could use your account in such a way that the actions they perform will seem as if they were performed by you. If such actions involve playing pranks or engaging in illegal activities, you could lose your computer privileges—or worse.

MANAGING PROGRAMS

An important operating system function—and the one that most dramatically affects an operating system's overall quality—is the way it manages program execution. In the early days of personal computing, **single-tasking** could run only one application program at a time, which users found to be very inconvenient. To switch programs with a single-tasking operating system,

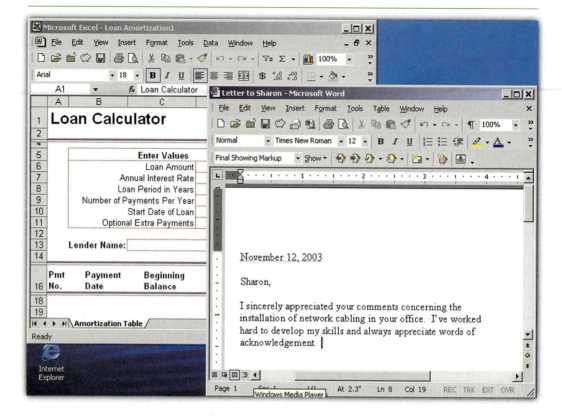

Figure 5.3

Multitasking operating systems enable a single user to work with two or more programs at once. Here the user is switching between a word processing application and a spreadsheet application.

you had to quit one program before you could start the second one.

Today, many users work with five or more applications in a single session. **Multitasking** operating systems enable a single user to work with two or more programs at the same time. In multitasking operating systems, the CPU doesn't actually run two programs at once; rather, it switches between them as needed. From the user's perspective, one application (called the **foreground application**) is active, while another (the **background application**) is inactive (see Figure 5.3). Such multitasking operating systems are now the norm.

A clear measure of the stability of an operating system is the technique it uses to handle multitasking. If one of the running programs invades another's memory space, one or both of the programs will become unstable or, at the extreme, **crash** (stop working).

In an early form of multitasking, **cooperative multitasking**, users could run two or more programs. The foreground application exercised control of the CPU until the program's task was finished. Only then did it relinquish the CPU to

other applications. But what happened if the foreground application crashed? The crashed program never relinquished the CPU. In consequence, the computer "froze," or "hung," and the user had to restart the computer, losing any unsaved work in any of the other applications. Microsoft Windows 3.1 and older versions of Mac OS used this type of multitasking.

A better and more recent type of multitasking, called **preemptive multitasking**, enables the operating system to regain control if an application stops running. You may lose any unsaved work in the application that crashed, but the failure of one application does not bring the whole system down. Personal computer operating systems that use preemptive multitasking include Linux, recent versions of Mac OS, and all current versions of Microsoft Windows.

A recent development in multitasking, **multithreading**, enables the computer to execute more than one task in a single program. To facilitate multithreading, programmers must divide a program into distinct tasks, called **threads**. For example, one thread can handle printing, while another handles file retrieval. With multithreading, users can work on one task in an application while other tasks keep running in the background.

Multithreading also brings benefits when more than one application is running. With multithreading, the background application's threads keep running even when the user is working with the foreground application. Personal computer operating systems that can handle multithreaded applications include Linux, Mac OS 8 and later versions, and Windows 95 and later versions.

Some operating systems are designed to facilitate **multiprocessing**, the use of two or more processors at a time. The Macintosh G4 with OS X is such a system. **Symmetric multiprocessing** (**SMP**), the easiest type of multiprocessing to implement, is designed to work with multithreading. With SMP, when a program needs to execute a thread, the operating system finds an idle processor and assigns the thread to this processor. Personal computer operating systems that support multiprocessing include Linux, Microsoft Windows NT, Microsoft Windows 2000, Microsoft Windows XP, and recent versions of Mac OS (beginning with Mac OS 8).

MANAGING MEMORY

Another operating system function is to manage the computer's memory. For example, the operating system gives each running program its own portion of memory, and—by means of cooperative or preemptive multitasking—attempts to keep the programs from interfering with each other's use of memory.

Most of today's operating systems can make the computer's main memory (RAM) seem larger than it really is. This trick is accomplished by means of **virtual memory**, a method of using the computer's hard disk as an extension of RAM. In virtual memory, program instructions and data are divided into units of fixed size, called **pages**. If memory is full, the operating system starts storing copies of pages in a hard disk file, called the **swap file**. When the pages are needed, they are copied back into memory (see Figure 5.4). The transferring of files from storage to memory and back is called **paging**.

Although virtual memory enables users to work with more memory than the amount installed on the computer's motherboard, the paging operations—

Figure 5.4

In virtual memory, program instructions and data are divided into units of fixed size, called pages. If virtual memory is full, the operating system starts storing copies of pages in a hard disk file called the swap file. When the pages are needed, they're copied back into memory.

called **swapping**—slow the computer down. Disks are much slower than RAM chips. For this reason, adding more RAM to your computer is often the best way to improve its performance. With sufficient RAM, the operating system makes minimal use of virtual memory.

The operating system and specialized hardware (called a **DMA controller**) team up to manage **direct memory access (DMA) channels**, a set of circuits that enable peripheral devices to access the computer's RAM directly, without having to go through the CPU. Before Plug and Play peripherals came into use, a common cause of system instability was users inadvertently configuring peripherals so that they competed for the same DMA channel. The result was a serious system instability called a **DMA conflict**. Plug and Play–compatible peripherals and operating systems are designed to ensure that DMA conflicts seldom occur.

HANDLING INPUT AND OUTPUT

A third operating system function involves dealing with input and output devices. These devices generate **interrupts**, signals that inform the operating system that something has happened (for example, the user has pressed a key, the mouse has moved to a new position, or a document has finished printing). The operating system provides **interrupt handlers**, miniprograms that kick in immediately when an interrupt occurs.

Communication between input or output devices and the computer's CPU is handled by **interrupt request (IRQ)** lines. Most PCs have a fixed number (16) of IRQs, numbered 0 through 15. If two devices are configured to use the same IRQ but aren't designed to share an IRQ line, the result is a serious system failure called an **IRQ conflict**. In most cases, an IRQ conflict makes the system so unstable that it cannot function. To remedy an IRQ conflict, you may need to shut down the computer and remove peripheral devices, one by one, until you determine which one is causing the conflict. Happily, Plug and Play–compatible operating systems and peripherals have made IRQ conflicts much less common.

Peripherals that handle input and output also require their own **input/output (I/O) port**, a circuit that enables the device to channel data into and out of the computer. As with IRQ lines, there are a fixed number of I/O ports available. Plug and Play–compatible operating systems and peripherals have eliminated most **port conflicts**, a serious system instability that occurs when two input/output devices attempt to use the same I/O port.

In Microsoft Windows, DMA, IRQ, and port conflicts, and other configuration problems can often be resolved by starting the computer in Windows' **safe mode**, an operating mode in which Windows loads a minimal set of drivers that are known to function correctly. Within safe mode, you can use the System Control Panel to determine which devices are causing the problem.

As you know, you can choose many brands and models of input and output devices. Because each brand and model of a given device has its own unique characteristics, the operating system needs **device drivers**. Device drivers are programs that contain specific information about a particular brand and model of input or output device. Most operating systems come with device drivers for popular input and output devices. Additional device drivers are supplied by the device manufacturers themselves.

PROVIDING THE USER INTERFACE

From the user's perspective, what makes or breaks an operating system is the quality of the **user interface**, the part of the operating system that you see and interact with. Sometimes the user interface is called the **shell**, suggesting the idea that the user interface (the shell) "surrounds" the operating system (the kernel within the shell). User interfaces typically enable you to do the following:

- Gain access (**log in**) to the system by providing a **user ID** (also called a **user name**) and a **password**. Many personal computers aren't secured in this way, but most can be.

- Start (**launch**) application programs.

- Manage disks and files. You can format new disks, display a list of files in a directory, create new directories, rename directories, delete empty directories, copy files from one directory or disk to another, rename files, and delete files.

- Shut down the computer safely by following an orderly shutdown procedure. (You shouldn't just switch the computer off; doing so may leave scrambled data on the computer's hard disk.)

Types of User Interfaces

The three types of user interfaces are command-line, menu-driven, and graphical interfaces (see Figure 5.5).

Command-line user interfaces require you to type commands using keywords that tell the operating system what to do (such as "format" or "copy"). You must observe rules of **syntax**, a set of regulations that specify exactly what you can type in a given place. For example, the following command

```
copy a:myfile.txt c:myfile.txt
```

copies a file from the disk in drive A to the disk in drive C, not the other way around.

Command-line operating systems aren't popular with most users because they require memorization, and it's easy to make a typing mistake. While the commands are usually very simple, such as *copy* and *paste*, some are more cryptic, such as *dir* to view the directory structure, and *md* to make a new directory. Some experienced users actually prefer command-line operating systems, however, because you can operate the computer quickly after you've memorized the keywords and syntax.

Menu-driven user interfaces enable you to avoid memorizing keywords and syntax. On-screen, text-based menus show all the options available at a given point. With most systems, you select an option with the arrow keys, and then press Enter. Some systems enable you to click the desired option with the mouse or to choose a letter with the keyboard.

Graphical user interfaces (**GUIs**, pronounced "gooeys") are by far the most popular user interface. In an operating

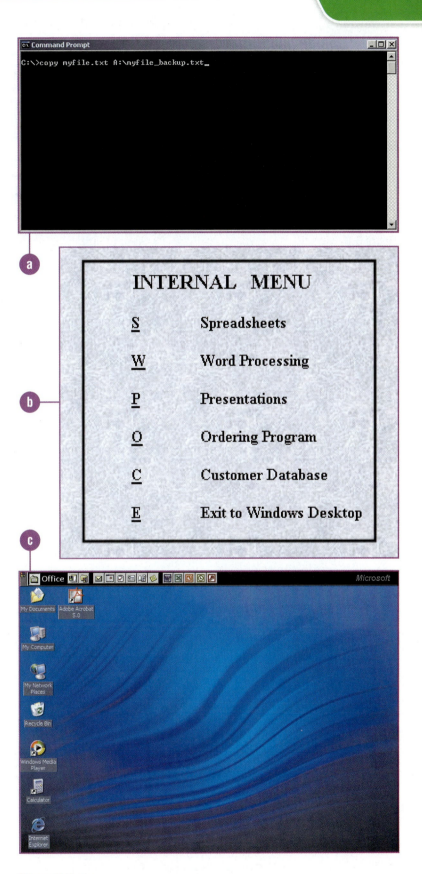

Figure 5.5 a–c

Examples of (a) command-line, (b) menu-driven, and (c) graphical interfaces.

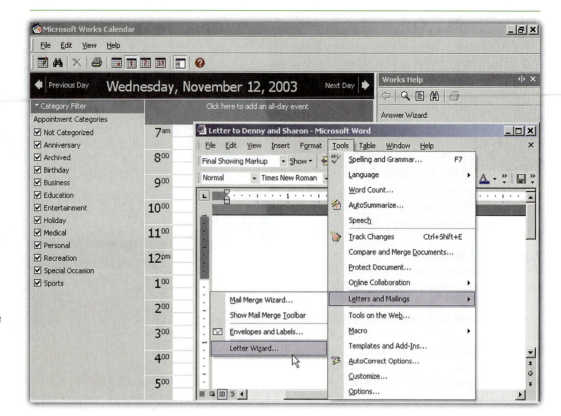

Figure 5.6
Programs run within sizeable on-screen windows, making it easy to switch from one program to another. Within programs, you can give commands by choosing items from pull-down menus.

Figure 5.7
A dialog box enables you to provide additional information that a program needs. This is the print dialog box.

system, GUIs are used to create the **desktop environment**, which appears after the operating system starts. In a desktop environment, computer resources (such as programs, data files, and network connections) are represented by small pictures, called **icons**. You can initiate many actions by clicking an icon. Programs run within sizeable on-screen windows, making it easy to switch from one program to another

(see Figure 5.6). Within programs, you can give commands by choosing items from pull-down menus, some of which display **dialog boxes**. In a dialog box, you can supply additional information that the program needs (see Figure 5.7). If a program needs to give you a warning message, you see an **alert box** that tells you what might happen if you proceed. Although GUIs are easy to use, they make heavy demands on a computer's processing circuitry and slow the computer down considerably.

Default and Alternative User Interfaces
Every operating system provides a **default user interface**, which accepts user commands and provides messages in response. But it's often possible to use a different user interface from the default one. For example, the operating system MS-DOS uses a command-line interface by default. But many programs are available that provide a menu-driven interface for MS-DOS. In the UNIX operating system, many users become confused because so many different shells are available. For example, the version of UNIX for Intel processors, Linux, can work with three different command-line user interfaces and dozens of graphical user interfaces.

DEBATES

Platform Passion: Macs versus PCs

As you almost certainly know, as a computer user, you have two major platforms to choose from: Macintosh and PC. The debate over which platform is best has raged on for years, and if market power is anything, PCs are winning by a landslide. But Apple hangs in there with its slew of adherents who choose to "think different."

What's the difference between the platforms? Although you'd never know from listening to people who love or hate Macs, there's not much difference, really. At least not in terms of power capacity. Still, the debate goes on.

On the one side, Mac lovers say their machines are easier to set up and use. Macs come with everything you need built right in—all you have to do is plug them in and you're on your way. Mac lovers also point to the fact that Apple has developed some incredibly advanced technology. (Even PC users will agree to that.) Apple offers its users cutting-edge, easy-to-use applications such as iMovie, iTunes, iPhoto, and iDVD. And Mac's FireWire technology spread to PCs first as an option and then as a standard.

It's not just the system and the software Mac users love. Most Macophiles love their one-button mice as well as their many shortcut keys. Not to mention the Apple design; many Mac adherents love the look of the Mac above all else. Today, you'll find Macs being used in most primary and elementary schools in the United States. (OS X is virtually crash-proof!) In addition, certain professions, such as publishing, advertising, and design, rely almost exclusively on Macs.

On the other hand, PCs still dominate, and the race isn't even close. PCs claim the largest chunk of the marketplace and are the choice of corporate America. And thanks to economies of scale, they also tend to be cheaper, in terms of both their hardware and software. Indeed, software is a big plus for PC users, who have far more to choose from than their Mac counterparts. Because so many more people buy the software, it tends to be better, and it is often developed and published more quickly than similar software for Macs. And as much as Mac lovers claim the one-button mouse is the way to go, PC users love their two-button mouse, which offers more choices in hand.

And as for design? Step aside, Mac. Make way for new PCs on the market. In the fall of 2002, Gateway introduced its new all-in-one computer that hopes to steal market share from Apple's iMac G4 (see Figure 5.8).

In recent years, Apple has tried to woo PC users by playing on the idea that Macs are easier to use. Meanwhile, Mac's OS X could improve the number of software products developed for Macs, and that includes games, a big reason PCs lead in the marketplace. However, as Apple moves into the PC market with its recent UNIX innovations, it may make itself more vulnerable to the viruses that have been mostly a PC headache in the past. In any case, Macs have a long way to go to catch up to PCs—and few users from either camp see that happening any time soon.

Figure 5.8 a&b
Gateway claims its all-in-one computer (a) is better and cheaper than its Mac counterpart (b).

CURRENTS

Exploring Popular Operating Systems: A Guided Tour

All of today's popular operating systems are strongly influenced by two very different predecessors: UNIX, and the first GUI-based operating system developed at Xerox's Palo Alto Research Center (PARC). In various ways, current operating systems represent variously successful attempts to pull together the ideas pioneered in these systems.

UNIX

Developed at AT&T's Bell Laboratories, **UNIX** is a pioneering operating system that continues to define what an operating system should do and how it should work. UNIX (pronounced "you-nix") was the first operating system with preemptive multitasking, and it was designed to work efficiently in a secure, centrally administered computer network. Other important UNIX innovations include the concepts of file directories and path names. UNIX also

supports multiprocessing, making it ideal for use with high-powered minicomputers equipped with several CPUs.

If UNIX is so great, why didn't it take over the computer world? One reason is the lack of compatibility among the many different versions, or flavors, of UNIX. Another reason is that it's difficult to use. UNIX defaults to a command-line user interface, which is challenging for new computer users. In the past few years, a number of GUI interfaces have been developed for UNIX, improving its usability (see Figure 5.9).

UNIX's greatest success lies in **client/ server computing**, a type of computer usage that is widely found in corporations today. In client/server computing, programs are broken into two parts, called the **client program** and the **server program**. The client program handles interaction with the user and is installed on users' desktop systems. The server program runs on a high-powered, centralized minicomputer that everyone on the network can access (if they have the appropriate security clearance). Examples of such programs include massive databases that track all of a company's financial data. UNIX-based client/server systems have enough sheer number-crunching capabilities to replace much more expensive mainframe systems, and they're very popular in corporations.

XEROX PARC AND THE FIRST GUI

While UNIX was defining how operating systems should manage computer resources, work at Xerox Corporation's Palo Alto Research Center (PARC) established how an OS should look. In the mid- to late- 1970s, PARC researchers originated every aspect of the now-familiar GUI interface, including the idea of the screen as a "desktop," icons, on-screen fonts, windows, and pull-down menus. Although Xerox released a GUI-based computer (called the Star) in 1981, the company was never able to capitalize on its researchers' innovations because the thrust of the company was and continues to be photocopying and printing devices—not computers and operating systems.

Figure 5.9
A number of GUI interfaces have been developed for UNIX in the past few years, improving the usability of this operating system.

MS-DOS

MS-DOS (or **DOS**, which is short for Disk Operating System) is an operating system for Intel-based PCs that uses a command-line user interface. Developed for the original IBM PC in 1981, MS-DOS was marketed by IBM in a virtually identical version, called PC-DOS. Like every operating system discussed in this chapter, MS-DOS shows the influence of UNIX. DOS commands for managing and navigating directories, for example, are almost identical to those of UNIX.

Because DOS was developed for early 16-bit Intel microprocessors, it can't take full advantage of the advanced capabilities of Intel's 32-bit microprocessors (beginning with the 80386). For example, DOS runs in the Intel processors' real mode, in which the operating system cannot prevent applications from invading each other's memory space (which causes crashes). In addition, DOS can work with only 640 KB of RAM at a time. Although some users still run DOS, its use is declining.

MAC OS

Just as MS-DOS brought key UNIX ideas to personal computing, **Mac OS** introduced the graphical user interface to the world. Closely modeled on the system developed at Xerox PARC, the original Macintosh operating system was released in 1984. It consisted of the operating system (called the System) and a separate shell (called the Finder). By the late 1980s, the Mac's operating system was the most technologically advanced in personal computing, but Apple Computer was unable to capitalize on its lead and the Mac OS (as it came to be called after System 7.5) lost market share to Microsoft Windows. Still, Mac OS is widely considered to be the easiest operating system for beginning computer users. In 1998, Apple was reinvigorated by the return of founder Steve Jobs. A new version of the operating system, called Mac OS X, was released in 2000 and brought Mac OS up to the technical standards of Microsoft Windows (see Figure 5.10).

MICROSOFT WINDOWS

Microsoft Windows is by far the most popular operating system. Over the years, it has gone through many iterations (see Figure 5.11), and it is now considered *the* operating system of PCs worldwide. In fact, Microsoft's dominance and business practices caught the attention of the United States government, along with that of many states who brought legal action against it in 2001-2002 for unfair or monopolistic behavior. Most of these actions have now been settled, but many believe that more action will come unless Microsoft changes the way it combines software into its operating environment. Even so, the Windows operating environment is and will remain the standard for years to come.

MICROSOFT WINDOWS 3.X

Early versions of Microsoft Windows did not attract much attention, even though they helped to introduce the GUI to PC users. However, the release of Windows 3.0 in 1990 (and subsequent versions of Windows 3.0, collectively known as **Microsoft Windows 3.x**) changed the

Figure 5.10
Released in 2000, Mac OS X brought Mac OS up to the technical standards of Microsoft Windows.

face of computing forever. Windows 3.0 was the first version of Windows to enable users to take full advantage of Intel's new 32-bit microprocessor, the 80386. This microprocessor offered a new processing mode, called **protected mode**, that enabled users to access virtually unlimited amounts of memory. And, most significant, it was the first GUI for the PC.

Microsoft Windows 95 and 98

Unlike the Windows 3.x generations, **Microsoft Windows 95** (called **Win 95** for short), released in 1995, was a true operating system, not merely a DOS application. Technically, Windows 95 was a major advance because it fully supported the 32-bit processing capabilities of the

Intel 80386 and later microprocessors. Despite its attractive features, Win 95 is best understood as a transitional operating system, poised between Windows 3.x (a 16-bit operating system) and Windows NT (a true 32-bit operating system with advanced features).

Microsoft Windows 98, or **Win 98**, released in 1998, was an improved version of Win 95 that offered better stability, improved Internet connectivity, and updated drivers for new peripherals, including DVD-ROM discs and devices that use universal serial bus (USB) port connections. Windows 98 was the first operating system to include a Web browser, Internet Explorer.

Microsoft Windows CE

Designed for hot-selling PDAs, **Microsoft Windows CE** is a "light" version of Windows. Unlike other PDA operating systems, Windows CE is designed to run simplified versions of Windows programs, such as Microsoft's own Office applications, which are available in "pocket" versions for Windows CE. This enables users to create documents on a PDA and transfer them to a desktop computer for further processing and printing.

For mobile computing, Windows CE includes an interactive scheduling calendar, an address book for contacts, e-mail, and Web browsing. By means of an automatic active synchronization program, users can quickly synchronize the corresponding utilities on their desktop

Windows Timeline

Year Released	Operating System	Version
1985	Windows	1.0
1987	Windows	2.0
1990	Windows	3.0
1992	Windows	3.1
1993	Windows	NT
1995	Windows	95
1998	Windows	98
2000	Windows	2000/ME
2001	Windows	XP

Figure 5.11

Figure 5.12
Windows CE brings Windows and Office functionality to the PDA.

computers. CE includes handwriting recognition and support for voice recording as well (see Figure 5.12).

Microsoft Windows NT

To go head-to-head with the powerful UNIX client/server systems that once dominated corporate computing, Microsoft developed **Microsoft Windows NT**. Unlike Windows 95 and Windows 98, Windows NT is a true 32-bit operating system that's specifically designed for client/server systems. To support client/server computing, Windows NT is made up of two components: Windows NT Workstation and Windows NT Server.

The Windows NT Workstation module is designed for individual desktop computers. On-screen, it looks like Win 95, but it isn't as easy to use; Windows NT is a sophisticated operating system oriented to business needs. It's faster than Win 95 and Win 98 (by as much as 30 percent). The real benefits of Windows NT Workstation emerge in a networked corporate environment, where NT desktops link to servers running Windows NT Server.

In a corporate network, Windows NT Server provides the following benefits:

Security Controls individual workstation access to networked resources, such as a database containing sensitive financial information.

Remote administration Enables the network administrator to set options remotely for each user's computer, such as specifying which applications the user can start.

Directory services Provides a "map" to all the files and applications available on the network.

Web server Makes Web pages available to internal intranet users or the external World Wide Web.

Microsoft Windows 2000

An updated version of Windows NT, **Microsoft Windows 2000** is offered in two versions: Microsoft Windows 2000 Professional (the successor to Windows NT Workstation) and Microsoft Windows

2000 Server (the successor to Windows NT Server). Both products offer better stability and more features than Windows NT, but the big gains are seen in the usability department. Both versions offer a feature-rich user interface, offering all the user-friendliness and entertaining features of Windows 98.

Microsoft Windows XP

Released in the fall of 2001, **Microsoft Windows XP** is the first Microsoft operating system family that uses the same underlying 32-bit code for all three versions (consumer, corporate desktop, and server). XP is short for "experience," reflecting Microsoft's view that users want computers with rich audio and visual features (see Figure 5.13). Microsoft Windows XP Home Edition, an improved version of Windows 2000 Professional designed for home users, replaces all previous versions of Windows designed for home users. Microsoft Windows XP Professional and Microsoft Windows XP Server are updated versions of the Windows 2000 Professional and Server products, respectively. XP Professional is designed for desktop computer users in networked corporate settings, while XP

Figure 5.13
Windows XP offers a graphically rich and relatively stable operating environment.

Destinations

Explore the features of Microsoft's latest Windows offerings at the Windows home page at **www.microsoft.com/ windows/default.mspx**.

For the latest news and developments in Linux, visit "Linux Today" at **http://linuxtoday.com**. Linux beginners can get assistance at Linuxnewbie.org at **www.linuxnewbie.org** and at Linux Start at **www.linuxstart.com**.

Server is designed to make information and services available on corporate computer networks.

Controversy surrounding the release of Windows XP focused on Microsoft's inclusion of numerous utilities and programs that formerly were not part of the operating system. These include Windows Messenger (in direct competition with America Online's Instant Messenger) and CD creation software (in direct competition with market-leading Roxio). According to Microsoft's critics, the inclusion of such products at the operating system level constitutes unfair competition; if consumers can get a utility for free with Windows XP, why should they buy it from one of Microsoft's competitors?

LINUX

A new "flavor" of UNIX, called **Linux** (pronounced "linn-ux"), is the fastest-growing operating system for Intel-based personal computers. (Versions of Linux have also been created for other PCs, including Macintoshes.) Linux is an **open-source software**, meaning its **source code** (the code of the program itself) is available for all to see and use. In fact, the Linux source code has been cooperatively and collaboratively developed by programmers from around the globe. According to one estimate, more than 257 million systems are running Linux (see Figure 5.14).

What makes Linux so attractive? Two things: it's powerful and it's free. Let's tackle "powerful" first. Linux brings all the maturity and sophistication of UNIX to the PC. Created in 1991 by a Finnish university student named Linus Torvalds, Linux has since been developed by thousands of the world's best programmers, who have willingly donated their time to make sure that Linux is a very good version of UNIX. According to Linux backers, they may have created the best version of UNIX in existence.

Linux includes all the respected features of UNIX, including multitasking, virtual memory, Internet support, multiprocessor support, and a graphical user interface. Recently, researchers at Los Alamos National Laboratories created a "bargain-basement supercomputer" by hooking up 68 microprocessors in a Linux-based system. The computer took only three days to assemble using off-the-shelf components. The result? One

Figure 5.14
Linux may soon be appearing on a computer near you.

EMERGING TECHNOLOGIES

IMPACTS

Could the Future Be Nothing But Net?

Standardized protocols and a universal common denominator are the hallmarks of the Information Age. Cyberspace transactions must share a common set of rules or there would be constant electronic chaos; and computing systems with differing operating systems and software must be able to share documents and data with each other, or there would be no value derived from using cyberspace. The following three profiles—of Marc Andreessen, Linus Torvalds, and Bill Gates—will help you to see what lies ahead in the Information Age (see Figure 5.15).

While an undergraduate at the University of Illinois in 1992, Marc Andreessen led a group of students to create Mosaic, the first graphical-interface Web browser. Mosaic was a point-and-click, user-friendly technology that became instantly popular; however, it was the school's property. Subsequently, Andreessen and others formed the Netscape Communications Corporation and created a new browser called Mozilla, which became Netscape Navigator. Within a year and a half of its introduction, Netscape became the most rapidly assimilated product in history, with 65 million users. Andreessen's vision is the cornerstone of the popularity and usability of the Web, and represents the first piece of our Information Age triad: universal interface.

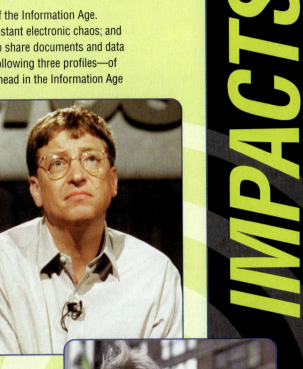

Around the same time that Andreessen was creating his browser, Finnish university student Linus Torvalds was working on a new operating system that he hoped would offer users a free alternative to UNIX. The story of Linux begins with Torvalds' being unable to afford to run UNIX on his home computer—starting prices for UNIX were $5,000, and it required a $10,000 workstation. So Torvalds decided to write his own version from scratch—something quite revolutionary. Operating systems are typically created by large teams of software engineers working for large corporations. That concept was turned upside down in 1991 when Torvalds introduced Linux, his freeware operating system, to the world.

Torvalds posted his fledgling operating system, named Linux version .02, on an Internet newsgroup and invited people to download it and make it better. Many people who downloaded Linux made modifications to the program. The community approach to Linux has made it a marvel of the computer world and has made Torvalds a folk legend. So, an open source code, universally available operating system is the second piece of our puzzle.

The story of Bill Gates and Microsoft is pretty well known. What you might not know is that on February 14, 2002, Bill Gates officially unveiled Microsoft's vision for the future: the .NET strategy, which is a comprehensive package of development tools aimed at facilitating the seamless sharing of documents and data across cyberspace. If Gates's vision comes to fruition, our third piece will be complete: any computer (using any operating system and software) will be able to share documents and data (in their native format) across cyberspace.

While Andreessen, Torvalds, and Gates could be looked at as professional adversaries, together they have thrown open the doors of computers and the Internet to everyday users. Their extraordinary Web browser, operating system, and software have become daily tools for millions—even billions—of ordinary people around the world. The future of the Information Age will be interesting!

Figure 5.15 a–c
(a) Bill Gates, (b) Marc Andreessen, and (c) Linus Torvalds

of the 500 fastest computers in the world, capable of performing 19.2 billion operations per second.

Linux is distributed using the Open Software Foundation's **General Public License** (**GPL**), which specifies that you can obtain and use Linux for free, as long as you don't turn around and try to sell it. In practice, most people buy a **Linux distribution**, a CD-ROM containing Linux and a collection of drivers, utilities, GUI interfaces, and application programs. Although most of the software on these CD-ROM discs is governed by GPL, what's being sold is the considerable effort that goes into collecting all the Linux drivers and utilities, organizing them coherently, and providing a setup utility that makes it easy for novices to get Linux running.

Although Linux is powerful and free, many corporate chief information officers (CIOs) shy away from adopting Linux precisely because it isn't a commercial product with a stable company behind it. Also, Linux can't run the popular Microsoft Office applications, which most corporate users prefer. But Linux is gaining acceptance.

The beauty of Linux, and its development model, is that it doesn't run on any particular type of computer: it runs on them all. Linux has been ported (translated) to run on systems as small as PDAs and as large as homegrown supercomputers. Another reason Linux is popular is because of a GPL-distributed free Web server called Apache, which is one of the most popular Web servers available. (A

Figure 5.16
A file manager such as My Computer enables you to organize your files and folders.

Web server is a program that makes Web pages available on the Internet.)

Because Linux is so powerful, many companies are finding that they can take disused Intel hardware, such as PCs based on the Intel 486, install Linux and Apache, and presto! They have a Web server that equals the performance of machines costing $10,000 or more.

System Utilities: Tools for Housekeeping

System utility programs (also called **utilities**) provide a necessary addition to an operating system's basic system-management tools. Sometimes these programs are included in the operating system, and sometimes they're provided by third-party suppliers. The following sections discuss the utilities considered essential.

FILE MANAGEMENT

Perhaps the most important of all system utilities is the **file manager**, a utility program that enables you to deal with the data stored on your disk (see Figure 5.16). The file manager enables you to perform various housekeeping operations on the files and folders created on your computer's storage devices.

As you learned in the special Spotlight feature "File Management" (directly following Chapter 1 of this book), your data (as well as the programs installed on your computer) is stored in **files**, which are labeled units in which related data is stored. For example, your first college essay could be stored in a file called essay1.doc. A filename such as this one often consists of two parts, the **filename** proper (essay1), and an **extension** (doc), separated by a period. The extension indicates the type of data that is contained in a file (in this case, the file is a Microsoft Word document). Files are organized using **directories** (also called **folders**). (For a more extensive discussion of file management, see the "File Management" Spotlight.)

FILE FINDERS

On a large hard disk with thousands of files, the task of finding a needed file can be time-consuming and frustrating if attempted manually. For this reason, most operating systems include a **file finder** utility, which enables you to search an entire hard disk for a file. In Microsoft Windows, Find enables you to search for files in a number of ways, including by name, date, and size (see Figure 5.17). A similar Mac OS utility, called Find File, offers the same features.

Figure 5.17
Use a file finder as a shortcut to finding a file.

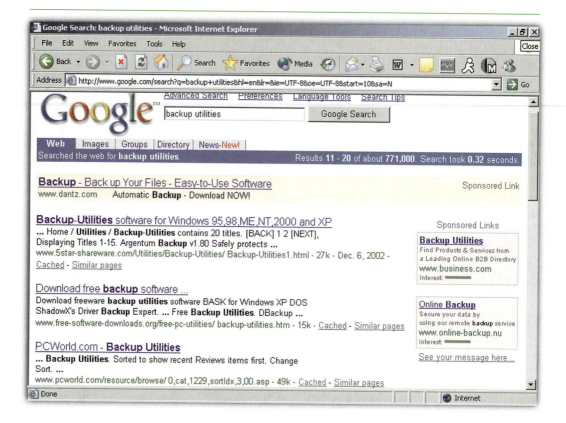

Figure 5.18
Backup utilities are an essential part of computing. You can search sites such as Google.com for useful links.

BACKUP UTILITIES

Backup utilities are an essential part of safe, efficient computer usage. They copy data from the computer's hard disk to backup media, such as tape cartridges or a Zip drive. Should the hard disk fail, you can recover the data from the backup disk (see Figure 5.18).

A backup begins with a **full backup**, in which a "mirror image" is made of the entire hard disk's contents. Subsequently, the software performs an **incremental backup** at specified intervals (such as once per day). In an incremental backup, the backup software copies only those files that have been created or changed since the last backup occurred. In this way, the backup media always contain an up-to-date copy of all programs and data. In the event of a hard disk or computer system failure, the backup tape can be used to restore the data by copying it from the tape to a new hard disk.

Even if you don't have backup software, you can still make backup copies of your important files: just copy them to a disk. When you finish working on an assignment, always copy the data to a disk, and put the disk away for safekeeping. Don't

ever rely on a hard disk to keep your only copy of a college paper.

ANTIVIRUS SOFTWARE

Antivirus programs protect a computer from computer viruses (see Figure 5.19). These programs work by examining all the files on a disk, looking for the telltale "signatures" of virus code. One limitation of such programs is that they can detect only those viruses whose "signatures" are in their databases. Most antivirus programs enable you to download the signatures of new viruses from a Web site. New viruses, however, appear every day. If your system becomes infected by a program that's not in the system's database, the program may not detect it. Due to this shortcoming, many antivirus programs also include monitoring programs that can detect and stop the destructive operations of unknown viruses.

Viruses are insidious and spread like wildfire. The worst kind are those that use the power of the computer to propagate themselves. Consider the following scenario. You're in a large lecture section of 100 students. Your teacher is very knowledgeable and you trust e-mail content that you receive from him or her. A former student of your professor receives an e-mail from a friend, opens it, and finds an attachment with an alluring filename, such as "Spring Break." The former student opens the attachment and notices that nothing seems to happen. Thinking nothing of it, the student goes about her Web browsing and homework assignments. The attachment, however, *is* doing something. It is sending a copy of itself to everyone in the student's e-mail address box—including your professor.

Your professor opens the mail from the former student and is pleased to find an attachment that apparently contains a picture of the student's spring break and so opens it. The attachment appears to do nothing, and the professor goes about his

or her business. Now, for the interesting part: Each of the 100 students in the class receives an e-mail from the professor. Each has no idea that the attachment is a virus, and most open it. Now the attachment is propagating to the e-mail address lists of each of the students. The attachment is received by parents, friends, professors, and fellow students. Many open the attachment, and the process accelerates very rapidly.

Some viruses do their damage immediately, while others hide themselves on your hard disk and then wait for a trigger time to do their work. Regardless, viruses spread quickly and can affect thousands, even millions, of users in a short period of time. This is why it's important that you install and use antivirus software. It only takes one nasty virus to cause you a lot of grief.

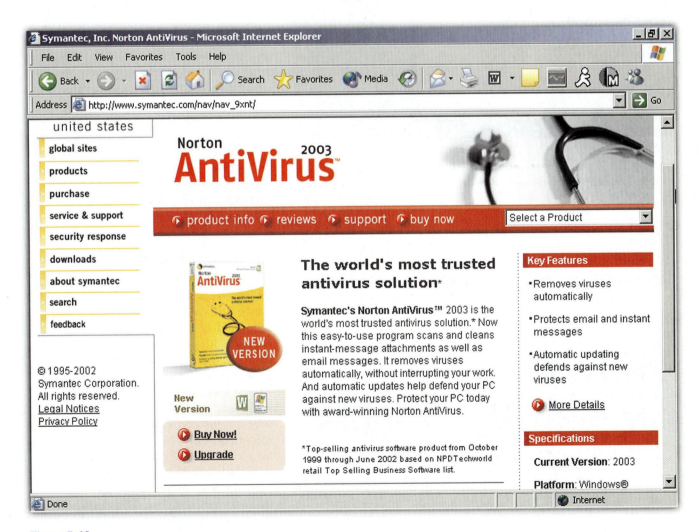

Figure 5.19
Norton AntiVirus is a utility that works by examining all the files on a disk, looking for the telltale "signatures" of virus code.

FILE COMPRESSION UTILITIES

To exchange programs and data efficiently, particularly by means of the Internet, **file compression utilities** are needed (see Figure 5.20). These programs can reduce the size of a file by as much as 80 percent without harming the data. Most file compression utilities work by searching the file for frequently repeated but lengthy data patterns and substituting short codes for these patterns. When the file is decompressed, the utility restores the lengthier pattern where each code is encountered. Popular compression utilities include WinZip for the PC and StuffIt for Macintosh systems.

Most compression utilities can also create **archives**. An archive is a single file that contains two or more files, stored in a special format. Archives are handy for storage as well as file exchange purposes because as many as several hundred separate files can be stored in a single, easily handled unit. WinZip combines compression and archiving functions.

Figure 5.20
A file compression utility enables you to create archives and compressed files.

Figure 5.21
Periodically, you should defragment your hard disk to ensure top performance.

DISK SCANNING UTILITIES

A **disk scanner** can detect and resolve a number of physical and logical problems that occur as your computer stores files on a disk. A physical problem involves an irregularity in the drive's surface, which results in a **bad sector** (a portion of the disk that is unable to store data reliably). The scanner can fix the problem by locking out the bad sector so that it's no longer used. Logical problems are usually caused by a power outage that occurs before the computer is able to finish writing data to the disk. **Disk cleanup utilities** can save disk space by removing temporary files that you no longer need.

FILE DEFRAGMENTATION PROGRAMS

As you use a computer, it creates and erases files on the hard disk. The result is that the disk soon becomes a patchwork of files, with portions of files scattered here and there. This slows the hard disk because the read/write head must go to several locations to find all of a file's data. A disk with data scattered around in this way is referred to as **fragmented**. Fragmentation isn't dangerous—the location of all the data is known, thanks to the disk's tracking mechanisms—but periodic maintenance is required to restore the disk's performance. **File defragmentation utilities** are used to reorganize the data on the disk so that it is stored in adjoining sectors (see Figure 5.21).

COMPUTERS IN YOUR FUTURE 2004

5.23

HOME | Takeaway Points | Key Terms and Concepts | Matching | Multiple Choice | Fill-In | Short Answer | Exercises/ Projects | Web Research | CHAPTER REVIEW

TAKEAWAY POINTS

- An operating system works at the intersection of application software, the user, and the computer's hardware. It manages programs, parcels out memory to applications, deals with internal messages from input and output devices, and provides a means of communicating with the user.

- Multitasking enables you to work with more than one program at a time. Preemptive multitasking is much safer to use than the earlier type, cooperative multitasking.

- The three basic types of user interfaces are command-line interfaces, menu-driven interfaces, and graphical user interfaces (GUIs). GUIs are the easiest to use, but some experienced users like the speed of command-line interfaces.

- UNIX is popular in high-end client/server systems, in which a powerful computer called a server makes data available to users through a computer network.

- Based on user interface ideas developed at Xerox Corporation's research center, the Mac OS (formerly called the System) introduced the GUI to personal computing.

- Early versions of Microsoft Windows were essentially MS-DOS applications, but Microsoft Windows 95 and 98 brought all the benefits of GUI and preemptive multitasking to PC users. Microsoft Windows NT Workstation and Windows NT Server are eating into UNIX's market share in client/server computing.

Windows 2000 is available in two versions: Windows 2000 Professional (the successor to NT Workstation) and Windows 2000 Server (the successor to NT Server). Windows XP is essentially the Windows NT operating environment tailored for the PC.

- Linux is an open-source version of UNIX that provides a great deal of power for free. It includes all of the respected features of UNIX, including multitasking, virtual memory, Internet support, multiprocessor support, and a GUI.

- Essential system utilities include backup software, file managers, file finders, disk scanning programs, antivirus software, file compression utilities, and defragmentation programs.

- A sound backup procedure begins with a full backup of an entire hard disk and continues with periodic incremental backups of just those files that have been created or altered since the last backup occurred.

- Antivirus programs protect a computer from computer viruses. They examine all files on a disk and look for signatures of virus code. It's extremely important that all computer users install antivirus software on their computer systems.

- A file that has data scattered around in portions here and there on a disk is called a fragmented file. File defragmentation utilities are used to reorganize the data on the disk so that it is stored in adjoining sectors.

CHAPTER REVIEW | Takeaway Points | Key Terms and Concepts | Matching | Multiple Choice | Fill-In | Short Answer | Exercises/ Projects | Web Research | HOME

KEY TERMS AND CONCEPTS

account
alert box
antivirus program
archive
authentication (login)
background application
backup utilities
bad sector
BIOS (basic input/output
    system) screen
booting
client program
client/server computing
CMOS (complementary
    metal-oxide semiconductor)
cold boot
command-line user interface
cooperative multitasking
crash
default user interface
desktop environment
device driver
dialog box
direct memory access
    (DMA) channel
directory (folder)
directory service
disk cleanup utility
disk scanner
DMA conflict
DMA controller
driver
emergency disk
    (boot disk)
extension
file
file compression utilities
file defragmentation utilities
file finder

file manager
filename
foreground application
fragmented
full backup
General Public License
    (GPL)
graphical user interface
    (GUI)
home directory
icon
incremental backup
input/output (I/O) port
interrupt
interrupt handler
interrupt request (IRQ)
IRQ conflict
kernel (supervisor program)
launch
Linux
Linux distribution
load
log in
Mac OS
memory resident
menu-driven user interface
Microsoft Windows
Microsoft Windows 3.x
Microsoft Windows 95
    (Win 95)
Microsoft Windows 98
    (Win 98)
Microsoft Windows CE
Microsoft Windows NT
Microsoft Windows 2000
Microsoft Windows XP
MS-DOS (DOS)
multiprocessing
multitasking

multithreading
nonresident
open-source software
operating platform
operating system (OS)
page
paging
password
Plug and Play (PnP)
port conflict
power-on self-test (POST)
preemptive multitasking
profile
protected mode
registry
remote administration
safe mode
security
setup program
server program
shell
single-tasking
source code
swap file
swapping
symmetric multiprocessing
    (SMP)
syntax
system administrator
system software
system utility program
    (utility)
thread
UNIX
user ID (user name)
user interface
virtual memory
warm boot (warm start)
Web server

HOME | Takeaway Points | Key Terms and Concepts | **Matching** | Multiple Choice | Fill-In | Short Answer | Exercises/ Projects | Web Research | **CHAPTER REVIEW**

MATCHING

Match each key term in the left column with the most accurate definition in the right column.

_____ 1. operating system

_____ 2. multitasking

_____ 3. multiprocessing

_____ 4. dialog box

_____ 5. alert box

_____ 6. disk scanner

_____ 7. emergency disk

_____ 8. interrupts

_____ 9. kernel

_____ 10. file viewer

_____ 11. file manager

_____ 12. Web server

_____ 13. icon

_____ 14. backup utilities

_____ 15. fragmented

a. an essential part of safe, efficient computer usage

b. a utility that can detect and resolve physical and logical problems on a disk

c. a miniprogram designed to give you a quick view of a file

d. enables a single user to work with two or more programs

e. essential portions of an operating system

f. signals that inform the operating system that something has happened

g. the use of two or more processors at a time

h. makes Web pages available to internal intranet users or the external World Wide Web

i. manages programs, parcels out memory, deals with input and output devices, and provides a means of interacting with the user

j. describes a disk or file whose data is scattered

k. allows users to supply additional information to a program

l. contains a reduced version of the operating system that can be used for troubleshooting purposes

m. a utility program that enables you to deal with the data stored on your disk

n. warns users what might happen if they proceed

o. graphical representation of computer resources

1 2 3 4 **5** 6 7 8 9 10 11 12 13 14 15 16

CHAPTER REVIEW

Takeaway Points | Key Terms and Concepts | Matching | Multiple Choice | Fill-In | Short Answer | Exercises/ Projects | Web Research | HOME

MULTIPLE CHOICE

Circle the correct choice for each of the following.

1. What does memory resident mean?
   a. A program that resides in memory at all times
   b. A program that monitors memory to make sure that it's used efficiently
   c. A measure of the amount of memory in a computer system
   d. Any program residing in memory

2. Which of the following is not something typically handled by the operating system?
   a. Managing programs
   b. Dealing with I/O devices
   c. Publishing Web pages
   d. Interacting with the user

3. Which of the following operating systems does not support multiprocessing?
   a. Windows 98
   b. Mac OS 8
   c. Linux
   d. Windows NT

4. Which version of Windows is designed for PDAs?
   a. Windows CE
   b. Windows NT
   c. Windows ME
   d. Windows PDA

5. Which of the following is a key component of a graphical user interface?
   a. Command words
   b. Icons
   c. Cursors
   d. Shell

6. Which company developed the first graphical user interface?
   a. Microsoft
   b. AT&T
   c. IBM
   d. Xerox PARC

7. An operating system's supervisor program is also known as what?
   a. Master
   b. Kernel
   c. General
   d. Boss

8. Which of the following operating systems is ideally suited for a networked corporate environment?
   a. Windows XP
   b. Windows 95
   c. Windows NT
   d. Windows 98

9. Which of the following is the first Microsoft operating system family that uses the same underlying 32-bit code for all three versions (consumer, corporate desktop, and server)?
   a. Windows 95
   b. Windows XP
   c. Windows 98
   d. Windows 2000

10. Linus Torvalds is credited with what?
    a. Developing multithreading
    b. Creating the Linux operating system
    c. Designing the first GUI
    d. Leading the team that wrote the first Mac operating system

COMPUTERS IN YOUR FUTURE 2004

5.27

HOME | Takeaway Points | Key Terms and Concepts | Matching | Multiple Choice | Fill-In | Short Answer | Exercises/Projects | Web Research | CHAPTER REVIEW

FILL-IN

In the blanks provided, write the correct answer for each of the following.

1. _____ user interfaces are the most popular interfaces.

2. When multiple programs are running on a computer, the one being used at the current time is known as the _____ application.

3. If an operating system uses virtual memory when memory is full, the operating system starts storing parts of memory in a _____ on the hard drive.

4. Files are organized using _____, which are also known as folders.

5. _____ enables network administrators to set options remotely for each user's computer.

6. _____ is a free and powerful operating system that brings all the maturity and sophistication of UNIX to the PC.

7. If a file's data is not stored in contiguous locations on a disk, it is said to be _____.

8. _____ programs are also known as vaccines.

9. A _____ is associated with the user name and contains a record of specific user performances.

10. _____ are programs that can reduce the size of a file by as much as 50 percent without harming the data.

11. An _____ is a single file that contains two or more files.

12. A _____ is a portion of a disk that is unable to store data reliably.

13. A file _____ indicates the type of data that is contained in a file.

14. _____ is an operating system for Intel-based PCs that uses a command-line user interface.

15. _____ enables the operating system to regain control if an application stops running.

SHORT ANSWER

1. Explain the purpose of the power-on self-test (POST). In addition to a computer system, do you know of any other systems that perform a POST?

2. When rebooting a computer, explain the difference between performing a cold boot and a warm boot. Describe what key(s) or button(s) are needed to initiate each.

3. What are the differences between multitasking, multithreading, and multiprocessing? Which, if any, of these have you used? Explain.

4. What is the purpose of a device driver? Have you ever had to install a device driver when connecting a new peripheral device to a computer? If you did, what was the device, and was the driver supplied by the operating system or by the device manufacturer?

5. Explain the differences between a full backup and an incremental backup. Which peripheral devices are commonly used for backups? Have you ever lost important files because you did not back them up? If you have done a backup, did you copy the entire disk or just selected files? When was the last time that you performed a backup?

1 2 3 4 5 6 7 8 9 10 11 12 13 14 15 16

COMPUTERS IN YOUR FUTURE 2004

PEARSON
Prentice Hall

5.28

CHAPTER REVIEW | Takeaway Points | Key Terms and Concepts | Matching | Multiple Choice | Fill-In | Short Answer | Exercises/Projects | Web Research | HOME

1 2 3 4 5 6 7 8 9 10 11 12 13 14 15 16

EXERCISES/PROJECTS

1. Considering the operating systems you use most often, and the functions that need to be performed by an operating system, what improvements can you envision? If you have used several versions of the same operating system, have you seen some of these improvements implemented when new versions are released?

2. Experiment with both a Macintosh computer and a PC. What version of each operating system did you use? Is it the latest release of the operating system? How are the two operating systems similar? Can you determine the strengths of each system? Which operating system do you prefer? Why?

3. Despite its cryptic commands, UNIX has remained a popular operating system for about 30 years. Many educational institutions have computers running this operating system, and, in fact, most Internet servers run the UNIX operating system. If you have used a UNIX computer, explain how and why you used it. Does your school have computers that use UNIX? If so, do you have an account? Can you get an account, or are the accounts restricted on these computers? Do you have an Internet service provider (ISP)? If you do, identify your provider and whether it uses UNIX to support customer Web sites.

4. List each of the Windows generations for both home and business/commercial use. Where is Windows CE used? What is significant about Microsoft's introduction of Windows XP?

5. Have you considered the purchase of a PDA? What companies manufacture PDAs? Some of these devices require special operating systems and application software. Go to a local computer store and "take one out for a test drive." Specifically, try out the operating system. Do these computers use a special version of Windows? If they use Windows, what version and release is it? How does this operating system compare with ones on a desktop or laptop computer? What are some of the differences between the two operating systems? Now that you have "kicked the keyboard" and taken a PDA out for a spin, explain why you would or would not purchase one.

COMPUTERS IN YOUR FUTURE 2004

5.29

HOME | Takeaway Points | Key Terms and Concepts | Matching | Multiple Choice | Fill-In | Short Answer | Exercises/Projects | Web Research | CHAPTER REVIEW

WEB RESEARCH

1. We discussed several system utility programs in this chapter. In this exercise, we'll examine file compression.

   Have you used a file compression program?

   • If you have, identify the brand name and version of this software application. Which operating system were you using? Did you find the file compression program simple or complicated to use? Would you recommend this product to someone else? Why or why not?

   • If you have not, visit the sites of two popular file compressors, WinZip at **http://winzip.com**, and StuffIt at **http://stuffit.com**. For which operating systems does each work? What are the current versions and manufacturers' suggested retail prices for each? Are free or evaluation versions available? Would you purchase one of these products? Explain why or why not.

2. We also discussed other system utility programs, such as antivirus programs, in this chapter. In this exercise, we'll examine these applications.

   Have you ever had to disinfect a file that was infected by a virus?

   • If you have, identify the brand name and version of the antivirus application you used and which operating system you were using. Were you able to successfully disinfect the file? Did you find the use of this program simple or complicated? Would you recommend this product to someone else? Why or why not?

   • If you have not, visit the sites of the two most popular antivirus applications, Norton AntiVirus at **www.symantec.com/nav**, and McAfee VirusScan at **www.mcafee.com/anti-virus**. For which operating systems does each work? What are the current versions and manufacturers' suggested retail prices of each? Are there free or evaluation versions available? Would you purchase one of these products? Explain why or why not.

3. So that you can answer the following questions, visit Microsoft's Windows XP site at **http://microsoft.com/windowsxp/default.asp** for information on the newest version of Windows.

   • Why would users of Windows NT/2000 upgrade to XP?
   • Why would users of Windows 95/98 upgrade to XP?
   • What other types of users will benefit from XP?
   • What are the minimum hardware requirements for XP?
   • What are the purchase and upgrade prices for XP?
   • Would you consider purchasing XP? Why or why not?

4. Use your browser to visit the site, **www.cnet.com**. Review an article that compares the Mac OS with the most current Windows operating environment. Which operating system did CNET conclude is the best one? Do you agree or disagree with its decision? Explain why.

5. Visit the Linux home page at **http://linux.com** and try the Linux 101 tutorial to learn more about this operating system.

   • What is the primary objective of this tutorial?
   • What is a dual-boot system, and what are the advantages and disadvantages of creating one? Why would or wouldn't you create a dual-boot system?
   • What is another name for the "root" user, and what is the purpose of having one?
   • What is the command to change your password?
   • What is the command to go to the home directory, and what is the command to see what is located in it?
   • What type of files are located in the /bin, /etc, and /usr directories?
   • Spend some time exploring the remainder of the tutorial. Do you feel that the tutorial met its primary objective? Explain why you would or would not install a UNIX system.

Application Software: Tools for Productivity

CHAPTER **6**

What You'll Learn . . .

When you have finished reading this chapter, you will be able to:

1. Differentiate between horizontal and vertical applications.

2. List the most popular types of horizontal applications.

3. Differentiate between commercial software, shareware, freeware, and public domain software.

4. Explain the concept of software versions.

5. Discuss the advantages and disadvantages of standalone programs, integrated programs, and suites.

6. Describe the essential concepts and skills of using application software, including installing applications, launching applications, understanding and using application windows, getting on-screen help, using menus and toolbars, and working with documents.

7. Discuss the advantages of Web integration.

The term **application software** refers generally to all the programs that enable you to *apply* the computer to the work you do. In this sense, application software is in contrast to system software, the programs that help the computer to function properly. Application software enables you to work efficiently with documents created in almost any line of work, including invoices, letters, reports, proposals, presentations, customer lists, newsletters, tables, and flyers. In this chapter, you'll learn how to make sense of the world of application software.

Horizontal and Vertical Applications

Application programs fall into two general categories: horizontal applications and vertical applications.

HORIZONTAL APPLICATIONS: GENERAL CONSUMER PROGRAMS

Horizontal applications are used *across* the functional divisions of a company and are also popular in the consumer market. The most popular horizontal applications are called **personal productivity programs**, which, as the name implies, help individuals do their work more effectively and efficiently. This category usually includes word processing software, spreadsheet programs, and database programs (see Figure 6.1).

Also considered personal productivity software are programs such as personal

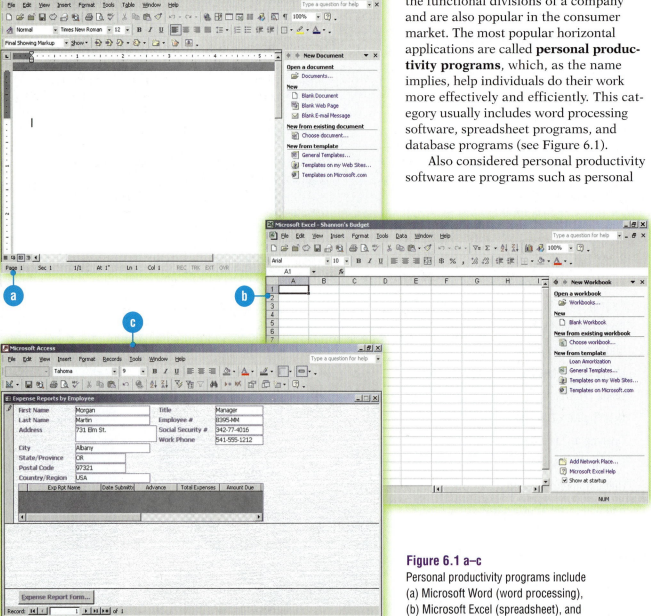

Figure 6.1 a–c

Personal productivity programs include
(a) Microsoft Word (word processing),
(b) Microsoft Excel (spreadsheet), and
(c) Microsoft Access (database).

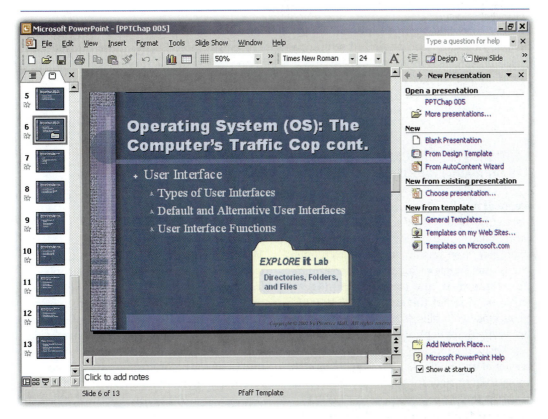

Figure 6.2
PowerPoint is a popular presentation graphics program.

information managers (for use with electronic address books and scheduling) as well as presentation graphics programs, which enable you to develop slides and transparencies for presentations. PowerPoint is an example of a popular presentation graphics program (see Figure 6.2).

A second type of horizontal software includes multimedia and graphics software, including professional desktop publishing programs (such as QuarkXPress), image-editing programs (such as Photoshop), and three-dimensional rendering programs (such as computer-aided design [CAD] programs).

A third type of horizontal software includes programs for using the Internet, such as e-mail programs, Web browsers, and videoconferencing software. (We'll discuss this software in more detail in Chapter 8.)

All three types of horizontal applications just mentioned—personal productivity, multimedia and graphics software, and Internet software—are likely to be found on business users' personal computers.

A fourth type of horizontal software includes programs developed for the home and educational markets, such as personal

Horizontal Application Software			
Personal Productivity Software	**Multimedia and Graphics Software**	**Internet Software**	**Home and Educational Software**
Word Processing	Professional Desktop Publishing Programs	E-mail Programs	Personal Finance Software
Spreadsheet		Web Browsers	Tax Preparation Software
Database	Professional Image-Editing Programs	Instant Messaging Software	Personal Desktop Publishing Programs
Presentation Graphics	Three-Dimensional Rendering Programs	Videoconferencing Software	Personal Image-Editing Programs
Personal Information Management			Home Design and Landscaping Software
	Video-Editing Programs		Computer-Assisted Tutorials
			Computerized Reference Information (such as Encyclopedias and Street Maps)
			Games

Figure 6.3

finance software, home design and land-scaping software, computerized reference information (such as encyclopedias and street maps), and games.

Figure 6.3 lists the various forms of horizontal application software.

VERTICAL APPLICATIONS: TAILOR-MADE PROGRAMS

Vertical applications are designed for a particular line of business or for a division in a company (see Figure 6.4). For example, programs are available to handle the billing needs of medical offices, manage restaurants, and track occupational injuries. Many of the estimated 350,000 programs available for Microsoft Windows are vertical applications.

Vertical applications designed for professional and business use often cost much more than horizontal applications. In fact, some of these programs cost $10,000 or more. The high price is due to the costs of developing the programs and the small size of most vertical markets.

If the right application isn't available, **custom software** might hold the key. Custom software requires the services of

a professional programmer (or programming team) and is even more expensive than vertical applications.

Commercial Software, Shareware, and Freeware

Most computer software is copyrighted, which means that you can't make copies for other people without infringing on the program's copyright (such infringements are called **software piracy** and are a federal offense in the United States). **Commercial software** is copyrighted software you must pay for before using. **Shareware** refers to copyrighted software that you can use on a "try before you buy" basis (see Figure 6.5). If you like the program after using it for a specified trial period, you must pay the registration fee or you violate the copyright. **Freeware** refers to copyrighted software given away for free, with the understanding that you can't turn

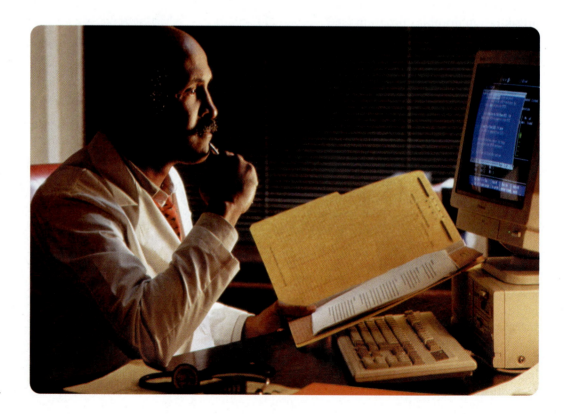

Figure 6.4
Medical offices use vertical applications to manage patient records.

around and sell it for profit. Included in the freeware category are programs distributed under the Free Software Foundation's **General Public License (GPL)**, such as the Linux operating system.

Very few programs are in the **public domain**; these programs are expressly free from copyright, and you can do anything you want with them, including modifying them or selling them to others. Public domain software typically includes games, loan analyzers, and other small utilities.

Software publishers sometimes offer **time-limited trial versions** of commercial programs on the Internet. You can download, install, and use these programs for free, but they are set to expire when the trial period ends. After the program expires, you can no longer use it.

Also available for free are **beta versions** of forthcoming programs. A beta version is a preliminary version of a program in the final phases of testing. Beta software is known to contain bugs (errors) and should be installed and used only with caution. Like time-limited trial versions, beta software is also set to expire after a set period of time.

More and more software is **copy-protected**, which means the program includes some type of measure to ensure that you don't make unauthorized copies of it. Copy protection schemes aren't popular with users because they often require extra steps to install and usually require a call to technical support if any program files become corrupted. Perhaps the loudest objection to copy-protected

Figure 6.5
Shareware is copyrighted software that you can use on a "try before you buy" basis. Tucows, launched in 1993, is renowned for its large library of shareware.

Figure 6.6
Many software publishers use the Internet to deliver software updates. For example, you can get free product updates to Microsoft Windows and Microsoft Office by accessing Microsoft's Web site.

Figure 6.7
Topical help is easy to find.

ETHICAL DEBATES

Software Piracy: "Warez" Can Get You into Big Trouble

It's called *warez*, and there's one important thing to know about it: it's illegal. The term *warez* (pronounced "wares") is widely used in the computer underground to describe illegal copies of commercial programs, such as Adobe Photoshop or Microsoft Office. Thanks to the Internet, trafficking in illegally duplicated software is rampant and increasing rapidly. According to a recent estimate, U.S. software firms lose $3 billion per year due to unauthorized software duplication; at this clip, the cost to the U.S. economy amounts to more than 100,000 jobs and $1 billion in lost tax revenues.

Much warez trafficking on the Internet takes place on Internet Relay Chat (IRC), in which it's harder to trace the actions of individuals. It's harder, but not impossible, as 25 individuals learned recently. All 25 were named in a lawsuit filed by the Business Software Association (BSA), an industry association that fights software piracy. The lawsuit's filing was accompanied by FBI-conducted raids at residences throughout the United States, in which computer equipment and software were confiscated. In addition to their civil liability under the lawsuit, each of the accused individuals is subject to up to $100,000 in civil penalties for *each* case of infringement that can be proven by prosecutors. Criminal penalties can include fines of up to $250,000 and jail terms of up to five years.

What about casual trading—just sharing programs without asking for money? That's illegal, too—and equally dangerous. Thanks to the No Electronic Theft (NET) Act, signed into law by President Clinton in 1997, it's no longer necessary for prosecutors to prove a profit motive in cases of criminal copyright infringement.

Despite enforcement efforts, software piracy is still rampant in the United States, where an estimated 25 percent of all business software programs in current use are thought to be illegally obtained. But the situation is much worse overseas. In China, as much as 96 percent of the software in current use is illegally obtained, thanks to the existence of several dozen large CD duplication factories that, until recently, operated with impunity. More recently, China's bid to gain entry into international trade associations has led to a crackdown against the duplication factories, but unauthorized software duplication is still the norm, rather than the exception. Unauthorized duplication is hurting China's emerging software industry, too; Beijing's Kingsoft Company, one of China's largest software producers, estimates that for every legal copy of its software, three pirated copies are in existence. As a result of piracy, the Chinese software market isn't growing and many publishers are driven into bankruptcy.

CURRENTS

software, though, is that the copy protection schemes are beginning to work. It is becoming difficult to "share" or "lend" a copy of major software programs with friends and family.

Copyright or not, you're always better off owning a legitimate copy of the software you're using. It's the right thing to do and offers you the greatest opportunity to derive benefit from the software. You're entitled to full customer support services should anything go wrong, as well as any add-ons or enhancements the company offers.

DISTRIBUTION AND DOCUMENTATION

Before the Internet came along, most software was available only in shrink-wrapped boxes. Now, many software

publishers are taking their cue from freeware and shareware publishers and are using the Internet as a means of distributing programs and program updates. Doing so is much cheaper than physically delivering a program in a box. Users of Microsoft Windows and Microsoft Office, for example, can get free product updates by accessing Microsoft's Web site (see Figure 6.6).

If you buy software in a shrink-wrapped package, you typically get at least some printed **documentation** in the form of tutorials and reference manuals that explain how to use the program. You'll also find **help screens** in the program that enable you to consult all or part of the documentation on-screen (see Figure 6.7). You may also find additional information at the software publisher's Web site.

Software Licenses and Registration

When you purchase a commercial or shareware program, you're not really purchasing the software, as you'll discover if you read the **software license** (a document distributed with the program). Generally, a license gives you the right to install and use the program on only *one* computer (see Figure 6.8). If you want to install the program on more than one computer, you must purchase additional licenses; otherwise, you violate the publisher's copyright.

Organizations such as colleges and universities often purchase **site licenses**, which enable them to install copies of a program on a specified number of computers. Site licenses offer large organizations licenses at a slightly reduced cost.

As for warranty, most software publishers will be happy to replace the program disk if it's defective, but that's it. The license expressly denies any liability on the publisher's part for any damages or losses suffered through the use of the software. If you buy a program containing bugs, and if these bugs wipe out your data, it's your tough luck. Or that's what software companies would like you to believe. In the past, these licenses haven't

stood up in court; judges and juries have agreed that the products were sold with an implied warranty of fitness for a particular use. Under consideration by U.S. state legislatures is a controversial model act, called the Uniform Computer Information Transactions Act (UCITA), which would give these licenses the force of law.

When you purchase a commercial or shareware program, you'll also be asked to **register** your software by filling out a registration form. (If your computer is connected to the Internet, you can sometimes do this online; otherwise, you have to mail the registration form to the software publisher.)

Generally, registration is worth the trouble. After you're registered, you'll receive automatic notification of software upgrades. Sometimes, you'll have a chance to upgrade to the new version at a price lower than the one offered to the general public.

Software Versions and System Requirements

You've no doubt noticed that most program names include a number, such as

Destinations

How will UCITA affect you? Learn more about the UCITA controversy at UCITA online at **www.ucitaonline.com**.

Figure 6.8
A software license gives you the right to install and use a program on only one computer. If you want to install the program on more than one computer, you must purchase additional licenses.

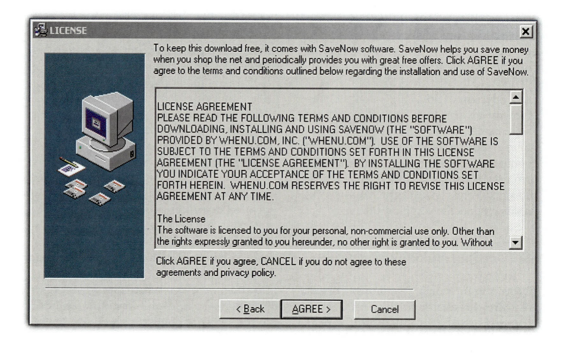

ETHICAL DEBATES

Digital Piracy: What's the Big Deal?

Most of us wouldn't consider walking into a store and stealing a laptop computer, right? But when it comes to software (or music or videos) for that laptop, well that's a different story. How many people do you know who have "borrowed" (that means stolen!) software, or who have downloaded copyrighted music off the Web illegally? If you ask around, you'll find that you're surrounded by users who don't see the big deal in stealing digital data.

Why is this? It may be that when you buy a computer or a CD, you buy a physical, tangible thing that you'll own. But when you buy software, you're only purchasing the right to *use* the software, not the copyright. So if you install software onto your computer and then install it onto a friend's computer, you're stealing. And if you download illegal music off the Web, you're stealing too. Just like you'd be stealing if you grabbed a laptop computer or CD off the shelf in a store. You may not see it that way, but the companies creating and distributing the software and other digital data do, as does the law.

Certainly, it's tempting for users to steal software and music. Consider a school system with 1,000 computers, all of which need to have Microsoft Word. Legitimate licensing could amount to quite a hefty bill, to say the least. Do you think it's okay for a school system to have unlicensed software on its computers? After all, the software is benefiting students. If you think the law bends for schools—and many school administrators do—think again. These same school administrators may one day be holding letters from software companies requesting an inspection to determine whether pirated software is running on their school's machines. If piracy is discovered, schools can face steep fines. Copyright infringement can even leave a school system bankrupt.

Maybe you're thinking, well, how about the school system just buys 500 copies of the software instead of the full 1,000. They're still paying for a lot of software, what's the big deal if they don't pay for it all? If you do a little calculating, though, you'll find that this kind of rationalization is expensive. Let's assume the value of each copy is $50 (not much considering the price of software these days). This means that the school is stealing $25,000 worth of software. Multiply that to include other schools in the district, state, country, and the world, and suddenly billions of dollars of programs are being stolen.

And when it comes to music, you may think it's no big deal to download your new favorite song off the Web, or to burn a copy of your friend's CD on your CD burner. Who isn't tempted by free music (especially college students who often already have to pinch a penny)? But what about the artist who wrote or performed the song? Or the record company that paid for the song to be produced, and all the other people down the line who rely on honest consumers to purchase the actual CD? Sure, the 15 dollars you've saved isn't much in the grand scheme of things for them, but if just 100,000 other people burn that same CD instead of buying it, that's a million and a half dollars of lost sales for your favorite artist.

Will you get caught? Maybe not. But technology offers us many ethical choices, and in the long run, digital piracy hurts us all.

6.0. Software publishers often bring out new versions of their programs, and these numbers help you determine whether you have the latest version. In a version number, the whole number (such as 6 in 6.0) indicates a major program revision. A decimal number indicates a **maintenance release** (a minor revision that corrects bugs or adds minor features).

When you buy software, your system will need to meet the program's **system requirements**, the minimum level of equipment that a program needs in order to run. For example, a given program may be designed to run on a PC with a Pentium microprocessor, a CD-ROM drive, at least 16 MB of RAM, and 125 MB of free hard disk space. If you're shopping for commercial software, you'll find the system requirements printed somewhere on the outside of the box. Although a program will run on a system that meets the minimum requirements, you'd be wise to exceed them, especially when it comes to memory and disk space.

Integrated Programs and Suites: The All-in-One Approach

Individual productivity applications, called **standalone programs**, are giving way to packages that combine two or more programs. **Integrated programs** offer all the functions of the leading productivity programs in a single, easy-to-use program. **Software suites** (also called **office suites**) combine individual programs in a box that may include as many as five or more productivity applications. Unlike integrated programs, software suites include separate programs, but they're integrated by means of a management tool (such as Microsoft Office Manager) that enables quick access to any of the suite's programs. Today, most personal productivity software is sold in office suites, such as Corel WordPerfect Office 2002, Lotus SmartSuite, and the market leader, Microsoft Office (see Figure 6.9).

Few standalone programs are top sellers in the personal productivity area, largely because buyers can often get the entire suite for little more than the cost of one of the individual programs.

Integrated programs such as Microsoft Works are generally aimed at beginning users. They offer easy-to-learn and easy-to-

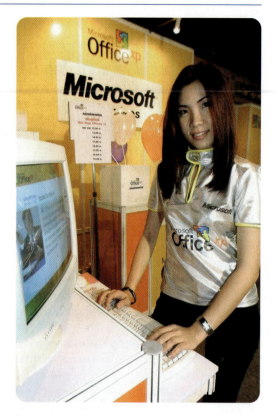

Figure 6.9
Microsoft Office is the most popular office suite.

use versions of basic productivity software functions. All the functions, called **modules**, share the same interface, and you can switch between them quickly. The individual modules, however, may be short on features compared with standalone programs or office suites. The lack of features may make these easy programs seem more difficult when you start exploring the program's more advanced capabilities.

Office Suites (Microsoft Windows)

	Microsoft Office	WordPerfect Office 2002	Lotus SmartSuite
Word Processing	Microsoft Word	WordPerfect	Word Pro
Spreadsheet	Microsoft Excel	Quattro Pro	Lotus 1-2-3
Database	Microsoft Access	Paradox	Lotus Approach
Presentation Graphics	Microsoft PowerPoint	Corel Presentations 10	Freelance Graphics
Person Information Managers (PIMs)	Microsoft Outlook	Corel Central	Lotus Organizer

Figure 6.10

Office suites typically include a full-featured version of leading word processing, spreadsheet, database, presentation graphics, and personal information manager (PIM) programs (see Figure 6.10). Ideally, the programs in an office suite offer some degree of interface consistency, but that's not always the case. In some suites, the programs were developed by two or more different companies, and it shows. The best suites include tools that enable you to switch quickly from one program to another. For example, Microsoft Office includes the Explorer bar, a toolbar that remains on your computer's desktop and enables you to start any Office program quickly.

The best office suites offer a **document-centric** approach, made possible by **object linking and embedding** (**OLE**). In a document-centric approach, your focus is the document you're creating; this can contain word processing text, presentation graphics, portions of a database, or data from a spreadsheet. When you select any of these components, the window changes to show the menus and toolbar relevant to the type of data you're working with. This process is made possible by OLE, which enables applications to exchange data and work with one another.

Using Application Software

Applications transform your computer into a useful tool for a huge variety of tasks, spanning the gamut of human activities. To use your computer successfully, you'll find it useful to acquire the essential concepts and skills of using application software, including installing applications, launching applications, understanding and using application windows, getting on-screen help, using menus and toolbars, and working with documents. The following sections briefly outline these concepts and skills.

INSTALLING APPLICATIONS

Before you can use an application, you must install it on your computer. **Installing** an application involves more than transferring the software from the distribution medium, such as a CD-ROM, to your computer's hard disk. The program must also be configured properly to run on your system. Installation software makes sure that this configuration is per-

Figure 6.11
In Microsoft Windows, you should always use the Add and Remove Programs utility to remove unwanted software.

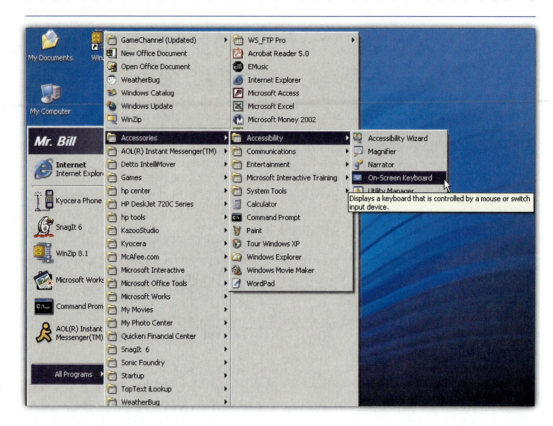

Figure 6.12
The Programs menu has a multitude of default programs you can select to launch.

formed properly. In Microsoft Windows, configuration includes making modifications to the **registry**, a configuration database that is stored within the Windows folder.

If the software was obtained from the Internet, you must first decompress it. Many programs from the Internet include decompression software; you simply launch the file you obtained, and the decompression occurs automatically.

If you later decide that you don't want to use an application, you shouldn't just delete it from your hard disk. You should **uninstall** the application using the Windows utility called Add and Remove Programs that is provided for this purpose (see Figure 6.11). Uninstalling not only removes the application's files from your hard disk, but also removes the program from the registry.

LAUNCHING APPLICATIONS

Once you have installed an application, you can **launch** it. When you launch an application, your computer transfers the program code from your computer's

hard disk to the memory, and the application's default window appears on-screen. To launch an application with Microsoft Windows, you can click the Start menu, point to Programs, and choose the application you want to launch (see Figure 6.12). In Mac OS, you locate the application's folder and double-click the application's icon.

UNDERSTANDING THE APPLICATION'S WINDOW

When the application appears on-screen (see Figure 6.13), you'll see some or all of the following features:

Title bar The **title bar** usually contains the name of the application as well as the name of the file you are working on, if any. If you haven't yet saved the file, you'll see a generic file name, such as Untitled or Document1. To reposition the window on-screen, drag the title bar. When the window is active, the title bar is highlighted. If the title bar isn't highlighted, click within the window to activate it.

Window controls Within the title bar, you'll also find **window controls**. These enable you to **maximize** the window (enlarge it so that it fills the whole screen), **minimize** the window (hide the window so that it's reduced to the size of an icon or button), **restore** the window (change to the preceding unmaximized size), and close the window once you've finished using it.

Window borders In Microsoft Windows, you can change the size of a window by dragging a vertical **window border** left or right, or a horizontal border up or down. If you click and drag a window corner, you can size the window horizontally and vertically at the same time. In Mac OS, click and drag the size box, which is positioned in the window's lower right corner, to size the window on-screen.

Menu bar The **menu bar** contains the names of **pull-down menus**, which are rectangular lists containing the names of the **commands** you can use with the application. A command performs a specific type of action, such as printing or formatting text. In Microsoft Windows, the menu bar is positioned beneath the title bar. In Mac OS, the menu bar is positioned at the top of the screen.

Toolbar The **toolbar** contains pictures, called **icons**, that depict the actions performed by the most commonly used commands. Some applications have more than one toolbar.

Application workspace The **application workspace** displays the document you are working on. In computing, a **document** is any type of product you create with the computer, including written work, an electronic spreadsheet, or a graphic. Most applications display a blank document by default when you launch them. If you wish to work on an existing document, you use the Open command to locate the document and load it into the workspace.

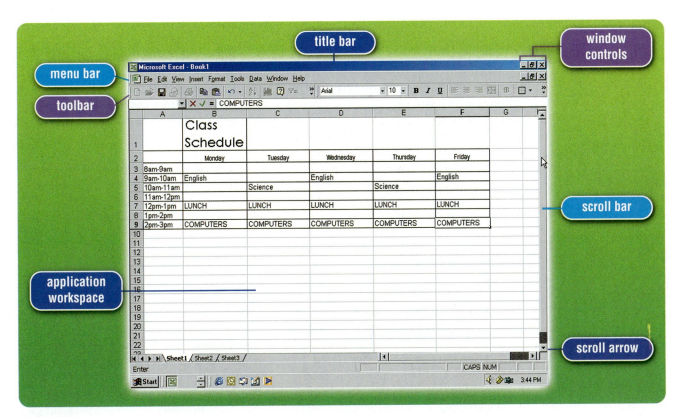

Figure 6.13
These window features are found in most Microsoft Windows applications.

Scroll bars, scroll boxes, and **scroll arrows** If the document with which you are working is larger than the application workspace, you'll see one or more **scroll bars**. A scroll bar provides tools that enable you to scroll through the document. The term **scroll** refers to the appearance of most documents on-screen; they seem to be continuous, like a roll of shelf paper. However, some programs enable you to view a multipage document using an on-screen representation of the printed page. In such applications, you may **page** through the document rather than scrolling. Whether you are scrolling or paging, you can use the **scroll box** and **scroll arrows** to move through the document. Typically, you can click the scroll arrows to move line-by-line; drag the scroll box to move larger distances.

Status bar The **status bar**, located at the bottom of the document window, displays information about the program as well as the program's messages to you, the user.

GETTING HELP

Most applications provide on-screen **help utilities**, which typically include a table of contents of frequently requested items and a searchable index to all available items (see Figure 6.14). Some applications provide animated assistants that enable you to type a question and view of list of possibly relevant responses. If the assistant annoys you, you can hide it.

UNDERSTANDING MENUS

Although applications organize menus in varying ways, many applications make use of the following standard menu names:

File On the **File menu**, you'll find options for creating new documents, opening existing documents, closing documents, saving documents, saving documents with a new file name or new location, printing documents, and quitting the application.

Edit On the **Edit menu**, you'll find options for deleting text, cutting text to a temporary storage location called the **clipboard**, pasting text from the clipboard to the cursor's location, undoing and redoing actions, and finding text within the document. In Mac OS, this menu also contains the Preferences options, which enable you to choose program preferences.

View The **View menu** contains options that enable you to choose how your document is displayed. Typically included are **zoom** options, expressed as a magnification percentage; **normal layout** (no pagination) or **page layout** (on-screen representation of pages as they will print); and options that enable you to hide or display toolbars.

Format The **Format menu** allows you to modify such features as the font style, paragraph settings, borders and shading, bullets and numbering, styles, and themes.

Tools The **Tools menu** typically includes useful utilities, such as a spell-checker. In Microsoft Windows, it also includes Options, a command that enables you to choose program preferences.

Help On the **Help menu**, you'll find the various options available for getting help with the program. If you are connected to the Internet, you may be able to access additional help resources on the Web.

CHOOSING PREFERENCES

Applications typically enable you to choose **preferences**, which are your choices for the way you want the program to operate (see Figure 6.15). Your choices can change the program's **defaults**, which are the settings that are in effect unless you deliberately

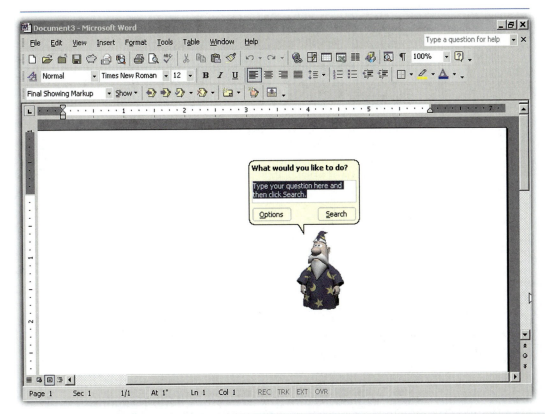

Figure 6.14
The Microsoft Office assistant can be an entertaining link to Help.

Figure 6.15
Most applications enable you to choose your preferences for program defaults.

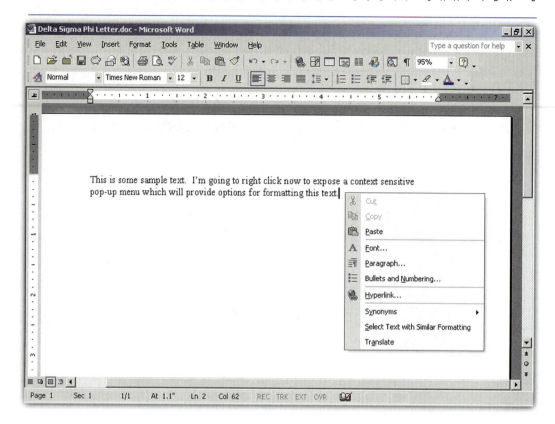

Figure 6.16
Popup menus display the options available for the context in which you displayed the menu.

override them. For example, Microsoft Word enables you to create a preference that allows you to display white text against a blue background, a setting that some writers find to be a bit easier on the eyes.

When you start working with a newly installed application, check the preferences menu for an option (usually called **autosave**) that automatically saves your work at a specified interval. With this option enabled, you'll be assured that you won't lose more than a few minutes' worth of work should the program fail for some reason.

USING POPUP MENUS

In addition to menus and toolbars, most applications enable you to display **popup menus**, also called **context menus** (see Figure 6.16). Typically, a popup menu appears when you click the right mouse button. (On the Macintosh, you can display a popup menu by holding the mouse button down.) Popup menus list the commands that are available for the area where you clicked the mouse button.

For example, if you right-click the application workspace within Microsoft Word, you'll see a menu of text-editing and text-formatting commands.

USING WIZARDS

To guide you through lengthy or complex operations, some applications display **wizards**. A wizard is a series of dialog boxes that guides you through a step-by-step procedure. When you finish making choices in one dialog box, click Next to go on to the next step (see Figure 6.17).

CREATING NEW DOCUMENTS

When you create a new document, you can start with a new, blank document or a **template** (see Figure 6.18). A template is a generic version of a document that has already been started for you. For example, word processing programs typically include templates for faxes, letters, memos, reports, manuals, brochures,

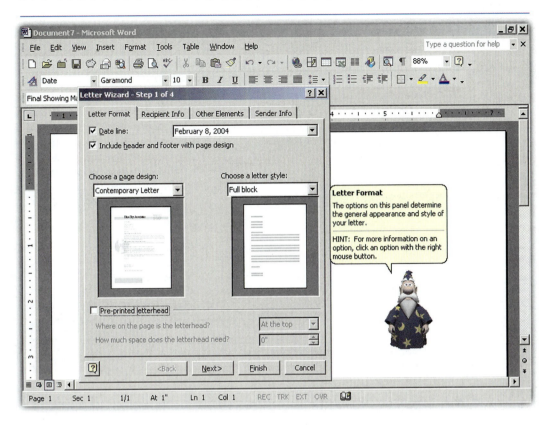

Figure 6.17
You might use a wizard to help you create a letter.

and many more. The template may include text, appropriate formats, graphics, or all of these.

OPENING AN EXISTING DOCUMENT

To **open** an existing document means to locate the document and load it into the application workspace. To do so, you'll use the Open dialog box. Figure 6.19 shows the typical appearance of an Open dialog box in Microsoft Windows. Begin by selecting the folder that contains the document. Next, highlight the document's name. Click OK to transfer the document to the application workspace.

SAVING YOUR WORK

Saving your work refers to the process of transferring the document from the computer's volatile memory to a nonvolatile storage device, such as a hard disk. In Microsoft Windows, documents are saved by default to a folder called My Documents.

When you save your work for the first time, you'll be presented with the **Save As** dialog box. First choose where you want to save your file. If you're a Windows user, you'll probably want to use drive C: or drive A:. If you're a Mac user, you can save

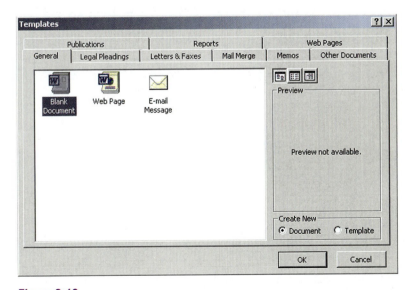

Figure 6.18
Templates provide consistent background content and formatting for standardized documents.

Figure 6.19
To open a document, begin by selecting the folder that contains the document. Then highlight the document's name, and click OK.

your file to your hard drive, your desktop, or to a disk. Next, choose or create a folder in which to store your file.

Once you've created a folder to save your file to, you'll need to give your document a **filename** (see Figure 6.20). This is the name that the storage device uses to

Figure 6.20
To save your document, choose a storage location and filename.

identify the file uniquely, so the name must differ from all the other filenames used within the same folder or directory. In Microsoft Windows, you can use up to 250 characters in a filename, and it's possible to use spaces. Filenames in Microsoft Windows cannot include any of the following characters: forward slash (/), backslash (\), greater than sign (>), less than sign (<), asterisk (*), question mark (?), quotation mark ("), pipe symbol (|), colon (:), or semicolon (;). In Mac OS, you can use up to 31 characters in a filename, including spaces and all characters except a colon.

Microsoft Windows filenames typically include a period and an **extension**, an addition to the filename of up to three characters in length. Typically, extensions are used to identify the type of data that the file contains, and sometimes the application that created the file. In Microsoft Windows, many applications automatically assign an extension when you save your document for the first time. For example, Microsoft Word automatically assigns the .doc extension. In Mac OS, extensions are not needed because Macintosh files include a code representing the name of the application that created the file. However, if you're a Mac user and you want to send files to PC users, it's a good idea to add the extension to the end of your filename to avoid conversion problems. Figure 6.21 lists the most commonly used extensions and their file types.

Once you've successfully saved your document, you can always save another copy elsewhere by using the Save As command. This command enables you to save the document using a new location, a new filename, or both.

Many computer users never figure out the difference between Save and Save As. It is actually quite simple: Save takes what is in memory and writes it to the same storage device and folder, with the same filename that it had when it was opened in the application. In other words, the content in memory replaces the content in storage. Save As, on the other hand, brings up a dialog box that offers all of the choices you had when you first saved a file. You may choose a different device or a different folder, or simply modify the filename. Modifying the filename is a good way to save various versions of your work—just in case something happens to what is in memory and you need to go back to a previous version.

QUITTING THE APPLICATION

When you've finished using the application, don't just switch off the computer. Quit the application by choosing the appropriate command from the File menu; by doing so, you ensure that the application will warn you if you've failed to save some of your work. In addition, you'll save the configuration choices you made, if any, while using the program.

SHUTTING DOWN YOUR SYSTEM

When you've finished using the computer, be sure to shut it down properly. In Microsoft Windows, click Start, and choose Shut Down. In Mac OS, click Special, and choose Shut Down. Don't just switch off the power without going through the shutdown procedure properly. If you switch the power off without shutting down, the operating system may fail to write certain

Commonly Used Extensions

Extension	File Type
.exe	Application
.doc	Microsoft Word
.xls	Microsoft Excel
.ppt	Microsoft Power Point
.mbd	Microsoft Access
.pdf	Adobe
.txt	SimpleText
.htm or .html	Web pages
.rtf	Files in Rich Text Format

Figure 6.21

system files to the hard disk. The next time you start the computer, the operating system will need to run the file checking utility to repair the resulting damage, which may take a few minutes to complete and could leave you with permanent damage to system or personal files.

An alternative to completely shutting down your system is to put it on **Standby**. In Microsoft Windows, Standby is a low-power state that allows you to restore your system to full power quickly without going through the lengthy boot process. In Mac OS, this option is called **Sleep**.

Web Integration: A New Way to Get the Word Out

The new wave in office suites is Web integration, which, for application software, means the capability to save your files in a form that contains the HTML codes that underlie Web documents. Why save in HTML? The answer boils down to one costly process: file conversion.

Many large organizations have been spending millions of dollars dealing with file incompatibility problems caused by the use of proprietary file formats. If you don't have Microsoft Word installed on your system, for example, you can't view a Word file unless you have a conversion program. The use of proprietary file formats imposes severe burdens, unless everyone in the company is using the same product. Even then, you get file incompatibility problems because software publishers introduce new file formats with new versions to support new features. Programs that can save data to HTML form eliminate file conversion costs because the file can be read by anyone with a Web browser.

File conversion costs come into play, too, when companies want to publish documents on the Web for use on the Internet or on internal corporate intranets. To put any document on the Web generally requires saving the document in plain ASCII text and then reformatting it from scratch for Web publishing. The capability to save documents in HTML format eliminates these costs.

On February 14, 2002, Microsoft formally unveiled its new long-term vision of the PC as a globally connected device (see Figure 6.22). The strategy is to accomplish the creation of universal communications between disparate and diverse computers and is called .NET (pronounced "dot NET"). .NET is a set of software technologies, according to Microsoft, "for connecting your world of information, people, systems, and devices." Microsoft hopes that .NET will increase software integration through the use of XML Web services, which are applications that connect to each other as well as to other applications via the Internet. There is no doubt that in the next five years there will be significant changes in the way we share communications and information with each other across the Internet.

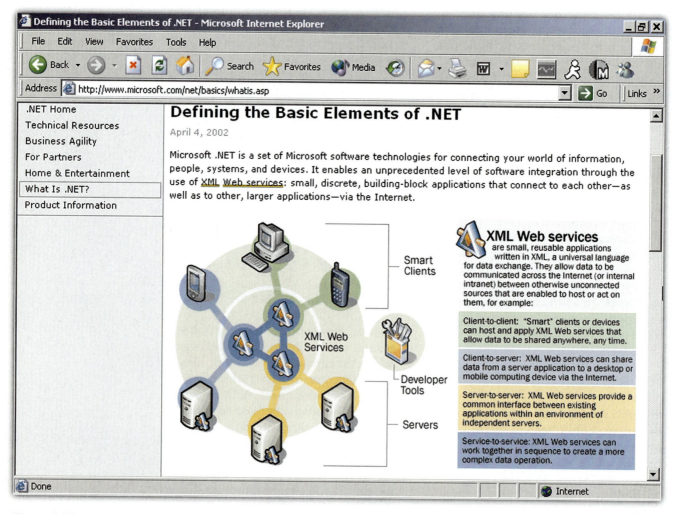

Figure 6.22

Visit Microsoft's Web site to learn more about the .NET strategy.

HOME | Takeaway Points | Key Terms and Concepts | Matching | Multiple Choice | Fill-In | Short Answer | Exercises/Projects | Web Research | CHAPTER REVIEW

TAKEAWAY POINTS

- Application software includes two categories of programs: horizontal and vertical.

- Horizontal programs are used across all the divisions of an organization and are also popular in the consumer market.

- Vertical programs are developed for use in a specialized field or business, such as a medical office or a restaurant.

- The four types of horizontal applications are personal productivity programs, multimedia and graphics software, Internet programs, and home/educational software.

- You must pay for commercial programs before you can use them. Shareware programs are copyrighted but distributed on a "try before you buy" basis. Freeware programs are copyrighted but available for free, as long as you don't turn around and sell them. Public domain programs are not copyrighted.

- In a software version, the whole number refers to a major program upgrade, and the decimal number refers to a bug fix (maintenance upgrade).

- Most people who want personal productivity software purchase an office suite because they can save money by doing so. Integrated programs are aimed at beginning users and may not include features some users will want later.

- To use your computer successfully, you need to learn the essential concepts and skills of using application software, including installing applications, launching applications, understanding and using application windows, getting on-screen help, using menus and toolbars, and working with documents.

- Programs that can save data to HTML eliminate file conversion costs because the file can be read by anyone with a Web browser.

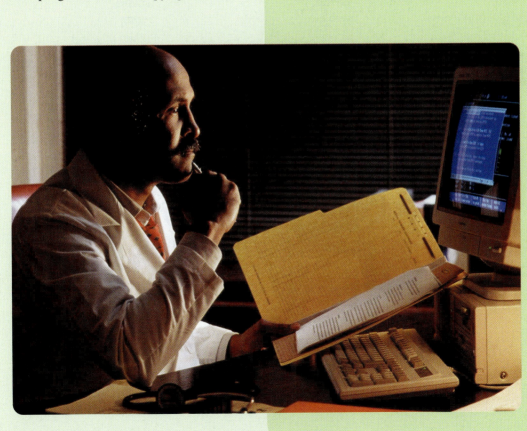

1 2 3 4 5 6 7 8 9 10 11 12 13 14 15 16

CHAPTER REVIEW | Takeaway Points | Key Terms and Concepts | Matching | Multiple Choice | Fill-In | Short Answer | Exercises/Projects | Web Research | HOME

KEY TERMS AND CONCEPTS

1 2 3 4 5 6 7 8 9 10 11 12 13 14 15 16

application software
application workspace
autosave
beta version
clipboard
close
command
commercial software
copy-protected
custom software
default
document
document-centric
documentation
Edit menu
extension
File menu
filename
Format menu
freeware
General Public License (GPL)
help utility
Help menu
help screen
horizontal application

icon
integrated program
install
launch
maintenance release
menu bar
module
normal layout
object linking and embedding
   (OLE)
open
page
page layout
personal productivity program
popup menu
   (context menu)
preferences
public domain
pull-down menu
register
registry
restore
Save As
saving
scroll

scroll arrow
scroll bar
scroll box
shareware
site license
software license
software piracy
software suite
   (office suite)
standalone program
Standby (Sleep)
status bar
system requirements
template
time-limited trial version
title bar
toolbar
Tools menu
uninstall
vertical application
View menu
window border
window controls
wizard
zoom

COMPUTERS IN YOUR FUTURE 2004

6.23

HOME | Takeaway Points | Key Terms and Concepts | **Matching** | Multiple Choice | Fill-In | Short Answer | Exercises/ Projects | Web Research | CHAPTER REVIEW

MATCHING

Match each key term in the left column with the most accurate definition in the right column.

_____ 1. application software

_____ 2. vertical application

_____ 3. horizontal application

_____ 4. time-limited software

_____ 5. site license

_____ 6. freeware

_____ 7. shareware

_____ 8. copy-protected software

_____ 9. documentation

_____ 10. status bar

_____ 11. popup menu

_____ 12. autosave

_____ 13. open

_____ 14. save

_____ 15. software piracy

a. software that is designed for a particular line of business or for a division

b. also known as a context menu

c. displays information about the program, as well as the program's messages to the user

d. all the programs that enable computer users to apply the computer to the work they do

e. copyrighted software that is free

f. printed materials in the form of tutorials and reference manuals that explain how to use a program

g. an option that allows you to save your work automatically at specified intervals

h. to locate the document and load it into the application workspace

i. copyrighted software that you can use on a "try before you buy" basis

j. infringing on a program's copyright by making copies for other people

k. trial versions of commercial software that are set to expire at the end of the trial period

l. software that is used across the functional divisions of a company

m. gives you permission to install copies of a program on a specified number of computers

n. to transfer a document from memory to a storage device such as a hard or floppy disk

o. includes some type of measure to ensure that you don't make unauthorized copies of the software

CHAPTER REVIEW

1 2 3 4 5 6 7 8 9 10 11 12 13 14 15 16

Go to **www.prenhall.com/ciyf2004** to review this chapter, answer the questions, and complete the exercises and Web research questions.

6.24

COMPUTERS IN YOUR FUTURE 2004

PEARSON
Prentice
Hall

| CHAPTER REVIEW | Takeaway Points | Key Terms and Concepts | Matching | Multiple Choice | Fill-In | Short Answer | Exercises/ Projects | Web Research | HOME |

MULTIPLE CHOICE

1 2 3 4 5 6 7 8 9 10 11 12 13 14 15 16

Circle the correct choice for each of the following.

1. Which of the following is a horizontal application?
   a. CAD software
   b. Software to manage a video store
   c. Motel management software
   d. Word-processing programs

2. What do you purchase when you buy a software program?
   a. The unlimited rights to the program and its source code
   b. The right to use the software in accordance with the publisher's software license
   c. A box and a distribution medium such as a disc or CD-ROM
   d. A warranty that guarantees the software will do what you want it to do

3. This menu is not part of the standard menu bar.
   a. File menu
   b. Edit menu
   c. Save menu
   d. Help menu

4. Microsoft Office is an example of what type of program?
   a. Standalone
   b. Integrated
   c. Software suite
   d. Vertical

5. What does OLE mean?
   a. Object linking and embedding
   b. Office library extensions
   c. Operations log entry
   d. Optional legal enhancements

6. Windows controls allow users to do which of the following?
   a. Maximize a window
   b. Minimize a window
   c. Close a window
   d. All of the above

7. Integrated programs contain these basic productivity software functions.
   a. Defaults
   b. Modules
   c. Templates
   d. Commands

8. Which of the following is not typically included in software suites?
   a. FTP client
   b. Word processing
   c. Database
   d. Spreadsheet

9. What are maintenance releases?
   a. Major revisions to an application
   b. Minor revisions to an application
   c. Entirely new versions of an application
   d. None of the above

10. The capability to save application files in HTML provides what benefit?
    a. A common format for sharing data with others
    b. The capability to publish on the Web
    c. No need to convert application files
    d. All of the above

COMPUTERS IN YOUR FUTURE 2004

6.25

HOME | Takeaway Points | Key Terms and Concepts | Matching | Multiple Choice | Fill-In | Short Answer | Exercises/ Projects | Web Research | CHAPTER REVIEW

FILL-IN

In the blanks provided, write the correct answer for each of the following.

1. _____ applications are typically more expensive than horizontal applications.

2. _____ software is expensive and requires the services of a professional programmer or programming team.

3. _____ is copyrighted software given away for free.

4. An _____ is an addition to a file-name that can be used to identify the type of data that the file contains, and some-times the application that created the file.

5. _____ allow you to choose the way you want a program to operate.

6. _____ software is copyrighted software that you must pay for before you can use it.

7. The _____ contains pictures, called icons, that depict the actions performed by the most commonly used commands.

8. The _____ usually contains the name of the application as well as the name of the file you are working on.

9. _____ combine individual programs in a box and are also called software suites.

10. If you want to install a program on a number of machines in your organization, you can purchase a _____.

11. A _____ is a preliminary version of a program in the final phases of testing.

12. A _____ is a generic version of a document that has already been started for you.

13. The _____ command enables you to save a document using a new file-name, a new location, or both.

14. To guide you through lengthy or complex operations, some applications display _____, which are a series of dialog boxes that guide you through a step-by-step procedure.

15. On the _____ menu, you will find options for deleting text, cutting and pasting text, finding text, and undoing and redoing actions.

SHORT ANSWER

1. Have you ever used a beta release of a soft-ware application? If you have, identify the name of the product and type of applica-tion. Since beta versions may contain errors, describe any problems that you encountered. Did you help the software producer by reporting the problems? What procedures did you follow to report the problems?

2. What are the differences between share-ware, freeware, and public domain soft-ware? Have you used any of these types of applications? If you have, identify the name of the product and type of application.

3. What are the benefits of registering your software? Do you regularly register your software applications? Explain why you do or do not follow this practice.

4. Have you needed to uninstall a software application? Identify the application, and explain why it was necessary to remove it. Sometimes an application is not completely uninstalled. Did your application uninstall completely? If not, what directories or files still remained?

5. Why should you use the operating system's Shut Down command to turn off your com-puter? Have you ever just turned off the power? Under what circumstances did you do that? What happened the next time you turned on the computer?

CHAPTER REVIEW

Takeaway Points | Key Terms and Concepts | Matching | Multiple Choice | Fill-In | Short Answer | Exercises/ Projects | Web Research

HOME

1 2 3 4 5 6 7 8 9 10 11 12 13 14 15 16

EXERCISES/PROJECTS

1. Did you ever see the old television series or movie *Mission Impossible*? There is a method of marketing software applications that is reminiscent of *Mission Impossible*. A full-function version of an application can be downloaded, installed, and run on your computer for free for a specified period of time. Although your computer will not self-destruct, the application will no longer function after the time interval expires. Have you used this method to evaluate software? Did you eventually purchase the full product? As a consumer, what do you think about this method of distributing and selling software?

2. Interview a faculty member from your major or intended major department to find out what career-specific applications are used by professionals in that discipline. Identify the discipline and type of applications, and explain how each application is used.

3. As you read in this chapter, a software license gives you the right to install and use a program on only *one* computer. If you want to install a program on more than one computer, you must purchase additional licenses. If you don't, you are in violation of the publisher's copyright. Read the software licenses that are provided with two major application software programs. Identify the product, version, and company. What do the licenses provide you? Are you protected by the licenses? Which product gives you more protection? How would you change them if you could?

4. Presentation software, such as PowerPoint, is an application that is typically included with office suites. This kind of software enables you to develop slides and transparencies for presentations. Do any of your instructors use presentation software in their classroom lectures or demonstrations? If they do, identify the application and explain why you like or dislike the software.

5. Businesses and institutions frequently use site licenses to purchase multiple copies of software applications. Contact your computing services to find out if your school uses this method of purchasing software. If it does, identify the applications for which site licenses are purchased. Is student home use of software applications included in the license? What is the primary advantage of purchasing site licenses for an application?

WEB RESEARCH

1. In July 1999, the National Conference of Commissioners on Uniform State Laws proposed the controversial Uniform Computer Information Transactions Act (UCITA) as the standard for state laws on software transactions. To learn more about this potential legislation, visit *InfoWorld's* UCITA Web site at **www.infoworld.com/ucita**. Identify two consequences that would result from passing this act. List the names of two organizations and two companies that support the UCITA, and list the names of two organizations and two companies that oppose it. Read the section about UCITA and national security. What is the problem with UCITA with regard to national security? Do you believe UCITA should be done away with? Explain why or why not.

2. Visit the Compaq Web site at **www.compaq.com/ products/software/info/swl_about.html** to read about software licensing. What is the difference between a personal use license and a concurrent use license? What is the purpose of license management? What is a PAK? Do you believe that software licensing is necessary? Explain why or why not.

3. Do you want some free or inexpensive software? Since the Internet is frequently used for distributing shareware and freeware applications, check out the DaveCentral Web site at **www.davecentral.com**. Expand one of the functional areas, and select an application that interests you. Describe the functional area, the name of the product, and how you will use it. If you downloaded and installed the application, what is your opinion of the quality of the product? Why do you think you did not find any applications such as word processing, spreadsheet, or database software?

4. Microsoft offers two applications suites: Office for business and higher education markets, and Works for home and K–12 educational customers. Which, if either, of these products does your school use? Did you use either of these when attending K–12 schools? You had an opportunity to explore Office in one of the Web Research exercises in the first chapter, and now you will learn about another of Microsoft's suites. Go to Microsoft's Works site at **http://works.msn.com** to learn about this product. What is the current version of the Works suite? Name the applications that are included in this version. Which are already available as free downloads from Microsoft's Web site? What components are included with Works Suite 2002? What is the estimated retail price of the Works suite? Explain why you would or would not purchase this product.

5. The major competitors of Microsoft Office are Corel WordPerfect Office 2002 and Lotus SmartSuite Millennium Edition 9.6.

   • Visit the Corel Web site at **www3.corel.com**. Identify the application areas and product names that are included in the professional version of Corel's office suite. What are the suggested full and upgrade prices? Are there different prices for digital and boxed versions? Is a free trial version available?

   • Visit the IBM Lotus Software Web site at **www.lotus.com**. Identify the application areas and product names that are included in the professional version of Lotus' office suite. What are the suggested full and upgrade prices? Is a free trial version available?

   • Explain why you would or would not purchase either of these products.

1 2 3 4 5 6 7 8 9 10 11 12 13 14 15 16

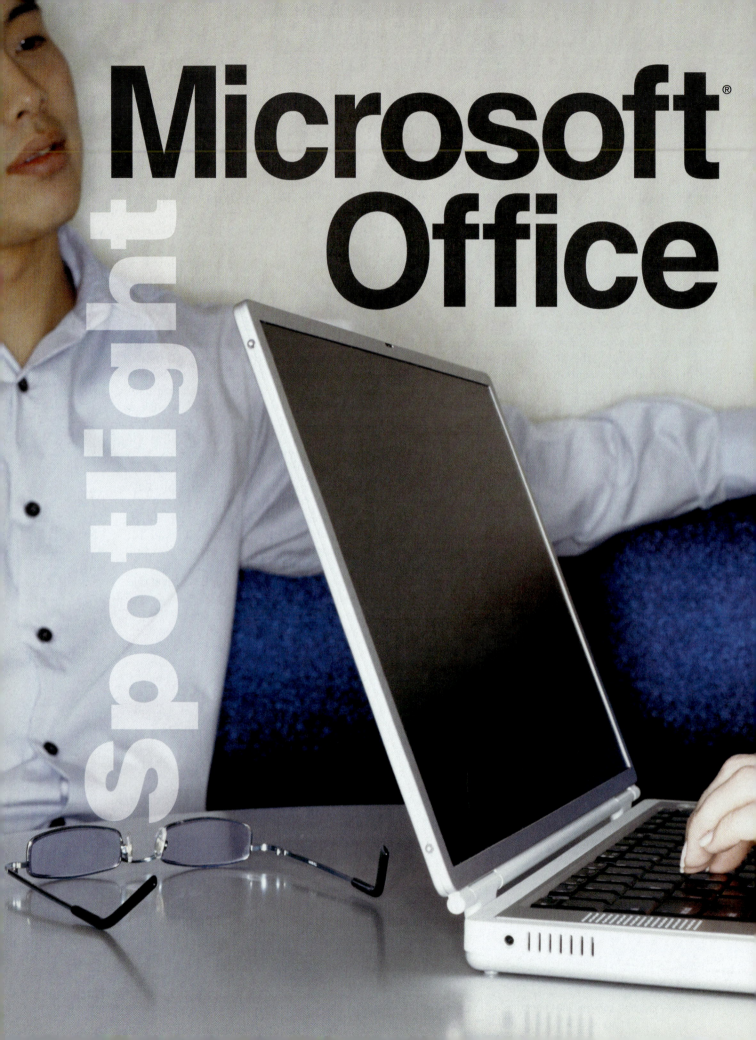

Microsoft® Office

Spotlight

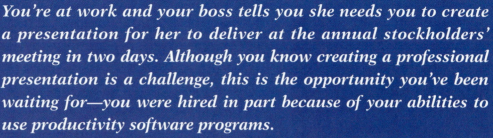

You're at work and your boss tells you she needs you to create a presentation for her to deliver at the annual stockholders' meeting in two days. Although you know creating a professional presentation is a challenge, this is the opportunity you've been waiting for—you were hired in part because of your abilities to use productivity software programs.

You get started right away by using Microsoft Access to generate reports that provide you with important information regarding your company's activities throughout the year. You then import the data you have extracted from Access into Microsoft Excel so that you can perform some statistical analysis and produce a number of key charts and graphs for stockholders. Now that you've got the background materials covered, you open Microsoft Word. Into your Word document, you copy your Excel charts and a number of the Access reports you have generated. You also type and format the meeting agenda that your boss will distribute to the attendees. Now comes

FIGURE 6A
Being able to use software programs such as those in Microsoft Office will help you gain a competitive edge in many careers.

the fun part: you open PowerPoint and create a professional, visually appealing presentation using the Word, Excel, and Access documents you've already created. As you put the finishing touches on your presentation—embedding an MP3 file into the introduction slide—you realize you've finally been able to use the skills you've worked so hard to acquire.

All of the programs you've used to help you create your presentation are components of a suite of software programs called **Microsoft Office.** *This Spotlight explores the various programs, features, and uses of Microsoft Office (see Figure 6A).*

Introducing Office

FIGURE 6B
Microsoft Office XP is the culmination of many generations of Office.

Microsoft was the first company to develop the concept of an *office* suite. A **suite** is an interconnected bundle of programs that share resources with each other and are designed to help workers accomplish the tasks they perform in a typical office environment. If Microsoft Windows is your desktop, then Microsoft Office is the set of tools that you typically use at work.

It all began in the early 1990s when Microsoft started bundling two standalone programs: Word and Excel. Word was the word processing program that Microsoft used to compete with the early market leader, WordPerfect. Likewise, Excel competed with Lotus 1-2-3. Soon, both Word and Excel left their competition far behind.

Before suites came along, you could only buy **standalone programs**. A standalone program is a program that is complete unto itself—fully self-contained. Standalone programs required a lot of storage overhead, however. For example, if you purchased Word and installed it and then purchased Excel and installed it, neither program would know about the other, nor would they share any resources such as menus, drivers, graphics libraries, and tools. Obviously, this was a very inefficient way to install and use software when the programs had so many features they could share.

When Microsoft recognized that its programs could share all of these features if they were bundled together, Office was born. At first, the bundled programs shared only the menu system and toolbars. Eventually, however, the programs were able to share graphics libraries, drawing tools, and print drivers.

Office became truly **integrated** (integrated programs share common resources) when the applications began sharing objects with each

other through something referred to as **object linking and embedding** (**OLE**). OLE allows software applications to share or get data and objects from each other using **linking** and **embedding**. When an object, such as a graphic or a paragraph, is *embedded*, it is simply copied into a program. When an object is *linked*, the linked object is dependent upon, or linked to, the source file. If the object changes in the source file, it changes in the destination file as well. For example, if you have an Excel chart linked to a Word memo and you change the data in the Excel chart, the chart will be updated in both the Excel file and the Word file because they are linked.

Microsoft Office is sold in three versions: Standard, Professional, and Developer. The Standard version includes Word, Excel, Outlook (for managing e-mail and contacts), and PowerPoint. (Office for the Macintosh uses a program called Entourage for managing e-mail and contacts.) The Professional version includes the Standard version programs as well as Access and the FrontPage Web site creation and management program. It also includes additional tools and documentation for building, deploying, and managing Office-based solutions. The Developer version includes everything in the Professional version as well as a Visual Basic programmer's tool set and other programs that are used in creating and managing Office files. Released in 2001, Office XP is the most recent version of Office on the market (see Figure 6B).

In summary, Office is a group of software programs that share common resources and that work together or separately to help workers accomplish the tasks they perform in an office environment.

THE SHARED OFFICE INTERFACE AND TOOLS

Microsoft programs share a common **user interface**, the method through which users interact with the computer system.

The topmost area of each program interface is called the **title bar**. It includes the program icon, the name of the file that is open in the program, and the minimize, restore, and close buttons. The bottom part of the program interface, called the **status bar**, contains specific information about your activities within the program, such as the current page number and number of pages in your document (see Figure 6C).

The shared interface also includes the menu bar and toolbars. The **menu bar** is made up of pull-down menus that include top-level headings such as File, Edit, View, Insert, Format, Tools, and Help. When you click a menu heading, a pull-down list appears, allowing you to choose among a number of tasks that you can complete. For instance, you might choose the File menu and then the Open command to bring up the Open dialog box.

Toolbars consist of icons that act as shortcuts to using the pull-down menus (see Figure 6D). For instance, if you click the printer icon on the standard toolbar, your file is sent directly to the printer. (If you work on a Mac and click the printer icon, the print dialog box appears.) The printer icon takes the place of the File, Print, OK menu sequence you would use via the menu bar.

Two toolbars, the **Standard toolbar** and **Formatting toolbar**, are loaded by default in each Office application. The Standard toolbar includes icons that allow you to open, close, print, spellcheck, copy, paste, and save your file, as well as several more options. The Formatting toolbar

FIGURE 6C
The title and status bars provide information about the program and allow you to resize the program window on your desktop.

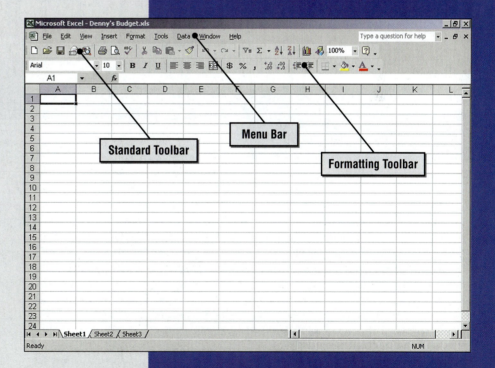

FIGURE 6D
Toolbars include icons that act as shortcuts to program menu choices. The shortcuts tend to use default options automatically, whereas menu bar sequences often allow you to make choices about the function or feature you're invoking.

FIGURE 6E
The Clip Organizer is an efficient
way to insert images.

includes icons that allow you to choose the document font, font size, style (bold, italics, or underlined), indentation, and bullet style, among other options. Dozens of other toolbars are available within the various Office applications, and you can also customize your own toolbars to suit your needs. To access the various toolbars, select View, Toolbars from the menu bar.

Other Shared Resources and Features
Office applications share a number of other resources, including the

Clip Organizer, print drivers, and the Office Clipboard. Recent versions of Office offer such shared features as the task pane and smart tags.

The **Clip Organizer** is a repository of clip art and images that you can insert into a document or presentation (see Figure 6E). Whereas the standalone programs each accessed their own separate gallery of images, in Office, all the applications share the same gallery. You can access the Clip Organizer by selecting Insert, Picture, Clip Art from the menu bar.

Another shared feature of Office applications is the **print driver**. (When you install a printer, some of the files that are placed on

your hard drive are called print drivers. Print drivers contain the printer's instruction set.) In the early days of computing, you needed to select a printer for each application you wished to use. Today, print drivers are installed from the Windows operating environment Control Panel and are shared by all of the programs installed on your PC. The Macintosh OS has always had this feature, but it wasn't available for the PC until Microsoft recognized that the operating environment, rather than the program, should control the printer.

Yet another shared feature in Office applications is the **Office**

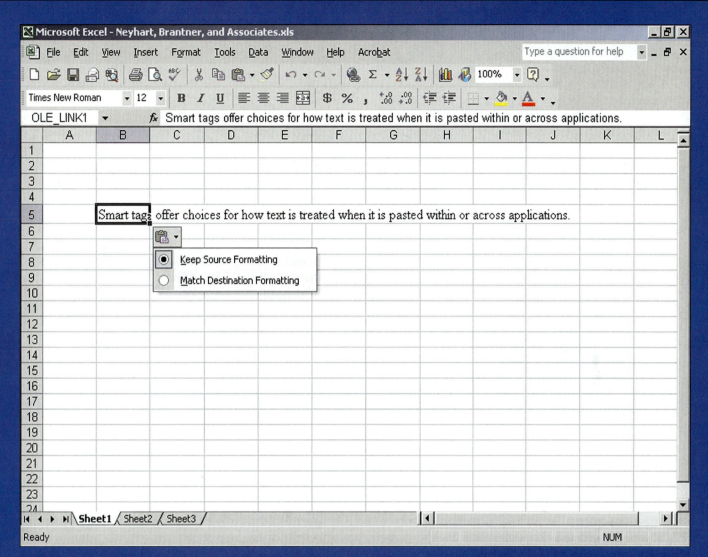

Clipboard. The Clipboard temporarily stores in memory whatever you've cut or copied from a document, and makes those cut or copied items available for use within any Office application. For example, you can create a financial summary in Excel, then copy it to the Clipboard, and then paste it into Word. (You don't have to physically copy the item to the Clipboard—the Clipboard is just the name for the PC's temporary storage location for your copied or cut items.)

Another shared feature, which first appeared in Office XP, is the **task pane**. The task pane usually appears on the right side of the window whenever an application is first opened. It contains options for opening work, creating new work, and formatting work, among other things. You can close the task pane by clicking the X in the top right corner, and open it again by choosing View, Task Pane from the menu bar.

Most Office applications also have **smart tags** (see Figure 6F). Smart tags are icons that are attached to items that you've pasted, or text and data that the program recognizes as a place where you might want to choose different options. When you click a smart tag, a small menu of choices appears. For example, when you

copy text from one place in a Word document and paste it to another place, or if you switch over into an Excel spreadsheet and paste the text there, a smart tag appears, listing options for how the pasted text should be treated. In this example, the options would be to keep the formatting from Word or change the formatting to that of the destination cell in Excel.

You can turn off both the task pane and the smart tags features by selecting Tools, Options, View from the menu bar.

Microsoft Word

Microsoft Word is a very powerful word processing program. In fact, it's so powerful that it rivals software made especially for desktop publishing. As with other Office applications, its interface includes the title bar, Standard toolbar, Formatting toolbar, and status bar. The remainder of the screen is basically a blank sheet of paper upon which you can create documents (see Figure 6G).

Using Word at its most basic level is extraordinarily simple; you just type text into the Word document and press the print button on the Standard toolbar to send your document to the printer. However, Word also includes a number of other features that can enhance your ability to present your thoughts in a formal way. For example, you can embed pictures, graphics, charts, tables, and other objects into your document. You can work with columns and set tabs to align text. You can print your document in portrait or landscape orientation. It's almost true

that if you can imagine it, you can do it in Word.

If you're using a PC, the files that you create in Word include the .doc extension by default. (If you're using a Mac, no such extension is needed.) Word can also save your documents as plain text (.txt), Web pages (.htm), Rich Text Format (.rtf), or in a format that can be read by previous versions of Word and competing products, such as WordPerfect.

Word also comes with a library of **templates**. Templates are document frameworks that are created once and intended to be used

FIGURE 6G

The Word interface is very simple and intuitive.

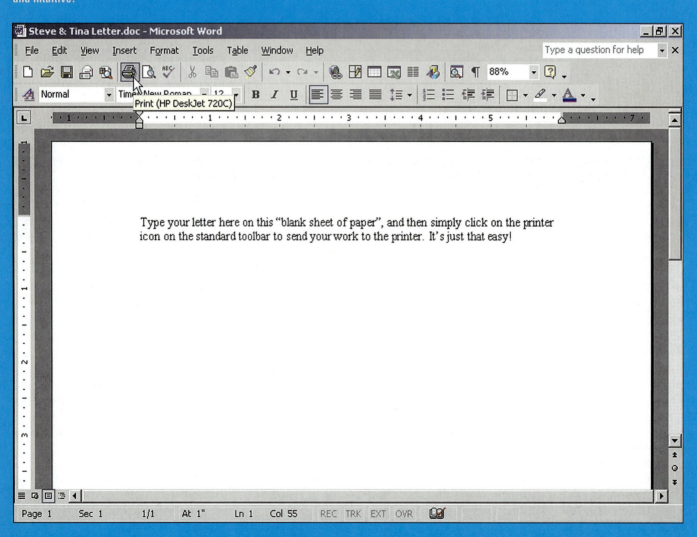

many times (see Figure 6H). A memorandum template is a good example. Templates are stored in a special folder that you access by selecting File, New from the menu bar while you have Word open.

In addition to the templates that Microsoft provides, you can also save files as templates yourself. For example, if you use the same format repeatedly in your college papers, you can save your paper format as a template. That way, next time you write a paper, you won't have to recreate all of the margins or indentations. To create a template, open the file

you'd like to save as a template and simply select File, Save As from the menu bar. From the dialog box that appears, select Template from the Save As Type pull-down menu at the bottom of the dialog box. Now, every time you wish to use your template, you can access it by selecting File, New from the menu bar.

Now that you're familiar with the basic Word menus and toolbars, you're ready to move on to other Office applications. The following sections will introduce you to Excel, Outlook, Access, and PowerPoint.

FIGURE 6H
Templates are very useful for providing a standardized framework for new documents.

Microsoft Excel

Microsoft Excel is the most popular spreadsheet program in the world. The primary function of a spreadsheet program is to store and manipulate numbers. Spreadsheets either record things that have actually happened or predict things that might happen through a method called **modeling**. Projected income statements are a good example of spreadsheet modeling. You plug in your assumptive values, and the model provides the prediction. If your assumptions are correct, the model will closely match the actual outcome. If not, then you can learn from your experience and perhaps make better assumptions in the future.

Excel's user interface is very similar to that of Word. One major difference is that in Excel, the menu bar has a choice for Data, whereas Word has a choice for Tables. The Standard and Formatting toolbars are almost identical. Like Word, Excel has a status bar at the bottom of the screen, along with scroll bars that enable you to move your view vertically and horizontally.

In Excel, each file is called a **workbook**. A workbook may contain as many as 255 **sheets**. Each sheet is composed of **columns** and **rows**, the intersection of which is called a **cell** (see Figure 6I). The columns in a spreadsheet are identified by the letters of the alphabet, and the rows by numbers. Spreadsheets have a fixed maximum size, which is 256 columns wide (column A through column IV) and 65,536 rows deep. A cell, then, is identified by its column letter and then its row number. For example, A1, B3, and AC342 each represent an individual cell. A **range** (two or more cells selected

FIGURE 6I

Spreadsheets are composed of cells, on sheets, in workbooks.

at the same time) of cells is identi-fied by the addresses of the top left and bottom right cells, separated by a colon. For example, the range from cell A1 to cell D5 would be represented as A1:D5.

Cells are the fundamental spreadsheet element and are used for storing text, numbers, and formulas. Text entries are also referred to as **labels**. Labels are used to identify numeric entries and the results of **formulas**. For example, you might type the label "First month's rent" in cell A5 and then place the value "$650" next to it in cell B5. Formulas come in two types: mathematic expressions and functions. Excel interprets a cell entry as a formula if the entry is preceded by the equals sign (=). In a **mathematic formula**, the mathematic order of operations is followed; that is, things in parentheses are acted upon first, followed by exponen-tiation, multiplication, division, addition, and subtraction. For example: $=6*(4–2)/3+2$ is equal to 6 because 4 minus 2 is 2, and 6 times 2 is 12, and 12 divided by 3 is 4, and 4 plus 2 is 6.

The other type of a formula is called a **function**. Functions are a very powerful type of formula because they include the ability to perform operations on multiple inputs. As an example, the pay-ment function is able to take the rate of interest, time period, and amount borrowed to produce the payment amount on a loan. Like mathematic formulas, functions begin with the equals sign. However, they then list the name of the func-tion, such as PMT for payments, and finally an **argument set**, which is placed within parentheses. An argument set contains the passable parameters or variables in a function. In the loan example above, the argument set contains

the rate of interest, the time period of the loan, and the amount borrowed. For example $=PMT(.06,48,18000)$ would return the payment for a loan of $18,000 at an interest rate of 6 percent for 48 months.

Excel also has features for creating **charts**, which are simply a graphical representation of data (see Figure 6J). Charts are based upon data sets and the labels that identify the data. There are two primary kinds of charts: **bar charts** (which show each element in comparison to the other elements in a numeric way) and **area charts** or **pie charts** (which show each element as a percentage of the sum of all the elements). Several other tools are also available for developing, managing, and assess-ing data. You can create pivot tables and charts or sorted reports with subtotals, and you can use the database feature to extract infor-mation from your data set.

To learn more about creating charts and reports in Excel, consult the online help at **www.microsoft.com** or the Excel Help wizard.

Let's now move on to a program that will help you communicate with others and manage your busy schedule: Outlook.

Microsoft Outlook

Microsoft Outlook is an e-mail and organizational communications tool you can use to send and receive mail, maintain a personal calendar, schedule meetings with coworkers, and store information about your personal contacts. Figure 6K shows the Outlook interface.

When you use the e-mail function of Outlook, you obviously need to know the recipient's e-mail address. E-mail addresses are composed of two parts: the name of the mailbox owner and the address where the mailbox resides. Mailbox addresses follow the same syntax as Web addresses, usually a server name followed by the domain type. For example, an e-mail address might look like president@whitehouse.gov.

Outlook also has an auto-complete feature that suggests the completion of an address you've already used as you type on the To: line. For example, if you begin typing the address myfriend@yahoo.com, the auto-complete feature suggests the complete address when you type the third letter, f, in myfriend. If the suggestion is correct, press the Enter key to insert the address. If the suggestion is not what you intend, then simply keep typing the correct address.

One feature of Outlook that is very helpful is the ability to create folders, which you can use to organize your saved e-mail messages. For example, you could create a Family folder for family mail, a separate folder for each of your classes, and perhaps a Friends folder for personal messages you've received from friends. Placing mail that you've read into these folders will then help you keep your inbox uncluttered.

FIGURE 6K
The Outlook calendar is a good way to manage your busy college schedule.

Microsoft Access

You may find the Outlook calendar helpful in managing all of the activities associated with school, work, and socializing. The calendar is very easy to use and even features an alarm to alert you 10 or 15 minutes before a scheduled event.

The best way to learn how to use Outlook is to experiment with it. Also remember that you can use the Help program to learn how to use the various features Outlook includes. You'll be surprised at just how easy it is to manage Outlook.

Let's now examine a more complicated program: Microsoft Access.

Microsoft Access, which is available in the Professional and Developer Office suites, is a **database management system** (**DBMS**). Two types of databases exist: flat file and relational. A **flat file database** is simply a database that has only one **table** (a table is composed of columns and rows that hold data). A **relational database**, on the other hand, is one in which there is more than one table. Access is a relational DBMS.

The Access interface is similar to that of Word and Excel, but is also different in many ways. The opening interface includes the menu bar, a grayed-out Standard

toolbar, and the task pane on the right-hand side (see Figure 6L). In Access, you must always be working on an existing database or you must be creating a new one. There is no default blank database screen analogous to the blank document in Word or the blank worksheet in Excel.

Access is designed to work with and manage **data**. Data are raw facts that become information when they are organized in such a way so as to be useful and provide

FIGURE 6L

The Access opening interface is rather stark in comparison to Word and Excel.

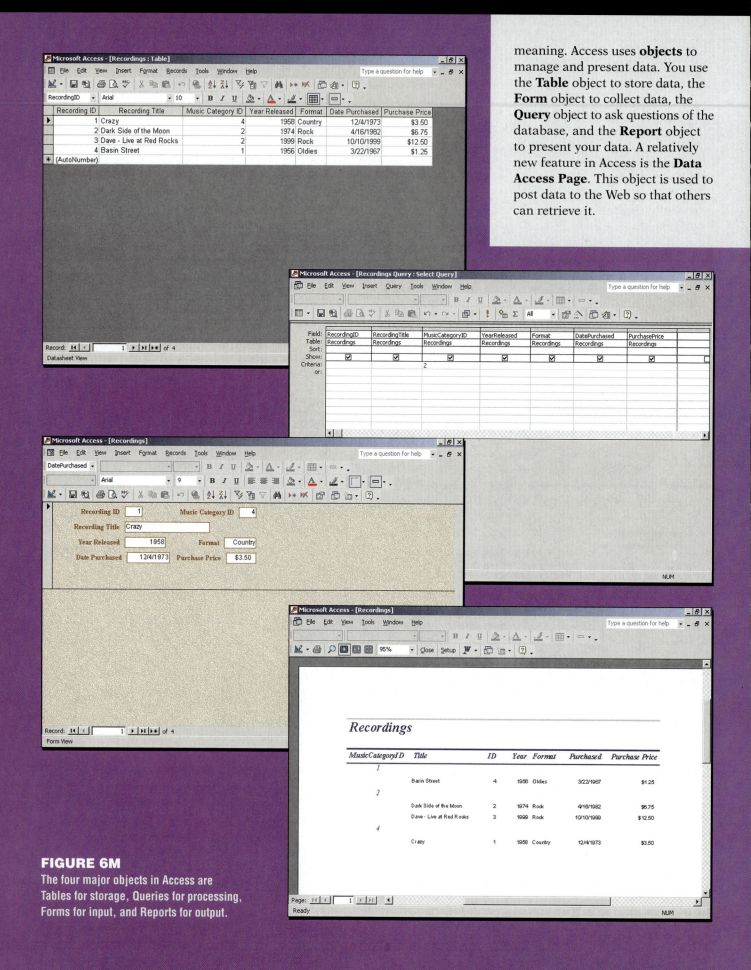

meaning. Access uses **objects** to manage and present data. You use the **Table** object to store data, the **Form** object to collect data, the **Query** object to ask questions of the database, and the **Report** object to present your data. A relatively new feature in Access is the **Data Access Page**. This object is used to post data to the Web so that others can retrieve it.

FIGURE 6M
The four major objects in Access are Tables for storage, Queries for processing, Forms for input, and Reports for output.

Access is capable of importing data from many sources, including, of course, Microsoft Excel. If the data isn't imported, then a form is usually used for data entry. Forms should be organized so that the data entry operator can easily move from one field to the next in a logical order. The order of fields on the form should match the order of fields on the document that the data entry operator is viewing. Or, in the case of face-to-face or phone interactions, the order of fields should match the logical order in which to collect the data. For instance, first name, then middle initial, then last name, then date of birth, and so on.

To be useful, the data must usually be processed using the Query object. Let's say you have a data set that includes the names and addresses of family, friends, and business associates. You want to send a mailing to only your family to let them know how school has been going. To find the names and addresses of your family members, you would run a query on your data set and set the filtering parameter to include only those names that have a field entry under the field name "family." In a large organization with a multi-table database that has tens of thousands of records, queries are very important.

When you use Access, you need to present the results of your query in a manner that is not only useful but is professional in appearance—in short, you must design a report. The Report object is the only object that most of us see. We receive reports from databases all the time. Junk mail, a utility bill, and unsolicited e-mail are all reports that are generated from massive data sets. Figure 6M shows an example of a Table, a Form, a Query, and a Report.

Access is the only Office program that doesn't include the Save As feature to save files. You

may use Save As to save an *object* within your database, but you can't save an open database to another location or give it another name. This can be a concern because Access is a complex program and it's possible you'll make mistakes that can cost you a lot of lost time and energy if you have to restore your entire database back to the way it was before you made the mistake. Most database managers, therefore, create intermediate copies of their work, just in case something goes wrong with the copy they're working on.

Let's look at an example. When you work in an application such as Word, the work you accomplish is all in memory until you initially save it to disk. Once you've saved your work to disk, the subsequent work you perform is in memory until you either save over the work you'd saved before (using the Save command), or choose a new folder and/or filename for your added work (using the Save As command). As you just learned, because you can't use the Save or Save As command in Access, if you make a mistake, the work you have in memory is often the same as the

work you have on disk. Access doesn't continually save everything you do, but it writes to disk often enough to make it very difficult to predict whether your actions have been recorded over your previously saved work. This means that it's possible for you to lose your entire database if you don't have a backup copy. The solution is to always make a copy of your work *before* a work session and then work on that copy.

Database concepts are very simple: you capture data, store them, manipulate them, and create a report. To learn more about how to use Access, visit the online help provided at **www.microsoft.com**. You can also use the Access wizards to learn how to create the objects that you'll need to manage whatever projects you may undertake.

Let's now look at a program that's a favorite among many college students: PowerPoint.

Microsoft PowerPoint

Microsoft PowerPoint is a popular program used to create and deliver presentations. PowerPoint opens to a blank slide that is in the Title slide format (see Figure 6O). A Title slide has two text boxes: the top box is for the title of your presentation, and the bottom box is for a subtitle or your name. The task pane on the right side of the screen allows you to choose to open an existing presentation, a blank presentation, or a presentation using a design template, or to use a wizard.

If you're looking to create a PowerPoint presentation from scratch, the wizard feature is a wonderful tool. It includes presentation categories for home and business projects, as well as the Carnegie Coach. The Carnegie Coach provides presentations on a wide variety of topics—everything from selling your ideas to introducing and thanking a speaker. The coach suggests the content, and you simply customize it with the details for your particular presentation.

It's very easy to get caught up in all of the bells and whistles available in PowerPoint. Ultimately, though, *you* are the presenter and therefore *you* must command your audience. A good PowerPoint presentation should serve as a backdrop to a good presentation (see Figure 6P).

Be forewarned: presentations almost never look the same on a video projector as they do on your computer screen. With this in mind, it's a good idea to try out your presentation in the room

FIGURE 6O
The initial PowerPoint screen features the outline pane on the left, a blank title slide in the center, and the task pane on the right.

where you'll give it. If you allow yourself plenty of time, you'll be able to change the design template to colors that will work best in the room. Professional presenters often purchase high-end digital light projectors and use them to project their presentations, thus eliminating the variability found in using whatever system is installed in the room.

Summary

Microsoft Office offers versatility, flexibility, and customization for your desktop. The tools, templates, wizards, and integration will serve you well in communicating your ideas to others.

Networks: Communicating and Sharing Resources

CHAPTER **7**

What You'll Learn...

When you have finished reading this chapter, you will be able to:

1. List the three main types of computer networks.

2. Discuss the ways that connecting computers increases the value of an organization's information technology investment.

3. Explain the importance of protocols in a computer network.

4. Contrast circuit switching and packet switching networks and explain their respective strengths and weaknesses.

5. Distinguish between peer-to-peer and client/server LANs.

6. Name the most widely used LAN protocol and discuss its benefits.

7. Identify three business applications of WANs.

Fast forward a few years, and imagine yourself building a house. Everyone in your five-person family wants a computer, a printer, and an Internet connection. You could pay for five computers, five printers, and five Internet accounts. Or you could pay for five computers, one really good printer, one Internet account, and inexpensive local area network (LAN) hardware that enables everyone to share the printer and Internet connection. If you think the LAN route makes sense, you've just joined the huge and growing number of people who've discovered the benefits of computer networking.

Businesses of all sizes are already convinced that networking is a great idea. They're spending billions of dollars annually on computer networking equipment. The benefits go far beyond saving money on shared peripherals. Networks enable organizations to create massive, centralized pools of information, which are vital to performing their mission. And networks enable people to communicate and collaborate in ways that aren't possible without some means of connecting the computers they're using (see Figure 7.1).

Although computer networking is increasingly important, most people consider this topic to be highly technical. As this chapter makes clear, however, the *concepts* of computer networking are easy to understand. As an informed and literate computer user, you need to know enough about networking to understand the benefits and possibilities of connecting computers. In addition, learning about computer networking is a good idea for anyone looking for a job these days; employers like to hire workers who grasp networking concepts. This chapter explains the essential concepts of computer networking and teaches the basic networking terms you'll need to discuss the subject intelligently.

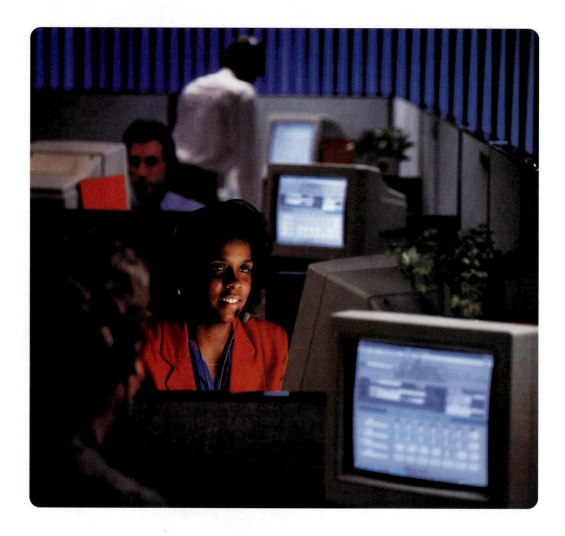

Figure 7.1
Computer networks enable users to create common pools of data, which employees can access to obtain the information they need.

Introducing Computer Networks: Synergy at Work

As composers working individually, former Beatles John Lennon and Paul McCartney penned many fine songs. But most rock critics agree that their solo efforts can't match the magic that happened when Lennon and McCartney worked together. This magic is called **synergy**. Synergy occurs when the performance of two or more components working together exceeds the performance of the same components working alone. And as you'll see in this chapter, the term *synergy* sums up nicely what happens when you connect two or more computers.

TYPES OF COMPUTER NETWORKS: LANS AND WANS

A **computer network** links two or more computers so that they can exchange data and share resources, including expensive peripherals such as high-performance laser printers. Computer networks fall into three categories: local area networks (LANs), metropolitan area networks (MANs), and wide area networks (WANs). There's quite a bit of overlapping within each description, but suffice it to say that one of the three definitions will describe the type of network you're using.

- A **local area network** (**LAN**) uses direct cables or localized wireless radio or infrared signals to link computers within a small geographic area, such as a building or a group of buildings. A home network is one example of a LAN. It comprises two or more computers that communicate with each other and with peripheral devices such as a printer or cable modem.

- A **metropolitan area network** (**MAN**) uses high-speed fiber-optic lines or cables to connect computers located at various places within a major urban region. For example, a Scottish MAN, called FatMAN, links universities in Scotland with 155 Mbps fiber-optic cables.

- A **wide area network** (**WAN**) uses long-distance transmission media, including telecommunications networks, to link computers separated by a few miles or even thousands of miles. The Internet is a wide area network open to public use. (As you'll see, other WANs, including some that use the same technology that the Internet uses, aren't public.)

Although the Internet is technically a wide area network, the term *WAN* is generally used to refer to other long-distance networks, called **public data networks** (**PDNs**), that are leased to business and government customers. PDNs offer the security and guaranteed bandwidth that the Internet can't yet ensure. This chapter discusses LANs, PDNs, and other WANs that businesses use.

NETWORKING SYNERGIES IN A NUTSHELL

What's the point of having a computer network? When you connect two or more computers, you see gains in every aspect of computing:

- **Reducing hardware costs.** Computer networks enable users to share expensive equipment and reduce costs. In a LAN, for example, dozens of users can share a single high-capacity printer. In a WAN, users of underpowered computers can connect to a supercomputer, which can rapidly perform centralized processing.

- **Enabling shared applications.** Computer networks enable users to share software. For example, **network versions** of applications are designed to be installed on a high-powered computer, called a **file server**, that makes these applications available to more than one user at a time. For example, at Platt Electric Supply, an

Oregon-based industrial electric supply firm, sales representatives upload orders from notebook computers to an order-tracking program installed on the company's file server. After installing the network, employees found that they had up to 20 percent more time to focus on their customers' needs.

- **Building massive information resources.** Computer networks enable users to create common pools of data, which employees can access to obtain the data they need. At publisher Prentice Hall, for example, a company-wide network makes a vast archive of illustrations available to book designers and greatly reduces the amount of time spent tracking down appropriate photographs for textbooks and other publishing projects.

- **Connecting people**. Computers create powerful new ways for people to work together. For example, **groupware** applications enable workers to create a shared calendar for scheduling purposes. Team members can see instantly who's available at a given day and time. What's more, these people don't have to work together in the same building. They could be located at various places around the world and still function effectively as a team.

Network Fundamentals

A computer network's basic components include **physical media** such as cables, switches, or routers that guide messages to their destination, and **standards** (called **protocols**) that specify how computers can communicate over the network. The following sections introduce these network fundamentals; subsequently, you'll learn more specifics about how LANs and WANs work.

PHYSICAL MEDIA

Most people think of computer networks in terms of cabling, but the physical medium is actually the least important part of a computer network. To be sure, some media place restrictions on the amount of data that can be transferred through a network, but even the simplest and least expensive cable can transfer as much as 1.5 Mbps. Network signals can traverse any type of telecommunications medium, including telephone lines, coaxial cable, microwave relay systems, satellites, wireless (radio and infrared), and fiber-optic cable. Often, a single message travels over several different physical media before arriving at its destination.

SWITCHING AND ROUTING TECHNIQUES

Networks can work with an amazing variety of physical media. But how does the message get through the maze of cables to the right place? Who sorts the mail en route? Networks funnel messages to the correct destination using two basic technologies, called circuit switching and packet switching.

Circuit Switching
In **circuit switching**, the network creates a physical, end-to-end circuit between the sending and receiving computers. Circuit switching works best when it is essential to avoid delivery delays. That's why circuit switching is ideally suited to voice and real-time videoconferencing. In a circuit switching network, high-speed electronic switches handle the job of establishing and maintaining the connection.

Packet Switching
In **packet switching**, an outgoing message is divided into data units of a fixed size, called **packets** (see Figure 7.2). Each packet is numbered and addressed to the destination computer. The sending computer pushes the packets onto the network, where they're examined by **routers**. Routers are computer-based devices that examine each packet they detect. After reading the packet's address, the router consults a table of possible

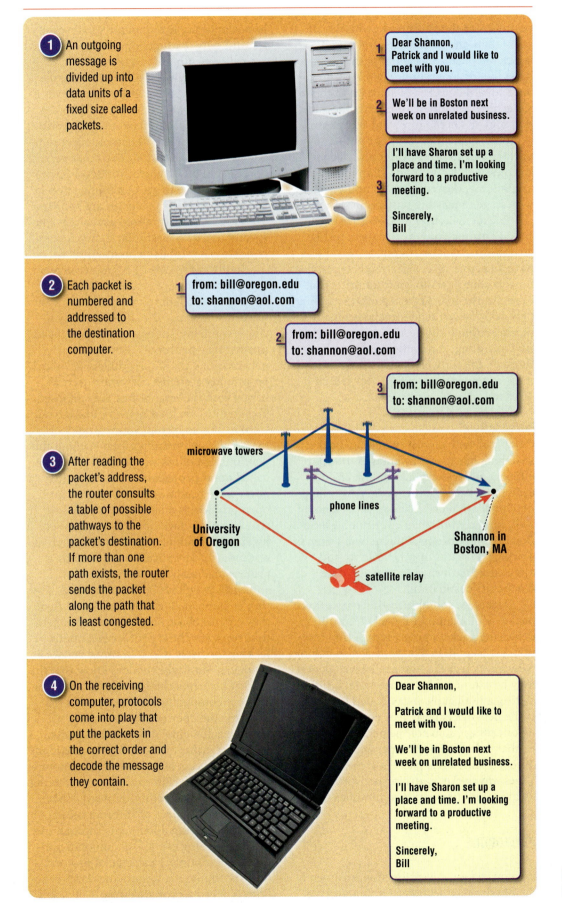

1 An outgoing message is divided up into data units of a fixed size called packets.

1. Dear Shannon, Patrick and I would like to meet with you.

2. We'll be in Boston next week on unrelated business.

3. I'll have Sharon set up a place and time. I'm looking forward to a productive meeting.

   Sincerely,
   Bill

2 Each packet is numbered and addressed to the destination computer.

1. from: bill@oregon.edu
   to: shannon@aol.com

2. from: bill@oregon.edu
   to: shannon@aol.com

3. from: bill@oregon.edu
   to: shannon@aol.com

3 After reading the packet's address, the router consults a table of possible pathways to the packet's destination. If more than one path exists, the router sends the packet along the path that is least congested.

microwave towers

phone lines

University of Oregon

Shannon in Boston, MA

satellite relay

4 On the receiving computer, protocols come into play that put the packets in the correct order and decode the message they contain.

Dear Shannon,

Patrick and I would like to meet with you.

We'll be in Boston next week on unrelated business.

I'll have Sharon set up a place and time. I'm looking forward to a productive meeting.

Sincerely,
Bill

Figure 7.2
Packet Switching

pathways to the packet's destination. If more than one path exists, the router sends the packet along the path that is most free of congestion. There's no guarantee that the packets will arrive in the same order that they were sent, but that's no problem; on the receiving computer, protocols come into play that put the packets in the correct order and decode the message they contain. If any packets are missing, the receiving computer sends a message requesting retransmission.

Packet switching networks are often called **connectionless** because, unlike switched networks, it's not necessary to have an active, direct electrical connection for two computers to communicate. For example, the Internet is a packet switching network; you can send somebody an e-mail message even if the destination computer isn't operating. If the message doesn't get through, the software keeps trying to send it for a set period of time, after which it gives up.

Which Is Best?

Compared with circuit switching, packet switching has many advantages. It's more efficient and less expensive than circuit switching. What's more, packet switching networks are more reliable. A packet switching network can continue to function even if portions of the network aren't working. Routers may be able to find alternative pathways so that the data reaches its destination.

Packet switching does have its drawbacks. As it examines a packet, a router delays the packet's progress by a tiny fraction of a second. In a huge packet switching network such as the Internet, a given packet may be examined by many routers, introducing a noticeable delay called **latency**. If the network experiences **congestion** (overloading), some of the packets may be further delayed, and the message can't be decoded until all its packets are received. That's why packet switching networks aren't ideal for real-time voice communication.

PROTOCOLS

What makes a network function isn't merely the physical connections. Of fundamental importance are the standards that specify how the network functions. These standards are called **protocols**.

What are protocols? They're like the manners you were taught when you were a child. When you're growing up, you're taught to say certain fixed things, such as "It's nice to meet you" when you meet someone in a social situation. The other person replies, "It's nice to meet you too." Such exchanges serve to get communication going. Networking protocols are similar. They are fixed, formalized exchanges that specify how two dissimilar network components can establish communication.

In the early years of computer networking, protocols were zealously guarded trade secrets of computer hardware manufacturers. Because they are owned by a single company, such protocols are called **proprietary protocols**. But these early networks had the same problem as other proprietary systems: customers weren't happy with the restrictions they imposed. You couldn't set up a network unless you were willing to buy all your equipment from the same manufacturer. Without the development of nonproprietary protocols, called **open protocols**, networking may never have become so widespread. An open protocol is a networking standard that has been developed and published by an independent organization, such as a standards committee organized by a professional association.

Open protocols benefit everyone. After they're published, companies know that they can purchase networking equipment that supports these protocols without locking themselves in to a single vendor's products. Similarly, vendors know that the market for networking products will grow as more companies offer equipment that supports the open protocols.

A specific type of network may use dozens of protocols, which cover the many different aspects of routing data communications correctly. For example, the Internet uses well over a hundred protocols that specify every aspect of Internet usage, such as retrieving documents through the Web or sending e-mail to a distant computer. The complete package of protocols that specify how a specific network functions is called a **protocol suite**. Collectively,

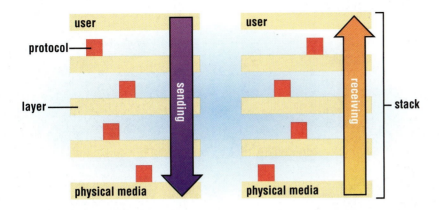

Figure 7.3

A network message starts at the top of a stack of layers and moves down through the various layers (protocol stack) until it reaches the bottom, or physical medium. On the receiving end, the process is reversed.

a protocol suite specifies the network's overall design, called the **network architecture**. The term *architecture* may sound daunting, but in the next section, you'll learn that the basic idea isn't much more complicated than a layer cake.

NETWORK LAYERS

Networks aren't easy to design because they're complex systems, and a lot can go wrong. To make network design easier, engineers divide a network architecture into separate **layers**, each of which has a function that can be isolated and treated separately from other layers. Because each layer's protocols precisely define how each layer passes data to another layer, it's possible to make changes within a layer without having to redesign the entire network.

The Protocol Stack

How do layers work? To understand the layer concept, it's helpful to remember that protocols are like manners, which enable people to get communication going. Let's look at an example.

Suppose you're using a Web browser, and you click a link that looks interesting. Now imagine that each protocol is a person, and each person has an office on a separate floor of a multistory office building. You're on the top floor, and the network connection is in the basement. When you initiate your request, your browser calls the person on the next floor down, "Excuse me, but would you please translate this Web page request into a form the Web server can process?" The person on the floor below replies, "Sure, no problem," and then calls the person on the *next* floor down. "If it isn't too much trouble, would you please put this translated message in an envelope and address it to such-and-such computer?" And so it goes, until the message finally reaches the physical transmission medium that connects the computers in the network.

At the receiving computer, precisely the opposite happens. The message is received in the basement and is sent *up*. It's taken out of its envelope, translated, and finally handed up to the top floor, where it's acted on.

To summarize, a network message starts at the top of a stack of layers and moves down through the various layers until it reaches the bottom (the physical medium). Because the various layers are seen to be vertically arranged like the floors in an office building, and because each is governed by its own protocols, the layers are called a **protocol stack**. On the receiving end, the process is reversed: the received message goes up the protocol stack. First, the network's data envelope is opened, and the data is translated until it can be used by the receiving application. Figure 7.3 illustrates this concept.

computer 2

accounting

computer 3

computer 1

personnel

sales and marketing

computer 4

server for daily sales records

laser printer

keyboard and monitor for server

Figure 7.4
LANs transform an organization's hardware into what seems to users like one gigantic computer system.

Local Area Networks (LANs): Limited Reach, Fast Connections

LANs don't travel far—the maximum geographic reach of a LAN is about one mile—but they're fast. Even the least expensive LANs can transfer data at 10 Mbps, and speeds of 100 Mbps or more are increasingly common. The newest LAN technology, called **Gigabit Ethernet**, can transfer data at the amazing rate of 1,000 Mbps (that's 1 gigabit per second).

LANs transform an organization's hardware into what seems to users like one gigantic computer system. From any computer on the LAN, you can access any data, software, or peripherals (such as fax machines, printers, or scanners), as long as the network administrator has made these resources accessible (see Figure 7.4).

Like all networks, LANs have all the basic network components—cabling, protocols, and a mechanism for routing information to the correct destination. As you'll see in the following sections, LANs require that connected computers have special hardware and software. LANs are primarily differentiated by the networking model they use (peer-to-peer or client/server), as well as their cabling, protocols, and spatial design (topology).

NETWORKING HARDWARE: NETWORK INTERFACE CARDS (NICS)

To connect to a LAN, a computer must be equipped with special hardware and software. In the hardware department, a computer needs a **network interface card** (**NIC**) to work with a LAN, unless this circuitry is part of the computer's design (see Figure 7.5). NICs are expansion boards that are made to fit into a computer's expansion slots. Some NICs are designed to work with a specific type of LAN cabling and protocol, but others can work with more than one type.

When a PC is connected to a LAN, the PC is called a **workstation**. The term

Figure 7.5
Some NICs are designed to work with a specific type of LAN cabling and protocol, but others work with more than one type.

node is used to describe any computer or peripheral (such as a printer) that's connected to the network. Every node on the LAN has a unique name that's visible to LAN users, as well as a unique, numerical network address.

NETWORKING SOFTWARE

Each computer on the LAN must also be equipped with additional system software that enables the computer to connect to the network and exchange data with other computers. Most operating systems, including UNIX, Linux, Windows, and Mac OS, now include such software in standard installations. You can set up a simple LAN, called a peer-to-peer network, by using this software, but you'll need additional software to set up a client/server network. Let's examine the differences between these two types of LANs.

Peer-to-Peer Networks

In a **peer-to-peer network** (**P2PN**), all the computers on the network are equals—that's where the term *peer-to-peer* comes from—and there's no file server. In **file sharing**, each computer user decides which, if any, files will be accessible to other users on the network. Users may also choose to share entire directories, or even entire disks. They can also choose to share peripherals, such as printers and scanners.

Peer-to-peer networks are easy to set up; people who aren't networking experts

workstation 2

fax machines
(shared resources)

workstation 1

fax server

file server
(shared hard disk)

print server

workstation 4

laser printer
(shared resource)

workstation 3

workstation 5

Figure 7.6
A client/server network includes one or more file servers as well as networked workstations.

do it all the time, generally to share an expensive laser printer or provide Internet access to all the workstations on the LAN. Peer-to-peer networks tend to slow down with heavy use, however, and keeping track of all the shared files and peripherals quickly becomes confusing. For this reason, peer-to-peer LANs aren't suitable for networks that connect more than one or two dozen computers.

Client/Server Networks

The typical corporate LAN is a **client/server network**, which includes one or more file servers as well as networked workstations (see Figure 7.6). The file server on a client/server network is a high-capacity, high-speed computer with a large hard disk capacity. It contains the **network operating system** (**NOS**), the software required to run the network. The server also contains network versions of programs and large data files. **Clients**—all the computers that can access the server—send requests to the server. The client/server model works with any size or physical layout of LAN and doesn't tend to slow down with heavy use.

A network operating system, such as Novell Corporation's NetWare or Microsoft's Windows NT Server, is a complex program that requires skilled technicians. Network operating system services include:

- File directories that make it much easier to locate files and resources on the LAN

- Automated distribution of software updates to the desktop computers on the LAN

- Support for Internet services such as the Web and e-mail

MEDIA

LANs use a variety of physical media to carry network signals:

Twisted pair The same type of wire used for telephones, **twisted pair** uses two insulated wires twisted around each other to provide a shield against electromagnetic interference, which is generated by electric motors, power lines, and powerful radio signals. The best type of unshielded twisted pair, called **category 5** (**cat-5**), can support data transfer rates of 100 Mbps or more.

Coaxial cable Familiar to cable TV users, **coaxial cable** consists of a center wire surrounded by insulation, which is then surrounded by a layer of braided wire. The braided wire provides a shield against electrical interference.

Fiber-optic cable A type of cable that transmits data in the form of light pulses, fiber-optic cable can carry more data and for longer distances than twisted pair or coaxial cable. A recent innovation in fiber-optic cables is the use of colored light. Instead of carrying one message in a stream of white light impulses, this technology allows for the use of colored impulses. The result is that a single fiber-optic strand can carry multiple signals simultaneously. Eight colors were available in 2000, 16 in 2001, 32 in 2002, and the projection is that there will be 256 colors in use by the turn of the decade.

Infrared If you use a television remote control, you're already familiar with the **infrared** wireless signaling technique. No wires are required, but the transmitter and receiver must be in line of sight or the signal is lost. Infrared signals work within a maximum of about 100 feet.

Radio Most **wireless LANs** (**WLANs**) use a **radio transmission** technique that ensures security by spreading the signal over a seemingly random series of frequencies. Only the receiver knows the series, so it isn't easy to eavesdrop on the signals. Radio-based wireless LAN signals can traverse up to about 1,000 feet.

Wireless LANs come in handy when users must move around a building instead of staying put. In Veterans Administration hospitals, for example, wireless LANs help hospital personnel track the distribution of controlled substances, a job that's both time-consuming and prone to error

without the computer's help. Now nurses use bedside computers, connected to the network through wireless signals, to track the use of these substances. Many campuses also are installing wireless LANs to serve students seamlessly as they move around campus.

LAN TOPOLOGIES

The physical layout of a local area network is called its **topology**. What's at stake here isn't just the arrangement of computers in space; topologies provide a solution to the problem of **contention**, which occurs when two workstations try to access the LAN at the same time. Contention sometimes results in **collisions**, the corruption of network data caused by two workstations transmitting simultaneously.

The earliest LANs used a **bus topology**, also called a daisy chain, in which the network cable forms a single bus to which every workstation is attached (see Figure 7.7a). At the ends of the bus, special connectors called terminators configure the end of the circuit. To resolve the contention problem, bus networks use some type of **contention management** technique, which specifies what happens when a collision occurs. (A common technique is to abandon any data that could have been corrupted by a collision.) The underlying design is simple, but bus networks are unwieldy in practice; it's difficult to add users in the middle of the circuit.

A **star topology** solves the expansion problems of the bus topology by introducing a central wiring concentrator, called a **hub** (see Figure 7.7b). Adding users is simple; you just run a cable to the hub and plug the new user into a vacant connector. Star networks also generally use contention management to deal with collisions.

A **ring topology** has all nodes attached in a circular wiring arrangement. This topology makes possible a unique way of preventing collisions (see Figure 7.7c). A special unit of data called a **token** travels around this ring. A workstation can transmit only when it possesses the token. Although ring topology networks are circular in that the token travels a circular path, they look more like star networks because all the wiring is routed to a central hub.

a. Bus Topology
The network cable forms a single bus to which every workstation is attached.

b. Star Topology
This network introduces a central wiring concentrator called a hub. It's easy to connect new users by running a cable to the hub.

c. Ring Topology
All the nodes are attached in a circular wiring arrangement.

Figure 7.7 a–c
Most networks use a bus, star, or ring topology.

EMERGING TECHNOLOGIES

CURRENTS

Sharing Wireless Communities

As cyberspace becomes populated by more and more of the world, the questions posed related to computer ethics become more complex. Should there be new rules for today's wireless world? For example, many people argue that compensation for use rather than access is ethical—that is, you should have to pay for each user on a DSL line, not for the DSL line itself. Others think that if you've subscribed to a DSL line, you should be able to share that line with whomever you see fit.

Imagine the following scenario: You recently decided to pay for fast Internet access by subscribing to an expensive DSL provider. You also bought an inexpensive router and now share your bandwidth free of charge with your roommate. You're even thinking of sharing it with your apartment building. Why not—it won't cost you anything more. After all, you paid for the access and you're not profiting yourself by offering it free to others. Surely there's nothing wrong with that.

Well, there is something wrong with it, in fact. For one, most DSL providers wouldn't allow it, and, more important, you'd be breaking the law even if you didn't earn any money by sharing your bandwidth.

Can bandwidth ever be shared legally? It might be in the case of business access to the net. There are those who are working on trying to build legal free wireless communities. One idea is to ask businesses to give away a little of their unused bandwidth so that "community members" can access the Internet using laptops and other wireless devices for free. In such communities, users have to be within a certain distance of the server in order to take advantage of the free bandwidth, but that range can be as far as a city block or more. Proponents of this idea suggest that businesses could offer the access at off-peak, after business hours. In order to make such ideas legal, businesses would pay a higher flat fee for their bandwidth on the condition that it may be offered freely.

This idea is already taking off. In New York City, for example, NYCWireless provides free "hotspots" of Internet access in parks, coffee shops, and building lobbies. Other cities are following suit. Sharing bandwidth certainly makes for a unique way for companies and governments to give back to the community. And free wireless access in cities may prove to be the next Internet frontier. Who knows, perhaps in the future, businesses will choose their locations based on which cities offer a free wireless zone to their residents.

As you may have guessed, the trick will be to make free wireless network communities safe and secure from malicious users and from those who would bog down the system with hefty downloads. In order for these networks to be feasible, they'll need to allow users access as well as prevent nasty network activities. Whether free networks piggy-back off existing commercial networks or are created through altogether separate, new, independent networks, look for these wireless Internet communities in the future.

Popular Lower-Layer LAN Protocols

Protocol Name	Data Transfer Rate	Physical Media	Topology
LocalTalk	230.4 Kbps	Shielded twisted pair (phone connector cords)	Bus
Ethernet (10base5 and 10base2)	10 Mbps	Coaxial cable	Bus
Ethernet (10baseT)	10 Mbps	Twisted-pair cable	Star
Fast Ethernet (100baseT)	100 Mbps	Twisted-pair or fiber-optic cable	Star
Gigabit Ethernet	1,000 Mbps	Fiber-optic cable	Star
IBM Token Ring Network	4–16 Mbps	Twisted pair	Star

Figure 7.8

Destinations

To learn more about the Ethernet, check out Charles Spurgeon's Ethernet Web site at **www.ethermanage.com/ ethernet/ethernet.html**. The site covers all the Ethernet technologies used today and includes a practical guide for do-it-yourselfers.

Destinations

For the latest news about LANs, check out *LAN Times*, the premier trade journal in this area. LAN Times Online is located at **www.lantimes.com**.

LAN TECHNOLOGIES

Although several LAN technologies specify functions at the lower layers of the protocol stack (see Figure 7.8), by far the most popular LAN standard is **Ethernet**, originally developed in the 1970s by Bob Metcalfe and other researchers at Xerox Corporation's Palo Alto Research Center (PARC). The various versions of Ethernet are used by approximately 80 percent of all LANs. Although early versions of Ethernet (called 10base2 and 10base5) used coaxial cable in bus networks, the most popular versions today are Ethernet star networks that use hubs and twisted pair wire. Two versions are available: **10baseT** (10 Mbps) and **Fast Ethernet** (100 Mbps, also called **100baseT**). The equipment to create a 10baseT Ethernet for five PCs can cost as little as $200. As we mentioned earlier, the newest LAN technology, Gigabit Ethernet, can transfer data at speeds as high as 1,000 Mbps.

Perhaps the simplest LAN technology is **LocalTalk**, the networking system built into every Macintosh computer. You can quickly create a LocalTalk network by buying some LocalTalk connectors and ordinary telephone cables.

LAN PROTOCOLS

LAN technologies such as Ethernet specify the nuts and bolts of the lower layers, including the physical and data link layers. These layers can work with a variety of higher-level protocols, which handle the network, transport, and higher layers. Following are examples of such higher-layer protocols:

AppleTalk Apple Computer's **AppleTalk** protocol provides the network routing and addressing functions for all Macintosh networks, whether they use LocalTalk, Ethernet, or token ring networks at lower layers.

IPX/SPX IPX and **SPX** are the network and transport layer protocols used for Novell NetWare networks.

NetBEUI The **NetBEUI** protocols (pronounced "net-boo-ee") define Microsoft Windows NT–based networks.

TCP/IP (Transmission Control Protocol/ Internet Protocol) These are the core Internet protocols. Like AppleTalk, TCP/IP can be used with a variety of lower-level protocols, such as Ethernet. A LAN that uses TCP/IP is called an intranet, a term that suggests that it's an Internet designed for internal use in an organization.

A single network can run more than one higher-level protocol at a time. Many LANs run IPX/SPX to access file servers, AppleTalk provide support for the Macintoshes connected to the network, NetBEUI to connect with Windows NT servers, and TCP/IP for Internet access.

Wide Area Networks (WANs): Long-Haul Carriers

Local area networks enable an organization to share computing resources in a single building or group of buildings. But a LAN's geographic limitations pose a problem. Today, most organizations need to share computing resources with distant branch offices, employees who are traveling, and even people outside the organization, including suppliers and customers. This is what wide area networks (WANs) are used for—to link computers separated by even thousands of miles.

Outside contact is increasingly important. In the early 1990s, the 80/20 rule was often used for network planning purposes: 80 percent of the network traffic would occur on internal LANs, while only 20 percent would go outside. Today, the rule is closer to 50/50, and WANs are growing at an incredible rate.

Why don't companies simply use the Internet to link to the outside world? They do, but the Internet has two major limitations: poor security and service interruptions due to network overload. Companies are increasingly using the Internet for low-security operations, as well as for exchanging data that isn't time-critical. But they're reluctant to use the public Internet for exchanging financial data or any other types of data that must arrive on time.

HOW WANS WORK

WANs are like long-distance telephone systems. In fact, much WAN traffic is carried by long-distance voice communication providers, such as AT&T, MCI, and Sprint. Like long-distance phone carriers, WANs have what amounts to a local access number, called a point of presence (POP), and long-distance trunk lines, called backbones (see Figure 7.9).

Point of Presence (POP)

To carry computer data over the long haul, a WAN must be locally accessible. For this reason, WANs make a **point of presence**

(**POP**) available in as many towns and cities as possible. A point of presence is a WAN network connection point that enables customers to access the WAN by means of a local analog telephone call (using a modem) or a direct digital hookup that enables a continuous, direct connection. One WAN, called Tymnet, has over 1,000 local points of presence in the United States.

The following physical media are often used to create permanent digital connections from an organization to a POP:

- A 56 Kbps **leased line** is a specially conditioned telephone line that enables continuous, end-to-end communication between two points. The earliest type of permanent digital

Figure 7.9

WANs are like long-distance telephone systems. In fact, a lot of WAN traffic is carried by long-distance voice communication providers.

connection, 56 Kbps leased lines have declined in popularity as services such as ISDN and ADSL become more widely available.

- ISDN services offer connections ranging from 56 to 128 Kbps (Basic Rate ISDN) or 1.5 Mbps (Primary Rate ISDN) using ordinary twisted pair telephone lines.

- ADSL and related Digital Subscriber Line (DSL) technologies are expected to provide 1 Mbps access, again using ordinary twisted pair telephone lines.

- Larger organizations, such as Internet service providers, corporations, and universities, connect using a leased **T1** line. This is a costly service that isn't affordable for individuals and small businesses.

- A new local connection service, called a **permanent virtual circuit** (**PVC**), uses a type of packet switching known as **frame relay**. Similar to leased 56 Kbps lines and leased T1 lines, a PVC establishes point-to-point data communication, but the use of packet switching enables more than one user's data to traverse the line simultaneously. Accordingly, costs are lower than they are for private leased lines.

Backbones

The high-capacity transmission lines that carry WAN traffic are called **backbones**. Some are regional, connecting towns and cities in a region such as southern California or New England. Others are continental or even transcontinental in scope.

Whatever their scope, backbones are designed to carry huge amounts of data traffic; cross-country Internet backbones, for example, can handle nearly 2.5 gigabits per second, and much higher speeds are on the way. A current U.S. government-funded research project is constructing a backbone network that will operate at speeds of 9.6 gigabits per second. Some WANs use circuit switching network technology, but most use packet switching.

HOW WANS ARE ORGANIZED

Most WAN traffic travels over connections leased from WAN service providers. The Internet is a WAN of massive proportions; backbone providers receive compensation by charging fees to Internet service providers (ISPs), who in turn sell subscriptions to individual and organizational Internet users.

As we mentioned earlier, a public data network (PDN) is a for-profit data communications network available for use on a per-byte-transmitted fee basis. PDNs charge hefty fees, but they can assure good security and can guarantee that bandwidth (network capacity) is available when it's needed.

Large corporations, banks, and governments may construct private data networks, which aren't open to the public or to any other users. These are the most secure WANs, but they're also the most expensive to operate. An alternative developed in the 1980s, called the **virtual private network** (**VPN**), consists of lines that are exclusively leased to a single company, thus ensuring excellent security.

WAN PROTOCOLS

Like any computer network, WANs use protocols. The oldest packet switching protocol for WAN usage, called **X.25**, is optimized for dial-up connections over noisy telephone lines and is still in widespread use. Local connections generally offer speeds of 9.6 to 64 Kbps. X.25 is best used to create a point-to-point connection with a single computer. It is widely used for automated teller machines and credit card authorization devices. New protocols designed for 100 percent digital lines, such as Switched Multimegabit Data Service (SMDS) and Asynchronous Transfer Mode (ATM), enable much faster data transfer rates (up to 155 Mbps).

WAN APPLICATIONS

WANs enable companies to use many of the same applications you use on the Internet, such as e-mail, conferencing, document exchange, and remote database access. This section focuses on the

MARKETING BLUNDERS

IMPACTS

The PARC Mystery:
Why Did Xerox Not Take Advantage of Its Own Innovations?

It's one of the most amazing feats of sheer technical brilliance in the history of computing—and indeed, in the history of any technology. In the early 1970s, a talented team of researchers at Xerox Corporation's Palo Alto Research Center (PARC) invented just about every major technology that you'll find in today's desktop computers. Yet Xerox failed to recognize what the PARC researchers had achieved and couldn't market any of their innovations successfully. The story of Xerox PARC is carefully studied to this day by business management students hoping to avoid what is commonly seen as Xerox's colossal marketing blunder. Was it really a blunder—or were the PARC researchers simply ahead of their time?

Here are a few highlights of what the PARC researchers came up with:

- The graphical user interface (GUI), replete with pull-down menus, dialog boxes, on-screen fonts that look the way they'll print, and on-screen graphic images
- Proved the usability of the mouse within a GUI
- Laser printers and the Postscript page description language
- Desktop publishing software and what-you-see-is-what-you-get (WYSIWYG) word processing software
- The Ethernet networking standard for local area networks

All these technologies came to fruition in Xerox's Star computer system, a 1974 desktop computer system with 512 KB of RAM and a brilliant, page-white display. Xerox attempted to market the Star as a breakthrough product, one that would enable collaborating workgroups to share their work by means of a high-speed, local area network and produce beautifully printed documents. But Xerox sold very few Stars—and, in the coming years, other companies took the PARC researchers' innovations to market and made billions.

Where did Xerox go wrong? Part of the problem was the Star's high cost; each fully equipped Star system cost more than $10,000. Bear in mind, there was no economy of scale at this point, and because the system was entirely new, everything to build it had to be done the first time by Xerox, which increased the cost. Yet Xerox probably would have failed to market the Star successfully even if it could have been manufactured for half that sum. The reason? When Xerox marketers tried to explain what the Star was supposed to do, nobody had the faintest idea what they were talking about. In those days, the cutting edge of office technology consisted of electric typewriters and photocopying machines. The leap to today's computer systems was simply too great for people to appreciate.

If you're still skeptical, consider that an entire decade elapsed before Apple Computer was able to win market acceptance for the Macintosh, a PARC-influenced system—and Apple was unable to win more than 10 percent of the total computer marketplace. The PARC researchers' ideas didn't win full acceptance until the release of Microsoft Windows 95 and 98, more than 20 years after the original innovations took place.

To understand what happened at Xerox, it's good to remember a favorite saying of famous American industrial designer Raymond Loewy, whose accomplishments include the 1961 Studebaker Avanti. If you're looking for the right design, said Loewy, choose the one that's the "most advanced yet most acceptable" to the public. PARC's technology was just far too advanced for public acceptance in the early 1970s.

Still, it's a good thing that PARC's management didn't take Loewy's maxim to heart. They might have directed PARC researchers to work on less advanced technology. In this case, Xerox's loss translated into enormous gains for computer users worldwide.

ways to take advantage of a WAN's superior security.

LAN-to-LAN Connections

In corporate information systems, WANs are often used to connect the LANs at two or more geographically separate locations. This use of WANs overcomes the major limitation of LAN technology: its incapability to link computers separated by more than a few thousand feet. New services from WAN service providers such as AT&T, Sprint, and MCI enable companies to connect their LANs at 100 Mbps, the same data transfer rate used in most companies' internal systems. With these connections, users get the impression that they're using one huge LAN that connects the entire company and all its branch offices.

Transaction Acquisition

When you make a purchase at retail chain stores such as Sears or Starbucks Coffee, information about your transaction is instantly relayed to central computers through WANs. That's because the "cash register" the clerk uses is actually a computer, called a **point-of-sale** (**POS**) **terminal**, that's linked to a data communications network (see Figure 7.10). The acquired data is collected for accounting and also analyzed to reveal changing sales patterns.

Electronic Data Interchange (EDI)

A set of standards that specify how companies can set up business-to-business financial transactions, **electronic data interchange** (**EDI**) is widely used to speed ordering, invoicing, and payments. If two companies have compatible systems, they can establish a connection through which company A sends a purchase order to company B by means of EDI—computer to computer. When company B ships the product, company B sends an invoice by EDI to company A. Company A can then pay by electronic funds transfer through its bank. The entire operation occurs without any paper changing hands.

If two companies don't have compatible systems, they can use an intermediary EDI company to change the code so that the two companies can communicate. Very large manufacturing companies often require as a condition of purchase that their suppliers have EDI systems compatible with the company's system. The buyer can order parts to be delivered just in time to be used. This capability enables the buyer to shorten the length of time between buying the parts and selling the finished product and receiving payment.

EDI can reduce a company's costs, but the technology is cumbersome and comes with high start-up costs.

Figure 7.10
POS terminals are fast becoming a part of a company's ability to know its customers.

HOME | Takeaway Points | Key Terms and Concepts | Matching | Multiple Choice | Fill-In | Short Answer | Exercises/ Projects | Web Research | CHAPTER REVIEW

TAKEAWAY POINTS

- Computer networks link two or more computers so that they can exchange data and share resources.

- The three types of computer networks are local area networks (LANs), metropolitan area networks (MANs), and wide area networks (WANs).

- Computer networks can reduce hardware costs, enable users to share applications, create the means to pool all of an organization's mission-critical data, and foster teamwork and collaboration.

- Computer networks require physical media, but their most important component consists of the protocols that define how network devices can communicate with each other.

- A network requires many protocols to function smoothly. When a computer sends a message over the network, the application hands the message down the protocol stack, where a series of protocols prepares the message for transmission through the network. At the other end, the message goes up a similar stack.

- Circuit switching creates a permanent, end-to-end circuit that is optimal for voice and real-time data. Packet switching does not require a permanent switched circuit and can funnel more data through a medium with a given data transfer capacity. But packet switching introduces slight delays that make the technology less than optimal for voice or real-time data.

- A peer-to-peer LAN doesn't use a file server and is most appropriate for small networks. Client/server networks offer network navigation tools, shared applications, shared databases, groupware, and e-mail, but trained technicians are required to configure and maintain them.

- By far the most widely used LAN protocol is Ethernet, which is available in 10 or 100 Mbps star topology configurations that use hubs and twisted pair wiring. The newest LAN technology, Gigabit Ethernet, can transfer data at the rate of 1,000 Mbps.

- Businesses use WANs for LAN-to-LAN connections, transaction acquisition, and electronic data interchange.

1 2 3 4 5 6 7 8 9 10 11 12 13 14 15 16

CHAPTER REVIEW | Takeaway Points | Key Terms and Concepts | Matching | Multiple Choice | Fill-In | Short Answer | Exercises/ Projects | Web Research | HOME

1 2 3 4 5 6 7 8 9 10 11 12 13 14 15 16

KEY TERMS AND CONCEPTS

10baseT
AppleTalk
backbone
bus topology
category 5 (cat-5)
circuit switching
client
client/server network
coaxial cable
collision
computer network
congestion
connectionless
contention
contention management
electronic data interchange
    (EDI)
Ethernet
Fast Ethernet (100baseT)
fiber-optic cable
file server
file sharing
frame relay
Gigabit Ethernet
groupware

hub
infrared
intranet
IPX/SPX
latency
layers
leased line
local area network (LAN)
LocalTalk
metropolitan area network
    (MAN)
NetBEUI
network architecture
network interface card (NIC)
network operating system
    (NOS)
network version
node
open protocol
packet switching
packet
peer-to-peer network (P2PN)
permanent virtual circuit
    (PVC)
physical media

point-of-sale (POS) terminal
point of presence (POP)
proprietary protocol
protocols
protocol stack
protocol suite
public data network (PDN)
radio transmission
ring topology
router
standards (protocols)
star topology
synergy
T1
TCP/IP (Transmission
    Control Protocol/
    Internet Protocol)
token
topology
twisted pair
virtual private network (VPN)
wide area network (WAN)
wireless LAN (WLAN)
workstation
X.25

COMPUTERS IN YOUR FUTURE 2004

7.21

HOME | Takeaway Points | Key Terms and Concepts | **Matching** | Multiple Choice | Fill-In | Short Answer | Exercises/ Projects | Web Research | CHAPTER REVIEW

MATCHING

Match each key term in the left column with the most accurate definition in the right column.

_____ 1. network operating system (NOS)

_____ 2. metropolitan area network (MAN)

_____ 3. protocols

_____ 4. TCP/IP

_____ 5. groupware

_____ 6. peer-to-peer network

_____ 7. routers

_____ 8. clients

_____ 9. token

_____ 10. packets

_____ 11. latency

_____ 12. bus topology

_____ 13. topology

_____ 14. collision

_____ 15. node

a. all the computers that access the server

b. applications that enable workers to create a shared calendar for scheduling purposes

c. a computer or peripheral that is connected to the network

d. a network where all the computers are equal

e. a special unit of data that travels around the ring in a ring topology

f. computer-based devices that examine each packet they detect

g. delay in packet transmission due to router examination

h. data units of fixed size that are used with packet switching networks

i. the use of high-speed fiber-optic lines to connect computers located at various places within a major urban region

j. standards that specify how the networks function

k. the core Internet protocols

l. also known as a daisy chain

m. the physical layout of a local area network

n. software required to run the network

o. the corruption of network data caused by two workstations transmitting simultaneously

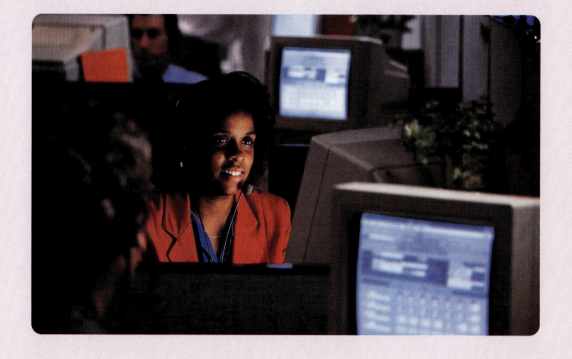

CHAPTER REVIEW | Takeaway Points | Key Terms and Concepts | Matching | Multiple Choice | Fill-In | Short Answer | Exercises/ Projects | Web Research | HOME

1 2 3 4 5 6 7 8 9 10 11 12 13 14 15 16

MULTIPLE CHOICE

Circle the correct choice for each of the following.

1. Which of the following is not a computer network?
   a. Local area network (LAN)
   b. Leased-line area network (L^{2}AN)
   c. Wide area network (WAN)
   d. Metropolitan area network (MAN)

2. Which technology enables networks to funnel messages to the correct destinations?
   a. Circuit switching
   b. Packet switching
   c. Both a and b
   d. None of the above

3. What is the set of standards used to specify how companies set up business-to-business financial transactions?
   a. Point of sale (POS)
   b. Electronic data interchange (EDI)
   c. Permanent virtual circuit (PVC)
   d. Virtual private network (VPN)

4. To connect to a LAN, a computer must be equipped with which of the following?
   a. Network interface card (NIC)
   b. Backbone
   c. Both a and b
   d. None of the above

5. Which of the following LAN media carries more data for longer distances?
   a. Infrared
   b. Coaxial cable
   c. Twisted pair
   d. Fiber-optic cable

6. Which of the following is not a LAN topology?
   a. Ring
   b. Star
   c. Hub
   d. Bus

7. What do you call a for-profit data communications network available for use on a per-byte-transmitted fee basis?
   a. Virtual private network (VPN)
   b. Public data network (PDN)
   c. Peer-to-peer network (P2PN)
   d. Client/server network (CSN)

8. Which of the following is a WAN network connection point that enables customers to access the WAN through a local phone call?
   a. Point of presence (POP)
   b. Leased line
   c. Permanent virtual circuit (PVC)
   d. Frame relay

9. Which of the following is the most popular LAN standard?
   a. IPX/SPX
   b. NetBEUI
   c. Ethernet
   d. Synchronous Optical Network (SONET)

10. Which of the following is the oldest and most widely used packet switching protocol for WAN usage?
   a. 10baseT
   b. Category 5 (cat-5)
   c. X.25
   d. T1

HOME | Takeaway Points | Key Terms and Concepts | Matching | Multiple Choice | Fill-In | Short Answer | Exercises/ Projects | Web Research | CHAPTER REVIEW

1 2 3 4 5 6 7 8 9 10 11 12 13 14 15 16

FILL-IN

In the blanks provided, write the correct answer for each of the following.

1. A computer _____ links two or more computers together to enable data and resource exchange.

2. A _____ uses direct cables, localized wireless radio, or infrared signals to link computers within a small geographic area.

3. When a PC is connected to a LAN, the PC is called a _____.

4. A _____ is a PC expansion board needed to connect a computer to a LAN.

5. In _____, an outgoing message is divided into data units of a fixed size called packets.

6. _____ wires are used in LANs because they support data transfers of 100 Mbps or more.

7. A _____ is a high-capacity, high-speed computer with a large hard disk capacity.

8. The earliest LANs used a _____ topology.

9. An _____ is a networking standard that has been developed and published by an independent organization such as a standards body.

10. The high-capacity transmission lines that carry WAN traffic are called _____.

11. A _____ uses a type of packet switching known as frame relay.

12. In a peer-to-peer network, _____ allows users to decide which computer files, if any, are accessible to other users on the network.

13. _____ protocols are owned by a single company.

14. A _____ uses long-distance transmission media, including telecommunications networks.

15. In _____, the network creates a physical, end-to-end circuit between the sending and receiving computers.

SHORT ANSWER

1. Explain why a mainframe with terminals and printers is not considered a computer network.

2. Explain the difference between peer-to-peer and client/server networks.

3. What are the differences between local, metropolitan, and wide area networks?

4. Name three types of LAN topologies, and describe how they work.

5. Explain the similarities and weaknesses of an infrared wireless connection and a television remote control.

6. Explain the differences between circuit switching and packet switching. What are the advantages of each method?

Go to www.prenhall.com/ciyf2004 to review this chapter, answer the questions, and complete the exercises and Web research questions.

EXERCISES/PROJECTS

1. Visit a campus computer lab and determine what network topology is used. In addition to computer workstations, what other devices are connected to the network? What types of physical media are used to connect the computers and other peripherals in this lab? If your school has more than one lab, what physical media are used to interconnect the labs? How does your school connect to the Internet?

2. Interview some of your instructors and see if they use groupware for scheduling or for participating in collaborative efforts with others. Have you used groupware? If you have, explain how you used this software.

3. If you were responsible for setting up a network for a company that had offices in five different states, how would you do it? What part would the Internet play in your plans?

4. The number of households that have more than one computer is increasing, and families want to share resources among them. One of these resources is the Internet connection. Although the newer versions of Microsoft Windows use software to allow two computers to share an Internet connection, consumers with high-speed connections such as cable or DSL can use hardware in the form of a router to share Internet access. Go to a local computer store and investigate cable/DSL routers. What are the number of ports and prices for these devices? What physical medium is used to connect the devices to the router? Can a printer be shared using a router? What type of network topology is used? What additional hardware is needed to network computers to the router? If you had a high-speed connection and multiple computers, would you purchase a router? Why or why not?

5. Many homes with cable television service have more than one television set. Connecting multiple televisions requires the use of "splitters" to divide the incoming signal and send it to each television set. Some new houses are constructed with coaxial cable running to multiple rooms, but how are multiple television sets connected in older homes? Unfortunately, this usually requires drilling holes in walls, floors, or ceilings or even running cables on the exterior of the residence, and some homeowners and landlords don't like doing this. The same connection problem exists with home computer networks. Fortunately, there's an alternative to running networking cables: using a wireless access point. Go to a local computer store and investigate wireless networking. What are prices for these devices? How does the wireless connection speed compare with a wired one? What type of network topology is used? What additional hardware is needed to network computers to the wireless access point? If you had a home network, would you consider this networking alternative? Why or why not?

HOME | Takeaway Points | Key Terms and Concepts | Matching | Multiple Choice | Fill-In | Short Answer | Exercises/ Projects | Web Research | CHAPTER REVIEW

1 2 3 4 5 6 7 8 9 10 11 12 13 14 15 16

WEB RESEARCH

1. The last two questions in the Exercises/ Projects section deal with a router for sharing an Internet connection and a wireless access point for connecting computers. Visit CNET at **www.cnet.com** to see if you can purchase a wireless router to do both. What are the connection speeds of a wireless router? What type of network topology is used? What additional hardware is needed to network computers to the wireless router? If you had a home network with Internet access, would you consider purchasing a wireless router? Why or why not?

2. The textbook discusses Gigabit Ethernet technology that allows LAN connection speeds of 1,000 Mbps or 1 Gbps. Go to the "10 GEA" site at **www.10gea.org/Tech-whitepapers.htm** to learn about this promising technology. What does 10 GEA mean, and when was it formed? Name three of the founding member organizations. What is the name of the new standard that is being developed? When is ratification of the new standard expected? What types of companies, organizations, or institutions do you think will use this technology?

3. Assume that you have both a desktop and a laptop computer and you wish to network them together. To do this, you need network interfaces for each computer. Go to **www.pricegrabber.com** to find the best price for a network card for a desktop and a laptop computer. What are the prices for each? Why do you think the cards for a laptop are

more expensive? Many desktop computers and laptop computers now include automatic built-in network connectivity. Locate and name specific desktop and laptop models that have internal networking capability. If you currently have a desktop or laptop computer, does your computer have internal networking capability?

4. Because of their small size, personal digital assistants (PDAs) are popular mobile computing devices. Do you own, or have you considered buying, a PDA? Go to **www.dartek.com/Browse/index.cfm** to find information on PDAs. What are the most popular methods for networking a PDA to a desktop computer? Which of these methods require additional PC hardware? Is the use of the word *networking* correct? Explain why it is or is not.

5. One of the oldest and most widely used network operating systems is Novell NetWare. Visit the Novel site at **www.novell.com**. What is the latest version of NetWare? In addition to LAN software, what Internet features does NetWare support? What are the initial purchase and upgrade costs for a small system that supports a server and five workstations? What products qualify for competitive upgrades? In addition to English, name three other languages for which NetWare is available. Does NetWare support Macintosh and UNIX-based computers? Does your school use any Novell networking software?

The Internet:
The Network of Networks

CHAPTER **8**

What You'll Learn...

When you have finished reading this chapter, you will be able to:

1. Define the Internet and discuss why it's so popular.

2. Differentiate the Internet from online services and the Web.

3. Explain the difference between client and server software.

4. List the most popular Internet services and explain what they do.

5. Define the elements of Internet addresses, including domain names.

6. Discuss the use of Internet-based networks within large organizations.

7. List the initiatives underway to improve the Internet's performance.

As you're well aware, the **Internet** is a global computer network with hundreds of millions of users worldwide, and it's growing like crazy (see Figure 8.1). According to one estimate, more than 300,000 new Web pages appear every week, and the total amount of information available on this worldwide network doubles each year. But defining the Internet as a fast-growing global network understates its significance. We're witnessing the birth of the first major mass medium since television; more than 60 percent of U.S. residents between the ages of 16 and 34 are Internet users. What's more, the Internet isn't simply a new mass medium; it's the *first* mass medium that involves computers and uses digitized data. And it's more interactive than TV, radio, and newspapers, which limit user interaction to content selection. With the Internet, people can create information as well as consume it. For this reason, it's the first truly democratic mass medium, one that allows ordinary people to add their own content to the growing mass of information available online.

Computers and digitization affect this new medium's possibilities in another important way: the potential for **media convergence**, the unification of *all* earlier media (including newspapers, TVs, radio, and telephones). Former U.S. Vice President Al Gore coined the term **Information Superhighway** to describe this phenomenon of media convergence. The Internet is already a major source of breaking news, rivaling such traditional sources as newspapers and television. And according to a recent estimate, more than five percent of all long-distance voice telephone calls will one day travel over the Internet, creating a $9 billion industry and posing a genuine threat to the traditional public switched telephone network (PSTN).

Traditional media aren't going to go away soon, but you can count on one thing: the Internet is transforming almost everything we do, including communicating, obtaining information, learning, looking for jobs, and keeping up with a career or a profession (see Figure 8.2). And it's equally indispensable for businesses; **electronic commerce** (**e-commerce**), facilitated by the Internet, has created a market worth billions. Just what *is* this network, and why is it growing at such an explosive rate?

Understanding the Internet: The Network of Networks

To understand the Internet, it's important to begin with a solid grasp of just what differentiates the Internet from other networks that traverse huge distances, such as wide area networks (WANs). And here's the most important point: technically, the Internet is best defined as *the* overarching network of networks.

In this network of networks, every connected computer can directly exchange data with any other computer on the network. The local area networks (LANs), WANs, and computers connected to the Internet are maintained by large organizations, such as corporations and universities, as well as by **Internet service providers** (**ISPs**), which sell Internet

Destinations

Looking for a radio station? Try "Live Radio" on the Internet at **www.live-radio.net**. This site lists more than 1,500 live Internet radio stations worldwide. You need a player to listen to radio over the Internet, but you can download one for free. Radio station home pages have links that enable you to obtain the software you need.

Figure 8.1

The Internet is the framework upon which we create cyberspace.

Figure 8.2
The Internet is rich with informative and entertaining sites.

subscriptions to the public (see Figure 8.3). Today, hundreds of thousands of networks and more than 50 million computers are connected to the Internet.

A GALACTIC NETWORK

The Internet was first envisioned by Massachusetts Institute of Technology (MIT) scientist J. C. R. Licklider in August 1962. President Roosevelt's science advisor during World War II, Licklider headed the first computer research program at the Defense Advanced Research Projects Agency (DARPA), as it was then known, a unit of the U.S. Department of Defense. In a series of historic memos, Licklider spoke of a "galactic network," a globally interconnected network through which any computer could directly access any other and exchange data. That's precisely what the Internet accomplishes.

Since it enables direct and immediate contact with any other computer on the network, the Internet bears some similarity to the telephone system (although the Internet

works on different principles). Every Internet computer has an **Internet address**, or **IP address** (similar to a phone number), and it can directly exchange data with any other Internet computer by "dialing" the other computer's address. The Internet works on packet switching principles rather than the circuit switching principles of the telephone system. Still, the Internet does for computers what the telephone system does for phones: it enables any Internet-connected computer to connect almost instantly and effortlessly with *any* other Internet-connected computer anywhere in the world. The Internet is an incredible achievement: an enormous, worldwide information space in which every connected computer has its own unique address.

INTEROPERABILITY

If the Internet merely allowed any one of millions of computers to exchange data with any other, it would be quite an achievement. But the Internet does more. It enables any connected computer to

Figure 8.3
LANs and computers connected to the Internet are maintained by corporations, universities, and Internet service providers.

Windows PC

mainframe

Internet

UNIX

Macintosh

Figure 8.4
The interoperability provided by the Internet removes the distinctions among different hardware and operating systems, allowing users on all different platforms to work with each other.

operate a remote computer by sending commands through the network. One key to the Internet's success is that such commands work even if the remote computer is a different brand and model. Called **interoperability**, this remarkable characteristic of the Internet comes into play every time you use the network. When you access the Web with a Macintosh, for example, you contact a variety of machines that may include other Macintoshes, Windows PCs, UNIX machines, and even mainframe computers. You don't know what type of computer platform you're accessing, however, and it doesn't make any difference. (A **platform** is a distinct type of computer that uses a certain type of processor and operating system, such as an Intel-based Windows PC.) In other words, the Internet is a **cross-platform network** (see Figure 8.4).

The Internet's cross-platform capability helps explain the network's popularity. No network could match the Internet's success if it forced people to use just one or two types of computers. Many home computer users have PCs, but others have Macintoshes or dozens of additional types of computers. All too many businesses have invested haphazardly in Windows PCs, UNIX workstations, and Macintoshes,

only to find that, in the absence of the Internet, these computers don't work together well. Almost magically, the Internet enables these computers to exchange data and even to control each other's operations. As you'll see later in this chapter, this is a major reason for the explosive popularity of **intranets**, internal networks that use Internet technologies.

LEAVE THE LOWER LAYERS TO THE LANS AND WANS

The Internet connects millions of LANs, but a key Internet design principle is that LANs don't all have to work the same way to connect to the Internet. The Internet protocols—standards that define how the Internet works—don't define the lower, nuts-and-bolts networking standards needed to transmit data physically over a certain transmission medium. Instead, the Internet leaves this up to whatever network the Internet data is traveling on. This is an important key to the Internet's success because it means that an organization doesn't have to change its internal computer network to connect to the Internet. In the same way, Internet data can travel over any type of WAN.

THE INTERNET VS. ONLINE SERVICES

What's the difference between the Internet and an **online service**, such as MSN or America Online? An online service provides a proprietary network that offers e-mail, chat rooms, discussions, and fee-based content, such as magazines and newspapers (see Figure 8.5). To enable users to access the service, an online service distributes software that runs on users' computers, makes the connection to the service, and guides them through the available content and activities. As the Internet grew in popularity during the late 1990s, online services began to offer Internet access in an attempt to keep existing customers and attract new ones. While retaining their proprietary network and custom content, they have become Internet service providers (ISPs).

Web services such as MSN, AOL, and Yahoo! are called **portals.** A portal is a gateway that provides a conveniently organized subject guide to Internet content, fast-breaking news, local weather, stock quotes, sports scores, and e-mail (see Figure 8.6).

Figure 8.5
An online service like America Online provides a proprietary network that offers e-mail, chat rooms, discussions, and fee-based content, such as magazines and newspapers.

Figure 8.6
A portal such as Yahoo! is a gateway that provides a conveniently organized subject guide to Internet content, news, local weather, stock quotes, and much more.

THE INTERNET'S HISTORY

Where did the Internet come from? As we mentioned earlier, the Internet's origins date to Licklider's idea of a galactic network, which led to 1960s-era work on packet switching theory at MIT. The Internet is also based on studies at a private-sector military think tank, California-based Rand Corporation, that called for the construction of a military network that could continue to function even if enemies knocked out portions of the network. Rand researchers had independently concluded that a packet switching network offered the best chance of survivability in wartime. Under the leadership of Lawrence G. Roberts at DARPA, these researchers formulated the specifications for the Advanced Research Projects Agency Network, **ARPANET**. In 1968, the agency requested bids for development work.

With DARPA's leadership and funding, university and corporate researchers developed the technologies we use today, including routers, WANs, and Internet protocols (standards). ARPANET went online in September 1969 and connected four computers located in California and Utah. Although ARPANET access was initially restricted to universities or research centers with U.S. Defense Department contracts, the network grew rapidly. ARPANET became an international network in 1973, with the addition of computers at defense-related sites in England and Norway. By 1981, ARPANET connected 213 computers.

By 1984, it connected 1,000 computers, and by 1987, this figure had risen to 10,000. Universities lacking ARPANET access were clamoring to get it.

The Importance of Communication

Why did ARPANET grow so quickly? One reason is that network users came to see the network as an indispensable means of communication. Although ARPANET's designers thought the network would be used to exchange research data, users saw the network as a communications medium. Invented in 1972 by ARPANET researcher Ray Tomlinson, e-mail quickly became the most popular use of ARPANET. Researchers used e-mail and e-mail discussion groups to stay in touch with colleagues at other institutions. Researchers who lacked ARPANET access felt left out, so they pressured their universities to join the network.

From ARPANET to Internet

The ARPANET was a testbed network, designed to serve as the development platform for packet switching technology. The original ARPANET protocols had many deficiencies. As ARPANET researchers Robert Kahn and Vincent Cerf addressed the network's shortcomings, they created the Internet protocols that are now in use throughout the world. On January 1, 1983, the Internet protocols went online for the first time.

As Internet technology took shape, ARPANET moved steadily away from its military origins. In 1982, the civilian (ARPANET) network was separated from the military (MILNET) portions. Supervision of ARPANET passed to the U.S. National Science Foundation (NSF), which subsidized ARPANET to aid university researchers. NSF financed the construction of a new long-distance data transmission network, called NSFnet. The old ARPANET backbone was decommissioned in 1990, having performed its research function with spectacular success. Collectively, the NSFnet backbone and the various regional networks connected to it became known as the Internet.

The Rise of a New Mass Medium

In the early 1990s, the Internet was still primarily a university network, used mainly for communication and file exchange. By the late 1990s, it was on its way to becoming a new mass medium of global proportions (see Figure 8.7).

Two factors spurred this transformation. The first is the World Wide Web, developed in 1989. The first graphical **Web browsers** (which enable hypertext to become "live" on your computer screen), developed in 1994, transformed the Internet into something more than a communication and file exchange network: it became a medium for discovering and exploring information that even novices could enjoy. A second factor was the 1995 elimination of barriers to commercial activity on the Internet. Before 1995,

Destinations

If you'd like to learn more about Internet history, the best place to start is the Internet Society's "Internet Histories" page at **www.isoc.org/ internet/history**. The Internet Society is a professional organization for anyone interested in supporting the Internet's technical development.

Figure 8.7
Worldwide Internet Use

commercial traffic was forbidden on the taxpayer-funded NSFnet backbone. When NSF shut down the backbone and eliminated all Internet subsidies, commercial Internet development took off.

Who controls the Internet today? Like the world telephone system, the Internet is a huge information space made up of thousands of privately owned computers and networks, all of which agree to implement the Internet protocols and share

resources on the network. A variety of organizations are responsible for different aspects of the network. For example, the World Wide Web Consortium (W3C), based in Cambridge, Massachusetts, issues standards related to all aspects of the Web. Standards organizations cannot force vendors to follow these standards, but most Internet vendors understand that everyone loses if the standards aren't followed.

Internet Software: Clients and Servers

The Internet is *the* network of networks, but a network without software and applications wouldn't attract millions of users. What makes the Internet so appealing for many is the variety of ways people can use it. Made possible by special software, these uses are called Internet services.

An **Internet service** is best understood as a set of standards (protocols) that define how two types of programs, a **client** and a **server**, can communicate with each other through the Internet. A client, such as a Web browser, runs on the user's computer. Following the service's protocols, the client requests information from a server program, which is located on some other computer on the Internet. On the Web, content is made available by means of more than one million **Web servers**, located on computers all over the world. Other services require different types of servers (and different client programs).

To make use of the most popular Internet services, you need several client programs. That's why the two leading browsers, Netscape Navigator and Microsoft Internet Explorer, are available as part of software suites that include several popular clients in addition to the Web browser (see Figure 8.8). Figure 8.9 lists the clients available in both suites, as well as the services they support. (You'll learn more about these services in Chapter 9.) Most Internet users obtain additional client software to make use of services that these suites don't support, such as Internet Relay Chat (IRC). Figure 8.10 illustrates how to connect to the Internet via your browser.

Figure 8.8
Netscape Navigator and Microsoft Internet Explorer are the two leading browsers.

Clients Available in Popular Browser Suites

Client	Microsoft Internet Explorer Suite	Netscape Communicator
Web browser	Internet Explorer	Netscape Navigator
E-mail	Outlook Express	Netscape Messenger
Usenet	Outlook Express	Netscape Collabra
Internet telephony	Netmeeting	Netscape Conference

Figure 8.9

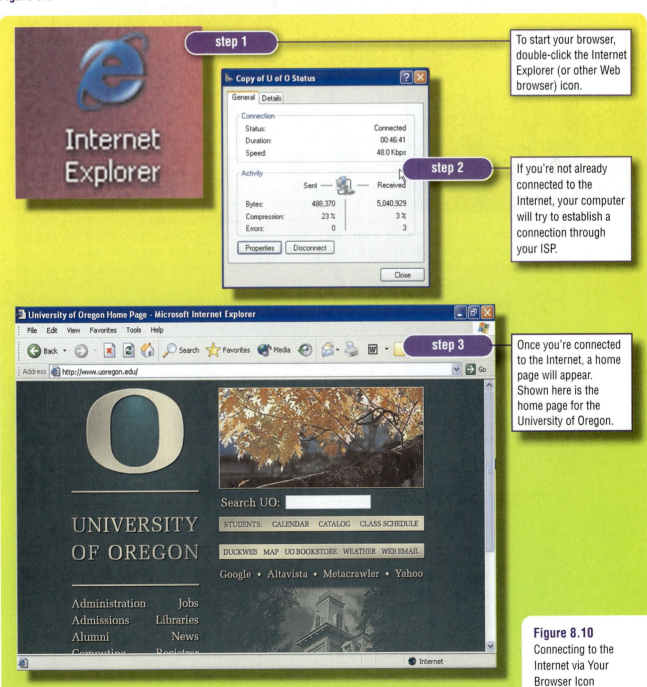

step 1

To start your browser, double-click the Internet Explorer (or other Web browser) icon.

step 2

If you're not already connected to the Internet, your computer will try to establish a connection through your ISP.

step 3

Once you're connected to the Internet, a home page will appear. Shown here is the home page for the University of Oregon.

Figure 8.10
Connecting to the Internet via Your Browser Icon

Exploring Internet Services

As we mentioned earlier, the Internet's capacity to work with many types of computers enables users of all popular computers—Macs, PCs, and UNIX systems—to access the Internet. After you're connected, you can take advantage of a lengthy and growing list of Internet services, described in this section.

Figure 8.11
E-mail is fast becoming indispensable.

E-MAIL: STAYING IN TOUCH

The most popular application on the Internet is **e-mail (electronic mail)** (see Figure 8.11). As you probably know, to send e-mail, you need to know the recipient's **e-mail address**. E-mail addresses include a unique cyberspace address for the recipient, such as **myname@someserver.com**. When you receive e-mail, you can reply to the message, forward it to someone else, store it for later action, or delete it. Usually, e-mail arrives in a few seconds, but it's stored on the ISP's computer until the recipient logs on and downloads the message. In addition to sending text messages, you can include attachments, such as a word processing document or a photo.

THE WORLD WIDE WEB: ACCESSING INFORMATION

Second in popularity only to e-mail, the World Wide Web is a global hypertext system implemented on the Internet. It's important to reread the last few words of the preceding sentence; the Web *uses* the Internet for its existence, but it's a separate entity. The Internet itself is the physical connections of millions of networks. The Web is the use of **hypertext** and Web browsers to share information within cyberspace.

The Web's hypertext provides an intuitive and fun way of browsing through information. In a hypertext document,

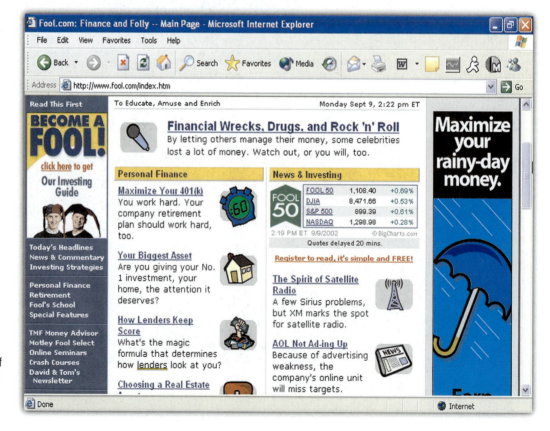

Figure 8.12
This site is an example of a Web page that features interesting hyperlinks and graphics.

UNWANTED E-MAIL

Spam: Can It Be Stopped?

Many e-mail users receive unsolicited e-mail advertising, called **spam**. This mail is sent by **spammers**, businesses that specialize in sending such mail. Spammers believe that they're doing only what direct marketing mail firms do: sending legitimate advertising. But they don't acknowledge a crucial difference between unsolicited postal advertising and spam. In postal advertising, the advertiser pays for the postage. In spam, the recipient pays the postage, in the form of Internet access fees. According to a coalition of Internet service providers, every Internet user is paying an average of $2 per month in additional fees because of costs directly attributable to the activities of spammers.

Most Internet users detest spam, and some find it so annoying that they stop using the Internet. For businesses, spam is a costly nuisance. On several occasions, spams on a gigantic scale have overwhelmed mail servers, resulting in impaired service for legitimate, paying customers.

Chances are that little or nothing of worth is being peddled: pornographic Web sites, phony get-rich-quick scams, bogus stock deals, rip-off work-at-home schemes, health and diet scams, and merchandise of questionable quality.

Can you filter out spam? You can try. Most spam, however, originates from a new account, which is almost immediately closed down after the service provider receives hundreds of thousands of outraged complaints. The spammer just moves on to a new account. Internet businesses like SpamCop will help to protect you from spam for a fee. In addition, software alternatives such as Spam Buster by Contact Plus Corporation and Spam Killer by McAfee let you set rules for limiting your inbox spam. Free software such as MailWasher and Mailshell help you clear spam automatically from your system. But there is so far no way to get rid of spam entirely.

Don't reply to spam or request to be "removed" from a spammer's mailing list. All you accomplish is verifying that your e-mail address is valid. A mailing list consisting of validated addresses is much more valuable than a "dirty" list, so all that will happen is that you'll get even more spam.

Increasingly, there are efforts to persuade legislatures—at both the state and federal levels—to pass laws against spam. Bills have been introduced in Congress, and the Senate's "CAN SPAM" act is aimed at deceptive e-mails, nonsolicited pornography, and marketing. One problem: the Direct Marketing Association (DMA) believes that the appropriate solution is an "opt-out" system, in which spammed e-mail users can request that the sender remove their names from the mailing list—but that's just what e-mail users have been trained not to do, out of fear that they'll receive even more spam than before. In addition, efforts to outlaw spam run afoul of free speech guarantees under the U.S. Constitution's First Amendment, which applies to businesses as well as individuals. States that attempt to outlaw spam, as Washington did, may find that their laws are thrown out of court because they inhibit interstate commerce. One solution: under consideration is a Congressional measure that would give Internet service providers the right to sue spammers for violating their spam policies.

For now, there's one thing for sure: if you haven't been spammed yet, you will be.

CURRENTS

---

certain words, called **hyperlinks**, are underlined or otherwise highlighted. When you click a hyperlink, your browser retrieves and displays the document associated with that hyperlink. This retrieval is possible because every Web page has its own unique address, called a **uniform resource locator** (**URL**), that specifies precisely where it is located on the Internet.

The Web is appealing not only because of its use of hypertext for browsing through information, but also because of its graphical richness, made possible by its integration of text and graphics. Increasingly, Web pages are as well designed as the pages of commercial magazines, and they often feature the quality fonts you'd associate with desktop publishing (see Figure 8.12).

FTP: TRANSFERRING FILES

FTP (**File Transfer Protocol**) provides a way to transfer files via the Internet. With an FTP client, you can transfer files from an FTP server's file directories in an operation called **downloading**. In **uploading**, you transfer files *to* the server and write them to a directory on the remote computer. FTP can transfer two types of files:

ASCII (text files) and **binary** (program files, graphics, or documents saved in proprietary file formats).

To use FTP, you need a user name and a password. An exception is called **anonymous FTP**. In anonymous FTP, files are made publicly available for downloading. It's called anonymous FTP because you log on by typing the word *anonymous* instead of a user name, and you supply your e-mail address as your password. The leading Web browsers, Microsoft Internet Explorer and Netscape Navigator, support file downloading from anonymous FTP sites, so you don't need any special skills to use anonymous FTP. Downloadable files are listed as hyperlinks; when you click such a hyperlink, downloading begins automatically.

Exercise caution when downloading executable program files and data files of unknown origin from the Web. (An **executable** program file is a file capable of running on your computer.) If you download software from a site that doesn't inspect files using up-to-date virus-checking software, you could infect your computer with a virus. Most Internet users believe that it's safe to download software from vendor sites (Web sites maintained by software companies) and from leading

shareware sites. However, you shouldn't download software to any computer that contains vital data. Also, be aware that many viruses are spread in the data files of productivity programs, such as Microsoft Word or Excel. These files may contain destructive viruses masquerading as **macros**, miniprograms that automatically carry out a series of program commands. If you download data files, be sure to check them with an antivirus program that can detect macro viruses.

Most downloadable software is **compressed**. In file compression, lengthy but frequently used data patterns are replaced with a short code, enabling compression software to reduce the size of program files by 50 percent or more. Compression enables faster downloads, but you must decompress the file after downloading it. In decompression, the compression software finds the short codes and replaces them with the longer data patterns. After decompressing the downloaded software, you can install it on your computer.

Some compressed files are designed to decompress automatically when you launch them; others require you to obtain and install decompression software. On Windows systems, the most widely used decompression software is WinZip

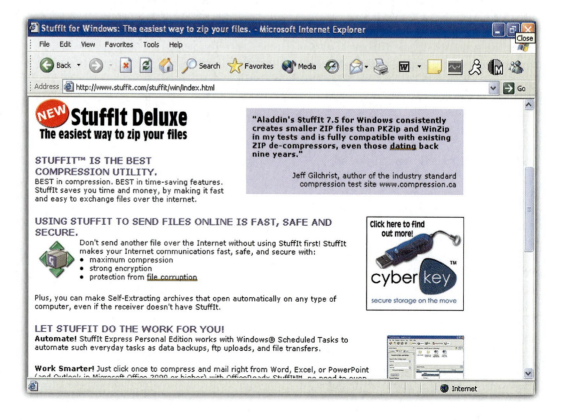

Figure 8.13

StuffIt is compression software used for both Mac and Windows systems.

Compression Software

Extension	Compression Software Needed
.exe	None; this file is designed to decompress itself automatically
.zip	WinZip (**www.winzip.com**) or ZipIt (**www.maczipit.com**)
.hqx	BinHex encoding; decompress with StuffIt Expander
.sit	StuffIt; decompress with StuffIt Expander

Figure 8.14

(**www.winzip.com**). To survive the trip over the Internet, Macintosh software is encoded using BinHex and may also be compressed with a compression program called StuffIt (see Figure 8.13). You can determine how a file was compressed by looking at the file's extension (see Figure 8.14).

You can easily download publicly accessible files by using a Web browser, but in some cases, you'll need an FTP client to upload files. If you'd like to publish your own Web pages, you need to use FTP to upload your pages to your ISP's Web publishing directories so that your pages are available to other Internet users. The best FTP clients enable you to work with remote file directories as if those directories were on your own computer.

USENET: JOINING ONLINE DISCUSSIONS

Usenet is a discussion system accessible through the Internet. It consists of thousands of topically named **newsgroups**, each of which contains **articles** that users have posted for all to see. Users can respond to specific articles by posting **follow-up articles**, and in time, a thread of discussion develops as people reply to the replies. A **thread** is a series of articles that offer a continuing commentary on the same general subject.

To access Usenet, you use a **Usenet client** that communicates with a **Usenet server** (also called an **NNTP server**). Usenet client software comes with most browser suites. To begin using your Usenet client, you download the entire list of newsgroups available on your ISP's server. Then you **subscribe** to the newsgroups you want to follow. When you open the newsgroup, your client downloads the current article list, which may contain anywhere from a few dozen to several thousand messages.

Usenet newsgroups are organized into categories called **hierarchies**. These categories are further divided into several

Standard Newsgroup Hierarchies

Hierarchy Name	Description of Topics Covered
comp	Everything related to computers and computer networks, including applications, compression, databases, multimedia, and programming
misc	Subjects that do not fit in other standard newsgroup hierarchies, including activism, books, business, consumer issues, health, investing, jobs, and law
sci	The sciences and social sciences, including anthropology, archaeology, chemistry, economics, math, physics, and statistics
soc	Social issues, including adoption, college-related issues, feminism, human rights, and world cultures
talk	Debate on controversial subjects, including abortion, atheism, euthanasia, gun control, and religion
news	Usenet itself, including announcements and materials for new users
rec	All aspects of recreation, including aviation, backcountry sports, bicycles, boats, gardening, and scouting

Figure 8.15

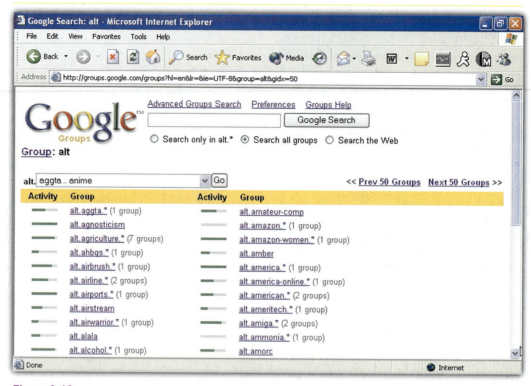

Figure 8.16
Anyone with the requisite technical knowledge can create an alt newsgroup, but servers aren't under any obligation to make them available. The Google Groups page carries a number of alt newsgroups.

Destinations

Learn the rules of netiquette by visiting "Dear Emily Postnews," the authoritative voice concerning Usenet manners, at **www.templetons.com/brad/emily.html**.

subcategories (also called hierarchies, if they include more than one newsgroup). These subcategories include the **standard newsgroups**, the **alt newsgroups**, and the **biz newsgroups**, each of which include additional subcategories and hundreds of newsgroups.

Standard newsgroups You're more likely to find rewarding, high-quality discussions in the standard newsgroups (also called **world newsgroups**), which can't be established without a formal voting procedure. Figure 8.15 lists the standard newsgroup hierarchies. Usenet servers are expected to carry all these standard newsgroups, with the exception of those in the talk hierarchy.

Alt newsgroups The alt hierarchy is much more freewheeling. Anyone with the requisite technical knowledge can create an alt newsgroup (which explains why so many of them have silly or offensive names), but servers aren't under any obligation to make them available (see Figure 8.16).

Biz newsgroups These newsgroups are devoted to the commercial uses of the Internet.

In addition to the standard and alt newsgroups, most servers carry many **local newsgroups**, which are created to suit the needs of a specific community, such as a university. Some of these are of interest outside their context, as well; for example, Symantec Corporation, a major software vendor, maintains the Symantec hierarchy. Technical support engineers monitor the groups and offer solutions to problems users encounter with Symantec products.

If you're sure you understand a newsgroup's mission, you can use your Usenet client to **post** your own messages. But be careful what you say on Usenet. When you post an article, you're publishing in a public medium. Although most Usenet servers erase messages more than a few days old, several Internet services store Usenet messages in Web-accessible archives.

Also, be aware that you'll be expected to follow the rules of **netiquette**, guidelines for good manners when you're communicating through Usenet. For example, some Usenet clients enable you to post messages using formatting, but this is considered bad manners because people who have text-only clients see a lot of meaningless formatting symbols. If you violate netiquette rules, you may receive **flames** (angry, critical messages) from other newsgroup subscribers.

LISTSERV: ELECTRONIC MAIL LISTS

A **listserv** is an automatic mailing list server developed by Eric Thomas for BITNET in 1986. When e-mail is addressed to a listserv mailing list, it's automatically broadcast to everyone on the list. The result is similar to a newsgroup or forum, except that the messages are transmitted as e-mail and are therefore available only to individuals on the list. Most colleges and universities manage listservs. The most common listserv program is called Majordomo, which is distributed as freeware.

IRC: TEXT CHATTING IN REAL TIME

Internet Relay Chat (**IRC**) is an Internet service that enables you to join chat groups, called **channels**, and get into real-time, text-based conversations. IRC servers typically make thousands of channels available; some cover a specific topic, whereas others are gathering places for groups of friends.

When you join a channel, you'll find that others are already there, chatting away, with their messages appearing on-screen (see Figure 8.17). Each message is prefaced with the participant's nickname. Sometimes IRC participants will send a special type of message, called an **action**, that describes a behavior (such as, "Walker shakes your hand"). Normally, your messages are seen by everyone in the channel, but it's possible to send a **whisper**, which is seen by only the one person to whom you send it.

Sometimes IRC isn't a friendly place. You may encounter various sorts of antisocial

Destinations

To get started with IRC, visit the IRChelp.org Help Archive at **www.irchelp.org**. You'll find lots of information devoted to making your IRC experience a rewarding one.

Figure 8.17
Chat rooms are now being used as online "classrooms."

behaviors, including **flooding** (sending repeated messages so that no one else can get a word in edgewise) and **nuking** (exploiting bugs that cause your computer to crash). Bear in mind, too, that some of the "people" in channels aren't people at all, but rather miniprograms called **bots**. Bots are illegal on some servers, but on others they're used to greet newcomers (and sometimes to harass them). Also, every channel has a channel operator who can kick you out of the channel for any reason, or none at all.

INSTANT MESSAGING: E-MAILING MADE FASTER

What's faster than e-mail and more convenient than picking up the phone? **Instant messaging (IM) systems** let you know when someone you know who also uses the IM system (a buddy or contact) is online. You can then contact this person

and exchange messages and attachments, including sound files.

To use IM, you need to install instant messenger software from an instant messenger service, such as AOL's Instant Messenger or Microsoft's Windows Messenger, onto your computer (see Figure 8.18). You can use IM systems on any type of computer, including handhelds. Many instant messenger services also give you access to information such as daily news, stocks, sports scores, and the weather. You can also keep track of your appointments. At this time, there is no standard instant messaging protocol, which means that you can send messages only to people who are using the same instant messaging service you are.

INTERNET TELEPHONY: REAL-TIME VOICE AND VIDEO

Although the Internet isn't ideal for real-time voice and video, you can place a "telephone" call to another Internet user, who must be online and have a computer equipped with a microphone and a sound card. If you and the person you're calling have a digital video camera, you can converse with real-time videoconferencing as well. Don't expect spectacular quality; you'll hear echoes and delays in the audio, and the picture will be small, grainy, and jerky. But there are no long-distance charges! You can try Internet telephony by using the clients supplied with the two most popular browsers.

In addition to Internet voice and video calls, Internet telephony products support real-time conferencing with such features as a shared whiteboard (a space where callers can draw simple graphics or share pictures), file exchange, and text chatting. Current technology doesn't enable you to videoconference with more than one caller at a time, but you can create an audio conference with as many users as you want (see Figure 8.19).

Until home users can obtain faster Internet connections, Internet telephony and videoconferencing will prove most useful on corporate intranets, where bandwidth (the number of bits per second that a channel can handle) is in ample supply.

Figure 8.18

An IM system lets you know when someone you know who also uses the IM system is online. You can then contact this person and exchange messages.

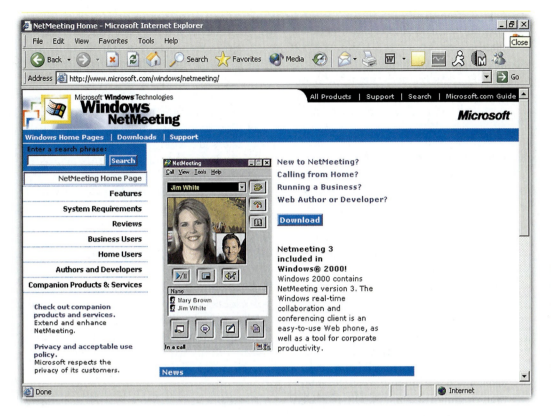

Figure 8.19
Microsoft NetMeeting's data conferencing features let you collaborate with a group of people—drawing on a shared whiteboard, sending text messages, and transferring data.

How the Internet Works: A Geography of Cyberspace

You don't need a degree in electrical engineering to understand the basics of how the Internet works. In this section, we'll explore the various components of the Internet, beginning with your computer.

CONFIGURING YOUR COMPUTER FOR INTERNET ACCESS

To connect to the Internet, your computer must support Internet networking protocols. Today, this support is built into popular operating systems, such as Mac OS, Microsoft Windows, and Linux. You also need communications equipment, such as a telephone, DSL, or cable modem, an ISDN adapter, or an Ethernet card, depending on how you're planning to access the Internet.

ACCESSING THE INTERNET

You can access the Internet in the following ways:

Shell access The least expensive type of Internet access, **shell access** requires a modem and a phone line. You get access to the shell (user interface) of a UNIX computer, enabling you to use text-based applications such as e-mail. UNIX knowledge is required for shell access. In this method, your computer isn't really connected to the Internet. You're using it as a terminal to access a computer that's connected to the Internet.

Dial-up access with Point-to-Point Protocol (PPP) Most home users access the Internet this way. You need a modem and an analog phone line, or an ISDN adapter and an ISDN telephone line. With this method, your computer is directly connected to the Internet, but it's usually assigned a temporary IP address. For this reason, you can't conveniently run server software on a computer connected to the Internet

Destinations

Looking for an ISP? A good place to start is The List, at **www.thelist.com**, a buyer's guide to ISPs. You can search for an ISP by area code or country.

with PPP; to run a server, you need a system that has a fixed IP address and a registered domain name (see "The Domain Name System," later in this chapter). Some ISPs use an older protocol, called SLIP, which isn't as efficient as PPP.

Digital Subscriber Line (DSL) Available in many urban areas, DSL connections offer high-speed access and a permanent online connection. DSL requires a special, digital telephone line. One drawback of DSL is that service doesn't extend more than a few miles from telephone switching stations (although this distance is being extended), so this service is often unavailable in rural areas.

Cable and satellite access Cable TV companies are increasingly offering Internet access at speeds much faster than dial-up modems. Satellite access enables fast downloads but requires a phone line and a modem for uploading data. Like modem access, these access methods give your computer a temporary IP address, so you can't run server programs in such a way that other Internet users can find your content.

LAN access If the company you're working for has a LAN, or if you're attending a university that provides Ethernet access in residence halls, you can access the Internet by means of the local area network. LAN access is generally much faster than dial-up access, but the performance you experience depends on how many LAN users are trying to access the Internet at the same time. With LAN access, your computer probably has a permanently assigned IP address, and you may be able to run server programs.

INTERNET SERVICE PROVIDERS (ISPS)

As we mentioned earlier, Internet service providers (ISPs) sell Internet subscriptions to home and business users (see Figure 8.20). For home users, they offer dial-up access. Many ISPs also provide direct connections for businesses using leased lines.

BACKBONES

To understand how data travels on the Internet, it's helpful to compare this journey to an interstate car trip. When you connect to the Internet and request access to a Web page, your request travels by local connections—the city streets—to your Internet service provider's local point of presence (POP). From there, your ISP relays your request to the regional **backbone**, a highway that connects your town to a larger metropolitan region. Your request then goes to a **network access point (NAP)**—a freeway on-ramp—where regional backbones connect to national backbone networks. And from there, the message gets on the national backbone network, the freeway. Near the destination, your message gets off the freeway and travels regional and local networks until it reaches its destination.

The Internet is becoming more complex every day as new backbone service providers expand the network and more ISPs sell this bandwidth to business and residential customers (see Figure 8.21). How is this growth accommodated? Because the Internet isn't centrally administered, the network couldn't work without its automated **routers** (physical switching devices), which route Internet messages to their

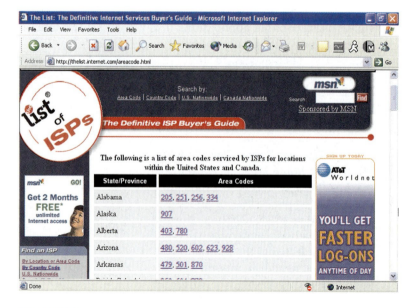

Figure 8.20
"The List" is a buyer's guide to ISPs that lists nearly 5,000 Internet service providers.

destinations. The Internet's routers are designed to share information with each other automatically. At any given moment, a router automatically possesses up-to-date information about the portion of the network to which it is directly connected. For this reason, new service providers can extend the Internet without obtaining permission from anyone. All that's needed is a registration process, which we'll discuss later in the chapter.

As local service providers extend the Internet, traffic grows rapidly. Backbone service providers are expanding capacity at a breakneck speed; for example, AT&T is doubling its Internet capacity every three months or so. Still, Internet experts worry that backbone service providers won't be able to construct bandwidth capacity rapidly enough to keep up with the Internet's burgeoning growth.

THE INTERNET PROTOCOLS (TCP/IP)

A network isn't just the physical transmission media that carry its signals, but also the protocols (standards) that enable

devices connected to the network to communicate with each other. The Internet protocols, collectively called **TCP/IP**, are open protocols that define how the Internet works. TCP/IP is an abbreviation for the two most important Internet protocols: the Transmission Control Protocol (TCP) and the Internet Protocol (IP). However, more than 100 protocols make up the entire Internet protocol suite, including the many protocols that define the Internet services we discussed previously in this chapter.

Internet Protocol (IP)

Of all the Internet protocols, the most fundamental is the **Internet Protocol (IP)**. IP defines the Internet's addressing scheme, which enables any Internet-connected computer to be uniquely identified. An Internet address (IP address) is a four-part number, with the parts separated by periods (such as 128.254.108.7). The IP protocol is a connectionless protocol. This means that with IP, two computers don't have to be online at the same time to exchange data. The sending computer just keeps trying until the message gets through.

Destinations

Explore the Internet's physical structure at "An Atlas of Cyberspace," located at **www.cyber-geography.org/atlas/atlas.html**. This site is maintained by Martin Dodge at the Centre for Advanced Spatial Analysis, University of London.

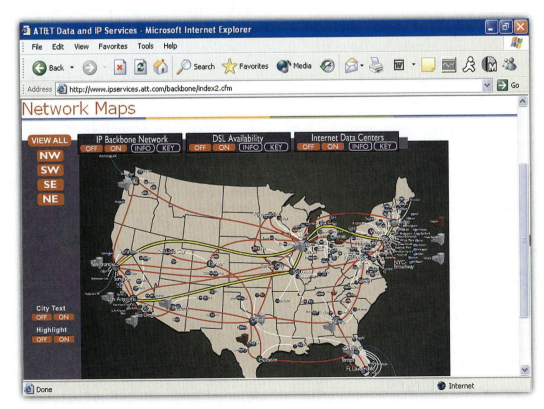

Figure 8.21
AT&T IP Services provides a backbone network in the United States.

Transmission Control Protocol (TCP)

Some Internet services (such as the Web) need two computers to communicate with each other. The **Transmission Control Protocol** (**TCP**) defines how one Internet-connected computer can contact another and exchange control and confirmation messages. You can see TCP in action when you're using the Web; just watch your browser's status line. You'll see messages such as "Contacting server," "Receiving data," and "Closing connection."

THE DOMAIN NAME SYSTEM

Because IP addresses are difficult to type and remember, the Internet uses a system called the **Domain Name System** (**DNS**). DNS enables users to type an address that includes letters as well as numbers. For example, MSN.com has the numeric address 207.68.172.246. You could type the numeric address into your browser, but most of us find that it's much easier to use text names. A process called **domain name registration** enables individuals and organizations to register a domain name with a service organization called the **InterNIC**. Within large organizations, administrators can assign internal domain names without having to go through the InterNIC.

How do domain names work? The secret lies in computers called **domain name servers** (also called **DNS servers**). These computers maintain up-to-date lists that match local domain names with the correct IP addresses. Suppose you want to access the computer that houses the Internet Explorer home page at Microsoft. When you request this page, your local ISP's domain name server contacts Microsoft's domain name server and asks for this computer's IP address. In this way, you always get the correct IP address, even if Microsoft moves the content to a different machine.

Domain names can tell you a great deal about where a computer is located. For computers located in the United States, **top-level domain** (**TLD**) **names** (the *last* part of the domain name) indicate the type of organization in which the computer is located (see Figure 8.22). Outside the United States, the top-level domain indicates the name of the country in which the

Destinations

See for yourself how the domain name service works. Access the "NSLOOKUP" page at **www.infobear.com/nslookup.shtml** and type a domain name such as **www.microsoft.com**. Click the run button and you'll see a message showing the IP address associated with the domain name you typed.

Common Top-Level Domain Names

TLD	Used By
com	Commercial businesses
edu	Educational institutions
gov	Government agencies
mil	Military
net	Network organizations (such as Internet service providers)
org	Non-profit organizations

Figure 8.22

New Top-Level Domain Names

TLD	Used By
aero	Air-transport industry
biz	Businesses
coop	Cooperatives
info	Unrestricted use
museum	Museums
name	Individuals
pro	Accountants, lawyers, physicians, and other professionals

Figure 8.23

computer is located, such as ca (Canada), uk (Great Britain), and jp (Japan).

Recently, the Internet Corporation for Assigned Names and Numbers (ICANN) expanded the number of top-level domains to include those listed in Figure 8.23.

For more information on the Internet Corporation for Assigned Names and Numbers, visit **www.icann.org**.

Intranets: Using TCP/IP Inside the Enterprise

The Internet has developed into a mature technology, and millions of people know how to access and exchange information using Internet e-mail, Web browsers, FTP, and discussion groups. And that's precisely why so many companies are building internal networks based on TCP/IP. Called **intranets**, these networks enable users to use the same familiar tools they use on the Internet. However, these networks are intended for internal use only and aren't accessible from the external Internet. To insulate the intranet from unwanted external accesses, computers equipped with **firewall** software screen incoming data, while allowing selected insiders to access external resources (see Figure 8.24).

Intranets are transforming the way organizations produce and share information. Because it's so easy to create a Web page, companies can distribute Web publishing duties throughout the enterprise. Previously, the IS department would have to make information available; now every department can maintain its own Web page, making its resources available to everyone. By moving expensive print-based publications, such as employee manuals and telephone books, to the internal Web, companies can realize enormous savings and greatly reduce the amount of trash that goes to local landfills.

Some companies open their intranets to selected allies, such as research labs, suppliers, or key customers. Called **extranets**, these networks use the external Internet for connection, but the data traverses the Internet in encrypted form, safe from prying eyes.

The Future of the Internet

Imagine a billion Internet users by 2015. What's more, hundreds of millions of people will be connecting with super-fast connections, using technologies such as cable modems and ADSL (Asymmetric Digital Subscriber Line). ADSL is a type of Digital Subscriber Line service for Internet access that enables download speeds of 1.5 Mbps. Can the Internet handle this growth? According to Internet experts, key changes must take place to ensure that the Internet doesn't become overwhelmed by its own success.

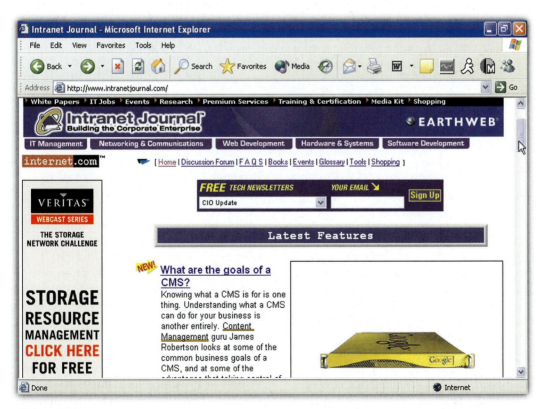

Figure 8.24
Intranet Journal offers advice and news on corporate intranet design and security.

ETHICAL DEBATES

IMPACTS

What's Hiding on Your Computer? Spyware, Adware, and Pop-Ups

By now you know the dangers of viruses, those insidious files that can damage your computer system. You've probably also heard of **cookies**, electronic files that are deposited on your hard disk when you visit certain Web sites. But do you know what else may be hiding on your computer? Ever heard of spyware or adware?

Spyware is Internet software that is placed on your computer without you knowing it. It helps outside organizations gather information about you (such as your login name and password) and then relays that information to the spyware source. Spyware usually enters your system through the Internet, often when you download software—most often shareware and freeware. Spyware may be launched by individuals, organizations, or the government. Some spyware is capable of recording every keystroke you type and every Internet address you visit. Spyware isn't necessarily always concerned with clandestine activity, but it's always a threat to your privacy.

If you've ever downloaded software and see a banner advertisement or pop-up, you've also downloaded a form of **adware**. Adware is like spyware only it's created specifically by an advertising agency to collect information about your Internet habits. Although ethically questionable, shareware and freeware creators sometimes allow advertisers to tag along and have their adware downloaded onto your computer at the same time you download software.

Spyware and adware are so commonplace that if you've ever downloaded anything from the Internet, you probably have some form of spyware or adware hiding on your computer.

How can you get rid of spyware and adware? One company, Lavasoft (**www.lavasoftusa.com**), offers a free spyware removal utility called Ad-aware that scans your memory, registry, and hard drives for known spyware and eliminates it safely. Because new spyware is created all the time, you should use the utility frequently to scan your system.

And if you hate pop-ups, an Internet privacy company called Panicware (**www.panicware.com**) has a Pop-Up Stopper program that can take care of these annoyances for you. The program lets you adjust the intensity of the pop-up stopping. (Be warned however: if you download the Pop-Up Stopper but need to use pop-up utilities for online quizzes, for example, the utility can keep such pop-ups from functioning properly.) Both Pop-Up Stopper and Ad-aware have free download versions, but advanced versions, with more options, can be purchased for a small fee.

Knowing that these privacy intrusions exist, and that there is something you can do about them, is an important defense. As you make your way through the Net, know that there are people watching you, and consider taking proactive steps to protect your privacy.

MORE INTERNET ADDRESSES

The IP protocol allows for a total of approximately four billion unique IP addresses, but that's not enough. The reason has to do with the way the four-part IP addresses (such as 128.254.207.8) are broken up into distinct categories, called **classes**. Class A supports up to 127 large networks with up to 16 million addresses for each; class B supports up to 16,000 networks with up to 65,000 addresses for each; and class C supports 2 million networks with 254 addresses each. There aren't enough class A or B networks, and class C networks are too small. The solution lies in a new version of the Internet Protocol, called **IPv6**, but existing Internet equipment must be modified to work with the new protocol.

MORE BANDWIDTH

Internet 2 (**I2**) is a collaborative effort between more than 120 U.S. universities, several U.S. Government agencies, and leading computer and telecommunications companies. It's a project of the University Corporation for Advanced Internet Development (UCAID). The I2 project is developing and testing high-performance network and telecommunications techniques. These improvements will eventually find their way to the public Internet. To test I2 ideas, universities participating in I2 are establishing **gigabits per second Points of Presence** (**gigaPoP**). These network connection points link to various high-speed networks that federal government agencies have developed.

HOME | Takeaway Points | Key Terms and Concepts | Matching | Multiple Choice | Fill-In | Short Answer | Exercises/ Projects | Web Research | CHAPTER REVIEW

TAKEAWAY POINTS

- The Internet is the network that connects hundreds of thousands of local area networks (LANs), creating a global medium in which millions of computers can directly dial each other and share resources.

- Internet protocols do not specify low-level network characteristics, so Internet data can travel on any type of network. In addition, networks don't have to be altered to carry Internet data.

- The Internet's popularity stems from its capability to foster communication, the fact that it can work with virtually all types of computers and networks, and the development of user-friendly tools such as Web browsers.

- Online services market a proprietary network that offers free and fee-based content, e-mail, and chat groups. As the Internet grew in popularity during the late 1990s, online services began to offer Internet access. While retaining their proprietary network and custom content, they have become Internet service providers (ISPs).

- Internet services are defined by protocols. Software includes clients (programs that access information) and servers (programs that deliver requested information).

- Popular Internet services include e-mail (communication), the World Wide Web (information browsing), FTP (file exchange), Usenet, listserv, instant messaging, Internet Relay Chat (text chatting), and Internet telephony (phone calls through the Internet and videoconferencing).

- An Internet address (IP address) is a four-part number that uniquely identifies one of the millions of computers connected to the Internet. A domain name is an easy-to-type and easy-to-remember equivalent of the numerical address.

- Intranets enable companies to set up internal communication and information systems that use familiar Internet tools, such as e-mail and Web browsers. They also enable companies to distribute publication tasks and save money by decreasing print publications.

- Tomorrow's Internet will feature a larger address space and higher bandwidth on backbone networks. It will be much more crowded but, hopefully, faster.

1 2 3 4 5 6 7 **8** 9 10 11 12 13 14 15 16

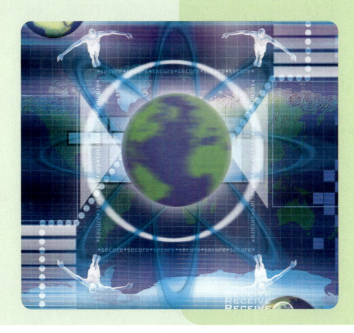

CHAPTER REVIEW | Takeaway Points | **Key Terms and Concepts** | Matching | Multiple Choice | Fill-In | Short Answer | Exercises/Projects | Web Research | **HOME**

KEY TERMS AND CONCEPTS

action
adware
alt newsgroups
anonymous FTP
ARPANET
article
ASCII
backbone
binary
biz newsgroups
bot
cable access
channel
classes
client
compressed
cookie
cross-platform network
Digital Subscriber Line (DSL)
domain name registration
domain name server
     (DNS server)
Domain Name System (DNS)
downloading
electronic commerce
     (e-commerce)
e-mail (electronic mail)
e-mail address
executable
extranet
firewall

flame
flooding
FTP (File Transfer Protocol)
follow-up article
gigabits per second Points of
     Presence (gigaPoP)
hierarchy
hyperlink
hypertext
Information Superhighway
instant messaging (IM) system
Internet
Internet 2 (I2)
Internet address (IP address)
Internet Protocol (IP)
Internet Relay Chat (IRC)
Internet service
Internet service provider (ISP)
InterNIC
interoperability
intranet
IPv6
LAN access
listserv
local newsgroup
macro
media convergence
netiquette
network access point (NAP)
newsgroup
nuking

online service
platform
point-to-point protocol (PPP)
portal
post
router
satellite access
server
shell access
spam
spammer
spyware
standard newsgroups
     (world newsgroups)
subscribe
thread
top level domain
     (TLD) name
Transmission Control
     Protocol (TCP)
TCP/IP
uniform resource locator
     (URL)
uploading
Usenet
Usenet client
Usenet server
     (NNTP server)
Web browser
Web server
whisper

HOME | Takeaway Points | Key Terms and Concepts | **Matching** | Multiple Choice | Fill-In | Short Answer | Exercises/ Projects | Web Research | **CHAPTER REVIEW**

MATCHING

Match each key term in the left column with the most accurate definition in the right column.

_____ 1. Internet
_____ 2. portal
_____ 3. DSL
_____ 4. browser
_____ 5. local newsgroups
_____ 6. platform
_____ 7. DNS servers
_____ 8. netiquette
_____ 9. executable
_____ 10. TCP/IP
_____ 11. binary
_____ 12. shell access
_____ 13. Internet Relay Chat
_____ 14. Internet service
_____ 15. bots

a. guidelines for good manners when you are communicating through Usenet

b. newsgroups created to suit the needs of a specific community

c. miniprograms

d. a technology that links LANs into large, distance-conquering technology

e. open protocols that define how the Internet works

f. a distinct type of computer that uses a certain type of processor and operating system

g. the least expensive type of Internet access, requiring a modem and a phone line

h. a gateway that provides a conveniently organized subject guide to Internet content and free e-mail

i. a set of standards that define how two types of programs can communicate with each other through the Internet

j. program files, graphics, or documents saved in proprietary file formats

k. an Internet service that enables the user to join chat groups

l. transformed the Internet into something more than a communication file and exchange network

m. offers high-speed access and a permanent online connection

n. computers that maintain lists that match local domain names with correct IP addresses

o. a file capable of running on your computer

CHAPTER REVIEW: 1 2 3 4 5 6 7 8 9 10 11 12 13 14 15 16

MULTIPLE CHOICE

Circle the correct choice for each of the following.

1. Which of the following networks best describes the functional structure of the Internet?
   a. Metropolitan area network (MAN)
   b. Cross-platform network
   c. Local area network (LAN)
   d. Client/server network

2. Which of the following is a client program?
   a. Hypertext
   b. ARPANET
   c. Internet address
   d. Web browser

3. Which of the following Web services provides free e-mail access?
   a. ARPANET
   b. Portals
   c. Listservs
   d. Usenet

4. This is the top-level domain name frequently used by ISPs.
   a. .gov
   b. .edu
   c. .net
   d. .com

5. IRC is an acronym for this.
   a. Internet Research Commission
   b. Internet Ready Communication
   c. Internet Relay Chat
   d. Internet Report Committee

6. Which of the following is absolutely necessary to connect to the Internet?
   a. A computer that supports the network access point protocols
   b. Communications equipment such as a modem or ISDN adapter
   c. Shell access
   d. LAN access

7. Which of the following is an internal network, based on TCP/IP, that gives users the same familiar tools they use on the Internet?
   a. Local area network (LAN)
   b. Intranet
   c. Extranet
   d. Firewall

8. Which of the following lets you know when someone you know is online?
   a. Client software
   b. Internet Explorer
   c. Online services
   d. Instant messaging systems

9. Which of the following provides the slowest Internet connection?
   a. Dial-up access
   b. Digital Subscriber Line (DSL)
   c. Cable access
   d. LAN

10. Debates on controversial subjects are covered in which newsgroup hierarchy?
    a. Comp
    b. Misc
    c. Talk
    d. News

| HOME | Takeaway Points | Key Terms and Concepts | Matching | Multiple Choice | Fill-In | Short Answer | Exercises/ Projects | Web Research | CHAPTER REVIEW |

FILL-IN

In the blanks provided, write the correct answer for each of the following.

1. A _____ is the unique address assigned to every Web page.

2. An _____ provides a proprietary network that offers e-mail, chat rooms, discussions, and fee-based content.

3. A _____ is a gateway that provides a conveniently organized subject guide to Internet content.

4. _____ are internal networks that are based on the TCP/IP protocol.

5. _____ are networks that use the external Internet to allow selected users access to corporate intranets.

6. _____ provides a way for users to transfer files via the Internet.

7. _____ sell Internet subscriptions to home and business users.

8. _____ is a collaborative effort among universities, government agencies, and leading computer and telecommunications companies.

9. _____ means transferring files from a remote server to your computer, and _____ means transferring files from your computer to a remote server.

10. _____ is the most popular service of the Internet.

11. An _____ is a four-part number that is separated by periods.

12. The unification of all earlier media, including newspaper, TV, radio, and telephone, is called _____.

13. Most home users access the Internet by using the _____ protocol.

14. _____ defines how one Internet-connected computer can contact another and exchange control and confirmation messages.

15. _____ enables individuals and organizations to register domain names with the InterNIC.

SHORT ANSWER

1. What is the difference between an Internet address and a domain name?

2. What is the difference between client and server software? Give an example of each.

3. Explain the difference between downloading and uploading files. Have you used the Internet to transfer files? What types of files did you transfer? What type of software did you use? Explain why it is dangerous to download executable (.exe) files.

4. Do any of your instructors use the Internet to distribute class materials? If they do, describe what software you need to access their materials and the types of materials that they distribute. What do you think of this method of delivering class materials?

5. Do you submit any of your assignments electronically? That is, have you submitted an assignment to a "drop-box," in the body of e-mail message, or as an e-mail attachment? If you have, describe the method, the assignment, and the course in which you used electronic submissions.

1 2 3 4 5 6 7 **8** 9 10 11 12 13 14 15 16

CHAPTER REVIEW

Takeaway Points | Key Terms and Concepts | Matching | Multiple Choice | Fill-In | Short Answer | Exercises/Projects | Web Research

HOME

EXERCISES/PROJECTS

1. Frequently, the IP addresses of an organization's Internet computers begin with the same several digits. For example, all the computers at Buffalo State College begin with 136.183.xxx.xxx, and the last two sets of numbers usually denote the building and individual computers. Stop by your school's computing services and find out if your institution has a common set of IP address for its computers. If it does, what are the common digits? Now go to one of your school's Windows-based networked computers to determine its IP address. Go to Start, select Run..., in the Open textbox type "winipcfg," and click the OK button. What is the IP address of this computer? Does it begin with the common set of digits?

2. Have you created a personal Web page? If you have, describe the server (IP address, domain name, and operating system); Web page content (personal page, class assignment page, and so on); and the software you used to create the page (text editor, HTML editor, and so on).

3. Have you participated in a chat room? If you haven't, join one and answer the following questions:

   • What software did you use?

   • How did you find the chat group?

   • What is the title of the discussion or its content area?

   • What are your personal feelings about chat rooms?

4. Although present Internet bandwidth does not support high-quality videoconferencing, it provides varying qualities of telephony. Besides computer-to-computer voice communication, you can also make computer-to-telephone connections. Visit the dialpad Internet site at **http://dialpad.com**. Sign up for the free calls, and make some local and long-distance calls. What was the quality of the phone conversations? What type of connection—modem, satellite, ISDN, xDSL, cable, or LAN—did you use? How does the speed of the connection affect the quality of the call?

5. Internet users are frequently frustrated by slow telephone connections. If you're connecting to the Internet using a conventional phone line, how fast is your modem? Although there may be faster connection options, they're also more expensive. Let's examine another telephone-related service. Contact your local phone company to learn about Integrated Services Digital Network (ISDN). What are the transfer rates, installation charges, and monthly fees? Based on the increased speed and increased cost, why would, or would you not, use ISDN?

HOME	Takeaway Points	Key Terms and Concepts	Matching	Multiple Choice	Fill-In	Short Answer	Exercises/ Projects	Web Research	CHAPTER REVIEW

WEB RESEARCH

1. Internet 2, or I2, is a collaborative effort among educational institutions, government agencies, and computer and telecommunications companies to increase Internet bandwidth. Visit the I2 site at **www.internet2.edu**. Presently, how many university members are there? Does your school belong to I2? If not, locate and identify the nearest institution that does. What are the annual membership fees and estimated annual institutional costs to participate in I2? What are the annual membership fees and estimated annual corporate partnership costs to participate in I2? Name two corporate partners and two corporate sponsors. In addition to I2, the U.S. government also sponsors its own advanced Internet initiative. Identify this initiative and list two governmental agencies that participate in it and in I2.

2. Have you thought about getting your own domain name? What would you like it to be? Visit the site **http://register.com** and try different top-level domain names (.com, .net, .org, and so on) to see if they're available. If they are, what is the annual registration cost? If the domain names are already taken, who owns them, when did they acquire them, and when do they expire? What is the minimum bid amount that can be offered to purchase domain names? Visit the Web sites and describe their content.

3. When you mail a letter, it doesn't necessarily travel directly from your nearest post office branch to the one nearest the destination address. For example, a letter mailed from Brunswick, Georgia, to Palo Alto, California, may not be placed on a direct flight between those two cities. Similarly, connections between a client and server aren't direct. Using a freeware version of NeoTrace's ping application, trace the communication paths between your computer and selected servers. Go to the NeoTrace site at **www.networkingfiles.com/ PingFinger/Neotraceexpress.htm**. Download, install, and register NeoTrace Express. Use the LIST command to determine the IP address of the server and how many intermediate computers were used to make the connections, the MAP command to list the cities between your computer and the servers, and the REGISTRANT command to obtain the name of the administrative contact. Connect to the following servers:

   - **www.uoregon.edu**
   - **www.whitehouse.gov**
   - **www.mcafee.com/myapps/neoworx/default.asp**
   - one of your school's servers (using an off-campus computer as the client)

4. Telephone companies offer consumers three tiers of Internet service—public switched telephone network (PSTN), Integrated Services Digital Network (ISDN), and Digital Subscriber Line (DSL). You are familiar with PSTN, and ISDN was examined in Question 5 in the Exercises/Projects section of this chapter, so we now focus our attention on DSL. Actually, there is a series of xDSL services—ADSL, SDSL, and IDSL. Unlike conventional telephone service, which is available to almost any home, DSL service is limited by the distance from the central office (CO) or switching station to your home. Do you have DSL? Go to the DSL Reports at **www.cognigen.net/speakeasy** to see if you qualify for this service. How far are you from the CO? Which, if any, of the xDSL services can you get? If you are able to get xDSL service, name at least one ISP that partners with the phone company to provide this service. What are the transfer rates, installation charges, and monthly fees? Based on the increased speed and increased cost, why would, or would you not, use DSL?

1 2 3 4 5 6 7 8 9 10 11 12 13 14 15 16

The World Wide Web and Electronic Commerce

CHAPTER **9**

What You'll Learn...

When you have finished reading this chapter, you will be able to:

1. Explain the concept of hypertext.

2. Contrast Web browsers and Web servers.

3. Explain the parts of a URL.

4. Name the browser navigation buttons and their functions.

5. Contrast Web subject guides and search engines.

6. Explain how search operators can improve Web search results.

7. Evaluate the reliability of information on a Web page.

8. Define business-to-business e-commerce and explain why it's moving to the Internet.

9. List the fastest growing public e-commerce applications and explain why customers like them.

Imagine an information source that contains billions of documents, each of them almost instantly accessible by means of the computer sitting on your desk. And imagine, too, that this information source is growing at an astonishing rate, with thousands of new documents appearing every day. This resource contains a wealth of useful information, and it's all available when you access the Internet. You guessed it, it's the World Wide Web.

Almost all college students have been on the Web—it's hard to imagine students these days not having heard of a Web page, a URL, or a Web link. But no matter how familiar you are with this part of the Internet, it's important that you fully understand the concepts behind the Web and Web browsers, how to effectively use the Web for research, and how to evaluate the quality of the information you retrieve. This chapter discusses these and other topics, helping you become an even more fluent Web user.

Figure 9.1

Increasing numbers of Internet users are turning to the Web to research product purchases, medical decisions, and current events.

The Web: An Indispensable Information Resource

Second in popularity only to e-mail, the **World Wide Web**, although in existence only since 1993, is already an indispensable information resource. Each day, millions of Internet users turn to the Web to research product purchases, medical decisions, current events, and much more (see Figure 9.1). In this section, you'll learn the fundamental concepts of the Web, starting with the concept of hypertext.

THE HYPERTEXT CONCEPT

Hypertext is a way of presenting information so that the *sequence* of the information—the order in which it is read—is determined by the reader. Hypertext works by means of **hyperlinks** (also called **links**). If you've spent any time on the Web at all, you know what links are—those underlined or highlighted words that you can click to bring another document into view (see Figure 9.2).

Authors who write hypertext documents use hyperlinks to connect to additional documents that readers can consult. In doing so, they create concise documents, called **chunks**, that contain many links instead of trying to explain everything in one place. Here's an example:

> Art historians consider Monet to be an Impressionist.

As you read this sentence, you can click the underlined text if you want to know more about either Monet or Impressionism.

Creating a hypertext system on your own is a lot of work because you have to create a separate page explaining every concept for which you've created a link. That's why hypertext remained relatively obscure until the Web came along.

A **hypermedia** system enables you to retrieve multimedia resources, such as sounds and movies, as well as text. The Web

Figure 9.2
In hypertext, you follow the links to related information.

is a **distributed hypermedia system**. In this system, the responsibility for creating content is distributed among many people. And the more people who create content, the easier hypertext development becomes. For example, if someone has created a document about Monet and another person has created a document about Impressionism, you can link to these documents instead of writing them yourself.

The Web's distribution of content-creation responsibilities does have a drawback: you can link to any page you want, but you can't guarantee that the page's author will keep that page on the Web. The author can delete it or move it, and the author isn't under any obligation to notify other authors who have included links to the page. For this reason, **stale links** (also called **broken links**), which are links to documents that have disappeared, are common on the Web.

WEB BROWSERS AND WEB SERVERS

Like other Internet services, Web software includes clients (Web browsers) as well as servers (Web servers).

Web Browsers
A **Web browser** displays a Web document and enables you to access linked documents. When you click a hyperlink, the browser sends a message to a Web server, asking the server to retrieve the requested information and send it back to the browser through the network. Browsers also contain navigation tools that enable you to return to previously viewed pages and to

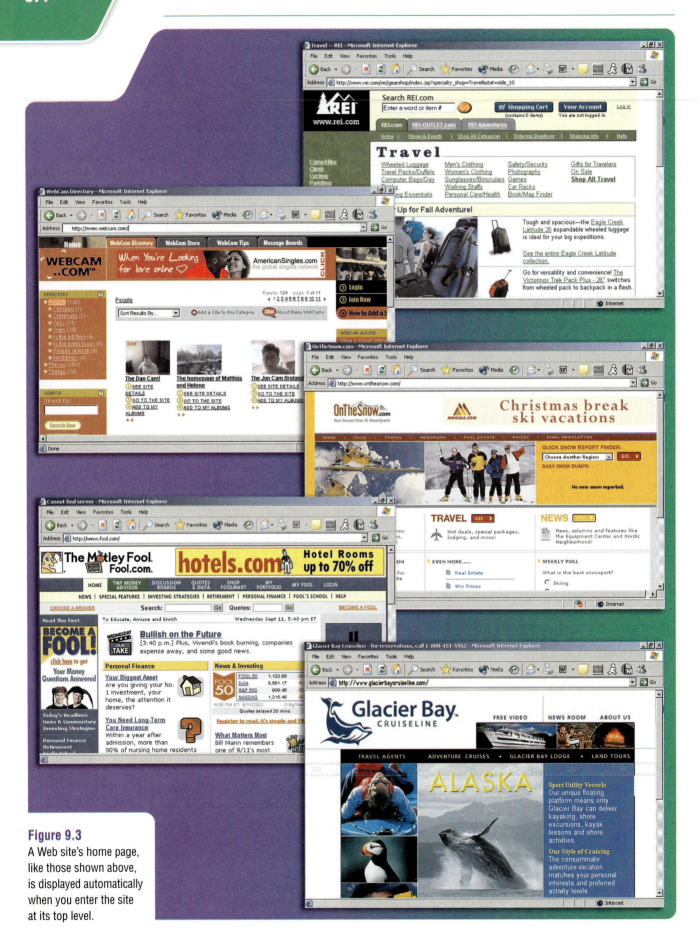

Figure 9.3

A Web site's home page, like those shown above, is displayed automatically when you enter the site at its top level.

bookmark (mark) favorite sites so that you can access them quickly.

The first Web browsers were **text-only browsers** that couldn't display graphics. The first successful **graphical browser**, Mosaic, helped launch the Web on the road to popularity. Unlike text-only browsers, graphical browsers can display GIF and JPEG graphics as well as text. Developed by the National Center for Supercomputing Applications (NCSA) at the University of Illinois, Mosaic was followed by two commercial products, Netscape Navigator and Microsoft Internet Explorer, which have since captured virtually the entire browser market.

Web Servers

A **Web server program** waits for browsers to request a Web page; when the server receives a request for a specific resource, it looks for the requested file and sends it to the browser. If the file isn't found, the server sends an error message.

You've undoubtedly visited many Web sites by now. These collections of related Web pages typically contain an **index page** (also called a **home page**), a default page that's displayed automatically when you enter the site at its top level. Figure 9.3 shows the home pages for several Web sites.

Simple Web servers are easy to operate, but you need programming skills to configure and maintain the industrial-strength servers that host popular Web sites. These complex servers use scripts and programs to enhance interactivity and provide access to information stored in databases.

WEB ADDRESSES (URLS)

To make the Web work, an addressing system is needed that precisely states where a resource (such as a Web page) is located. This system is provided by **uniform resource locators** (**URLs**), a standard for describing the location of resources on the Web. You've seen plenty of URLs, which look similar to that in Figure 9.4.

A complete URL has four parts:

Protocol The first part of a complete URL specifies the Internet standard to be used to access the document. For the Web, it's the **Hypertext Transfer**

Protocol (**HTTP**). Most browsers can also access information using FTP (File Transfer Protocol) and other protocols. The protocol name is followed by a colon and two slash marks (//). With most Web browsers, you can omit the *http://* protocol when you're accessing a Web page by typing its address. For example, you can access **http://www.prenhall.com/ciyf2004** by typing **www.prenhall.com/ciyf2004**.

Server The second part of a complete URL specifies the name of the Web server on which the page is located. Early Web servers adopted the name "WWW," and this is why so many Web addresses contain the WWW. As time has passed, the convention of using WWW as the Web server name has become less common. Included in the second part of a complete URL is the top-level domain name. The **domain** is the three-letter extension (such as .com or .edu) representing the type of group or institution that the Web site represents.

Path The third part of a complete URL specifies the location of the document on the server. It contains the document's location on the computer, including the names of subfolders (if any).

Resource Name The last part of a complete URL gives the filename of the resource you're accessing. A resource is a computer file, which might be an HTML file, a sound file, a movie file, a graphics file, or something else. The resource's extension (the part of the filename after the period) indicates the type of resource it is. For example, HTML documents have the .html or .htm extension.

Many URLs don't include a resource name because they reference the server's

Figure 9.4
A complete URL has four parts: protocol, server, path, and resource name. This is the URL for the default Internet Explorer home page.

default home page. If no resource name is specified, the browser looks for a file named *default* or *index*. If it finds such a file, it loads it automatically. For example, **www.microsoft.com/windows/ie** displays the default Internet Explorer home page. Other URLs omit both the path name and the resource name. These URLs reference the server's home page. For example, **www.microsoft.com** displays Microsoft's home page on the Web.

WEB PROTOCOLS

Like other Internet services, the Web involves communication between clients and servers. As we mentioned earlier, the exact format of this communication is specified by the Hypertext Transfer Protocol (HTTP). This protocol specifies the format of URLs as well as the procedure clients and servers follow to establish communication.

WEB PAGE DESIGN TOOLS

To create a Web page, Web authors use a **markup language** called the **Hypertext Markup Language** (**HTML**). A markup language is a set of codes, called **elements**, that authors can use to identify portions of a document, such as a title or a heading. Most elements have two codes, called a **start tag** and an **end tag**, that surround the marked-up text. The following illustrates HTML markup for a level 1 (major) heading, a paragraph of text, and an indented quotation:

```
<H1>This is the text of a major
heading.</H1>

<P>This is a paragraph of text.
Most browsers display paragraph
text with a blank line before
the paragraph and flush left
alignment.</P>

<BLOCKQUOTE>This is an indented
quotation. Most browsers dis-
play blockquote material with
an indentation from the left
margin.</BLOCKQUOTE>
```

A document marked up with HTML contains nothing but plain text (ASCII text) and is easy to exchange on a cross-platform network. When browsers access the document, they read the markup and position the various portions of the document in accordance with the browser's formatting settings.

HTML's simplicity is an important reason for the Web's popularity—anyone can learn how to create a simple Web page using HTML. As a result, it's possible for millions of people to contribute content to the Web. In fact it may be easier than you imagine; Microsoft Word, Excel, Access, and PowerPoint allow you to save Web-ready documents in HTML format.

Browsing the Web

The two most popular graphical Web browsers are Netscape Navigator and Microsoft Internet Explorer (see Figure 9.5). Learning to use one of these programs effectively is an essential component of computer and information literacy.

EXPLORING YOUR BROWSER'S WINDOW

Although browsers vary somewhat, you'll find the following features in the two most popular programs:

Navigation buttons On the browser's toolbar, you'll find frequently used navigation buttons (Back, Forward, Home, and Refresh) that play an important role in Web navigation. You'll learn more about these tools later in the chapter.

Address toolbar (also called the **Location toolbar**) This toolbar contains a text box that indicates the URL of the page you're viewing. If you type a URL here and press Enter, the browser takes you to that location.

Program icon This icon, located in the top right corner of the browser, displays an animation when the browser is attempting to download information from the Web.

Status bar Located at the bottom of the screen, the status bar shows you messages about what the program is doing.

Within the application workspace area, you see the page that's located at the URL indicated in the Address toolbar. If the page is longer or wider than the window, you'll also see scrollbars.

USING THE DEFAULT START PAGE

When you start your Web browser, you see the program's **default start page**. This page is located at the browser vendor's home server (AOL, Microsoft, and so on) and generally offers the services you'd expect from a Web portal, such as free e-mail, a subject guide to the Web, stock

Figure 9.5 a&b
(a) Netscape Navigator and (b) Microsoft Internet Explorer are the two most popular graphical Web browsers.

quotes, news, weather, and sports. You can customize your browser by changing the default start page. You might also decide to use the *default blank* default page choice, which doesn't load a page at all but waits for you to type in an address. You can find the default page setting in Internet Explorer under the Tools, Internet Options menu.

If you get lost while exploring the Web, click the Home button on the browser's toolbar. This button redisplays the default home page (see Figure 9.6).

Figure 9.6
If you get lost while exploring the Web, click the Home button on the browser's toolbar.

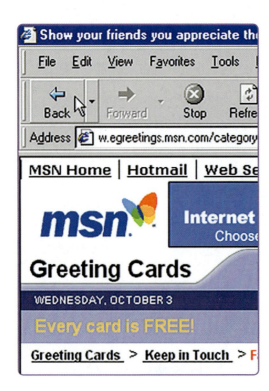

Figure 9.7
Click the Back button to return to a page you just viewed.

ACCESSING WEB PAGES

To access a Web page, you can do any of the following:

- **Click a hyperlink.** Hyperlinks are usually underlined, but sometimes they're embedded in graphics or highlighted in other ways, such as with shading or colors. To tell whether a given portion of a Web page contains a hyperlink, position your mouse pointer over it and watch for a change in the pointer's shape. Most browsers indicate the presence of a hyperlink by changing the mouse pointer to a hand shape.

- **Type a URL in the Address box (Internet Explorer) or Location box (Netscape Navigator).** You don't need to type http://. Watch for spelling errors, and don't insert spaces. A common mistake is typing a comma instead of a period to separate the components of a URL.

- **Click a button on the Links toolbar.** Both major browsers come with predefined links on a toolbar, which contains buttons linked to Web pages. You can customize this toolbar with pages you frequently access.

USING THE BACK AND FORWARD BUTTONS

To return to a Web page you just viewed, click the Back button (see Figure 9.7). To return to pages more than two or three clicks back, right-click the Back button and choose the page's name from the drop-down menu. (On a Macintosh, position the pointer over the Back button and hold down the mouse button until the menu appears.) After you've clicked the Back button, you can click the Forward button to go forward in the list of pages you've viewed.

USING NAVIGATION AIDS

When you're exploring a Web presentation that includes many pages, you'll probably find that the author has provided navigation aids, such as a column of subject links positioned on the left or right of the page (see Figure 9.8). You can use these aids to explore the various pages of this presentation.

USING THE HISTORY LIST

As you browse the Web, your browser keeps a list of the pages you've accessed, called the **history list**. If you'd like to return to a previously viewed site and can't find it by clicking the Back icon, you can consult the history list and choose the page from there (see Figure 9.9). In Microsoft Internet Explorer, you can access this list by clicking the History button on the toolbar. In Netscape Navigator, you choose the History option from the Communicator menu.

CREATING FAVORITES AND BOOKMARKS

You'll soon find some Web pages you'll want to return to frequently. To accomplish this easily, you can save these pages as Favorites (Internet Explorer) or Bookmarks (Netscape Navigator) (see Figure 9.10). After you've saved these pages as Favorites or Bookmarks, you see the names of these pages in the Favorites menu or the Bookmarks menu.

In either program, you'll find that your list of favorite sites soon becomes unwieldy. You'll need to use the program's Favorite or Bookmark organization tools to categorize them by creating and naming folders. After you do this, the Favorites or Bookmarks menu shows folder names, and submenus pop up when you select a folder name.

Finding Information on the Web

Although browsing by means of hyperlinks is easy and fun, it falls short as a means of information discovery. Web users soon find themselves clicking link after link, searching for information that they never find. If you can't find the information you're looking for after a bit of browsing, try *searching* the Web. Although Web search

Figure 9.8

Some Web pages include navigation aids, such as a column of subject links positioned on the left or right of the page.

clickstream

As you spend time on the Web, you leave a **clickstream** in your wake. A clickstream is a trail of Web links that you have followed to get to a particular site. Internet merchants are quite interested in analyzing clickstream activity so they can do a better job of targeting advertisements and tailoring Web pages to your liking.

Figure 9.9
The history list is very helpful if you've been doing lots of browsing.

Figure 9.10
You'll soon find some Web pages you'll want to return to frequently. To accomplish this easily, you can save these pages as Favorites (Internet Explorer) or Bookmarks (Netscape Navigator).

tools are far from perfect, knowledge of their proper use (and their limitations) can greatly increase your chances of finding the information you want.

UNDERSTANDING INFORMATION DISCOVERY TOOLS

You've no doubt heard of search tools such as Google, Yahoo!, AltaVista, and Lycos. What many Web users don't realize is that these tools differ, and some are more suitable for some purposes than others. Understanding these differences will help you increase your chances of success when you search for information on the Web.

USING SUBJECT GUIDES

Most search services offer a **subject guide** to the Web, grouping Web pages under such headings as Business, News, or Travel (see Figure 9.11). These services don't try to include every Web page in the subject

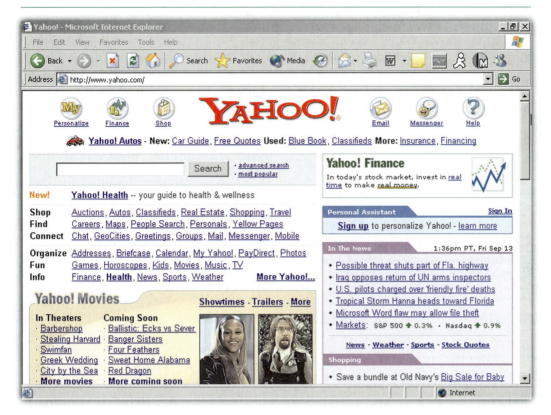

Figure 9.11

Yahoo! is one of the most extensive subject guides.

categories. Instead, they offer a selection of high-quality pages that they believe represent some of the more useful Web pages in a given category. If you're just beginning your search for information, a subject guide is an excellent place to start.

USING SEARCH ENGINES

If you can't find what you're looking for in a Web subject guide, you can try searching databases that claim to index the full Web. Called **search engines**, these services don't actually maintain databases of every Web page in existence, but the leading ones are known to have indexed about one-third of them (see Figure 9.12). That's an enormous pool of information, and chances are that by using these services, you'll find information relevant to the subject you're looking for. Unfortunately, few people know how to use these services effectively. All too often, people try search engines only to see a lengthy list of irrelevant material.

Using the Web to research a paper? Visit "A Student's Guide to Research with the WWW," created by Craig Branham of St. Louis University, at **www.slu.edu/ departments/english/ research**.

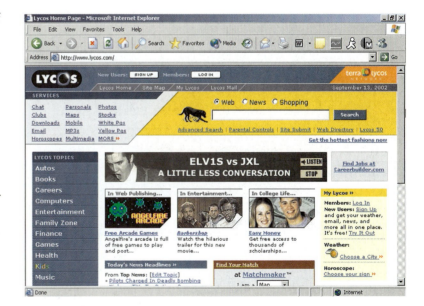

Figure 9.12

Lycos is a popular search engine.

To use a search engine, you type one or more words that describe the subject you're looking for. Generally, it's a good idea to type several words (four or five) rather than one or two; most Web searches produce far more results than you can use.

Why do search engines sometimes produce unsatisfactory results? The problem lies in the ambiguity of the English language. Suppose you're searching for information on the Great Wall of China. You'll find some information on the ancient Chinese defensive installation, but you may also get the menu of the Great Wall of China, a Chinese restaurant, information on the Great Wall hotel in Beijing, and the lyrics of a song titled "Great Wall of China" by Billy Joel.

Although you can improve search effectiveness by learning the search techniques we'll discuss later in the chapter, Web searches will continue to be hampered because there remains no framework to describe the content of documents. If such a framework existed, Web authors could describe their documents using such terms as *historical* or *commercial.* Searches would be much more effective because you could specify the *type* of document you want, not just the content it should contain. Several proposals for such frameworks have been made, but no standard exists yet.

Specialized Search Engines

Full Web search engines generally don't index specialized information such as names and addresses, job advertisements, quotations, and newspaper articles. To find such information, you need to access **specialized search engines**. Examples of such specialized search engines include CareerBuilder.com, a database of over 400,000 jobs, and Infoplease.com, which contains the full text of an encyclopedia and an almanac (see Figure 9.13).

Using Search Techniques

By learning a few search techniques, you can greatly increase the accuracy of your Web searches. One problem with Web search services is that each uses its own unique set of **search operators**, symbols or words that you can use for advanced searches. A trend toward standardization, however, means that some or all of the following techniques will work with most search services. To find out which ones you can use with a given search service, look for a link to a page explaining search options.

Figure 9.13 a&b
(a) CareerBuilder.com is a specialized search engine that adds more than 110,000 job listings each week. (b) Infoplease.com, another specialized search engine, contains the full text of an encyclopedia and an almanac.

INCLUSION AND EXCLUSION

In many search engines, you can improve search performance by specifying an **inclusion operator**, which is generally a plus (+) sign. This operator states that you don't want a page retrieved unless it contains the specified word. By listing several key terms with this search operator, you can exclude many pages that don't contain one or more of the essential terms. The following, for example, will retrieve only those pages that contain all three of the words mentioned:

+kittens +care +Siamese

If the list of retrieved documents contains many items that you don't want, you can use the **exclusion operator**, which is generally a minus (–) sign. For example, the preceding search retrieves many classified ads for Siamese kittens. You can exclude them by preceding the term *classified* with the exclusion operator, as follows:

+kittens +care +Siamese –classified

WILDCARDS

Many search engines enable you to use **wildcards** (symbols such as ? and * that take the place of one or more characters in the position in which they are used). Wildcards help you improve the accuracy of your searches. In the preceding example, many unwanted pages contain the word *classifieds* and aren't excluded by the singular *classified*. The following example using the asterisk wildcard excludes any document containing the words *classified* or *classifieds*:

–classified*

PHRASE SEARCHES

Another way to improve the accuracy of your searches involves **phrase searching**, which is generally performed by typing a phrase within quotation marks. This tells the search engine to retrieve only those documents that contain the exact phrase (rather than some or all of the words anywhere in the document).

BOOLEAN SEARCHES

Some search engines enable you to perform **Boolean searches**. These searches use keywords (AND, OR, and NOT) to link the words you're searching for. By using Boolean operators, you can gain more precise control over your searches. Let's look at a few examples.

The AND, OR, and NOT Operators
When used to link two search words, the AND operator tells the search service to return only those documents that contain both words (just as the plus sign does). For example, the search phrase "Jamaica AND geography" returns only those documents that contain both terms. You can use the AND operator to narrow your search so that it retrieves fewer documents.

If your search retrieves too few documents, try the OR operator. For example, the search phrase "pottery OR ceramics" retrieves documents that contain either or both of these words. (Most search engines will return both without the OR operator.)

To exclude unwanted documents, use the NOT operator. This operator tells the search engine to omit any documents containing the word preceded by NOT (just as the minus sign does). For example, the search phrase "kittens NOT cats" retrieves pages that mention kittens, but not those that mention cats.

The NEAR Operator
Some search engines have a **proximity operator** (usually called NEAR), which enables you to specify that the two linked words appear close together (such as within 10 words of each other). Consult the search service's help page to find out whether such an operator is available and if so, what it's called and how it works. The following example phrase retrieves only those documents that contain *browser* and *performance* within a few words of each other:

browser NEAR performance

Destinations

The leading search engines include Google (**www.google.com**), HotBot (**www.hotbot.lycos.com**), AltaVista (**www.altavista.digital.com**), GoTo.com (**www.overture.com**), Excite (**www.excite.com**), and Go.com (**www.go.com**). Most of these also offer subject guides.

If you're using Web sources in a college paper, you'll need to cite your sources. "A Style Sheet for Citing Internet Resources: MLA Style," located at **www.lib.berkeley.edu/TeachingLib/Guides/Internet/Style.html**, shows how to cite Internet sources using the Modern Language Association style, which is widely used in the humanities. For the American Psychological Association citation style for Internet sources, see "The Columbia Guide to Online Style: APA-Style Citations of Electronic Sources," located at **www.columbia.edu/cu/cup/cgos/idx_basic.html**.

Using Parentheses

Many search engines that support Boolean operators enable you to use parentheses to **nest** Boolean expressions. When you nest an expression, the search engine evaluates the expression from left to right, and the material within parentheses is resolved first. Such expressions enable you to conduct a search with unmatched accuracy. Consider this example:

> **(growth OR increase OR development)**
> **NEAR (Internet or Web)**

This search retrieves any document that mentions the words *growth*, *increase*, or *development* within a few words of *Internet* or *Web*.

Evaluating the Information You've Found

After you've found information on the Web, you'll need to evaluate it critically. Anyone can publish information on the Web; Web pages are not subjected to the fact-checking standards found in newspapers or magazines, let alone the peer review process that safeguards the quality of scholarly and scientific publications. Although you can find excellent and reliable information on the Web, you can also find pages that are biased and self-serving. You'll even encounter information that can be described only as the product of unbalanced minds. Beware!

RULES FOR CRITICALLY EVALUATING WEB PAGES

As you're evaluating a Web page, carefully note the following:

Author Who is the author of this page? Is the author affiliated with a recognized institution, such as a university or a well-known company? Is there any evidence that the author is qualified with respect to this topic? A page that isn't signed may signal an attempt to disguise the author's lack of qualifications.

Sources Does the author cite his or her sources? If so, do they appear to be from recognized and respected publications?

Server Who provides the server for publishing this Web page? Who pays for this page?

Objectivity Does the presentation seem balanced and objective, or is it one-sided?

Style Is the language objective and dispassionate, or is it strident and argumentative?

Purpose What is the purpose of this page? Is the author trying to sell something or push a biased idea? Who would profit if this page's information were accepted?

Accuracy Does the information appear to be accurate? Is the page free of sweeping generalizations or other signs of shoddy thinking? Do you see many misspellings or grammatical errors that would indicate poor educational background?

Currency Is this page up-to-date? When was it last maintained?

LOCATING MATERIAL IN PUBLISHED WORKS

Remember that the Web is only one of several sources you can and should use for research. Your best sources of information are respected publications, which you'll likely find in the library. You can use the Internet, however, to locate publications, then obtain them in your college's library. Check your library's home page to find out what Internet services are available. Also, visit Ingenta (**www.ingenta.com**), a free database service that enables you to search for quality articles from more than 25,000 published magazines and journals (see Figure 9.15). After you

TECHNOLOGICAL PIONEERS

Faces Behind the Web

The Web is the second-largest single part of the Internet and is growing daily. Millions of users browse millions of pages, all sharing information freely and openly.

It wasn't always that way, however. In the world of computing, the Web is not that old. It started as the brainchild of Tim Berners-Lee, a researcher at CERN in Geneva, Switzerland (see Figure 9.14). Although many of the concepts behind the Web were laid out in a paper Berners-Lee authored at CERN in 1980, it wasn't until 1989 and 1990 that the protocols and programs were developed to make the Web a reality.

The original Web browsers were text-oriented programs designed for the UNIX environment. This approach more than fulfilled the development goals of Berners-Lee, who saw the Web as a way for researchers to communicate and collaborate. The lack of a graphical interface, however, was in stark contrast to the overwhelming success of Windows, the operating system that was taking the desktop by storm.

In late 1992, two programmers at the National Center for Supercomputing Applications (NCSA) at the University of Illinois developed a new browser called Mosaic. The lead programmer on the project was an undergraduate student named Marc Andreessen. While working at the university's physics research lab, Andreessen saw the potential for bringing multimedia together with the capability to link global resources. At the time, the world had between 30 and 50 Web servers, but that didn't stop the development of Mosaic. The development effort consisted of many all-night sessions to get the C code put together and debugged. The result was released to the public as a free download in 1993. It became extremely popular due to its easy-to-use point-and-click interface, and it was quickly recognized as state-of-the-art technology.

Figure 9.14
The Web started as the brainchild of Tim Berners-Lee.

In late 1993, Andreessen moved to California and accepted a job with Enterprise Integration Technologies. After three short months, Andreessen met with Jim Clark, founder of Silicon Graphics, and the two formed a company named Netscape Communications Corporation. The focus of their company was the infant Web, and they decided to create a commercial Web browser that anyone could use.

Andreessen assembled a team of six programmers, who developed the original Netscape Navigator between May and July of 1994. After some testing and refinement, the product was released to the world in October 1994.

Navigator featured several improvements over the original Mosaic; the biggest improvement was continuous document streaming, which meant users could view documents as they were being downloaded.

Netscape followed an unorthodox distribution program for its software: the company gave it away. When released, Navigator was available for free download for educational and nonprofit uses. Others could use it for a time but then agree (on the honor system) to pay a modest licensing fee. In this respect, Netscape was following the popular distribution model of thousands of shareware authors.

The marketing model followed by Netscape was wildly successful. From the humble beginnings of Netscape in 1994, the company grew into a powerhouse with annual revenues in excess of $525 million. Netscape was subsequently purchased by America Online, where Andreessen worked briefly as the company's chief technology executive.

CURRENTS

search, you'll see article lists and titles. You can then obtain the source in the library or online.

AUTHORITATIVE SOURCES ONLINE

Some respected magazines and journals have established Web sites that enable you to search back issues, giving you the best of both worlds: the power and convenience of the Internet, plus material that's more reliable than the average Web page. The following respected publications provide a valuable public service by providing free access to their back issue archives:

- *Christian Science Monitor*
  (**www.csmonitorarchive.com**)

- *Time* magazine
  (**www.time.com/time/magazine/archives**)

- *Scientific American*
  (**www.sciam.com**)

Understanding Electronic Commerce

Electronic commerce, or **e-commerce**, is broadly defined as the use of telecommunications or the Internet to carry out business of any type. E-commerce isn't new; companies have used wide area networks (WANs) to do business with suppliers for years. What *is* new is that, thanks to the Internet and inexpensive PCs, e-commerce has become accessible to anyone equipped with an Internet connection and a Web browser (see Figure 9.16).

Increasingly, Internet users are shopping online, opening online bank accounts, and trading stocks online. In total dollars, e-commerce is still in its infancy—currently, 99 percent of retail sales occur in traditional, brick-and-mortar stores—but it's growing. By 2005, online retail sales are

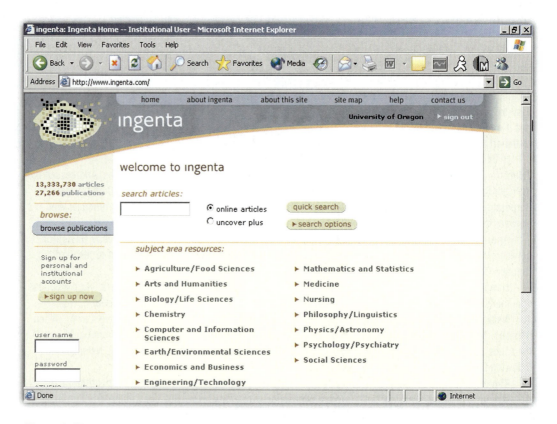

Figure 9.15

Need reliable information? Ingenta is a free database service you can use to search for quality articles from more than 25,000 published magazines and journals.

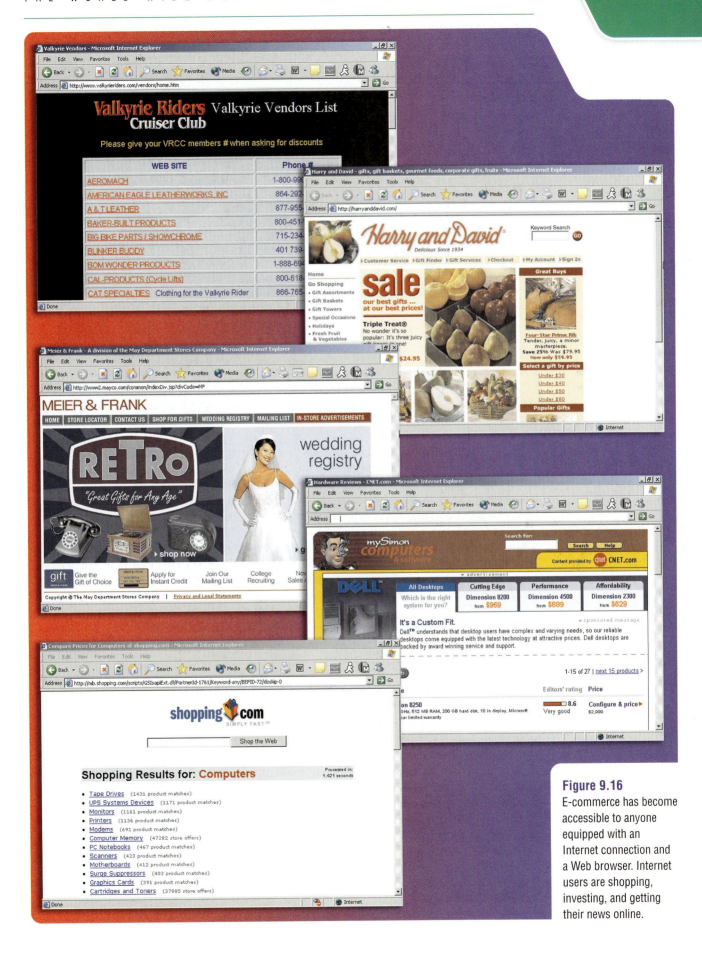

Figure 9.16
E-commerce has become accessible to anyone equipped with an Internet connection and a Web browser. Internet users are shopping, investing, and getting their news online.

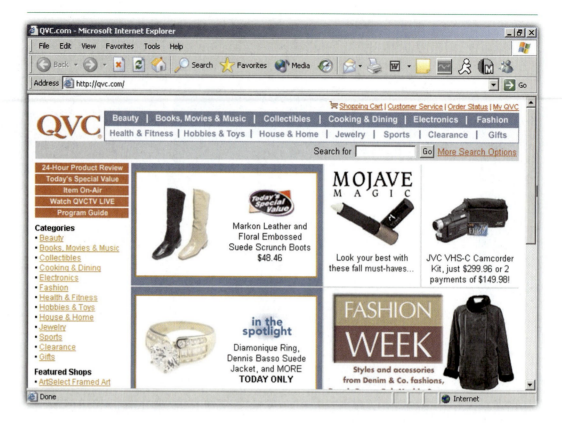

Figure 9.17
Online research and shopping are changing the face of business.

expected to reach five percent of the total U.S. figures. That's paltry compared with the mail-order business, but it's worth remembering that the mail-order business had to start from zero, too. According to a Microsoft Corporation executive, within a generation—25 to 30 years—approximately one-third of all consumer transactions will occur on the Internet, in the context of a massive global electronic marketplace for goods and services. Some of us are much more skeptical, but the shift in purchasing practices and patterns will be interesting to watch.

BUSINESS-TO-BUSINESS E-COMMERCE

Although most people think of online shopping when they hear the term *e-commerce*, much of e-commerce's projected growth involves business-to-business links that customers won't see. **Business-to-business (B2B) e-commerce** involves one business providing another business with the materials and supplies it needs to conduct its operations. Today, business-to-business e-commerce requires companies to lease network capacity from a **value-added network (VAN)**, which charges a hefty

per-byte fee. What's more, VANs aren't flexible; if a local dial-in (called a **point of presence [PoP]**) doesn't exist, you can't connect without incurring long-distance charges.

To exchange financial information and other business related data, firms use a data standard called **electronic data interchange** (**EDI**). EDI requires partnering firms to collaborate to customize the various EDI documents, and it's a huge job. Despite the hassles of EDI, business-to-business commerce has been growing at a 15 to 20 percent annual clip.

ONLINE SHOPPING

Online shopping is made possible by the security and encryption features built into popular browsers. According to a recent survey, fewer than half of Web users have bought something online, but this percentage is growing each year. What's more, the same survey revealed that nearly three-quarters of Internet users used the Internet to research potential purchases before making them, even if they subsequently bought them in an old-fashioned real-world store. Businesses are concluding

E-COMMERCE

Are Ads Keeping the Internet Free?

You've probably seen digital billboards, called banner ads, peppered throughout the Web pages you visit on the Internet. In fact, if you spend any time on the Web at all, it's nearly impossible to avoid them. How do these ads work? When you click a banner ad, you're taken to another page or site. When the page loads onto your screen, it electronically records how you arrived there. The advertising company then gives the site from which you clicked anywhere from a penny to as much as fifty dollars if a sale occurs as a result of your click.

Not all clicks have to result in a sale in order for them to be profitable for the sponsoring Web site. Some ads operate on a "pay-per-click" basis in which the advertiser that places the ad pays the sites that generate clicks a certain amount of money per click. "Click-through" systems count the number of hits a site receives on a hit counter. Advertisers pay the sites that generate the clicks only if sales rise in relationship to the rise in hits to the advertised site.

Another common way for a site to earn money is to become a "sponsored" site. Often, sponsors are large companies that agree to provide financial assistance to small companies or organizations in exchange for advertising space on their site. The site being sponsored benefits not only from the support offered by the advertiser, but also because the advertiser's logo may lend the site an air of legitimacy. However, as many sites have found only too late, just because a large company sponsors you doesn't mean you're guaranteed payment. Some very promising sponsor sites, like Pet.com and Toys.com, have ended up dropping off the face of the Internet, sometimes leaving sites they've sponsored in the lurch and without paying their sponsorship commissions.

Although they can be annoying, banner ads do serve a purpose on the Web. In fact, some Web experts say that without them, some sites on the Web would become a thing of the past. Why? Because many of the sites rely on the meager amounts generated by such ads and sponsorship deals. So, you may just want to consider turning off that banner-ad-blocking software when you visit your favorite small sites. Or, the next time you are asked to "Please visit our sponsor to keep this site free," you might want to see what a click has to offer. In doing so, you may possibly be keeping your favorite site in business.

IMPACTS

that they must be on the Internet or they'll soon be out of business (see Figure 9.17).

One of the tremendous advantages of online shopping is the low capital investment needed to set up shop. For less than $1,000, a startup can open a Web storefront and start selling products online. Don't make plans to drop out of college and set up shop just yet, though. Obviously, not every business succeeds on the Internet— something that was made painfully clear to the many people who lost their jobs in the dot-com crash in the late 1990s. What works best? The big winners thus far are Amazon.com, Autobytel.com (an online automobile information provider that enables car buyers to avoid showroom shakedowns), and eBay. Shoppers are looking for information about products that they can then go and buy locally, products that are unavailable locally, and price discounts due to volume. If you do have an idea for an online business,

research the Web to see if your idea is already out there. Learn from others before jumping into a new venture. Having a Web site does not mean that you have a Web *presence*.

Least successful of all e-commerce ventures are attempts to bring traditional retailing concepts to the Internet. Business experts believe part of the problem lies in poor customer service. Would-be customers are afraid something will go wrong with their order and they won't be able to talk to anyone about it. For this reason, **click-and-brick** stores—retailers that have both an online and a traditional retail store presence—are winning the consumer's confidence. Why? Shoppers can return products locally or talk to an actual human being if there's something wrong with an order.

There's another reason for the click-and-brick strategy's success: customers like to use the Internet to research products before they buy. Although less than three percent of new car sales are made online, more than 40 percent of new car buyers researched their purchase on the Internet.

The Web won't come close to taking over traditional store presence for other reasons as well. Most people enjoy the gratification they receive when they can obtain their purchased item immediately at a store.

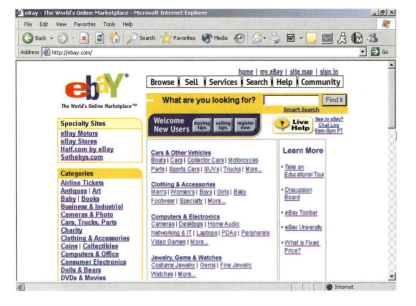

Figure 9.18 a&b

(a) Autobytel.com and (b) eBay are two highly successful online businesses that put customers in direct contact with incredibly rich sources of information.

In addition, shipping costs often make Web purchases more expensive. In fact, many things are not economical to ship—big-screen televisions, refrigerators, and most furniture, to name a few—no matter what the price discount. Michael Dell, on the other hand, has made a fortune by offering high-quality PCs strictly by Internet and phone sales, so it all depends.

So what *does* work? The online shopping successes give people something they can't get elsewhere. Amazon.com enables readers to choose from a massive inventory, most of which can be delivered to the customer's doorstep in two or three days. In addition, the site is rich in information, including reviews submitted by customers. And in 2002, the Web site started offering free shipping on orders over a certain amount of money. If you search for a book on Amazon.com, you'll find it—if it exists—and you'll probably find other books that will interest you. Autobytel offers great prices and a way to avoid haggling with dealers, an experience that virtually all car buyers detest. Finally, eBay puts collectors in contact with nearly one million other collectors worldwide; the site holds more than 10 million electronic auctions per month (see Figure 9.18).

If one word could sum up what all these sites share, it's **disintermediation**. All three of these online success stories take intermediaries—booksellers, car salesmen, and auctioneers—out of the picture. These sites put customers in direct contact with incredibly rich resources of information. They enable customers to make their own choices without being restricted to stock on hand (or a salesperson's interference).

SECURE ELECTRONIC TRANSACTIONS (SET)

What about credit card fraud at online shopping sites? To protect both merchants and customers, Visa, MasterCard, and American Express got together to create an online shopping security standard called **Secure Electronic Transactions** (**SET**). SET's goal is to create a security infrastructure using **digital certificates** for merchants and customers. A digital certificate is an electronic code that offers legitimacy to the business/customer relationship. Both the company and the customer need to satisfy registration requirements to obtain a certificate. To ensure that the certificates are valid, both certificates would have to be endorsed by a third-party **certificate authority** (**CA**). But very few online merchants are currently interested in SET because it requires customers to use cumbersome plug-in programs, which aren't popular with browser users.

Something like SET may be needed to get electronic commerce rolling, but it's overkill right now. Amazon.com reports that very few of its millions of customers have experienced any problems with credit card fraud. And just to make sure that consumers have full confidence, the company promises to cover the full $50 of your personal liability should someone make fraudulent use of your credit card.

ONLINE BANKING

In **online banking**, you can use a Web browser to access your accounts, balance your checkbook, transfer funds, and even pay bills online (see Figure 9.19). Currently, online banking offers a competitive advantage in attracting new customers. It's now a necessary and expected service, like ATMs.

Banks implement online banking in different ways. One method makes use of checkbook programs such as Microsoft Money or Intuit's Quicken, enabling customers to balance their checkbooks automatically. The drawback, however, is that you have to access your online banking account from the computer that has all the Money or Quicken data, and this data could be examined by anyone with access to your computer. An advantage is that Money and Quicken offer powerful features for budgeting your money and analyzing your spending habits.

Easier to use are Web-based systems that require only one program: a Web browser. All the data is stored on the bank's computer, not your own, which means you can access your account anywhere. Web-based online banking is also much easier to use. (So far, however, the Web-based systems don't offer advanced features such as budgeting and spending

analysis.) What's in it for the banks? Plenty. Bank branches and tellers cost a lot of money.

Many people who would like to use online banking are concerned about losing their money. As long as you follow certain precautions, however, you have little need for concern. Online banking is much safer than using an ATM.

When you access an online banking account, be sure you're doing so in your browser's **secure mode**. In the secure mode, the browser uses encryption to communicate with the bank's server. Check your browser's documentation to find out where the secure mode icon appears and what it looks like. Also, be sure you're using the highest-level **128-bit domestic-level encryption**, which is invulnerable to decoding. Above all else, keep your password safe.

Another concern is the security of the bank's **electronic vault**, a mainframe computer that stores account holders' information. Because no computer system is totally secure, it's reasonable to feel concerned that an intruder could gain access to the vault and steal your money. Still, the threat is small. Online banks use state-of-the-art security systems, including firewalls (see Figure 9.20). An additional security measure is **active monitoring**, in

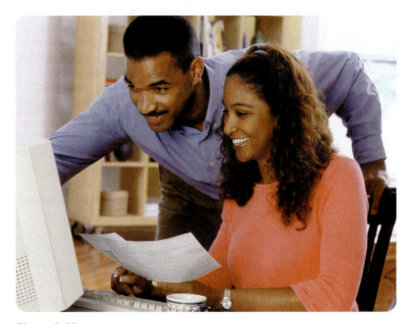

Figure 9.19

Online banking allows customers to access their accounts and balance checkbooks online. Some 12 million households make regular use of online banking.

Figure 9.20
Wachovia Corporation uses security measures such as encryption, filters, and firewalls to ensure their customers' online banking is secure.

which a security team constantly monitors the vault for the telltale signs of unauthorized access.

ONLINE STOCK TRADING

Another area of e-commerce experiencing rapid growth is **online stock trading**. *Rapid* probably isn't strong enough; available only since 1996, online stock trading now accounts for one out of every six stock trades, making it easily the fastest growing application in consumer-based e-commerce. Offering secure connections through the customer's Web browser, online stock trading sites enable investors to buy and sell stocks online, without the aid of a broker (see Figure 9.21).

The attraction of online stock trading can be summed up in one word: cost. Traditional, full-service brokerages charge up to $100 per trade; discount brokerages charge about $50. But the most aggressive e-traders have cut the charges to $10 per trade or less. E-traders can offer such low prices because the trading is automatic—no human broker is involved—and because they can make money on the side by earning money on investors' accounts.

There are two concerns worth mentioning: security and timeliness. The issue of making secure trades isn't really any different from the general issue of online security. All financial institutions such as banks and brokerages use secure connections. This doesn't mean that transactions can't be intercepted or redirected, but millions of dollars are transacted online every day without incident. Online trading of stocks is regulated by the Securities and Exchange Commission in the same way other methods of trading are. Most brokerages use trade confirmation methods that help to ensure that all trades are transacted properly.

Timeliness is an issue only if there is a delay in completing a transaction and that delay causes you to miss an opportunity that you wanted to take advantage of. Delays can be caused by a multitude of things, such as power outages, dropped connections, computer overload, and batch processing. On the other hand, most online transactions take place in a timely manner and without delay.

There is a downside to online trading, according to investment professionals. Online trading appeals to an amateur investor's worst instincts—namely, buying

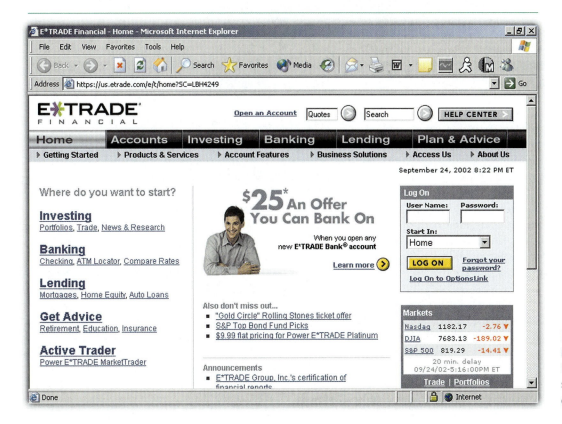

Figure 9.21
E-trading sites enable investors to buy and sell stocks online without going through a broker.

when the market's at its peak of enthusiasm (and prices are also at their peak) and then selling when prices start to drop. This translates to buying high and selling low. You don't make money that way; you lose money. That's true even when, overall, the market is going up. Most investment counselors believe that amateurs are well advised to avoid frequent trading (sometimes called day-trading). Also, when the market plunges, electronic investors often receive a rude shock: due to overloaded Internet servers, they can't unload their stocks until the market hits the bottom.

ONLINE TRAVEL RESERVATIONS

Another area of e-commerce experiencing rapid growth is **online travel reservations.** Sites such as CheapTickets.com and Expedia.com allow you to book flights, hotels, and car rentals online, as well as help you find the cheapest fares based on your trip parameters (see Figure 9.22). Sites such as these allow you to purchase **e-tickets** so that you can quickly check in at airport terminals by using small self-serve kiosks. In fact, e-tickets cost 10 to 15 dollars less than standard, paper-copy tickets.

In addition, nearly every hotel and car-rental agency is now online, and you can often check room or car availability and book a reservation without making a single call. And if you're looking for backpacking trails at a national park, you're sure to find plenty of free information using any search engine.

Figure 9.22
Sites such as CheapTickets.com are popular among travelers.

CHAPTER REVIEW | Takeaway Points | Key Terms and Concepts | Matching | Multiple Choice | Fill-In | Short Answer | Exercises/ Projects | Web Research | HOME

1 2 3 4 5 6 7 8 9 10 11 12 13 14 15 16

TAKEAWAY POINTS

- Millions of Internet users turn to the Web to research current events, general information, product information, scientific developments, and much more.

- In hypertext, related information is referenced by means of links instead of being fully explained or defined in the same location. On the Web, authors can link to information created by others.

- The Web is an Internet service that involves the use of a client (the browser) and a Web server, which retrieves documents requested by clients.

- A URL consists of the protocol (such as http://), the server (such as www), the path (such as /windows/ie), and the resource name (such as default.htm). URLs enable Web authors to state the exact location of a resource available on the Internet.

- To create Web pages, Web authors use Hypertext Markup Language (HTML).

- Web subject guides index a limited number of high-quality pages, whereas full Web search engines enable you to search huge databases of Web documents.

- Most Web searches retrieve too many irrelevant documents. You can improve search results by using inclusion and exclusion operators, phrase searches, and Boolean operators.

- Anyone can publish anything on the Web. Don't accept any information you find until you have critically evaluated the author's credentials and purpose for publishing the page.

- Most e-commerce involves business-to-business links that currently require value-added networks (VANs) and electronic data interchange (EDI). Many businesses are moving these transactions to the Internet to take advantage of the Internet's flexibility, widespread availability, and ease of use.

- Online shopping succeeds when it gives people something they can't get in traditional retail stores, such as an enormous selection or a way to avoid aggressive sales personnel.

- Online banking enables customers to use a Web browser to access their accounts, balance checkbooks, transfer funds, and pay bills online. Online banking is growing rapidly, although some potential users are concerned about security.

- One of the most rapidly growing forms of e-commerce is online trading, but most investors would be well advised to stick with their investments rather than buying or selling too frequently.

- Making online travel reservations is a popular way to use the Web. Travelers like the ease of e-tickets, which allow them to check in quickly at the airport terminal.

HOME | Takeaway Points | Key Terms and Concepts | Matching | Multiple Choice | Fill-In | Short Answer | Exercises/ Projects | Web Research | CHAPTER REVIEW

KEY TERMS AND CONCEPTS

128-bit domestic-level
  encryption
active monitoring
Address toolbar
  (Location toolbar)
bookmark
Boolean search
business-to-business (B2B)
  e-commerce
certificate authority (CA)
chunk
click-and-brick
clickstream
default start page
digital certificate
disintermediation
distributed
  hypermedia system
domain
electronic commerce
  (e-commerce)
electronic data
  interchange (EDI)
electronic vault

elements
end tag
e-ticket
exclusion operator
graphical browser
history list
home page
hyperlink
hypermedia
hypertext
Hypertext Markup
  Language (HTML)
Hypertext Transfer
  Protocol (HTTP)
inclusion operator
index page
markup language
navigation button
nest
online banking
online stock trading
online travel reservations
path
phrase searching

point of presence (PoP)
program icon
protocol
proximity operator
resource name
search engine
search operators
Secure Electronic
  Transactions (SET)
secure mode
server
specialized search engine
stale link (broken link)
start tag
status bar
subject guide
text-only browser
uniform resource
  locator (URL)
value-added network (VAN)
Web browser
Web server program
wildcards
World Wide Web

1 2 3 4 5 6 7 8 9 10 11 12 13 14 15 16

MATCHING

Match each key term in the left column with the most accurate definition in the right column.

_____ 1. World Wide Web

_____ 2. hypertext

_____ 3. hypermedia

_____ 4. Secure Electronic Transactions (SET)

_____ 5. index page

_____ 6. subject guide

_____ 7. program icon

_____ 8. certificate authority (CA)

_____ 9. Web server

_____ 10. wildcard

_____ 11. Web site

_____ 12. electronic commerce

_____ 13. Hypertext Transfer Protocol (HTTP)

_____ 14. click-and-brick

_____ 15. markup language

a. the use of telecommunications or wide area networking to carry out financial transactions

b. also known as the default page or home page for a Web site

c. a program that waits for browsers to request a Web page

d. groups Web pages under similar headings such as Business, News, or Travel

e. third-party organization that validates digital certificates

f. a set of codes that authors can use to identify portions of a document for a Web page

g. a collection of related Web pages

h. retailers that have both an online and a traditional retail store presence

i. a way of presenting information so that its sequence is left up to the reader

j. the protocol that specifies the format of URLs as well as the procedure clients and servers follow to establish communication

k. displays an animation when the browser is attempting to download information from the Web

l. symbols that you can use, along with words, for advanced searches

m. an online shopping security standard

n. an indispensable information resource on the Internet

o. enables users to retrieve multimedia resources such as sound and movies, as well as text

MULTIPLE CHOICE

Circle the correct choice for each of the following.

1. Links to documents that have disappeared are known as what?
   a. Unknown links
   b. Tenuous links
   c. Hyperlinks
   d. Stale links

2. If you click the Home button in a Web browser, what happens?
   a. The home page of the site you are visiting is displayed.
   b. The browser helps you create a home page.
   c. The default startup page for the browser is displayed.
   d. The displayed page becomes your home page.

3. Which of the following are not typically indexed in full Web search engines?
   a. Resource information
   b. Job advertisements
   c. Magazines
   d. News stories

4. When using a search engine, a minus sign is an example of what?
   a. An exclusion operator
   b. An addition operator
   c. A mathematical operator
   d. An inclusion operator

5. Which of the following is a commonly used wildcard character?
   a. Plus sign
   b. Slash
   c. Minus sign
   d. Asterisk

6. A complete URL does *not* contain which one of the following?
   a. Protocol
   b. Server
   c. Path
   d. Author

7. Which of the following is the markup language commonly used by Web authors?
   a. SGML
   b. XML
   c. HTML
   d. DHTML

8. Which of the following is *not* a Boolean operator?
   a. AND
   b. NEAR
   c. NOT
   d. NOR

9. Which of the following is a common browser navigation button?
   a. Back
   b. Save
   c. Insert
   d. Bold

10. Business-to-business e-commerce relies on which data standard?
    a. Point of presence (PoP)
    b. Electronic data interchange (EDI)
    c. Value-added networks (VANs)
    d. Secure Electronic Transaction (SET)

CHAPTER REVIEW
1 2 3 4 5 6 7 8 9 10 11 12 13 14 15 16

CHAPTER
REVIEW

Takeaway
Points

Key Terms
and Concepts

Matching

Multiple
Choice

Fill-In

Short
Answer

Exercises/
Projects

Web
Research

HOME

FILL-IN

In the blanks provided, write the correct answer for each of the following.

1. To create a Web page, Web authors use a _____ that is called _____.

2. The first Web browsers were _____ that could not display graphics.

3. The Web is a _____ system, where the responsibility for creating content is distributed among many people.

4. If you can't find what you are looking for using a Web subject guide, you can try a _____, such as Lycos or AltaVista.

5. A browser's _____ list keeps a list of the Web pages that you've accessed.

6. _____ are underlined or highlighted words that you can click to bring another document into view.

7. _____ are used to nest Boolean expressions, enabling you to phrase search questions accurately.

8. _____ searches use key words such as AND, OR, and NOT.

9. Some search engines have a _____, which enables you to specify that the two linked words appear close together.

10. When doing a _____, you enclose a phrase within quotation marks.

11. A _____ is standard for describing the location of resources on the Web.

12. A _____ is an online shopping security standard used to protect both merchants and customers.

13. When you access an online banking account, be sure you're doing so in the browser's _____.

14. An additional security measure is _____, in which a security team constantly monitors the electronic vault for signs of unauthorized access.

15. Business-to-business e-commerce requires companies to lease network capacity from a _____ network.

SHORT ANSWER

1. What is the difference between a Web server and a Web browser?

2. What are some rules of thumb for evaluating content on the Web?

3. Online stock trading now accounts for one out of every six stock trades, making it one of the fastest growing consumer-based applications of e-commerce. Why has online stock trading been so successful? What are the potential pitfalls of online trading?

4. Have you purchased an item from a merchant over the Internet? Describe the item, the merchant, and the method of payment. Would you use the Internet to make another purchase? Explain why or why not.

5. Now that you have completed this chapter, you should be able to conduct more effective searches. List three search engines that you use most frequently to find information on the Internet, and explain why you prefer these search engines over the others.

HOME | Takeaway Points | Key Terms and Concepts | Matching | Multiple Choice | Fill-In | Short Answer | Exercises/ Projects | Web Research | CHAPTER REVIEW

EXERCISES/PROJECTS

1. Explain the difference between a browser's history list and Favorites (Internet Explorer) or Bookmarks (Netscape Navigator). Have you used either one? Explain how you used them. Did you know that you can place very frequently visited Web sites in your Links Toolbar (Internet Explorer) or in your Personal Toolbar (Netscape Navigator)? Select one of these two browsers and explain how you can place links to Web sites in the appropriate toolbar. If you have never done this, use the browser's help feature to learn how.

2. The two leading browsers are Internet Explorer and Netscape Navigator. Which of the browsers do you prefer to use and why? What version are you currently using? What are the latest versions of Internet Explorer and Netscape Navigator?

3. Internet sales are not limited only to items that are sold by merchants. Individuals can also use the Internet to buy and sell new or used items, and one of the most popular methods is through an online auction. Have you used the Internet to buy or sell an item? If you have participated in an online auction, identify the auction, describe the item, and tell whether you successfully sold or purchased it. Describe how the payment was made and how the item was shipped. Explain why you would or would not use an Internet auction to sell or purchase another item. (If you have not participated in an online auction, you can explore an auction site as part of one of the Web Research questions.)

4. Use the Internet to find two potential jobs in the field of your current or intended major. List the URLs of the sites that list the positions, and describe each job—the organization, location, necessary qualifications, benefits, salary, and so on. Explain why you feel that your major coursework does or does not prepare you to assume either of these two positions.

5. As institutions begin to offer distance learning courses, student access to library materials becomes a critical issue. Since students may not be able to visit an institution's library physically, how will they read relevant materials? One method is to make full-text versions of books and periodicals available online. Visit your school's library (either physically or electronically) and determine whether it offers online reference materials. Does your library provide these materials directly, or does it use a third party to provide these services? Can you read the online materials from off-campus as well as on-campus? Are the materials accessible only to faculty and students? If so, how do they gain permission to view the materials?

1 2 3 4 5 6 7 8 9 10 11 12 13 14 15 16

WEB RESEARCH

1. Are you in the mood to do a little shopping? Visit eBay at **http://ebay.com**, and track the sale of an item. Select and describe an item that you wish to purchase. There are two methods for finding your item.

   - You can select a general category and then refine your search by selecting successive subcategories.
   - You can enter a description of the item in the search textbox and then click the Search button.

   Try both methods. Which method do you prefer? How many items met your criteria? If the number is too large, refine your criteria. View the list of items and sellers, and select a specific item. Identify the item, the seller, the first bid, the current bid, the bid increment, the number of bids, and the amount of time left in the auction. Click the bid history link, and identify the bidders and how many bids they have submitted. Click the view comments in seller's Feedback Profile link to see the seller's rating. What is the seller's overall number of positive, neutral, and negative ratings? Based on buyer activity and the seller's profile, determine the amount of money that you would initially bid for this item. Track the bidding of this item until the auction closes, and increase your imagined bid as necessary. When the auction ends, determine whether you would have been the successful bidder. If not, what was your maximum bid, and what was the final bid? Would you consider actually bidding for items in an online auction?

2. Online stock trading is one of the fastest growing applications in consumer-based e-commerce. To see why, visit E*TRADE, one of the most popular online trading sites, at **www.etrade.com/global.html**. What was the last level of the NASDAQ, DJIA, S&P 500, and 30-year bonds? Although you will not formally open an account online, look at the steps that are needed to open one. (Enter the requested information, but don't accept the agreement!)

   - **Step One** What are the three nonretirement personal account types? How are they funded, and what are the minimum amounts?
   - **Step Two** What personal information is needed?
   - **Step Three** What information is needed to create your investment profile?
   - **Step Four** What is the final step?

   What are the five areas in which you can invest your money? You may be surprised that you're not going to "play a stock market game" by investing a specified amount of money for one or two weeks and then tracking your gains or losses. Why do you think you weren't asked to do this?

3. Suppose one of your instructors requires you to write a research paper for his or her class. Besides referencing printed sources found in books and periodicals, you can use the Internet to find information. However, before using Internet materials, you should critically evaluate them. Since citing Internet-based sources is not the same as citing traditional references, visit UC Berkeley's "Library style" site at **www.lib.berkeley.edu/TeachingLib/ Guides/Internet/Style.html** to learn how to properly cite Internet and electronic resources. What are the three general content areas and corresponding style sheets discussed on this site? Although there are minor differences, what are the main components of citations for:

   - WWW sites?
   - E-mail messages?
   - Online databases?

   Why do you think that the date the site was last accessed is always included? Have you already had an occasion to "cite a site" in a paper? If you have, list the title of your paper and the style you used.

4. Use the search techniques discussed in this chapter to locate two sites that sell papers. Identify the URLs of these sites, how you find a specific topic, and the costs of purchasing a paper. Do these sites post any disclaimers about students using their papers? Do they provide sample writings? What is the quality of the paper?

   Do you know anyone who has purchased an online paper? Discuss the ethics of using one of these sites to purchase a research or term paper.

   (Warning: You should also know that there are software applications and Web sites that instructors can use to see if students have gotten a paper from online sites.)

SPOTLIGHT

Multimedia &
Virtual Reality

You're on the Web and decide you want to learn more about multimedia, so you go to www.nasa.gov/gallery/ to see what NASA has to offer (see Figure 9A). Your professor posts a PowerPoint presentation and an audio track of his lecture, which you watch from the Web when you're free later that night. You take a break from studying and visit the pool tables at Yahoo!, watching the cue move on the screen as the other player lines up her shot. You do all of this, of course, from your own computer. Welcome to the world of multimedia.

Multimedia has been around for a while, but it's much easier to implement with computer and Internet technology—an obvious point if you think about the difficulties of delivering real-time video with the morning newspaper. In fact, multimedia is what makes the Web so popular.

In this spotlight, you'll learn how professional graphic artists develop their work using the tools of digital media production—a booming field in which artistic and professional opportunities abound. You'll also consider the fascinating and often disturbing potential of computer-based multimedia to draw us into immersive, computer-based environments, such as three-dimensional virtual realities that you can explore endlessly, graphics-intensive action and role-playing games, communities of simulated people that exist only on the Internet, and much more.

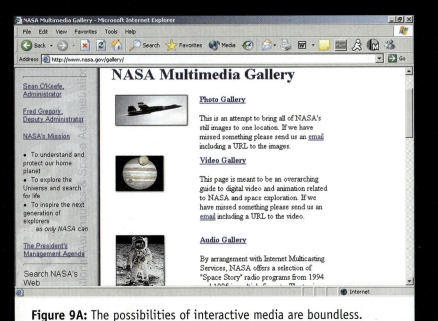

Figure 9A: The possibilities of interactive media are boundless.

INTRODUCING MULTIMEDIA

You've heard of it before, but what exactly *is* **multimedia**? The standard definition is any presentation that involves two or more media, such as text, graphics, or sound (see Figure 9B). By this ho-hum definition, any TV show or movie is a multimedia experience. What makes multimedia *exciting* is another characteristic altogether: interactivity. In **interactive multimedia**, users can choose their own path through the presentation. The interactive dimension makes computer-based multimedia a non–couch-potato technology; instead of sitting back and letting someone else determine the presentation's flow, you're in control.

Figure 9B: Multimedia presentations involve two or more media. Such presentations are now the norm in professional settings.

9.A

Interactivity has helped make the Web popular; in fact, the Web could be viewed as a gigantic multimedia presentation. Most Web pages include graphics along with the text, and many also offer animations, videos, and sounds. The Web's navigation method, called **hypertext**, enables users to browse as they please. (In a hypertext world, you choose where you want to go by clicking a link to another document.) By blending multimedia with the Web, **hypermedia** becomes possible. In hypermedia, media other than text become the vehicle for navigating to new material. On many Web pages, for instance, you can click parts of a graphic to access a different page.

Multimedia Hardware

Just a few years ago, most personal computers needed additional equipment to run multimedia presentations. Today, this equipment—a sound card, a CD- or DVD-ROM drive, and speakers—is standard issue. If you want to go into serious multimedia production, you may need additional equipment, such as a pen-based graphics tablet, stereo microphones, a digital camera, and a video adapter. If you enjoy playing games, you'll want a 3-D video accelerator, which is an add-on video adapter that works with your current video card. For surround sound, you'll need a sound card capable of producing the surround effect. And, while you're at it, pick up a few extra speakers and a subwoofer.

Multimedia Applications

Multimedia is used for any computer application in which text alone won't do. Arguably, this category includes just about *every* computer application, because graphics, sounds, animations, and video can often do a more effective job of involving the user (and conveying information) than text alone.

Multimedia is a prerequisite for computer games of all kinds, but it's also finding growing use in computer-based education (CBE), distance learning, and computer-based training (CBT). Hot sellers in the CD/DVD-ROM market include multimedia versions of reference works, such as dictionaries (which include recordings that tell you how to pronounce difficult words), encyclopedias (replete with sound and video clips from famous moments in history), and how-to guides (which use multimedia to show you how to do just about anything around the home) (see Figure 9C).

In businesses, multimedia can be seen not just in multimedia presentations using PowerPoint and other software. It's also finding its way into **information kiosks** (automated presentation systems used for public information or employee training), **simulations** (which help companies avoid dangerous and often expensive real-life experiments), and even into corporate databases (see Figure 9D). For example, one major wholesale electronics firm is developing an object-oriented database to store complex images of engineering designs, which can't be stored in a text-only database. By making these designs accessible to buyers, the firm can help them determine quickly whether a given design is appropriate for their needs.

Figure 9D: In businesses, multimedia is finding its way into presentations, information kiosks, and training systems.

Figure 9C: DVD-ROM versions of reference works such as the *Encyclopædia Britannica* offer users not just text, but photos, maps, video clips, audio clips, and more.

MULTIMEDIA SOFTWARE: INTRODUCING THE CAST

If multimedia is a show, then a multimedia presentation involves some or all of the following cast members: bit-mapped graphics, vector graphics, edited photographs, rendered three-dimensional images, edited videos, and synthesized sound. In the following sections, we'll discuss each of these cast members and look briefly at some of the software used to create multimedia productions.

Compression and Decompression (Codecs)

Computers can work with art, photographs, videos, and sounds, but they can do so only when these multimedia resources are stored in digitized files. These files, however, require huge amounts of storage space. For example, an average-sized hard disk might store only 30 or 40 audio CDs, and there wouldn't be much room left for system software or applications. To reduce the size of multimedia files, most software uses compression/decompression algorithms called **codecs**.

Codecs use two different approaches to compression, called **lossless compression** and **lossy compression**. In lossless compression, the original file is compressed so that it can be completely restored, without flaw, when decompression occurs. In lossy compression, the original file is processed so that some information is permanently removed. However, you probably won't notice the loss. Lossy compression techniques eliminate information that isn't perceived when people see pictures or hear sounds, such as very high notes and frames from a video that are above the number needed to eliminate the flicker effect.

Figure 9E: Paint programs are used to create bit-mapped graphics, which are composed of tiny dots, each corresponding to one pixel on the computer's display.

A great site to check out to learn more about multimedia and graphics software is About's "Graphic Software" at **http://graphicssoft.about.com**.

Paint Programs

Paint programs are used to create **bit-mapped graphics** (also called **raster graphics**), which are composed of tiny dots, each corresponding to one pixel on the computer's display (see Figure 9E). Professional paint programs such as Fractal Design Painter enable you to create beautiful effects, even if you're not good at art! Although paint programs enable artists to create pictures easily, the resulting bit-mapped image is difficult to edit. To do so, you must zoom the picture so that you can edit the individual pixels, and enlargement may produce an unattractive distortion called the *jaggies*.

Although most monitors can't display more than 72 dots per inch (dpi), paint programs can create and store bit-mapped graphics at higher resolutions, which can make a big difference in their appearance when they're printed.

Just how many colors you can display depends on the amount of video RAM in your system. The more colors shown on-screen, the more memory is required to store them. A file that stores eight bits of color information per pixel can display a **color depth** of only 256 colors. For realistic color photographs, a color depth of 16.7 million colors is needed (24 bits per pixel).

Paint programs can save your work to a variety of file formats, including the following standard formats:

Graphics Interchange Format (GIF) GIF (pronounced "jiff" or "giff") is a 256-color file format that uses lossless compression to reduce file size. It's best for simple images with large areas of solid colors. Because this file format is a Web standard, it's often used for Web pages.

Joint Photographic Experts Group (JPEG) The JPEG (pronounced "jay-peg") format can store up to 16.7 million colors and is best for complex images, such as photographs. This image format is also a Web standard. The JPEG file format uses lossy compression to reduce file size.

Portable Network Graphics (PNG) PNG (pronounced "ping") is a new alternative to GIF that doesn't require companies to pay a royalty for the lossless compression technique used.

Windows Bitmap (BMP) BMP is a standard bit-mapped graphics format developed for Microsoft Windows. Compression is optional, so BMP files tend to be very large.

Image Editors

Image editors are sophisticated versions of paint programs designed for editing and transforming—but not creating—complex bit-mapped images, such as photographs. These programs make use of automated image processing algorithms to add a variety of special effects to photographic images. They also enable skilled users to doctor photographs in a way that leaves few traces behind.

Leading image editors such as Adobe Photoshop have been used by professional design studios for years (see Figure 9F), but image editors may soon capture a wider market due to the booming market for digital cameras. Programs such as Adobe's PhotoDeluxe are designed for beginners who want to perform the most common image enhancement tasks quickly and easily and then print their pictures on a color printer. Among the image processing tasks that PhotoDeluxe can perform are removing red-eye from flash snapshots and adjusting the picture's overall color cast.

Figure 9F: Adobe Photoshop is an image editor that has been used by professional design studios for years.

Drawing Programs

Drawing programs are used to create **vector graphics**, in which each on-screen object is stored as a complex mathematical description. What this means, in practice, is that every object in a vector graphic can be independently edited and resized without introducing edge distortions, the bane of bit-mapped graphics. To compose an image with a drawing program, you create independent lines and shapes; you can then add colors and textures to these shapes. Because the resulting image has no inherent resolution, you can choose any size you want. The picture will be printed using the output device's highest resolution.

Professional drawing programs, such as Macromedia Freehand and Adobe Illustrator, save files by outputting instructions in the **PostScript** language, which is an automated **page description language** (**PDL**). A page description language is a programming language capable of precisely describing the appearance of a printed page, including fonts and graphics. PostScript is an established PDL standard widely used in desktop publishing.

To print PostScript files, you need a printer equipped with its own microprocessor and an interpreter capable of decoding PostScript instructions. PostScript graphics files are saved to the **Encapsulated PostScript** (**EPS**) format, which encapsulates the PostScript in a file that also contains a bit-mapped thumbnail image of the enclosed graphic. (The thumbnail image enables you to see the graphic on-screen.)

One drawback of drawing programs lies in the lack of Web support for vector graphics. Several proposals have been made for adopting a standard, and we should see one in the next few years.

Animation Programs

When you see a movie at a theater, you're actually looking at still images shown at a sufficiently high **frame rate** (images per second) so that the eye is tricked into seeing continuous motion. Like a movie, an **animation** consists of a series of still images displayed at a frame rate high enough to create the illusion of movement. Animators create each of the still images separately. In computer animation, the computer provides tools for creating the animation as well as running it.

It's easy to create a simple animation using the GIF graphics file format, which enables programs to store more than one image in a GIF file. Also stored in the file is a brief script that tells the application to play the images in a certain sequence and to display each for a set period of time. Because Web browsers can read GIF files and play the animations, **GIF animations** are common on the Web (see Figure 9G).

Professional animation programs provide more sophisticated tools for creating and controlling animations, but they create proprietary files. To view these files on the Web, you need a special viewer such as Macromedia's Flash Player or Shockwave Player (see Figure 9.H).

3-D Rendering Programs

A **3-D rendering** program adds three-dimensional effects to computer graphic objects. The results are strikingly realistic and can be rotated in any direction to achieve just the result the artist is looking for.

In the past, rendering software required a high-powered engineering workstation, but today's top desktop computers are up to the task. One rendering technique, **ray tracing**, adds amazing realism to a simulated three-dimensional object by adding variations in color intensity that would be produced by light falling on the object from multiple directions (which is the norm in the real world).

Video Editors

Video editors enable you to modify digitized videos, such as videos imported from a video camera by means of a video capture board. With a video editor, you can cut segments, resequence the video, add transitions, compress the file, and determine the video's frame rate (the number of still images displayed per second).

Figure 9G: The Ulead.com GIF animator is a popular Web animation product.

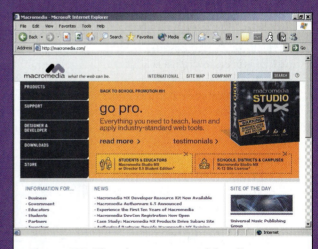

Figure 9H: When it comes to multimedia, Macromedia.com is one of the hottest sites on the Web. The Macromedia Flash Player and Shockwave Player are the most popular rich-content media players on the Internet. And Macromedia's Studio MX media development kit, released in late 2002, is a powerful tool for developing multimedia Internet applications.

Video editors also enable you to save video files to some or all of the following video file formats:

Moving Picture Experts Group (MPEG) MPEG is a family of video file formats and lossy compression standards for full-motion video. The most recent version, MPEG-2, offers resolutions high enough to fill a monitor's screen at speeds of up to 60 frames per second (fps). MPEG-2 is the video format used by DVD-ROM discs, and MPEG-2 videos include CD/DVD-quality audio.

QuickTime QuickTime is a video file format developed by Apple Computer. The latest version, QuickTime-6 Pro, plays full-screen, broadcast-quality video as well as CD/DVD-quality audio and is widely used in multimedia CD-ROM productions.

Video for Windows The native video file format for Microsoft Windows (often called AVI because these files use the .avi file name extension), this format isn't adequate for fullscreen, broadcast-quality video.

Because a huge amount of data must be stored to create realistic-looking video on a computer, all video file formats use compression/decompression (codec) techniques. For the best playback, special video adapters are also required. These adapters have hardware support for decoding videos at high speed.

To make video available on the Internet, **streaming video** formats have been developed. These formats enable the video picture to start playing almost immediately after the user clicks the video link. (With nonstreaming video, the user has to wait for the entire file to be transferred to the user's computer before playing begins.) Streaming video formats rely on compression, low frame rates, and small image

size to deliver video over the Internet, which does not have sufficient **bandwidth** (signal-carrying capacity) to disseminate broadcast-quality video. A variety of competing streaming video formats are available; the most popular format is RealNetworks' RealVideo format.

Audio Software

For capturing and processing sound for multimedia presentations, a variety of programs are available, including sound mixers, compression software, bass enhancers, synthesized stereo, and even on-screen music composition programs. You won't see any tape recorders in today's recording studios—just computers!

Digital audio **waveforms** (recorded live sounds or music) can be saved in a variety of file formats. Here are the most popular ones:

MP3 A sound file format with almost unbelievable characteristics: using MP3 (also known as MPEG-3), you can compress CD-quality digital audio by a factor of 12:1 with no perceptible loss in sound quality.

Sun/Next (AU) Sounds A low-fidelity monaural format developed for Sun and NeXT workstations and now widely used due to the small size of AU files. It's often used to distribute sample sounds over the Internet.

WAV Sounds The default Microsoft Windows sound file format (called WAV due to the .wav extension used to store these sounds). WAV sounds can be saved with a variety of quality levels, including low-fi mono all the way up to CD-quality stereo. WAV sounds usually aren't compressed, so they tend to take up a lot of disk space.

A new digital format, called **Ogg Vorbis**, is an even faster format than MP3. Ogg files are also about 20 percent smaller than MP3 files, so you can fit more of them onto your hard disk or MP3 player.

Streaming audio formats are available that enable Internet-accessed sounds to start playing almost immediately after the user clicks an audio link. The most popular streaming audio format, RealAudio, can deliver voice-quality audio over modem connections.

You'll also encounter **Musical Instrument Digital Interface** (**MIDI**) files, which don't contain waveforms. Instead, they contain a text-based description designed to drive **synthesizers**, electronic devices that simulate musical sounds. Sound cards have built-in synthesizers.

Figure 9I: The Windows Media Player is handy for burning CDs and for creating MP3 files.

MULTIMEDIA AUTHORING SYSTEMS: WRITING THE SCRIPT

Now that you've met the cast of multimedia productions, take a look at the tools you use to write the script. To create multimedia presentations, you use **authoring tools**. These tools enable you to specify which multimedia objects to use (such as text, pictures, videos, or animations), how to display them in relation to each other, how long to display them, and how to enable the user to interact with the presentation. To take full advantage of an authoring tool's capabilities, it's often necessary to learn a **scripting language** (an easy-to-learn programming language). A leading authoring package is Macromedia Director.

Commercial authoring tools such as Macromedia Director save output in proprietary file formats. To view Macromedia presentations on a Web site, it's necessary to download and install a **plug-in program** (software that extends a browser's capabilities). Some users are bothered by having to download viewers and so the Web's standards-setting body, the World Wide Web Consortium (W3C), recently approved the **Synchronized Multimedia Integration Language** (**SMIL**), a simple multimedia scripting language designed for Web pages. If SMIL is supported by Web browsers, Internet users will be able to enjoy enhanced multimedia without having to download programs.

VIRTUAL REALITY: TOWARD THE HOLODECK?

You've probably seen one of the episodes of *Star Trek: The Next Generation* where the crew takes some time off in the Holodeck, an immersive virtual reality environment. (One of the standard plots is that the crew gets trapped in the Holodeck and has to fight for their lives against virtual creatures that suddenly become deadly.) **Virtual reality** (**VR**) refers to the creation of an immersive, three-dimensional world that appears as if you can actually go inside and explore it.

Enhancing the Immersive Experience: VR Hardware

Displayed on a two-dimensional computer screen, virtual reality environments are lots of fun; you use navigation controls that enable you to walk around—or fly, if you prefer—in the simulated world. But virtual reality comes into its own when you don a **head-mounted display** (**HMD**), a helmet-like contraption equipped with stereo LCD displays (see Figure 9J). You can then physically explore what appears to be a complex virtual environment, even though you're really walking around in a big, empty room.

The most advanced (and expensive) immersive technology to date is the **Cave Automatic Virtual Environment** (**CAVE**), which projects stereo images on walls to give the illusion of a virtual environment. To create the illusion of objects inside the environment, explorers wear special shutter glasses that alternately block the left and right eyes in synchrony with the projection sequence, which similarly alternates between left and right stereo vision seen from the person's location. The effect is so realistic that explorers can't tell the difference between real and simulated objects in the room unless they touch them.

Figure 9J: Virtual reality refers to the creation of a three-dimensional world that appears as if you can go inside and explore it. Navigation controls enable you to walk around or fly within the simulated world.

Bringing VR to the Internet: VRML

On the Web, virtual realities can be created by means of the **Virtual Reality Modeling Language** (**VRML**, pronounced "vir-mal"). VRML enables programmers to define the characteristics of Web-accessible, three-dimensional worlds, through which visitors can journey.

To visit a VRML site on the Web, you'll need to equip your Web browser with a VRML plug-in, such as the Microsoft VRML Viewer for Internet Explorer, or WorldView (Intervista Software), a VRML plug-in for Netscape

Navigator. After installing the plug-in and accessing a VRML "world" (a Web site with the .wrl extension), you can walk (or "fly") through the three-dimensional construct.

In some virtual worlds, you'll see other explorers who are virtually represented by means of an **avatar**, a graphical representation of a computer user who is exploring the world. You can choose your own avatar and interact with other users' avatars.

Practical Applications of VR

What's the use of virtual reality? For consumers, the answer is simple: games. Almost all top-selling computer games offer three-dimensional virtual realities. But virtual reality (VR) isn't all fun and games (see Figure 9K). In the military, VR systems are being used to train fighter pilots and combat soldiers. In architecture, VR simulations enable clients to preview and walk through an architect's design. In medicine, VR is being used to train surgeons in delicate and dangerous surgical techniques. In manufacturing, VR is being used to analyze complex, three-dimensional structures to make sure that they have been correctly designed and can be manufactured in a cost-effective way.

Figure 9K: In medicine, VR simulation is being used to train surgeons in new techniques.

COMPUTER GAMES

By any standard, computer games are big business. In the United States, they bring in sales at a clip of $6 billion per year, and the market shows no signs of shrinking.

This highly profitable industry got its start in the 1970s, when the earliest computer video games (such as Pong) appeared in bars and gaming arcades. Next, video games came to the living room with the advent of Atari, Nintendo, and Sega console game players, which are special-purpose computers designed to display their output on a TV screen. Games soon migrated to personal computers—and from there, to the Internet.

The VR Factor

Taking a cue from virtual reality, the hottest computer games offer three-dimensional, graphical environments that players can explore. They've helped to fuel explosive growth in the computer gaming market. One of the earliest three-dimensional, VR-type games, Doom, has sold over 2.7 million copies, and it's believed that some 20 million copies of the game are in use worldwide.

3-D games have also driven computer video card manufacturers to new feats of technical innovation; today's 3-D video cards offer sophisticated, ultra-fast graphics processing that, only a few years ago, would have required a supercomputer to equal.

A new wrinkle on the gaming scene is **multiplayer online gaming**, an Internet-based gaming service that enables players to engage other characters—and in this case, they're controlled by other players rather than by the computer. Combining a rich, graphical virtual environment with multiplayer thrills, these services are attracting increasing numbers of users. There's a technical problem, though, caused by the Internet's inherent latency, which can cause characters to freeze up momentarily—or even disappear, if the user's connection is lost. (Latency is caused by the random nature with which packets travel the Internet. Humans perceive even the slightest lag in timing, so this imperfection in the delivery of sound and images is a challenge for developers.)

Too Much Violence?

Computer gaming isn't universally admired. More than one-third of all games fall into the action category; among these, the most popular are so-called "splatter" games, which emphasize all-out violence of an especially bloody sort. Parents and politicians express the concern that kids who play these games may be learning aggressive behaviors that will prove dysfunctional in real life—and they may be right.

In a study, 210 college students were observed before and after playing an especially violent computer game. Researchers found the students were more hostile and reacted more aggressively after playing the game. Another study found that young men who played violent computer games during their teenage years were more likely to commit crimes.

Fears concerning the impact of violent computer games were heightened by the Columbine High School tragedy in 1999, in which two Littleton, Colorado, teenagers opened fire on teachers and fellow students before committing suicide. Subsequently, investigators learned that the boys were great fans of splatter games such as Doom and Quake, and may have patterned their massacre after their gaming experiences.

Still, psychologists disagree on the effect of violent computer games. Some point out that they're little more than an extension of the World War II "combat" games that kids used to play on street corners before the television—and the computer—came along. Others claim that violent video games provide an outlet for aggression that might otherwise materialize in homes and schools.

One thing's for certain: computer games keep getting more violent. In the past few years, the video game industry has released a slew of new titles that offer a smoother gaming experience, particularly when you're connected to the Internet in multiplayer mode—and, of course, much more

realistic beheadings, amputations, and disembowelments.

MUDs

Popular among gamers for years has been the non–computer-based Dungeons and Dragons role-playing game, in which players can take on the personalities and powers of fantasy characters, including elves, sorcerers, and muscle-bound adventurers, as they interact with other players. Role-playing games are a natural for Internet-connected computers, which enable players to participate even if they're not physically present in the same room. Although several types of Internet-mediated role-playing games exist, they're generally called **MUDs**, an acronym for **multiuser dungeons**.

MUDs and their various offshoots offer users a text-only environment, consisting (generally) of a number of rooms—sometimes

thousands of them—inhabited by various online characters. You can ask for a description of the room, a list of players present in the room, and additional facts. You interact with other players by means of text chatting, very much like the chat rooms on America Online or the channels to be found on Internet Relay Chat (IRC).

If MUDs are text-only, what's so engrossing about them? Just ask the regulars. It's a matter of using your imagination. Most MUDs focus on themes derived from popular books (such as Roger Zelazny's *Amber* novels or Anne McCaffrey's *Pern* series), TV and movies (such as *Star Wars*), or role-playing games. Within a MUD, you can construct a persona for yourself, build a fantasy environment around you, and share the experience with other players.

MUDs aren't necessarily all fun and games. On most MUDs, player killing is allowed or tolerated, which means that your character might suddenly get zapped. You'll have to invent a new character, and you may lose all the possessions and powers your character has acquired. In addition, women often complain that male players harass them online to the point that they give up and log off.

Graphical MUDs

The latest MUD development, **graphical MUDs (gMUDs)**, brings the virtual environment to life with three-dimensional, graphical environments (see Figure 9L). Many are directly accessible online with no special equipment other than a Web browser, but a new trend is a commercial gMUD that relies on a locally installed game package to speed up processing. Examples include Ultima Online and EverQuest. Players fork over up to $40 for the locally installed software and $10 or more per month for online usage.

Figure 9L: Graphical MUDs like EverQuest bring the virtual environment to life with three-dimensional, graphical environments.

Telecommunications: Exchanging Data via the Telephone System

CHAPTER 10

What You'll Learn . . .

When you have finished reading this chapter, you will be able to:

1. Explain the limitations of the public switched telephone network (PSTN) for sending and receiving computer data.

2. Discuss how modems transform digital computer signals into the analog tones suited for the telephone system.

3. Define *bandwidth* and discuss the bandwidth needs of typical users.

4. List two digital telephony standards that can bring digital connections into homes and offices using existing wiring.

5. Provide examples of how convergence is blurring the boundaries among popular communication devices, including phones, computers, and TVs.

6. Discuss the prospects for telephony through the Internet.

Suppose you're on a trip and need to access your e-mail, but you don't have your laptop with you. No problem, you just use your Web-enabled cell phone to retrieve your messages. As for sending e-mail messages back: no problem, you can do this too with most messaging devices. Back at home, you hop on your ultra-fast DSL connection to download and upload files. The whole time, you're experiencing the realities of **telecommunications.** Defined broadly, this term refers to the transmission of information of any type using the telephone system. In this chapter, we'll discuss an important aspect of telecommunications: the transmission of computer data through the telephone system.

Although you use the telephone system to send and receive computer data all the time, it's important to understand the phone system's limitations for this purpose. As you'll learn in this chapter, most telephone connections in homes and offices offer analog service, which isn't ideal for data communication. You'll also learn why analog connections are still so common and how this situation is changing as more and more new digital telephone services become available. **Digital telephony** uses all digital protocols—the telephones are digital, and the transmission is all handled digitally. We'll discuss digital telephony throughout this chapter.

Destinations

To learn more about PSTN and fast-breaking new telecommunications technologies, a great place to start is HelloDirect.com's Get Informed tutorials at **http://telecom.hello-direct.com/docs/Tutorials/default.asp**.

Understanding the Telephone System

Let's start with the beginning: the **public switched telephone network** (**PSTN**), derisively (and somewhat unfairly) called the Plain Old Telephone Service (POTS) by some computer users. The derision comes from the fact that most telephone lines provide an analog connection, based on standards that date back more than a century (see Figure 10.1). As you'll see, though, it's not true that the PSTN is an entirely analog network. In this section, you'll learn enough about how PSTN works to realize that it's on the verge of becoming a truly digital network, which will mean big, positive changes for data communication.

QUALITY OF SERVICE

Any discussion of the telephone system should begin with praise for its accomplishments. Today's telephone system uses advanced switching technology to create an end-to-end circuit between *any* two telephones in the world. What's amazing about this system is the number of telephones that can be directly and almost instantly connected; nearly a half a billion telephones are connected to the global telephone system today, and most are accessible by means of direct dialing (see Figure 10.2). In the United States alone, nearly a billion telephone calls are made *every day*. Despite infrequent service outages, PSTN is able to pull off these feats with a guaranteed **quality of service** (**QoS**): when you need to make a call, you can, and the audio quality is good.

LOCAL EXCHANGE CARRIERS (LECS)

Telephone services are provided by **local exchange carriers** (**LECs**), also called **telcos**, which provide directly wired services to the homes and offices of subscribers. This network of local connections is called the **local access and transport area** (**LATA**). Within the LATA,

10.1

connection, based on standards that date

Figure 10.2
Nearly a half a billion telephones are connected to the global telephone system today, and most are accessible by means of direct dialing. In the United States alone, nearly a billion telephone calls are made every day.

you can place a call without accessing a long-distance carrier.

Let's explore the local exchange by starting with your home telephone. Most home telephones in use today are **analog** devices, which transmit and receive a continuously changing electrical signal that matches the acoustics of the human voice. These telephones are linked to **subscriber loop carriers** (**SLCs**) by means of copper wires, called **twisted pair**, that are twisted around each other to prevent interference (called **noise**) from electrical circuits (see Figure 10.3). An SLC is a small, waist-high installation that connects as many as 96 subscribers; you've probably seen one in your neighborhood. The area served by an SLC is called the **local loop**.

In most local exchanges in the United States, only the local loop is still stuck with analog technology, due largely to the fact that nearly all existing buildings were originally constructed with built-in twisted-pair wiring. In order for the local loop to change over to digital lines, all of this wiring would have to be redone—an expense that is simply too great. From the SLC on, though, the telephone system is increasingly a digital network. The SLC transforms local analog calls into digital signals, routing them through high-capacity, fiber-optic cables to the **local exchange switch**, which is also based on digital technology capable of handling thousands of calls. The local exchange switch is located in the local telephone company's central office.

twisted-pair cable

Figure 10.3
Twisted-pair cable refers to inexpensive copper cable that's used for telephone and data communications. The cable is twisted to prevent interference from electrical circuits.

Figure 10.4
Fiber-optic cables consist of thin strands of glass that transmit data by means of pulses of light.

Figure 10.5
Communications satellites are often permanently positioned with respect to the earth to provide specific area coverage.

LONG-DISTANCE TRANSMISSION MEDIA

If you place a call outside the local transport area, an **interexchange carrier (IXC)**—a long-distance telephone company—comes into play. In the United States, long-distance service is open to competition.

A variety of transmission carriers are used to provide regional and long-distance service between local telephone exchanges, including the following:

Copper wire Specially conditioned copper wires called **T1 carriers** can handle as many as 24 voice calls simultaneously or up to 1.544 Mbps of computer data.

Fiber-optic cables Fiber-optic cables consist of thin strands of glass that transmit data by means of pulses of light (see Figure 10.4). **T3 carriers** can handle 672 voice calls or 43 Mbps of computer data.

Microwaves High-frequency radio waves called **microwaves** handled much of the long-distance telephone service before the recent growth of fiber-optic networks. Because microwaves must travel in a straight line, relay stations are built at a distance of approximately every 30 miles (the line-of-sight distance to the horizon) or closer if the terrain blocks transmission.

Satellites Essentially microwave relay stations suspended in space, communications satellites are positioned in **geosynchronous orbits**, which match the speed of the earth's rotation and therefore are permanently positioned with respect to the ground (see Figure 10.5).

Because long-distance lines must handle thousands of calls simultaneously, techniques called **multiplexing** have been developed to send more than one call on a single line. The electrical and physical characteristics of copper wire place a limit of 24 multiplexed calls per wire, but fiber-optic cables can carry as many as 48,384 digital voice channels simultaneously. In contrast to the analog local loop, most long-distance carriers use digital signals

CHANGING TIMES

Universal Service: No More Access for Everyone?

It's called universal service—and thanks to the rise of Internet telephony, it may very well be coming to an end. An outgrowth of Depression-era New Deal legislation, universal service has long been a cornerstone of U.S. telecommunications policy.

In the telecommunications industry, universal service ensures that people in all parts of the country have equal access to "reasonably priced" telephone services (see Figure 10.6). But there's just one problem: it's much more expensive to provide telephone service in lightly populated rural areas, where wires must be strung dozens or hundreds of miles just to serve a few houses. To pay for local phone service, long-distance companies collect surcharges from their customers, and kick back most of these surcharges to local telephone companies in the form of **access fees**. In turn, the local telephone companies use these fees to hold down the cost of residential telephone services.

But all that's changing. Thanks to the U.S. Telecommunications Act of 1996, **competitive access providers (CAPs)** can sell direct access to the long-distance market without paying access fees—and that's one of the reasons Internet telephony is booming. Internet telephony service providers (ITSPs) such as Net2Phone don't pay access fees. According to conventional long-distance providers, that isn't fair. Long-distance, regional, and local telephone companies want the U.S. Congress to hit ITSPs with access fee charges—or abandon the idea of universal service altogether.

The 1996 Telecommunications Act does give telephone companies a break; the legislation calls for gradual reductions in access fees until they're completely eliminated. But it doesn't let consumers off the hook; universal service must still be paid for, somehow, and the Telecommunications Act extended the concept of universal service to digital-based services such as the Internet. For now, consumers are taking the hit, as you'll discover if you examine your next phone bill: there's a welter of incomprehensibly named taxes, such as the Presubscribed Interexchange Carrier Charge, the Federal Access Charge, the FCC line charge, state-imposed Universal Service charges, and—chances are—several more. The various taxes and fees can add up to 60 percent to the cost of your monthly phone bill.

At least there's one tax you won't be paying any more. In 2000, the U.S. Congress voted to terminate the Federal Excise Tax on telephone service—a tax that was initially created in 1898 to pay for the Spanish-American War.

Figure 10.6
The Universal Service Administrative Company is a nonprofit organization dedicated to providing underserved regions of the United States with access to affordable telecommunications.

IMPACTS

so that they can pack the greatest number of calls in a single circuit.

STANDARDS AND REGULATIONS

The public switched telephone network isn't purely a technological creation. It's based also on internationally recognized standards and important legal and political principles.

Standards
Because telephone services are offered by thousands of companies in hundreds of countries, standards are needed to ensure that one company's subscriber can communicate with another's. Telephone and other telecommunications standards are governed by the Geneva, Switzerland-based **International Telecommunications Union** (**ITU**), a division of the United Nations.

Universal Service
In the United States, the concept of **universal service** underlies the legislation that regulates telephone service. This concept recognizes that telephone service is vital to public safety and economic welfare, but it also recognizes that profit-seeking telephone companies will not provide service in unprofitable areas (such as remote rural locales) unless they're provided with financial incentives. Telecommunications laws specify that subscribers and phone companies should pay access fees and other fees to pay for the construction and maintenance of telephone systems in remote or otherwise unprofitable areas. Universal service isn't an issue in most other nations, where telephone service is a state-run monopoly.

Common Carrier Immunity
Another important concept underlying the telephone system is **common carrier immunity**. A **common carrier** is a transportation or communications company that provides vital public services; in return, legislation holds these carriers immune from civil or criminal liability for the actions of individuals who misuse these services. If you make a harassing telephone call, for example, you, not the phone company, are personally liable.

Deregulation
In the United States, an important development in telephony is **deregulation**, in which laws and regulations circumscribing telephone company actions have been altered or eliminated. In 1983, a court decision broke up telephone monopoly AT&T and created a competitive market for long-distance services. AT&T was restricted to providing long-distance service; local telephone service would be provided by **Regional Bell Operating Companies** (**RBOCs**), also called Baby Bells, which retained a monopoly in their service areas. The Telecommunications Act of 1996 deregulated RBOCs, exposing them to local competition while enabling them to compete for long-distance service.

MORE WAYS TO ACCESS THE SYSTEM

As you've already learned, most phones are analog devices tied to the local loop's twisted-pair wiring. That's unsatisfactory for many, so alternative ways have been devised to gain access to telephone services, such as private branch exchanges, wireless (cellular) telephones, and leased lines.

Private Branch Exchange (PBX)
As we mentioned earlier, most of the phones in the local loop are analog devices, prone to noise and interference. Digital phones, however, offer noise-free transmission and high-quality audio. You've probably already used a digital phone: large organizations, such as corporations and universities, typically install their own internal digital telephone systems, called **private branch exchanges** (**PBXs**). By using a PBX, an organization avoids the high cost of paying for a line to the local telephone company's exchange switch for each employee. Calls to the outside must be translated into analog signals to connect to the PSTN.

Cellular Telephones
The PSTN isn't the only analog phone technology around. Increasingly popular are **cellular telephones**, which enable subscribers to place calls through a **wireless communications system** (see Figure 10.7).

Destinations

To learn more about the ITU and international telecommunications standards, visit the ITU's home page at **www.itu.int**.

Destinations

The home page of one of the most technically innovative RBOCs, Pacific Bell (**www.pacbell.com**), is packed with information and tutorials about cutting-edge telecommunications services for homes and businesses.

A wireless communications medium uses radio or infrared signals.

World War II proved the usefulness of the walkie-talkie, a wireless communications service that enables mobile, two-way communication. But a walkie-talkie signal weakens and finally disappears if you get out of range of the transmitting unit. In 1971, AT&T discovered a way to solve this problem: build a network of automatic repeating transmitters (called **cell sites**), each of which would broadcast a signal throughout a limited geographic area, called a **cell**. As a caller moves from one area to another, a new cell site automatically steps in to keep the signal strength strong. All cell sites are connected to a **mobile telephone switching office** (**MTSO**), which in turn is connected to the standard PSTN telephone system (see Figure 10.8). Originally (and still predominantly) an analog system, cellular telephone service

Figure 10.7
Cellular telephones enable subscribers to place calls through a wireless communications system.

Figure 10.8
As a caller moves from one area to another, a new cell site automatically steps in to keep the signal strength strong. All cell sites are connected to a mobile telephone switching office (MTSO), which in turn is connected to the standard PSTN telephone system.

was introduced commercially in 1983. Current projections indicate that by 2005, more than 500 million people will be using cell phones worldwide.

Leased Lines

To get around the analog limitations of the local loop, companies that need long-distance data communication obtain **leased lines**. These specially conditioned telephone lines provide direct digital access to long-distance carriers. Unlike switched local connections, leased lines are permanently connected and always available.

THE PSTN IN PERSPECTIVE

Let's put this all into perspective. Because the PSTN forces computer users to transform digital data into analog form, it's of limited use for data communication. The analog connections are vulnerable to line noise and can't surpass a theoretical limit of 56 Kbps for analog services on twisted pair. But most people don't realize that the PSTN in advanced industrial countries is already a predominantly *digital* network, as you've just learned. In the last mile of service delivery, the local loop causes the problem, which is why it's called the **last mile problem**. The solution is easy, you say. Just rip out the twisted pair and put in fiber-optic cable. But as we mentioned earlier, the cost to replace all the twisted pair that currently delivers phone service to homes and offices worldwide would be upwards of $325 billion. That's not going to happen anytime soon.

Figure 10.9
A modem transforms digital signals into analog form for transmission through the telephone network.

Modems: From Digital to Analog and Back

As long as your telephone company is still using analog equipment in the local loop, all your messages, whether voice or data, must be sent as analog sounds that fall within the range of the human voice. Linking two computers through the analog telephone system requires that both computers be equipped with **modems**, devices that transform digital signals into analog form for transmission through the telephone network (see Figure 10.9).

HOW MODEMS WORK

Using a process called **modulation**, a modem transforms the computer's digital signals into analog tones that can be conveyed through the telephone system. On the receiving end, the process used is **demodulation**, in which the other modem transforms this signal from analog back to digital. Modems can play both roles, modulation and demodulation, which is where the name *modem* comes from: it's short for modulator/demodulator (see Figure 10.10).

Two types of modems are available: internal and external. An **internal modem** is designed to fit in one of your computer's expansion slots. It gets its power from the computer's expansion bus. An **external modem** has its own case and power supply. For this reason, external modems are slightly more expensive.

ASYNCHRONOUS COMMUNICATION

Modems use a method of networking called **asynchronous communication**. In this method, data is sent one bit at a time, in a series (one after the other). So that the receiving computer can tell where one byte ends and the next one begins, start bits and stop bits are added to the data. This networking method is called asynchronous because the start and stop bits eliminate the need for some kind of

telephone lines use analog transmission

Figure 10.10

A modem transforms the computer's digital signals into analog tones that can be conveyed through the telephone system.

synchronization signal. In **synchronous communication**, data exchange requires a synchronization signal that identifies the units of data being exchanged.

MODULATION PROTOCOLS

To establish communications, modems must conform to standards called **modulation protocols.** These protocols, set by international standards organizations, ensure that your modem can communicate with another modem, even if the second modem was made by a different manufacturer.

Several modulation protocols are in common use. Each protocol specifies all the necessary details of communication, including the **data transfer rate**. This is the rate at which the two modems can exchange data. The rate is measured in **bits per second (bps)**. You may encounter the term **baud rate** when a modem's data transfer rate is discussed. The baud rate is the maximum number of changes that can occur per second in the electrical state of a communications circuit. Note that the technical definitions of baud rate and bps rate differ. The correct measurement of a modem's data transfer rate is the bps rate.

Modem protocols are governed by the International Telecommunications Union (ITU). The most recent modulation protocol, called **V.90**, enables modems to communicate at a maximum rate of 56 Kbps. (In practice, V.90 modems rarely achieve speeds higher than 42 Kbps.) The protocol also includes standards for data compression and error checking. The previous protocol, **V.34**, enables a rate of 28,800 bits per second. An earlier standard, V.32 bis, established a rate of 14,400 bps. Standards before V.32 regulated communication at 9600, 2400, 1200, and 300 bps.

Two modems can communicate only if both follow the same modulation protocol. If your modem follows the V.34 protocol, your modem can't communicate at 28,800 bps unless the modem on the other end observes the same protocol. Most modems, however, can **fall back** to a lower rate. When a modem attempts to establish a connection, it automatically negotiates with the modem on the other end. The two modems try to establish which protocols they share, and then they use the fastest rate that both modems have. If a computer with a 9600 bps modem is connected to a computer with a 14,400 bps modem, data is transferred between the two computers at 9600 bps.

Figure 10.11
Facsimile transmission enables you to send an image of a document over the telephone lines to anyone who has a fax machine. If your computer has a fax modem, you can send and receive faxes from your computer instead of a fax machine.

FAX

Facsimile transmission—or **fax**, as it's popularly known—enables you to send an image of a document over the telephone lines (see Figure 10.11). The sending fax machine makes a digital image of the document. Using a built-in modem, the sending fax machine converts the image into an analog representation so that it can be transmitted through the analog telephone system. The receiving fax machine converts the analog signals to digital signals, converts the digital signals to an image of the document, and prints that image.

Fax usage didn't take off until the ITU established modulation protocol standards for facsimile transmission years ago. These standards differ from modem protocols. Fax protocols govern transmission at 9.6 Kbps (V.29) and 14.4 Kbps (V.17).

Some modems, called **fax modems**, support fax as well as data modulation protocols. If your computer has a fax modem, you can send and receive faxes from your computer instead of a fax machine. However, you'll need a scanner too if you want to fax something that's printed or sketched on paper.

Digital Telephony: Living with Twisted Pair

Because twisted-pair wiring will be with us for many years, engineers have developed a number of interim digital telephony technologies that make use of twisted-pair wiring. Sometimes called **last mile technologies**, these solutions include digital telephone standards (such as ISDN and DSL) that can use twisted-pair wiring, as well as technologies that dispense with the local loop entirely, such as cable and satellite systems.

To understand new digital telephone technologies, you'll find it helpful to learn how engineers express the data transfer capacity (called **bandwidth**) of a given transmission medium. This section introduces the bandwidth concept and goes on to examine the new technologies that can deliver digital telephone service directly to homes and offices.

BANDWIDTH

For digital communication, a transmission medium's bandwidth is measured in kilobits per second (Kbps), megabits per second (Mbps), or gigabits per second (Gbps). Bandwidth is determined by the method used to represent and transmit data via the transmission medium, subject to an upper limit imposed by the physical characteristics of the medium.

So how much bandwidth do you need? For text, you can get by with a slow modem (such as a 28.8 Kbps modem). That rate, however, is too slow for the Web (unless you're *really* patient). Exploring the Web is a more pleasant proposition at 128 Kbps. But even 128 Kbps is far too slow for tomorrow's digital services, such as digital television, on-demand movies, and videoconferencing. These services require **broadband** digital transmission, conventionally defined to refer to connections with speeds of at least 1.5 Mbps. Network-based delivery of high-quality videoconferencing requires a bandwidth of at least 10 Mbps, the speed of a slow hard disk or standard Ethernet local area network (see Figure 10.12). High-definition television (HDTV), an emerging standard for digital TV, requires a bandwidth of 11 Mbps.

Broadband digital connections aren't expected to be widely available soon. According to one estimate, by 2005 only about five percent of households in the United States will have digital connections operating at speeds of 1.5 Mbps or greater.

LAST MILE TECHNOLOGIES

Thanks to the Telecommunications Act of 1996, local telephone services are facing competition for the first time. Cable TV companies, satellite firms, and other phone companies are invading their turf and offering improved service. In response, local phone companies are increasingly offering digital telephone services, including ISDN and ADSL. In this section, you'll learn what's available and what's coming as phone companies finally solve the last mile problem by delivering digital telephony directly to homes, offices, and businesses.

Figure 10.12
Network-based delivery of high-quality video-conferencing requires a bandwidth of at least 10 Mbps.

Integrated Services Digital Network (ISDN)

Integrated Services Digital Network (ISDN) is an ITU-defined standard that provides digital telephone and data service. Three types of ISDN services follow:

Basic Rate ISDN (BRI) Designed for home and small business users, this service offers one or two 64 Kbps channels, as well as a 16 Kbps signaling channel. If you obtain service with both 64 Mbps channels, you can connect your computer at 128 Mbps; the service automatically cuts back to 64 Mbps when a voice call arrives. BRI can use twisted-pair wiring.

Primary Rate ISDN (PRI) Designed for organizations, this service includes 23 channels operating at 64 Kbps each, as well as one signaling channel. PRI requires a T1 carrier (1.544 Mbps).

Broadband ISDN (BISDN) Still on the drawing boards, this high-bandwidth technology can't work with twisted pair; it requires fiber-optic cable. Data transfer capacities vary, with a maximum bandwidth of 622 Mbps.

Basic Rate ISDN (BRI) is widely available in the United States, Japan, and Europe. The cost of an ISDN line is often two to three times that of an analog phone line, but there's a payoff. With 128 Kbps ISDN services, you get two telephone numbers with one ISDN account; you can use one for computer data and another one for voice or fax. When you're using the connection for computer data only, the system automatically uses both data channels to give you the maximum data transfer rate; if a phone call comes in, the connection automatically drops back to 64 Kbps to accommodate the incoming call. What's more, connection is nearly instantaneous; unlike analog connections with a modem, there's no lengthy dial-in procedure and connection delay.

To hook up computers to BRI or PRI ISDN lines, you need an **ISDN adapter** (also called a **digital modem**, although ISDN modems aren't actually modems). ISDN adapters are 100 percent digital. Increasingly, small businesses and even

homeowners are installing ISDN-capable **routers**, which enable them to link the ISDN circuit to a local area network (LAN). Using an ISDN router, a small business can connect as many as 32 desktop computers and provide all with on-demand Internet service.

ISDN is the first widely available digital telephone service, but it may have a limited life, thanks to Digital Subscriber Line technologies.

Digital Subscriber Line (DSL)

Digital Subscriber Line (DSL, also called **xDSL)** is a blanket term for a group of related technologies, including **Asymmetric Digital Subscriber Line (ADSL)**. Already available in major metropolitan markets, ADSL is akin to ISDN in that it uses existing copper wiring. But ADSL is much faster: typically, up to 1.5 Mbps when you're downloading data and up to 256 Kbps when you're uploading data. (Note that downloading speeds are much faster than uploading speeds; the discrepancy explains why the service is called asymmetric. ADSL isn't the best choice if you need to upload huge amounts of data.) DSL technologies are capable of higher bandwidth, but local loop wiring problems limit DSL to 1.5 Mbps (or less).

To connect to a DSL line, your computer needs a DSL "modem," as well as a DSL phone line and a DSL service subscription. One problem is that DSL service isn't standardized, so you'll need to select a modem that's compatible with your telephone company's particular type of DSL service. Standardization efforts are underway, however, and these efforts will reduce the cost and complexity of DSL installations.

DSL isn't likely to be available in rural areas anytime soon. To connect with DSL, your computer must be positioned within a few miles of a local switching station.

SONET

Requiring fiber-optic cable, **Synchronous Optical Network (SONET)** promises to break bandwidth restrictions wide open. The slowest SONET standard calls for data transfer rates of 52 Mbps; some enable rates of 1 Gbps or faster. Outside the United States, SONET is known as

Synchronous Digital Hierarchy (SDH). SONET is expected to provide the fiber-optic cable services for Broadband ISDN (BISDN), but this service isn't expected to benefit homes and small businesses.

Alternatives to Digital Telephony

Protected from local competition until 1996, local telephone companies have been slow to offer high-bandwidth digital telephone services. Now they're facing competition from satellite and cable TV systems and even the local power company.

DIRECT BROADCAST SATELLITE (DBS)

Digital satellite systems, called **Direct Broadcast Satellite (DBS)**, use an 18- or 21-inch reception disk to receive digital TV signals broadcast at a bandwidth of 12 Mbps. Increasingly, DBS operators offer Internet access as well as digital TV service, but at much lower bandwidth. Currently, Hughes Network Systems offers satellite Internet access at 400 Kbps, but there's a rub. Satellite systems can't handle uploaded data, so you'll still need a modem and telephone line to send requests to the server and to upload files.

CABLE MODEMS

Currently, the leading contender in the high-bandwidth sweepstakes is your local cable TV company, which has probably already wired your home with **coaxial cable** (see Figure 10.13). In contrast to twisted pair, coaxial cable makes it easy to achieve very-high-bandwidth data communication. What's more, about 73 million homes in the United States now subscribe to cable TV service, and an additional 35 million are within easy reach of cable systems.

Does the cable TV industry's huge installed base of coaxial cable hold the key to high-bandwidth digital service delivery? Not yet. The cable TV system

was designed as a couch-potato service, in which customers would sit back and choose from a fixed number of channels. So most cable systems are designed to run signals in one direction only: toward the house, not away from it. But data communication requires two-way communication. Only about one-eighth of the homes in the United States have cable service delivery that's capable of two-way data communication; the cable industry is busily upgrading the rest of its infrastructure to provide this capability. And increasingly, they're offering data communications services—specifically, Internet access.

For computer users, these services offer data transfer rates that leave ISDN in the dust and rival those of DSL. **Cable modems** now deliver data at bandwidths of 500 Kbps to 1 Mbps or more, depending on how many subscribers are connected to a local cable segment. You'll hear figures

Figure 10.13

In contrast to twisted pair, coaxial cable makes it easy to achieve very-high-bandwidth data communication.

CURRENTS

EMERGING TECHNOLOGIES

The Bright Future of Bluetooth™

One of the difficulties in getting any technology to work together with another technology is compatibility. If the devices' platforms, software, or wiring are different, you may just be out of luck. But what if all technology manufacturers could agree to a standard and worked together to make sure that the standard was implemented?

That idea is becoming a reality in the form of a new short-range wireless communications technology called **Bluetooth**. Named after the infamous 10th-century Viking Harold Bluetooth, who united Denmark and Norway, the Bluetooth technology was first conceived by Swedish cell phone giant Ericsson (see Figure 10.14). Bluetooth technology relies on a network called a piconet, or a PAN (a personal area network), that allows all kinds of devices—desktop computers, mobile phones, printers, pagers, PDAs, and more—within a certain range of each other to communicate automatically and wirelessly.

Using Bluetooth-enabled devices, you can wirelessly send files from your desktop computer to your printer or to a friend's laptop. You can buy concert tickets online, download the electronic tickets into your Bluetooth-enabled PDA, and then link to the Bluetooth-enabled scanner at the concert house instead of presenting a ticket. You can even equip the devices in your own home (such as light fixtures and microwave ovens) with a Bluetooth chip and use your cell phone or other device as a remote control, wirelessly telling your appliances what to do and when.

Already, companies like Apple, Microsoft, Ericsson, IBM, Intel, Lucent, Nokia, Toshiba, 3Com, and Motorola have banded together to support Bluetooth's radio frequency connection. In fact, more than a thousand companies in Bluetooth's Special Interest Group (SIG)—ranging from software developers to consumer electronics manufacturers—are working toward the goal of taking this inexpensive radio chip technology and making all technology able to communicate with each other, cable free.

How exactly does Bluetooth work? Bluetooth-enabled devices identify each other using identification numbers that are unique to each device. When these devices are within a certain range of each other (usually 30 feet or so), they automatically "find" and link to one another. You don't have to worry about being connected to Bluetooth devices you don't want to connect to either: the device requires that you confirm a connection before making it final. Up to eight Bluetooth-enabled devices can be connected to each other in a piconet at any one time, and, unlike infrared technologies, Bluetooth doesn't require a direct line of sight to be connected. Because the frequency used by Bluetooth devices changes often, Bluetooth devices never use the same frequency at the same time, and won't interfere with each other.

Bluetooth advocates (especially in Japan and Europe, where it's already popular) have been saying for years that Bluetooth technology is the wave of the future. Already, the automobile industry and other heavy industries are finding ways to improve their production and their products by using wireless remote features. Time will tell whether Bluetooth will catch on with general consumers and change the way our devices communicate.

Figure 10.14
To learn even more about the possibilities of Bluetooth, visit www.bluetooth.com.

stating that cable modems are capable of bandwidths of 30 Mbps or more, but this bandwidth must be divided among the 2000 or more subscribers in the cable company's equivalent of the local loop.

ELECTRICAL POWER SYSTEMS

Yes, you read the heading correctly. Data communications can be sent over electrical power lines. Recent research has solved the problem of noise and interference generated by power fluctuations and surges. Current technology enables data transfer rates of 1 Mbps, comparable to DSL and cable modems. This approach, however, isn't readily compatible with the U.S. power grid. It's expected to attract users in Asia and Europe, which lack the U.S. tradition of unlimited local telephone service and use power systems more amenable to data communication delivery. Some technical problems still need to be solved, however. In a Manchester, England, test of this delivery method, researchers found that street light poles acted as transmitting antennas and interfered with local radio reception.

Convergence: Is It a Phone or a Computer?

The phone system is going digital, as you've just learned, and that's enabling new technologies that carry computer data over voice lines. At the core of this process, however, is a more fundamental change: **digitization**, the transformation of all the media we've been discussing into digital systems. Digitization enables **convergence**, a process of technological morphing in which previously distinct devices lose their sharply defined boundaries and blend together (see Figure 10.15). This section explores some of the dimensions of computer-telephony convergence. As you'll see, it's creating some interesting hybrids.

THE EVERYTHING PC

It *looks* like a computer, but it's much more: it's also an audiophile-quality stereo, a TV, a DVD player, and even an answering machine. That's the pitch for a new series of multimedia-enhanced PCs that combine huge monitors (27 or even 31 inches), DVD drives, high-fidelity speakers with surround sound, and voice-capable 56 Kbps modems. Equipped with a microphone and the right software, you can even use this PC to place free, long-distance phone calls over the Internet, as explained subsequently. This could be the ultimate machine for cramped dorm rooms!

TV INTERNET SET-TOPS

You're sitting in front of your TV, and your eyes never leave the screen. The show you're watching is boring, so you spend some time checking your e-mail and surfing the

Web-enabled pager

Web-enabled cell phone

messaging device

Figure 10.15
Digitization enables convergence, a process of technological morphing in which previously distinct devices lose their sharply defined boundaries and blend together.

Figure 10.16
MSN® TV allows you to access the Internet using your television set as a display.

Destinations

MSN® TV Service (**www.webtv.com**) explains MSN® TV service options and explains how MSN® TV can enhance the TV viewing experience.

Web. While you're on the Web, you check an interactive channel guide featuring your local cable TV listings, jump to some TV-related Web sites, and finally find something worth watching. All these tasks are accomplished on your TV set, thanks to **MSN® TV** (formerly **WebTV**), an Internet service that you access using an inexpensive **set-top appliance** that enables you to access the Internet using your TV as a display (see Figure 10.16). To navigate the Web, you use a wireless keyboard or a remote control unit.

PERSONAL COMMUNICATION SERVICE (PCS)

Digitization is bringing the same rapid change to cellular phone service that you're seeing in other media. **Personal Communication Service** (**PCS**) refers collectively to a group of related digital cellular telephone service technologies that are rapidly supplanting analog cellular services.

Digital cellular phones offer noise-free sound and improved coverage, but that's just the beginning. PCS offers protection from eavesdropping and cellular phone fraud, two problems that plague analog cellular technologies. It also offers a spate of new, computer-based telephony services, such as voice recognition technology that enables users to screen incoming calls or to place calls without dialing a phone number. In short, PCS enables computers and cellular phones to be combined, and the result is a profusion of technologies that transform the way we communicate.

PCS is transforming mobile computing into a reality for millions of people. Because PCS technology is digital, it's much more amenable to data communication than analog cellular services. It's possible to access the Internet by means of a modem connected to an analog cellular phone, but data transfer rates are as low as 4 Kbps due to line noise and poor connections. Emerging PCS standards will enable speeds of up to 384 Kbps for downloads.

INTERNET TELEPHONY

Internet telephony is the use of the Internet for real-time voice communication. Unlike the public switched telephone network, the public Internet doesn't establish a point-to-point, switched connection with a guaranteed quality of service. It was never designed for real-time use. When you place telephone calls over the public Internet, network congestion often causes garbled messages, delays, and echoes. Still, using the Internet for phone calls has a major advantage over using the public switched telephone network (PSTN): providers can route dozens, hundreds, or even thousands of calls over the same circuit.

You can place calls via the Internet in a variety of ways. To place free long-distance calls, you'll need a computer equipped with a microphone, speakers, an Internet connection, and a telephony-enabled program such as Microsoft's NetMeeting. Your calls are limited to people using similarly equipped computers—and they need to be online.

What about placing a call to an ordinary telephone? You can't do it for free. However, **Internet telephony service providers** (**ITSPs**) such as Net2Phone are stepping into the act by offering computer-to-phone and phone-to-phone services that use the Internet for long-distance transmission (see Figure 10.17). Rates are cheap, but the quality isn't always what subscribers expect.

Still, the basic idea of Internet telephony has an enormous advantage: because the Internet doesn't rely on switches to route messages, it's cheaper to operate. According

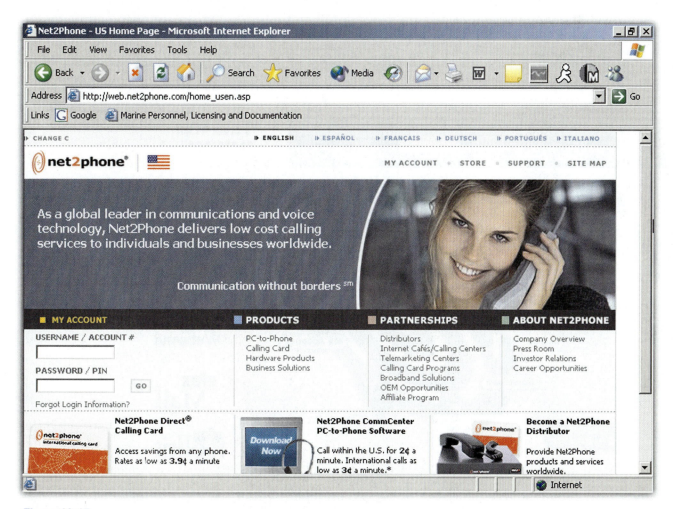

Figure 10.17

Net2Phone is an Internet telephony service provider that offers computer-to-phone and phone-to-phone services that use the Internet for long-distance transmission.

to one estimate, routing data over a switched network costs more than three times as much as sending the same data over a switch-free computer network such as the Internet. New technologies, such as advanced compression, are making Internet telephony sound better, but you'll still run into delays when you're calling over the public Internet.

Because it's cheaper to build telephone networks with Internet technology than with switching circuits, some experts believe that the term *telecommunications* will become obsolete. Computer data won't be routed over voice networks. Instead, voice will be routed over computer networks, the only type of network that will exist once obsolete switching technology is dismantled.

INTERNET FAXING

If the Internet isn't perfect for voice calls, it has none of those shortcomings for faxes. Faxes don't have to be delivered in real time, like voice does, so slight service delays don't cause a problem.

How does Internet faxing work? You need an Internet connection and an account with an Internet fax service provider (see Figure 10.18). From a fax machine or computer, you send the fax through the Internet to the fax service provider, which then automatically routes the fax through the Internet to a local telephone near your fax's destination. The service isn't free, but it's 25 to 50 percent cheaper than sending the fax through the phone system.

Figure 10.18
eFax.com is just one of the many Internet fax service providers available on the Web.

HOME | Takeaway Points | Key Terms and Concepts | Matching | Multiple Choice | Fill-In | Short Answer | Exercises/ Projects | Web Research | CHAPTER REVIEW

TAKEAWAY POINTS

- The public switched telephone network (PSTN) is predominantly digital, except for the local loop, which uses low-bandwidth twisted-pair wire connected to analog telephones.

- To send digital data over the telephone system, it's necessary to modulate the signal (transform it into analog form). On the receiving end, the signal must be demodulated (transformed back into digital form). Modems (modulators/ demodulators) perform this service.

- The term *bandwidth* refers to the data transfer capacity of a communications channel and is measured in bits per second (bps).

- Modulation protocols are standards that define how modems work. The latest protocol is called V.90, and it enables data transfer rates of up to 56 Kbps.

- 56 Kbps isn't sufficient for real-time video-conferencing or other advanced multimedia applications. For these applications, bandwidths of 1 Mbps or more are needed for good quality.

- ISDN and ADSL are two digital telephony services that can bring digital service directly to homes and offices using twisted-pair wiring. Basic ISDN services can provide data transfer rates of up to 128 Kbps; ADSL provides 1 Mbps or more.

- Digitization is blurring the boundaries between phones, computers, and TVs. MSN® TV brings Internet capabilities to TV viewing, and PCS enables high-bandwidth data communications through cellular telephones.

- In Internet telephony, voice is routed over the public Internet or private networks constructed using Internet standards. However, these networks can't guarantee PSTN's quality of service.

1 2 3 4 5 6 7 8 9 10 11 12 13 14 15 16

CHAPTER REVIEW | Takeaway Points | Key Terms and Concepts | Matching | Multiple Choice | Fill-In | Short Answer | Exercises/ Projects | Web Research | HOME

KEY TERMS AND CONCEPTS

access fees
analog
Asymmetric Digital
    Subscriber Line (ADSL)
asynchronous communication
bandwidth
Basic Rate ISDN (BRI)
baud rate
bits per second (bps)
Bluetooth
broadband
Broadband ISDN (BISDN)
cable modem
cell
cell site
cellular telephone
coaxial cable
common carrier
common carrier immunity
competitive access provider
    (CAP)
convergence
copper wire
data transfer rate
demodulation
deregulation
digital telephony
Digital Subscriber Line
    (DSL or xDSL)
digitization
Direct Broadcast
    Satellite (DBS)

external modem
fall back
facsimile transmission (fax)
fax modem
fiber-optic cable
geosynchronous orbit
Integrated Services Digital
    Network (ISDN)
interexchange carrier (IXC)
internal modem
International
    Telecommunications
    Union (ITU)
Internet telephony
Internet telephony service
    provider (ITSP)
ISDN adapter (digital modem)
last mile problem
last mile technologies
leased line
local access and transport
    area (LATA)
local exchange carrier (LEC)
local exchange switch
local loop
microwave
mobile telephone switching
    office (MTSO)
modem
modulation
modulation protocols
MSN® TV (WebTV)

multiplexing
noise
Personal Communication
    Service (PCS)
Primary Rate ISDN (PRI)
private branch exchange
    (PBX)
public switched telephone
    network (PSTN)
quality of service (QoS)
Regional Bell Operating
    Companies (RBOCs)
router
satellite
set-top appliance
subscriber loop
    carrier (SLC)
synchronous communication
Synchronous Digital
    Hierarchy (SDH)
Synchronous Optical Network
    (SONET)
T1 carrier
T3 carrier
telecommunications
telcos
twisted pair
universal service
V.34
V.90
wireless communications
    system

| HOME | Takeaway Points | Key Terms and Concepts | Matching | Multiple Choice | Fill-In | Short Answer | Exercises/ Projects | Web Research | CHAPTER REVIEW |

MATCHING

Match each key term in the left column with the most accurate definition in the right column.

_____ 1. local exchange carrier

_____ 2. broadband

_____ 3. universal service

_____ 4. coaxial cable

_____ 5. wireless

_____ 6. leased lines

_____ 7. fall back

_____ 8. bandwidth

_____ 9. cell

_____ 10. microwave

_____ 11. fiber-optic cables

_____ 12. PBX

_____ 13. quality of service

_____ 14. asynchronous communication

_____ 15. modulation

a. specifically conditioned telephone lines that provide direct digital access to long-distance carriers

b. a communications medium that uses radio or infrared signals

c. a process that describes a modem transforming a computer's digital signals into analog tones

d. the ability of a modem to connect at a rate slower than its maximum

e. the geographic area in which wireless signals are broadcast

f. data transfer capacity

g. high-frequency radio wave transmissions that are limited to line-of-sight distances

h. a method of networking in which data is sent one bit at a time in a series

i. provides directly wired services to the homes and offices of subscribers

j. thin strands of glass that transmit data by using pulses of light

k. a medium used by cable companies for wiring homes

l. an organizational internal digital telephone system

m. a concept that recognizes that telephone service is vital to public safety and economic welfare

n. the expectation of completing a quality audio phone call

o. digital transmissions in excess of 1.5 Mbps

1
2
3
4
5
6
7
8
9
10
11
12
13
14
15
16

CHAPTER REVIEW

Takeaway Points | Key Terms and Concepts | Matching | Multiple Choice | Fill-In | Short Answer | Exercises/ Projects | Web Research | HOME

MULTIPLE CHOICE

Circle the correct choice for each of the following.

1. Which of the following provides basic telephone services?
   a. Operators
   b. Local exchange carriers (LECs)
   c. Cable modems
   d. International Telecommunications Union

2. Which of the following is not a transmission medium used to provide regional and long-distance service between local telephone exchanges?
   a. Microwaves
   b. Fiber-optic cables
   c. Common carrier
   d. Copper wire

3. What does POTS stand for?
   a. Pretty Old Telephone System
   b. Plain Old Telephone Service
   c. Partially Operative Telephone Switching
   d. Progressive Open Telecommunications Standard

4. Who governs modem protocols?
   a. United States government
   b. Federal Communications Commission (FCC)
   c. International Telecommunications Union (ITU)
   d. WWW Consortium

5. What does DBS stand for?
   a. Digital Band Service
   b. Direct Binary Satellite
   c. Digital Broadband Service
   d. Direct Broadcast Satellite

6. When someone makes a cellular phone call, all the cell sites are connected to which of the following?
   a. Public switched telephone network (PSTN)
   b. Mobile optical network (MONET)
   c. Mobile Digital Subscriber Line (MDSL)
   d. Mobile telephone switching office (MTSO)

7. What is multiplexing?
   a. A multiple screen movie theater
   b. Many interconnected networks
   c. The ability to transmit more than one call on a single line
   d. The ability to send data and faxes with a single device

8. Which of the following services requires broadband digital transmission?
   a. Digital television
   b. Faxing
   c. Sending e-mail
   d. None of the above

9. This is the use of the Internet for real-time voice communication.
   a. Internet telephony
   b. Personal Communications Service
   c. Internet faxing
   d. Convergence

10. Which of the following technologies requires fiber-optic cable and promises to break bandwidth restrictions wide open?
    a. Cable modems
    b. Synchronous Optical Network (SONET)
    c. Direct Broadcast Satellite
    d. MSN® TV

HOME | Takeaway Points | Key Terms and Concepts | Matching | Multiple Choice | **Fill-In** | Short Answer | Exercises/ Projects | Web Research | CHAPTER REVIEW

FILL-IN

In the blanks provided, write the correct answer for each of the following.

1. _____ refers to the transmission of information of any type through the telephone system.

2. _____ provide directly wired services to subscribers' homes and offices.

3. A network of local connections is called the _____.

4. _____ has been developed to send more than one call on a single line.

5. _____ is the use of the Internet for real-time voice communication.

6. _____ are set by international standards organizations to ensure that your modem can communicate with another modem, even if the second modem was made by a different manufacturer.

7. _____ protects communications companies from civil or criminal liability for the actions of individuals who misuse their services.

8. The rate by which two modems exchange data is measured in _____.

9. If your computer is equipped with a _____, you can send and receive faxes from your computer.

10. Long-distance telephone companies are also known as _____.

11. A _____ enables you to access the Internet using your television as a display.

12. Communication satellites are placed in _____ orbits, which match the speed of the earth's rotation.

13. Even though they are not modems, _____ are also called digital modems.

14. _____ offer computer-to-phone and phone-to-phone services that use the Internet for long-distance transmission.

15. _____ refers collectively to a group of related digital cellular telephone service technologies.

SHORT ANSWER

1. A computer must have a fax modem and a scanner to fully function as a fax. Explain why the scanner is needed.

2. In terms of the "last mile problem," explain the limitations of the public switched telephone network (PSTN) for sending and receiving computer data.

3. Explain the difference between the terms *modulation* and *demodulation*. A modem must be able to perform which of these? Explain why.

4. The copper wires that connect telephones in your home, and your home to a service loop carrier (SLC), usually consist of pairs of twisted wires. Explain why these wires are twisted.

5. Explain why only a small percentage of cable companies are capable of supporting two-way data communication.

Sidebar tabs: 1 2 3 4 5 6 7 8 9 10 11 12 13 14 15 16

Go to **www.prenhall.com/ciyf2004** to review this chapter, answer the questions, and complete the exercises and Web research questions.

CHAPTER REVIEW | Takeaway Points | Key Terms and Concepts | Matching | Multiple Choice | Fill-In | Short Answer | Exercises/Projects | Web Research | HOME

1 2 3 4 5 6 7 8 9 10 11 12 13 14 15 16

EXERCISES/PROJECTS

1. Examine your most recent telephone bill. What are the various surcharges and taxes? What percentage of your bill is for local calls, long-distance calls, and surcharges and taxes? Is your long-distance company the same as your local one? Are your telephone bills available online? Can you pay them online?

2. Do you own, or have you considered owning, a cellular phone? Contact two communications companies that provide cellular service in your area. What are their various rate plans? Do any of these plans include long distance? Do the two companies that you contacted provide Internet access? If they do, describe which Internet services they support and their associated costs.

3. Have you sent or received a facsimile transmission using a computer? Was the fax sent or received from another computer or from an actual fax machine? Could you tell the difference? What was the name of the fax software application that you used? Describe the process for sending and receiving the fax. If you sent a fax, describe how you created the document. If you received a fax, did you print it? Why or why not?

4. Many people have negative feelings about the use of cellular phones. They may be irritated by the careless use of cell phones in public places or concerned about their dangerous use by people driving motor vehicles. Which states have banned drivers from using handheld cell phones? See if you can determine the policies on cellular phone use in aircraft, trains, hospitals, movie theaters, restaurants, and the classrooms on your campus.

5. If you live in a highly populated area, you may already have cable television access for your home. Some cable companies also offer one-way (download-only) Internet service through this cable. However, this service still requires the use of a modem and a telephone connection for uploading. Unfortunately, only a fraction of the cable companies can provide the two-way data communication that is needed for full cable Internet access. Contact your local cable company to see if you are one of the lucky cable users who can get a two-way Internet cable connection. What additional hardware is needed for Internet cable connections? What is the monthly cost of this service? Do you already have a two-way Internet cable connection? If not, explain why you would or would not consider this high-speed option to telephone service.

HOME | Takeaway Points | Key Terms and Concepts | Matching | Multiple Choice | Fill-In | Short Answer | Exercises/ Projects | Web Research | CHAPTER REVIEW

WEB RESEARCH

1. In the last Exercise/Project question, we examined cable as a high-speed alternative to telephone-based Internet access. However, cable is not readily available in rural or other low-population areas. But, given a clear view of the southern sky, many of these areas are prime candidates for Direct Broadcast Satellite (DBS). Visit the StarBand Web site at **www.starband.com/index.htm**. Why do DBS systems require a clear view of the southern sky? Unfortunately, the major weakness of DBS systems is their inability to upload data. The StarBand DBS system by StarBand Communications allows two-way high-speed Internet access. Identify the additional hardware that is necessary to use the StarBand system with a computer. What are the initial hardware costs, installation charges, and monthly service fees? Explain why you would or would not consider using one of these DBS systems for high-speed access. Can these systems also be used to receive television signals?

2. OnStar is a multifaceted communications system that offers a broad range of services. Visit their Web site at **www.onstar.com/ flash.html**. What is the primary function of the OnStar system? Name four automotive manufacturers who supply vehicles with OnStar systems. What are the costs and services provided with the basic and premium service plans? Do you know anyone who has OnStar? What do they think about this service? Would you consider purchasing a vehicle with OnStar? If you would, which plan would you select?

3. Have you tried MSN® TV (formerly known as WebTV)? Visit the MSN® TV site at **http://resourcecenter.msn.com/access/MSNTV/ default.asp** to explore this communications medium.

   - What is needed to connect an MSN® TV?
   - What are the manufacturer's suggested retail prices for the two receivers? Explain which, if either, you would purchase and why.
   - What are the six service plans? Explain which, if any, you would purchase and why.

4. One of the newest technologies in mobile communications is 3G, which stands for *third generation*. Visit the Webopedia site at **http://webopedia.com** to learn about this new technology. What were the first generations of mobile phones? Although you may think that Sprint created the term "PCS," what organization actually did? What organization developed the specifications for 3G? The present speed for using a cellular phone to connect a computer to the Internet is only 14.4 Kbps. What are the expected transmission rates for 3G connections? When are 3G systems expected to be available? Explain why you would or would not consider purchasing or upgrading to a 3G phone.

5. Go to the gps4fun site at **http://gps4fun.com** to examine sophisticated satellite-based communications systems called Global Positioning Systems (GPSs). Who owns the collection of satellites that make up the GPS? How many GPS satellites are there, and how high do they orbit? How does a GPS receiver determine its position? How accurate is a GPS? List a civilian, military, and commercial use of a GPS. Do you know anyone who owns a GPS? Have you tried one? Find a specific model GPS and its price, and explain how you would use it.

1 2 3 4 5 6 7 8 9 10 11 12 13 14 15 16

Computer Crime and Security

CHAPTER **11**

What You'll Learn . . .

When you have finished reading this chapter, you will be able to:

1. Explain how attackers and intruders can gain entry to computer systems and harm or destroy data.

2. List ways you can help system administrators keep a computer system safe from unauthorized access and computer viruses.

3. Identify the stereotypes of people who are most likely to attack or harm computer systems, and explain their motives.

4. List the types of losses caused by computer system intrusions and attacks.

5. List and explain the tools and techniques used to defend computer systems against intruders and attackers.

In this chapter, you'll learn why computer crime is on the rise, and why improvements in computer security are needed. You'll learn about the tools and tricks attackers use to invade computer systems and steal or destroy computer data. You'll meet some of the people who are behind computer attacks, and learn about the motives that underlie their sometimes devastating actions. You'll also examine the techniques security experts use to defend systems from intrusion and attack.

Scope of the Problem

Not all of the dangers posed to computer systems are caused by malicious, conscious intent. A **computer security risk** is defined as any event, action, or situation—intentional or not—that could lead to the loss or destruction of computer systems or the data they contain. For example, many people fail to make backup copies of their data, even though they know perfectly well that they should. A hard disk failure could lead to a devastating loss of data. Neglect of this sort is a serious computer security risk, and its consequences include loss of college papers, loss of data, and lost business. But such risks should be distinguished from **computer crimes**, actions that violate state or federal laws. The term **cybercrime** is often used to describe crimes carried out

by means of the Internet, and a new legal field, called **cyberlaw**, is emerging in order to track developments in this areas.

Computer Crime and Cybercrime: Tools and Tricks

Anyone who wants to invade or harm a computer system can make use of a variety of tools and tricks, which are summarized in this section. Pay close attention: you'll learn several facts that could help you avoid becoming a victim.

TRICKS FOR OBTAINING PASSWORDS

The most publicized computer security problems stem from **unauthorized access**, in which an unauthorized intruder gains entry to a supposedly secure computer system. Typically, computer systems use some type of **authentication** technique—usually plaintext passwords—to protect the system from uninvited guests. It isn't difficult, though, to guess or obtain a password. Once in, the hackers often attempt to obtain the entire system password list so that they may access user accounts and do their mischief.

Techniques used to obtain passwords include the following:

Password guessing Computer users too often don't understand the need to choose secure passwords. They choose a password that's easily guessed, such as "password." Other popular passwords are "qwerty" (the first six letters of the keyboard), obscene words, personal names, birthdays, celebrity names, movie characters such as Frodo or Gandalf, and the names of cartoon characters such as Garfield.

Shoulder surfing In a crowded computer lab, it's easy to peek over someone's shoulder, look at their keyboard, and obtain the person's password. Watch out for **shoulder surfing** when you're using an ATM machine, too.

Figure 11.1
Dumpsters can hold treasure troves of information for intruders.

Packet sniffers A **packet sniffer** is a program that examines all the traffic on a section of a network. The program examines the data stream and looks for passwords, credit card numbers, and other valuable information.

Dumpster diving Companies may unthinkingly discard documents that contain lists of user IDs and even passwords. In **dumpster diving**, intruders go through an organization's trash in the hope of finding such documents (see Figure 11.1). It's wise to use a shredder!

Social engineering Imagine that you work for a large corporation and you get a call from a person who claims to be your network administrator. You're told, "We have a problem with our mail backup system. I need your password right now to save your mail." Without

NATIONAL SECURITY

IMPACTS

Tracking an Intruder

If you've ever visited the National Aeronautics and Space Administration (NASA), you know that getting anything closer than a binocular view of a space shuttle is impossible, unless you have top security clearance. In August 2002, however, a hacker known as "RaFa" was able to get a lot much closer view of NASA space shuttles—without even leaving his computer. The 23-year-old downloaded about 43 MB of data from a top-security NASA server, including a 15-slide PowerPoint presentation of a future shuttle design.

Previous front man of the hacker group World of Hell, known for defacing Web sites until it disbanded in 2001, RaFa supposedly used an anonymous FTP (File Transfer Protocol) vulnerability to hack the design plans and engineering drawings for the next generation of space shuttles. RaFa proceeded to send the drawings to a reporter for the *ComputerWorld* Web site as proof that the NASA site was insecure. Because of International Trafficking in Arms Regulations (ITAR), making this sort of document available to foreign markets is restricted, and could have political and military ramifications.

Although NASA didn't experience any direct financial loss from RaFa's activities, many companies do lose money through hack attacks. In a recent survey conducted by *Information Week*, more than half of the surveyed U.S. and Canadian companies reported financial losses averaging in excess of $100,000 due to computer fraud. Seventeen companies reported losses of more than $1 million as the result of a single security incident. Since many companies are reluctant to report losses out of fear that their customers will lose confidence in their security procedures, the losses are probably much greater than reported. In short, computer crime is a serious problem, and it's getting worse.

As the NASA case indicates, more is at stake than just financial loss. Consider this: if someone could invade NASA's site, what's to stop foreign intelligence services from mounting similar attacks from abroad? NASA's investigators and government officials are concerned about the possibility of someone hacking into NASA or other government computers in order to change documents. This has the potential of causing larger, far-reaching problems. The Internet, after all, is a global network. Advanced industrial economies are increasingly dependent on networked information systems to support vital infrastructures, such as finance, energy, and transportation. According to some experts, an enemy could bring the United States to its knees by means of electronic warfare without firing a single shot (see Figure 11.2).

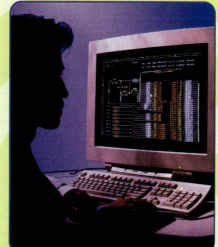

Figure 11.2
Many unauthorized intrusions by hackers go undetected, and the attackers are never caught.

As for RaFa, he claims he didn't realize the national security ramifications of his hacking. He is now portraying himself as an "investigative hacker" looking into the vulnerability of home and business systems for the good of consumers. RaFa may have changed his ways, but many hackers continue to do damage, threatening the growth of e-commerce, and even our national security.

realizing what you're doing by answering, you're giving an intruder a means to gain entry to a secure system. You're a victim of **social engineering**, a form of deception designed to get people to divulge sensitive information.

Superuser status Multiuser operating systems such as UNIX and Windows NT provide system administrators with **superuser status**, enabling them to access and modify virtually any file on the network. If intruders are able to obtain superuser status, they can obtain the passwords of everyone using the system.

Another widely used technique involves exploiting well-known holes in obsolete e-mail programs, which can be manipulated to disclose a user's password. Competent system administrators know better than to run these programs, but a tight job market and a huge increase in the number of networked systems often make it difficult to find well-trained people. As a result, many computer systems are run by undertrained people who leave gaping holes for intruders.

SALAMI SHAVING AND DATA DIDDLING

Most computer crime is an inside job. In **salami shaving**, a programmer alters a program so that it subtracts a very small amount of money from each account—say, two cents—and diverts the funds to the embezzler's account. Ideally, the sum is so small that it's never noticed. In a business that handles thousands of accounts, an insider could skim tens of thousands of dollars per year using this method.

In **data diddling**, insiders modify data so that it's difficult or impossible to tell that they've stolen funds or equipment. In some cases, data diddling requires little more expertise than altering accounts or database records to disguise illegal activities. A Colorado supermarket chain learned a great deal about data diddling recently when it discovered nearly $2 million in unaccounted losses. Subsequently, the chain's computer manager and two clerks were arrested on suspicion of embezzlement. Although the highest salary they earned was $32,000, they had each purchased expensive new

cars (including a Dodge Viper) and made several trips to Las Vegas, where they flashed wads of cash—$20,000 or more.

FORGERY

Basic shortcomings in the Internet's technical design enable knowledgeable users to make data appear to come from one place when it's really coming from another. There are even "anonymizer" sites and programs that strip the sender's tracking data from a message and then resend the message. Pranksters can easily originate forged e-mail messages, which can do a great deal of harm if the forgery is undetected. Spammers (marketers who send unsolicited e-mail) use this technique to disguise the origin of their messages.

SECURITY LOOPHOLE DETECTION PROGRAMS

Intruders can use a variety of programs that automatically search for unprotected or poorly protected computer systems and notify them when a target is found. They can also use **SATAN**, a security loophole analysis program designed for use by system administrators. In the wrong hands, the program can tell an intruder how to get into a poorly secured system.

COMPUTER VIRUSES

A **computer virus** resembles a living virus in frightening ways. Like real viruses, computer viruses require a host (such as a program file), and they're designed to make copies of themselves.

How does a computer get infected by a virus? Typically, virus infections spread when somebody inserts a disk containing an infected program into a computer, and then starts the infected program. You might also get a virus by downloading an infected program from the Internet. Either way, starting the infected program causes the virus to start copying itself. The virus attaches itself to other programs and soon infects much or all of the software on your computer. Should you copy a program on your computer to a disk and give it to someone, the infection spreads again (see Figure 11.3).

Although many viruses are best categorized as nuisances or pranks, all consume system memory and slow the computer's processing speed, and some damage data. In the prank category is the Wazzu virus, one of the most widespread in virus history, which randomly relocates a word in a Microsoft Word document and sometimes inserts "wazzu" into the text. Still others—such as Disk Killer, authored by an individual who calls himself The Computer Ogre—are far more malicious: Disk Killer wipes out all of the data on your hard drive.

The viruses we've been describing are called **file infectors** because they attach themselves to a program file. When the program is executed, the virus spreads to other programs on the user's hard disk. Most viruses are file infectors.

A second and far more serious type of virus is called a **boot sector virus**. A boot sector virus also propagates by means of an infected program, but it installs itself on the beginning tracks of a hard drive, where code is stored that automatically executes every time you start the computer. Unlike file infectors, boot sector viruses don't require you to start a specific program to infect your computer: starting your system is sufficient. Boot sector viruses also may lead to the destruction of all the data stored on your hard drive.

A third type of virus, called a **macro virus**, takes advantage of the automatic command execution capabilities (called **macros**) of productivity software, such as word processing and spreadsheet programs. Before macro viruses came along, the only type of file that could be infected by viruses (and cause them to spread) was an **executable file**, a file containing a program that can run on a given computer platform (such as Microsoft Windows or Mac OS). The virus couldn't spread unless somebody ran the program. What's scary about macro viruses is that they infect data files, which are files containing the data created with an application program such as Microsoft Word. Many people exchange data files; in fact, they often must exchange data files to do their jobs. For example, most on-the-job writing you'll do will involve collaboration with one or more coworkers. When you exchange drafts of a report, will you infect your computer?

Viruses pose a serious threat to computer systems (see Figure 11.4). More than 20,000 computer viruses are in existence, and more are being written each day. In U.S. companies, they're causing serious financial losses. Two of the most famous and devastating viruses, the Melissa virus of 1999 and the Love Bug virus of 2000, are estimated to have cost businesses and individuals worldwide more than $10 billion in lost data, computer repairs, lost work time, and lost sales. A particularly nasty virus, called SirCam, appeared in the fall of 2001 and spread so rapidly that the Internet and many corporate networks

Figure 11.3
Computer viruses can be passed from one computer to another on floppy disks and over networks.

were all but brought to a standstill. And the threat is growing. Computer virus authors are hard at work trying to "improve" their programs. Some new viruses are self-modifying so that each new copy is slightly different from the previous one, making it difficult to protect your computer.

Most computer viruses spread by means of e-mail attachments. An **e-mail attachment** is any computer file that is included with an e-mail message. If you receive an e-mail message containing an attachment, your e-mail program displays a distinctive icon, such as a paper clip, informing you that the message contains an attachment (see Figure 11.5). You may also see a dialog box asking whether you want to open the attachment. Don't do so unless you're sure the attachment is safe.

Which attachments are risky to open? Worst of all are executable files. You can tell an executable file by its extension, the short part of the file name on the right side of the period. In Microsoft Windows, .exe, but they can also be named .com, .bin, or .bat. But you can't be sure that a file is executable by its extension alone. The best policy is to check the file with an antivirus program before you open it.

You should also be wary of opening Microsoft Office documents, such as Microsoft Word (.doc) and Microsoft Excel (.xls) files. These files may contain macro viruses.

Should you open a Word or Excel document that you have received from someone you trust? Bear in mind that even trusted friends and coworkers may not be aware that their computers are infected with a virus. Always run attachments through an antivirus program, just to be sure. This is a case where the old adage "an ounce of prevention is worth a pound of cure" holds true.

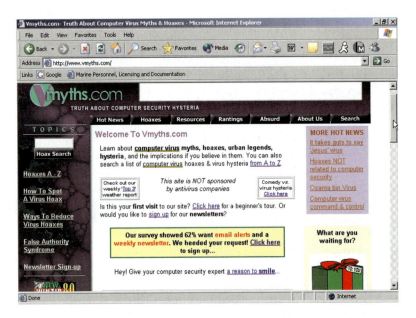

Figure 11.4
Web sites such as Vmyths.com offer information on computer viruses and debunk the myths surrounding them.

MORE ROGUE PROGRAMS

Viruses aren't the only type of rogue program. Other destructive programs include time bombs, worms, and Trojan horses.

A **time bomb**, also called a **logic bomb**, is designed to sit harmlessly on a system until a certain event or set of circumstances causes the program to become active. Disgruntled programmers may create a time bomb designed to detonate after they've left a firm's employment, for example.

A **worm** resembles a computer virus in that it can spread from one computer to another. Unlike a virus, however, a worm can propagate over a computer network, and it doesn't require an unsuspecting user to execute a program or macro file. It takes control of affected computers and

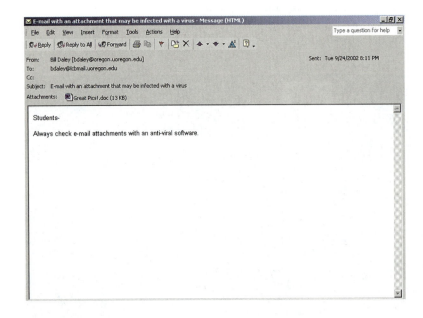

Figure 11.5
E-mail attachments are often carriers of viruses.

uses their resources to attack other network-connected systems.

A **Trojan horse** is disguised as a useful program, but it contains hidden instructions to perform a malicious task instead. Sometimes a Trojan horse is disguised as a game or a utility program that users will find appealing. Then, when the users begin running the game, they discover that they have loaded another animal entirely. A Trojan horse may erase the data on your hard disk or cause other irreparable damage.

Meet the Attackers

Who wants to harm computer systems and computer users? As you'll see, a surprising variety of people can cause security problems, ranging from people with too much time on their hands to hardened criminals, such as the Russian intruders who recently made off with $10 million from Citibank. Motives vary, too. Some attackers are out for ego gratification and don't intend any harm. Others are out for money, others are on a misguided crusade, and still others are just plain malicious.

The variety of attackers is a problem in itself. When intruders try to break into a system, administrators can't be sure initially where the problem is coming from. In 1998, U.S. Defense Department computers were besieged during a Gulf military action, and newspapers jumped to the conclusion that the attacks originated in Iraq and were intended to stymie the military's activities. The culprits turned out to be two California boys under the direction of a teenage computer intruder in Israel!

CRACKERS, CYBERGANGS, AND VIRUS AUTHORS

The most celebrated intruders are computer hobbyists and computer experts, for whom unauthorized access is something of an irresistible intellectual game. The press tends to call all these hobbyists hackers, but this term is actually too broad. In this section, you'll learn better-focused terms to refer to computer users who try to break into computer systems.

Hackers are computer hobbyists who enjoy pushing computer systems (and themselves) to their limits. They experiment with programs to try to discover **undocumented features**, capabilities that aren't mentioned in the systems' manuals. They modify systems to obtain the maximum possible performance. And sometimes they try to track down all the weaknesses and loopholes in a system's security. When hackers attempt unauthorized access, they rarely damage data or steal assets. Hackers generally subscribe to an unwritten code of conduct, called the **hacker ethic**, that forbids the destruction of data. For hackers, unauthorized access is an intellectual diversion or game. (As you'll learn later in this chapter, the people who have to secure systems against hacker attacks don't think it's a game.) Hacker motives include ego gratification: hackers form communities, with a pecking order defined in terms of an individual's reputation for hacking prowess (see Figure 11.6).

Crackers (also called **black hats**) are hackers who, like Darth Vader in *Star Wars*, have turned to the "dark side." They become obsessed (often uncontrollably) with gaining entry to highly secure computer systems. Like hackers, they generally don't intend to harm or steal data, but the frequency and sophistication of their attacks cause major headaches for system administrators.

Techtalk

phreaking
When a computer or other device is used to trick a telephone system, it's called "phreaking." When successful, a phone phreak will be able to make free telephone calls or have calls charged to a different account. Either way, they break into the phone system and steal time from the phone company.

Figure 11.6
Many Web sites, including Hackers.com, are dedicated to the field of hacking.

A Pentagon official recently disclosed that the U.S. Department of Defense computer systems experience more than 1,000 detected unauthorized access attempts per day, and that as many as 96 percent of such attempts evade detection. Cracking appears to be one form of **computer addiction**: many crackers confess that they feel compelled to return to cracking even if they've made an effort to stop.

Like hackers, crackers are obsessed with their reputation in the hacking and cracking communities. To document their feats, they often leave calling cards, such as a prank message, on the systems they penetrate. Sometimes these traces enable law enforcement personnel to track them down.

Cybergangs bring crackers together by means of the Internet and physical meetings. The group dynamics reinforce their immature and often destructive aims.

Hackers and crackers can cause major headaches, but both should be distinguished from criminals who seek to steal money or valuable data by gaining unauthorized access to computer systems. However, anyone who tries to gain unauthorized access to a computer system is probably breaking one or more laws.

Computer virus authors are typically teenage males whose programming ability is much more developed than their ethical conscience. They want to see how far they can push the boundaries of virus software. Often, they see no harm in what they're doing. They claim that all technological progress is inevitable, and that somebody else would eventually create the programs they write. Most eventually stop writing viruses after they've matured a bit and found something more worthwhile to do with their time.

Some virus authors appear to be motivated by a twisted moral crusade—specifically, a campaign to rid the world of the Microsoft Corporation, which has long been detested by the hacker community. In the twisted logic of some virus authors, Microsoft deserves to be attacked because, they believe, its products fail to protect users adequately from computer security risks. However, their attacks have yet to harm Microsoft. Instead, they've penalized millions of innocent computer users, many of whom have suffered devastating losses of data.

More than a few hackers and crackers have turned pro, offering their services to companies hoping to use hacker expertise to shore up their computer systems' defenses. (This practice is called **ethical hacking**, and those who undertake this type of hacking are called **white hats**.)

However, without doubt, some hackers have crossed the line from hacking and cracking to intentional computer crime. This prospect sounds scary, but a far greater threat exists inside the organizations that house computer systems, as the next section explains.

DISGRUNTLED EMPLOYEES

Computer intrusions make headlines, but a much greater security risk stems from disgruntled employees. According to one estimate, 80 percent of all data loss comes from company insiders. Unlike intruders, employees have many opportunities to sabotage a company's computer system, often in ways that are difficult to trace. They may discover or deliberately create security holes called **trap doors**, which, after leaving the firm, they can exploit to

Figure 11.7
Trap doors enable people to access a company's computers without being detected.

get even with the company (see Figure 11.7). They can then divulge the company's trade secrets to a competitor or destroy crucial data.

A Texas firm recently learned the peril posed by disgruntled employees the hard way. Before leaving the firm, a fired programmer planted a time bomb (a destructive program) that wiped out 168,000 critical financial records.

SPIES

Corporate computer systems contain a great deal of information of interest to competitors, including product development plans, customer contact lists, product specifications, manufacturing process knowledge, cost data, and strategic plans. According to computer security experts, **corporate espionage** is on the rise—so sharply that it may soon eclipse all other sources of unauthorized access.

How do spies gain entry to a corporation's computers? Some get help from hackers and crackers. More often, though, the perpetrators are ex-employees who have been hired by a competing firm precisely because of their knowledge of the computer system in their previous place of employment. As we just mentioned, sometimes employees who are planning to leave one company will create a trap door that enables them to access the company's computers without detection after they've left the company and joined another.

Hacking and cracking skills are no longer the only means available for snooping on a company's data. In the mid-1980s, Wim van Eck, a Dutch electronics researcher, proved that it's possible to reconstruct the words on a computer display terminal from a distance by decoding the terminal's radio frequency emissions. What's even scarier is that the necessary device can be assembled from inexpensive, off-the-shelf components and mounted in an innocent-looking van.

The espionage threat goes beyond national borders. Nations bent on acquiring trade secrets and new technologies are also trying to break into corporate computer systems. According to a recent estimate, the governments of more than 125 countries are actively involved in industrial espionage.

SWINDLERS

The Internet is the latest playground for con men, swindlers, and fraud artists, and it's a serious problem. Much of the problem is the same old garbage that telemarketing "boiler rooms" dished out in years past, such as bogus work-at-home opportunities, illegal pyramid schemes, chain letters, risky business opportunities, bogus franchises, phony goods that won't be delivered, overpriced scholarship searches, and get-rich-quick scams. Today, the distribution media of choice include e-mail, Internet chat rooms, and Web sites.

Estimates of the scope of the problem vary, but the U.S. National Consumer's League believes that consumers are losing millions of dollars on a variety of Internet scams—and the figure is growing by leaps and bounds. Here's a sampler:

Rip and tear A Seattle man recently posted ads for Barbie dolls and other goods on the leading Internet auction site, eBay.com, collected more than $32,000 in orders, and never delivered any goods—a type of swindle known to law enforcement as **rip and tear**, because the swindlers move to a new state once their activities are uncovered. The perpetrators believe that law enforcement won't be concerned with the relatively small amounts involved in each transaction. In another of a growing number of rip and tear scams on Internet auction sites, a San Diego man was recently charged with duping Internet users out of more than $60,000 for Beanie Babies that were never delivered.

Pumping and dumping In **pumping and dumping**, crooks use Internet stock trading sites, chat rooms, Usenet discussions, and e-mail to sing the praises of worthless companies in which they hold stock—and after the share prices go up, they dump the stocks and make a hefty profit. This activity is, of course, illegal under U.S. security laws.

Bogus goods Two Miami residents were recently indicted on charges of mail and wire fraud after selling hundreds of "Go-boxes," which purported to turn red traffic lights to green. The boxes, which were actually nothing more than strobe lights, were sold for between $69 and $150. Such bogus goods are offered with frightening regularity by spammers.

SHILLS

Internet auction sites such as eBay are among the hottest on the Web, but they're attracting cybernetic versions of the same scams long perpetrated at live auctions (see Figure 11.8). A **shill** is a secret operative who bids on another seller's item in order to drive up the price. The practice made headlines recently when an abstract painting's price shot from 25 cents to $135,805 after speculation that the work was a long-lost canvas by the renowned artist Richard Diekenborn. In this case, the shill was the seller, who used a different e-mail address to bid up his own offering. In response, the auction site cancelled the sale and suspended the seller's account.

The practice may be more common than Internet auction sites are willing to admit. A group of sellers can band together, drive up each other's prices, and post glowing reviews of each other's selling and

delivery practices. There's actually nothing illegal about any of this, as long as each member of the ring actually purchases the items if they should, by chance, win the auction. Shill bidding may also be close to impossible to detect. The telltale patterns can be detected only by piecing through bidding records, but most auction sites, such as eBay, retain the records for only 30 days.

If shill bidding is indeed a widespread practice, it's big business. Auction sales likely exceed $10 billion per year, and the largest auction site, eBay, receives more than 1,000 bids per minute on more than five million items listed for sale.

CYBERSTALKERS AND SEXUAL PREDATORS

One of the newest and fastest growing of all crimes is **cyberstalking**, defined as the use of the Internet, e-mail, and other electronic communication media to harass or threaten a person repeatedly (see Figure 11.9). You can read about many cases of cyberstalking in newspapers every year. Recently, for example, a San Diego university student terrorized five female classmates for more than a year, sending them hundreds of violent and threatening e-mails. In an Internet chat room, a 16-year-old boy was contacted by a woman who asked him to make a videotape of himself being tied up and tickled. When the boy refused, the woman bombarded him with e-mails—more than 30,000 of them—demanding the videotape and threatening to tell the boy's parents. A former security guard used the Internet to terrorize a woman who refused his sexual advances. He impersonated his 28-year-old victim in Internet chat rooms, posting messages that she fantasized about being raped. On at least six occasions, the women received visitors—sometimes at night—who said they were there to rape her.

Cyberstalking has one thing in common with traditional stalking: most perpetrators are men, and most victims are women, particularly women in college. One in every eight women attending college has been followed, watched, phoned, written, or e-mailed in ways that they found obsessive and frightening.

Figure 11.8
Web sites such as eBay attract shills, secret operatives who bid on another seller's item in order to drive up the price.

Children are at risk from online sexual predators, who are much more numerous than most parents realize. According to a study conducted by the National Center for Missing and Exploited Children, about one in every five kids has received invitations to engage in sexual activities while participating in Internet discussions. Online predators may encourage children to run away from home or meet them while their parents are away. Help is available, however. Later in the chapter you'll read about a volunteer group called CyberAngels whose mission it to make cyberspace a safer place for children (see Figure 11.10).

INFORMATION WARFARE

Imagine a war as some experts portray it. Without a shot being fired, the United States is thrown into economic chaos and forced to make major concessions to a foreign adversary. How? By means of **information warfare**, the use of information technologies to corrupt or destroy an enemy's information and industrial infrastructure.

A concerted enemy attack would include **electronic warfare** (the use of electronic devices to destroy or damage computer systems), **network warfare** (hacker-like attacks on the nation's network infrastructure, including the electronic banking system), and **structural sabotage** (attacks on information systems that support transportation, finance, energy, and telecommunications). However, don't leave out old-fashioned explosives directed at computer centers. According to one expert, a well-coordinated bombing of only 100 key computer installations in the United States could bring the country's economy to a grinding halt. We've learned a lot about redundant backup systems and the resiliency of the U.S. monetary system since the September 11, 2001, attacks. But we're still vulnerable and must develop ways to protect our computer systems and infrastructure.

How big is the threat? According to experts, information warfare is inevitable, but defenses are sorely lacking. A recent U.S. Department of Defense study disclosed that military systems were attacked a quarter of a million times in 1995, and

that number has surely grown since then. As a test in 1995, a Defense Department tiger team conducted 38,000 attacks of their own. They were successful 65 percent of the time, and 63 percent of those attacks escaped detection. Former U.S. Deputy Attorney General Jaime Gorelick warns of a "cyber equivalent of Pearl Harbor" if the United States does not take steps to prepare for electronic attack.

Even if no enemy nation mounts an all-out information war on the United

Figure 11.9
In cyberstalking, a person uses the Internet, e-mail, or other electronic communication media to harass or threaten another person.

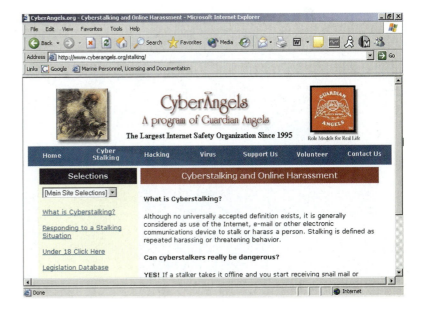

Figure 11.10
Cyberangels is just one of a growing number of anticyberstalking victim assistance programs.

States, **information terrorism** is still increasingly likely. Thanks to the world-wide distribution of powerful but inexpensive microprocessors, virtually anyone can construct electronic warfare weapons from widely available materials. These weapons include high-energy radio frequency (HERF) guns and electromagnetic pulse transformer (EMPT) bombs, which can damage or destroy computer systems up to a quarter of a mile away. A van loaded with such devices could cruise down Wall Street and bring chaos to the stock market.

If this scenario sounds frightening, remember that information technology is a double-edged sword. Information technology gives despots a potent weapon of war but also undermines their power by giving citizens a way to organize democratic resistance. In Russia, for example, e-mail and fax machines played a major role in the failure of the 1989 military coup.

What's at Stake?

Breaches of computer security can be costly, even when no harm has occurred. As our entire economy and infrastructure move to networked information systems, the potential costs grow higher every day.

Figure 11.11
For security measures, users should lock their doors and turn off their computers. In some cases, it may be wise to secure hardware to desks to prevent theft.

CONSUMPTION OF STAFF TIME

Even if intruders do no damage, they still cost companies money. When an intrusion occurs, the computer staff must drop everything they're doing and focus on the problem. After they've secured the system against the intruder, they must consider how they'll stop the next attack. They may spend days or weeks on the problem. It's no wonder that security currently accounts for an estimated three to five percent of all corporate expenditures on information systems.

DOWNTIME

Ostensibly harmless security breaches also cost money when an intrusion occurs and system administrators shut down the system rather than risk data loss. Financial losses may also include the loss of customers who may be put off by slow service.

When rogue programs propagate by means of the Internet and affect thousands of systems, staff time and downtime add up. Think about it: hundreds of thousands— if not millions—of workers and homes receive the virus. Time must be spent to eradicate the virus and repair damage. Software often has to be reinstalled, backup files have to be retrieved to replace damaged files, and systems have to be checked to ensure that the virus has not affected their performance. And, all the while, productivity is being lost. Downtime is a very serious consideration indeed!

FRAUD AND THEFT

Physical theft of computer equipment is a huge and growing problem, and it's particularly difficult to trace (see Figure 11.11). An estimated 85 percent of computer thefts are inside jobs, leaving no signs of forced physical entry. In addition, it's difficult to trace components after they've been taken apart and reassembled. Particularly valuable are the microprocessor chips that drive computers. Employees at several large corporations have arrived at work only to find that their computers won't start. The problem? Overnight, somebody went through every computer in the building and pried out the processors. **Memory shaving**, in which knowledgeable thieves remove some of a computer's RAM chips but leave enough so that the computers are able to start, is harder to detect. The crime might not be detected for weeks.

ADVERSE PUBLICITY

You may be surprised to learn that, according to one estimate, more than 40 percent of all computer crimes go unreported. Why? Suppose you're running a bank. You've lost $1 million due to computer theft. What's going to cost you more, covering the loss or telling the world that depositors' money isn't safe? Mum's the word.

According to news reports, computer attackers are taking advantage of adverse publicity fears by blackmailing financial institutions. In London, cybergangs have reportedly extorted nearly $650 million from banks in the past few years after demonstrating to senior executives that the gangs could completely wipe out the banks' information systems.

VANDALISM

A surprising number of Web servers aren't properly secured, enabling any knowledgeable outsider to replace the existing content with prank material. This happens to people who ought to know better. One especially famous case occurred in 1996, when the CIA Web site was penetrated by a group of Swedish hackers who altered the home page to say "Welcome to the Central Stupidity Agency."

CHARACTER ASSASSINATION

Forged messages and Web pages can cause embarrassment and worse. A university professor in Texas was recently attacked with thousands of e-mail messages and Usenet postings after someone forged a racist Usenet article in his name. In Beijing, a student almost lost an $18,000 scholarship when a jealous rival forged an e-mail message to the University of Michigan turning it down. Fortunately, the forgery was discovered and the scholarship was reinstated, but only after a lengthy delay. And, reportedly, there exists a Microsoft Word macro virus that sends copies of a victim's Word documents to 23 different Usenet newsgroups under subject lines like "New Virus Alert!," "Important Princess Diana Info," and "How to find child pornography."

LOSS OF PRIVACY

If computer intruders make off with sensitive personal information, the potential for harm multiplies. In one Florida intrusion, a cracker made off with confidential medical records on 8,000 carriers of HIV. In another case, employees of the U.S. Social Security Administration used their computer access privileges to gather Social Security numbers and other information on 11,000 U.S. citizens and sold this information to criminals specializing in credit card fraud.

RISKS TO PUBLIC SAFETY

Perhaps the greatest threat posed by security breaches is the threat to human life. And, as computers are increasingly incorporated into safety-critical systems, such as air-traffic control, the threat increases.

This threat nearly became a reality when a 14-year-old recently knocked out phone and radio service to a regional airport's communications tower. Although the hacker didn't realize he had accessed an airport computer and meant no harm, his actions paralyzed the airport's computer system and forced air-traffic controllers to rely on cellular phones and battery-powered radios to direct airplanes. Fortunately, the attack came when traffic was light. Had the airport's computers gone down in the midst of peak traffic, the outcome might have been tragic.

Should information terrorism or information warfare materialize, it could cause catastrophic harm. By paralyzing transportation and power infrastructures, attackers could completely disrupt the distribution of electricity, food, water, and medical supplies.

DENIAL OF SERVICE

By exploiting some of the most troubling flaws in the Internet's basic structure, hackers have learned how to launch another type of assault: a **denial of service (DoS)** attack (also called **syn flooding**, due to technical details concerning the attack method). In such an attack, attackers bog down an Internet server so that it becomes overloaded and can't function. When this happens, customers become unhappy, orders can't be taken, and business suffers.

Playing It Safe

What can we do to protect computer systems and users from attackers? This section discusses several measures that safeguard computer systems, but it's important to remember that none of them can make a computer system 100 percent secure. A tradeoff exists between security and usability: the more secure the system, the less useful it becomes due to the restrictions imposed by the security tools. There are no totally secure computer systems.

PROTECTING COMPUTERS FROM POWER-RELATED PROBLEMS

Some of a computer's enemies aren't human, as you'll learn to your dismay—if you haven't already. Consider this: you've just spent three hours typing a college paper on your laptop. You hear a thunderstorm in the background, but you keep working anyway. Suddenly, it's dark—the power's gone. And so is your work, unless you saved it. If you're very unlucky, you may also have suffered irreparable damage to your system.

Power surges and **power outages** present serious threats to any computer system. Often caused by lightning storms, power surges can destroy sensitive electronic components, and outages carry the threat of data loss. To safeguard against data loss caused by surges and outages, some application programs offer an **autosave** feature, which backs up your work at a specified interval (such as every 10 minutes). That way, should you experience a power outage, you'll lose no more than 10 minutes of work. You can also equip your system with an **uninterruptible power supply** (**UPS**), a battery-powered device that goes to work instantly when it detects an outage or critical voltage drop (see Figure 11.12). Large-scale computer systems have their own electrical generators that step in when the power fails.

CONTROLLING ACCESS

As you've learned, many security problems originate with purloined passwords. Passwords can be easy to guess or steal. If even one password has been guessed or stolen, system administrators can't be certain whether the user currently logging on is an authorized user or an intruder bent on destroying data.

The term *authentication* refers to the method used to verify that the users who are logging on really are the people they say they are. Most computer systems authenticate users by means of a **user name** (also called **user ID**), which is linked to the user's real name and other contact information, and a **password**. Typically, these systems require users to select their own passwords—and that is the source of a serious computer security

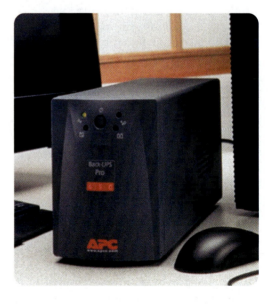

Figure 11.12
A UPS is a battery-powered device that provides power to your computer for a limited time during a power outage.

risk. As mentioned at the beginning of the chapter, too many users choose passwords that are easy to guess, such as "password" or some variation on their name. If an intruder can guess your password, the intruder can gain access to the computer system—and any damage that results will appear to have been perpetrated by you, not the intruder.

What's a good password? You shouldn't use any variation of your name or any word that can be found in a dictionary. The best passwords are at least eight characters in length, combine upper- and lowercase letters, and include one or more numbers.

Callback systems can ensure that the person attempting to gain access to a computer is calling from a recognized telephone on specific days of the week and during certain hours. In a callback system, the user calls the computer and enters his or her account number and password, after which the computer terminates the connection. The computer verifies the user ID and password, the day, and the time of day. The computer then calls the user back at the telephone to which that user is assigned.

Callback systems help to reduce insider crime, but they're useless for public access systems, which still rely mainly on password authentication. New approaches require users not only to *know* something (such as a password or PIN number), but to *have* something as well. You're probably familiar with this approach because it's used in automated teller machines (ATMs): you must have your ATM card and know your PIN number, or you can't get your money.

In **"know & have" authentication**, users can be required to use **tokens**, which are handheld electronic devices that generate a logon code. Increasingly popular are **smartcards**, credit card–sized electronic devices with their own internal memories (see Figure 11.13). In tandem with a supplied PIN number, a smartcard can reliably establish that the person trying to gain access has authorization to do so, unless the owner carelessly writes the PIN number on the card itself. (As many as one-fourth of all ATM card holders do this, according to banking security experts.)

The most secure authentication approach is called **biometric authentication**, which uses a variety of techniques, including voice recognition, retinal scans,

Figure 11.13
Smartcards are credit card–sized devices with their own internal memories.

fingerprint scans, and face and hand recognition. If this sounds like something so futuristic that it belongs only in *Star Trek*, you may be surprised to learn that such systems are already in widespread use (see Figure 11.14).

Figure 11.14 a-c
Biometric authentication devices such as (a) retinal scanners, (b) fingerprint scanners, and (c) hand geometry readers are already in widespread use.

your organization's PCs

corporation network

FIREWALL

Internet

Figure 11.15
A firewall permits an organization's internal computer users to access the Internet, while placing severe limits on the ability of outsiders to access internal data.

Figure 11.16
Information you want to keep away from unauthorized people must be either withheld from them or encrypted.

USING FIREWALLS

As you've learned, the Internet provides a new way for intruders to gain access to computer systems. Perhaps the best defense against such attacks is to pull the plug on the Internet connection, but few organizations want to do this. Instead, they try to insulate internal computers by means of a **firewall** (see Figure 11.15). A firewall is a computer program that generally runs on its own dedicated computer. A properly configured firewall permits an organization's internal computer users to access the external Internet, while placing severe limits on the ability of outsiders to access internal data. Firewalls are a necessity, but they have a major shortcoming: they provide no protection against insider pilferage.

Because increasing numbers of home users are opting for "always on" broadband connections such as cable modems or Digital Subscriber Line (DSL), they're experiencing increased computer security risks. **Personal firewalls** are programs or devices that are designed to protect home computer users from unauthorized access.

USING ENCRYPTION

Because no foolproof means exist to protect all data from unauthorized access, it makes sense to make data unreadable to everyone except authorized eyes. This is precisely what **encryption** is for. In a nutshell, encryption takes the original data and scrambles it through the use of a key, which is also held by the receiver of the message, who uses the key to unencrypt it upon receipt. (We'll discuss encryption in more detail in Chapter 12.)

Many programs are available that enable computer users to encrypt computer data. By using encryption, companies can store sensitive data in scrambled form, so that even if an intruder were to steal the data, it wouldn't make any sense (see Figure 11.16).

Consumers can use encryption, too. Web browsers are designed to use encryption automatically when users contact secure shopping sites on the Internet. However, many Web users don't realize that the default **40-bit encryption** used by Web browsers is inadequate. The strength of an encryption technique is measured by the number of bits used in the key to encode the secret messages. For a good level of protection, **128-bit encryption** is needed. Due to U.S. restrictions on the export of strong encryption technology, however, 128-bit encryption is available only by downloading and installing an upgrade module. If you're using a Web browser for online shopping, be sure to do so.

USING ANTIVIRUS PROGRAMS

Antivirus programs, often called **vaccines** or **virus checkers**, are available for all types of computers (see Figure 11.17). Most antivirus programs use a pattern-matching technique: they examine program and data files, looking for the telltale code patterns of virus code (the **virus signature**). This technique has two major drawbacks: antivirus programs can't find new viruses that aren't in their virus databases, and they can't deal with new types of viruses that alter themselves to evade detection. To cope with these shortcomings, the better antivirus programs offer frequent updates and include programs that monitor system functions to detect virus activities.

Adhering strictly to a few guidelines can help you reduce the risk of contracting or spreading a virus. Whenever you've used a disk on another system or your disk contains files from another system, you should check the disk for viruses. Any time you download files from the Internet or bulletin board systems, carefully screen the files for viruses. If you're using Microsoft Word or other popular productivity programs, disable macros or upgrade to the latest program version, which may offer protection against macro viruses.

BACKING UP DATA

Even if you take every precaution mentioned here, it's still possible to suffer a data loss. To minimize the effect of such a loss, computer personnel and users should back up programs and data regularly. Backups should be stored away from the computer system so that, in the event of a fire or flood, they don't suffer the system's fate.

Full backups of everything stored on the computer should be made at least once each month. **Incremental backups**, which back up only those files that have been changed since the last incremental backup, should be made regularly, too—in a business environment, once or more per day.

Large organizations should also establish a written **disaster recovery plan**. The plan should have complete detailed instructions and include an alternate computing facility that can be used for emergency processing until a nonoperational computer can be repaired or replaced.

Figure 11.17

Norton AntiVirus is a utility that works by examining all the files on a disk, looking for the telltale "signatures" of virus code.

CURRENTS

INTERNET SECURITY

CyberAngels: Protecting Children in Cyberspace

Are there angels in cyberspace? A couple in Fanwood, New Jersey, has a ready answer to this question, and it's an emphatic yes! After their computer-addicted 13-year-old daughter ran away from home after a fight, the couple began to suspect that she had fled to the residence of an adult man who had been romancing the child online—so they contacted CyberAngels (**www.cyberangels.org**), a voluntary organization of thousands of Internet users worldwide. The group's purpose: to protect children in cyberspace.

Formed in 1995, CyberAngels was started by Curtis Sliwa, the founder of the Guardian Angels (the volunteer organization that patrols inner-city streets wearing red berets). As a radio call-in program host in New York, Curtis received a call from a woman who wanted to know what he would do to keep the Internet safe. Understanding that the fledgling cyberspace had the potential to be very dangerous for kids, Curtis asked a few Guardian Angels to create a cyberneighborhood watch. He called the group CyberAngels.

The group initially helped women who were being harassed online. As the Internet grew, CyberAngels started to search for and report online child pornography. In the late 1990s, under the leadership of Parry Aftab, the group became larger, earning the respect of law enforcement agencies, Internet users, and the Internet industry for its many accomplishments. In May 2002, Aftab resigned, but CyberAngels is still going strong.

Today, CyberAngels' volunteers scour the Internet for online predators, cyberstalkers, and child pornographers, and they've been responsible for a number of arrests. One group of volunteers, called Cybermoms and Dads, monitors chat rooms, a favorite Internet hangout of adults hoping to entice kids into sexual liaisons. The group's elite unit, called Net Patrol, is a small group of highly trained investigators who search for missing children, identify online sexual predators, locate and expose child pornography sites, and assist local police departments in prosecuting sexual predators. Each volunteer snares as many as four cyberstalkers a week.

CyberAngels receives nothing short of adulation from the thousands of families the organization has assisted, but some people lump CyberAngels together with right-wing, moralistic groups that are intent on imposing censorship on the Internet. However, the CyberAngels mission statement clearly affirms the group's belief that the Internet should be self-regulating and that further censorship isn't needed. What is needed, CyberAngels says, is more parents who are willing to supervise their children's online activities.

And what about the New Jersey couple? Their daughter is home, thanks to CyberAngels. The group successfully used its network of contacts to identify the child's contact.

AVOIDING SCAMS

To avoid being scammed by Internet fraud, follow these tips:

- Do business with established companies that you know and trust.

- Read the fine print. If you're ordering something, make sure it's in stock and that the company promises to deliver within 30 days.

- Don't provide financial or other personal information or passwords to anyone, even if the request sounds legitimate.

- Be skeptical when somebody in an Internet chat room tells you about a great new company or great stock.

PREVENTING CYBERSTALKERS

While you're online you can protect yourself against cyberstalkers. Follow these tips:

- Don't share any personal information, such as your real name, in chat rooms. Use a name that is gender- and age-neutral. Do not post a user profile.

- Be extremely cautious about meeting anyone you've contacted online. If you do, meet in a public place and bring friends along.

- If a situation you've encountered online makes you uncomfortable or afraid, contact the police immediately. Save all the communications you've received.

COMPUTERS IN YOUR FUTURE 2004

11.19

HOME | Takeaway Points | Key Terms and Concepts | Matching | Multiple Choice | Fill-In | Short Answer | Exercises/Projects | Web Research | CHAPTER REVIEW

TAKEAWAY POINTS

- Most unauthorized computer access goes undetected and the perpetrators are never brought to justice.

- Financial losses due to computer attacks and intrusions are increasing rapidly.

- The Internet enables intruders to attack computer systems from almost anywhere in the world.

- Intruders have little difficulty obtaining passwords to computer systems, thanks to poor user practices in choosing passwords.

- Computer viruses are no longer limited to program files. They can infect the automated command sequences (called macros) within user documents, enabling them to spread rapidly.

- Although the press sensationalizes hacker and cracker attacks, most computer crime is committed by disgruntled employees.

- As crucial energy, transport, and financial infrastructures become increasingly dependent on networked information systems, the risk of electronic warfare rises.

- Even if crackers intend no harm, targeted companies can suffer huge losses due to downtime and consumption of staff time.

- Physical theft of computers and microprocessors is increasing rapidly, in part because it's difficult to trace stolen systems.

- Computer systems need tighter authentication using methods such as callback systems, smartcards, or biometric authentication.

- To protect your own data, you should back up your data regularly, disable macro features of productivity programs, and run an antivirus program regularly.

KEY TERMS AND CONCEPTS

40-bit encryption
128-bit encryption
antivirus program
   (vaccine or virus checker)
authentication
autosave
biometric authentication
bogus goods
boot sector virus
callback system
computer addiction
computer crime
computer security risk
computer virus
computer virus author
corporate espionage
crackers (black hats)
cybercrime
cybergang
cyberlaw
cyberstalking
data diddling
denial of service attack
   (DoS or syn flooding)
disaster recovery plan

disgruntled employee
dumpster diving
e-mail attachment
electronic warfare
encryption
ethical hacking
executable file
file infector
firewall
full backup
hacker ethic
hackers
incremental backup
information terrorism
information warfare
"know & have"
   authentication
macro
macro virus
memory shaving
network warfare
packet sniffer
password
password guessing
personal firewall

power outage
power surge
pumping and dumping
rip and tear
salami shaving
SATAN
shill
shoulder surfing
smartcard
social engineering
structural sabotage
superuser status
time bomb
   (logic bomb)
token
trap door
Trojan horse
unauthorized access
undocumented feature
uninterruptible power
   supply (UPS)
user name (user ID)
virus signature
white hat
worm

COMPUTERS IN YOUR FUTURE 2004

11.21

HOME | Takeaway Points | Key Terms and Concepts | **Matching** | Multiple Choice | Fill-In | Short Answer | Exercises/ Projects | Web Research | CHAPTER REVIEW

MATCHING

Match each key term in the left column with the most accurate definition in the right column.

_____ 1. packet sniffer
_____ 2. social engineering
_____ 3. SATAN
_____ 4. shill
_____ 5. Trojan horse
_____ 6. time bomb
_____ 7. cracker
_____ 8. firewall
_____ 9. token
_____ 10. macro virus
_____ 11. hacker ethic
_____ 12. rip and tear
_____ 13. uninterruptible power supply (UPS)
_____ 14. smartcard
_____ 15. antivirus program

a. an unwritten code of conduct that forbids the destruction of data

b. a computer program that places severe limits on the ability of outsiders to access internal data

c. use the Internet to offer something for sale but never deliver the item

d. a form of deception designed to get people to divulge sensitive information

e. a program that examines all the traffic on a section of the network

f. a security loophole analysis program designed for use by system administrators

g. a handheld electronic device that generates a logon code

h. a virus that contains hidden instructions to perform a malicious task

i. a battery-powered device that goes to work instantly when it detects an outage or critical voltage drop

j. a secret operative who bids on another seller's auction item in order to drive up the price

k. a credit card–sized electronic device with its own internal memory

l. a hacker obsessed with gaining entry to highly secure computer systems

m. a virus that sits on a system until a certain event or set of circumstances causes the program to be active

n. often called a vaccine

o. a virus that takes advantage of automatic command execution capabilities

CHAPTER REVIEW | Takeaway Points | Key Terms and Concepts | Matching | Multiple Choice | Fill-In | Short Answer | Exercises/ Projects | Web Research | HOME

1 2 3 4 5 6 7 8 9 10 11 12 13 14 15 16

MULTIPLE CHOICE

Circle the correct choice for each of the following.

1. Which of the following is not a technique used to obtain passwords?
   a. Guessing
   b. Dumpster diving
   c. Social engineering
   d. Encryption

2. Which of the following describes a programmer's altering a program so that it subtracts a very small amount of money from each account?
   a. Salami shaving
   b. Data diddling
   c. Unauthorized access
   d. Packet sniffing

3. What are most viruses?
   a. File infectors
   b. Boot sector viruses
   c. Worms
   d. Time bombs

4. These are computer hobbyists who enjoy pushing computer systems to their limits.
   a. Crackers
   b. Trojan horses
   c. Hackers
   d. Cybergang members

5. This is the act of praising a worthless company to increase its stock value and then selling owned shares.
   a. Dumpster diving
   b. Pumping and dumping
   c. Ripping and tearing
   d. Shilling

6. Some application programs offer this feature to protect against data loss caused by power surges and outages.
   a. Uninterruptible power supply
   b. Surge protection
   c. Autosave
   d. Denial of service

7. How often should individuals make full backups of their computer data?
   a. Hourly
   b. Daily
   c. Monthly
   d. Quarterly

8. What is the most secure authentication approach?
   a. Encryption
   b. Biometrics
   c. Digital certification
   d. Firewalls

9. A firewall is usually used to protect a local area network from which of the following?
   a. Smoke damage
   b. Unauthorized access through the Internet
   c. Electronic funds transfer
   d. Buggy programs

10. Which of the following is not a type of access control?
    a. Callback system
    b. Password
    c. UPS system
    d. Locking door

COMPUTERS IN YOUR FUTURE 2004

11.23

HOME | Takeaway Points | Key Terms and Concepts | Matching | Multiple Choice | Fill-In | Short Answer | Exercises/ Projects | Web Research | CHAPTER REVIEW

FILL-IN

In the blanks provided, write the correct answer for each of the following.

1. Computer systems typically use some type of _____ technique for protection against unauthorized access.

2. Crimes carried out by means of the Internet are known as _____.

3. In _____, insiders modify data so that it's difficult to tell that they've stolen funds or equipment.

4. A(n) _____ installs itself at the beginning of a hard drive where code is stored and automatically executes every time you start the computer.

5. In a computer network, a(n) _____ takes control of affected computers and uses their resources to attack other network-connected systems.

6. _____ bring crackers together by means of the Internet and physical meetings.

7. _____ is the use of information technologies to corrupt or destroy an enemy's informational and industrial infrastructures.

8. _____ uses one of a variety of techniques, including voice recognition, retinal scans, and thumbprints.

9. _____ can ensure that a person attempting to gain access to a computer is calling from a recognized telephone.

10. _____ is the science of scrambling messages so that nobody but the intended recipient can read them.

11. _____ is any event, action, or situation—intentional or not—that could lead to the loss or destruction of computer systems or the data they contain.

12. A(n) _____ file contains a program that can run on a given computer platform, such as Microsoft Windows or Mac OS.

13. Disgruntled employees may discover or create security holes called _____ that, after leaving the firm, they can exploit to get even with the company.

14. _____ is using the Internet, e-mail, and other electronic communication media to repeatedly harass or threaten a person.

15. Attackers use _____ to bog down an Internet server so that it becomes overloaded and cannot function.

SHORT ANSWER

1. What are some of the techniques an intruder can use to obtain passwords?

2. Describe the differences between time bombs, worms, and Trojan horses.

3. Explain how macro viruses work and why they are potentially so dangerous.

4. Name some of the common types of passwords that users choose. Why are these poor choices?

5. Describe who typical computer virus authors are, and explain why they create viruses.

Chapter Review: 1 2 3 4 5 6 7 8 9 10 11 12 13 14 15 16

CHAPTER REVIEW

| Takeaway Points | Key Terms and Concepts | Matching | Multiple Choice | Fill-In | Short Answer | Exercises/ Projects | Web Research |

HOME

EXERCISES/PROJECTS

1. Have you ever lost data because of a power failure? Prevention Protection against this and other power-related problems can be achieved by using an uninterruptible power supply (UPS). At one time, UPS devices were used only by companies to protect their corporate computers. However, with prices falling below $100, users of personal computers can also protect their computers. Contact a local computer retailer to get information about uninterruptible power supplies. Besides loss of power, what other calamities does a UPS protect against? In addition to the computer, what peripherals can be connected to a UPS? What peripherals should not be connected to a UPS and why? How long does the battery backup last? Is autosave software provided with the UPS? Explain why you would or would not purchase a UPS.

2. How do students at your school obtain computer accounts? How are passwords initially assigned, and how do users change them? Does your computer system disallow the use of common words as passwords? What is the minimum number of characters required in a password? What are some of the tricks intruders can use to obtain passwords? Have any unauthorized persons gained access to your computer account? If they did, do you know how they obtained your password? Did they alter or destroy any of your files? Were you able to find the identity of the intruder(s)?

3. How does your school prevent theft of computer hardware from laboratories and "smart" classrooms? Identify the security devices. Check with campus security to find out how successful these security systems have been. Individual users must also be conscious of security measures. How can an individual protect his or her computer from theft? Have you personally had a computer stolen, or do you know people who have had theirs stolen? Describe the circumstances that led to the theft. Was it avoidable?

4. Who are the most common victims of cyberstalking? Who are the most common perpetrators? Have you been, or do you know anyone who has been, cyberstalked? What did the cyberstalker do? If the stalker was identified, what actions were taken?

5. Locate a newspaper or magazine article about a computer crime. Write a brief paper that includes the following:

   • Correct citation of the article and author

   • Type of computer crime and the name of the company or organization that was victimized

   • Person committing the crime and the relationship to the company or organization

   • How the computer thief was detected and caught and his or her punishment

WEB RESEARCH

1. A recent newspaper article reported that due to the events of September 11, 2001, some people were surprised that the flightTRACKER feature of TRIP.com is still working. Visit the Web site at **www.trip.com**. What does flightTRACKER do, and what information does it provide? What are the search criteria? Now that you know about this site, explain how you would use it. Explain why TRIP.com should or should not continue to offer this service.

2. As one of the leading antivirus software producers, the Symantec Corporation maintains a virus information site. According to the Web site, **www.symantec.com**, what are two of the latest virus threats and two of the top virus threats? Virus names are strange but have a definite pattern. Using the virus naming convention, what do you know about the fictitious virus named "WM.Bogus.B@mm"? What is a polymorphic virus? Like hurricanes, viruses are identified by categories, with Category 5, or CAT 5, being the most severe. What three criteria are used to determine a virus's category? Give a brief definition of each. As one would expect, a CAT 5 virus ranks high in all three criteria. What determines a CAT 3, or Moderate, threat? Not all reported viruses are real. Name a hoax virus.

3. Users can protect their personal computers by using firewalls. A firewall can be implemented through software, hardware, or a combination of both. Two of the leading software applications, McAfee Personal Firewall and Norton Personal Firewall, are designed for personal computers running various Windows operating systems. Visit the McAfee Web site at **www.mcafee.com/myapps/firewall/default.asp** and the Symantec Web site at **www.symantec.com/sabu/nis/npf**.

According to these sites, why should you purchase firewall software? What is the annual subscription for McAfee's firewall application, and what are purchase and upgrade prices for Norton's firewall application? Read both product descriptions and find additional Web sites to get "independent" evaluations of these products. Identify the URLs of these additional review sites, and explain which firewall application you would purchase, and why.

4. How do we protect children who are using the Internet? Visit the Cyberangels Web site at **http://cyberangels.org**. What is their mission? What are the major areas in which their work falls? Cyberangels provides online forms to report what activities? Is your state one of those that has enacted a cyber-stalking law? Name three of the national and international law enforcement agencies with which Cyberangels works. Explain the difference between blocking software and filtering software, and discuss their weaknesses. Explain why you would or would not become a volunteer for this organization.

5. Was your school affected by the W32.Nimda.A@mm virus? If it was, how were the files on your school's servers disinfected? Specifically, what server software was vulnerable to attack by this virus? What software applications helped spread the virus? Which client platforms were susceptible to this virus?

   If your personal computer was infected, what antivirus program did you use to disinfect the computer? Do you regularly use Internet Explorer? If you do use it, you could have reduced the possibility of receiving the virus by disabling JavaScript. How do you do this? Explain why you would or would not want to disable JavaScript.

Privacy and Encryption

CHAPTER **12**

What You'll Learn . . .

When you have finished reading this chapter, you will be able to:

1. Explain the threat to privacy posed by the sale of sensitive personal information on the Internet.

2. Define anonymity and discuss how it can be abused.

3. Describe how technological developments are eroding privacy and anonymity.

4. Explain the reasons why many employers feel that they need to monitor their employees' computer usage.

5. State why U.S. security officials believe public key encryption poses a threat to U.S. security, both foreign and domestic.

6. Describe the U.S. government's proposed key recovery plan, and explain why it threatens the growth of Internet commerce.

The phone rings, and it's a collection agency. They're demanding immediate payment for a $5,000 stereo system bill that's past due. You can't believe what you're hearing—you always pay your bills on time, and what's more, you haven't purchased any stereo equipment lately. What's going on?

It's **identity theft**, one of the fastest-growing crimes in the United States and Canada. In identity theft, a criminal obtains enough information about you to open a credit account in your name and then maxes it out, leaving you with the bill. Although laws limit liability for fraudulent charges to $50, victims of identity theft have found themselves saddled with years of agony. The bad marks on their credit reports prevent them from buying homes, obtaining telephone service, and even getting jobs. Many victims of identity theft state that the crime ruined their lives, at least for a little while.

What do criminals need to pull off an identity theft? They need only your address, Social Security number, and a little more information, such as the addresses you've lived at for the past few years. How does somebody get this information? Thanks to the Internet, it's easy—too easy, say privacy advocates. Dozens of Web sites sell individuals' Social Security numbers for as little as $6 each (see Figure 12.1). Is it any surprise that U.S. law enforcement officials say that identity theft is the fastest-growing type of crime and is already the leading type of consumer fraud?

Privacy and Encryption

Defined by U.S. Supreme Court Justice Louis Brandeis in 1928 as "the right to be left alone," **privacy** refers to an individual's ability to restrict or eliminate the collection, use, and sale of confidential personal information.

Computer databases and the Internet are combining to erode privacy to an unprecedented degree. For example, many Web sites sell the information they collect on site registration forms. This information joins a wealth of similar information streaming in from dozens of additional sources, including supermarkets, drug stores, telephone surveys, vacation contest applications, local government agencies, and many more. All this information finds its way into huge marketing databases, which aim to collect so much information about a given consumer that companies will be able to predict which products the consumer is most likely to buy. In the United States, few laws regulate the sale of collected personal information to third parties. As a result, U.S. citizens lack the privacy protections found in most European nations.

At the same time that computer technology is making it easier to invade others' privacy, it's also providing new means of defending yourself against such invasions. **Encryption** refers to a coding or scrambling process by which a message is rendered unreadable by anyone except the intended recipient. A person who uses the latest encryption technology to scramble e-mail messages can be reasonably certain that the message will remain secret. Strong, unbreakable encryption is needed for electronic commerce—otherwise, money could not be safely exchanged on the Internet. But the potential for encryption's misuse troubles law enforcement and defense agencies. Criminals, including drug dealers and terrorists, can use encryption to hide their activities. In the aftermath of the September 11, 2001, terrorist attacks, U.S. officials revealed that the terrorist network had used encrypted e-mail to help keep their plans and activities secret.

Figure 12.1
Web sites can sell your Social Security number to anyone they please.

Privacy in Cyberspace

Of all the social and ethical issues raised by the spread of widely available, Internet-linked computers, threats to privacy and anonymity are among the most contentious. This section introduces the basic concepts of privacy and anonymity, and shows how technology is eroding these basic rights.

Some people say that privacy isn't a concern unless you have something to hide. But this view is naive. It ignores the fact that individuals, governments, and corporations sometimes collect and use information in ways that harm people unnecessarily, even if you don't have anything to hide.

One example: stalking; another of the fastest-growing crimes. Thanks to the easy availability of residential address information on the Internet, victims of stalkers are finding it difficult to avoid being located by their stalkers. A particular brand of stalking, cyberstalking, occurs when a person repeatedly harasses someone (usually a woman) by using an electronic form of communication, such as e-mail.

Consider another example: DNA. As scientists unlock the genetic code, your DNA will reveal a great deal of information about you, including your susceptibility to alcoholism, cancer, heart disease, and many other genetically influenced diseases that are very expensive to treat. If this information falls into the wrong hands, it could adversely and unfairly affect your chances of obtaining employment and health insurance. At most, one's genes reveal a propensity, usually only a very slight propensity, to develop a disease. People with such propensities generally lead healthy, productive lives. To exclude them from employment or health insurance benefits, privacy advocates insist, is odious and unjust.

THE PROBLEM: COLLECTION OF INFORMATION WITHOUT CONSENT

Few people believe that privacy should be absolute. People are willing to divulge information when their consent is asked and when they see a need for doing so. When you apply for a loan, for example, the bank can reasonably ask you to list your other creditors so that it can determine whether you'll be able to repay your loan.

But most people are much less comfortable about divulging information when they see no clear need to do so—which is why marketers often solicit such information using tactics that can only be termed deceptive. For example, people often supply revealing personal information when they fill out product sweepstakes entry forms and warranty registration cards. The forms or cards often tell consumers that the company needs the information in order to serve them better. However, what the company doesn't tell consumers is that this information will be sold to database marketing firms.

Much more information is collected from public agencies, many of which are under a legal obligation to make their records available to the public upon request. Again, this information is collected without your knowledge or consent. It finds its way into computerized databases—thousands of them—that track virtually every conceivable type of information about individuals (see Figure 12.2). You are probably aware of credit reporting databases, which track your credit history. Other databases include information such as your current and former addresses, your current and former

Figure 12.2

Thousands of electronic databases track virtually every conceivable type of information about you. In the United States, you have no recourse against those who collect sensitive personal information.

employers, other names you've used (and your previous name, if you're married and use a different name now), current and former spouses, bankruptcies, lawsuits, property ownership, driver's license information, criminal records, purchasing habits, and medical prescriptions.

THE INTERNET FACTOR

Who accesses this information? Most of the **database vendors** (companies that maintain these databases) claim that they sell their information only to bona fide customers such as lending institutions, prospective employers, marketing firms, and licensed private investigators. They maintain that their databases don't pose a threat to the privacy of individuals because they are highly ethical firms that would not release this information to the general public. However, these database vendors also state that, once the information is sold, they have no control over what someone else does with it.

According to privacy activists, what happens to information after it's sold is precisely the problem. Before the Internet came along, it was much more difficult for ordinary individuals to gain access to sensitive personal information, and doing so cost more money. Thanks to the Internet, it's much easier and much cheaper. Try browsing the Internet for "Social Security numbers." As we mentioned earlier, you'll find dozens of sites placed on the Web by private investigators who offer to find someone's Social Security number for a small fee, which can easily be charged to your credit card. Sites such as InfoUSA.com offer information such as estimated income, marital status, buying habits, and hobbies for more than 120 million U.S. households. And this data could be accessed by jealous coworkers trying to get some dirt on you, stalkers hoping to track you down, and thieves who want to go on a shopping spree in your name.

PROTECTING PRIVACY: BASIC PRINCIPLES

How should governments protect the privacy of their citizens? Privacy advocates agree that the key lies in giving citizens the

right to be informed when data is being collected about them—and what's more, the right to refuse to participate if they so desire. In the European Union, a basic human rights declaration gives all citizens the following privacy rights:

- Consumers must be informed when information is being collected about them. They must be told exactly what information is being collected and how it will be used.

- Consumers must be allowed to choose whether they want to divulge the requested information and to choose the uses that are made of this information.

- Consumers must be allowed to remove information about themselves from marketing and other databases, upon request.

As we've mentioned, in general, U.S. citizens don't enjoy these same rights. Apart from the Fair Credit Reporting Act (FCRA), which provides limited privacy protection for credit information, no comprehensive federal law governs the privacy rights of U.S. citizens. Instead, privacy is protected by a patchwork quilt of limited federal and state laws and regulations. However, most of these laws regulate what government agencies can do. Except in limited areas covered by these laws, little exists to stop people and companies from acquiring information about you and selling this information to someone else. In addition, at your place of work, you have no privacy when you are using your employer's computer system.

ANONYMITY

In Vernor Vinge's classic science fiction novella *True Names*, computers are everywhere—but anonymity is illegal. The term **anonymity** refers to the ability to convey a message without disclosing your name or identity.

A society in which anonymity is illegal would provide the perfect foundation for a totalitarian police state—a proposition that Adolf Hitler personally endorsed. "In the Third Reich," a Nazi apologist conceded, "there is no such thing as a private individual." In a democracy, anonymous speech functions as an important means by which people can make unpopular viewpoints heard without fear of reprisal.

To be sure, anonymity can be abused. Anonymity frees people from accountability, and, as a result, they may abuse the privilege of anonymous speech. In particular, they may engage in **defamation**, the act of injuring someone's reputation by making false and malicious statements. When defamation occurs in writing, the term **libel** is used. Anonymous communications can also be used to threaten and harass, or to spread false and misleading information.

Still, the U.S. Supreme Court recently held that anonymity—despite its unpalatable aspects—must be preserved. In a democracy, what is essential is that citizens have access to the full range of possible ideas, so that they are best equipped to make decisions for themselves. By freeing authors from the need to be accountable for anonymous works, the Court argued, there is a potential that false or misleading ideas will be brought before the public, but the price is worth paying.

How Is Technology Eroding Privacy and Anonymity?

Computers and the Internet enable marketing firms, snoops, and government officials to harness all the power of technology in order to collect information in ways that are hidden from the user's view. The same technology is also making it increasingly difficult for citizens to engage in anonymous speech. In this section, these two points are illustrated by looking at two technologies that are in increasingly common use: cookies and global unique identifiers (GUIDs).

COOKIES

Imagine that you're shopping in your local supermarket. You notice that a clerk is following your every move and making detailed notes about which products you're examining, how long you look at them, and which

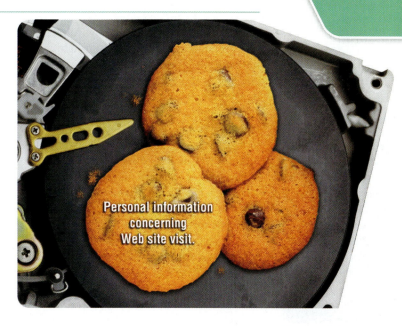

products you buy. Would this constant surveillance make you uncomfortable? If so, you'd better think twice about shopping on the Web. Thanks to cookies, that's exactly what virtually all online retail sites are doing (see Figure 12.3).

Cookies are small files that are written to your computer's hard disk by many of the Web sites you visit. Essentially, cookies provide Web sites with a way of recording information so that it's available for future browsing sessions at the same site.

In many cases, cookies are used for legitimate purposes. For example, Internet retailing sites use cookies to implement "shopping carts," which enable you to make selections and then return to the online store for more browsing and shopping. What troubles privacy advocates is the use of cookies to gather data on Web users' browsing and shopping habits without their consent.

Several Internet **ad networks**, such as DoubleClick, Inc., use cookies to track users' browsing actions across thousands of the most popular Internet sites. When you visit a Web site that has contracted with one of these firms, a cookie containing a unique identification number is deposited on your computer's hard drive. This cookie is used to track your browsing habits and preferences as you move among the hundreds of sites that contract with the ad network. As you visit another site, the cookie is detected, read, and matched with a profile of your previous browsing activity. On this basis, the

Figure 12.3
Cookies are small files, written on your computer's hard disk by Web sites, that provide Web sites with a way of recording information about your browsing habits.

Destinations

To see an online demonstration of how ad banner tracking can be paired with user names through site registrations, visit Privacy.net's demonstration page at **www.privacy.net/track**.

Destinations

For more information on Microsoft .NET Passport, visit **www.passport.net**.

ad network selects and displays a **banner ad**, a rectangular advertisement which is not actually a part of the Web page you are viewing, but is instead separately supplied by the ad network (see Figure 12.4)

In response to concerns that their tracking violates Internet users' privacy, ad network companies claim that they do not attempt to link the collected information with users' names and addresses. However, current technology would enable these firms to do so—and some privacy advocates fear that some of them already have. What kind of information can be transmitted to Internet ad networks such as DoubleClick? You'd be surprised:

- your e-mail address

- your full name

- your mailing address (street, city, state, and ZIP code)

- your phone number

- transactional data (names of products purchased online, details of plane trip reservations, and search phrases used with search engines)

In early 2000, DoubleClick put any doubts about its intentions to rest. The firm shelled out $1 billion to purchase Abacus Direct, a marketing database company that possessed detailed information on 120 million U.S. households. DoubleClick announced that it would begin a new program to combine its Internet and Abacus databases. Consumers who dislike such monitoring could "opt out" of the tracking by visiting the company's Web site, according to the firm.

DoubleClick's announcement made few friends for the firm. What resulted was a massive public outcry, a series of lawsuits, and the threat of an investigation from the U.S. Federal Trade Commission (FTC). After the firm's stock dropped precipitously in a massive bad-news sell-off, the company's CEO, Kevin O'Connor, admitted that he had made a mistake, and vowed to hold off on linking names to Internet browsing habits until a "national consensus" on privacy emerged.

What's wrong with collecting information about a person's browsing habits? Internet marketing firms explain that, if they do collect such information, they could provide a "richer" marketing experience, one that's more closely tailored to an individual's interests. Privacy advocates reply that, once collected, this information could become valuable to others—including future employers. If you visited a number of sites specializing in information concerning worker's compensation, would this browsing behavior mark you as a "high risk" job candidate?

GLOBAL UNIQUE IDENTIFIERS (GUIDS)

A **global unique identifier (GUID)** is a unique identification number that is generated by a computer hardware component or a program. Privacy advocates have discovered several instances in which popular computer components or programs made GUIDs available in such a way that anonymous usage of the Internet would become more difficult, if not impossible:

- To provide a better foundation for e-commerce, Intel Corporation designed a GUID into its Pentium III processors. The GUID could be used, the company said, to positively identify shoppers—an important step in the fight against

Figure 12.4
Banner ads can be tailored to match your customer profile.

online fraud. But analysts discovered that the Pentium III GUID can be accessed by Web servers, which holds out the threat that any site you visit on the Web could learn your identity. In response to a public outcry, Intel redesigned the Pentium III processor so that the GUID is turned off by default.

- A programmer who used a network traffic analysis device discovered that RealNetworks' RealJukeBox player was sending information back to the company when users accessed streaming audio or video content on the Internet, or played an audio CD. The information included the user's name, e-mail address, and a description of the content being viewed.

- Microsoft Word 97 and Excel 97 embedded GUID information in every document users created with these applications. This information could have been used to trace an anonymous document back to a particular computer used on a university or corporate network.

Companies that introduce GUIDs into their products generally conceal this information from the public. When forced to admit to the use of a GUID, the firms typically remove the GUID-implanting code or enable users to opt out of their data collection systems. Advocates of online anonymity insist that these companies are missing the basic point: users, not corporations, should determine when and how they divulge their identities to third parties.

In 2001, Microsoft introduced the **.NET Passport** as part of its new .NET strategy (see Figure 12.5). Using a .NET Passport profile, users can store personal information that, if they choose, will automatically be shared when they sign in to Web sites so that participating sites can provide them with personalized services. One advantage of .NET Passport is that you at least have an opportunity to manage your profile. In addition, Microsoft has a privacy policy agreement with .NET Passport-affiliated vendors that is designed to protect your privacy. Will it? We'll see. It is often very difficult to manage the integrity of a personal identification system that has many partners with many different interests.

Is Self-Regulation Sufficient?

As the previous sections illustrate, technology poses a threat to basic privacy rights precisely because computer systems enable government and corporate snoops to automate the collection of marketing data—and what's more, the same systems also make it increasingly impossible to disguise one's identity so that such collection cannot take place. Still, marketing industry spokespeople and lobbyists argue that the U.S. government should not impose laws or regulations designed to protect consumers' privacy. They argue that the industry should be left free to regulate itself.

Privacy advocates counter that technology has outpaced the industry's capability to regulate itself, as evidenced by the widespread availability of highly personal information on the Internet.

In addition, many of the most aggressive Internet-based marketing firms have no ties to or previous experience with traditional industry associations, such as the Direct Marketing Association (DMA), which claims to enforce a basic code of ethics among the companies that belong to the association. The DMA takes steps to ensure

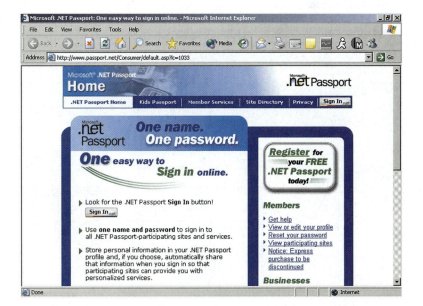

Figure 12.5
.NET Passport allows you to manage a single user profile that identifies you to partner Web sites.

that confidential information doesn't fall into the wrong hands and that consumers can opt out of marketing campaigns if they wish (see Figure 12.6). However, opt-out systems on the Internet are already used for fraudulent purposes. For example, e-mail spammers typically claim that recipients can "opt out" of mass e-mail marketing campaigns. But recipients who respond to such messages succeed only in validating their e-mail addresses—and the result is often a major increase in the volume of unsolicited mail.

Consumer fears regarding the use of information collected by Web sites may even be impeding the growth of e-commerce. According to a recent survey by *Business Week* magazine, consumers not currently using the Internet cite privacy concerns as their primary reason for not going online. But online businesses don't seem to be getting the message. According to a recent study, more than two-thirds of the most popular commercial Web sites displayed "privacy policy" pages that explained how they intended to collect and use personal information about site visitors—but only 10 percent of these sites gave visitors any meaningful control over the use of this information. Given that 82 percent of surveyed Internet users strongly object to the sale of their personal information, it's hardly surprising that the Internet retail sector is growing more slowly than anticipated.

PROTECTING YOUR PRIVACY ONLINE

According to privacy advocates, the reality of Internet marketing shows that self-regulation has failed. Faced with such abuses, Internet users overwhelmingly agree—by a ratio of three to one—that the U.S. government needs to adopt laws that will safeguard basic privacy rights. Until that time, it's up to you to safeguard your privacy on the Internet. To do so, consider the following:

- Browse anonymously by surfing from sites such as "The Anonymizer" (**www.anonymizer.com**) or "The Cloak" (**www.the-cloak.com**) (see Figure 12.7).

- Disable cookies on your Web browser or use cookie management software, such as Junkbuster (**www.junkbusters.com**).

- Use a "throw-away" e-mail address from a free Web-based service such as Hotmail (**www.hotmail.com**) for the e-mail address you place on Web pages, mailing lists, chat rooms, or other public Internet spaces that are scanned by e-mail spammers.

Figure 12.6
The Direct Marketing Association takes steps to ensure that consumers can opt out of marketing campaigns if they wish.

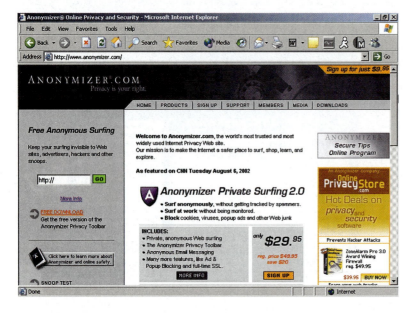

Figure 12.7
The "Anonymizer" enables you to surf the Web anonymously.

- Tell children not to divulge any personal information to strangers online without first asking a parent or a teacher for permission.

- Don't fill out site registration forms unless you see a privacy policy statement indicating that the information you supply won't be sold to third parties.

Privacy at Work

Increasingly, employees are given e-mail accounts and Internet connections at work. They can't do business without them. According to a recent study, 80 percent of 1,000 surveyed employees in Fortune 500 firms say that e-mail has replaced "snail mail" for the majority of their business correspondence. But the Internet can be a time waster, too. Many companies are finding that they lose a great deal of money and time each year due to employees browsing the Web or sending personal e-mails when they should be working.

Employers are naturally concerned about getting their money's worth from employees. For this reason, more than three-quarters of large U.S. employers routinely monitor employees' phone calls, e-mail, Web browsing habits, and computer files—and about one company in four has fired an employee based on what they've found. Other companies are enforcing strict policies prohibiting employees from sending personal e-mail or browsing the Web at all.

But the snooping is done for other reasons, too. Companies are concerned about employees who may offer trade secrets to competitors in the hope of landing an attractive job offer. Another concern is sexual harassment lawsuits. Employees who access pornographic Web sites or circulate offensive jokes via e-mail may be creating a hostile environment for other employees—and that could result in a huge lawsuit against the company.

Yet computer technology enables employers to monitor nearly everything an employee does, and many employees wonder whether the monitoring goes too far. While you're working with your employer's phone and computer systems, virtually everything you do may be monitored—right down to the keystrokes you type at the keyboard. Automated software combs your e-mail for words such as "boss" and "jerk." Software that takes snapshots of your computer screen can defeat privacy measures such as encryption. At what point does employer snooping represent an unjustifiable intrusion into an employee's private affairs?

In the United States, few laws protect employees from intrusive monitoring. In extreme cases, an employer may be reading employee e-mail, listening to phone conversations, and even viewing an exact copy of the computer screen the employee is looking at (see Figure 12.8). These measures are direct and invasive, but they're a sign of the times.

When you're at work, remember the following rules:

- Unless you have specific permission, don't use your employer's telephone system for personal calls. Make all such calls from a pay telephone.

- Never use the e-mail account your employer gives you for personal purposes. Get your own account with an Internet service provider (ISP), and be sure to send and receive all personal mail from your home computer.

Destinations

Take a look at the software your boss may be using. Called Spector (**www.spectorsoft.com**), this program provides employers with a report of everything employees do online by taking hundreds of screen snapshots per hour.

Figure 12.8

Software from companies such as SpectorSoft provides people with a way to monitor your computer activity.

- Assume that everything you do while you're at work—whether it's talking on the phone, using your computer, taking a break, or chatting with coworkers—may be monitored and recorded.

The Encryption Debate

An encrypted (coded) message cannot be read by anyone except the intended recipient. Until recently, encryption was used only by intelligence services, militaries, and banks. But powerful encryption software is now available to the public, and U.S. law enforcement officials aren't happy about it.

ENCRYPTION BASICS

To understand encryption, try this simple exercise: take a short message, such as "I love you." Before it is encrypted, a readable message such as this one is called **plaintext**. For each character, substitute the letter exactly 13 positions to the right in the alphabet of 26 letters. (When you reach the end of the alphabet, start counting from the beginning.) This procedure is an example of an **encryption key**, a formula that is used to make a plaintext message unreadable. After applying the key, you get a coded message, called **ciphertext**, that looks like this:

```
V YBIR LBH
```

It looks like gibberish, doesn't it? That's exactly the idea. Nobody who intercepts this message will be able to tell what it means. Your intended recipient, however, can tell what the message means if you give him or her the decoding key: in this case, counting

13 characters to the left (see Figure 12.9). When your recipient gets the message and decrypts it, your message reappears:

```
I LOVE YOU
```

Congratulations! You just encrypted a message and your recipient decrypted it. You began with a readable message, called plaintext, and then encrypted the message by using the encryption key, a formula that specifies how to scramble the message so that no one can read it but the intended recipient. The recipient decrypts the message by applying the same encoding key, except in reverse. Called **rot-13**, this encryption technique is sometimes used in chat rooms or Usenet discussions to hide adult language from children's eyes. The "rot" in rot-13 is short for *rotation*, the method used to scramble the characters. For encryption, characters are rotated 13 positions right in the alphabet; for decryption, they are rotated 13 positions left. Several other simple encryption methods exist, including transposition (switching the order of characters), substitution (replacing some characters with others), expansion (inserting characters within existing text), and compacting (removing certain characters).

For centuries, machines have been used to reduce or eliminate the need to conduct the encryption and decryption of messages manually. Thomas Jefferson invented a simple encryption device that implemented a variety of rotation-based encryption techniques. In the two world wars of the twentieth century, combatants used sophisticated encryption devices in order to hide their communications from enemy eyes.

Encryption techniques that use the same key for encryption and decryption are called **symmetric key encryption algorithms**. Thousands of symmetric key encryption algorithms are in common use. (An **encryption algorithm** is a step-by-step

Decoding key for "I Love You"																									
A	B	C	D	E	F	G	H	I	J	K	L	M	N	O	P	Q	R	S	T	U	V	W	X	Y	Z
1	2	3	4	5	6	7	8	9	10	11	12	13	14	15	16	17	18	19	20	21	22	23	24	25	26

Figure 12.9

method for encrypting and decrypting a message.) In the United States, a commonly used symmetric key encryption system is the **Data Encryption Standard** (**DES**), which was developed by U.S. security agencies.

THE PROBLEM OF KEY INTERCEPTION

As you may have already concluded, rot-13 isn't a secure encryption method. If you study the ciphertext, you can find the key. Banks and military intelligence agencies use much more complex keys to encrypt their messages. Some of these keys are so complex that the world's most powerful computer would have to analyze the ciphertext for several hundred years to discover the key. The term **strong encryption** refers to encryption methods that are very difficult or impossible to break.

But there is a much easier way to defeat any symmetric key encryption system: steal the key (see Figure 12.10). Symmetric key encryption systems require the key to be transmitted to the recipient before messages can be decrypted. For example, banks deliver decryption keys using trusted courier services, while militaries use trusted personnel or agents. But keys can be stolen. Sometimes, trusted personnel turn out to be criminals—or, in war, double agents, who give the decryption key to one's enemies but deliver it as if nothing had happened.

This major vulnerability of symmetric key encryption, called **key interception**, has played an important role in military history. Some scientists and military historians believe that the outcome of the Second World War might have been much different if the Allies had not been able to intercept or break the encryption systems used by the Axis powers (Germany and Japan).

PUBLIC KEY ENCRYPTION

Now that you understand the problem of key interception, you're prepared to grasp why public key cryptography is considered one of the greatest (and most troubling) scientific achievements of the twentieth century. In brief, **public key encryption** uses two different keys: an encryption key (called the **public key**) and a decryption

key (called the **private key**). People who wish to receive secret messages publish their public key—for example, by placing it on a Web page or including it with a Usenet posting. When the public key is used to encrypt a message, the message becomes unreadable. The message becomes readable only when the recipient applies his or her private key, which nobody else knows.

Do you see why public key encryption is such a major breakthrough? Recall that symmetric key encryption requires the sender to transmit the key through an insecure medium. But public key encryption requires no such transmittal. Users of public key encryption systems never give their private key to anyone. This doesn't mean that public key encryption is invulnerable. For instance, a spy could break into an official's home and obtain the private key from the official's computer. However, the fact that the private key does not need to be transmitted makes key interception much more risky and difficult.

Because it allows two parties who have not previously met to exchange secret messages, public key encryption is an essential foundation of electronic commerce. When you visit a secure site on the Web, for

Figure 12.10

One way to break a code is to steal the key.

Destinations

For more information concerning public key encryption, visit the RSA Laboratories' "Frequently Asked Questions on Cryptography" page at **www.rsasecurity.com/ rsalabs/faq/ references.html**.

example, your Web browser provides your public key to the Web server; in turn, the Web server provides the site's public key to your Web browser. Once a secure communication channel has been created, your browser displays a distinctive icon, such as a lock, on the status bar. You can now supply confidential information, such as your credit card number, with a reasonable degree of confidence that this information will not be intercepted while it is traveling across the Internet.

Compared with symmetric key encryption, public key encryption is **computationally intensive** (it places a heavy burden on a computer's CPU). For this reason, public key encryption is normally used only at the start of a secret communication session. Public key encryption creates a secure channel, through which symmetric encryption keys can be transmitted safely. Once the symmetric encryption keys have been exchanged, the rest of the communication session relies on the symmetric key technique, which is much less demanding on CPUs.

KEY LENGTH

Like symmetric key encryption, public key encryption is vulnerable to **cryptanalysis** (code breaking). One code-breaking technique, called the **brute force method**, tries every conceivable decryption key— millions or billions of them—until the solution is found. One way to defeat brute force attacks involves using a lengthy encryption key. **Key length** is the term used to describe the length (in bits) of an encryption key.

The longer the key, the stronger the encryption. A key length of 40 bits is highly vulnerable to brute force attack; a desktop computer can find the solution within a day or two. A key length of 56 bits was formerly thought to be reasonably safe for Web shopping and other nonmilitary or non-banking exchanges. A desktop computer would need a year or two to break a message encrypted with a key length of 56 bits. However, code breakers can use the Internet to link dozens, hundreds, or even thousands of computers into a massive code-breaking machine. Using such techniques, a message encrypted

with a 56-bit key can be decoded in a matter of hours.

Safe electronic commerce requires a key length of at least 128 bits. However, chances are good that your Web browser is not currently configured to use 128-bit encryption. You may need to visit the browser's home page in order to obtain the 128-bit upgrade.

PUBLIC KEY ENCRYPTION ALGORITHMS

Numerous public key encryption algorithms have been developed. The oldest, called the **Diffie-Hellman algorithm**, is named after the two inventors of public key encryption. In widespread use is the **RSA encryption algorithm**, also named after its inventors (Rivest, Shamir, and Adleman). The U.S. government has developed its own public key encryption algorithm, called **Fortezza**. However, it is not in widespread use because U.S. officials refuse to disclose the underlying algorithm to cryptographers. As a result, cryptographers cannot determine whether Fortezza is safe to use.

DIGITAL SIGNATURES AND CERTIFICATES

Public key encryption enables people who have never met to exchange secret messages, but it can do much more. Because public key encryption creates a secret channel through which information can be sent securely, it can be used to implement **digital signatures** (a technique used to guarantee that a message has not been tampered with) and **digital certificates** (a technique used to validate one's identity, like showing your driver's license when you cash a check).

Digital signatures can be used with non-encrypted and encrypted messages alike. A digital signature uses the recipient's public key to encrypt a mathematical value, called a **hash key**, that uniquely describes the message's content. When the message is received, the recipient's computer generates its own hash key. Then it compares the two. If the message has been altered in any way, the recipient's computer sounds an alarm and warns the recipient that the message may have been tampered with—possibly with malicious or fraudulent intent—since it was sent. Digital signatures are an important foundation of e-commerce because they enable people to determine whether a received message or document is authentic and undisturbed.

Although they are not yet in widespread use, many experts believe that digital certificates are vital to the future of electronic commerce. They enable parties engaged in Internet-mediated transactions to confirm each other's identity. Digital certificates can be obtained from a **certificate authority** (**CA**). For example, an employer may become a CA in that it provides digital certificates to its employees. The employees must, in turn, provide the digital certificate in order to access the company's computer resources. Public certificate authorities, such as Verisign, sell digital certificates to the public. However, few Internet users have obtained digital certificates. To be considered valid, such a certificate should be issued only after the CA has seen positive identification, such as a driver's license or birth certificate. This cannot be done via the Internet; thus, a trip to the CA's office is required. But such offices are few and far between.

A more convenient way to implement digital certificates uses the **web of trust** system. In the web of trust system, you obtain a digital certificate from a trusted friend, who knows you personally. You, in turn, give your friend a certificate. Both of these certificates may be further certified by a friend who knows both of you. Each certificate says, in effect, "I know these people, and they really are who they say they are." Because a group of people could easily conspire to forge new identities for themselves, the web of trust model isn't suitable for electronic commerce. But it works well in small, tightly knit communities, such as one of programmers who collaborate on the Internet, in which some of the participants know each other personally.

Clearly, CA-issued digital certificates should be more widely used. Currently, credit card fraud—the use of stolen credit card numbers—is a major problem for Web vendors and credit card companies alike. Like gas station clerks, Web shopping sites check with your credit card

supplier to make sure that your account is valid and that your card hasn't been reported as stolen. Even so, the vendor can't be certain that your Web shopping order is really coming from you rather than from a criminal who obtained your name, credit card number, address, and expiration date after rummaging through your trash can.

TOWARD A PUBLIC KEY INFRASTRUCTURE (PKI)

As you've learned in this chapter, public key encryption is already in widespread use. If you've ever visited a secure Web site, you've used it yourself. But safe electronic commerce requires digital signatures and digital certificates, too. They're not widely used. One reason, mentioned earlier, is the inconvenience of having to visit the certificate authority's office in order to prove your identity.

To facilitate electronic commerce, experts believe a public key infrastructure based on trusted certificate authorities is needed. A **public key infrastructure** (**PKI**) is a uniform set of encryption standards that specify how public key encryption, digital signatures, and CA-granted digital certificates should be implemented in computer systems and on the Internet. Although there are numerous contenders, no dominant PKI has emerged.

What explains the slow development of a public key infrastructure? One reason involves the fear, shared by many private citizens and businesses alike, that a single, dominant firm will monopolize the PKI and impose unreasonable fees on the public. Recently, Microsoft announced its .NET initiative, a wide-ranging plan to move many computing resources, including file storage and software distribution, to the Internet. A key component of this initiative is Microsoft's Passport system, which we discussed earlier. The Passport system implements a Microsoft-developed PKI. Because so many people use Microsoft operating systems, Microsoft is in perhaps the best position to implement a PKI. But consumers and businesses fear that Microsoft will use its operating system monopoly and Passport for unfair purposes, such as driving Microsoft's competitors out of business and imposing artificially high costs on the emerging electronic economy.

PUBLIC SECURITY ISSUES OF STRONG ENCRYPTION

Another reason for the slow development of a public key infrastructure is that governments may step in to regulate public key encryption—or at the extreme, outlaw its use entirely. As you've already learned, public key encryption enables two people who have never physically met to exchange unbreakably secure messages. This capability is as beneficial to drug dealers and terrorists as it is to legitimate, law-abiding citizens and businesses.

The danger is real. Just one year before the terrorist attack on the World Trade Center, U.S. Federal Bureau of Investigation Director Louis Freeh told the U.S. Congress that "the widespread use of robust unbreakable encryption ultimately will devastate our ability to fight crime and prevent terrorism. Unbreakable encryption will allow drug lords, spies, terrorists, and even violent gangs to communicate about their crimes and their conspiracies with impunity." In light of the terrorists' use of public key encryption—

specifically, Pretty Good Privacy (PGP) (see Figure 12.11)—Freeh's warning now seems prophetic. Soon after the bombing, there were calls in the U.S. Congress to outlaw public key encryption.

Why is public key encryption so dangerous? In brief, public key cryptography can be used not only for e-mail messages but also for telephone conversations. It promises to put the FBI out of the wire-tapping business. That's good news for terrorists, drug dealers, and organized crime. According to Freeh, court-ordered wiretapping is the most effective way to detect terrorist plots and wide-ranging criminal conspiracies, both of which pose real and growing danger to public safety and welfare.

Recognizing that public key encryption is vital to the emerging electronic economy, U.S. law enforcement and security agencies don't recommend that public key encryption be outlawed. Instead, they recommend that the U.S. Congress pass laws requiring the use of a public key algorithm or a public key infrastructure that would enable investigators to eavesdrop on encrypted communications.

If public key encryption is virtually unbreakable, how would such a scheme work? U.S. government agencies have proposed three alternatives.

The first, the **Clipper Chip**, is a microprocessor that could be used to encrypt voice or data communications, but in such a way that investigators could intercept and decode the messages (see Figure 12.12). The chip would have encrypted messages with a **back door**, a secret decoding mechanism, which would have enabled investigators to decrypt messages without having first obtained the private key. Cryptography experts warned that this approach would endanger electronic commerce; attackers might figure out how to open the back door, which would make encrypted messages just as visible to them as they would be to investigators. The Clipper Chip proposal collapsed after an expert cryptographer discovered, relatively easily, how to open the back door.

The former Clinton administration proposed a **key escrow plan**, in which a user's private key would be held by an independent key escrow agency and divulged

Figure 12.11

MIT manages a Web site for the distribution of Pretty Good Privacy software. This free encryption program is widely recognized as a viable alternative to commercial products.

Figure 12.12
The Center for Democracy and Technology maintains information on Clipper Chip–type technology.

to investigators only when a valid court order was produced. However, this plan has met with criticism as well. The key escrow agency would have to store the keys on its computer systems, which might not be adequately secured. The agency's employees would be vulnerable to bribes from criminals, as well as pressure from government investigators, who might try to obtain private keys without going through the lengthy court order process. Even if the key escrow system worked perfectly, it would still function too slowly to aid investigators dealing with fast-breaking situations, such as a terrorist attack.

In 1998, FBI director Freeh called for a new back door–based encryption system. Called **key recovery**, this back door would be built into encryption software, rather than implemented by means of a microprocessor chip. This would enable encryption product vendors to fix vulnerabilities such as the one discovered in the Clipper Chip. By eliminating the cumbersome key escrow bureaucracy, the key recovery system would function much faster and, for this reason, is more attractive to investigators. According to law enforcement officials, some type of key escrow system is needed to fight illegal drugs and terrorism. After the World Trade Center bombing, bills were introduced in the U.S. Congress that mandated stiff penalties for the use of encryption lacking key recovery features.

But the social and economic costs of a key escrow system would be very high, according to the system's critics. Criminals and terrorists already have strong, unbreakable encryption technology, and it would be virtually impossible to detect or eliminate its use. Law-abiding citizens would be most likely to suffer if the use of key recovery software were mandated by law, critics say. Such a system would leave citizens open to illegal monitoring for political reasons. Civil liberties advocates point out that, in the past, the U.S. government has too frequently used wiretapping for political purposes. During the 1960s, Dr. Martin Luther King, Jr., was routinely wiretapped on the pretext that he posed a risk to national security. Former President Richard M. Nixon used illegal wiretaps to track the activities of his political opponents and the reporters and other individuals on his "Enemies List." Would a future Nixon monitor e-mail, looking for evidence of political dissent? According to critics of key recovery, the government's proposals are similar to asking U.S. citizens to install a live video camera in their homes, which could be activated if investigators suspected criminal activity.

A key recovery system could be very costly in another way, too. It may impede the development of e-commerce, which some see as the key to continued U.S. economic growth. Corporations and banks will not wholeheartedly embrace electronic commerce without strong, secure encryption, but cryptography experts are wary of key recovery systems. As mentioned earlier, the U.S. government's public key

NATIONAL SECURITY

Navajo Code Talkers

Suppose you're a Japanese intelligence officer in World War II, and you're trying to intercept U.S. Marine communications in the Pacific. If you succeed, you'll know where the Americans are planning their next amphibious attack, and you'll give your country a tremendous advantage. However, the messages you're hearing are in some kind of code that you can't figure out.

What was the secret of U.S. Marine communications in the Pacific? A formidable secret weapon: the Navajo language and several hundred Navajo code talkers, who served with great distinction in the Pacific from 1942 to 1945. Transmitting coded messages in their native language, they served in all six Marine divisions, including Marine Raider battalions and Marine parachute units (see Figure 12.13).

Navajo code talkers played a decisive role in the United States' Pacific victory. Major Howard Connor, 5th Marine Division signal officer, worked with six Navajo code talkers during the invasion of Iwo Jima, which historians regard as the Pacific war's turning point. Working around the clock, the code talkers sent and received hundreds of messages, all without error. In fact, Connor declared that were it not for the Navajos, the Marines would never have taken Iwo Jima.

Who came up with the idea of using the Navajo language for secret communications? It was Philip Johnston, the son of a missionary and a fluent Navajo speaker who was raised on a Navajo reservation. Johnston knew that no dictionary of the Navajo language existed at that time and that the language was exceptionally difficult to learn. To express meanings in Navajo, you must learn a complicated syntax, including subtle tone generations that can alter a word's meaning. Knowledge of Navajo requires many years of training and direct exposure. Compounding the difficulty was the fact that code talkers used a special, memorized vocabulary consisting of Navajo translations of military and naval terms. These code words wouldn't make any sense even to a native Navajo speaker (for example, a submarine was an iron fish, while a fighter plane was a hummingbird).

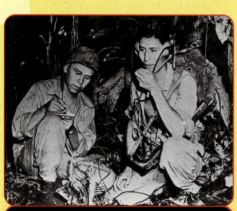

Figure 12.13
Several hundred Navajo code talkers served with great distinction in the Pacific from 1942 to 1945.

After the war ended, the chief of Japanese Intelligence, Seizue Arisue, confirmed that the Japanese were never able to break the code, even after they captured a Navajo soldier and made him listen to the transmissions. Through the use of an ancient language and its application to modern needs, code talkers helped ensure the security of American forces at the height of the Pacific war.

In July 2001, President George W. Bush presented the four surviving members of the original 29 Navajo code talkers (and relatives of the other 25) with the Congressional Gold Medal. Commenting on the long delay in recognizing the code talkers' achievements, President Bush affirmed the nation's gratitude "for all time" as symbolized by the medals, which represent the highest honor the United States can bestow. One motivation for Congress's timing may have been the 2001 release of *Windtalkers*, a film directed by John Woo and starring Nicholas Cage. In the film, a war-battered soldier is asked to guard Navajo code talkers, with whom the soldier develops a warm relationship.

CURRENTS

encryption algorithm Fortezza includes key recovery capabilities, but the government won't disclose the algorithm to cryptographic researchers, who are therefore unable to say whether the algorithm is secure. Until cryptographers are reasonably certain that an encryption algorithm is safe to use, businesses will not use it to transfer anything other than trivial amounts of money.

EXPORT RESTRICTIONS

Since the outcomes of most of the twentieth and twenty-first century's military conflicts have been influenced or even decided by the contestants' ability to transmit secret messages, U.S. security agencies have every reason to fear the proliferation of strong encryption algorithms. Currently, the U.S. government encryption technologies are considered munitions (arms), which means that strong encryption tools cannot be exported without a license under the U.S. Department of Commerce's International Traffic in Arms Regulations (ITAR). Each application for an export license is required to go through a lengthy and expensive process that can take months or even years to complete.

What is a strong encryption tool? As you've already learned, it all boils down to bit length. Banks require 128-bit encryption for online banking. The ITAR restrictions, however, define 56-bit encryption tools as munitions, even though such tools are vulnerable to brute force attacks. Currently, the U.S. Department of Commerce will grant permits for exporting programs containing 56-bit encryption tools, but only if the company promises to develop key recovery tools for domestic surveillance.

Even U.S. government officials admit that ITAR will not stop the spread of encryption technologies to other countries. The other countries already have them. The regulations serve only to keep U.S. firms from competing in what could be a lucrative international marketplace for software products containing strong encryption. According to the U.S. Economic Strategy Institute, the total cost to the U.S. economy of continuing export controls on strong encryption products could hit $35 billion.

THE ACADEMIC ANGLE

U.S. researchers have long held the world lead in cryptography, but many of these researchers warn that the United States may soon lose its advantage in this area. U.S. security officials have tried to stop cryptographic researchers from publishing their research or presenting papers at conferences where foreigners were in attendance.

Recently, corporations have exerted pressure on university researchers in an attempt to stop them from disclosing the results of their research. These companies are implementing encryption-based **copyright management infrastructures** (**CMIs**), which enable vendors of copyrighted digital media, such as e-books, digital music recordings, and digital videos, to track and control the use and copying of their products after consumers purchase them. A 1998 law called the **Digital Millennium Copyright Act** (**DMCA**) imposes stiff penalties, including fines of up to $500,000 and 10 years in a federal penitentiary, for anyone convicted of disclosing information about how a CMI works.

Fearing that they will continue to be hounded by government security personnel and threatened with lawsuits, more than a few leading cryptographic researchers have decided that cryptographic research is too dangerous to pursue and have turned to other areas of interest.

THE GLOBAL DIMENSION

Outside the United States, few countries place restrictions on the use of encryption technologies. It is interesting to note that the few that do—including China and Singapore—are among the world's most authoritarian or totalitarian regimes. Until recently, an exception was France, which formerly had the world's most stringent controls on encryption technologies. However, France has recently relaxed its restrictions to enable French software companies to take advantage of the growing encryption marketplace.

Destinations

To read the latest news and perspectives about cryptography issues, visit the Center for Democracy and Technology's "Crypto Debate" page at **www.cdt.org/crypto**.

IMPACTS

ETHICAL DEBATE

Is the Government Watching You?

Are U.S. national security agencies running an automated privacy-invasion system that spans the entire globe, one that's capable of eavesdropping on phone calls, faxes, or e-mails anywhere on the planet? No, this isn't an *X-Files* rerun. Rumors about the existence of such a system have been floating around since 1988. U.S. security agencies strongly deny the existence of such a system, but there's increasing evidence that something like Echelon actually exists—not the least of which is the fact that several participating governments, including Australia and New Zealand, have confirmed the existence of at least some type of globe-spanning system for monitoring data transmissions.

What is Echelon? According to journalists and researchers who are trying to uncover the truth about the alleged global spying system, Echelon is a Cold War–era system that is designed to intercept and search phone calls, fax and Telex transmissions, e-mail messages, Internet downloads, and satellite data transfers worldwide—some three billion messages per day, according to one estimate. Operated jointly by the United States, the United Kingdom, Canada, Australia, and New Zealand, the system uses ground-based listening devices and up to 120 satellites to intercept messages. It also uses sophisticated, artificial intelligence–based software to comb through the huge volume of intercepted messages, looking for words and phrases such as "bomb," "terrorist," "Saddam Hussein," and other information of interest to intelligence agencies. Using these data-screening technologies, Echelon operators can allegedly home in on specific organizations, individuals, and places at will.

If Echelon actually exists, is it such a bad thing? Most people would readily agree that the world isn't a particularly peaceful place, and countries need effective intelligence to protect their interests. Still, almost anyone familiar with the emerging facts about Echelon will find grounds for concern. In the United States, the agency most deeply involved in Echelon, the National Security Agency (NSA), is prohibited from spying on U.S. citizens. However, Echelon critics believe that the NSA intercepts and scans up to 90 percent of the data transmitted on the domestic Internet, in direct violation of the agency's charter.

Europeans are alarmed by the prospect that Echelon has been used for industrial espionage. According to an accusation made by French government officials, Echelon was used to eavesdrop on a 1995 contract offer made by the European Airbus consortium to a prospective customer, and the information was passed on to U.S. aerospace giant Boeing—which subsequently used the information to win the contract.

The NSA denies these and other allegations concerning Echelon. It insists that the concept of a globe-spanning system capable of reading billions of messages per day is "sheer fantasy." Scholars who study the intelligence community tend to agree with the NSA. The technology probably doesn't exist to reliably transcribe millions of intercepted telephone calls into text. In fact, a former NSA director confessed that he had "wasted" millions of dollars of taxpayers' money trying to develop such a technology, only to meet with failure. Critics of the NSA portray it as a dysfunctional, overly bureaucratic agency that is, if anything, woefully out of touch with the latest technology.

But Echelon's critics aren't convinced. In one of the most damaging revelations to date, the NSA conceded that the agency had obtained and compiled more than 1,000 pages of information on Diana, Princess of Wales, prior to her death in an automobile accident. Just how the NSA obtained this information, and what it contains, is unknown—but some of the information was indeed obtained from "intercepted messages," according to an NSA spokesperson.

Does Echelon really exist? According to an investigative committee of the European Parliament, the existence of the system is "no longer in doubt." However, the committee believes that Echelon isn't as powerful or pervasive as Echelon's critics fear. Still, the committee had a word of advice for European computer users: encrypt your e-mail.

HOME | Takeaway Points | Key Terms and Concepts | Matching | Multiple Choice | Fill-In | Short Answer | Exercises/ Projects | Web Research | CHAPTER REVIEW

1 2 3 4 5 6 7 8 9 10 11 12 13 14 15 16

TAKEAWAY POINTS

- Because the United States has no comprehensive federal regulations protecting an individual's privacy, highly sensitive personal information, such as Social Security numbers, is now for sale on the Internet. Many Web sites collect personal information without informing their visitors.

- Anonymity refers to the ability to convey a message without disclosing one's name or identity. We hold anonymity as a personal freedom in the United States, but anonymity may free people from accountability, and they may abuse the privilege of anonymous speech. Using the cloak of anonymity, someone may injure another's reputation by making false and malicious statements. Anonymous communications can also be used to threaten and harass, or to spread false and misleading information.

- Computers and the Internet enable marketing firms, snoops, and government officials to harness all the power of technology in order to collect information in ways that are hidden from the user's view. For example, cookies are small files that are written to your computer's hard disk by many of the Web sites you visit. Cookies provide Web sites with a way of recording information so that it is available for future browsing sessions at the same site.

- A global unique identifier (GUID) is a unique identification number that is generated by a computer hardware component or a program. Privacy advocates say that GUIDs make anonymous usage of the Internet difficult, if not impossible.

- Because large U.S. employers want to make sure that they're getting their money's worth from employees, many of them routinely monitor employees' phone calls, e-mail, Web browsing habits, and computer files. Companies are concerned about potential sexual harassment lawsuits and employees who offer trade secrets to competitors.

- Public key encryption uses two different keys: an encryption key (called the public key) and a decryption key (called the private key). People who wish to receive secret messages publish their public key. When the public key is used to encrypt a message, the message becomes unreadable. The message becomes readable only when the recipient applies his or her private key, which nobody else knows.

- U.S. security agencies fear that public key encryption will prevent them from detecting the activities of terrorists, drug dealers, and organized crime syndicates.

- Key length is the term used to describe the length (in bits) of an encryption key. The longer the key, the stronger the encryption. A key length of 40 bits is highly vulnerable to brute force attack; a key length of 56 bits was formerly thought to be reasonably safe for Web shopping and other non-military or non-banking exchanges. However, safe electronic commerce requires a key length of at least 128 bits.

- A public key infrastructure (PKI) is a uniform set of encryption standards that specify how public key encryption, digital signatures, and CA-granted digital certificates should be implemented in computer systems and on the Internet. Although there are numerous contenders, no dominant PKI has emerged.

- Encryption software containing key recovery features would enable investigators to read secret messages, but financial institutions fear that these features would open security holes.

CHAPTER REVIEW

| Takeaway Points | Key Terms and Concepts | Matching | Multiple Choice | Fill-In | Short Answer | Exercises/ Projects | Web Research | HOME |

1 2 3 4 5 6 7 8 9 10 11 12 13 14 15 16

KEY TERMS AND CONCEPTS

ad network
anonymity
back door
banner ad
brute force method
certificate authority (CA)
ciphertext
Clipper Chip
cookie
computationally
    intensive
copyright management
    infrastructure (CMI)
cryptanalysis
Data Encryption Standard
    (DES)
database vendor

defamation
Diffie-Hellman algorithm
digital certificate
Digital Millennium Copyright
    Act (DMCA)
digital signature
encryption
encryption algorithm
encryption key
Fortezza
global unique identifier
    (GUID)
hash key
identity theft
key escrow plan
key interception
key length

key recovery
libel
.NET Passport
plaintext
privacy
private key
public key
public key encryption
public key infrastructure
    (PKI)
rot-13
RSA encryption
    algorithm
strong encryption
symmetric key
    encryption algorithm
web of trust

COMPUTERS IN YOUR FUTURE 2004

12.21

HOME | Takeaway Points | Key Terms and Concepts | **Matching** | Multiple Choice | Fill-In | Short Answer | Exercises/Projects | Web Research | CHAPTER REVIEW

MATCHING

Match each key term in the left column with the most accurate definition in the right column.

_____ 1. privacy
_____ 2. anonymity
_____ 3. libel
_____ 4. cookies
_____ 5. banner ad
_____ 6. global unique identifier (GUID)
_____ 7. encryption algorithm
_____ 8. public key encryption
_____ 9. cryptanalysis
_____ 10. Clipper Chip
_____ 11. key length
_____ 12. digital signature
_____ 13. defamation
_____ 14. hash key
_____ 15. encryption

a. a step-by-step method for encrypting and decrypting a message
b. the encoding of messages
c. code breaking
d. the ability to convey a message without disclosing one's name or identity
e. a mathematical value that uniquely describes a message's content
f. a new encryption method that doesn't require the message's receiver to have received the decoding key in a separate transmission
g. a microprocessor that could be used to encrypt voice or data communications
h. small files written to your computer's hard disk by many of the Web sites you visit
i. a rectangular advertisement that appears on a Web site
j. an identification number that is generated by a computer hardware component or a program
k. an individual's ability to keep personal and family business away from prying eyes
l. a technique used to guarantee that a message has not been tampered with
m. injuring someone's reputation by making false and malicious statements
n. the number of bits in an encryption key
o. written defamation

CHAPTER REVIEW: 1 2 3 4 5 6 7 8 9 10 11 12 13 14 15 16

MULTIPLE CHOICE

Circle the correct choice for each of the following.

1. A recipient uses which of the following to read an encrypted message?
   a. Private key
   b. Public key
   c. Digital certificate
   d. Certificate authority

2. Database information is commonly collected through which of the following sources?
   a. Loan applications
   b. Product registration cards
   c. Web sites
   d. All of the above

3. The Fair Credit Reporting Act provides which of the following?
   a. Federal laws governing the privacy rights of U.S. citizens
   b. Limited privacy protection for credit information
   c. Extensive privacy protection for credit information
   d. None of the above

4. This is the act of injuring someone's reputation by making false and malicious statements.
   a. Defamation
   b. Anonymity
   c. Perjury
   d. Libel

5. Which of the following uses cookies to track a user's browsing actions across thousands of popular Internet sites?
   a. Banner ads
   b. GUIDs
   c. Ad networks
   d. E-mail messages

6. What is rot-13?
   a. An acronym for rapid online translation
   b. A federal statute that protects user anonymity
   c. An encryption technique
   d. A database vendor

7. What is a coded message called?
   a. RTF text
   b. Cybertext
   c. Plaintext
   d. Ciphertext

8. This is one of the fastest-growing crimes in the United States and Canada.
   a. White collar crime
   b. Laptop theft
   c. Identity theft
   d. Software duplication

9. What encryption key length is currently required for electronic commerce?
   a. 40
   b. 128
   c. 64
   d. 56

10. What maximum encryption key length is currently approved for export under U.S. regulations?
    a. 40
    b. 128
    c. 64
    d. 56

HOME	Takeaway Points	Key Terms and Concepts	Matching	Multiple Choice	Fill-In	Short Answer	Exercises/Projects	Web Research	CHAPTER REVIEW

FILL-IN

In the blanks provided, write the correct answer for each of the following.

1. The major vulnerability of symmetric key encryption is _____.

2. The term _____ refers to one's ability to convey a message without disclosing a name or identity.

3. Several Internet ad networks use _____ to track a user's browsing actions across thousands of popular Internet sites.

4. Defamation in written form is called _____.

5. A(n) _____ is not actually a part of the Web page you're viewing, but is separately supplied by the ad network.

6. _____ is the most widely used digital signature and certificate system.

7. _____ is an encryption technique that's sometimes used in Usenet discussions.

8. The Clinton administration proposed a _____, in which a user's private key would be held by an independent agency and divulged to investigators only when a valid court order was produced.

9. The U.S. government has developed its own public key encryption algorithm called _____.

10. A(n) _____ is someone who is authorized to issue a digital certificate.

11. A(n) _____ is a commonly used symmetric key encryption system developed by United States security agencies.

12. A(n) _____ is a technique used to validate one's identity, like showing your driver's license when you cash a check.

13. A(n) _____ is a microprocessor that could be used to encrypt voice or data communications, but in such a way that investigators could intercept and decode the messages.

14. A(n) _____ enables vendors of copyrighted digital media, such as e-books, digital music recordings, and digital videos, to track and control the use and copying of their products after consumers purchase them.

15. A(n) _____ is a uniform set of encryption standards that specify how public key encryption, digital signatures, and CA-granted digital certificates should be implemented in computer systems and on the Internet.

SHORT ANSWER

1. What privacy rights do citizens have in the European Union? Do you think U.S. citizens should enjoy the same rights? Why or why not?

2. Do you believe that the database vendor industry can adequately and effectively regulate itself? If not, who should regulate it?

3. What steps can you take to ensure your privacy online?

4. Explain how public key encryption methods work.

5. Explain how the brute force code breaking method works.

CHAPTER REVIEW | Takeaway Points | Key Terms and Concepts | Matching | Multiple Choice | Fill-In | Short Answer | Exercises/ Projects | Web Research | HOME

1 2 3 4 5 6 7 8 9 10 11 12 13 14 15 16

EXERCISES/PROJECTS

1. Identify which browser you use most often. What are the different cookie settings? What is the current cookies status on your computer? (Hint: if you are not sure, click the browser's Help button and enter "cookies.") Describe how to switch the cookie settings. What cookie setting do you prefer? Explain why.

2. To counteract brute force code attacks, strong encryption is used, and so both Internet Explorer and Netscape Navigator provide 128-bit encryption versions for domestic use. However, due to the International Traffic in Arms Regulations (ITAR), United States government encryption technologies are considered munitions. Consequently, only 56-bit versions are generally available for international users. Currently, the United States Department of Commerce grants permits for exporting programs containing 56-bit encryption tools, but only if the company promises to develop key recovery tools for domestic surveillance. Identify which browser and version you use most often, and how many bits are used for encryption. (Hint: if you are not sure, you may have to visit the browser's home page.) Explain how your browser indicates that you have connected to a secure site. This is especially important when making an online purchase and paying by a credit card. Have you ever made purchases online? Were they always at secure sites? If not, let's hope any future purchases will be!

3. You have undoubtedly received unsolicited e-mail messages. Who or what companies sent these? Sometimes, these messages give recipients the option to cancel all further mailings. Have you received any messages with this option? Did you reply that you wished to be removed from future mailings? As we mentioned in the chapter, recipients who respond to such messages succeed only in validating their e-mail address—and the result will be a major increase in the volume of unsolicited mail. If you did reply, did you notice any increase in unsolicited mail?

4. A few years ago, New York State began to use its E-ZPass system to collect tolls at selected bridges and tunnels in the New York City area. Instead of stopping at a toll booth to pay, users could drive through special toll lanes and have their toll fees deducted from their E-ZPass accounts. A small transmitting device placed on the inside of the windshield registers the vehicle's presence at the toll lane. A monthly statement shows the exact time, location, and lane when the vehicle was charged a toll. Presently, this system has been expanded to include the entire New York State Thruway system, as well as selected toll roads in neighboring states. E-ZPass authorities and others can now monitor a vehicle's movements by knowing when and where it enters and leaves the system. On an episode of the television show *Law and Order*, the detectives were able to trace the whereabouts of a suspect's car by using this information. By monitoring the time and location when a vehicle enters and leaves the thruway, authorities can determine the driver's average speed. From a privacy standpoint, what are your feelings about the E-ZPass system? Explain why you would or would not use this service.

5. A recent newspaper article reported that a customer was fined by a car rental company for speeding. Although he was not cited for a speeding violation by any police agencies, his credit card was charged a penalty. His rental car was equipped with a vehicle positioning system that reports the location of the vehicle. This feature allowed the company to determine the speed at which the driver was traveling. These types of systems are also used by some long-distance trucking companies to monitor the movements of their trucks. From a privacy standpoint, what are your feelings about these systems? What are the advantages of using these systems?

HOME | Takeaway Points | Key Terms and Concepts | Matching | Multiple Choice | Fill-In | Short Answer | Exercises/ Projects | **Web Research** | **CHAPTER REVIEW**

WEB RESEARCH

1. Use the Federal Trade Commission's Web site located at **www.ftc.gov** to see what information you can learn from the Internet about the Fair Credit Reporting Act. When was the FCRA first enacted, and when was it last amended? What are your rights under this act? There are numerous references to "CRA." What do these letters represent, and what is their purpose? What is the usual time period for removal or correction of inaccurate or unverified information? What are the time limitations on outdated information? What is the maximum fee that can be charged for a credit report? Have you ever requested a copy of your credit report? If you have, what was the name of the company that provided it, and what was their fee for this service? Explain why you feel that this act does or does not provide adequate protection of consumers' rights.

2. Military organizations have used encryption methods for many years. During World War II, the German military forces used Enigma encoding machines, which where sophisticated devices that roughly resembled typewriters. It appeared that the allies were unable to break the code used by these machines. The theme of the fictional movie *U-571* was the capture of the submarine U-571 and the recovery of an Enigma machine. The greatest secret of World War II was the breaking of the Enigma code by Allied forces. Visit PBS's *NOVA* Web site at **www.pbs.org/wgbh/nova** to learn the truth about these cipher machines. How many years did the breaking of the Enigma machine code remain a classified secret? What was the name of the person who led the Station X team that broke the Enigma code? What was the real location of Station X? What were the backgrounds of these code breakers? Enigma machines were mechanical devices that used wheels and rings that could easily be changed. What made code breaking so difficult was the sheer number of combinations of wheel orders and ring settings. What were the number of wheel orders and ring settings, and how many pairings did these produce? Why didn't the code breakers use the brute force method described in the text?

3. What is a Web bug? Help stamp out bugs by visiting the Bugnosis Web site at **www.bugnosis.org**. What foundation supports Bugnosis? Their anti–Web bug software is limited to what browser and which versions? What is the cost of this software? After downloading and installing Bugnosis, visit the sites that are reported to have Web bugs. Which, if any, of these sites no longer have Web bugs? Why would a site no longer use a Web bug?

4. SpectorSoft Corporation is identified in this chapter as a company that produces software that monitors and records all activities on a personal computer. Visit the company's Web site at **http://spectorsoft.com**. In addition to employees, this software is designed to monitor the activities of what two other groups? Identify the three products that SpectorSoft distributes, and explain their differences and identify their prices. List the contents of two of the "Did you know" banners that appear on the Web site. It may be easy to be offended by the use of this software, so explain why someone would purchase and use it.

5. Visit the Web site **http://serendipity.magnet.ch/hermetic/crypto/echelon/echelon.htm** to find information about the Echelon surveillance system. Identify at least three sources of information about this system. Since anyone or any organization can publish Web pages, in addition to reading the material that is presented, see what you can find about the person or organization that published it. Based on the material presented in the text and your exploration of the Internet, write a brief paper that includes the following:

- The URLs and a description of the publishers of the material

- A discussion of the existence or nonexistence of Echelon

- A reason to oppose Echelon

- A reason to support Echelon

- Your thoughts about Echelon

1 2 3 4 5 6 7 8 9 10 11 **12** 13 14 15 16

STANDARDS
OF
INFORMATION AGE
CONDUCT

Computers raise new issues in which right and wrong aren't always easy to discern. For example, computer use can cause **moral dilemmas**, in which people run into difficulty when they try to figure out how the existing rules apply to a new situation. Morals are important because they serve as the principles by which we live.

A new branch of philosophy called **computer ethics** deals with computing-related moral dilemmas and also defines ethical principles for computer professionals. **Ethics** is the branch of philosophy concerned with determining what's right and wrong. With ethics, we have a framework into which we can place dilemmas so that we can make decisions.

This spotlight examines computer ethics, starting with issues in which right and wrong are easy to discern.

Spotlight Ethics

Avoiding Computer-Related Legal Problems

Every day, newspapers carry stories about people losing their jobs (and even going to jail) due to acts committed on computers while they're at work. In many cases, the offenders used company computers to browse the Web and send personal e-mail on company time, or to commit crimes such as cyberstalking or distributing pornography. Most organizations have an acceptable use policy for computer use within the company. Be aware that the use of the a computer for non-business-related tasks is generally outlawed within an organization.

What other kinds of things can cause computer users problems? Let's start with a problem that gets many college students into serious trouble: plagiarism.

PLAGIARISM

The term we often use in discussing rights of writers is **intellectual property**. The use of someone else's intellectual property is called **plagiarism.** Plagiarism predates computers; in fact, it has been around for thousands of years. But computers—and especially the Internet—make the temptation and ease of plagiarism even greater. It's not only very easy to copy and paste from the Internet, many sites are set up specifically to sell college-level papers to the lazy or desperate.

Imagine this scenario. It's four in the morning, and you have a paper due for your nine o'clock class. While searching for sources on the Internet, you find a Web site with a

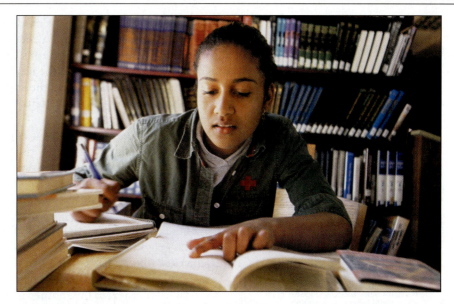

FIGURE 12A: At some colleges, plagiarism can get you thrown out of school on the first offense.

nice little essay on your topic. There's no copyright notice. In fact, it seems as though the author *wants* people to copy it (although maybe for a small price).

What's wrong with downloading the text, reworking it a bit, and handing it in? Plenty.

Plagiarism is a serious offense. How serious? At some colleges, the first offense can get you thrown out of school (see Figure 12A). Furthermore, even if your actions are not discovered now, someone could find out later, and the evidence could destroy your career.

The more well known you are, the more you're at risk of your plagiarism being detected. Take noted historian and Pulitzer Prize–winning author Doris Kearns Goodwin, for example. In 2002, she was accused of plagiarizing part of her best-selling 1987 book *The Fitzgeralds and the Kennedys*. Although she claimed her plagiarizing was inadvertent and due to inadequate research methods, she suffered a large decline in credibility and even felt obligated to leave her position at the PBS news program *NewsHour with Jim Lehrer*. It took 15 years for Goodwin's plagiarism to come to light. Keep in mind that college instructors often are able to detect plagiarism in college papers in about 15 seconds.

Does this mean you can't use the Internet source you found? Of course not. But to do so you must follow certain citation guidelines. In college writing, it's fine to make use of someone else's effort as long as you use your own words and give credit where credit is due. If you use a phrase or a few sentences from the source, use quotation marks. Attach a bibliography, and list your sources. For Internet sources you should list the Web site's URL, the date the article was published (if available), the date and time you accessed the site, the name of the article, and the author's name.

Plagiarism may cause legal problems, too. Plagiarizing copyrighted material is called **copyright infringement**, and if you're caught red-handed, you can be sued and may have to pay damages in addition to compensating your victim for any proven financial losses due to your theft of the material. If you're tempted to copy anything from the Web, bear in mind that the United States is a signatory to international copyright regulations, which specify that an author does *not* need to include an explicit copyright notice to be protected under the law.

FIGURE 12B: The Software Publisher's Association (SPA) is trying to raise consciousness about software piracy.

SOFTWARE PIRACY

You've just copied a computer program. It seems that everyone's doing it. Did you do something wrong?

Not necessarily. Some programmers place their products in the **public domain**, which means anyone is free to copy the program, or even modify it, if they want. However, don't assume that a program is in the public domain unless you see a note (often in the form of a "read me" text file) that explicitly identifies the file as copyright free.

Some software is made available under the provisions of the Free Software Foundation's **General Public License** (GPL). This license specifies that anyone may freely copy, use, and modify the software, but no one can sell it for profit. Much Linux software, for example, is available under the provisions of GPL.

Unlike public domain software, **shareware** programs are copyrighted. (When a work is copyrighted, you can't copy or modify it without asking permission.) You can, however, freely copy trial versions of shareware programs. Shareware authors make evaluation versions of their programs available on a try-before-you-buy basis. When the evaluation period expires, you must pay the **registration fee** or delete the software from your disk. If you continue using the software past this date without paying the fee, you're violating the author's copyright.

Most commercial software is copyrighted; to use it, you must purchase the program. What you're really purchasing is a **software license**, which outlines what you can and can't do. Generally, software publishers grant you the right to make **backups** of the program disks. You may also be allowed to install the software on multiple machines, as long as it's clear that you're only using one copy of the software at a time.

Increasingly, software is becoming **machine dependent**. This means that the program captures a machine ID during the installation process and writes that ID back to the installation disc or to the software company server during the mandatory online registration process. Should you attempt to install the program on another machine, the code will be checked and the installation will terminate.

Organizations with many computers can buy software for all their computers at a reduced price per unit. This agreement, called a **site license**, is a contract with the software publisher; the contract allows multiple copies of software to be made for use in the organization. Taking copies outside the organization violates the contract.

The copying and use of copyrighted software is rampant amongst college students and within organizations. Software manufacturers are working very hard to develop **copyright protection schemes** to thwart the illegal use of their programs. Although early versions of these schemes caused slowdowns on legitimate users' machines, recent versions do not do so. The solution to the problem, perhaps, is for individuals to do the right thing and purchase every program they use. This isn't always easy, as a "free" copy can be very attractive, but doing the right thing tends to pay off in the long run.

Now that you understand the various ways in which software publishers make programs available, you can tell whether you're guilty of **software piracy** (see Figure 12B). All of the following actions are illegal:

Incorporating all or part of a GPL-licensed program in a commercial program that you offer for sale.

Continuing to use a shareware program past the evaluation program's expiration date, even though you didn't pay the registration fee.

Violating the terms of a software license, even if you've paid for the program. For example, many licenses forbid you to install and use more than one copy at a time, so you're guilty of an infringement if you have copies of the same program on your desktop and notebook computers.

Making copies of site-licensed programs for your personal use at home.

Giving or selling copies of commercial programs to others.

How serious is software piracy? Very serious. The industry loses billions of dollars a year in revenues, and if you're caught, you may be charged with a felony. If you're convicted of a felony, you could spend time in jail, lose the right to vote, and ruin your chances for a successful career.

Do you have pirated programs on your computer? The police aren't likely to storm into your residence hall and take you away, kicking and screaming. Most software piracy prosecutions target individuals who are trying to distribute or sell infringing copies or companies that have illegally made multiple copies for their employees. At Bates College, students were arrested after investigators discovered that they were distributing copies of Microsoft Office 2000 from a Web site based on the college's server; they were charged with aggravated invasion of computer privacy, a crime that carries a maximum sentence of five years in prison, a $5,000 fine, or both. If you have any pirated software, you should remove these programs from your computer right away for one simple reason: it's illegal.

If you still don't see the need to delete pirated software from your computer, consider this: it's very, very wise to become accustomed to a zero-tolerance approach to pirated software. If you're caught with an infringing program at work, you could lose your job. A company can't risk retaining employees who expose the firm to prosecution.

COPYRIGHT INFRINGEMENT

Increasing numbers of Internet users seem to believe that sharing illegally made copies of copyrighted music is permissible because so many people are doing it. But it's not. At the University of Oregon, a student was charged with criminal copyright infringement—a federal crime—after making thousands of MP3s available on his Web site. He faced potential penalties of up to three years in prison and $250,000 in fines. At Carnegie Mellon University, 71 students were disciplined for posting illegally duplicated music files on their sites. Stories like this are now commonplace.

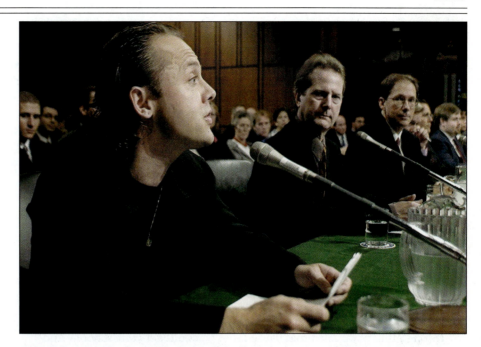

FIGURE 12C: Bands like Metallica fought to have illegal downloads banned from the Internet. In 2000, Metallica sued Napster, a once-popular site for free music downloads. Thanks to lobbying by Metallica and other musicians, free downloads are harder to find on the Web.

Copyright violators are endlessly creative when it comes to rationalizing their illegal behavior. You may hear that it's okay to download a copyrighted MP3 file as long as you keep it no longer than 24 hours, but that's false. If you upload music copied from a CD you've paid for, you're still violating the law. Spreading a band's copyrighted music around isn't justified by saying it's "free advertising"; if the group wants advertising, they'll arrange it themselves (see Figure 12C). And don't fall into the trap of thinking that sharing MP3s is legal as long as you don't charge any money for them. You're still taking royalties away from copyright holders, and it's still illegal.

You'll often hear people use the term **fair use** to justify illegal copying. The fair use doctrine does justify *limited* uses of copyrighted material without payment to or permission from the copyright holder, but it is sharply limited. The fair use doctrine holds that a *brief* selection from a copyrighted work may be excerpted for the purposes of commentary, parody, news reporting, research, and education. Such excerpts are short—generally, no more than five percent of the original work—and they shouldn't compromise the commercial value of the work. In general, the reproduction of an entire work is almost never justifiable by means of the fair use doctrine.

Plagiarism & Copyright Infringment

Introducing Ethics

As we mentioned earlier, ethics is the branch of philosophy concerned with determining what's right and wrong, especially in the context of moral dilemmas. An **ethical principle** is a principle that helps people find their way through moral dilemmas.

As this spotlight's opening suggests, computers cause new moral dilemmas by pushing people into unprecedented situations. Computer ethics explores the ways that ethical principles can be used to think through the moral dilemmas caused by computer use.

MORAL DILEMMAS

It's easy to say that you don't need to worry about ethics; you'll just do the right thing. But that's just the trouble with moral dilemmas. When you're in one, it's difficult to tell what's right and what's wrong, even if you're the most moral person around.

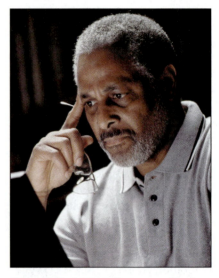

FIGURE 12D: Ethics is the branch of philosophy concerned with determining what's right and wrong, especially in the context of moral dilemmas.

Moral dilemmas arise in two situations:

- **When it's not clear which, if any, moral rule applies.** Can you imagine an electronic love triangle? That's just what existed after an incident on the WELL, a computer network based in northern California. A male user had been involved in electronic romances with at least two female users. Neither woman was aware of the other, and none of these people had ever met. Do real-life courtship rules apply to an online chat group? Are these relationships real?

- **When two or more rules apply, and they conflict.** You've just discovered that your friend is making and selling CDs containing pirated copies of your school's site-licensed software. You've told your friend that it's wrong and he should stop, but he persists. The copies could get your school—and your friend—in a lot of trouble. What's more important: your loyalty to your friend or your obligations to your school?

Moral dilemmas aren't fun. When you find yourself in the middle of one, it's a lonely feeling—people disagree about what you should do. Ethical principles come in handy because they help you think through your options.

FIGURE 12E: When you find yourself in the middle of a moral dilemma, it can be difficult to tell what's right and what's wrong.

ETHICAL PRINCIPLES

Over the centuries, philosophers have come up with many ethical principles. To some, it's disconcerting to find that these principles sometimes conflict. In the end, though, an ethical principle is only a tool you can use to think through a difficult situation. You must make your choice and live with the consequences.

Three of the most useful ethical principles are:

- **An act is ethical if, were everyone to act the same way, society as a whole would benefit.** Here's a good argument against software piracy. If everyone stole software, programmers would have little incentive to develop innovative programs. When we refuse to tolerate software piracy, everyone wins.

- **An act is ethical if it treats people as an end in themselves, rather than as a means to an end.** If the cybernetic two-timer had spent more time thinking about the fact that people with feelings were on the other end of the chat line, he might not have been so eager to play his little game. In this view, the fact that the relationships took place by means of the computer becomes irrelevant. He was using the relationships as a means to an end—his own ego gratification, perhaps.

From this perspective, what he did is unethical.

- **An act is ethical if impartial observers would judge that it is fair to all parties concerned.** As we mentioned earlier, a few years ago, software publishers were so concerned about software piracy that they implemented copyright protection schemes in their programs. Although these schemes prevented unauthorized duplication of the programs, they slowed down users' computers and left them without any convenient recourse if the software was lost due to a hard disk crash. Is it fair to punish legitimate users to prevent others from engaging in criminal activity?

THINKING THROUGH MORAL DILEMMAS

If you find yourself in a moral dilemma related to computer use, talk to people you trust. Make sure you have all the facts. Think through alternative courses of action, based on different principles. Find a solution that you can be proud of. Not sure what that means? Here's a handy, practical guide:

> You'd be proud to tell your parents or friends what you did.
>
> If you were in someone else's shoes, you'd have to admit that your action was fair.
>
> If you did it at work, your company's customers would agree that you did the right thing and they'd be even more eager to buy your company's products.
>
> You wouldn't mind reading about your action on the front page of your hometown newspaper.

Computer Ethics for Computer Users

How do these ethics concepts apply to you, the college computer user? They all boil down to one word: respect. Use campus computers in a way that shows respect for yourself, for others, and for academic integrity:

- **Respect yourself.** If you obtain an account and password to use the campus computer system, don't give your password to others. They could do something that gets you in trouble. In addition, don't say or do anything on the Internet that could reflect poorly on you, even if you think no one will ever find out.

- **Respect others.** Obviously, you shouldn't use a computer to threaten or harass anyone. You should also avoid using more than your share of computing resources, such as disk space. If you publish a Web page on your college's computers, remember that your page's contents affect the college's public image.

- **Respect academic integrity.** Always give credit for text you've copied from the Internet. Ask permission before you copy pictures. Don't copy or distribute software unless the license specifically says you can.

Your college probably has its own code of conduct for computer users. Read it carefully, and follow the rules.

TEN COMMANDMENTS FOR COMPUTER ETHICS

The Computer Ethics Institute of the Brookings Institution, located in Washington, D.C., has developed the following "Ten Commandments" for computer users, programmers, and system designers:

1. Thou shalt not use a computer to harm other people.
2. Thou shalt not interfere with other people's computer work.
3. Thou shalt not snoop around in other people's files.
4. Thou shalt not use a computer to steal.
5. Thou shalt not use a computer to bear false witness.
6. Thou shalt not copy or use proprietary software for which you have not paid.
7. Thou shalt not use other people's computer resources without authorization or proper compensation.
8. Thou shalt not appropriate other people's intellectual output.
9. Thou shalt think about the social consequences of the program you write or the system you design.
10. Thou shalt use a computer in ways that show consideration and respect for your fellow humans.

NETIQUETTE

General principles such as the "Ten Commandments for Computer Ethics" are useful for overall guidance, but they don't provide specific help for the special situations you'll run into online—such as an unwanted sexual advance in a MUD (multiuser dungeon game). As a result, computer and Internet users have developed a lengthy series of specific behavior guidelines for the various Internet services available, such as e-mail, mailing lists, Usenet, Internet Relay Chat (IRC), MUDs, and MOOs (MUD object oriented). Called **netiquette**, these guidelines provide specific pointers on how to show respect for others—and for yourself—while you're online.

Here's a sample, based on Arlene Rinaldi's "Netiquette Home Page" (**www.fau.edu/netiquette/net/netiquette.html**) and other Internet sources:

- **Mailing lists.** After you join a mailing list, read the discussion for a couple of days to see what kinds of questions are welcomed and how to participate meaningfully. If the list has a FAQ "Frequently Asked Questions" document posted on the Web, be sure to read it before posting a question to the list; it may already have been answered in the FAQ. Bear in mind that some people using the list may not speak English as their native tongue, so don't belittle people for spelling errors. Don't post inflammatory messages; never post in anger. If you agree with something, don't post a message that says "Me too"—you're just wasting everyone's time. If you need to unsubscribe from the list, don't post messages requesting that somebody do this for you; find out how to send the correct command to the list server.

- **E-mail.** Check your e-mail daily, and respond promptly to the messages you've been sent. Download or delete messages once you've read them so that you don't exceed your disk usage quota. Remember that e-mail isn't private; you should never send a message that contains anything you wouldn't want others to read. Always speak of others professionally and courteously; e-mail is easily forwarded, and the person you're describing may eventually see the message. Check your computer frequently for viruses that can propagate by means of e-mail messages. Keep your messages short and to the point; focus on one subject per message. Don't type in all capital letters; this comes across as SHOUTING. Spell-check your e-mail as you would any other written correspondence, especially in professional settings. Watch out for sarcasm and humor in e-mail; often, it fails to come across as a joke. Be mindful when you request a return receipt; some people consider this to be an invasion of privacy.

- **Internet Relay Chat (IRC).** Learn what commonly used IRC abbreviations such as BRB "Be Right Back" mean so that you don't pester others to explain them. In a new channel, listen to the discussion for a while so you can figure out how to join in meaningfully. Don't flood the channel with text so that others can't communicate, and lay off the colors, beeps, and scripts that interfere with the flow of dialogue. Don't harass other users with unwanted invitations. If somebody tells you to type in a command, don't do it—it may be a trick. Learn how to use the ignore command if someone is bothering you.

Computer Ethics for Computer Professionals

Suppose you hire an engineer to build a bridge. Within months, it falls down, injuring several people. It turns out that your so-called engineer never took any courses in bridge construction. And as you investigate further, you learn that the engineer received a 15 percent kickback from a heartily recommended contractor who sold you substandard materials. You probably wouldn't have very much confidence in the next engineer you hire.

CODES OF CONDUCT AND GOOD PRACTICE FOR CERTIFIED COMPUTING PROFESSIONALS

The essential elements relating to conduct that identify a professional activity are:

- A high standard of skill and knowledge

- A confidential relationship with people served

- Public reliance upon the standards of conduct in established practice

- The observance of an ethical code.

FIGURE 12F: Excerpt from the Code of Ethics of the Institute for Certification of Computing Professionals.

As this example suggests, no profession can stay in business for long without a rigorous (and enforced) code of professional ethics. That's why professional engineers subscribe to ethical **codes of conduct**. Many such codes exist; they're developed by professional associations, such as the Association for Computing Machinery (ACM). These codes expressly forbid actions such as those undertaken by this engineer. Figure 12F is an excerpt from the Code of Ethics of the Institute for Certification of Computing Professionals.

SAFETY FIRST

The field of computer ethics tries to specify ethical codes for computing professionals. Most of these codes closely resemble engineering ethical codes, and for good reason. Like engineers, computer professionals create products that affect many people and may expose them to risk of personal injury or even death. Increasingly, computer systems and computer programs figure prominently in safety-critical systems, including transportation monitoring systems (such as air-traffic control) and critical patient monitoring.

At the core of every engineering or computer code of ethics, therefore, is a professional person's highest and indispensable aim: to preserve and protect human life and to avoid harm or injury. If we, the public, are to trust professional people, we must be able to believe that they have the inner virtue needed to protect our safety and welfare—even if doing so means the professional person suffers financially.

ADDITIONAL ETHICAL RESPONSIBILITIES

Safety is important, but the public has a right to expect additional ethical responsibilities in a professional person. Professionals in any branch of computing should also have the following qualities:

- **Competence.** Professionals keep up with the latest knowledge in their fields by reading professional journals, attending conferences, and taking refresher courses as needed. In addition, professionals perform services only in their areas of competence. They make sure all their work meets the highest possible standards of quality.

- **Responsibility.** Professionals are loyal to their clients or employers. They don't disclose confidential information concerning a project, even if they leave a client or firm's employment. Professionals are also honest: if a project seems likely to fail, they say so. They turn down work if accepting it would place them in a conflict of interest.

- **Integrity.** Professionals express opinions only when they're based on fact. They are impartial in their judgment and don't change their judgment in response to external pressure.

THE ACM CODE OF CONDUCT

Of all the computing associations' codes of conduct, the one developed by the Association for Computing Machinery (ACM) is considered the most

innovative and far-reaching. According to the ACM code, a computing professional:

1. Contributes to society and human well-being

2. Avoids harm to others

3. Is honest and trustworthy

4. Is fair and takes action not to discriminate on the basis of race, sex, religion, age, disability, or national origin

5. Honors property rights, including copyrights and patents

6. Gives proper credit when using the intellectual property of others

7. Respects the right of other individuals to privacy

8. Honors confidentiality

Like previous engineering codes of conduct, the ACM code places public safety and well-being at the top of the list. Unlike previous codes, it adds a new and important dimension of professionalism: active intervention to prevent sexual, racial, and other forms of discrimination.

PROGRAMMER LIABILITY

Even the most ethical programmer can produce a program with errors (see Figure 12G). Most complex programs have so many possible combinations of conditions that to test for every combination isn't feasible. In some cases, the tests would take years; in other cases, no one could think of a test for all the possibilities. All experienced programmers know that all programs of any size have bugs. If the program results in injury or death, who's at fault?

Consider the following situation. An airplane flying in poor visibility uses a computer to guide the plane, which is a common occurrence. The air-traffic control system is also computer-based. The plane crashes. The investigation discloses minor bugs in both computer programs. If the plane's computer had been dealing with a person in the tower rather than a computer, or if the air-traffic control program had been interacting with a human pilot, the crash would not have occurred. Where does the liability lie for the loss of life and property?

Because bugs are inevitable and programmers can't predict all the different ways programs interact with their environment, most computer experts believe that it's wrong to single out programmers for blame. Software companies are at fault, too, if they fail to test and document their products. And the organization that buys the software may share part of the blame, too, if they fail to train personnel to use the system and understand its possible shortcomings.

Recognizing these facts, a new field called **software engineering** attempts to apply the principles of mainstream engineering to software production. Among other things, these principles call for an external, impartial review of a project at various stages before completion. Computer scientists are also working on **fault-tolerant systems**, which can keep working even if they encounter a glitch.

COMPUTER ETHICS IN BUSINESS

A business or organization must protect its data from loss and damage, from misuse and error, and from unauthorized access. Otherwise, the organization is not serving its clients effectively.

To protect data from loss, an organization must have proper **backup procedures**. Backup procedures involve making copies of data files for protection against data loss. Without backup procedures, an organization may place its customers' information at risk. What would happen to a bank, for example, if it lost all its data and didn't have backups?

Protecting data from misuse or error is difficult for any organization. Misuse can arise, for example, from not using the appropriate software or not using the software properly.

Data that hasn't been properly maintained can have serious effects on the individual or organization it relates to. Errors in data can and do occur. It is the ethical responsibility of the organization dealing with the data to ensure that its data is as correct as possible.

Another type of data misuse occurs when an employee or company fails to keep data confidential. A breach of confidentiality occurs when an employee looks up data about a person in the database and uses that information outside the specific job. For example, according to a recent press report, some IRS employees routinely looked up the tax returns of neighbors and celebrities. Thanks to a public outcry, such actions are now grounds for termination.

Companies may punish employees for looking up customer data, but many of them think nothing of selling it to third parties. A mail-order company, for example, can gain needed revenue by selling customer lists to firms trying to market related products. Privacy advocates believe that it's unethical to divulge customer data without first asking the customer's permission.

WHISTLE-BLOWING

What happens when a company's profit-seeking goals conflict with a computer professional's code of conduct? For example, the ACM Code of Ethics tells computing professionals to respect people's privacy. What if you're

FIGURE 12G: Who was liable for the loss of the European Space Agency's $3 billion Ariane missile in 1996? How do you think these individuals or organizations should be held accountable?

hired to write software that gathers information about customers without their knowledge?

People who have lived through situations like this agree that none of the options are attractive. You can quit and look for another job. You can refuse to perform the requested task, but you'll probably be fired. If the requested task poses a danger to the public or appears to be illegal, you can report the company's intentions to regulatory agencies or the press, an action called **whistle-blowing**. Although some laws exist that protect whistle-blowers, most wind up unemployed—and permanently blacklisted. And what if your whistle-blowing actions cause the government to shut down your company, harming not only you but all your coworkers as well? Often, there's no clear-cut solution.

As this discussion illustrates, codes of ethics don't solve every ethical problem. They provide needed guidance, but they can't save everyone from moral dilemmas.

TEST YOUR ETHICAL SENSE

1. A music fan sets up a Web site about his favorite band. On his site, he posts photos he's downloaded from other sites, as well as the song lyrics of all the band's songs. He doesn't obtain permission for the photos or lyrics, but figures this is fine since his site only serves to promote the band he loves. Has he acted ethically?

2. An employee at a small nonprofit organization often uses her home computer to do work for her organization. In order to complete her work from home, she copies the software program she uses at work to her home computer. The only time she ever uses the software is when she is performing work for the organization. Has she acted ethically?

3. A high-school history teacher finds a Web site that covers the topic of the American Revolution perfectly. She prints all the pages of the site and makes copies of them, giving one to each member of her class. Has she acted ethically?

4. A graphic designer is creating a brochure for a local weight-loss center. The brochure contains a number of before and after photos of people who have lost weight. The weight-loss center asks the graphic designer to digitally alter one of the after photos so that the woman in it appears to have lost more weight than she actually has. The graphic designer complies, figuring that the woman did lose weight, so a little image-editing is not a big deal. Has she acted ethically?

5. Software often includes security holes. A software company proposes legislation that makes it illegal for anyone other than the company that owns the code to reveal security holes in proprietary code. The company claims that the proposed legislation should become law because widespread knowledge of security holes may allow hackers to create an unsafe environment for users. Is it ethical for software companies to "hide" their security holes from customers in this way?

6. A network administrator at a large corporation is asked to check the e-mail of employees occasionally to determine whether they are using corporate e-mail services for personal use—something that is strictly forbidden during work hours. While scanning the subject lines of e-mails, the network administrator finds one that includes his own name. Knowing that he is up for a promotion and being curious as to whether the e-mail contains any information about it, he opens the e-mail. He instead discovers his coworkers are planning a surprise birthday party for him. Has he acted ethically in opening the e-mail?

7. A college student is suspicious that his residence hall roommate is using his computer when he's not around. He installs and hides a live Web cam and hides it on his bookshelf without telling his roommate, and periodically checks the Web cam's broadcast from his friend's computer in another room. Has he acted ethically in installing a Web cam without telling his roommate?

8. A programmer on a mission-critical project is constantly being pressured by his boss to work faster to complete his project. His boss is under the gun from management to finish the project on time and under budget, no matter what. After the programmer repeatedly tells his boss that he needs more time to complete the project safely, he is told he must finish the project within one month or he may be fired. Wanting to keep his job, he rushes to complete the work, knowing that it may possibly contain errors. Has the programmer acted ethically? Has his boss?

9. Online file-sharing sites continue to be popular Internet attractions. Detractors claim that such sites make it easy for users to violate copyright laws. The sites themselves claim that they don't support copyright violations; they simply allow users to share files. Are the users who exchange files on such sites acting ethically? Are the creators of such file-sharing software and Web sites acting ethically? What about those who want to prevent such sites from existing at all?

10. A computer tech person working at a campus repair center finds child pornography on a computer he is repairing. He knows that possession of child pornography is illegal and that he should contact the authorities. However, he also knows he shouldn't have been looking at the contents of the customer's hard drive so closely, and may lose his job if his employer finds out he did. He doesn't report his discovery to the police. Instead, he permanently erases all the files containing child pornography from the customer's hard drive. Has he acted ethically?

Databases and Information Systems

CHAPTER **13**

What You'll Learn . . .

When you have finished reading this chapter, you will be able to:

1. Recognize the potential uses of a database program.

2. Describe the basic components of a database.

3. Describe the basic capabilities of a good database program.

4. Distinguish between flat file and relational database programs and explain the advantages and disadvantages of each.

5. List the three basic characteristics of a computerized information system.

6. List the four functions of managers.

7. Identify the characteristics of valuable information.

8. Describe the major types of computerized information systems used in today's organizations.

9. Describe how the retail sector is taking advantage of computer databases to increase sales and gain a competitive edge.

Destinations

For more information on data warehousing, see the Data Warehousing Institute's home page at **www.dw-institute.com**.

Information isn't useful if you're buried in it. For computers to deliver on the promise to help us cope with information more efficiently, they must cut information down to a manageable size. And that's precisely what database programs are designed to do. **Database programs** store data so that you can quickly locate, organize, and display (or print) information you need while keeping unwanted information out of your way.

Because database programs are so valuable, they're found on all types of computers, large and small. Regular computer users set up personal databases to organize music, names and addresses, research notes, and more. In businesses, **information systems** are used to make key information available to employees, managers, executives, and customers.

Some of these business databases are very large. In large corporations, a trend has emerged toward ever-larger databases called **data warehouses**, which are capable of storing all the information that a corporation possesses. The payoff could be huge. Lucent Technologies in Murray Hill, New Jersey, for example, is reported to have saved $10 million the first day a new data warehouse went into operation—the software found $10 million worth of transactions that had been shipped without follow-up billing. The company previously used smaller, separate databases for billing and shipping, and nobody ever discovered the foul-up.

Understanding database and information systems concepts is a prerequisite for membership in an information society. No matter what line of work you pursue, you'll almost undoubtedly wind up working with databases and information systems sooner or later (see Figure 13.1).

Database Concepts: The Essentials

The term **data** means any unorganized text, graphics, sound, or video that haven't yet been processed by a computer. For example, the SETI Institute, a nonprofit research center, uses the Arecibo radio telescope (based in Puerto Rico) to scan the skies for signs of extraterrestrial intelligence. Programmed to "listen" to more than 28 million radio channels, the radio telescope produces huge amounts of data—but they mean nothing until they're processed by computers. The telescope produces so much data, in fact, that the SETI Institute has appealed for help from home computer users, who can download an application called SETI@home. Working like a screensaver, the program automatically downloads SETI data and analyzes the data while the user's computer is idle.

Information is data that have been processed so that they're organized in a way that people find meaningful and useful. The SETI Institute's computers—as well as those of participants in the SETI@home project—are looking for narrow-band radio signals. Unlike naturally occurring radio signals, narrow-band signals require a consciously constructed transmitter. The computers comb through huge amounts of data. If a narrow-band signal is found, the computers alert the SETI staff. On several occasions, the SETI computers indicated that a narrow-band signal appeared to be coming from a distant star, but the researchers haven't been able to locate these signals again. So, the data that are collected by SETI program computers are analyzed, and the resulting information is the output that states whether the data meet the criteria of a narrow-band signal or not.

A **database** is any collection of data stored in a way that enables people to add, find, sort, group, summarize, and print the data. Database programs, called **database management systems** (**DBMSs**), make these tasks easy to perform.

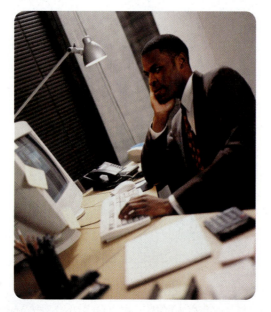

Figure 13.1
Understanding database and information systems concepts is a must for many careers.

As you'll learn in this chapter, databases are essential to today's businesses. They can even save lives. In London, England, a database of road traffic accidents reveals where accidents are most likely to happen, enabling traffic authorities to focus their safety improvements on the most dangerous intersections. Thanks to the database, accidents have been reduced by more than 15 percent—which means that, every year, this database is directly responsible for saving as many as 800 lives and preventing 8,000 serious injuries.

The Hierarchy of Data

In a database, data is constructed from the bottom up, like the layers of a cake. At the lowest level is the **bit**, a 1 or a 0, which is the smallest unit of data that the computer can store. The next level up is made up of **characters** (including letters, numbers, and special symbols), which require bits to represent them.

The next layer is **fields**. A field is a separate area designed to store a certain type of data. In the London traffic accident database, for example, one field records the exact location of each accident. A field has a name, called a **field name**, which describes the type of data that should be entered into the field. So, in the London case, the field name for the accident scene would be "Location." Fields contain items that are of the same type. For example, the field named First_Name holds only first names. An easy way to remember this is to think of a field of corn or a field of wheat. Neither of these fields would contain anything but a single type of crop. Simply put, fields contain things that are alike.

Fields are designed to accept only a certain type of data, called the **data type**. Common data types include text, numbers, currency, and dates. One data type, called a **logical data type**, allows only a "yes" or "no" value. Other data types have been developed for large units of text (called **memos**) and nontextual data (called **objects**). Examples of objects include pictures, sounds, and videos. The latest databases can handle very large objects, called **BLOBs** (**binary large objects**), of several megabytes or more in size.

Except for fields containing memo and object data types, each field has a specified field size. For example, a field for one of the U.S. states is two characters in length, such as MN for Minnesota.

Some fields are designed to display a **default value**, such as today's date, in a field designed to accept the date on which the data were recorded.

The next level up from fields is the **record**, which contains a group of related fields. In the London traffic accident database, for example, a record might include all known facts about an accident, including the names and ages of those involved, the model and age of each car involved, weather conditions at the time, and much additional information. All this information in a record is about the one accident that the record describes. You might remember this by thinking of a record as a *recording* of a person, place, thing, or event.

Within a record, one of the fields is identified as the **key field** (also called the **primary key**). This field contains a code, number, name, or some other information that uniquely identifies the record. In your school's records, for example, chances are you're identified by your student identification number. When you register for courses or request transcripts, you must supply this number so that the computer operators can find your data.

Near the top of the data hierarchy is the **data file**, also called a **table**. A data file is a collection of related records. A database consists of one or more related data files (see Figure 13.2).

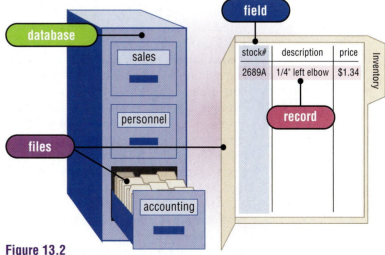

Figure 13.2

A database consists of one or more files. A file is made up of records, and within a record, you find information organized into distinct fields.

Introducing Database Management Systems

As the term implies, a database management system (DBMS) is designed to help people work with all aspects of data. But a DBMS wouldn't be of much use if it contained errors or made confidential data available to people who weren't authorized to see it. In this section, you'll learn what database management systems are designed to do and why.

DATA INTEGRITY

The term **data integrity** refers to the validity of the data contained in a database. Data integrity can be compromised in many ways, including input typing errors, hardware malfunctions, and data transmission errors. To avoid data integrity errors, database programs use **data validation** procedures, which define acceptable input ranges for each field in a record. If the user tries to input data that's out of this range, an error message is displayed.

Several types of data validation are commonly used. An **alphabetic check** ensures that only alphabetical data (the letters of the alphabet) are entered into a field. Similarly, a **numeric check** ensures that only numbers are entered. A **range check** verifies that the entered data fall within an acceptable range. For example, a U.S. ZIP code must not exceed 99999. A **consistency check** examines the data entered into two different fields to determine whether an error has been made. For example, a Web page that asks you to create a user name and password for yourself typically asks you to type your password twice. If there is a discrepancy between the two typed passwords, you're asked to type them again. This ensures that you've typed the password correctly. A **completeness check** determines whether a required field has been left empty. If so, the database program prompts the user to fill in the needed data.

DATA INDEPENDENCE

The term **data independence** refers to the separation of data from the programs that use the data. The whole concept of a database management system supports the notion of data independence since it represents a system for managing data separately from the programs that use the data. In contrast, it is possible to write applications in which the data being processed is actually represented in the program's source code. This data-dependent approach is very inflexible because it makes it difficult to modify the data and also makes the data inaccessible to other programs.

AVOIDANCE OF DATA REDUNDANCY

Data should be entered once—and only once. **Data redundancy** (repetition of data) is a characteristic of poorly designed systems. For example, in many companies, customer names and addresses may appear in two different, unrelated databases. This not only doubles the amount of work needed to update the customer's records should the customer move, but also increases the chance of an error. Will the data be typed the same way twice? If the data is entered differently, some of the data will be unavailable upon retrieval.

DATA SECURITY

The data stored in a database shouldn't be accessible to people who might misuse it, particularly when the collected data are sensitive. Sensitive data include data about people, such as their health records, and data about an organization's finances. Equally important is the protection of data against loss due to equipment failure or power outages. Regular backup procedures are needed so that the data can be restored after an equipment failure.

DATA MAINTENANCE

Good database management also involves having a system in place for data maintenance. This system includes procedures for adding records, updating records, and deleting records.

Types of Database Programs

Two types of application software have been developed to work with database files: file management programs that can work with only one file at a time, and database management systems that can work with several separate files at a time. This section describes both types of software.

FILE MANAGEMENT PROGRAMS

A **file management program** enables users to create customized databases and to store and retrieve data from these databases. File management programs come in handy when an individual or small business needs to set up a computerized information storage and retrieval system. The owner of a baseball card store, for example, could create a database of available baseball cards for customer reference.

Because file management programs are less complex than database management systems, they're also less expensive and easier to use. The ease of use comes at a price, though. File management programs create **flat files**. (You can also create a flat file database with Microsoft Excel.) Flat files can be accessed sequentially when most of the records need to be processed, accessed randomly to retrieve a specific record, or sorted so that the records can be accessed sequentially in a different order. The data stored in a flat file cannot, however, be linked with data in other files.

DATABASE MANAGEMENT SYSTEMS

A database management system (DBMS) can link data from two or more data files. A DBMS is usually more expensive and more difficult to learn than a file management program. The most widely used type of DBMS is called a relational database.

In a **relational database**, data in several files is related through the use of a common

key field. Each record in the file has the same key field but unique key field contents, enabling the field to be used to identify a record. The computer uses this key field as an index to locate records without having to read all the records in the files. As mentioned earlier, your student ID is often the key field for your records at your school. Note: in computer science, the term *relational database* has a more restricted meaning, but this meaning isn't relevant to the way the term is understood in the general computer industry.

A relational DBMS is best envisioned as a collection of two-dimensional tables. Each table corresponds to a data file. Each row in the table corresponds to a record, and each column corresponds to a field. A relational database structure can link a customer table and an accounts payable table, for example, through the use of a common field, such as a customer account number field. The user can then request a report consisting of fields from both the customer record and the accounts payable record (see Figure 13.3). To keep track of the tables that make up the database, the DBMS uses a **data dictionary**. The data dictionary contains a list of the tables the database contains, along with details concerning each table, including field names, field lengths, data types, and validation settings.

What's the advantage of using a relational DBMS instead of a file management program? Before DBMS software came along, it wasn't unusual for companies to have dozens of database files with incompatible formats. Since some of the same data appeared in different files, this violated the rule of avoiding data redundancy (data typed in two or more places), and because

Figure 13.3
In this Microsoft Access database, eight tables are related by means of common fields.

IMPACTS

BUSINESS PRACTICES

How Do Companies Use Data Mining?

You've heard of *data mining*—the process managers use to explore data to discover previously unknown patterns—but what exactly *is* data mining, how do businesses use it, and which businesses profit most from the information they gleam?

Imagine you're a manager at a large retail sales corporation. You want to find out what your top-selling items are, where these items are sold the most (in what part of the country and in which stores), and to whom they are sold (the demographics of the buyers). Your guess is that if you can uncover the relationships between what was sold, where, and when, you might better be able to market your products and predict sales in other locations. In order to track down that information, you "mine" your company's databases. As a manager, you hope that such data mining will help you uncover relationships in your databases that you may not have found otherwise.

Data mining is thus the discovery of information. In making use of this information, managers employ statistical analysis and modeling, which they can use to better understand their customers and their market, as well as to predict future trends. In a sense, managers using data mining are similar to gold prospectors panning for a few precious nuggets of gold. Finding an important nugget of information can make the difference between boom or bust.

Retail leader Wal-Mart is one company that takes advantage of data mining. Its data warehouse stores primitive data for the huge enterprise, including precise records of what was sold, for what price, and when, in all its retail stores. Wal-Mart's data warehouse is designed with no *particular* purpose in mind, but that's the point: data warehouses are intended to support data mining's exploration and discovery of data patterns that aren't obvious even to experienced managers and executives.

Another company that uses data mining is Delta Airlines. Before it started to mine its data, Delta had difficulty making heads or tails of the data it collected. And because Delta's old data weren't in one central database, it used to take days or weeks for users on the Web to get answers to information requests. Now, with the help of National Cash Register (NCR) technologies and solutions, users can get more specific and accurate results from Delta's Web site in just minutes. Delta also uses the data to better determine who its most profitable customers are—and the results have surprised Delta executives. Finally, data mining has helped Delta in recent troubled times to decide how best to sell it services to customers, hoping to keep the airline running well into the future.

---

it multiplied the possibilities for errors, it also violated the rule of data integrity. With relational database programs, it's possible to design the database using two or more tables so that data redundancy is eliminated. This process is called **normalization**.

Object-oriented databases are the newest type of database structure and are starting to gain in popularity. In an object-oriented database, the result of a retrieval operation is an object of some kind, such as a document. Within this object are miniprograms that enable the object to perform tasks, such as display a graphic. Object-oriented databases can incorporate sound, video, text, and graphics into a single database record. This type of database is well suited for multimedia applications. A search of a health-related database, for example, could display a document that included pictures of healthy foods, videos of exercise techniques, and recorded lectures from health professionals.

DATA WAREHOUSING AND DATA MINING

A data warehouse is not intended to replace database management systems developed to support the functional divisions of an organization, such as marketing or accounting. Instead, a data warehouse supplements them by bringing all the data together into a massive database (often containing one trillion bytes of data or more). Using a technique called **drill-down**, managers can view performance data for the entire firm, and then drill down to lower levels (sales, regions, offices, individual salespeople), viewing summaries at each level. By means of a data exploration technique called **data mining**, managers also can explore data in an attempt to discover previously unknown patterns (see Figure 13.4). Less ambitious data warehouse projects, intended to support one division of an organization rather than the entire enterprise, are called **data marts**.

Client/Server Database Systems

A **database server** is a professionally administered program that runs on a local area network (LAN) and is designed to respond to external requests for data. A database server is not designed to be easy to use—and that's because users never contact the server directly. To access the data in the database, users run a **client** program, a user-friendly program that enables them to add data to the database, maintain existing records, perform queries, and generate reports. Because these database systems draw a distinction between the database server and client, they're often called **client/server systems**. They're designed so that many users—hundreds or even thousands of them—can access the database simultaneously. Examples of database servers include the market-leading DB2 (IBM) and Oracle (Oracle Corporation).

The clients of most database servers frame query requests using a **query language** called **SQL** (pronounced "sequel"). Short for **Structured Query Language**, SQL enables users to phrase simple or complex requests for data in a way that the server can understand. SQL isn't difficult to learn. However, most users prefer to use clients that provide more user-friendly tools for constructing SQL queries. One such client is Microsoft Access. With Access, you can build queries that, in the background, are transformed into SQL queries, which can be sent to a database server. In sum, Access can be used to build local databases. It can also be used as a client to access database servers.

The Internet Connection: Going Public with Data

The latest trend in database software is **Web-database integration**, a name for a variety of techniques used to make information stored in databases available through Internet or intranet connections. Web-database integration enables customers of the express shipping giant FedEx to access shipping information through its Web site (see Figure 13.5). You don't have to learn SQL or any other query language to use this or similar sites. The Web server accepts your input and translates it into a query sent to the database. The database responds with the requested information, and the server generates a new Web page on the fly, containing the information you've requested.

Many companies are venturing into online commerce by making enormous internal resources available to the public through

Figure 13.4

Nuggets is a data mining system from Data Mining Technologies.

Figure 13.5

The FedEx tracking system allows you to track a package from pickup, through each transfer point, to delivery.

the Internet. At AMP, a Pennsylvania-based electronics components manufacturer, an enormous online catalog of nearly 90,000 components is made accessible by means of a Web server linked to an Oracle relational database. The payoff for AMP is an annual savings of $2 million in expenses related to catalog production, telephone calls, and customer support.

Employees with knowledge of Web-database integration skills are in high demand. Such skills include knowing how to configure and maintain a Web server, such as Apache (the market leader) or Microsoft's Internet Information Server (IIS), how to write scripts (short programs) that tell the server how to interact with the database software, and how to design and maintain the database.

Information Systems: Tools for Global Competitiveness

Smart businesses know that information systems aren't merely a cost center. Viewed properly, information systems are a value center, a wealth-producing asset that enables a firm to compete more effectively on a global scale. Let's take a closer look at information systems: what they are, how they relate to business organizations, and how advanced information technologies are reshaping the corporate landscape.

COMPUTERIZED INFORMATION SYSTEMS: SERVING AN ORGANIZATION'S NEEDS

You already know that an information system processes data to produce information. This information is useful for providing quality customer service (and for other needs, too, as you'll see in a moment). But what does the "system" part mean?

A **system** is a collection of components purposefully organized into a functioning whole to accomplish a goal. Systems occur in nature, but what we're talking about are **artificial systems**, systems deliberately constructed by people to serve some pur-

pose. Systems are all around us. The air transport system, for example, is a complex system that does a remarkably good job of safely delivering millions of people to their destinations every day.

At the core of the system concept lies the recognition that various parts of the system need to be modified or adapted so they'll function together smoothly. (After all, you wouldn't want to fly on an airplane that had the wrong type of wing installed.) A second important concept about systems is that they have a **life cycle**: they are born, go through a process of maturation, live an adult life, and become obsolete to the point that they have to be modified or abandoned. Figure 13.6 summarizes the stages of a system's life cycle. If you think about yesterday's transportation systems, such as canals or the Pony Express, you'll see it's obvious that systems outlive their usefulness.

At this point, we could be talking about any kind of system, including a manufacturing system (such as an assembly line). What's special about information systems lies in their provision of essential information services to **organizations**, which are collections of resources (personnel and equipment) organized so that they can provide a product or a service. Essential services provided by information systems include recording and keeping track of **transactions** (exchanges of goods, services, or funds), assisting decision makers by providing them with needed facts and figures, and providing documentation needed by customers and suppliers. No organization, not even a small one, can function without an information system of some kind, even if it isn't computer-based. All businesses, for example, are required to keep detailed business records for tax purposes.

Computerized information systems make use of the computer's special capabilities—namely, accepting input in the form of represented data, processing that data to produce information, and disseminating this information throughout the organization. Computerized information systems don't consist merely of computers and software. They also include some method of representing the data essential to the organization, the trained personnel who operate the system, and the procedures these people must follow to ensure that the system functions properly.

A complete definition of a **computerized information system (CIS)** recognizes

System Life Cycle

Life Cycle Stage	Key Tasks
Preliminary design stage	Identifying system development goals
Detailed design stage	Designing specific components
Fabrication, assembly, integration, and test stage	Putting it all together
Production and customer support stage	Using the system
Termination and disposal stage	Retiring the system

Figure 13.6

all these characteristics. A computerized information system:

- Provides essential services to organizations, including processing transactions and keeping exact records

- Collects mission-critical data, processes these data, stores the data and the results of processing, and disseminates information throughout the organization

- Includes data, hardware, software, trained personnel, and procedures

the firm's primary activities, such as providing services or making products. For example, consider a one-person taxi business: the CEO collects the fares, pays the bills, keeps the books, and drives the taxi.

In biology, when you compare a one-celled creature with more complex organisms, you can see a big difference: complex creatures develop specialized groups of cells, called organs, that perform specialized functions. The same goes for organizations. When an organization grows to the point that the founder can't handle all the tasks alone, specialized divisions appear to handle each of the organization's core functions (see Figure 13.7). Consider what happens

Understanding Complex Organizations: The Power Pyramid

How can information systems help organizations achieve their goals? This question can't be answered unless you begin by considering how organizations are structured. Most information systems are designed to fit into existing organizational structures and to support their activities. Some new information systems are being designed to make organizations even more efficient.

FUNCTIONAL DIVISIONS OF AN ORGANIZATION

In a one-person organization, only one person (usually the founder) deals with money matters, handles sales and marketing, keeps essential records, and supervises

Figure 13.7

In an organization, specialized divisions handle each of the organization's core functions. The information systems division manages all of the organization's computerized information systems.

when that one-person taxi company grows into a fleet of 300 vehicles. Chances are that the company will have separate people focusing on the following:

Finance Deal with money: getting it, tracking it, spending it, and accounting for it to external stakeholders and tax agencies. A taxi business with 300 vehicles needs at least one full-time accountant and a part-time bookkeeper or two.

Marketing and sales Promote the organization's product or service and arrange sales with customers. In the taxi business, for example, someone has to handle high-profit ventures such as providing limousines for weddings.

Human resources Hire and train new employees, deal with pay and benefits, and track employee performance. Finding and keeping good drivers is a big job.

Operations Perform the organization's primary function, such as manufacturing a product or delivering a service. In the taxi business, someone has to make sure that the drivers know where to go and guarantee that they actually get there.

Information systems Manage the organization's computerized information systems, including planning and purchasing new systems, providing user training and support, and dealing with day-to-day operational problems. A taxi business is an information-intensive job, which is why today's fastest-growing taxi companies use computer-based systems and state-of-the-art communications systems.

All organizations, including nonprofit organizations and government agencies, tend to develop this functionally differentiated structure, which is sometimes called the **traditional organizational structure**.

CHAIN OF COMMAND

An organization develops because one person can't handle all the work. As an organization grows, the same development takes place with regard to management-related tasks. In a large organization, the CEO hires senior managers who can handle a division such as finance or marketing. To senior managers, the CEO delegates not only the responsibility to manage these divisions properly, but the power to do so effectively. After delegating responsibility and power to senior management, the CEO doesn't have to worry about the time-consuming details of making these divisions work. The CEO's job is to worry about big-picture issues, such as where the organization should go in the future and how it's likely to be affected by trends in the organization's external environment.

The delegation of responsibility proceeds down the organizational ladder. The senior managers of each division hire middle managers, who are responsible for subdivisions. Middle managers may further delegate responsibility to operational managers, who directly supervise nonmanagement personnel (production workers, clerical workers, and other employees). Note that this structure has a few people at the top and lots at the bottom. For this reason, it's called a pyramid (see Figure 13.8). And because this organizational structure is a chain of command, with lots of power at the top and little at the bottom, it's also called a hierarchy.

What do all these managers do? **Managers** decide how best to use the

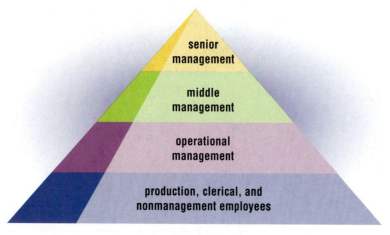

Figure 13.8
The delegation of responsibility in an organization resembles a pyramid. Divisional senior managers hire middle managers, who may delegate responsibility to operational managers. Operational managers supervise nonmanagement personnel.

organization's resources, including money, equipment, and people, so that the organization achieves its goals efficiently. All managers perform some or all of the following management functions:

Planning Establishing goals and creating a strategy to achieve these goals

Organizing Putting resources together so that the goals are achieved

Leading Communicating goals and motivating people to achieve them

Controlling Assessing whether the goals are being met and taking corrective action if necessary

Although all managers perform most or all of these functions, they do so in varying ways. Those in senior management (including the CEO) are more concerned with high-level planning and leadership. They make **strategic decisions** concerning the organization's overall goals and direction. Middle managers focus on planning their division's goals and organizing resources to achieve them. They make **tactical decisions** about how best to organize resources to achieve their division's goals. Operational managers focus on leadership and control, and they make **operational decisions** concerning localized issues (such as an inventory shortage) that need immediate action (see Figure 13.9).

Characteristics of Valuable Information

Before we discuss how information systems are used in organizations, it's important that you understand a few things about information in general. For one, not all information is valuable, a fact you'll appreciate after doing some research on the Internet (see Figure 13.10). To be valuable, information must be:

Accessible You can find it quickly and easily.

Accurate You're confident that it doesn't contain errors.

Complete The information doesn't omit anything important.

Economical The benefit exceeds the cost of producing the information.

Relevant It's related to the task you're trying to perform.

Reliable It's there every time you need it.

Secure Unauthorized people can't access the information.

Simple It doesn't overwhelm you.

Timely It's there when you need it.

Verifiable If necessary, you can confirm the facts and figures by double-checking them.

Figure 13.10
Not all information is valuable, and all too often, we're overwhelmed with more information than we can use.

Types of Management Decisions

Managers	Decisions	Type
Senior managers	Strategic decisions	Determining the organization's goals and direction
Middle managers	Tactical decisions	Deciding how to organize resources to achieve their division's goals
Operational managers	Operational decisions	Deciding how to handle localized issues requiring immediate action

Figure 13.9

TECHNIQUES OF INFORMATION REDUCTION

As pioneering computer scientist Grace Hopper stressed throughout her career, computers are indispensable, but they also pose the threat of producing too much information (**information overload**). It's important to control information to keep it from overwhelming people in an organization. With an information system, the following **control methods** are possible:

- Routing information so that it goes to only those people who really need to see the information

- Summarizing information so that decision makers do not drown in the details

- Enabling selectivity so that people with specific information needs can get that information (and ignore the rest)

- Eliminating unnecessary information (exclusion) so that it doesn't take up time

Now that you understand what makes information valuable, and why organizations need to control the flow of information, let's move on to the various ways information systems are used in organizations.

Information Systems in Organizations: A Survey

To meet the information needs of an organization's employees, many different systems have been developed. In a very small business, a single computer might meet all of the business's information needs. Larger organizations supplement single-user systems with minicomputers, mainframe computers, local area networks (LANs), and wide area networks (WANs). Some of these larger systems are designed to assist **workgroups** (teams of two or more people working on the same project); others are **enterprise-wide systems**, available throughout an organization (including all of the organization's branch offices).

TRANSACTION PROCESSING SYSTEMS

A **transaction processing system** (**TPS**) (also called an **operational system** or a **data processing system**) handles an organization's day-to-day accounting needs. It keeps a careful, verifiable record of every transaction involving money, including purchases, sales, and payroll payments. In businesses that sell products, a TPS is often linked with an inventory control system so that sales personnel will know whether an item is in stock. Transaction processing systems date to the earliest years of business computing, and the cost savings they introduced helped create a huge market for business computers. A TPS saves money by automating routine, labor-intensive record keeping.

Early transaction processing systems used **batch processing**, in which the data were gathered and processed at periodic intervals, such as once per week. With the rise of timesharing systems in the 1970s, **online processing** systems were developed. These systems enabled operations personnel to enter transaction data and see totals and other results immediately.

Transaction processing systems provide useful tools for employees, such as sales and human resource personnel, but they're useful for managers, too. A well-designed TPS can produce periodic **summary reports** that provide managers with a quick overview of the organization's performance. They can also provide **exception reports** that alert managers to unexpected developments (such as high demand for a new product).

MANAGEMENT INFORMATION SYSTEMS

A **management information system** (**MIS**) is a computer-based system that supports the information needs of different levels of management. This type of system is designed to help management make informed decisions. Most management information systems are designed to work with transaction processing systems. They produce reports that tell middle managers how well they are meeting their goals (see Figure 13.11).

Although management information systems continue to play an important role in organizations, they have drawbacks. They generate predefined reports that may not contain the information a manager wants.

Figure 13.11
A management information system produces reports that tell middle managers how well they're meeting their goals.

The information may not be available when it's needed, and it might also be buried within reams of printouts.

DECISION SUPPORT SYSTEMS

A **decision support system (DSS)** addresses the deficiencies of management information systems by enabling managers to ask questions that can't be answered by fixed, predefined MIS reports. For example, a retail chain manager can ask how an advertising campaign affected sales of advertised versus nonadvertised items. Many DSS applications enable managers to create simulations that begin with real data and ask what-if questions, such as, "What would happen to profits if we used a shipper who could cut our packaging costs by two percent, but who would sometimes cause slight delivery delays?"

Online analytical processing (OLAP) provides decision support by enabling managers to import rich, up-to-the-minute data from transaction databases. For example, analysts at Pizzeria Uno, a chain of more than 100 pizza stores, obtain and analyze all the sales information from each of the firm's stores every morning. As a result, they can quickly spot trends that may be emerging in customer preferences and employee performance.

EXECUTIVE INFORMATION SYSTEMS

An **executive information system (EIS)**, also known as an **executive support system (ESS)**, supports management's strategic planning function. Though similar to a DSS, an EIS is designed to support decisions made by top-level management that will affect the entire company.

An EIS filters critical information (including information about the firm's external environment) so that overall trends are apparent, and presents this information in an easy-to-use graphical interface. For instance, you might create a report that compares the company inventory levels with the average of the industry. Little training is required to use these systems.

EXPERT SYSTEMS

An **expert system** is a software package that deals with knowledge rather than information. Expert systems help in formulating a decision in the way an expert in the field might (see Figure 13.12). Expert systems operate using principles of artificial intelligence (a field that attempts to endow a computer with intelligence). Expert systems are helping to improve service in one area in which organizations sometimes perform an unsatisfactory job: providing technical support for customers.

KNOWLEDGE MANAGEMENT SYSTEMS

Organizations are increasingly aware that knowledge is a valuable asset and are turning to technology to help them capture the knowledge employees create. A variety of information technologies are being used to create **knowledge management systems**, which capture such knowledge and make it available where it's needed. This process doesn't have to be high-tech: at Columbia/HCA, a nationwide hospital chain, a team visits each hospital and writes a report on the most successful business processes (best practices) found at each site. The reports are then made available on the company's internal Web server.

COMPUTER-SUPPORTED COOPERATIVE WORK

Organizations that have networks can use **groupware**, software that provides computerized support for the information

Destinations
To learn more about workflow management, visit the Workflow Management Coalition's home page at **www.wfmc.org**.

Figure 13.12
A sample expert system. This Web site brings together artificial intelligence and Web technology to create an interactive system for whale watchers to identify observed whales.

needs of workgroups. Groupware applications are collectively known as **computer-supported cooperative work** (**CSCW**). These applications include electronic mail, videoconferencing, group scheduling systems, customizable electronic forms, real-time shared applications, and shared information databases (see Figure 13.13).

The first successful groupware, Lotus Notes, was designed to run on client/server systems. Newer groupware products, such as Microsoft Exchange and new versions of Lotus Notes, are designed to run on intranets and extranets. They make groupware applications available to workgroups that work at geographically separated offices, and even enable organizations to bring in group members who work for other organizations (such as affiliated research labs).

WORKFLOW AUTOMATION

In many companies, important documents must go through a series of personnel for approval. For example, in an engineering firm, an engineer may prepare a proposal for an external contract. The proposal then goes to the engineer's supervisor for review and approval. The document may need to be seen by several other people until it's finally approved and sent. **Workflow automation** can greatly speed this process by automatically sending a document to the next person who needs to see and approve it.

BUSINESS PROCESS REENGINEERING

Business process reengineering (**BPR**), also known as **reengineering**, refers to the use of information technology to bring about major changes and cost savings in an organization's structure. At the core of reengineering is the principle that information technology (IT) doesn't bring big payoffs if you simply automate existing work processes. The key to big payoffs lies in using IT to *change* existing processes.

In BPR, designers ignore an organization's functional divisions and focus instead on work processes: activities that have an identifiable output and a value to the organization's customers. For example, product development is a process that often involves many functional divisions, including marketing, engineering, procurement, and finance. By using information technology such as groupware, an organization can be redesigned around work processes rather than functional divisions. The work is then carried out by a **cross-functional team**, in which team members perform functions that were formerly separated out among the company's functional units.

Reengineering can lead to big payoffs, but a high proportion of early BPR projects failed. Many companies came to see reengineering as a means of **downsizing**, and employees learned to fear and resist BPR efforts.

Computers and Databases in the Retail Sector

In the retail sector, computers are indispensable for traditional applications such as automating the checkout process. But some companies have also figured out how to use computers and databases for strategic purposes: getting an edge on their competitors. These companies have grown rapidly and have made fortunes for their shareholders.

AT THE CHECKOUT STAND

Today's cash registers are really computers—specifically, **point-of-sale (POS) terminals** (see Figure 13.14). Clerks check items out by passing them over an optical scanner, which reads the item's **universal product code (UPC)** encoded on a label or a tag (see Figure 13.15). The UPC is encoded with a series of bars of varying widths and spacing. Use of the UPC has resulted in faster processing of items and fewer price errors. The latest POS terminals are fully integrated with a **credit card authorization** system, which automatically originates a call to a **call center**, a computer-based telephone routing system that connects to an authorization service, and cranks out an authorization number. Thanks to the volume of credit card authorization calls, firms that make call center equipment have watched their market grow from virtually nothing

25 years ago to a worldwide $200 billion bonanza today.

Because point-of-sale terminals produce digitized data, they're useful for more purposes than determining the customer's

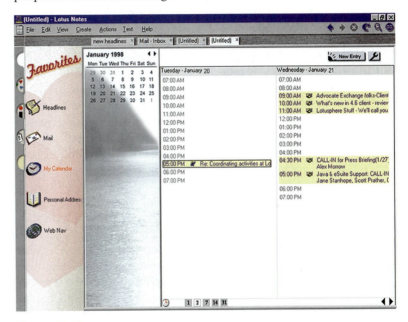

Figure 13.13
Groupware applications such as Lotus Notes are collectively known as computer-supported cooperative work (CSCW).

Figure 13.14
The latest POS terminals are fully integrated with a credit card authorization system.

Figure 13.15
The UPC has resulted in faster processing of items and fewer price errors.

bill. POS terminals are linked to the store's inventory database. When a customer buys an item, the database is automatically updated to reflect the lowered stock level. When the level gets too low, the software originates a restocking order.

POS terminals are also used as marketing devices. If a customer buys a particular brand of coffee, the terminal produces a coupon for a discount on a competing brand. Another feature is to list the total of the discounts that were recorded for items purchased. Marketers believe that creating a sense of well-being at the point of sale will subliminally influence the customer to associate the store with good feelings, causing the customer to come back in the future.

Chain stores link their POS terminals to central computer systems using **public data networks** (**PDNs**). Disney, however, is taking POS data to the airwaves. At Walt Disney World, POS terminals at hundreds of retail carts supply data to company computers using wireless communications, a means of linking computers by radio signals. As a result, the Lion King cart never runs out of those cute stuffed animals, and that means bigger profits.

POS terminals can also help reduce losses due to bad checks and credit card fraud. **Check-screening systems** read a check's account number and access a database containing the numbers of delinquent accounts. These systems help reduce bad-check losses by up to 25 percent, translating into big savings for retail firms. According to one estimate, banks and retailers lose a staggering $58 billion annually due to bounced checks and check fraud.

Signature capture systems enable stores to capture a customer's signature digitally by having the customer sign the receipt on a pressure-sensitive pad using a special stylus. What's the point? The system cuts down on credit card disputes. With a receipt signed by the customer, the store can prove that the purchase was made. This system isn't popular with consumers, however, due to fears that a dishonest employee could use the captured signature for fraudulent purposes. **Photo checkout systems** access a database of customer photos and display the customer's picture when a credit card is used. In a New York test, this system cut credit card fraud by 94 percent.

SUCCESS STORIES

What Makes Wal-Mart So Successful?

Suppose your parents put $1,000 into Wal-Mart stock in 1970, when the company's stock was first offered to the public, and set the shares aside for the child they planned to have. You turn 18, your trust fund comes due, and guess what? You're a multimillionaire!

What's the secret of Wal-Mart's amazing success? Business analysts point to the retail chain's smart strategy of locating in populous but underserved semirural markets, good customer service, profit-sharing plans for employees (who are called associates), and low prices. Most of all, some say, Wal-Mart's innovative use of information technology is responsible for the company's success. Wal-Mart has poured billions of dollars into state-of-the-art information technology.

What's so special about the way Wal-Mart uses computers? For Wal-Mart, computers aren't simply a means to perform a task, such as keeping an inventory database up-to-date. Far more important, computers are a means of creating and cementing relationships with suppliers, the key business partner in any retail business. Instead of seeing suppliers as adversaries, Wal-Mart views them as partners and makes valuable information available to them, such as what's selling and what's not in its huge chain of retail stores. Wal-Mart collects this information by means of sophisticated checkout scanners, which quickly alert managers when sales patterns develop.

In addition, Wal-Mart opens its inventory database to suppliers and tells them, "When you see that we're getting low on something, ship it." By transferring the inventory maintenance responsibility to suppliers and creating the computer systems needed to do this, Wal-Mart cut inventory restocking time from the industry average of six weeks to just 36 hours. The result? When shoppers go to Wal-Mart, they find what they're looking for. That translates into customer loyalty and huge profits.

Not everyone is happy with Wal-Mart's success. In the suburbs and rural areas that Wal-Mart management favors for new stores, the coming of a new Wal-Mart generally spells the end of small, family-run businesses that cannot compete with Wal-Mart's pricing. In that respect, Wal-Mart's low prices don't come without costs of their own.

HOME | Takeaway Points | Key Terms and Concepts | Matching | Multiple Choice | Fill-In | Short Answer | Exercises/ Projects | Web Research | **CHAPTER REVIEW**

TAKEAWAY POINTS

- Database software transforms data into information by showing just the information required for a task. Information is data that are organized in such a way that they provide meaning and are useful.

- A database is a collection of data stored in an organized way. A database file is made up of records, which are units of information about a person, place, thing, or event. Each record has one or more fields. Fields are made up of characters. Each field stores a certain type of data.

- A good database system ensures data integrity (validity of the data), promotes data independence (usefulness with more than one application), avoids data redundancy (entry of the same data in two or more places), ensures data security (protection from loss of confidentiality), and provides procedures for data maintenance (procedures for adding, updating, and deleting records).

- File management programs work with only one database file, called a flat file, at a time. As a result, they can't eliminate data redundancy. Relational databases work with two or more database files, called tables, at a time. The data in the various tables can be related by means of common fields. Through a process called normalization, it is possible to design a relational database so that data redundancy is eliminated.

- A computerized information system (CIS) is a system that provides essential services to organizations by collecting, processing, storing, and disseminating mission-critical data. The system includes data, hardware, software, trained personnel, and procedures.

- Managers plan, organize, lead, and control. Senior management is primarily concerned with planning and leading; middle managers focus on planning and organizing; and operational managers focus on leadership and control.

- Managers and many employees need information that is accessible, accurate, complete, economical, relevant, reliable, secure, simple, timely, and verifiable.

- Information systems include the transaction processing system (TPS), the management information system (MIS), the decision support system (DSS), the executive information system (EIS), the knowledge management system, groupware, workflow routing, and business process reengineering (BPR). Increasingly, data warehousing is seen as a way to provide all these systems with rich data.

- More and more companies are using databases for strategic purposes. These companies have grown rapidly and have made fortunes for their shareholders. Point-of-sale (POS) terminals are linked to a store's inventory database, allowing managers to quickly know which products are selling and which are not. Check-screening systems also access a database to determine whether an account is fraudulent or delinquent.

1
2
3
4
5
6
7
8
9
10
11
12
13
14
15
16

CHAPTER REVIEW

| Takeaway Points | Key Terms and Concepts | Matching | Multiple Choice | Fill-In | Short Answer | Exercises/Projects | Web Research | HOME |

KEY TERMS AND CONCEPTS

1 2 3 4 5 6 7 8 9 10 11 12 13 14 15 16

alphabetic check
artificial system
batch processing
bit
BLOB (binary large object)
business process
   reengineering (BPR)
   (or reengineering)
call center
character
check-screening system
client
client/server system
completeness check
computerized information
   system (CIS)
computer-supported
   cooperative work (CSCW)
consistency check
control method
credit card authorization
cross-functional team
data
data dictionary
data file (table)
data independence
data integrity
data mart
data mining
data redundancy
data type
data validation
data warehouse

database
database management
   system (DBMS)
database program
database server
decision support
   system (DSS)
default value
downsizing
drill-down
enterprise-wide system
exception report
executive information
   system (EIS)
executive support
   system (ESS)
expert system
field
field name
file management program
flat file
groupware
information
information overload
information system
key field (primary key)
knowledge management
   system
life cycle
logical data type
management information
   system (MIS)
manager

memo
normalization
numeric check
object
object-oriented database
online analytical
   processing (OLAP)
online processing
organization
photo checkout system
point-of-sale (POS) terminal
public data network (PDN)
query language
range check
record
relational database
signature capture system
strategic decision
Structured Query
   Language (SQL)
summary report
system
tactical decision
traditional organizational
   structure
transaction processing
   system (TPS)
transaction
universal product
   code (UPC)
Web-database integration
workflow automation
workgroup

| HOME | Takeaway Points | Key Terms and Concepts | Matching | Multiple Choice | Fill-In | Short Answer | Exercises/ Projects | Web Research | CHAPTER REVIEW |

MATCHING

Match each key term in the left column with the most accurate definition in the right column.

_____ 1. field

_____ 2. flat file

_____ 3. normalization

_____ 4. information system

_____ 5. data

_____ 6. primary key

_____ 7. workgroup

_____ 8. database

_____ 9. computer-supported cooperative work

_____ 10. client/server

_____ 11. data warehouse

_____ 12. bit

_____ 13. data validation

_____ 14. management information system (MIS)

_____ 15. batch processing

a. a field that is used to uniquely identify each record in a table

b. a system that processes data to produce information

c. information stored in this cannot be linked to data in other files

d. a system that's designed so that many users can access data simultaneously

e. a system in which data are gathered and processed periodically

f. a database of databases

g. a process that eliminates data redundancy

h. a computer-based system that supports the information needs of different levels of management

i. any unorganized text, graphics, sound, or video that haven't yet been processed by a computer

j. an area in a database designed to store a certain type of data

k. defines an acceptable input range for each field in a record

l. any collection of data stored in a way that enables the user to add, find, sort, group, summarize, and print the data

m. groupware applications that include e-mail, videoconferencing, and shared information databases

n. the smallest unit of data that the computer can store

o. a team of two or more people working on the same project

CHAPTER REVIEW: 1 2 3 4 5 6 7 8 9 10 11 12 13 14 15 16

CHAPTER REVIEW | Takeaway Points | Key Terms and Concepts | Matching | Multiple Choice | Fill-In | Short Answer | Exercises/ Projects | Web Research | HOME

1 2 3 4 5 6 7 8 9 10 11 12 13 14 15 16

MULTIPLE CHOICE

Circle the correct choice for each of the following.

1. This makes up a database file.
    a. Characters
    b. Fields
    c. Records
    d. Text

2. Which of the following is analogous to a record in a database?
    a. A single card in a card catalog
    b. A single phone number from the phone book
    c. A single drawer in a filing cabinet
    d. A single book on a bookshelf

3. This specifies the type of information allowed to be stored in a field.
    a. Data type
    b. Character
    c. Record
    d. Variable

4. If a ZIP code is entered in a field intended for a phone number, it violates which principle of good database design?
    a. Data independence
    b. Data redundancy
    c. Data integrity
    d. Data security

5. If a database contains the same information more than once, it is an example of what?
    a. Data independence
    b. Data security
    c. Data integrity
    d. Data redundancy

6. This software package deals with knowledge rather than information.
    a. Executive support system (ESS)
    b. Decision support system (DSS)
    c. Expert system
    d. Knowledge integrated system (KIS)

7. Which of the following people typically makes strategic decisions for an organization?
    a. Middle manager
    b. CEO
    c. Operational manager
    d. Supervisor

8. This is a data processing system that handles an organization's day-to-day accounting needs.
    a. Enterprise processing system (EPS)
    b. Transaction processing system (TPS)
    c. Batch processing system (BPS)
    d. Online analytical processing system (OLAP)

9. An object-oriented database is well suited for which type of application?
    a. General application
    b. Horizontal application
    c. Financial application
    d. Multimedia application

10. What is the latest trend in database software?
    a. Data warehousing
    b. Web-database integration
    c. Object-oriented design
    d. Stand-alone modules

COMPUTERS IN YOUR FUTURE 2004

PH it
shaping generation IT

13.21

HOME | Takeaway Points | Key Terms and Concepts | Matching | Multiple Choice | Fill-In | Short Answer | Exercises/Projects | Web Research | CHAPTER REVIEW

FILL-IN

In the blanks provided, write the correct answer for each of the following.

1. A(n) _____ is any collection of information stored in some organized way.

2. A(n) _____ check determines whether a required field has been left empty and, if so, the database program prompts the user to fill in the needed data.

3. A(n) _____ program enables users to create customized databases and to store and retrieve data from these databases.

4. In a(n) _____ database, data in several files is related through the use of a common key field.

5. Data _____ are intended to collect data in a primitive, less organized way than traditional databases.

6. _____ enables managers to explore data in an attempt to discover previously unknown patterns.

7. Smaller data warehouse projects designed for use in a single division of an organization are called _____.

8. An organization suffers from _____ when it is overwhelmed with more information than it can effectively or efficiently use.

9. A(n) _____ supports management's strategic planning function.

10. A(n) _____ saves money by automating routine, labor-intensive record keeping.

11. _____ allow managers to find information-based answers to questions that can't be answered with fixed, predefined reports.

12. _____ can greatly speed an approval process by automatically sending a document to the next person who needs to see and approve it.

13. The use of information technology to implement major changes and cost savings in an organization's structure is known as _____.

14. _____ are information technologies that capture knowledge and make it available where it's needed.

15. A(n) _____ is a professionally administered program that runs on a local area network (LAN) and is designed to respond to external requests for data.

SHORT ANSWER

1. What are the qualities of a good database?

2. What are the two major types of database programs?

3. What is a key field, and how does it work in a relational database?

4. What is the purpose of data warehousing and data mining?

5. Explain why a pyramid is an appropriate representation of the structure of a business organization. What are the management levels, and what are the responsibilities of managers at each level?

6. What are the three characteristics of a computerized information system (CIS)?

Chapter review tabs: 1 2 3 4 5 6 7 8 9 10 11 12 13 14 15 16

EXERCISES/PROJECTS

1. Preventing erroneous data from being entered into a database is extremely important. Identify and describe the five data validation procedures that should be performed when entering data. Which of these have you encountered when entering data on the Internet? Explain the circumstances and what error message or response you received.

2. Identify and briefly describe the nine characteristics of valuable information. Go to your school's main Web site to determine how many of these characteristics are implemented on their site. Identify those characteristics that you believe are not, and explain why you listed them.

3. Does your school library provide browser-based online access to its reference material databases? Can patrons access the materials from both on-campus and off-campus? In addition to standard card catalog information—like author, title, and publication date—can you access full-text versions of materials? Can anyone access these full-text materials, or is access limited to faculty, staff, and students? If access to some materials is limited, how do faculty, staff, and students identify themselves as legitimate users?

4. The administration of an academic institution also follows the organizational pyramid structure. Identify the titles and names of the senior, middle, and operational "managers" at your school. Are you familiar with any of these names? Which, if any, of these managers do you recognize on sight? Have you ever met or spoken to any of them?

5. Many schools have an Office of Instructional Advancement (or some other similar title) that includes areas such as development, finance/accounting, news services, and fund-raising. Since this is an important activity, this office is frequently headed by a vice president. What is the formal title of this office at your school? Contact this office and determine whether they use a management information system (MIS) to aid in their efforts. If they do, identify the name of the product(s) and how this software is used.

HOME | Takeaway Points | Key Terms and Concepts | Matching | Multiple Choice | Fill-In | Short Answer | Exercises/Projects | Web Research | CHAPTER REVIEW

1 2 3 4 5 6 7 8 9 10 11 12 13 14 15 16

WEB RESEARCH

1. Because of the enormous growth in the amount of information that is available, software known as intelligent software agents has been developed to help users gather and analyze information. Visit BotSpot's Web site at **http://botspot.com** to learn about this software. What is another name for intelligent software agents? Other than e-mail, data mining, and shopping, name three of the categories of agents. Describe what the following software agents do: snoop, NetSumm, and DestinationRx. Find, categorize, and describe a software agent that you would personally use.

2. Another type of assistive software application is an expert system. Take the tutorial at eXpertise2Go's Web site, **http://expertise2go.com**. What is an expert system? What are the three methods for delivering advice without the expert's presence? What are the two parts to a rule? Define forward and backward chaining. A typical rule-based expert system integrates what three components? What kinds of problems make good candidates for expert systems? In what area were some of the first expert systems developed?

3. At one time, expressing database queries was a difficult task. Users could not simply enter, "Who lives in the South?" Instead they had to frame their requests using the specific syntax (grammar) of the database they were using. With the development of SQL (Structured Query Language), they were able to use a common set of commands for a variety of different SQL-based databases. However, this still required users to learn the SQL syntax. Many Web-based databases are designed to ask users a series of questions and display the results without users having to learn how to form queries. By visiting Sprint's Web site at **http://sprint.com** and answering some questions, you are going to investigate their service areas, their plans, and their mobile phone options.

   Do you live in a Sprint PCS service area? If so, look at the various service plans. (Be sure to select the All Plans tab.) As you can see, changing the number of phones used in the Family Plans causes different rates to be displayed. Overall, which plan is the best one for you? What additional features are included with Sprint's basic service? Now let's find a phone.

   Before you decide which phone to purchase, you need to answer a few questions. What is a dual-band phone, and do you need one? What is a "Wireless Internet Ready" phone, and do you need one? Explain which phone best matches your needs.

4. In this question, you're going to further examine decision support systems (DSSs). Go to the DSSResources Web site at **http://dssresources.com** to learn more about these software applications. What is the definition of a DSS given on this Web site? Is this definition consistent with the one given in the text? Most of the DSS research centers are located at educational institutions. Which one is nearest to you? Research is not limited to just the United States; name an international DSS site and the country in which it is located. Follow one of the DSS company links and do the following:

   - List the company and its URL.
   - Name and describe its DSS product.
   - Identify whether it is designed for general business use or for a specific application.

5. You are going to use the Internet to see what additional information you can learn about online analytical processing (OLAP). When using the Internet, you have to be careful to obtain current information. Therefore, when answering the following questions, be sure the Web pages that you use were created/modified no earlier than last year. Find suitable site(s) and provide the following information:

   - List URL(s) and their creation/modification date(s).
   - Name a company that produces an OLAP.
   - Name the OLAP product and describe its purpose.
   - Identify whether it is designed for general business use or for a specific application.

Systems Analysis and Design

CHAPTER **14** OUTLINE

What You'll Learn . . .

When you have finished reading this chapter, you will be able to:

1. Explain what systems analysts do.

2. Discuss the reasons for the widespread use of the systems development life cycle (SDLC).

3. List the SDLC's five phases.

4. Describe the classic mistakes of failed information systems development projects.

5. Discuss the activities in each of the SDLC's five phases.

You may wonder what studying systems analysis has to do with computers. Well, actually, quite a bit. You see, it's in the analysis of information systems that we can create new ways of doing things. This is particularly pertinent today as we're at the very beginning of a new age in human history: the Information Age. Those who understand the fundamentals of this new age will be those who can capitalize on its characteristics, least of which is the systematic management of information. This chapter explores what's going on behind the scenes in the Information Age.

Creating a computerized information system isn't something to take lightly. The benefits are great, but so are the risks. A poorly planned information system can eat up profits, anger customers, and even cause companies to go bankrupt. Unfortunately, poor results are all too common. According to a recent study published in *PC Week*, nearly one-third of information projects are abandoned before completion because it's apparent that the project will fail. The price tag for these failures could be $80 billion or more.

Is it too much to ask that information systems be finished on time and within budget and that they perform their

intended job? Admittedly, information systems development is a difficult challenge, and it's not made any easier by the fact that every case is unique. (For example, a pizza delivery company needs a different information system than does a pharmaceutical firm or an auto maker.) In addition, users and clients may have difficulty communicating their needs clearly, leading to products that don't satisfy them. And too many times, estimates are overly optimistic, typically by as much as 20 to 30 percent. Building an information system takes longer than most people care to admit.

In the face of such chaos, it makes good sense to try to get organized. **Systems analysis** is a field of knowledge concerning information systems development. Systems analysts learn from previous development efforts and formulate strategies for improved planning, organization, control, and execution of information systems development projects. They have developed an organized procedure for planning and building information systems, called the systems development life cycle (SDLC), which is the focus of this chapter.

The Information Age is all about managing data to provide information, entertainment, and systems to support our

Figure 14.1
Systems analysts must talk to a variety of users and understand their needs. They must involve users in the project so that users feel a sense of ownership.

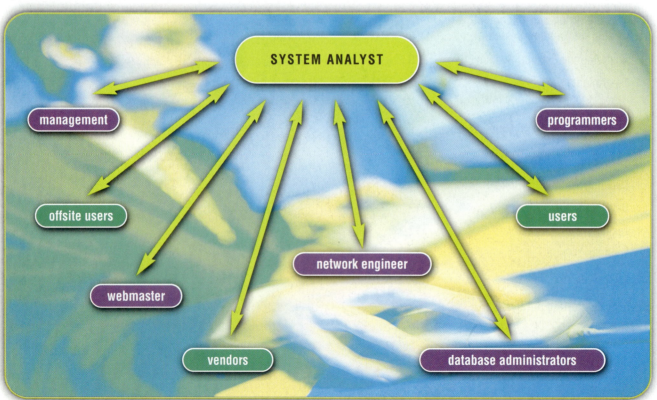

society's many activities. With that said, let's now turn our attention to the exciting field of systems analysis.

Systems Analysts: Communication Counts

Computer professionals called **systems analysts** are problem-solving professionals who work with users and management to determine an organization's information system needs (see Figure 14.1). They define the requirements needed to modify an existing system or to develop a new one. Systems analysts don't ordinarily do the development; rather, they identify and evaluate alternative solutions, make formal presentations to management, and assist in the development of the system after an option has been chosen.

Much of a systems analyst's job involves communication, including listening skills. Systems analysts must understand the organization's mission, including its strategic goals. They must talk to users and understand their needs. They must involve users in the project so that users feel some ownership of the project. They must keep in close contact with project team members so that they know how the project is doing. They must write voluminous documentation that explains, at every step, what was performed, why and how it was performed, and who did it.

The Systems Development Life Cycle: A Problem-Solving Approach

In the early years of business computing, information systems development was a disorganized, ad hoc process, frequently producing discouraging results. Systems

typically were delivered late, went over their budgets, and didn't provide the services users expected. The **systems development life cycle** (**SDLC**) approach was developed to improve the quality of information systems. By encouraging an organized approach to problem solving, the SDLC can produce better information systems, but it's no substitute for creativity and intelligence.

THE FIVE PHASES OF THE SDLC

At the core of the SDLC model is a simple idea: you shouldn't go on to the next step until you're certain that the current one has been performed properly. Figure 14.2 depicts the five phases (steps or stages) of the SDLC. Each phase is intended to address key issues and to produce **deliverables** (outcomes), which form the input for the next phase.

Note that several different versions of the systems development life cycle exist; some of these versions identify more phases than others, and some use different names for the individual phases. The five-part process described here represents what is common practice.

AVOIDING MISTAKES

Systems analysts have learned, often through bitter experience, to avoid the classic mistakes of failed projects. Built into the SDLC model are the following essentials of systems development wisdom:

- **User involvement is crucial.** Users include any person for whom the system is built, and that may include customers if, for example, you're creating a public Web site. Users are the ultimate judges of the system's usability, although they may not know how to express their needs coherently. Without user involvement, the system may not meet users' needs, and they may then resist or even sabotage the new system.

- **A problem-solving approach works best.** To create an effective system, you must identify the problem, place the problem in context, define the

Figure 14.2
The Five Phases of the Systems Development Life Cycle

IMPACTS

EMERGING TECHNOLOGIES

Telemedicine: Can Computers Save Lives?

Can computers save lives? Doctors who are leading the field of *telemedicine*—which combines computers and doctors to provide "computerized" health care—are proving that they can.

You can think of telemedicine as a long-distance house call, without the doctor being present. Imagine you live in a rural area and are visiting your local physician. After consulting with her about a health problem, she recommends that you immediately consult with a specialist, although you're miles away from one. No problem. Using telemedicine, your physician communicates with a "telephysician" specialist to treat you. The specialist doesn't have to be in the same city, state, or country as you and your doctor are. Instead, your local physician uses an interactive computer and video conferencing software to send the telephysician the information he or she needs—your health records, x-rays, CT scans, and so on. The telephysician downloads your files, looks at them, and then returns his or her diagnosis to your local physician. With the specialist's opinion, your doctor is able to offer a course of treatment.

Telemedicine is catching on (see Figure 14.3). Physicians at one of the world's leading telemedicine centers, the University of North Carolina (UNC) Medical Center, for example, often use computer network connections and sophisticated imaging technologies to extend a specialist's expertise into rural and remote areas. In one recent case, a young child living in an isolated rural community suffered a brain hemorrhage and couldn't be moved. By linking with other physicians via the Internet and videoconferencing connections, a local surgeon uploaded x-rays of the girl's brain and consulted with a UNC neurologist. The surgery was a success.

"TeleStroke" telemedicine programs are also being used throughout the United States to help stroke patients. Remote telephysician specialists can view patients' brain scans, providing care to those who don't live close to a stroke recovery center. With the TeleStroke program, patients get expert attention regardless of their location. It is hoped that stroke-related complications will diminish when more high-quality remote care is made available to stroke victims. And such applications of telemedicine have substantial trickle-down effects: with improved treatment care, fewer patients need home nursing.

Figure 14.3
Innovations in medical support systems will bring us a future that was impossible to even think of 25 years ago.

Although telemedicine sounds great, some major problems will have to be solved before its use becomes widespread. For example, state licensing programs forbid doctors to practice medicine outside the state in which they're licensed. Insurance companies may pay for teleconsulting, but not for the expenses incurred when a physician forwards your medical records, x-rays, and so on to the telephysician. And if a patient is misdiagnosed and then claims that a face-to-face meeting would have prevented the misdiagnosis, a malpractice lawsuit could result. Without regulation to address these and other issues, telemedicine will grow only slowly—and within state lines.

solution, examine alternative solutions, and choose the best one. Without this approach, the new system may not fully address the underlying shortcomings of the existing system.

- **Good project management skills are needed.** Many failed development projects are characterized by unrealistic expectations, overly optimistic schedules, and lack of solid backing from management, as well as people's inability to make decisions and stick with them, lack of control over insertion of new but unnecessary features, and interference from problem personnel. A poorly managed project may become so chaotic that cancellation is necessary.

- **Documentation is required.** The term **documentation** refers to the recording of all information pertinent to the project, which is stored in a **project notebook** (which may or may not be based on a computer system). The documentation enables everyone connected with the project to understand all the decisions that have been made. Documentation shouldn't be put off until the end of the project, at which time important information or key personnel might not be available. Without documentation, the system can't be properly supported or modified (especially after key development personnel have left).

- **Use checkpoints to make sure the project is on track.** At the end of each phase, the project must be critically and independently evaluated to make sure it's on track. An organization shouldn't be afraid to cancel the project (or repeat a phase) if results aren't satisfactory. Some of the worst development disasters occur when the project team conceals the fact that the system couldn't possibly work.

- **Design for growth and change.** If no room is left on a crucial data input screen, what happens when the firm introduces new products with more features? The system should be designed so that it won't break down

or require a major redesign in the event of change (including unanticipated increases in usage). Failure to anticipate change and growth could make the entire system useless in short order.

Avoiding mistakes doesn't guarantee success. On the other hand, making mistakes may very well guarantee failure!

THE WATERFALL MODEL

Although the systems development life cycle calls for a step-by-step process, it's not always wise to keep going if work in a later stage turns up problems with the work performed in an earlier one. For example, in the systems analysis phase, the team may discover that the problem hasn't been formulated correctly. The **waterfall model** builds correction pathways into the model that enable a return to a previous phase (see Figure 14.4). It's the most widely used way to implement the systems development life cycle.

Let's now look at phase 1 of the SDLC.

Phase 1: Identifying the Problem and Opportunities

In phase 1 of the SDLC, an organization recognizes the need for an information system, defines the problem, identifies opportunities for change, and assesses the project's feasibility. The result is a project proposal submitted to senior management. If this phase is performed well, it assures that the right information system will be built, and, just as important, it assures that the wrong system won't be built.

RECOGNIZING THE NEED FOR THE SYSTEM

New information systems (or modified ones) result from a recognition of deficiencies in performance (such as slow response

Figure 14.4
The waterfall model builds into the model correction pathways that enable a return to a previous phase. It's the most widely used implementation of the systems development life cycle.

time), information quality (out-of-date information, inaccuracy), economics (high operating costs), security (vulnerability to break-ins), efficiency (wasting of time, generation of too much paper), or service (difficulty of use, forcing people to do things in an awkward way). Even if the current system doesn't have obvious deficiencies, it might still be judged worthwhile to replace it if a redesigned system could generate new business opportunities.

To get the project going, someone makes a formal request to the organization's information technology steering committee, which generally includes representatives from senior management, information systems personnel, users, and middle managers. The steering committee reviews requests and decides which ones to address.

If a project is approved, the steering committee appoints a project team. Goals for the first phase, planning, include determining the nature of the problem, examining alternative solutions, studying the project's feasibility, and creating a proposal for the overall project.

DEFINING THE PROBLEM

To solve a problem, you must first understand it. But that's not always as easy as it might seem. Problems can be masked by symptoms. A *symptom* is an unacceptable or undesirable result, whereas a *problem* is the underlying cause of the symptom. For example, people might complain about a symptom, such as the time it takes to get a response from the computer when entering a transaction. Users may demand more powerful computers. But the slow response time is just a symptom. If the problem lies in the slow speed of network transmission, it's a waste of money to buy faster computers!

Determining the exact problem is often a difficult task. Ideally, the problem definition stage identifies the features that need to be added to the information system to make it acceptable to users. Although users must be involved in defining the problem, they're not accustomed to looking at information systems in a structured, unbiased way. The systems analyst talks to as many users as possible, and slowly a picture emerges of what these people do, when they do it, how they do it, and why they do it (see Figure 14.5). The analyst then derives from these facts a recommendation for new system features (if an existing system will be modified) or for a new system built from scratch.

IDENTIFYING OPPORTUNITIES

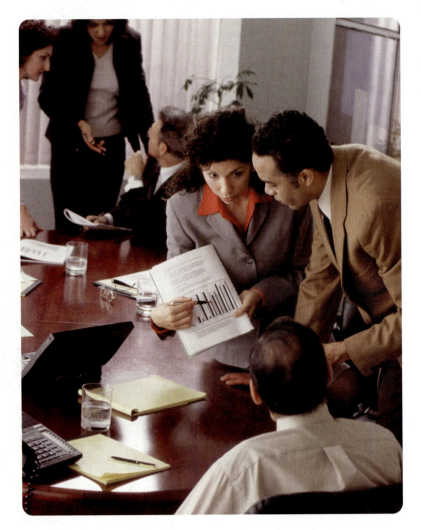

Figure 14.5
To determine the exact problem, the systems analyst must talk to as many users as possible to discover what they do, when they do it, how they do it, and why. The analyst then recommends new system features or an entirely new system.

After the problem has been identified and the system requirements have been specified, the project team looks at a range of possible solutions, including internally developed systems, off-the-shelf software, and externally contracted solutions (called outsourcing). If the project team believes that a solution exists, the project proceeds.

DEVELOPING A PLAN

When an appropriate solution has been identified, the project leader formulates a **project plan**. The plan identifies the project's goal and scope and specifies all the activities that must be completed for the project to succeed. For each activity, the plan specifies the estimated time that the project will require, as well as the estimated costs. The plan also identifies activities that must be completed before new ones can begin and indicates which activities can occur side-by-side. Project plans are often graphically summarized by means of a **Gantt chart**, a type of bar chart that shows how the activities are performed over time. Project management software (such as Microsoft Project) provides an excellent means of developing and modifying project plans (see Figure 14.6).

DETERMINING FEASIBILITY

A feasible project can be completed successfully. Feasibility has three dimensions: technical, operational, and economic.

A project that's **technically feasible** can be accomplished with existing, proven technology. For example, consider a project that requires speech recognition. Although computers are getting much better at recognizing and transcribing human speech, they do make errors. If the error rate is unacceptable, the project isn't feasible until speech recognition technology is improved.

A project that's **operationally feasible** can be accomplished with the organization's available resources. If some of the project's goals include changes beyond the organization's control (such as regulations in a foreign country), the project isn't operationally feasible.

The question of whether the project is **economically feasible** is usually answered by a **cost/benefit analysis**. The costs are the *expected* costs to develop and run the new system. The purpose of cost estimates is to help clarify what the system is going to do.

The benefits include both tangible savings and intangible benefits. **Tangible savings** include labor costs, services, and materials that are needed with the current system but can be eliminated if the new system is installed. It's common to sell a new system to a company's management based on **intangible benefits**. These benefits may include increased sales due to improved customer services or to managers having better information on which to base decisions. Bank managers, for example, may decide to install an automated teller machine (ATM) because they believe that many people won't deal with a bank that doesn't have one. Avoiding the loss of sales that would occur as a result of not installing the new system is an intangible benefit.

In many companies, managers request a study of the proposed system's **return on investment** (**ROI**). The money invested in the system should produce a return that is greater than alternative investments, such as putting the money in the bank.

PREPARING THE PROJECT PROPOSAL

At the conclusion of phase 1, the project leader writes a project proposal that

id	task name	duration	jan	feb	mar	apr	may	jun	jul	aug
1	planning	3w	1/26 ▬ 2/13							
2	analysis	10w		2/9 ▬▬▬▬▬ 4/17						
3	design	11w			3/23 ▬▬▬▬▬ 6/5					
4	implementation	4w						6/5 ▬▬ 7/3		

Figure 14.6
A Gantt chart is a graphical summary of project plans that indicates activities performed over a period of time.

CURRENTS

NATIONAL SECURITY

The U.S. Air Traffic Control System: Is It Really Safe to Fly?

Throughout the world, many large-scale organizations are facing a crisis brought on by **legacy systems**, information systems based on older-generation computers that can't handle today's demands. Replacing these systems isn't easy. For example, they may rely on programs written in computer languages that are no longer actively used. And all too often, the systems are so complex that the cost of upgrading them is beyond the organization's means.

One of the best examples of an overloaded, obsolete information system is the U.S. air traffic control (ATC) system. The FAA runs the ATC system and hires and trains air traffic controllers. Given the ATC's importance, it's nothing short of amazing, say the FAA's critics, that in many areas the system is still using 30-year-old computers that break down with alarming frequency. Some of the FAA's computers are so old that they can be found in only one other place: computer museums.

So *is* it safe to fly? Although many Americans still feel uneasy about flying post–September 11, 2001, these fears have nothing to do with air traffic control systems. When failures in these systems occur, there is usually no immediate threat to public safety because backup systems step in to help controllers track aircraft locations. However, these backup systems are often slow and cumbersome to use, and controllers must increase spacing between flights to ensure safety. The result is flight delays. The FAA concedes that equipment failures cause air traffic slowdowns that cost airlines $5 billion annually (see Figure 14.7).

Why has the FAA been so slow to update these critical systems? It's easy to point the finger of blame at plodding management and unresponsive bureaucrats. The biggest problem, however, lies in the enormous challenges of dealing with outmoded legacy systems, antiquated information systems that can't keep up with increased demand. Just because these systems are old doesn't mean they're simple. The FAA's 250 computer systems run 23 million lines of code written in 50 different computer languages. What's worse, these systems and languages are so out-of-date that it's increasingly difficult to find qualified technicians and programmers who can help in the migration to modernized equipment.

Figure 14.7
The FAA concedes that the failures of outdated computer equipment result in air traffic delays that cost airlines $5 billion each year.

Faced with a complex, safety-critical legacy system that's deteriorating rapidly, what should management do? One option is to design a completely new system, with new software and new computers. But shockingly few large-scale software projects succeed. Studies show that at least one-fourth of all large-scale software development projects are so riddled with bugs that they're eventually abandoned; the successful ones overshoot their schedules by 50 percent. Of these, as many as three-quarters are operating failures that don't fully function as they were originally intended.

Currently, FAA officials are in the process of implementing a modernization program that makes use of old software running on new machines and, therefore, avoids the delays and cost overruns typically associated with new, massive software development programs.

introduces the nature of the existing system's problem, explains the proposed solution and its benefits, details the proposed project plan, and concludes with a recommendation. In response, management decides whether to continue the project.

Phase 2: Analyzing and Documenting the Existing Information System

In phase 2 of the SDLC, the systems analyst or the systems development team determines precisely what the new system should accomplish. Here, the emphasis is placed on *what* the system should do, not *how*. (That comes later.) This phase includes two steps: analyzing the existing system and determining the needs of the new system.

ANALYZING THE EXISTING SYSTEM

A study of the existing system (whether computerized or manual) helps determine which activities currently being performed should be continued in the new system. This step can be simple if the current system is well documented. Unfortunately, most systems are not well documented, and that's especially true of updates to an original system. A major part of the analysis of the existing system, then, is to document it. If the original system is computerized, the current hardware needs to be examined to see whether it's adequate to do the job.

An unexpected but valuable benefit of the systems analysis phase is that it often points out problems that weren't fully identified in phase 1. This analysis may be the first time a group of people has sat down in the same room and talked about the actual process. The discussion can result in new insights, and problems that were not part of the preliminary investigation can be solved.

DETERMINING THE NEW SYSTEM'S REQUIREMENTS

After the existing system has been exhaustively documented, the new system's requirements are precisely stated. The requirements state the innovations that need to occur for the system to be acceptable to users. Here again, user involvement is crucial. Systems analysts obtain information about system requirements through interviews, surveys, and observations of the system's current uses.

Phase 3: Designing the System

In contrast to the previous phase, phase 3 of the SDLC, the system design phase, is concerned with *how* the new information system will work. This phase isn't concerned with the nitty-gritty details of how the software will be coded. Instead, this phase's deliverable is a **logical design** that provides an overall picture of how the new system will work. Here, the project team uses the same tools developed to describe the existing system, such as entity relationship diagrams, data flow diagrams, and data dictionaries. The team begins by specifying how the new system's output will look; this is specified first because the output drives the rest of the design.

During this phase, it's important that analysts think about the system's logical requirements and don't start thinking about what can be accomplished (and what can't) with existing information systems and software. Such thinking might prevent them from realizing that they may need to create an entirely new type of system, one that's never been developed before. This is the reason phase 3 is clearly separated from phase 4, in which attention turns to the system's physical implementation. These two phases must be rigorously kept separate.

To describe the new information system, analysts can use **structural analysis and design tools**. These methods of graphical analysis help convey the analysts' findings to managers, programmers, and users alike. An **entity relationship diagram (ERD)** shows all the entities (organizations, departments, users, programs, and data) that play roles in the system (see Figure 14.8). A **data flow diagram** shows how data moves through the existing system using a set of graphical symbols (see Figure 14.9). Also specified are the details of how this data is processed.

Team members create a **project dictionary**, which explains all the terminology relevant to the project; they also develop a **data dictionary**, which precisely defines the type of data that is inputted in the system. The goal of this phase of the project is to specify in exact terms what data flows into the system, where it goes, how it's processed, who uses it, how it's stored, what data-entry forms are involved, and what procedures people follow.

Two recent approaches, prototyping and computer-aided software engineering (CASE), are helping to improve the design phase. In **prototyping**, also called **joint application development (JAD)**, a

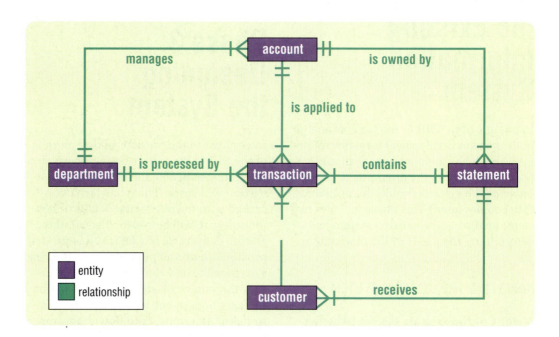

Figure 14.8
An entity relationship diagram depicts all the entities that play roles in the system.

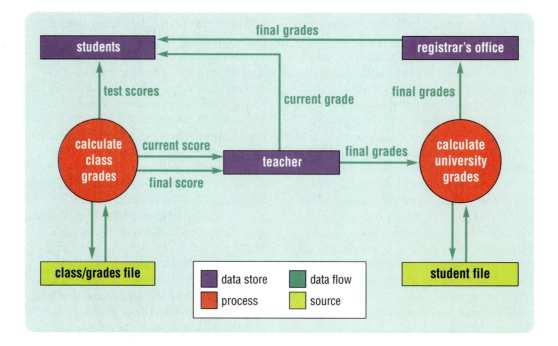

Figure 14.9
A data flow diagram shows how data moves through the existing system.

small-scale mock-up, or prototype, of the system is developed and shown to users (see Figure 14.10). The prototype is developed at an early stage and isn't intended to be fully functional. It provides just enough functionality so that users can give feedback. The advantage of prototyping lies in the fact that users don't have to imagine what the system specifications mean in terms of a working system. They can experience the system and thus find problems or enhancements that they may not have considered otherwise.

The second tool, called **computer-aided software engineering** (**CASE**), can help automate the often tedious task of documenting entity relationships and data flows in a complex new system. Most CASE tools include project management, data dictionaries, documentation support, and graphical output; some even generate prototype code automatically (see Figure 14.11). CASE software, however, is expensive, requires extensive training, and is difficult to use.

Phase 4: Implementing the System

In phase 4 of the SDLC, the system implementation phase, the project team and management decide whether to create the physical system using internal expertise or to purchase it from outside vendors. Hardware must be purchased and installed, and programs must be written. The system must be exhaustively tested, and users must be trained. When the team is confident that the new system is ready for use, the conversion to the new system takes place.

DECIDING WHETHER TO BUILD OR BUY

After the new system's requirements and logical design have been specified, the project team faces the **build-or-buy decision**: should the new system be developed in-house or purchased from an outside vendor? If the decision is made to outsource the project, the project team sends out a

request for quotation (**RFQ**) or a **request for proposal** (**RFP**). An RFQ is used if the specific components have been identified. An RFP is used if the project team wants a computer vendor or a **value-added reseller** (**VAR**) to select the system components. VARs are independent companies that combine and install equipment and software from several sources.

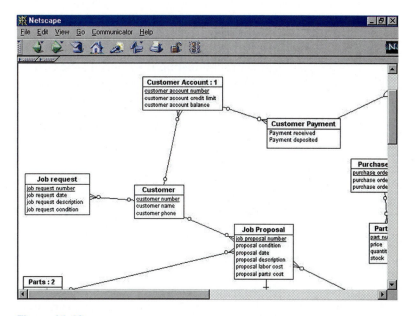

Figure 14.10

Through prototyping, users don't have to imagine what the system specifications mean in terms of a working system. Instead, they can experience the system and find problems with it.

Figure 14.11

PowerBuilder is a CASE tool that delivers a complete 4GL (fourth-generation language) environment for building traditional client/server and multitier distributed applications.

DEVELOPING THE SOFTWARE

To develop the software required for the new system, programmers use the **program development life cycle (PDLC)**. Like the systems development life cycle, the PDLC is a step-by-step procedure that helps programmers develop good software. We'll look at the PDLC in more detail in Chapter 15.

TESTING

Thorough testing is essential. The two basic types of testing are application testing and acceptance testing. In **application testing**, the programs are tested individually and then tested together. In **acceptance testing**, users evaluate the system to see whether it meets their needs and functions correctly. It's essential that errors or problems be detected before the system is released for use in the organization.

TRAINING

A computerized information system includes not only computer hardware and software, but also knowledgeable users and procedures. A successful conclusion to the project requires training users to use the new system effectively. The best training methods involve sitting users down with the new system in one-on-one training sessions. Users will also need manuals that include tutorials as well as reference information. Increasingly popular is **computer-based training (CBT)**, a form of computer-based education that uses multimedia, animation, and programmed learning to teach new skills. CBT has an added advantage: it is not usually time or place dependent. This means that the training is available whenever an employee has the time to access a computer terminal or workstation.

CONVERTING SYSTEMS

After the new system has been tested, conversion to the new system occurs. System conversion can be performed in any of the following ways:

- A **parallel conversion** involves running both systems for a while to check that the new system produces answers at least as good as those of the old system. This type of conversion is the safest; the old system can carry the load until any problems with the new system are cleared up. This conversion is also the most expensive, however, because the work is duplicated.

- In a **pilot conversion**, one part of the organization converts to the new system while the rest of the organization continues to run the old system. When the pilot group is satisfied with the new system, the rest of the organization can start using it.

- A **phased conversion** occurs when the new system is implemented in different time periods, one part at a time. After one part of the new system is running, another piece is implemented.

- A **direct conversion**, sometimes called a **crash conversion**, requires stopping the old system and then starting the new system. A direct conversion is the most risky but may be necessary in some situations.

Phase 5: Supporting the System

In the final phase of the SDLC, the new system receives ongoing evaluation to ensure that it has met its intended needs and works correctly. A **post-implementation system review** determines whether the system has met its goals. After conversion, widespread use may reveal errors that were not detected during testing; these must be corrected. In addition, changes will be needed as the business environment changes. For example, changes may be needed in data entry forms to deal with an expanded product line. In time, the system may be found to be so deficient that a new round of systems development must take place—and the systems development life cycle begins anew.

HOME | Takeaway Points | Key Terms and Concepts | Matching | Multiple Choice | Fill-In | Short Answer | Exercises/ Projects | Web Research | CHAPTER REVIEW

TAKEAWAY POINTS

- We have entered the Information Age. Those who understand the fundamentals of information management will be poised to exploit new opportunities.

- Systems analysts help determine an organization's information system needs by working closely with both users and management.

- Systems analysts can avoid mistakes by involving users, using a problem-solving approach, applying project management skills, keeping thorough documentation, using checkpoints to make sure the project is on track, and designing the system so there is room for growth and change.

- The systems development life cycle (SDLC) was developed to impose order on earlier, haphazard development processes. It breaks information systems development down into discrete stages, each of which must be successfully completed before the project moves on to the next phase.

- The SDLC's five phases are identifying problems and opportunities, analyzing and documenting existing systems, designing the system, implementing the system, and supporting the system.

- In phase 1 of the SDLC, the organization recognizes the need for an information system, defines the problem, identifies opportunities for change, and assesses the project's feasibility.

- In phase 2 of the SDLC, the systems analyst determines what the new system should accomplish by analyzing the existing system and determining the needs of the new system.

- In phase 3 of the SDLC, the systems analyst determines how the new system will work.

- In phase 4 of the SDLC, the management team decides whether to build or buy a new system, develops the software, tests the system, and trains users.

- In phase 5 of the SDLC, the new system receives ongoing evaluation to ensure that it has met the organization's needs and works properly.

- Each phase of the SDLC provides a deliverable, which serves as the input to the next phase. These deliverables are a project proposal, a graphical analysis of the current information system, a graphical and detailed analysis of the new information system, a finished and tested product, and a post-implementation review.

 1
 2
 3
 4
 5
 6
 7
 8
 9
 10
 11
 12
 13
 14
 15
16

CHAPTER REVIEW | Takeaway Points | Key Terms and Concepts | Matching | Multiple Choice | Fill-In | Short Answer | Exercises/Projects | Web Research | HOME

KEY TERMS AND CONCEPTS

1 2 3 4 5 6 7 8 9 10 11 12 13 14 15 16

acceptance testing
application testing
build-or-buy decision
computer-aided software
    engineering (CASE)
computer-based training (CBT)
cost/benefit analysis
crash conversion
data dictionary
data flow diagram
deliverable
direct conversion
documentation
economically feasible
entity relationship
    diagram (ERD)

Gantt chart
intangible benefit
joint application
    development (JAD)
legacy system
logical design
operationally feasible
outsourcing
parallel conversion
phased conversion
pilot conversion
post-implementation system
    review
program development life
    cycle (PDLC)
project dictionary

project notebook
project plan
prototyping
request for proposal (RFP)
request for quotation (RFQ)
return on investment (ROI)
structural analysis
    and design tools
systems analyst
systems analysis
systems development
    life cycle (SDLC)
tangible savings
technically feasible
value-added reseller (VAR)
waterfall model

COMPUTERS IN YOUR FUTURE 2004

14.15

HOME | Takeaway Points | Key Terms and Concepts | **Matching** | Multiple Choice | Fill-In | Short Answer | Exercises/Projects | Web Research

MATCHING

Match each key term in the left column with the most accurate definition in the right column.

_____ 1. systems analysis

_____ 2. systems development life cycle

_____ 3. waterfall model

_____ 4. post-implementation system review

_____ 5. return on investment (ROI)

_____ 6. data flow diagram

_____ 7. Gantt chart

_____ 8. data dictionary

_____ 9. pilot conversion

_____ 10. direct conversion

_____ 11. application testing

_____ 12. acceptance testing

_____ 13. project dictionary

_____ 14. computer-based training

_____ 15. operationally feasible

a. describes how money invested in the system should produce a return greater than alternative investments

b. shows how data moves through an existing system

c. requires stopping the old system and starting the new system

d. education that uses multimedia, animation, and programmed learning to teach new skills

e. the field of knowledge concerning information systems development

f. describes a project that can be accomplished with the organization's available resources

g. precisely defines the type of data that is inputted in the system

h. an approach used to improve the quality of information systems

i. explains all terminology relevant to the project

j. builds correction pathways into the model that enable a return to the previous phase

k. time-based activity bar graph

l. an evaluation in which users see if the system meets their needs and functions correctly

m. testing in which programs are tested individually and then tested together

n. determines whether the new system has met its goals

o. one part of an organization converts to the new system while the rest of the organization continues to run the old system

CHAPTER REVIEW

1 2 3 4 5 6 7 8 9 10 11 12 13 **14** 15 16

CHAPTER REVIEW | Takeaway Points | Key Terms and Concepts | Matching | Multiple Choice | Fill-In | Short Answer | Exercises/ Projects | Web Research | HOME

1 2 3 4 5 6 7 8 9 10 11 12 13 **14** 15 16

MULTIPLE CHOICE

Circle the correct choice for each of the following.

1. SDLC is an acronym for this.
   a. Secondary dynamic life cycle
   b. Simple data linear compression
   c. Systems development life cycle
   d. Synchronous data line current

2. Prototyping is also known as which of the following?
   a. Phased conversion
   b. Outsourcing
   c. Joint application development (JAD)
   d. System design

3. Recognition of which of the following is not essential to sound systems development?
   a. Hiring value-added resellers
   b. Good project management skills
   c. Documentation
   d. User involvement

4. Which of the following does not need to be part of a project plan?
   a. Résumés of key personnel
   b. Goal
   c. Scope
   d. Necessary activities

5. What is a VAR?
   a. An abbreviation for the variables used in systems analysis
   b. An acronym for Value Added Resources
   c. A graphical method for showing projected implementation time lines
   d. An independent company that combines and installs equipment and software from several sources

6. Which of the following tools is not a structural analysis and design tool?
   a. Entity relationship diagram
   b. Gantt chart
   c. Data flow diagram
   d. Project dictionary

7. What describes a project that can be accomplished with the organization's available resources?
   a. Technically feasible
   b. Operationally feasible
   c. Economically feasible
   d. Resource feasible

8. CASE is an acronym for which of the following?
   a. Computer-assisted system engineering
   b. Community action for system engineering
   c. Computer and system enterprises
   d. Computer-aided software engineering

9. System training is a part of which development phase?
   a. Phase 1
   b. Phase 2
   c. Phase 3
   d. Phase 4

10. Which type of system conversion involves running two systems simultaneously to ensure that the new system produces output similar to or better than the old system?
    a. Direct conversion
    b. Parallel conversion
    c. Pilot conversion
    d. Phased conversion

COMPUTERS IN YOUR FUTURE 2004

14.17

HOME | Takeaway Points | Key Terms and Concepts | Matching | Multiple Choice | Fill-In | Short Answer | Exercises/ Projects | Web Research | CHAPTER REVIEW

FILL-IN

In the blanks provided, write the correct answer for each of the following.

1. _____ is a field of knowledge concerning information systems development.

2. _____ is the use of externally contracted solutions.

3. The _____ builds into the SDLC process correction pathways that enable a return to a previous phase.

4. Contracting for goods and services external to an organization is called _____.

5. Project plans are often graphically summarized by means of a(n) _____.

6. A(n) _____ diagram shows all the entities that play roles in the system.

7. A(n) _____ is used to explain all the terminology relevant to a project.

8. Another name for joint application development (JAD) is _____.

9. A(n) _____ determines whether it is economically feasible to undertake a project.

10. A(n) _____ conversion occurs when the new system is implemented in different time periods, one part at a time.

11. The _____ identifies the project's goal and scope, and specifies all the activities that must be completed for the project to succeed.

12. A project that is _____ can be accomplished with existing, proven technology.

13. _____ include labor costs, services, and materials that are needed with the current system but can be eliminated if the new system is installed.

14. _____, or outcomes, form the input for the next phase in the SDLC.

15. Whether the new system will be developed in-house or purchased from an outside vendor is call the _____.

SHORT ANSWER

1. What are the five phases of the SDLC?

2. Why is it important to document the existing system, regardless of whether it's computerized?

3. What are the advantages of prototyping at an early stage in the development of a system?

4. What are the advantages and drawbacks to using a CASE system?

5. Identify the seven essentials of systems development. Explain which one you feel is most important.

1 2 3 4 5 6 7 8 9 10 11 12 13 14 15 16

Go to **www.prenhall.com/ciyf2004** to review this chapter, answer the questions, and complete the exercises and Web research questions.

CHAPTER REVIEW

Takeaway Points | Key Terms and Concepts | Matching | Multiple Choice | Fill-In | Short Answer | Exercises/ Projects | Web Research | HOME

1 2 3 4 5 6 7 8 9 10 11 12 13 **14** 15 16

EXERCISES/PROJECTS

1. What are the four types of system conversions? Which is the most expensive, and which is the most risky? If your school were going to change its student accounts, registration, and financial aid systems, which method of conversion would you want it to use? Explain why. Visit a campus office that uses one of these systems, and find out when and how the current system was implemented. Did the office use the implementation method that you preferred?

2. Does your school have a computer studies department? Typically these departments are identified as computer science (CS), computer information systems (CIS), or management information systems (MIS). If it does, what is the actual title of the department? Look at a school catalog to see if the department offers any systems analysis courses. What, if any, are the prerequisites for the systems analysis courses? Find the name of an instructor, and contact him or her to find and identify what software tools are used in the course.

3. Individuals who do systems analysis and design are usually called systems analysts. Check the classified section of a Sunday edition of a local large-city newspaper to see if there are job openings for systems analysts. List the job qualifications, such as academic degree, required skills, work experience, and so on. What is the salary range for systems analysts? Are these positions with local or out-of-town companies? Are you interested in becoming a systems analyst?

4. Describe the current process at your school's library for finding, reading, and checking out a book or periodical. Can this system be improved? What improvements would you suggest? What would be the tangible savings and intangible benefits of implementing your system changes? Congratulations! You're using some systems analysis and design methods!

5. Suppose a company will decide after a systems analysis whether to purchase software or have programmers write software for it. What are the advantages and disadvantages of each approach?

HOME | Takeaway Points | Key Terms and Concepts | Matching | Multiple Choice | Fill-In | Short Answer | Exercises/ Projects | Web Research | **CHAPTER REVIEW**

WEB RESEARCH

1 2 3 4 5 6 7 8 9 10 11 12 13 **14** 15 16

1. In this exercise, you're going to examine a large-scale system upgrade. Buffalo State College is in the final stages of implementing a comprehensive upgrade to its student information services. This includes enhancements and integration of services such as admissions, registration, financial aid, and student accounts. Visit the college's Web site at **www.buffalostate.edu** to answer the following questions. What does the acronym SABRE mean? What is the timeline for implementation of the SABRE project? Much of the design and development for SABRE is being outsourced to what company? Which method of conversion is being used to change from the old system to the new system? During the analysis phase of the SDLC, systems analysts obtain information about system requirements through interviews, surveys, and observations of the system's current uses. Several meetings were held with students, and 21 "Wouldn't it be nice if" registration features were voiced. If you were a student at the college, which five features would you consider the most important? Which of the 21 features are implemented on your school's registration system?

2. One of the CASE tools discussed in the textbook is PowerBuilder software. Visit the PowerBuilder Web site at **www.sybase.com/ home**. What company created this tool, and what is the current version of PowerBuilder? PowerBuilder is a tool for developing applications in what environments? As for many software applications, a trial version of PowerBuilder is available. After how many days does the trial version expire? Identify a city, a state, a U.S. government organization, and a college or university that has used PowerBuilder. As discussed in the text, CASE tools are expensive, require extensive training, and are difficult to use. What are the upgrade and purchase prices for this development tool? PowerBuilder training sessions are conducted nationwide. In days, what are the shortest training sessions and the longest? Name two non-U.S. cities in which PowerBuilder training is offered.

3. One of the tools described in this chapter is the waterfall model of development. Some computer professionals believe that the waterfall model is inadequate. You can learn about alternatives to the waterfall model in several articles published in the online version of the *Software Development Magazine* at **www.sdmagazine.com**. Use the site's search engine to find articles on the "waterfall model." Name one or more alternatives to the waterfall model, and identify the one that is the most supported in the articles. Describe, in your own terms, your choice of at least one alternative method to the waterfall model.

4. You read in the text that a Gantt chart is a type of bar chart that shows how activities are performed over time. Use the Internet as an information resource, and locate three software applications that create Gantt charts. Identify the manufacturer, the specific product name, and the cost of each application. Identify the products that offer free trial versions and the length of the trial periods. Based on the product descriptions, do you think you could learn how to use one of these applications? Explain why or why not.

5. What are the five phases of the software development life cycle that are listed in the text? What questions are asked during each phase? As mentioned in the text, there are several different versions of the SDLC. Some versions identify more phases than others and use different names for individual phases. Use the Internet to find three other definitions for the SDLC. For each, identify the URL, the number of phases, and the title of each phase. Explain why you agree or disagree with the author's statement that the five-part SDLC described in the text represents the common practice.

next
salesperson
name
sales

get first

print salesperson
commission

get next
salesperson
name, sales

print total
commission

end of
data

print total
commission

A

Programming Languages and Program Development

CHAPTER **15**

What You'll Learn . . .

When you have finished reading this chapter, you will be able to:

1. Explain what a programming language is.

2. Contrast machine language and assembly language.

3. Discuss the benefits of a high-level programming language.

4. List the measures taken to improve third-generation languages.

5. Identify the shortcomings of early languages and explain how object-oriented languages attempt to remedy these shortcomings.

6. List several popular programming languages and explain their advantages and disadvantages.

7. List the six phases of the program development life cycle (PDLC) and explain why the PDLC is needed.

8. Explain why top-down programming makes programs easier to debug and maintain.

9. List the three basic types of control structures.

10. Differentiate between syntax errors and logic errors in programs.

Where does software come from? It's an old dream to get computers to write software automatically, but this dream hasn't come true (yet). Computer software comes from the efforts of computer programmers, who work individually or in groups. They use programming languages to do their job.

What's a programming language? It's not a natural language, like the ones people speak. Rather, it's an artificial language, one that's deliberately created to tell the computer what to do. Typically, a programming language consists of a vocabulary and a set of rules (called **syntax**) that the programmer must learn. The vocabulary and rules are used to write a program, which in most cases must be translated before a computer can run it.

What's the best programming language? If you ask this question of 10 computer people, chances are you'll get five different answers. The truth is that there isn't any one language that's best for all programming purposes. Every language has its advantages and disadvantages. The question is, which language is the right one for the job?

In this chapter, you'll learn how to make sense of the world of programming languages. You'll learn how these languages developed, and you'll take a look at today's hottest languages. You'll also learn how programs are developed by means of the **program development life cycle** (**PDLC**), an organized method of software development that bears many similarities to the systems development life cycle (SDLC) discussed in Chapter 14. The PDLC is part of the SDLC's implementation phase.

If you don't plan to learn programming, this chapter will help you understand what all the debate is about and will help you play a more informed role in the companies for which you work. And should you decide to give programming a try, you'll get the background you need to select a good language to learn.

First-Generation Languages: 0s and 1s

The earliest computers didn't have a programming language, if the term is taken to suggest a vocabulary that makes programming easy for humans. Computers had to be programmed in the computer's language, also known as machine language.

Machine language consists of binary numbers—0s and 1s—that directly correspond to the computer's electrical states. While tedious for humans to work with, machine language is the only programming that the computer can understand directly, without translation. The program must be written in accordance with the special characteristics of a given processor. Each type or family of processor requires its own machine language. For this reason, machine language is said to be **machine-dependent** (or **hardware-dependent**).

In the computer's first generation, programmers had to use machine language because no other option was available. Programmers had to know a great deal about the computer's design and how it functioned. As a result, programs were few in number and lacked complexity.

Although only a few people program directly in machine languages today, they're still in use. More recent programming languages give programmers easier ways to write programs, but the code they write must still be translated into machine language to execute on a given processor.

Second-Generation Languages: Using Mnemonics

The first programming language to break programmers' dependence on machine language was **assembly language**. Assembly language closely resembles machine language in that it's machine-dependent and closely tied to what goes on inside the computer. For this reason, it's called a **low-level language** (one that's not far removed from machine language in terms of its level of abstraction).

To program in assembly language, programmers still need to know exactly how the computer works. However, assembly language doesn't force programmers to program in binary. Instead, it enables programmers to use brief abbreviations for program instructions, as well as familiar, base-10 (decimal) numbers. The abbreviations are called **mnemonics** (pronounced "nih-MON-icks"). For example, the mnemonic COMPARE A, B tells the processor to compare the data stored in memory locations A and B.

Before an assembly language program can be run on a computer, it must be translated into machine language. As it is written, the program is a text file called **source code**. The source code is translated into machine language by an **assembler**.

Assembly language is still used sometimes, especially when it's important to make a short program that runs as fast as possible. A good assembly language programmer knows how to write a program for fast execution on a given processor.

Third-Generation Languages: Programming Comes of Age

Due to the difficulty of using machine and assembly language, **third-generation languages** were developed. Although these languages are still **procedural languages** in that they tell the computer what to do and how to do it, they are also high-level. **High-level languages** eliminate the need for programmers to understand the intimate details of how the computer processes data. They enable programmers to create programs at a high level of abstraction compared with machine and assembly language. For example, the programmer can write an instruction using familiar English words

such as PRINT or DISPLAY. Each such instruction sums up many lines of assembly or machine code. Third-generation languages are much easier to read, write, and maintain than assembly language.

COMPILERS AND INTERPRETERS

Writing in a third-generation language, programmers create source code, just as they do when they write in assembly language. To be used on a specific type of computer system, this source code must be translated using a compiler or an interpreter (see Figure 15.1).

A **compiler** is a translation program that translates all the source code into **object code**, a file that contains instructions in (or close to) a specific computer's machine language. With some compilers, it's necessary to use a program called a **linker** or **assembler** to transform the object code into an **executable program** (a program that runs on a certain type of computer). When the compiler translates the code, it checks the code for errors. If any errors are found, the program identifies the error's location and prints a **program listing** (a printout of the source code) that highlights the location and likely cause of the error.

An **interpreter** doesn't produce object code. Instead, it translates one line of the source code at a time and executes the translated instruction. Although interpreters run programs more slowly than programs compiled into object code, they're helpful tools for learning and **debugging** (ridding a program of errors, called **bugs**). As the program executes line-by-line, the programmer can see exactly what each line does.

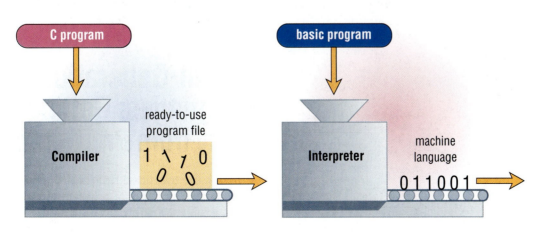

Figure 15.1
A Compiler and an Interpreter

For most programming languages, a programmer can use both an interpreter and a compiler. The interpreter comes in handy during program development. When the program is finished, it's compiled for efficient use.

SPAGHETTI CODE AND THE GREAT SOFTWARE CRISIS

Although early third-generation languages such as Fortran and COBOL represented a major improvement over assembly and machine languages, they introduced a problem. To enable programs to branch to new locations (depending on whether a condition was met), early third-generation languages used GOTO statements. This wasn't a problem for simple, short programs, but the advances of third-generation languages enabled programmers to tackle more ambitious projects. In a lengthy program, the use of many GOTO statements resulted in **spaghetti code**, which was code that was difficult to follow, and, in consequence, the programs were prone to error (see Figure 15.2).

The attempt to create larger and more complex programs led to the **software crisis** of the 1960s. Programs were not ready on time, exceeded their budgets, contained too many errors, and didn't satisfy customers. A study during the mid-1960s found that COBOL programmers were able, on average, to produce only 10 error-free lines of code per day of work.

STRUCTURED PROGRAMMING LANGUAGES

One response to spaghetti code problems focused on improving the management of software development. Another response focused on improving the languages themselves. The earliest (late 1960s) product of such efforts was the concept of **structured programming** and languages that reflected structured programming concepts.

In structured programming, GOTO statements are forbidden, and programmers are required to construct a program using logical elements called **control structures**. For example, program branching is handled by an IF-THEN-ELSE control structure (called a **selection control structure**), rather than a GOTO statement. These elements are grouped in a block with an END statement, which results in more readable code that's much easier to debug. Examples of structured languages include Algol and Pascal.

MODULAR PROGRAMMING LANGUAGES

By the 1970s, it was clear that structured programming languages, although better than their predecessors, weren't able to solve the problems encountered in the even larger development projects underway at that time. This led to the development of the **modular programming** concept. In a modular language, the program is divided into separate modules, each of which takes care of a specific function that the program has to carry out. Each module requires a specified input and produces a specified output, so the programming job can be easily divided among members of the programming team. An important principle of modular programming is called **information hiding**. The author of one module doesn't have to be concerned with the details of what's inside another module. This information can remain hidden (and other programmers can ignore it) as long as a given module generates output in the specified form.

Figure 15.2
In a lengthy program, the use of many GOTO statements resulted in spaghetti code, which was code that was difficult to follow and, consequently, the programs were prone to error.

Fourth-Generation Languages: Getting Away from Procedure

Although the transition from the second to the third generation of programming languages is reasonably clear, the same can't be said for the transition to **fourth-generation languages**. Various types of programming languages have been claimed to be "fourth-generation," including **report generators** (languages for printing database reports) and **query languages** (languages for getting information out of databases). What these languages share is that they are **nonprocedural**; that is, they don't force the programmer to consider the procedure that must be followed to obtain the desired result. For example, in **Structured Query Language**, or **SQL** (pronounced "sequel"), you can ask the following question of the data in a database:

```
SELECT employee-name
FROM employee-salary-table
WHERE salary > 50000
AND position = 'Engineer'
```

In everyday terms, this request is to "Get the names of all engineers who make more than $50,000." Note that this question isn't totally nonprocedural; you still have to know quite a bit about how the database is structured. (For example, you have to specify which table the information should come from.) The ultimate nonprocedural language would be **natural language**, the everyday language that people speak, but computers will need to be endowed with artificial intelligence before they can decode natural language.

Object-Oriented Programming: Component Reusability

Although fourth-generation languages have given nonprogrammers useful tools for extracting information from databases, they aren't general-purpose programming languages. Programmers have continued to use third-generation languages. Structured and modular programming help programmers do a better job, but they have not revolutionized programming. What's needed is **component reusability**, the capability to develop well-designed program modules that perform a specific task, such as handling print output. If component reusability can be achieved, programmers could quickly construct a program by combining ready-to-use modules, in a process that would take a fraction of the time required to develop these modules from scratch.

ELIMINATING THE PROGRAM VERSUS DATA DISTINCTION

A more recent approach to programming, called **object-oriented programming** (**OOP**), is achieving the dream of component reusability. It does so by introducing a different philosophy of program design.

In traditional programming, the program and data are kept separate. If the data must change—because, for example, a company decides that it needs to start tracking the exact time of orders as well as the date—all programs that access this data must also be changed. That's an expensive, time-consuming process.

In object-oriented programming, the problem of having to update many programs is solved by doing something unprecedented: eliminating the distinction between programs and data. In OOP, the data is stored along with all the program procedures needed to access and use the data. If another program accesses the data, it immediately learns which procedures are available, including any new ones. This eliminates the need to go through and change many programs just because of some little change in the data. As explained in the next section, the term *object* is used to describe the units that store data along with the procedures available to access and use the data.

OBJECTS

An **object** is a unit of computer information that contains data as well as all the procedures or operations (called **methods**) that can process or manipulate this data. The object also contains information that defines its **interface**, or its means of exchanging messages with other objects. For example, one object can ask another object, in effect, "What methods do you have available?" and the object will describe them. With object-oriented programming, information hiding becomes a reality.

Users (or other objects) don't have to know anything about the specifics of how the object was implemented internally. (In object-oriented programming, information hiding is called **encapsulation**.)

Here's an example to illustrate what an object is. Suppose you're running a bike shop, and you've created an object called **DASHER**. This object contains all the data about Dasher bicycles (including inventory, pricing information, and performance characteristics). It also contains all the methods that can be used to process the data. You can use a program (which is itself an object) that can query **DASHER** to find out which methods are available. You'll find out that you can choose from many methods, including totaling the number of Dasher bicycles on hand, updating the inventory, listing available accessories, or computing a sale price that includes specified accessories.

Note that object-oriented programming encourages the programmer to start thinking *from the beginning* about the real-world environment in which the program will function. Proponents of object-oriented programming believe that this focus leads to more usable software.

Figure 15.3
DASHER, SPEEDO, and ZOOM-310 are subclasses of the BIKES object. They all inherit the BIKES object's properties.

CLASSES

An important feature of object-oriented programming is the concept of **class**, a category of objects. In the DASHER example just given, the DASHER object is a type of a broader, more abstract category of objects called BIKES. In other words, it's a **subclass** of the BIKES class. The BIKES class is a **superclass** of DASHER because it's more abstract and generic. Other lines of bikes carried by the same bike shop are SPEEDO and ZOOM-310. Objects exist for these, too, and they, like DASHER, are subclasses of BIKES.

INHERITANCE

One of the major objectives of object-oriented programming is reusability, the capability to create an object and then reuse it whenever it's needed. By means of inheritance, possibilities for object reuse are multiplied.

Inheritance refers to an object's capacity to "pass on" its characteristics to its "children," or subclasses. To create objects for the bike shop, a programmer begins by creating the BIKES object. This object is then copied and modified to make the DASHER, SPEEDO, and ZOOM-310 objects, all of which inherit the BIKES object's properties (see Figure 15.3).

RAPID APPLICATION DEVELOPMENT (RAD)

Because objects can be so easily reused, object-oriented programming enables a fast method of program development, called **rapid application development** (**RAD**). In RAD, a programmer works with a library of prebuilt objects that have been created for a huge variety of applications.

MIDDLEWARE (OBJECTS ACROSS THE ENTERPRISE)

One of the most appealing possibilities of object-oriented programming lies in its suitability for use in computer networks. Suppose you have hundreds, or even thousands, of objects accessible on the network, and each one contains data, as well as the knowledge of how to use that data. It would be nice to be able to access these objects. But to do so, **middleware** is needed. The term *middleware* refers to standards that define how programs can find objects and query (ask) them about what kinds of goodies they contain.

Middleware is a fairly new concept, and the standards are still maturing. One leading standard is the **Common Object Request Broker Architecture** (**CORBA**). CORBA defines how objects can communicate with each other across a network, even if the objects are written in dissimilar programming languages. For example, oil giant Chevron uses CORBA to give nearly 3,000 employees access to a variety of databases, which are written in many different languages. By means of the **Internet Inter-Orb Protocol** (**IIOP**), CORBA capabilities can be built into Web browsers, which transform them into tools for requesting information from objects.

CORBA isn't the only middleware standard. Microsoft Corporation is pushing its own standard, called **Component Object Model** (**COM**), which works best where companies are running nothing but Windows machines.

A Guide to Programming Languages: One Size Doesn't Fit All

In this section, you'll find a guide to the most popular programming languages in use today. As you'll see, each program has its pros and cons for particular purposes. A major part of programming success involves choosing the right language for the job.

COBOL AND FORTRAN: FOR SOME PEOPLE, RETRO RULES!

Imagine it's 1959. Cars have big fins. Dwight Eisenhower is the president of the United States. Hawaii becomes a state.

And computer programmers are using COBOL and Fortran.

Now fast-forward. It's the beginning of the twenty-first century. Guess what? More than 50 percent of computer programmers are still using COBOL and Fortran. Are these really good languages, or do people have trouble learning new ones?

COBOL
COBOL is one of the earliest high-level programming languages, dating all the way back to 1959. It gets very little respect in university computer science departments. In fact, a leading computer scientist stated in 1982 that the teaching of COBOL should be made a criminal offense. Nonetheless, **Common Business-Oriented Language** (**COBOL**) is the most widely used business programming language in the world. What's more, thousands of jobs are available for COBOL programmers, and businesses are competing to hire COBOL talent. Why?

COBOL's success lies in the simple fact that it's a proven way to tackle the huge job of dealing with a large organization's accounting information, including inventory control, billing, and payroll. In addition, COBOL has some features that more recent programming languages would do well to imitate. For example, COBOL requires programmers to write in a style that explains what the program is doing at each step of the way. Anyone who knows COBOL can look at someone else's program and quickly figure out how it works.

That's what COBOL boosters say. Detractors say COBOL's longevity has more to do with the surprising survival of **legacy** (obsolete) mainframe computer systems, where COBOL programming dominates. Like other legacy programming languages, COBOL has been updated with structured and even object-oriented versions, so there's a clear path to the future.

Fortran
Fortran, short for formula translator, is yet another survivor from the 1950s. It is so well suited to scientific, mathematical, and engineering applications that even after all this time it's very difficult to pry it out of engineers' hands. In many engineering schools, protracted battles arise over which programming language to teach engineering students; the computer science

Destinations

Want to find out what kinds of jobs are available for COBOL programmers? Try **www.coboljobs.com/public/default.asp**.

people want to teach C++ (which we'll get to in a bit), and the engineers want to teach Fortran.

What's so great about Fortran? The answer's in the name: "formula translator." If you need to solve a complex engineering equation, no other programming language comes close to Fortran's simplicity, economy, and ease of use. Fortran is most likely to be replaced not by another programming language, but by a formula-solving program such as Wolfram Research's Mathematica, which can transform equations into complex (and often beautiful) graphics that reveal underlying mathematical patterns.

STRUCTURED AND MODULAR LANGUAGES

COBOL and Fortran still have their places in mainframes and engineering shops, but large-scale program development requires structured and modular languages. The following languages are in widespread use among professional developers and software firms.

Ada

A programming language incorporating modular programming principles, Ada is named after Augusta Ada Byron (1815–1852), who helped nineteenth-century

TECHNOLOGICAL PIONEERS

Y2K: A Story of a Visionary Ahead of His Time

Some visionaries are way ahead of their time, particularly when it comes to software development. Sometimes these people raise issues that don't seem important at the time, and they're ignored by people around them. With the help of hindsight, it's easy to look back and see that everyone should have listened.

A case in point is Bill Schoen. A programmer working in Detroit, Schoen was the first to publicly point out what later became known as the Y2K problem. You no doubt remember the Y2K problem. Ever wonder what all the fuss was about? Well, it all boiled down to storage: the storage of just two characters, the numbers 1 and 9. From 1959 until the mid- to late 1980s, almost all COBOL programs were written with storage places for a two-digit year—the 19 was assumed. Forms and reports included the 19 in addition to whatever year between 0 and 99 that was in the data set. By using this method, only the last two digits of the year needed to be stored, not the 19. Schoen had the foresight to bring the issue up in 1983. At the time, everyone thought that if there was a problem, it would be solved as old programming code faded away and new programs were developed.

Schoen was so passionate about the problem he foresaw that he devised a solution, quit his job, and formed the world's first Y2K consulting firm, Charmar Enterprises. The COBOL routine to correct the Y2K problem was developed on his Commodore 64 (an early personal computer) and named the Charmar Correction.

With his solution in hand, Schoen set out on a one-man crusade. He made numerous presentations and tried to get software companies to come up with their own solutions. He tried to gain media exposure for the problem but ended up with only a single article in print. At one point, Schoen made a management presentation about the problem to one of his clients, which also happened to be one of the world's largest corporations. The company subsequently canceled Schoen's contract and ignored the issue.

Eventually, Schoen dropped the price of the Charmar Correction to less than a thousand dollars. Many companies still scoffed at his predictions and were too concerned with their quarterly earnings to focus on a problem that was 16 or 17 years away.

Much to Schoen's dismay, his predictions and solutions weren't well received by the computer world. His efforts led to only two sales of the Charmar Correction, and even those companies did not implement it systematically throughout their organizations. After a year of near universal rejection, Charmar Enterprises closed its doors in 1984, and Schoen went back to programming at Ford Motor Company.

According to Schoen, a few simple corrections in the early 1980s could have solved 95 percent of the programming problems and averted the need to spend so much money in what turned out to be a race against time. The Y2K problem has been characterized by Schoen as "the biggest technical screw-up in history." Many computer programmers and engineers would likely agree with him on that point, even though it was not seen as such in the early 1980s. On December 31, 1999, at the stroke of midnight, no one was sure what would happen to computing systems that were set up to assume that the year began with the digits 19. As it turned out, most institutions had made the necessary adjustments to their programs. Meanwhile, many COBOL programmers made a lot of money in the late 1990s, thanks to the "screw-up" Schoen had predicted years before.

inventor Charles Babbage conceptualize what could have been the world's first digital computer (see Figure 15.4). Ada's popularity is due in part to its role as the required language until 1996 for most U.S. Defense Department projects. Major advantages of Ada include its suitability for the reliable control of real-time systems (such as missiles). For example, the U.S. Navy's Seawolf submarine uses more than five million lines of Ada code running on more than 100 Motorola processors.

BASIC

BASIC (Beginner's All-Purpose Symbolic Instruction Code) is an easy-to-use, high-level programming language available on many personal computers. Developed at Dartmouth College in the mid-1960s to teach programming basics to beginners, BASIC has become a language that many hobbyists use to create simple programs. It's also widely taught in high schools and some colleges in beginning programming courses. Many educators, however, believe that the original versions of BASIC teach flawed programming skills, due to BASIC's reliance on GOTO statements. More recent versions of BASIC incorporate the principles of structured, modular, and object-oriented programming.

BASIC was designed as an interpreted language so that beginners could create a program in an interactive mode, run the program, test it, and debug it. Interpreted languages are conducive to learning programming, but they run much more slowly than compiled programs. As a result, professional programmers avoided using BASIC. Newer versions of BASIC have added compilers.

Visual Basic (VB)

Is BASIC a kid's language, something you grow out of? Better think twice. Microsoft's **Visual Basic** (**VB**), developed in the early 1990s, is one of the world's most widely used program development packages. In the United States, it's part of the programming tool kit of more than 50 percent of the country's 2.4 million professional programmers. The company has sold more than one million licenses for Visual Basic 6.0. What's the secret to Visual Basic's success? It's by far the most successful rapid application development (RAD) tool in

Figure 15.4
Nineteenth-century inventor Charles Babbage, working in conjunction with Augusta Ada Bryon, is credited with conceptualizing what might have been the world's first digital computer.

Destinations

If you want to learn more about the life and times of Augusta Ada Byron and her contributions to computer history, check out **www.cs.yale.edu/ homes/tap/Files/ ada-bio.html**.

existence for Microsoft Windows applications, and Windows is the operating system used on an estimated 80 percent of the world's computers (see Figure 15.5).

Using an **event-driven** programming model, in which the program is designed to wait for the user to do something (such

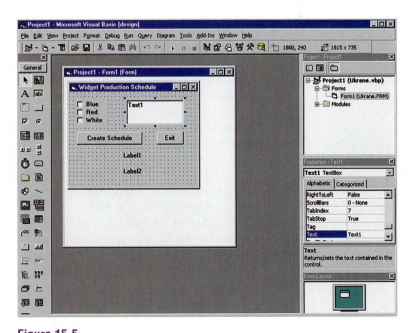

Figure 15.5
Visual Basic enables a programmer to develop an application quickly by designing the graphical user interface on-screen as the first step in program development.

Destinations

If you're thinking about a career in computer science or professional programming, C++ is the language to learn. For more information on C++, see the C++ Virtual Library at **www.desy.de/user/ projects/C++.html**.

as click the mouse button), Visual Basic enables a programmer to develop an application quickly by designing the graphical user interface on-screen as the *first* step in program development. Each on-screen control, such as a text box or a radio button, can then be linked to a brief BASIC program that performs an action. The programmer doesn't have to worry about any of the code that generates the great looking user interface: that's all handled automatically by the Visual Basic compiler, which creates an executable program capable of running on its own. Using Visual Basic, even a novice programmer can develop an impressive application in short order.

A huge variety of accessory tools enable Visual Basic programmers to accomplish tasks quickly, such as building interfaces to databases and increasing the functionality of Web pages. **VBScript**, a **scripting language** based on Visual Basic, was created for writing **scripts** (short programs) that can be embedded in Web pages. A script isn't compiled; it's interpreted by the Web browser, line by line.

ActiveX controls are miniprograms (mainly written in Visual Basic) that can be downloaded from Web pages and used to add functionality to Web browsers. However, VBScript and ActiveX controls require users to be running Microsoft Windows and Microsoft Internet Explorer.

Pascal

Pascal, named after seventeenth-century mathematician Blaise Pascal, is a high-level programming language that encourages programmers to write well-structured programs. Pascal has gained wide acceptance as a teaching language and is available in interpreted and compiled versions.

Like most older programming languages, Pascal has been updated to reflect new approaches to programming. An object-oriented version of Pascal provides the foundation for **Delphi**, a compiler created by Borland International that closely resembles Visual Basic. However, Delphi hasn't been able to match Visual Basic's success.

C

C is a high-level programming language developed by AT&T's Bell Labs in the 1970s. C combines the virtues of high-level programming languages with the efficiency of an assembly language. Using C, programmers can directly manipulate bits of data inside the processing unit. As a result, well-written C programs run significantly faster than programs written in other high-level programming languages. However, C is difficult to learn, and programming in C is a time-consuming activity.

OBJECT-ORIENTED (OO) LANGUAGES

Structured and modular languages are the workhorses of software development, but they're not the cutting edge. That honor goes to object-oriented (OO) languages.

Smalltalk

Developed in the early 1970s at Xerox Corporation's Palo Alto Research Center (PARC), the home of the graphical user interface (GUI) and many other key innovations in computing, **Smalltalk** is considered by many to be the only "100 percent pure" object-oriented programming language. Although the language is not often chosen for professional software development, more than a few corporations have chosen Smalltalk for mission-critical applications (including American Airlines, Federal Express, and Texas Instruments). But Smalltalk is facing stiff competition from another object-oriented language: Java (described below).

C++

A more recent version of C, **C++**, was developed at Bell Labs in the 1980s. C++ incorporates object-oriented features but doesn't force programmers to adhere to the object-oriented model (see Figure 15.6). Thanks to this flexibility and the fast execution speed of compiled C++ programs, the C++ language is in widespread use for professional program development. Software giant Microsoft Corporation uses C++ for application development.

Java

Suppose you ask the computer industry's version of the magic mirror, "Who's the fairest of them all?" The answer will come quickly: Java. Developed by Sun Microsystems, **Java** is an object-oriented, high-level programming language with a new twist (see

Figure 15.7). According to Java backers, it's the world's first truly **cross-platform programming language**, a language that enables you to "write once, run anywhere." And it's gained acceptance faster than any programming language in the history of computing. (Note that Microsoft launched its answer to Java on February 14, 2001, with its official kickoff of the .NET initiative. **XML**, a cross-platform markup language, has Java in its sites. The next few years will be very interesting as the battle heats up!)

Developed for consumer electronic devices, Java is a simplified version of C++ (and is much easier to learn than C++). But the feature "write once, run anywhere" is what's attracting attention. How is it possible to write one program and run it on any computer? As you've learned, language translators (compilers or interpreters) transform source code into executable programs, which are designed to run on a specific type of computer. But Java programs are designed to run on any computer in widespread use today, including computers using the Windows, Mac OS, or UNIX operating systems. The secret to this remarkable capability is the **Java Virtual Machine**, which needs to be installed on any computer that runs Java. The Virtual Machine is a program execution environment that provides a "home away from home" for Java, no matter what type of computer it's running on.

Why is this capability so attractive? The answer is simple: reduced costs. Many companies are struggling with the fact that they've acquired computers helter-skelter over the years. They may have UNIX workstations, all kinds of Windows boxes, Macintoshes, and more. At the same time, they need to develop software tools that give all employees the ability to access mission-critical network resources. Java offers the possibility of writing only

one program that can run on all the computers in a firm, without the considerable expense of making several versions of the original program for each type of computer it needs to run on.

Java saves money in another way, too. When specially designed Java miniprograms (called **applets**) are made available through a network, employees can obtain a program by accessing a Web page, clicking a link, and downloading the Java applet. The applet is soon running on the employee's computer, and the distribution costs are next to nothing. That's a different situation from that of traditional programs, which must be installed and configured on each employee's machine.

Despite Java's considerable advantages, the language has many of the weaknesses characteristic of a young programming language that's still evolving. Downloaded applets pose a security risk, so they're limited to actions that don't involve storage devices. (To put this another way, Java applets run in a virtual "sandbox," where they can't get hold of any system features that could do damage.) Perhaps worst of all, though, is the fact that Java software is slow. Java programs aren't as slow as interpreted programs, but they're considerably slower than compiled programs.

JavaScript (ECMAScript)

Like VBScript, **JavaScript** is a scripting language designed for use on Web pages. Despite including "Java" in its name, JavaScript isn't based on Java. JavaScript was created by Netscape Communications. Recently standardized by the European Computer Manufacturers Association (ECMA), JavaScript is now properly known as ECMAScript. It's a simple, easy-to-learn language for writing scripts on Web pages, and it's in widespread use on the Web.

```
# include <iostream.h>

void main ()
{
    cout <<"Hello World!";
```

Figure 15.6
This is a simple C++ program that prints "Hello World!" to the screen.

```
class Hello World {
    public static void main (String args
})      {
        System.out.println ("Hello World!");
    }
```

Figure 15.7
An example of Java code. Java has gained acceptance faster than any programming language in computing history.

CURRENTS

TECHNOLOGICAL MILESTONES

PostScript and the Desktop Publishing Revolution

Programming languages allow humans to convey to machines what they want to accomplish. Many programming languages are on the market. Each has its strengths, weaknesses, proponents, and detractors.

One programming language that has been around for a while doesn't even need a computer to be useful—at least, not a computer in the traditional sense of the word. PostScript is a programming language that is used to describe how information should be printed on a page. In other words, it is a page description language. PostScript is used most often in printers but can be used in other types of output devices as well.

PostScript has its roots in work performed at Xerox's Palo Alto Research Center (PARC). Two researchers at the facility, John E. Warnock and Charles M. Geschke, developed the language. When Xerox failed to develop the potential of the language and settled on a different standard for page description, the two struck out on their own in 1982 to form Adobe Systems. In 1985, the first commercial product using PostScript—the Apple LaserWriter printer—was released to the world. The result was the birth of a revolution we have since termed desktop publishing.

Nothing about PostScript is mystical. By design, it is interpreted. Programming commands consisting of plain ASCII characters are sent to and acted upon by a processor in a device. For instance, one set of commands might describe margins for the page, and another set might detail the type of fonts to be used. Still others can be used to create graphic designs or special artwork. In all, several hundred PostScript commands handle everything from creating a simple dot on the page to creating detailed output.

The PostScript language is considered a device-independent language. It doesn't require a specific type of computer and can be implemented on any type of system. It has been embedded in printers, high-end typesetting equipment, and specialized manufacturing equipment. It can also be used to display information to a computer monitor.

Using special printer drivers, many programs can create output for PostScript devices. Programs such as word processors, spreadsheets, and graphics programs all typically generate PostScript output.

PostScript is a proprietary language owned and developed by Adobe. The company licenses the language to device manufacturers so that they can create PostScript interpreters for their output devices. The success of PostScript, and its worldwide adoption as a printing standard, have catapulted Adobe to the forefront of computing technology and ensured a place in computer history for Warnock and Geschke.

Introducing the Program Development Life Cycle

At the dawn of the modern computer era, no notion existed of managing the software development process. Programs were written for specific, well-defined purposes, such as calculating missile trajectories. If the program didn't work, the programmer corrected it, so this approach came to be known as **code-and-fix** (or "cut-and-run," as detractors put it).

When businesses began using computers for more complex purposes, problems arose. Often, it turned out that programmers didn't really understand what managers wanted a program to do, and

correcting problems often turned into an expensive, time-consuming nightmare. Other problems arose, too: programmers didn't document their programs well (if at all), and some developed idiosyncratic programming styles so that they could assure their continued employment, since no one else could figure out what their code did! These early programs were almost impossible to debug and maintain (especially if the original programmer had left the company).

To address these problems, the program development life cycle (**PDLC**) was introduced in the 1970s, and it is still in widespread use today. Like the software development life cycle, the PDLC provides an organized plan for breaking down the task of program development into manageable chunks, each of which must be successfully completed before programmers move on to the next phase (see Figure 15.8). Let's look at each of these phases.

PHASE 1: DEFINING THE PROBLEM

The first step in developing a program is to define the problem. This is a job for systems analysts, who provide the results of their work to programmers in the form of a **program specification** (or "spec"). The specification precisely defines the input data, the processing that should occur, what the output should look like, and how the user interface should look. Depending on the size of the job, the program development might be handled by a single individual or a team.

PHASE 2: DESIGNING THE PROGRAM

An architect doesn't design a home by going to the site with a bunch of boards and bricks. After the architect has determined the home buyer's needs, the next step is an architectural drawing—a plan drawn up on paper that can be reviewed and discussed until everything's right. Similarly, programmers create program designs. Like an architect's drawing, the program design specifies the components that make the program work.

Top-Down Program Design

Program design begins by focusing on the main goal that the program is trying to achieve and then breaking the program into manageable components, each of which contributes to this goal. This approach is called **top-down program design** (also called structured programming). The first step involves identifying the **main routine**, which is the program's major activity. From there, programmers try to break down the various components of the main routine into smaller **subroutines**, also called **modules**, until each subroutine is highly focused and accomplishes only one major task. Experience shows that this is the best way to ensure program quality. If a bug appears in a program designed this way, it's relatively easy to identify the module that must be causing the error.

Structured Design

Within each subroutine, the programmer draws on the programming equivalent of basic building materials, called **control structures**, to envision how the subroutine

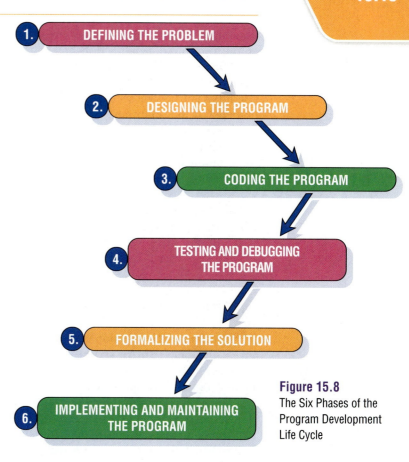

Figure 15.8
The Six Phases of the Program Development Life Cycle

1. DEFINING THE PROBLEM
2. DESIGNING THE PROGRAM
3. CODING THE PROGRAM
4. TESTING AND DEBUGGING THE PROGRAM
5. FORMALIZING THE SOLUTION
6. IMPLEMENTING AND MAINTAINING THE PROGRAM

will do its job. These are combined to create an **algorithm**. An algorithm is a step-by-step description of how to arrive at a solution. You can think of an algorithm as a recipe or a how-to sheet.

Three basic control structures, which are logical constructs that specify how the instructions in a program are to be executed, are available. Control structures are defined at a high level of abstraction and are relevant to all programming languages (except very old ones).

In a **sequence control structure**, instructions to the computer are designed to be executed (performed by the computer) in the order in which they appear. Sequence control structures provide the basic building blocks for computer programs. If you can imagine yourself as a computer, here's an example of a sequence to follow to obtain pizza:

```
Go to the phone.
Dial the pizza place.
Order the pizza.
Hang up.
```

In a **selection control structure**, (also called a conditional, or branch, control structure), the program branches to different instructions depending on whether a condition is met. Most conditions are based on IF...THEN...ELSE logic. If a condition is true, one set of instructions is executed. If the condition is not true, a different set of instructions is executed. Here's an example that includes a *very* important test: making sure you have enough money.

```
Open your wallet.
IF you have enough money,
    THEN   Go to the phone.
           Dial the pizza place.
           Order the pizza.
           Hang up.
    ELSE   Forget the whole thing.
```

A variant of the selection control structure is the **case control structure**. In a case structure, the condition is fundamental and each branch leads to its own, lengthy series of instructions. For example, the IRS processes tax returns differently depending on marital status. A coded field indicates whether the taxpayer is married filing a joint return, married filing separately, single, head of household, or widowed. A case selection can be used so that the computer can determine which of those five categories a taxpayer belongs to and then use the correct set of instructions to process the return.

In a **repetition control structure**, (also called a looping or iteration, control structure), the program repeats the same instructions over and over. The two types of repetitions are DO-WHILE and DO-UNTIL. In a DO-WHILE structure, the program tests a condition at the beginning of the loop and executes the specified instructions only if the condition is true. In a DO-UNTIL structure, the program executes the instructions, and then tests to see whether a specified condition is true. If not, the loop repeats.

Drawing on pizza once again, the following example illustrates a DO-WHILE structure:

```
WHILE there is still more
    pizza, gobble down pizza.
```

Note that a DO-WHILE structure doesn't guarantee that the action will be performed even once. If the initial test condition is false, the action doesn't occur.

Here's a DO-UNTIL structure:

```
DO gobble down pizza
UNTIL none remains.
```

Developing an Algorithm

Algorithms aren't restricted to computers. In fact, we use them every day. Most people do long division by following an algorithm.

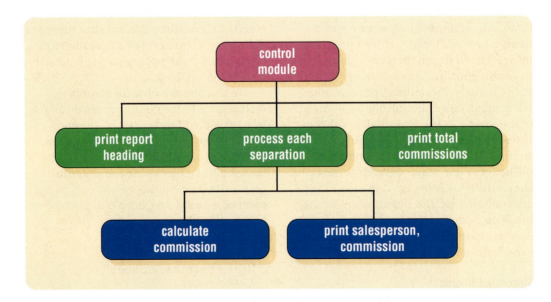

Figure 15.9
Each box, or module, in a structure chart indicates a task that the program must accomplish.

Here's another example: suppose that you want to determine your car's gas mileage. You probably do this by filling the tank and noting your mileage. The next time you get gas, you note the mileage again, determine the number of miles you drove, and then divide the miles driven by the amount of gas you put in. The result tells you your car's gas mileage, at least for the type of driving you did between these two tankfuls.

In programming, coming up with an algorithm involves figuring out how to get the desired result by **nesting** control structures. To get programs to do useful things, programmers nest control structures within each other. Here's an example that remedies some of the unhealthy implications of the examples in the previous section:

```
WHILE there is still more pizza,
Check to see whether you're
    still hungry.
IF you are still hungry,
THEN gobble down pizza.
ELSE put the rest in the fridge.
```

Program Design Tools

To help programmers develop well-structured programs, a variety of design tools exist.

Structure charts (also called **hierarchy charts**) show the top-down design of a program. Each box, or module, in the chart indicates a task that the program must accomplish (see Figure 15.9). The top module, called the **control module**, oversees the transfer of control to the other modules.

A **flowchart** is a diagram that shows the logic of a program. Programmers create flowcharts either by hand using a flowcharting template or on the computer. Each flowcharting symbol has a meaning. A diamond, for example, is used to indicate a condition, a rectangle is used for a process, and a parallelogram indicates an input or output procedure (see Figure 15.10).

Some programmers don't like flowcharting. **Pseudocode**, created in the 1970s as an alternative to flowcharts, is a stylized form of writing used to describe the logic of a program. Pseudocode can't be compiled or executed—it doesn't follow any formatting or syntax rules. Instead,

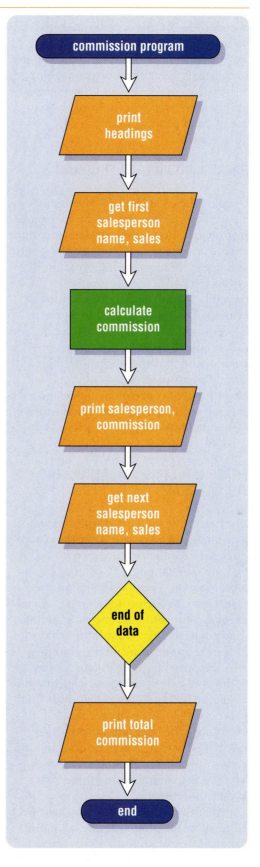

Figure 15.10

A flowchart is a diagram that shows the logic of a program. Each flowcharting symbol has a meaning.

pseudocode enables programmers to focus on basic algorithms without having to worry about the details of a programming language. Programmers are even able to write pseudocode without knowing what programming language they're going to use upon implementation.

PHASE 3: CODING THE PROGRAM

Creating the code involves translating the algorithm into specific program language instructions. The programming team must choose an appropriate programming language and then create the program by typing the code. The programmers must carefully follow the language's rules of syntax, which specify precisely how to express certain operations. For example, different programming languages specify basic arithmetic operations in different ways. Program development tools can check for **syntax errors** while the program is being written. Syntax errors must be eliminated before the program will run.

PHASE 4: TESTING AND DEBUGGING THE PROGRAM

The fourth step in a programming project is to eliminate all errors. After the syntax errors are eliminated, the program will execute. The output may still not be correct, however, because the language translator can't detect logic errors. A **logic error** is a mistake that the programmer made in designing the solution to the problem. For example, a programmer tells the computer to calculate net pay by adding (instead of subtracting) deductions to gross pay. The programmer must find and correct logic errors by carefully examining the program output. As we mentioned earlier, syntax errors and logic errors are collectively known as **bugs**. The process of eliminating these errors is known as **debugging**.

After the visible logic errors have been eliminated, the programming team must test the program to find hidden errors. However, it's not always possible to examine every outcome for each program condition. Inevitably, some errors will surface only when the system is put into use.

PHASE 5: FORMALIZING THE SOLUTION

Now the project is almost complete. The structure chart and pseudocode or flowchart developed during the design phase become documentation for others who will modify the program in the future. Other documentation should have been created as the program was being coded: lists of variable names and definitions, descriptions of files that the program needs to work with, and layouts of output that the program produces. All of this documentation needs to be placed together and saved for future reference.

The job isn't finished until the program is thoroughly documented. This requires writing a manual that provides an overview of the program's functionality, tutorials for beginning users, in-depth explanations of major program features, reference documentation of all program commands, and a thorough description of the error messages generated by the program. These manuals, along with the program design work, are known as **documentation**.

PHASE 6: IMPLEMENTING AND MAINTAINING THE PROGRAM

All that is left now is the sixth and last step: implementation. If the program has been developed for use by the company for which the programmers work, the program will still need to be tested by the users. The best-written program is useless if the user does not understand how to work with it. What's more, users will discover program errors that weren't caught in the testing phase, no matter how exhaustively the program was tested.

Even after a program is complete, it needs to be maintained and evaluated regularly. In **program maintenance**, the programming team fixes program errors that users discover. In periodic **evaluations**, the team asks whether the program is fulfilling its objectives. The evaluation may lead to modifications to update the program or to add features for the user. It may even lead to a decision to abandon the current system and develop a new one, and so the program development life cycle begins anew.

HOME | Takeaway Points | Key Terms and Concepts | Matching | Multiple Choice | Fill-In | Short Answer | Exercises/ Projects | Web Research | CHAPTER REVIEW

TAKEAWAY POINTS

- A programming language is an artificial language consisting of a vocabulary and a set of rules.

- The earliest (and lowest-level) programming language is machine language, the binary instructions needed to control a particular brand and model of processor.

- Assembly language is easier to use than machine language because the programmer can use symbols to sum up program instructions. However, the programmer still needs to know a great deal about how a particular brand and model of processor works.

- High-level languages (third-generation languages) free the programmer from having to know the details of processors, but these languages still require the programmer to specify the procedure to be followed to solve the problem.

- Fourth-generation languages free programmers from having to worry about the procedure to be followed to solve a problem, but most are restricted to accessing databases.

- To solve the "spaghetti code" problems of early third-generation languages, new languages appeared that emphasized structure and modularity.

- Because third-generation languages failed in their goal of total modularity and information hiding, object-oriented languages emerged. These languages achieve these goals by combining procedures and data.

- An object is a computer resource that contains data, as well as a variety of procedures for making use of this data.

- The program development life cycle (PDLC) is needed because previous, ad hoc programming techniques produced software that was riddled with errors and virtually impossible to debug or maintain. The PDLC is part of the SDLC's implementation phase (see Chapter 14).

- The PDLC's six phases are defining the problem, designing the program, coding the program, testing and debugging the program, formalizing the solution, and implementing and maintaining the program.

- Top-down programming makes programs easier to debug and maintain because program functions are divided into separate modules, each of which has a clear, simple function.

- Using the three basic types of control structures (sequence, selection, and repetition), a programmer can create an algorithm for performing any processing task. The use of these structures makes a program easy to read and maintain.

- The task of debugging a program requires finding and correcting not only syntax errors, which prevent execution, but also logic errors, which do not prevent execution but do produce incorrect output.

CHAPTER REVIEW

1 2 3 4 5 6 7 8 9 10 11 12 13 14 **15** 16

CHAPTER REVIEW | Takeaway Points | Key Terms and Concepts | Matching | Multiple Choice | Fill-In | Short Answer | Exercises/ Projects | Web Research | HOME

KEY TERMS AND CONCEPTS

ActiveX controls
algorithm
applet
assembler
assembly language
BASIC
bug
C
C++
case control structure
class
COBOL (Common
    Business-Oriented
    Language)
code-and-fix
Common Object Request
    Broker Architecture
    (CORBA)
compiler
Component Object
    Model (COM)
component reusability
control module
control structure
cross-platform
    programming language
debugging
Delphi
documentation
encapsulation
evaluation
event-driven
executable program
flowchart
Fortran

fourth-generation
    language
high-level language
information hiding
inheritance
interface
Internet Inter-Orb
    Protocol (IIOP)
interpreter
Java
Java Virtual Machine
JavaScript
legacy
linker
logic error
low-level language
machine language
machine-dependent
    (hardware-dependent)
main routine
method
middleware
mnemonics
modular programming
module
natural language
nesting
nonprocedural
object
object code
object-oriented
    programming (OOP)
procedural language
program development
    life cycle (PDLC)

program listing
program maintenance
program specification
programming language
pseudocode
query language
rapid application
    development (RAD)
repetition control structure
report generator
scripting language
script
selection control structure
sequence control structure
Smalltalk
software crisis
source code
spaghetti code
structure chart
    (hierarchy chart)
structured programming
Structured Query
    Language (SQL)
subclass
subroutine
superclass
syntax
syntax error
third-generation language
top-down program
    design programming
    (structured programming)
VBScript
Visual Basic (VB)
XML

HOME | Takeaway Points | Key Terms and Concepts | Matching | Multiple Choice | Fill-In | Short Answer | Exercises/Projects | Web Research

CHAPTER REVIEW

MATCHING

Match each key term in the left column with the most accurate definition in the right column.

_____ 1. low-level language

_____ 2. procedural language

_____ 3. interpreter

_____ 4. structured programming

_____ 5. algorithm

_____ 6. class

_____ 7. cross-platform programming language

_____ 8. logic error

_____ 9. debugging

_____ 10. syntax

_____ 11. C

_____ 12. top-down design

_____ 13. Fortran

_____ 14. encapsulation

_____ 15. COBOL

a. a category of objects

b. a mistake that a programmer can make in designing the solution to a problem

c. a step-by-step description of how to arrive at a solution

d. rules that specify precisely how to express certain operations

e. a language that tells the computer what to do and how to do it

f. a programming language that is well suited to scientific, mathematical, and engineering applications

g. the process of eliminating syntax and logic errors

h. constructing a program so that it uses logical elements; GOTO statements are forbidden

i. a language that is similar to machine language in terms of its level of abstraction

j. translates one line of source code at a time

k. a language that enables you to "write once, run anywhere"

l. a programming approach in which the focus is on the main goal that a program is trying to achieve; the program is broken into manageable components, each of which contributes to this goal

m. information hiding

n. the most widely used business programming language

o. a programming language developed by AT&T's Bell Labs in the 1970s

CHAPTER REVIEW: 1 2 3 4 5 6 7 8 9 10 11 12 13 14 15 16

CHAPTER REVIEW | Takeaway Points | Key Terms and Concepts | Matching | Multiple Choice | Fill-In | Short Answer | Exercises/Projects | Web Research | HOME

MULTIPLE CHOICE

Circle the correct choice for each of the following.

1. Which programming language can a computer understand directly without the need for translation?
   a. BASIC
   b. Assembly language
   c. Machine language
   d. C

2. In which generation of languages were procedural languages introduced?
   a. First
   b. Second
   c. Third
   d. Fourth

3. Which term is not used in object-oriented programming?
   a. Encapsulation
   b. Data set
   c. Class
   d. Method

4. What is inheritance?
   a. The capacity of an object to transfer characteristics to an object in a subclass
   b. How an object maintains cohesion from one program to another
   c. The capability of an object to be encapsulated in a class
   d. How concepts are passed from one language generation to the next

5. What is JavaScript now known as?
   a. VBScript
   b. LiveScript
   c. NetScript
   d. ECMAScript

6. This was not a problem evident in some early programming efforts.
   a. Lack of programming documentation
   b. Difficulty in debugging and maintaining code
   c. Idiosyncratic programming styles
   d. Using structured programming concepts to solve the problem of spaghetti code

7. This is not one of the six phases in the PDLC.
   a. Developing a prototype
   b. Formalizing the solution
   c. Specifying the problem
   d. Testing and debugging

8. What does OOP mean?
   a. Open ordered programming
   b. Ordinary operational programming
   c. Object-oriented programming
   d. Optimal organized programming

9. Which of the following is not a program design tool?
   a. Pseudocode
   b. Flowchart
   c. Structure chart
   d. Program specification

10. A repetition control structure is also known as which of the following?
    a. Selecting
    b. Looping
    c. Parsing
    d. Verifying

| HOME | Takeaway Points | Key Terms and Concepts | Matching | Multiple Choice | Fill-In | Short Answer | Exercises/ Projects | Web Research | CHAPTER REVIEW |

FILL-IN

In the blanks provided, write the correct answer for each of the following.

1. _____ consists of binary numbers that directly correspond to a computer's electrical states.

2. _____ are mini-Java programs that run over a network.

3. A(n) _____ is a translation program that translates all of the source code into object code.

4. _____ programming promises to achieve the dream of component reusability.

5. A(n) _____ is a unit of computer information that contains data, as well as all the procedures or operations that can process or manipulate the data.

6. In a(n) _____, the program branches off to different instructions depending on whether a condition is met.

7. A(n) _____ precisely defines the input data, the processing that should occur, what the output should look like, and how the user interface should look.

8. _____ show the top-down design of a program.

9. _____ is a stylized form of writing to describe the logic of a program.

10. A(n) _____ is a diagram that shows the logic of a program.

11. _____ enables a fast method of object-oriented programming program development.

12. _____ defines how objects can communicate with each other across a network, even if the objects are written in dissimilar programming languages.

13. _____ refers to standards that define how programs can find objects and query them.

14. _____ are miniprograms that can be downloaded from Web pages and used to add functionality to Web browsers.

15. Of the several computer languages discussed in this chapter, only _____ and _____ are named after people.

SHORT ANSWER

1. What are the major structured and modular languages being used today?

2. What are the six phases of the PDLC?

3. What are the elements of a program specification?

4. Identify the basic control structures used in program development, and explain the purpose of each.

5. Explain the differences between syntax errors and logic errors, and give an example of each type of error.

6. The translation of a high-level program to a machine level is done by applications known as compilers and interpreters. Distinguish between a compiler and an interpreter, and give an example of a compiled language and an interpreted language.

CHAPTER REVIEW

Takeaway Points | Key Terms and Concepts | Matching | Multiple Choice | Fill-In | Short Answer | Exercises/Projects | Web Research

HOME

1 2 3 4 5 6 7 8 9 10 11 12 13 14 15 16

EXERCISES/PROJECTS

1. Documentation is primarily created for what two groups? Describe the types of documentation that would be supplied for each group.

2. Does your school have a computer science (CS), computer information systems (CIS), or management information systems (MIS) department? If so, look at a school catalog to see what language is covered in the initial programming courses. If the language is not specified, then you will have to contact the department directly. What, if any, are the prerequisites for the programming courses? Are additional computer languages taught in subsequent courses? What are the additional languages?

3. Three program design tools were discussed in this chapter. Name and describe each. For which of these tools can a programmer use aids such as a template or special software? Identify which tool you would prefer to use if you were a programmer, and explain why.

4. Algorithms are not just used for writing programs. They can be used to describe many processes accurately. Design an algorithm that lists the correct steps to safely start and move a motor vehicle. Include at least one selection control structure, either branch or conditional.

5. Just as it is easier to read a report than it is to write a report, it is easier to read a program than it is to write one. One of the simplest computer languages is BASIC. In a paragraph, explain the purpose of the three lines of code below. Why was it necessary to divide by 100? If the input is 300, 6, 4, what is the resulting output? Are the parentheses necessary in the formula? Explain why they are or are not needed.

```
Input Principal, Rate, Time
Interest =
  (Principal * Rate * Time) / 100
Print Interest
```

| HOME | Takeaway Points | Key Terms and Concepts | Matching | Multiple Choice | Fill-In | Short Answer | Exercises/ Projects | Web Research | CHAPTER REVIEW |

WEB RESEARCH

1. Some of the more widely used computer languages were discussed in the text. In this exercise, you're going to learn more about these, as well as about some other languages by exploring the "Dictionary of Programming Languages" site at **http://users.erols.com/ziring/dopl.html**. Fortran was the first higher-level programming language. This text does not tell us when and where Fortran was developed. During what time period and by what company was it developed? Although COBOL applications are used for solving business problems, what organization was the major contributor to the development of this language? Why was the Y2K bug a problem, especially for programs written in COBOL? Two other early programming languages are Lisp and Logo. During what time period was Lisp developed? Lisp is described as the "undisputed king" of which research area? When and where was Logo developed? It is designed to teach programming and problem solving to what group?

2. Microsoft's Visual Basic is the leading programming language and rapid development environment for creating Windows-based applications. Let's look at the evolution of this product by doing some research on the Web. Visit the Microsoft Web site at **http://msdn.microsoft.com/vbasic**. In what year was Visual Basic first released? Although there were some interim versions, the next major revision allowed programmers to create 16-bit or 32-bit applications. In which year and with which version was this? What was the major emphasis of versions 5 and 6? What is the name given to the next generation of Visual Basic? What are some of the improvements implemented in this version? What is the cost of the new Visual Basic? Is any version of Visual Basic available on your campus? If so, what version is it?

3. In this chapter the author states that if you were to ask the computer industry's version of the magic mirror, "Who's the fairest of

them all?" then the answer would be Java. As you read in the text, Java was developed by Sun Microsystems in the 1990s. Visit the Sun Microsystems site at **http://java.sun.com** to answer the following questions. Explain what "bytecode" and the purpose of the Java Virtual Machine are. Applets are Java programs that run over the Web in a browser on the client's computer. What terms are used for Java programs that run on a server and for the traditional programs that run on an individual computer? Sun Microsystems offers free versions of Java. What is the title of this software, what is the current version, and for which platforms is it available? Are you interested in downloading a copy?

4. Mathematica is a relatively new programming language that was briefly mentioned in the text. This type of software is called a Computer Algebra System (CAS). Visit the Web site **www.wolfram.com/products/mathematica** to answer the following questions. What company produces Mathematica? On which platforms does it run, and what are the current educational prices? Is Mathematica or any other CAS used in any of your school's mathematics classes? If so, identify the CAS and course(s) in which it is used. Have you taken one of these courses and used a CAS?

5. As you have read, there are several different computer languages. A language that has been gaining in popularity is Perl. Research the Web site **www.perl.com** to answer the following questions. What do the letters in the name represent? What is the logo that is associated with Perl? What is the current version? Is Perl compiled or interpreted? Name two platforms on which Perl runs. What types of applications are written using Perl? Not only are many applications free, but so is Perl itself. Locate and identify the URL of a site where you can download a free copy of Perl. Are you interested in downloading a copy?

CHAPTER REVIEW 1 2 3 4 5 6 7 8 9 10 11 12 13 14 15 16

Careers and Certification

CHAPTER **16**

What You'll Learn . . .

When you have finished reading this chapter, you will be able to:

1. Describe the traditional information technology (IT) career paths.

2. Compare and contrast computer science (CS), systems engineering, and computer information science (CIS) curricula in colleges and universities.

3. Describe two settings in which most IT workers find employment.

4. List at least three typical job titles in information systems (IS) departments and vendor companies.

5. Identify the business skills IS managers want in new IT workers.

6. List the technical skills currently in high demand.

7. Discuss the positive and negative aspects of certification.

Figure 16.1
The Web is an indispensable resource for searching for a career in the IT industry.

In the coming years, companies will need many more skilled information technology (IT) workers than they're likely to find. According to United States government projections, companies right now are in the process of buying and putting into service as many as 800 million computers, at a cost of $7.5 trillion. These information systems are needed to help them remain competitive in the Information Age. What's more, companies will create an estimated 95,000 new information technology jobs each year, creating a huge demand for new, skilled IT personnel. By 2005, the service sector will need 158 percent more systems analysts, 142 percent more computer scientists and engineers, and 37 percent more programmers than they did five years earlier. One significant shortfall is the fact that United States colleges and universities are turning out only about 50,000 graduates with computer science, systems engineering, or computer information systems (CIS) degrees each year.

What this means for you is opportunity. If you have the right background and skills, you can find a job in the IT industry. With the high demand for skilled personnel, salaries are rising—off the charts, in some cases. Students straight out of college level computer science, systems engineering, and computer information systems programs are getting job offers in the $40,000 to $50,000 range.

Of course, as with any career, computing-related jobs aren't for everyone. IT careers are a particularly poor choice for anyone who dislikes acquiring new knowledge and skills: change, not continuity, is the norm. And today's job market has no such thing as job security. In a computer-related field, you'll probably work at as many as five or six different jobs before you retire.

Is a career in information technology for you? In this section, you'll take a closer look at the traditional path to the best IT careers, which require (at a minimum) a four-year college degree. Later in this chapter, you'll learn about new IT career paths that have been created by the strong demand for skilled IT workers as well as rapid technological change (see Figure 16.1). As you'll see, more ways are available than ever before to pursue a career in information technology.

Traditional Information Technology (IT) Career Paths

Ten years ago, most people got into IT careers by obtaining a computer-related bachelor's degree and landing a job with a corporate **information systems (IS) department** (see Figure 16.2) or a software development firm (see Figure 16.3),

also called a **vendor**. The four-year college degree was and is a prerequisite for the best jobs: in a recent survey, 83 percent of surveyed U.S. corporations stated that they require a four-year college degree for entry-level programming jobs.

Before the era of corporate downsizing and dramatic reductions in job security, IT workers could remain with a firm for many years, perhaps until retirement. They could climb the corporate ladder by earning advanced degrees in their fields or by moving into management. Today it's more likely that you'll reach a plateau with one company and move to another

Typical Job Titles and Responsibilities in a Corporate IS Department

Job Title	Responsibilities	Salary Range
Chief Information Officer (CIO)	Senior-level management position Defines the IS department's mission, objectives, and budgets and creates a strategic plan for the enterprise's information systems	$130,000 to $400,000
Director of Computer Operations	Middle management position Ensures overall system reliability	$90,000 to $125,000
Director of Network Services	Middle management position Ensures overall network reliability	$100,000 to $150,000
Network Engineer	Installs, maintains, and supports computer networks; interacts with users; and troubleshoots problems	$40,000 to $90,000
Systems Programmer/Administrator	Installs, maintains, and supports the operating system	$50,000 to $90,000
Client/Server Manager	Installs, maintains, and supports client/server applications	$50,000 to $90,000
Systems Analyst	Interacts with users and application developers to design information systems	$50,000 to $90,000
Programmer/ Analyst	Designs, codes, and tests software according to specifications	$40,000 to $75,000
Programmer	Writes code according to specifications	$40,000 to $60,000

Figure 16.2

Typical Job Titles and Responsibilities in a Software Development Firm

Job Title	Responsibilities	Salary Range
Director of Research and Development	Senior-level management position in charge of all product development activities	$140,000 to $200,000
Software Architect	Computer scientists who are challenged to create new, cutting-edge technologies	$95,000 to $150,000
Software Engineer	Manages the details of software development projects	$75,000 to $125,000
Systems Engineer	Assists the sales staff by working with current and prospective customers; gives technical presentations and supports products on-site	$55,000 to $100,000
Software Developer	Develops new programs under the direction of the software architect	$50,000 to $75,000
Customer Support Technician	Provides assistance to customers who need help with products	$40,000 to $90,000

Figure 16.3

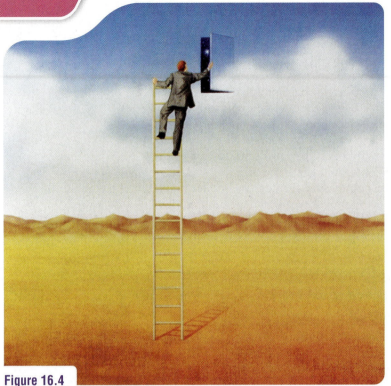

Figure 16.4

In traditional career paths, IT professionals could climb the corporate ladder by earning advanced degrees or by moving into management.

Destinations

Walden Personnel Testing Consulting provides employment skills testing and aptitude testing services to assess the competence of job applicants in Information Technology. For more information, visit **www.waldentesting. com/tests/skillcheck.htm**.

company that has room for you to grow. You may eventually make your way up the corporate ladder, or you may decide that there are enough chiefs in the world and be content as an IT professional.

Traditionally, to stay on top of trends, IT employees consulted trade and professional journals and attended professional conferences. Workers with business savvy and good communication skills could move into management (see Figure 16.4). If employees needed to acquire additional skills, the employer might arrange and pay for additional training. The traditional IT career path still exists, but it's changing. Let's look first at the components of a traditional IT career.

TRAINING FOR TRADITIONAL IT CAREERS

Reflecting the long-standing split in computing between science and business, education for traditional IT careers has been divided between two very different academic departments: computer science and computer information systems. In recent years, systems engineering has

provided a middle-ground approach, offering the rigor of an engineering approach combined with a real-world focus on the realities of information systems in contemporary business.

Computer Science

Computer science (**CS**) uses the principles of scientific and engineering research to improve computing. In general, computer science departments emphasize the theoretical rather than the practical aspects of computing, and they focus on cutting-edge technology and fundamental principles rather than teaching marketable skills. At most colleges and universities, computer science programs grew out of mathematics programs and are often housed in the engineering school.

Computer science training is highly technical and usually involves several semesters of higher mathematics such as calculus, as well as training in several programming languages and theoretical topics such as programming language structure, advanced computer graphics, artificial intelligence, and relational database design. Qualified CS graduates find that their theoretical and analytical skills make them attractive for jobs in cutting-edge software development firms. The skills of these graduates may also be needed by IS departments that are working with advanced technology or developing software in-house.

Computer Information Systems

Generally located in business schools, **computer information systems** (**CIS**) departments are often the mirror image of the CS department; they're focused on the practical rather than the theoretical and emphasize the skills that businesses need right now. Apart from work in programming and systems analysis, strongly emphasized are business smarts (including coursework in finance and marketing), first-rate communication skills, and the interpersonal skills needed for effective teamwork and leadership. With their business savvy and communication skills, CIS graduates are more likely to find jobs in corporate IS departments, but software development firms also need IT personnel who have excellent communication skills as well as technical ability (see Figure 16.5).

Figure 16.5
With their business savvy and communication skills, CIS graduates are more likely to find jobs in corporate IS departments.

Systems Engineering

The engineering discipline called **systems engineering** applies the scientific method to creating and maintaining quality systems, whether in business or in industry. Unlike other engineering disciplines, systems engineering looks at the whole picture, including the people and the organization as well as the technologies. The principles of systems engineering are useful for software development, systems analysis, and program development. Systems engineering students learn strong project management skills, and graduates are in high demand.

Electrical Engineering

The engineering discipline called **electrical engineering** (**EE**) offers a strong focus on digital circuit design as well as cutting-edge communication technologies. It's the primary choice if your interests lean more toward hardware than software.

TRADITIONAL METHODS OF CONTINUING EDUCATION

In traditional IT careers, professionals kept up with new technology by going to seminars, subscribing to computer periodicals, attending conferences and shows, and actively participating in a professional association.

Training Seminars

Computer-related seminars, usually lasting from one day to one week, are widely available. Typically, they're presented by the developer of a new hardware or software product or by a company specializing in training in a new technology (see Figure 16.6).

Figure 16.6
Typically, computer seminars are presented by the developer of a new hardware or software product or by a company specializing in training in a new technology.

Traditionally, companies view formal training as a wise investment and pay for training seminars. According to one study, a single hour of focused, professional instruction is worth six employee hours of ad hoc learning.

Computer Magazines, Newspapers, and Journals

Computer-related trade journals are an indispensable resource for IT professionals. Some, such as *Computerworld,* cover the entire spectrum of computer issues.

Others are aimed at a specific part of the computer industry, such as technology management (*InformationWeek*), networking (*LAN Times*), or office automation (*InfoSystems*). Over a hundred of these types of periodicals are in print. If you have a particular area of interest, you can probably find a periodical that reports late-breaking developments in your field. Most of these periodicals are also published on the Web. You can usually find one's site by simply adding .com to the name of the magazine.

Destinations

Most computer industry trade journals are published on the Internet as well as in print. At their Web sites, you can read current issues and search the publications' archives. A leading site is CMPnet, at **www.cmpnet.com**. This site contains *Byte, EE Times, InformationWeek, LAN Times, UnixWorld,* and many more.

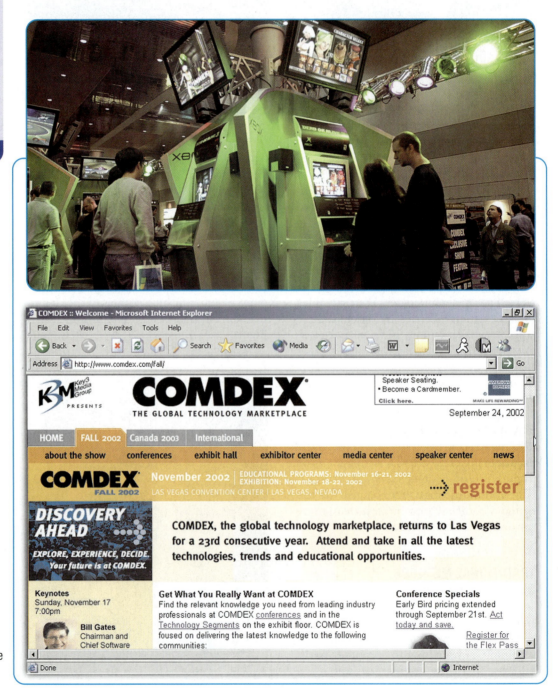

Figure 16.7
COMDEX is an annual event held in various locations around the world. To learn more about it, visit its Web site at **www.comdex.com**.

Figure 16.8
The Association for Women in Computing is dedicated to the advancement of women in the technology fields.

Conferences and Shows

One way to keep in touch with your profession is to attend conferences and trade shows. **Trade shows** are annual meetings in which computer product manufacturers, designers, and dealers showcase their products. Job fairs and on-the-spot interviews provide incentives for job seekers. Training seminars and product showcases provide many opportunities for skill and knowledge development.

The largest computer-related trade show is the annual COMDEX show in Las Vegas, Nevada (see Figure 16.7). With 4,000 members of the press and nearly one-quarter million attendees, COMDEX provides the perfect opportunity to roll out new products. COMDEX also sponsors well attended regional events. Growing in importance is NetWorld + InterOP, a spring Las Vegas show that focuses on Internet and networking technologies.

Professional Organizations

Joining one of the many professional associations can help you keep up with your area of interest, as well as provide valuable contacts for your career. Some associations have local chapters, and most offer publications, seminars, training, and conferences for members. Here are some of the most important organizations:

- **Association for Computing Machinery (ACM)** Focusing on computer science, this organization features many special-interest groups in such areas as databases, artificial intelligence, microcomputers, and computer graphics.

- **Association for Women in Computing (AWC)** This professional organization is devoted to promoting women in computing (see Figure 16.8).

- **Association of Internet Professionals (AIP)** This is the premier organization for Internet professionals.

- **Data Processing Management Association (DPMA)** This is the premier organization for CIS personnel and managers.

- **Network Professional Association (NPA)** This organization focuses on the professional advancement of

Destinations

Add TV to your list of bona fide ways to learn more about computers and technology. There's an entire channel devoted to the industry, called TechTV. The channel features shows on the Internet, cyber-crime, technology news, and new products. A listing of shows, as well as useful, non-broadcast information, can be found at the channel's Web site at **www.techtv.com**.

networking experts and offers a
non–vendor-based skills certification
program.

Jobs for Nondegreed IT Workers
In the traditional IT job picture, workers
who lack four-year college degrees generally find that they can't get the best IT
jobs, such as programming and systems
analyst positions. Nondegreed candidates
who possessed the needed qualifications,
however, could find jobs as data entry
clerks, help desk technicians, and technical writers. As you'll learn in the next section, this picture is changing.

New Information Technology (IT) Career Paths

IT careers are changing, driven both by
rapid technological change and by shifts
in the nature of today's businesses.
Increasingly, a four-year college degree
isn't sufficient to convince prospective
employers that would-be employees possess needed skills, since many of these
skills aren't yet widely taught in colleges
and universities.

ETHICAL DEBATES

Will You Ever Be Too Old to Have a Job in IT?
It's a story you'll hear quite often in Silicon Valley. A 45-year-old computer programmer lost his job at a major software firm, but before he was let go, he was asked to train his successor: a 22-year-old programmer from India, who is temporarily residing in the United States on an H1-B visa. Created by the U.S. Congress in response to the software industry's concerns about severe shortages of IT workers, the H1-B program enables qualified technical professionals from other countries to work in the United States temporarily.

Critics of the program charge that the worker shortage wouldn't exist if companies were willing to retrain older workers, and that the H1-B program facilitates what amounts to widespread age discrimination in the software industry. Countering this charge, industry spokespersons insist that it's far too expensive and time consuming to retrain older programmers who know nothing about today's cutting-edge technologies, such as Java and Web database interfaces. If they prefer younger programmers, these spokespersons insist, it's simply because younger programmers are more likely to have the skills they need.

Who's right? In the absence of reliable statistics, it's difficult to know for sure. According to one study, the unemployment rate for IT workers aged 50 and over is around 17 percent. However, another study came up with conflicting findings and suggested that the unemployment rate for older IT workers is in line with overall U.S. workforce figures. Another study found that, after 20 years, fewer than one in five programmers was still working in the profession—but this doesn't necessarily mean that these workers were let go. They may have moved into management, changed careers, or opened consulting businesses. So far, there have been no successful age discrimination lawsuits brought against the software industry.

The statistics don't tell the full story, but there's plenty of anecdotal evidence highlighting the difficulties older workers face. High-flying software and e-commerce companies tend to prefer younger, unmarried work-ers who have the enthusiasm and stamina to put in 80-hour work weeks. In such companies, workers with homes and families may be perceived as not completely dedicated. In addition, some of these companies are run by twenty-something millionaires who don't feel comfortable interviewing job candidates twice their age. After all, why hire older workers when talented, young H1-B workers are available—and will accept wages that are 30 percent lower than those received by U.S. workers? In addition, H1-B workers aren't very likely to protest poor working conditions or cause problems for management. Otherwise, if they lose their jobs, they'll very likely be required to leave the United States.

What's the lesson here? If you're interested in a career in the IT industry, you should be aware that today's hot skill set could be tomorrow's prescription for unemployment. You won't be able to rest on your achievements in college. Instead, you'll need to dedicate yourself to lifelong learning—and your career survival may depend on your ability to sense where technology's headed and what you should learn to make yourself indispensable.

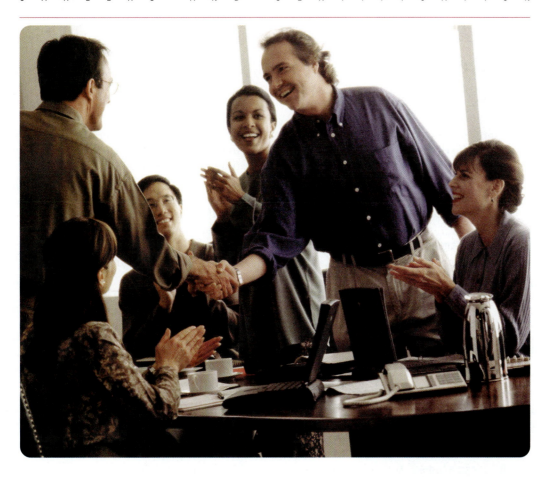

Figure 16.9
IT professionals work in teams with professionals from finance, marketing, and other corporate divisions.

As you'll see in this section, these skills include communication skills, business savvy, and technical skills in fast-emerging areas such as the Internet and Microsoft Windows NT. Some companies are hiring skilled applicants who don't have a four-year college degree as long as they can demonstrate that they possess the needed skills. In especially tight job markets, companies have even hired students who are still in high school. But, by lacking degrees, these employees are at risk of losing their jobs should their technological skills become obsolete. Nonetheless, most IT jobs still require a four-year college degree.

The changing patterns of employment have also affected IT careers. Today, IT workers can't rely on a company's paternalism to guide their career development, and they can't even count on keeping their jobs. Corporate downsizing, mergers, and acquisitions may put you out of work suddenly. For this reason, IT workers must become managers of their own careers. You may change jobs often, or you may forsake the job market altogether, preferring—as do increasing numbers of IT professionals—

to work as an independent contractor or consultant. Whichever path you choose, it's increasingly the worker's responsibility to obtain the training needed to keep up with fast-changing technology.

SOUGHT-AFTER BUSINESS SKILLS

Ten years ago, most IT jobs were internally focused. IT professionals worked inside companies. They created and supported computer services, such as payroll and inventory systems. But this picture is changing—and it's changing radically.

Today, driven by new network-based information systems, jobs increasingly combine an internal and an external focus. IT professionals are expected to work with a company's external partners and often with customers. They'll work in teams made up of people from different divisions of the enterprise (see Figure 16.9). Rather than performing a specific function, they're much more likely to work on a series of projects on which they'll use different skills. For all these reasons, today's businesses are looking for workers with the following "soft" skills in addition to "hard" technical knowledge:

Teamwork Increasingly, IT personnel are working in teams with workers from finance, marketing, and other corporate divisions. IT workers need to appreciate varying intellectual styles, work effectively in a team environment, and understand business perspectives.

Project management The ability to plan and budget a project—and especially to do so using project management software—is a plus in hiring decisions.

Communication Every employee needs communication skills now, even those who formerly worked internally and seldom had contact with people outside their departments. You'll need excellent writing and interpersonal skills, including the ability to give presentations using presentation graphics software.

Business acumen Information technology is now part of most companies' strategic planning, and IT employees are expected to possess some knowledge of business. The wise student takes courses also in general business subjects, including finance and marketing.

Older, experienced IT workers who suffer job losses due to downsizing may have difficulty finding employment if they don't possess these skills. In the past, you could focus on technology and ignore business and communication skills, but that's no longer true.

SOUGHT-AFTER TECHNOLOGY SKILLS

Businesses are also demanding new technology skills. Here's what's hot as of this writing:

Networking Skills related to networking include Ethernet, TCP/IP (Internet protocols), and LAN administration.

Microsoft Windows XP Expertise in managing the Office applications

and in working with Visual Basic continues to pay big rewards within organizations.

UNIX Despite the success of Windows, UNIX isn't going away. A strong demand exists for IT workers skilled in UNIX operating system configuration and maintenance, UNIX networking, and UNIX system programming.

TCP/IP Knowledge of the protocols underlying the Internet are in strong demand, both for external Web servers and for internal intranets.

Oracle Companies are looking for workers who have experience working with this company's products, including the Oracle relational database and client/server application tools.

C++ This object-oriented programming language is the language of choice for cutting-edge software development, both among vendors (software publishers) and corporate development shops.

Microsoft Visual Basic Rapid application development and code reusability make this language a winner for quick solutions.

Although a four-year degree in CS or CIS may fail to give you some of these desirable skills, the best preparation for a successful IT career still involves the invaluable theoretical background you get from a four-year college degree.

New Technologies, New Jobs

New technology brings not just more jobs, but new *types* of jobs (see Figure 16.10). For example, Web page design involves technical skills and knowledge in areas such as HTTP, HTML, CGI programming, and server configuration. But that's not enough. Increasingly, companies are looking for **Webmasters** (Web server managers and content developers) who understand marketing, advertising, and graphic design. What's required is not only technical skills and business smarts but artistic sensitivity, including some background in the aesthetics of design and color, coupled with a good deal of creativity (see Figure 16.11).

Although a bachelor's degree is still a prerequisite for IT careers in most companies, employers increasingly recognize that a degree alone may not guarantee that a new employee possesses needed skills. One reason: many of these new jobs are inherently cross-disciplinary, involving artistic or communication skills as well as top-notch technical ability. Existing CS and CIS programs may produce graduates who lack creativity, marketing knowledge,

graphic design experience, or communication abilities. For this reason, many companies are hiring students who have taken many computer courses but possess degrees in other fields, such as design, marketing, or English.

CERTIFICATION

The rapid change in information technology is creating a demand for new ways to ensure that employment applicants possess the skills they claim. In traditional IT careers, the four-year college degree assured a certain level of competence, but that's no longer entirely true. As we mentioned

New Jobs in Information Technology

Job Title	Responsibilities
Interactive digital media specialist	Uses multimedia software to create engaging presentations, including animation and video
Webmaster	Designs and maintains a Web server and related database servers
Web application engineer	Designs, develops, tests, and documents new Web-based services for Web sites
Web specialist	Works with internal and external customers to create high-quality content pages for Web sites

Figure 16.10

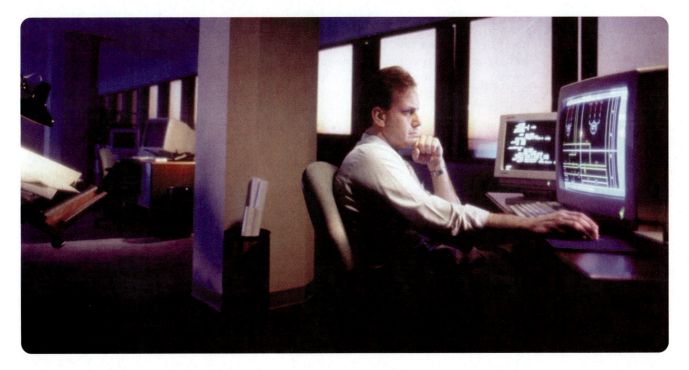

Figure 16.11
Webmasters must understand marketing, advertising, and graphic design.

Selected Certification Programs

Certification Program	Description
Microsoft Certified Systems Engineer (MCSE)	Microsoft Windows NT Server and BackOffice applications; operating system and network configuration and maintenance as well as LAN-based client/server development (Microsoft Corporation)
Microsoft Certified Systems Engineer (MCSE) + Internet	Microsoft Windows NT Server configuration and maintenance for Internet and intranet sites (Microsoft Corporation)
Microsoft Certified Solution Developer (MCSD)	Programming and application development with Microsoft development tools, such as Visual Basic (Microsoft Corporation)
Certified NetWare Engineer (CNE)	Novell networking and NetWare network operating systems (Novell Corporation)
Certified Java Programmer	Programming in Java (Sun Microsystems)
Certified Java Developer	Programming and application development in Java (Sun Microsystems)

Figure 16.12

earlier, many of the skills today's companies need are so new that they're not yet widely taught in colleges and universities, which often need as long as one or two years to alter their curricula. Certification is increasingly seen as a way that employers can assure themselves that newly hired workers can do necessary tasks.

In brief, **certification** is a skills and knowledge assessment process organized by computer industry vendors (and sometimes by professional associations). To obtain a certificate, you choose your preferred method of training; you can take courses at a college or a private training center, or study on your own using vendor-approved books, CD-ROM materials, or the Web. When you're ready, you take a tough, comprehensive examination. If you pass, you get the certificate (see Figure 16.12). Unlike a college degree, the certificate isn't good for life; to retain certification, you may need to take brush-up courses and exams periodically, sometimes as often as every six months.

Benefits of Certification

What's the payoff for job applicants? A certificate won't guarantee a job or even higher pay, but it does provide a benchmark that enables prospective employers to assess skills in an applicant pool. In areas of high demand, certification can translate into an increase of 10 to 15 percent in initial salary offers. Applicants who possess the Microsoft Certified Systems Engineer (MCSE) certificate may gain as much as $10,000 in starting salary.

What's the payoff for employers? Although the effect of certification hasn't been rigorously studied by independent investigators, vendors and trainers claim that employers who hire certified employees have less downtime and lower IT costs.

Risks of Certification

Certification entails some risks for employees and employers alike. The reason lies in the nature of the certification process, which emphasizes a form of learning that is both narrow (focused on a specific technology) and deep (rigorous and thorough).

For employees, certification requires that they devote a great deal of time and effort to a specific vendor's technology. But changing technology may make vendor-specific skills less marketable. If you're certified as a Novell NetWare technician, for example, you won't impress a prospective employer who's running a Windows NT network. And Windows NT has gained considerable market share at the expense of Novell NetWare systems. If you make a bad bet on which certificate to pursue, you could wind up with excellent skills in a technology that's considered to be obsolete.

For employers, hiring people with narrow training is a risk. Specifically, narrowly trained people may not be able

Techtalk

MOUS

One of the certifications any computer user can earn is MOUS certification. MOUS stands for Microsoft Office User Specialist and signifies a user's proficiency with Microsoft Office products such as Word, Excel, Access, and PowerPoint.

to adjust to rapidly changing technology. That's why it's a good idea to take as many CS and CIS courses as you can. With a solid theoretical foundation, you can learn new skills throughout your career. In itself, certification isn't a ticket to a high-paying job or a satisfying career. You'll prove most attractive to employers if you combine certification with a good college record, communication skills, and business courses. In addition, just having one skill isn't enough. Some companies expect employees to possess strong skills in as many as four or five areas.

The Effect of Computers on Overall Employment

Although computers are creating new job opportunities, they're also shifting labor demand toward skilled workers, particularly those with computer skills. As a result, skilled workers earn more, while the wages paid to unskilled workers have stagnated over the past 20 years. Partly in consequence, the gap between the rich and the poor has widened as educated, skilled workers have taken advantage of new, technology-based opportunities. Technology isn't the only cause of this trend; it's fueled also by the exodus of low-paying, unskilled jobs to foreign countries, where labor is cheaper. But the fact remains that computer and information literacy has never been more important to a person's future.

Technology is also eliminating some jobs by automating them out of existence. One purpose of advanced technology is to free people from drudgery and make work more efficient, but as a result, fewer workers may be required. For instance, computer-guided robots are taking over many manufacturing jobs that people once held (see Figure 16.13). This process is called **automation** (the replacement of human workers by machines).

The jobs most likely to be eliminated by computers involve repetitive, semi-skilled tasks. For example, the United States Postal Service eliminated nearly

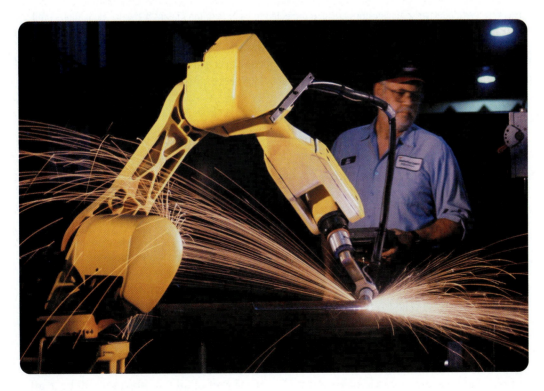

Figure 16.13
Computer-guided robots are handling many manufacturing jobs that people once held.

CURRENTS

CAREER LANDSCAPES

Will Your Dream Job in IT Be There When You Arrive?

In the world of technology, especially, nobody knows what the future will bring. That can feel a little troubling for future job seekers attempting to acquire today the skills they'll apply tomorrow. Will the job of your dreams be around when you're looking for employment? Does it even exist yet? How do you prepare for an uncertain career landscape?

Learning about computers and getting a bachelor's degree is a step in the right direction, as is keeping up with emerging technologies. Nobody wants to head down a path toward an occupation that won't even exist in five years. Staying abreast of job trends is an excellent way to ensure you're heading in the right direction. Where do you find such information? The Bureau of Labor Statistics (BLS), located at **www.bls.gov**, is a good place to start.

As we look to the year 2010, research indicates that many computer technology, programming, database, and networking jobs will continue to be in high demand. Both small and large companies will need computer specialists and administrators who can keep up with the fast-changing technology needed to keep them growing and competitive. This is especially important when integrating new and increasingly sophisticated technologies.

Computer software engineering is projected to be the fastest-growing occupation in the next five years, especially in the computer and data processing services industry. Software engineers will be needed to upgrade, manage, and modify computer systems to meet new Internet and e-commerce challenges. These engineers will continue to develop the ever-evolving Internet, company intranets, and a whole new age of Web applications. Software engineers with strong programming, systems analysis, interpersonal, and business skills are those who are most likely to succeed. Of course, the future will bring with it many new problems for software engineers to solve—problems we can't even think of because they don't exist yet.

Some IT experts predict that some of the programming needs in the United States will be met by overseas programmers, who tend to be cheaper than their American counterparts. Regardless, there will continue to be a need for good software programmers.

Because new technologies will continue to be incorporated into businesses, computer support specialists will be needed to aid in technical support for customers. System administrators, systems analysts, computer scientists, and database administrators are also projected to be among the fastest-growing occupations until 2010. And security specialists will be in high demand to protect data, communications, and technological investments. Companies will continue to seek individuals who are able to apply new technology and strategies efficiently. Those who not only know the technologies but also can communicate with employees, clients, and consumers using that technology will be the most effective job seekers. And in most IT positions, consulting will be a continuing trend.

Don't wait until the future arrives to find your technological niche. Plan ahead. Conduct research. Check the trends at the BLS site. Make sure your dream job of the future is there waiting for exactly you when you arrive.

100,000 jobs formerly held by workers who read and sorted envelopes. Today, automated equipment does most of the work with little, if any, human intervention.

When advancing technology makes an entire job category obsolete, **structural unemployment** has occurred. Structural unemployment differs from the normal up-and-down cycles of layoffs and rehires. People who lose jobs because of structural unemployment are not going to get them back. Their only option is to retrain themselves to work in other careers.

Who will survive—and flourish—in a computer-driven economy? The answer is simple. The survivors will be people who are highly educated, who know that education is a lifelong process, and who adapt quickly to change. Just consider this: according to the author of a recent book on career survival, half of all the jobs that will be available in 10 years don't even exist today.

COMPUTERS IN YOUR FUTURE 2004

16.15

HOME | Takeaway Points | Key Terms and Concepts | Matching | Multiple Choice | Fill-In | Short Answer | Exercises/Projects | Web Research | CHAPTER REVIEW

TAKEAWAY POINTS

- Traditionally, information technology (IT) careers required a four-year college degree in computer science (CS) or computer information systems (CIS). Employment was long term, and employers provided training if additional skills were needed.

- Training in computer science emphasizes the theoretical and cutting-edge aspects of computing. Training in computer information systems emphasizes more practical aspects of computing in business settings.

- IT workers typically find employment in corporate information systems (IS) departments and vendor companies.

- Today, recruiters are looking for teamwork, project management skills, communication skills, and business savvy as well as technical skills.

- Recruiters are looking for workers with knowledge and experience in networking, Microsoft Windows XP, UNIX, C++, and the Internet.

- Certification provides one means of demonstrating your skills to an employer, but it shouldn't take the place of a sound background in computer science or computer information systems.

CHAPTER
REVIEW

Takeaway
Points

Key Terms
and Concepts

Matching

Multiple
Choice

Fill-In

Short
Answer

Exercises/
Projects

Web
Research

HOME

1
2
3
4
5
6
7
8
9
10
11
12
13
14
15
16

KEY TERMS AND CONCEPTS

automation
certification
computer information
　systems (CIS)
computer science (CS)

electrical
　engineering (EE)
information systems
　(IS) department
structural unemployment

systems
　engineering
trade show
vendor
Webmaster

HOME | Takeaway Points | Key Terms and Concepts | **Matching** | Multiple Choice | Fill-In | Short Answer | Exercises/ Projects | Web Research

CHAPTER REVIEW

MATCHING

Match each key term in the left column with the most accurate definition in the right column.

_____ 1. computer science (CS)

_____ 2. project management

_____ 3. vendor

_____ 4. systems engineering

_____ 5. electrical engineering

_____ 6. Association for Computing Machinery

_____ 7. Webmasters

_____ 8. certification

_____ 9. automation

_____ 10. structural unemployment

_____ 11. computer information systems (CIS)

_____ 12. trade shows

_____ 13. Certified NetWare Engineer (CNE)

_____ 14. Oracle

_____ 15. training seminars

a. an organization featuring special interest groups in areas such as databases, microcomputers, and computer graphics

b. applies the scientific method to creating and maintaining quality systems

c. the replacement of human workers by machines

d. Web server managers and content developers

e. a software development firm

f. focuses on the practical rather than the theoretical, and emphasizes the skills that businesses need right now

g. planning and budgeting a project

h. occurs when advancing technology makes an entire job category obsolete

i. a skills and knowledge assessment process organized by computer industry vendors

j. offers a strong focus on digital circuit design, as well as cutting-edge communication technologies

k. training for new computer-related technologies

l. a company that is a major producer of relational database and client/server applications

m. uses the principles of scientific and engineering research to improve computing

n. Novell networking certification

o. periodic meetings in which computer product manufacturers, designers, and dealers showcase their products

1 2 3 4 5 6 7 8 9 10 11 12 13 14 15 16

MULTIPLE CHOICE

Circle the correct choice for each of the following.

1. Which of the following is not characteristic of the traditional career path in information technology (IT)?
   a. A computer-related bachelor's degree is a must.
   b. IT employees with business savvy and good communication skills could move into management.
   c. It is important not to stay with any one company for very long to have a successful career in IT.
   d. To keep up with trends, IT professionals read professional journals and attend conferences.

2. Which of the following is not a typical job title in a corporate IS department?
   a. Director of Computer Operations
   b. Software Architect
   c. Network Engineer
   d. Programmer/Analyst

3. Which of the following is not a typical job title in a software development firm?
   a. Director of Research and Development
   b. Software Engineer
   c. Client/Server Manager
   d. Customer Support Technician

4. This is not true of computer science departments.
   a. They focus on the theoretical, rather than the practical aspects of computing.
   b. They focus on the practical, rather than the theoretical aspects of computing.
   c. CS graduates are more likely than CIS graduates to find jobs in cutting-edge software development firms.
   d. CS uses the principles of scientific and engineering research to improve computing.

5. This is a traditional method of continuing education.
   a. Conferences
   b. Project management
   c. Professional organizations
   d. Both a and c

6. Which of the following is not a professional organization designed to help IT professionals keep up with their areas of interest?
   a. Association for Computers and Machines (AC&M)
   b. Data Processing Management Association (DPMA)
   c. Association for Women in Computing (AWC)
   d. Association for Computing Machinery (ACM)

7. Which of the following is not an IT professional association?
   a. Association of Web Professionals (AWP)
   b. Association for Computing Machinery (ACM)
   c. Association of Internet Professionals (AIP)
   d. Network Professional Association (NPA)

8. Which of the following is one of the hot technological skills mentioned in the chapter that businesses are demanding of employees?
   a. Certification
   b. Windows NT
   c. Visual Oracle
   d. Linux

9. Which of the following is not a new job in information technology?
   a. Webmaster
   b. Web specialist
   c. Systems analyst
   d. Interactive digital media specialist

10. Which of the following is a certification program?
    a. Association of Computer Machinery Certificate
    b. Certified NetWare Engineer
    c. Macintosh Certified Solution Developer
    d. Certified BASIC Programmer

HOME | Takeaway Points | Key Terms and Concepts | Matching | Multiple Choice | Fill-In | Short Answer | Exercises/ Projects | Web Research | CHAPTER REVIEW

FILL-IN

In the blanks provided, write the correct answer for each of the following.

1. Many years ago, most people got into IT careers by obtaining a computer-related degree and getting a job with a corporate _____.

2. _____ departments emphasize the theoretical rather than the practical aspects of computing.

3. _____ departments emphasize business coursework, interpersonal skills, and communications skills.

4. The premier organization for CIS personnel and managers is the _____.

5. _____ offers a strong focus on digital circuit design, as well as cutting-edge communication technologies.

6. The _____ engineering discipline applies the scientific method to creating and maintaining quality systems, whether in business or in industry.

7. When it comes to Web design, companies are increasingly looking for _____ who understand marketing, advertising, and graphic design.

8. _____ is a skill and knowledge assessment process that is organized by computer industry vendors.

9. The process in which computers replace human workers is called _____.

10. When advancing technology makes an entire job category obsolete, _____ has occurred.

11. _____ are periodic meetings in which computer product manufacturers, designers, and dealers showcase their products.

12. _____ is the ability to plan and budget with appropriate software tools.

13. _____ refers to certification in the use of Microsoft Office products.

14. _____ is a language that allows rapid application development and code reusability.

15. _____ is having knowledge of business concepts.

SHORT ANSWER

1. What are some of the typical job titles and responsibilities in a corporate IS department?

2. What are some of the basic differences between the computer science and computer information systems departments?

3. Describe in detail some of the traditional methods associated with continuing education.

4. Describe some of the typical job titles and responsibilities associated with the newest jobs in information technology.

5. What is certification? What are its benefits and risks?

6. What overall effect are computers having on employment?

1 2 3 4 5 6 7 8 9 10 11 12 13 14 15 16

EXERCISES/PROJECTS

1. Check the classified section of a Sunday edition of a local large-city newspaper to see how the job salaries compare with those given in Figures 16.2 and 16.3. The salary ranges given in the text are based on national averages. For each job description that you can find advertised, list those jobs that are above or near the top and those that are below or near the bottom of the figures cited in the book. Overall, are the salaries for IT positions in your area above or below the national standards? Explain why you think this is true.

2. Does your school have a computer information systems (CIS) department? If so, look at a school catalog (printed or online) to find information about its program. If you can't find answers to some of the following questions in the catalog, then you'll have to contact the department directly.

   What are the job titles for which graduates are prepared? If there are required courses in the areas of interpersonal communication, business knowledge, or the Internet, identify them by title. Is there an elective or a required course that allows students to intern with an IT company?

3. What type of education and training do you think a company would want for a software support technician?

4. Check local newspapers and telephone books to see if IT certification training is offered in your area. If it is, then contact the training center(s) so that you can answer the following questions. What are the names of the training companies? Do they offer training programs in any of the certifications—such as MCSE, MCSD, and CNE—that are described in the text? What is the duration and cost of these training sessions? Are there prerequisite skills for any of these sessions? After training, will they help you find a job?

5. IT professionals do not have to attend certification training sessions to learn new skills. They can study at home and then take a certification examination. Visit a bookstore and see what types of publications are designed to help professionals study for certification examinations. List the names of the certification programs, and the title, author, and price of the books. Select one of these texts and look at it in greater detail by examining the table of contents and selected pages. Does the book seem to provide IT professionals with background knowledge and content depth, or does it just focus on passing the examination? Explain which approach you would prefer if you were an IT professional, and why.

HOME | Takeaway Points | Key Terms and Concepts | Matching | Multiple Choice | Fill-In | Short Answer | Exercises/ Projects | Web Research | CHAPTER REVIEW

WEB RESEARCH

1. In the last two Exercises/Projects questions you learned how training seminars and printed materials are available to help prepare IT professionals to take certification examinations. Now you are going to search the Internet to see if you can find Web-based training. Select one of the recognized certification programs identified in the text—MCSE, MCSD, CNE, Certified Java Programmer, or Certified Java Developer—and find a site that has information about online courses. Identify the certification area, the URL, and the cost for a specific course. Can the actual certification examination be taken online? Did you find any references to other computer-related certification training? If so, name two of them.

2. Newspapers are not the only source for finding local or national jobs. Use the Internet to find a specific IT position in several different geographical areas. Identify the position, the URLs where you found the job information, and what the salaries are in the different areas. Identify an area where the salaries appear to be exceptionally high and an area where they appear to be exceptionally low. Why do you think the salaries are exceptional in those areas?

3. Besides attending meetings and reading printed materials, members of professional organizations can obtain information online. Discussion groups, also known as listservs, are forums where members can talk about a variety of issues. ISWorld Net at **www.isworld.org/isworld/isworldtext.html** maintains several online discussion groups for IS professionals. Name the current discussion groups that are supported by this organization. In which discussion group would your instructor discuss IS curriculum issues? In which groups are IS careers, both from a business and a computer science perspective, discussed? These forums are also frequently used to post job openings. In which discussion group would one place an advertisement for a faculty position?

4. The text identifies the following as "Sought-After Technology Skills": Networking, Microsoft Windows NT, UNIX, TCP/IP, Oracle, C++, and Microsoft Visual Basic. Go to your school's library Web site or the library Web site of a college of your choice to look at some online magazines and journals that professionals may read to find information on these key skills. Select one of the skills, and find a recent article that may be of interest to IS professionals. Identify the skill, the publication, the date, the title, and the author. Write a brief one-page, single-spaced review of the article. Submit the URL and your review to your instructor in whatever form (hard copy or electronic) is preferred.

5. As discussed in the preceding chapter, Visual Basic is an extremely popular language for rapidly designing Windows-based applications, and in this chapter you have learned that one of the traditional methods for professionals to continue their education is to attend training seminars. Suppose that you're an experienced programmer in other programming languages, and you wish to learn Visual Basic. Visit the Web site **www.appdev.com/schedule/home.asp** to find a beginner's training seminar in Visual Basic. Write a request to your manager justifying your attendance at the seminar. Be sure to include the location, length, and cost of the seminar and benefits to your company.

1 2 3 4 5 6 7 8 9 10 11 12 13 14 15 16

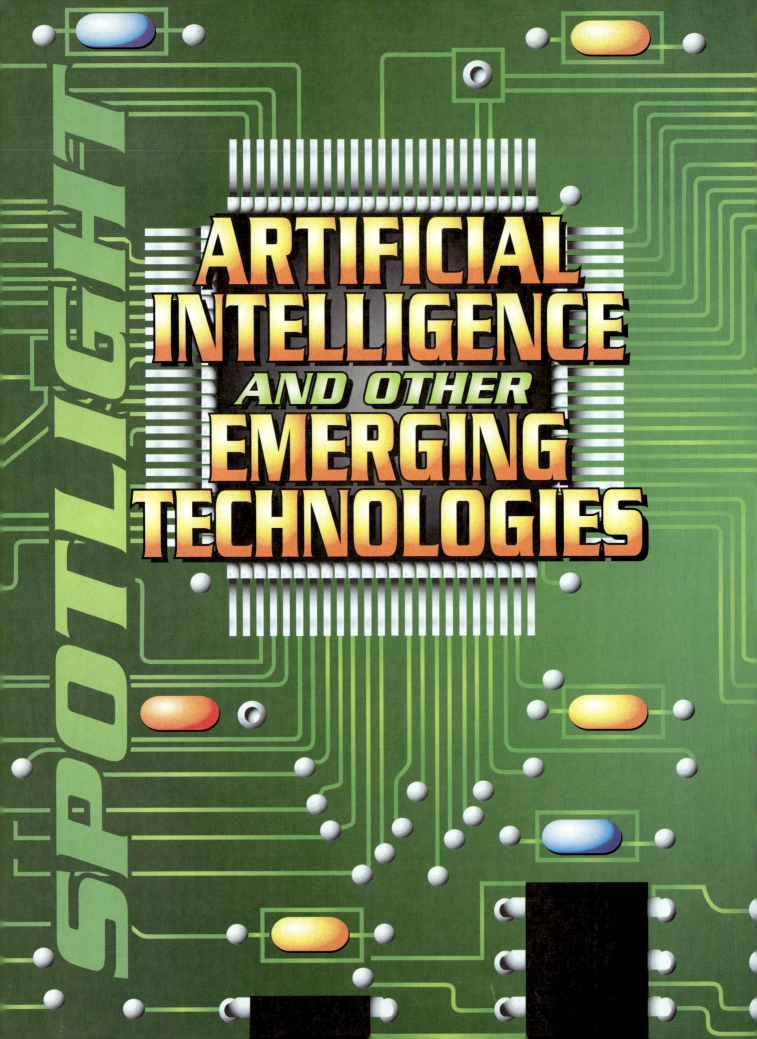

SPOTLIGHT

ARTIFICIAL INTELLIGENCE
AND OTHER
EMERGING TECHNOLOGIES

What will computers be like in the future?

It's easy to predict the future, but the hard part is getting it right, particularly where technology is concerned. Past predictions don't offer much comfort. In 1876, a Western Union official said, "The telephone has too many shortcomings to be seriously considered as a means of communication. The device is inherently of no value." A century later, the chairman of IBM stated that there was no reason anyone would want a computer in their home.

Predicting the future will never be an exact science, but it's possible to approach the task in an organized way. In the field called *future studies*, scholars rely on a variety of methods to develop more accurate predictions. One method, called *trend extrapolation*, identifies current trends and then projects them out into the future. In this spotlight, you'll look at the trends driving contemporary computing, and you'll explore what may happen if these trends continue for the next several decades. You'll also examine the potential impact of artificial intelligence (AI), should computer designers succeed in creating a truly intelligent machine.

Tomorrow's Hardware: Faster, Cheaper, Connected

Could the history of the next 50 years be described simply by stating two laws of technology and economics? Consider these:

- **Moore's Law** Intel Corporation Chairman Gordon Moore predicted more than 30 years ago that microprocessors and other miniature circuits would double in circuit density (and therefore in processing power) every 18 to 24 months. Moore's Law still holds true, and experts believe that the trend should continue for at least another decade, and perhaps for 20 more years, until the process of miniaturization of silicon components runs into physical barriers. If Moore's Law continues until the middle of this century, computers will be 10 billion times more powerful than today's fastest machines. Storage technology shows a similar trend: steep rises in capacity and steep declines in cost.

- **Metcalfe's Law** Ethernet inventor Bob Metcalfe predicts that the value of a computer network grows in proportion to the square of the number of people connected to it. Consider that a telephone line that connects two people is of limited value, but a telephone system that connects an entire city becomes an indispensable resource for every aspect of life. Under Metcalfe's Law, for example, a network with two people connected has a value of 4, but a network with four people connected has a value of 16. According to some predictions, the Internet will ultimately connect one billion users worldwide.

If you put these two laws together, you get a potent mixture: the computer industry is now giving us *networked* machines that double in power every 18 to 24 months, even as the networks they're connected to are rapidly growing in size.

As computers become faster, cheaper, and more valuable, they'll encourage the trend toward the digitization of all the world's information and knowledge—the entire storehouse

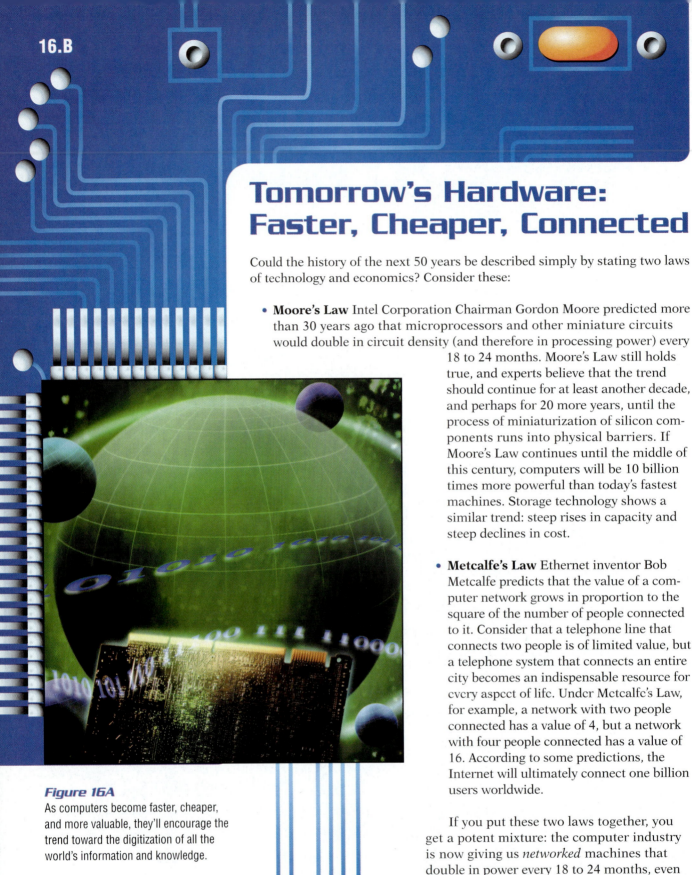

Figure 16A
As computers become faster, cheaper, and more valuable, they'll encourage the trend toward the digitization of all the world's information and knowledge.

of accumulated human experience (see Figure 16A). And as digitization proceeds, the result will be increasing convergence of all media, communication, and networking technologies; the boundaries between telephones, newspapers, radio, television, and computers will fade away.

THE SHORT TERM

In the next several years, you'll see Moore's and Metcalfe's Laws at work. Figure 16B lists the characteristics of a circa 2005 personal computer, based on the assumption that Moore's Law will remain in effect. Compare the computer of tomorrow with the computer of less than five years ago and the difference is astounding. Besides these performance improvements, you'll see some basic changes in the standard PC's hardware, such as an increase in the use of flat-panel LCD displays in place of bulky cathode ray tube (CRT) monitors. High-capacity, read/write optical drives will be standard equipment. New network technologies will bring megabit bandwidth to homes and offices.

The Typical Personal Computer: 1999 vs. 2005

Component	1999	2005
RAM	64 MB	1 GB
Processor speed (instructions per second)	400 million	7 billion
Circuit density (number of transistors)	7.5 million	125 million
Hard disk capacity	8 GB	135 GB
Average Internet connection speed (bits per second)	56,000	1 million

Figure 16B

THE LONG TERM

What will computing be like several decades from now? By 2020, Moore's Law predicts that all the components of unbelievably powerful computers will be accommodated on just one tiny mass-produced silicon chip. These chips will include super fast processors (capable of performing a trillion instructions per second), huge amounts of RAM, video circuitry—the works. And they'll cost less than $500. In some scenarios, they could cost as little as $100!

Recognizing the trends toward lower cost and miniaturization, some computer scientists speak of **ubiquitous computing**. (The term *ubiquitous* means *everywhere*.) In ubiquitous computing, computers are everywhere, and they fade into the background, providing computer-based intelligence all around us. Your car will inform you when it needs maintenance. Short on

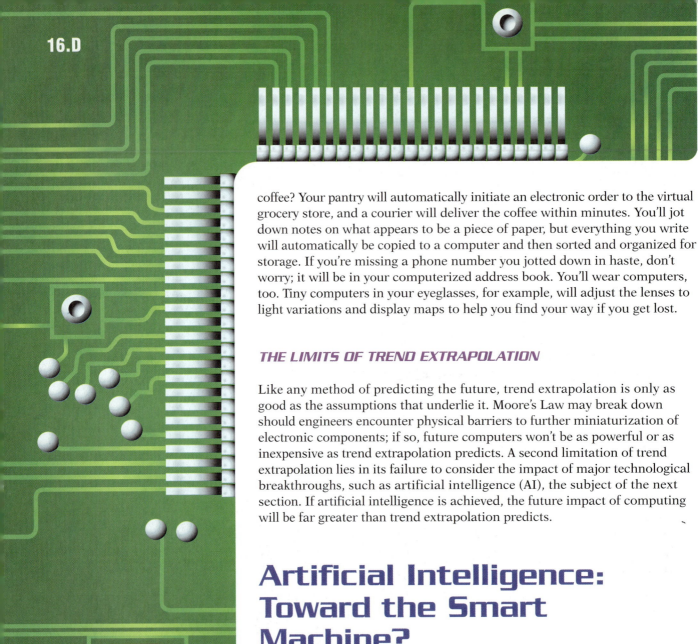

coffee? Your pantry will automatically initiate an electronic order to the virtual grocery store, and a courier will deliver the coffee within minutes. You'll jot down notes on what appears to be a piece of paper, but everything you write will automatically be copied to a computer and then sorted and organized for storage. If you're missing a phone number you jotted down in haste, don't worry; it will be in your computerized address book. You'll wear computers, too. Tiny computers in your eyeglasses, for example, will adjust the lenses to light variations and display maps to help you find your way if you get lost.

THE LIMITS OF TREND EXTRAPOLATION

Like any method of predicting the future, trend extrapolation is only as good as the assumptions that underlie it. Moore's Law may break down should engineers encounter physical barriers to further miniaturization of electronic components; if so, future computers won't be as powerful or as inexpensive as trend extrapolation predicts. A second limitation of trend extrapolation lies in its failure to consider the impact of major technological breakthroughs, such as artificial intelligence (AI), the subject of the next section. If artificial intelligence is achieved, the future impact of computing will be far greater than trend extrapolation predicts.

Artificial Intelligence: Toward the Smart Machine?

In the classic sci-fi adventure *2001*, a glitch in an intelligent computer's programming brings ruin and death to a manned expedition to Jupiter. Concluding that the ship's human crew represent a danger to the mission, the computer—named HAL 9000—decides to eliminate them. As envisioned in the film, HAL 9000 exhibits many of the characteristics of human intelligence, such as the ability to reason, to converse in **natural language** (ordinary human speech), and to formulate a plan or strategy. But HAL 9000 exists only in the imagination of science fiction writers.

The field that attempts to endow computers with intelligence is known as **artificial intelligence (AI)**, but it has met with only partial success due to the many formidable obstacles the field has encountered (see Figure 16C). As you'll see in this section, AI specialists have succeeded in creating special-purpose programs that exhibit some aspects of human intelligence, but these programs can't function intelligently outside the context for which they were designed.

What's in store for the future? Computer scientists are sharply divided between optimists who believe that these problems will be overcome and pessimists who believe that the underlying problems are so difficult that they're impossible to solve.

Let's start with the big question: just what *is* intelligence?

DEFINING INTELLIGENCE

Scientists and philosophers do not agree on the definition of *intelligence*, except for one point: intelligence has many components. An intelligent creature can do some or all of the following:

- Learn and retain the learned knowledge

- Reason on the basis of this knowledge

- Adapt to new circumstances

- Plan (develop strategies)

- Communicate

- Recognize patterns

Scientists still know very little about the human brain, but it's already clear that the brain is far more complex and works differently from any computer. The average adult's brain contains approximately 100 billion neurons (nerve cells) linked in complex, interconnected pathways; for any given operation, thousands of neurons may come into play. Operations are both electrical and chemical. Areas of the brain are known to govern specific functions, such as sensory input (vision and hearing, for example), speech, emotions, reasoning, and memory.

How does the human brain compare with a computer? Some speculative estimates are shown in Figure 16D. Compared with computers, the human brain accepts voluminous amounts of input and stores an unbelievable amount of data. In terms of processing, the human brain excels at pattern recognition (for example, recognizing faces and understanding speech), but it's a slow calculator. In contrast, computers accept much smaller amounts of input and do a poor job of recognizing patterns, but they can calculate rapidly and produce output much faster than humans can.

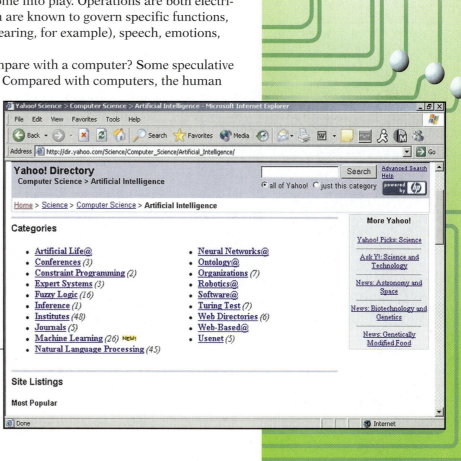

Figure 16C

Yahoo! features many categories with hundreds of links on the topic of artificial intelligence.

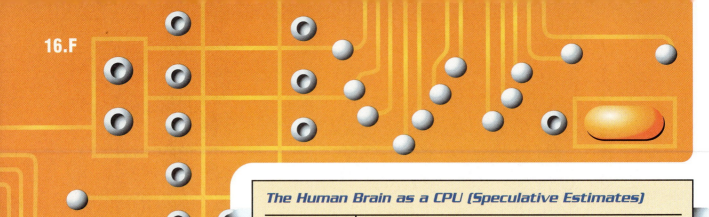

The Human Brain as a CPU (Speculative Estimates)	
Operation	**Estimated Speed or Capacity**
Input	Fast (1 gigabit per second). The human retina can achieve a resolution of approximately 127 million "pixels."
Processing	Fast for pattern recognition (10 billion instructions per second); slow for calculations (2–100 per second)
Output	Slow (speech: 100 bits per second)
Storage	Very large (10 terabytes), but retrieval can be uncertain

Figure 16D

THE TURING TEST

As you've just learned, there's no scientific consensus on what constitutes intelligence. So how do we tell whether a computer is intelligent? For British computer scientist Alan Turing, the answer is easy. A computer is intelligent if a team of unbiased judges can't tell the difference between computer-generated and human output.

Writing in the 1950s, Turing envisioned what AI specialists now call a **Turing Test** (see Figure 16E). In a Turing Test, a person sits at a computer and types questions. The computer is connected to two other hidden computers. At one, a human being reads the questions and types responses. At the other, a computer with no human assistant runs a program that also gives answers. If the person typing the question can't tell the difference between the human's answers and the computer's answers, Turing said, the computer is intelligent.

By Turing's standard, computers long ago passed the Turing Test. In the mid-1960s, Joseph Weizenbaum, a computer scientist at MIT, wrote a simple program called ELIZA. This program mimics a human therapist. If you type, "I'm worried about my girlfriend," the program responds, "Tell me more about your girlfriend." The program is actually very simple. If the user types a word on the program's built-in list, such as girlfriend, father, guilt, or problem, the program copies this word and puts it into the response. Even so, some people were fooled into thinking they were conversing with a real therapist.

ELIZA can't fool people for long, but today's programs are larger and more resourceful. In the First Annual Loebner Prize Competition (an annual competition designed to implement the Turing Test and award the most "human" computer), held at the Boston Computer Museum in 1991, ten human judges tried to determine which of eight display screens showed text produced by people and which ones displayed text produced by the computer. An advanced program called PC Therapist tricked half the judges into thinking that the program was a human being. The 1998 Loebner Prize winner, a program called Fred, is an even better chatter. Fred uses a number of tricks to evade questions you might ask in an attempt to trip up the programming. In 2000

Figure 16E
British computer scientist Alan Turing. According to most psychologists, the Turing Test's type-and-response method is too simplistic.

For more information on the Loebner Prize, visit www.loebner.net/Prizef/loebner-prize.html.

and 2001, the prize was won by Richard Wallace for his work on A.L.I.C.E., short for Artificial Linguistic Internet Computer Entity.

Does the Turing Test withstand scrutiny? According to most philosophers and psychologists, the Turing Test's type-and-response method is too simplistic. Many programmers have learned how to create a chat response program that can fool judges. The only intelligence that comes into play here is that of the human judges, who use their immense pattern recognition and memory capabilities to make sense of these program's sometimes odd responses.

BRUTE FORCE

The human brain excels at recognizing patterns; the computer excels at performing computations. Instead of trying to get a computer to work the way the human brain does, why not use the computer's calculation capabilities to simulate human intelligence? After all, what matters is the outcome, not the process.

That's exactly the reasoning behind an entire generation of chess-playing programs, which have long been pitted against human chess masters. These programs don't work the way human chess players do. They don't plan, strategize, or learn from experience. Instead, they examine each board position, calculate *all* the possible moves that can be made, and select the best one. This is called the **brute force** approach to artificial intelligence. A brute force technique relies on the computer's fast processing capabilities to repeat a simple operation until an answer is found.

Good chess-playing programs can easily defeat novice or intermediate players. Until 1997, no chess-playing program had ever defeated an international chess champion. But that changed on May 11, 1997, when an IBM-designed chess-playing system, called Deep Blue, defeated Russian chess master Garry Kasparov (see Figure 16F). Combining a supercomputer with specialized programming, Deep Blue can examine more than 200 million alternative plays per second. What's more, Deep Blue works without emotions, which may have hampered Kasparov. During the match, Kasparov was increasingly angered by what he saw as the IBM programmers' attempt to analyze Kasparov's game and to write a program specifically defeat *him*.

Is Deep Blue intelligent? Deep Blue's programmers are the first to deny that Deep Blue possesses anything like human intelligence. It's simply a very fast program that examines a chess situation and calculates the optimum move. What's more, it can't drive to the chess match, converse with the match's organizers (or even recognize who they are), or reach out and move the chess pieces on the playing board. Still, Deep Blue's success suggests that computers don't have to work the way the human brain does to exhibit some of the characteristics associated with intelligence.

Figure 16F
On May 11, 1997, Deep Blue defeated Russian chess master Garry Kasparov.

AI ACHIEVEMENTS

In the early years of AI research, computer scientists sometimes made exuberant predictions. In 1967, Marvin Minsky, one of the founders of AI research, declared that by the 1990s, computers intelligent enough to converse with humans and drive automobiles would be commonplace. Because today's typical computer lacks these capabilities, Minsky's prediction is often ridiculed. But Minsky might have the last laugh. Today's special-purpose AI systems may not combine all the attributes of human intelligence in a single system, but they can and do emulate human brain power in selected areas.

As long as you're not looking for a walking, talking computer that has all the attributes of human intelligence, Minsky's prediction rings surprisingly true. For example, PEGASUS, a spoken language interface connected to American Airlines' SABRE reservation system, enables subscribers to obtain flight information and make flight reservations by conversing with the computer through a telephone. And an onboard computer equipped with a video monitoring system recently drove a van from Washington, D.C., to San Diego, California, averaging 63 mph, 24 hours per day. The progress has been piecemeal but is nevertheless impressive. Let's look at some of AI's achievements.

NATURAL LANGUAGE

The term *natural language* refers to the speech people use every day. Computers would be much easier to use if they could understand natural language, whether the input was spoken or typed. For example, instead of looking through folder after folder in search of a missing file, imagine asking the computer, "Where's that file I created a couple of days ago? You know, the one in which I wrote about those two paintings we saw in my art history class?"

Despite years of effort to create natural language interfaces, computers are still not good at understanding what they hear and acting on this understanding. Much of what passes for a natural language interface amounts to word matching; for example, you can navigate a Macintosh's folders by speaking their names and giving a few simple commands, such as "Open" or "Close." Combined with software that can parse (decode) a sentence's grammatical structure, word matching programs can work well in areas with highly specialized vocabularies of a few thousand words.

Attempts to create natural language systems of more general capabilities have run into profound problems, such as the ambiguity of human language. The term *intelligence,* for instance, has at least four other senses, or meanings, besides the one we're talking about here; in the military, for example, *intelligence* means knowledge about the enemy. A program capable of understanding the various senses of a word would have to know a great deal about the world. For example, natural language software should be able to understand that "the day before Christmas" is December 24. The underlying problems are exceedingly complex and will require many more years of research to solve.

Natural language understanding may lie in computing's future, but major advances have been made in **speech recognition**, in which computers translate spoken speech into text (see Figure 16G). Previously, speech recognition software worked only if the speaker paused between words. New software is much better at continuous speech recognition (recognizing words spoken without a pause between them). Still, it often takes a long time for speakers to adjust their speech patterns to match the capabilities of the software. It isn't unusual for this process to be misstated; it is often said that the computer "learns" the speaker's speech pattern, but the fact is that the "learning" is on the part of the speaker, not the computer.

Continuous speech recognition is the first step toward a true natural language interface because such an interface would require the computer to recognize anyone's natural speech. With reliable speech recognition technology, the day is closer when you'll be able to control a computer solely by talking to it in ordinary speech.

Figure 16G

Major advances have been made in speech recognition and other technologies, allowing people with hearing or speech impairments to communicate with others using their computers. Stephen Hawking (above left) uses a computer to help him speak.

MACHINE TRANSLATION

In the 1960s, experts confidently predicted that **machine translation**—the use of computers to translate foreign language text automatically—could be achieved quite easily. But many problems emerged, including how to resolve ambiguity (for example, compare the word *pen* in the following two sentences: "My pen is in my pocket" and "Charlie is doing 25 to life in the pen"). After many years of work, automatic translation software is coming closer to the dream of machine translation. The software is fast—one program can translate 300,000 words per hour—but the results are riddled with errors. Still, the results are good enough to provide a working draft for human translators; some systems make only three to five errors for every hundred words translated.

EXPERT SYSTEMS

Will your next doctor be a computer? Research in **expert systems** attempts to formulate the knowledge of human experts according to if-then rules ("if you have a temperature, then you may have an infection"). These rules formally express the knowledge used by human experts as they reason their way to a conclusion. The process of eliciting these rules from human experts is called **knowledge representation**. Once elicited, the rules are captured in expert systems. Expert systems use these rules to reach a conclusion, the same way a human expert does.

An expert system relies on a **knowledge base**, a database of represented knowledge. To use the expert system, you supply information to the program.

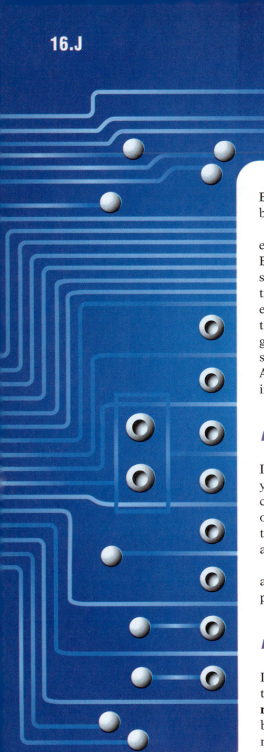

Based on the information you supply, the program consults its knowledge base and draws a conclusion, if possible.

Early proponents of expert systems thought that their programs would eventually replace human experts, but these predictions have not materialized. Expert systems work best where they're limited to sharply defined subjects, such as jet engine maintenance, planning and scheduling, diagnosis and troubleshooting of a specific device, or financial decision-making. However, expert system technology is making its appearance in application software, too. Microsoft Word uses rule-based reasoning to check documents for grammatical errors. MailJail, a junk e-mail detection accessory for Outlook, screens out unwanted or unsolicited e-mail, or spam. Created by Omron Advanced Systems, MailJail uses more than 600 rules to decide whether an incoming message is junk mail.

INTELLIGENT AGENTS

Imagine having a helper inside your computer, one that can converse with you, understand your needs, and offer assistance. These helpers, called **agents**, can sample conversations in thousands of newsgroups and recommend items of interest, find human experts who can solve specific problems, negotiate the best price for something you're trying to buy, or understand your interests and scout ahead for Web pages you'll want to see.

If you're using Microsoft Office software, you're probably familiar with an agent: the Office Assistant, an agent that springs into action when the program deduces that you're performing a certain type of action.

PATTERN RECOGNITION

Imagine a computer that can see in a way that goes beyond recording a digitized image. By means of a digital camera, computers equipped with **pattern recognition** software can process what they're seeing and draw connections between the patterns they perceive and patterns stored in a database. Pattern-recognizing computers are already used for security; a new type of video surveillance camera, for example, can detect shoppers with suspicious movement patterns and alert security personnel. Pattern recognition software is also playing an important role in data mining, discovering previously unnoticed trends in massive amounts of transaction data.

FUZZY LOGIC

The term **fuzzy logic** suggests inaccurate logic, but it refers to a type of logic that may prove *more* accurate than the type of yes/no, on/off logic that computers use. With fuzzy logic, it's possible to express a proposition with varying degrees of confidence about its truthfulness. Fuzzy logic helps make expert systems and other AI-based software work better by automating forms of reasoning that people use. An example of an application of fuzzy logic is the circuitry that enables a handheld video camera to adjust to jiggling and show a steady picture. The circuitry figures out what probably should and should not move and adjusts the image accordingly.

ROBOTS

Late at night, Dottie cleans the floors in a Richmond, Virginia, office building. The work is dull and repetitive, but she doesn't mind. She's never late to work, doesn't call in sick, and doesn't even receive a salary. Dottie is a robot, created by Cyberclean, a company that's going after a $50 billion industrial cleaning market. A **robot** is a computer-based device programmed to perform motions that can accomplish useful tasks. But can robots do so safely? Using video sensors, Dottie observes simple rules to avoid doing any damage, such as stopping and waiting if somebody walks in front of her. When her work is finished, she returns to her charging station.

Dottie and robots like her—such as AIBO and PaPeRo—are at the cutting edge of **robotics**, a field that has transformed industrial production (see Figure 16H). As early as 1997, the annual market for industrial robots passed the $1 billion mark. Increasingly, robots are performing tasks such as assembly, welding, material handling, and material transport (see Figure 16I).

Figure 16H
Robots such as AIBO and PaPeRo are at the cutting edge of the field of robotics. PaPeRo can interact with people, detect a person's presence, and even sense a person's mood and respond accordingly.

Figure 16I
Increasingly, robots are performing tasks such as assembly, welding, material handling, and material transport.

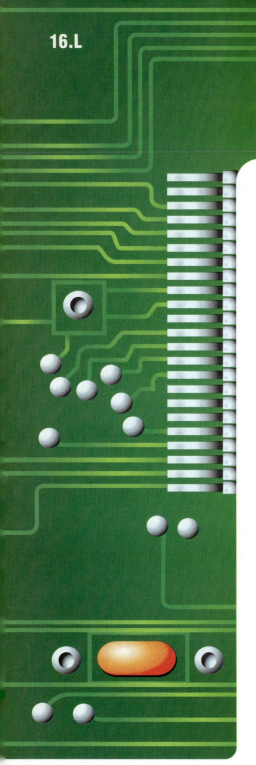

According to a recent estimate, more than one million industrial robots are in use, with more than half of them in Japan. Robots are in use in medicine, too. Rock-steady surgical robots are saving lives where natural hand tremors could lead to fatal consequences. Robots are also exploring hazardous environments, such as the radioactive ruins of the Chernobyl Unit 4 nuclear power plant.

So where's the all-in-one personal robot that will someday mow the lawn, clean the house, and shampoo the carpets? Most experts agree that such personal robots are a decade or so away. These robots are just too expensive for consumers right now, but that will change as technology advances and market demand grows.

STRONG AI

Although piecemeal advances in artificial intelligence are transforming the computers and software we use every day, the decades-old dream of creating a truly intelligent computer seems as far away as ever. What's been achieved so far is a semblance of intelligence within only highly restricted areas of knowledge, such as routing parts through a factory or making airline reservations. Is the dream of true machine intelligence still alive? Proponents of **strong AI** believe that it is and that the achievement of artificial intelligence is only decades away.

What is needed to achieve true artificial intelligence? Everyone agrees that an intelligent computer would need a high proportion of the knowledge that people carry around in their heads every day, such as the fact that Philadelphia is a city on the East Coast, and that East Coast cities can be unbearably hot in the summer. You use this type of knowledge constantly. If someone tells you, "My friend went to work in Philadelphia for the summer," you can respond, "She must not mind the heat!" But there's considerable disagreement about how this knowledge can be provided to a computer. Should humans provide such knowledge, or should computers learn it on their own? Two AI projects, Cyc and Cog, illustrate these two different approaches to knowledge acquisition.

CYC

In Austin, Texas, computer scientist Douglas B. Lenat and the Cycorp company are programming a computer called Cyc (pronounced "sike," from "encyclopedia") with basic facts about the world that everyone knows, such as "mountain climbing is dangerous" and "birds have feathers." The goal is to create a computer that knows as much as a 12-year-old. The challenge is that 12-year-olds know a great deal. Lenat's staff has spent more than 15 years feeding basic knowledge into Cyc—the computer now stores over 1.4 million rules—and they're many years away from achieving their goal. At some point, though, Cyc's designers say that the computer will be able to learn on its own, reading material from the Internet and asking questions when it can't understand something. Already, companies are using Cyc in various capacities, and the U.S. military has invested millions of dollars in Cyc, hoping to use the computer as a military intelligence tool.

COG

A different approach to strong AI is taken by MIT professor Rodney A. Brooks, who believes that Lenat is approaching the problem the wrong way. In the natural world, intelligence arose as organisms tried to survive. The path to artificial intelligence, Brooks argues, lies in creating robots that, unlike Cyc, have minimal preprogrammed knowledge. What they do have is massive sensory input (sight, hearing, and touch) coupled with artificially programmed "desires." For Brooks, intelligence isn't reasoning, but rather a set of behaviors acquired as organisms interact with their environment. To make his point, Brooks and his students have constructed a series of impressive insect-like robots that have learned how to crawl across fields strewn with boulders (and even steal soda cans from students' desks). Their latest projects are Cog—a humanoid robot that has a torso, a head, and two arms—and Kismet, a robotic head that can elicit emotional responses through its eyes and voice.

Figure 16J
The brain contains billions of neurons. In a neural net, thousands of computer processing units are connected in multiple ways, just as the neurons in the brain are connected.

NEURAL NETWORKS

Yet another approach to strong AI involves creating computers that mimic the structure of the human brain. Called **neural networks** (or neural nets), these computers are composed of hundreds or thousands of tiny processors that are interconnected in multiple ways, just like neurons in the human brain.

Although little is known about how the human brain works, its physical structure has been explored. Anatomists know that the brain contains billions of brain cells, called neurons (see Figure 16J). These neurons are connected by current-conducting nerve fibers called ganglia. Often, a single neuron has many ganglia attached to it, forming a dense and complex network of interconnections. Scientists believe that when people learn things, some connections are reinforced and grow stronger.

In a neural net, thousands of computer processing units are connected in multiple ways, just as the neurons in a brain are connected. Neural nets aren't programmed; they're trained. The net learns by trial and error, just the way humans do. An incorrect guess weakens a particular pattern of connections; a correct guess reinforces the pattern. After the training is finished, the neural net knows how to do something, such as operate a robot. Neural nets behave much the way brains behave. In fact, neural nets exhibit electromagnetic waves that are surprisingly similar to the brain waves in humans.

None of today's neural nets approaches the complexity of even a farm animal's brain, but more complex neural nets are planned.

Ordinary computers are good at solving problems that require linear thinking, logical rules, and step-by-step instructions. Neural nets are good at recognizing patterns, dealing with complexity, and learning from experience.

Neural nets are emerging from laboratories and finding their way into commercial applications. Right now, neural nets are comparing signatures made in banks with stored signatures, monitoring the state of aircraft engines, and predicting trends in the stock market.

GENETIC ALGORITHMS

Intelligence is a byproduct of evolution, through the mechanism of natural selection. So why not try to create artificial intelligence by creating laboratory conditions in which the most intelligent programs survive? That's the object of research on **genetic algorithms**.

According to evolutionary theories of biology, organisms try to survive. Occasional errors in the genetic code introduce mutations, leading to change. Sometimes these changes are advantageous and give the organism a better chance to survive. Organisms with an advantageous genetic code dominate because they have more opportunities to reproduce.

Genetic algorithm research mimics nature in the following way: A number of algorithms are placed into a computer environment and are given the potential to mutate in random ways. All the algorithms compete to try to solve a problem. Over time, one algorithm emerges as the best at tackling the problem. Where's the AI connection here? AI requires the creation of algorithms that can mimic the behavior of intelligent beings, but such algorithms are difficult to discover. Genetic algorithm techniques offer a new way to discover these algorithms.

Summary

What will be the nature of computers in your future? We know that they'll be fast, will have tremendous storage capacity, and will manage peripheral devices that will serve us in many ways. We are at the very beginning of an age: the Information Age. The one distinguishing thing about this age is that we know we're in it. Just think of what might have happened if educated people had known that they were at the beginning of the Industrial Revolution and could have envisioned the fantastic advances to come. Think what they could have accomplished had they only known! Today we know. We know that we are at the beginning of the Information Age.

Think. Think every day of the possibilities. There *are* computers in your future, and they'll help to provide you with the means for a successful and satisfying life. Enjoy the ride!

ILLUSTRATION CREDITS

CHAPTER 1

Figure 1.1
Top to bottom
    © Walter Hodges/Corbis
    Photo Disk, Inc.
    © LWA-Dann Tardiff/Corbis
    © Jose Luis Palaez/Corbis
    © Larry Williams & Assoc./Corbis

Figure 1.2
© R. W. Jones/Corbis

Figure 1.4a
© Reuters NewMedia/Corbis

Figure 1.4b
Courtesy of PaPeRo.

Figure 1.7
© Alain Mogues/Corbis Sygma

Figure 1.8l
Courtesy of Intel Corporation.

Figure 1.10a
Courtesy of Intel Corporation.

Figure 1.10b
Courtesy of Intel Corporation.

Figure 1.11b
Courtesy of International Business Machines
    Corporation. Unauthorized use not permitted.

Figure 1.13a
Courtesy of Iomega.

Figure 1.14 top left
© 2003 Apple Computer, Inc. All rights reserved.

Figure 1.15 top
Courtesy of Cray, Inc.

Figure 1.15b
second, third, and fourth
Courtesy of International Business Machines
    Corporation. Unauthorized use not permitted.

Figure 1.18
© Lester Leftkowitz/Corbis

Figure 1Q
© 2002 Urban Legends Reference Pages

CHAPTER 2

Figure 2.2a
© 2003 Apple Computer, Inc. All rights reserved.

Figure 2.2b
Courtesy of International Business Machines
    Corporation. Unauthorized use not permitted.

Figure 2.3a
© 2003 Apple Computer, Inc. All rights reserved.

Figure 2.3b
© 2003 Apple Computer, Inc. All rights reserved.

Figure 2.4
Courtesy of Intel Corporation.

Figure 2.6
Courtesy of Intel Corporation.

Figure 2.7
Courtesy of Giga Byte Technology.

Figure 2.13
Courtesy of Intel Corporation.

Figure 2.14
Courtesy of Intel Corporation.

Figure 2.15
Courtesy of Intel Corporation.

Figure 2.16
Courtesy of Advanced Micro Devices.

Figure 2.20
© AFP/Corbis

Figure 2.28
AP/Wide World Photos

CHAPTER 3

Figure 3.11b
Courtesy of International Business Machines
    Corporation. Unauthorized use not permitted.

Figure 3.11c
Courtesy of International Business Machines
    Corporation. Unauthorized use not permitted.

Figure 3.11e
Courtesy of International Business Machines
    Corporation. Unauthorized use not permitted.

Figure 3.11f
© Kim Kulish/Corbis Saba

Figure 3.11g
Courtesy of International Business Machines
    Corporation. Unauthorized use not permitted.

Figure 3.12
AP/Wide World Photos

Figure 3.13
AP/Wide World Photos

Figure 3.15
Courtesy of International Business Machines
    Corporation. Unauthorized use not permitted.

ILLUSTRATION CREDITS

Figure 3.17
© Reuters NewMedia, Inc./Corbis

Figure 3.18
Courtesy of International Business Machines
 Corporation. Unauthorized use not permitted.

Figure 3.20
© 2002 PhotoWorks, Inc.

Figure 3.21
© Mug Shots/Corbis

Figure 3.22
© 2002 EarthCam Inc.

Figure 3.23a
Courtesy of International Business Machines
 Corporation. Unauthorized use not permitted.

Figure 3.23b
© Reuters NewMedia, Inc./Corbis

Figure 3.25 top
© Michael Newman/Photo Edit

Figure 3.25 bottom
© Donald McDonald/Photo Edit

Figure 3.26
© Blake Little/Stone/Getty Images

Figure 3.30
Courtesy of International Business Machines
 Corporation. Unauthorized use not permitted.

Figure 3.32a
© Stocker Mike/Corbis Sygma

Figure 3.32b
AP/Wide World Photos

Figure 3.32c
© Hekiman Julien/Corbis Sygma

Figure 3.37
Fargo Electronics

Figure 3.38
Xerox Corporation

Figure 3.39a
Infocus

Figure 3.39b
Infocus

Figure 3.40
© Roger Ressmeyer/Corbis

Figure 3.41
Courtesy of Cannon.

Figure 3.42
© Reuters NewMedia, Inc./Corbis

CHAPTER 4

Figure 4.4a
Courtesy of International Business Machines
 Corporation. Unauthorized use not permitted.

Figure 4.8
Courtesy of Iomega.

Figure 4.10a
Courtesy of International Business Machines
 Corporation. Unauthorized use not permitted.

Figure 4.10b
Courtesy of International Business Machines
 Corporation. Unauthorized use not permitted.

Figure 4.17 center
Courtesy of International Business Machines
 Corporation. Unauthorized use not permitted.

Figure 4.17 left
Courtesy of Intel Corporation.

Figure 4.18
Courtesy of Advanced Computer and Network
 Corporation.

Figure 4.19
Courtesy of Iomega.

Figure 4.20
Seagate Technology, Inc.

Figure 4.21
© Michael A. Keller Studios/Corbis

Figure 4.22
Courtesy of International Business Machines
 Corporation. Unauthorized use not permitted.

Figure 4.24
Courtesy of International Business Machines
 Corporation. Unauthorized use not permitted.

Figure 4.26
Courtesy of International Business Machines
 Corporation. Unauthorized use not permitted.

Figure 4.27
Courtesy of International Business Machines
 Corporation. Unauthorized use not permitted.

Figure 4A
Courtesy of Intel Corporation.

Figure 4C-1
Courtesy of International Business Machines
 Corporation. Unauthorized use not permitted.

Figure 4C-2
© 2003 Apple Computer, Inc. All rights reserved.

Figure 4D
Courtesy of Intel Corporation.

Figure 4E
AP/Wide World Photos

ILLUSTRATION CREDITS

Figure 4F
© Mark Peterson/Corbis

Figure 4G
Courtesy of International Business Machines Corporation. Unauthorized use not permitted.

Figure 4H-1
© LWA-JDC/Corbis

Figure 4H-2
© Jose Luis Palaez, Inc./Corbis

Figure 4I
© Mark Richards/Photo Edit

Figure 4K
Tripp Lite Worldwide

Figure 4L
Courtesy of Intel Corporation.

CHAPTER 5

Figure 5.8a
Courtesy of Gateway Computers.

Figure 5.8b
© 2003 Apple Computer, Inc. All rights reserved.

Figure 5.15a
© Judy Griesediek/Corbis

Figure 5.15b
© James Leynse/Corbis Saba

Figure 5-15c
© James A. Sugar/Corbis

Figure 5.18
© 2002 Google, Inc.

Figure 5.19
© 2002 Symantec Corporation

CHAPTER 6

Figure 6.4
© Jose Luis Palaez, Inc./Corbis

Figure 6.5
© 2002 Tucows, Inc.

Figure 6.9
© AFP/Corbis

Figure 6O
Infocus

CHAPTER 7

Figure 7.1
© William Taufic/Corbis

Figure 7.6a
Courtesy of International Business Machines Corporation. Unauthorized use not permitted.

Figure 7.9
© Lester Lefkowitz/Corbis

Figure 7.10
© Chuck Savage/Corbis

Currents
© Bill Ross/Corbis

Impacts
Courtesy of Palo Alto Research Center.

CHAPTER 8

Figure 8.2b
©2002 CNET Networks, Inc.

Figure 8.2c
© 2002 Monster.com

Figure 8.2d
© 2002 Priceline.com, Inc.

Figure 8.2e
Reprinted with permission from Britannica.com. © 2002 by Encyclopedia Britannica, Inc.

Figure 8.4 bottom right
© 2003 Apple Computer, Inc. All rights reserved.

Figure 8.5
© 2002 America Online, Inc.

Figure 8.6
© 2002 Yahoo! Inc.

Figure 8.7
Image courtesy of Matrix NetSystems, Inc.

Figure 8.8a
© 2002 Netscape Communications Corporation. Screenshot used with permission.

Figure 8.10c
© 2002 University of Oregon

Figure 8.11
© Dennis Novak/Image Bank/Getty Images

Figure 8.12
© The Motley Fool, Inc.

Figure 8.13
© 2002 Aladdin Systems, Inc.

Figure 8.16
© 2002 Google, Inc.

Figure 8.20
© 2002 Jupitermedia Corporation

Figure 8.21
© 2002 AT&T

Figure 8.24
© 2002 Jupitermedia Corporation

CHAPTER 9

Figure 9.1a
© 2002 by Consumers Union of U.S., Inc., Yonkers, NY 10703. Used by permission. Log on to www.ConsumerReports.org.

ILLUSTRATION CREDITS

ILLUSTRATION CREDITS

Figure 10.15
Right, Courtesy of Motorola.
Center, Courtesy of Nokia.
Left, Courtesy of Motorola.

Figure 10.16
© Torchig Sion/Corbis Sygma

Figure 10.17
© 2002 Net2Phone, Inc.

Figure 10.18
© 2002 j2 Global Communications, Inc.

CHAPTER 11

Figure 11.1
CyberAngels

Figure 11.2
© Bill Varie/Corbis

Figure 11.4
© 2000 Rhode Island Soft Systems, Inc.

Figure 11.6
Hackers.com

Figure 11.8
These materials have been reproduced with the permission of eBay Inc. Copyright © eBay Inc. All rights reserved.

Figure 11.9
© Michael Boys/Corbis

Figure 11.11
Courtesy of Kensington Technology Group, a division of ACCO Brands, Inc.

Figure 11.12
American Power Conversion Corporation

Figure 11.13
© P. Franch/Corbis Sygma

Figure 11.14a
AP/Wide World Photos

Figure 11.14b
AP/Wide World Photos

Figure 11.14c
© Mark Peterson/Corbis Saba

Figure 11.16
© William Whitehurst/Corbis

CHAPTER 12

Figure 12.1
© 2002 DPI, Inc.

Figure 12.3
© Ralph A. Clevenge/Corbis

Figure 12.4
© 2001 AdDesigner.com

Figure 12.6
© 2002 The Direct Marketing Association

Figure 12.7
© 2002 Anonymizer.com

Figure 12.8
© 2002 SpectorSoft Corporation

Figure 12.12
© 2002 The Center for Democracy and Technology

Figure 12.13
© Bettmann/Corbis

Figure 12A
© Tom Stewart/Corbis

Figure 12B
Courtesy of the Software Publishers Association.

Figure 12C
© AFP/Corbis

Figure 12D
© Ed Wheeler/Corbis

Figure 12E
© Jim Erichs/Corbis

Figure 12G
© Alain Mogues/Corbis

CHAPTER 13

Figure 13.4
© 2000 Data Mining Technologies

Figure 13.5
© 2002 FedEx Corporation

Figure 13.10
© Ronnie Kaufman/Corbis

Figure 13.11
© Jose Luis Peleaz, Inc./Corbis

Figure 13.14
© Jeff Zaruba/Corbis

CHAPTER 14

Figure 14.3
© Peter Beck/Corbis

Figure 14.5
© Jose Peleaz, Inc./Corbis

Figure 14.7
© AFP/Corbis

CHAPTER 15

Figure 15.2
© Japack Co./Corbis

Figure 15.4
© Bettmann/Corbis

ILLUSTRATION CREDITS

CHAPTER 16

Figure 16.1a
© 2002 Monster.com

Figure 16.1b
© 2002 HotJobs.com

Figure 16.1c
© SoftwareJobs.com, Inc.

Figure 16.1d
© 2002 ComputerJobs.com, Inc.

Figure 16.1e
© 2002 by Dori Reuscher
   (http://certification.about.com), licensed
   to About Inc. Used by permission of About Inc.,
   which can be found on the Web at
   http://www.about.com. All rights reserved.

Figure 16.4
© Mendola/Brad Gaber/Corbis

Figure 16.5
© John Feingersh/Corbis

Figure 16.6
© Roger Ball/Corbis

Figure 16.7a
© 2002 Key3Media Events, Inc.

Figure 16.7b
AP/Wide World Photos

Figure 16.8
© AWC, Inc. 2002, http://www.awc-hq.org

Figure 16.9
© Robert Levine/Corbis

Figure 16.11
© John Erickson/Corbis

Figure 16.13
© II.David Seawell/Corbis

Figure 16A
© Rick Gayle/Corbis

Figure 16C
© 2002 Yahoo! Inc.

Figure 16E
Courtesy of Computer Museum History Center.

Figure 16F
AP/Wide World Photos

Figure 16G
AP/Wide World Photos

Figure 16H
Left, © Reuters NewMedia/Corbis

Figure 16H
Right, Courtesy of PaPeRo.

Figure 16J
© Michael Freeman/Corbis

ACRONYM FINDER

NOTE: SEE GLOSSARY FOR DEFINITIONS

3GL See third-generation language.

4GL See fourth-generation language.

ADSL See Asymmetric Digital Subscriber Line.

AGP See Accelerated Graphics Port.

AGV See automatic guided vehicle.

AI See artificial intelligence.

ALU See arithmetic-logic unit.

ASCII See American Standard Code for Information Interchange.

ATA See Advanced Technology Attachment.

AUP See acceptable use policy.

BIOS See basic input/output system.

BMP See Windows Bitmap.

BPR See business process reengineering.

bps See bits per second.

BRI See Basic Rate Interface.

CA See certificate authority.

CAD See computer-aided design.

CAI See computer-assisted instruction.

CAM See computer-aided manufacturing.

CAPE See computer-aided production engineering.

CASE See computer-aided software engineering.

cat-5 See category 5.

CAVE See Cave Automated Virtual Environment.

CBE See computer-based education.

CBT See computer-based training.

CCD See charge-coupled device.

CD-R See compact disc-recordable.

CD-ROM See compact disc read-only memory or CD-ROM drive.

CD-RW See compact disc-rewritable.

CIM See computer-integrated manufacturing.

CIS See computer information system.

CISC See complex instruction set computer.

CMI See computer-managed instruction.

CMI See copyright management infrastructure.

CMOS See complementary metal-oxide semiconductor.

COM See Component Object Model.

CORBA See Common Object Request Broker Architecture.

CPU See central processing unit.

CRT See cathode ray tube.

CS See computer science.

CSCW See computer-supported cooperative work.

CSS See Cascading Style Sheet.

CTD See cumulative trauma disorder.

CTS See carpal tunnel syndrome.

CVS See computer vision syndrome.

DBS See Direct Broadcast Satellite.

DIMM See dual inline memory module.

DMA See direct memory access.

DNS See domain name server.

DoS See denial of service attack.

DRAM See dynamic random access memory.

DSL See Digital Subscriber Line.

DSS See decision support system.

DTP See desktop publishing.

DTV See digital television.

DVD See digital video disc.

DVD-RAM See digital video disc-RAM.

DVD-ROM See digital video disc-ROM.

EBCDIC See Extended Binary Coded Decimal Interchange Code.

EDI See electronic data interchange.

EE See electrical engineering.

EIDE See Enhanced IDE.

EIS See executive information system.

EPIRB See Emergency Position Indicating Radio Beacons.

EPS See Encapsulated PostScript.

ERD See entity-relationship diagram.

ERMA See Electronic Recording Machine—Accounting.

ESS See executive support system.

FAT See file allocation table.

FED See field emission display.

FPU See floating-point unit.

GIF See Graphics Interchange Format.

GPL See General Public License.

GPS See Global Positioning System.

GUI See graphical user interface.

HGP See Human Genome Project.

HMD See head-mounted display.

HTML See Hypertext Markup Language.

HTTP See Hypertext Transfer Protocol.

IC See integrated circuit.

IDE See Integrated Drive Electronics.

IIOP See Internet Inter-Orb Protocol.

ILS See integrated learning system.

IM See instant messaging.

IMAP See Internet Message Access Protocol.

IP See Internet Protocol.

IS See information systems.

ISA See Industry Standard Architecture.

ISDN See Integrated Services Digital Network.

ISP See Internet service provider.

ITS See Intelligent Transportation System.

ITU See International Telecommunications Union.

IXC See interexchange carrier.

ACRONYM FINDER

JAD See joint application development.

JIT See job instruction training.

JIT See just-in-time.

JPEG See Joint Photographic Experts Group.

K See kilobyte.

KB See kilobyte.

L2 See level 2.

LAN See local area network.

LATA See local access and transport area.

LCD See liquid crystal display.

LEC See local exchange carrier.

LSI See large-scale integration.

M See megabyte.

MAN See metropolitan area network.

MB See megabyte.

MICR See magnetic-ink character recognition.

MIDI See Musical Instrument Digital Interface.

MIME See Multipurpose Internet Mail Extensions.

MIS See management information system.

MO See magneto-optic.

MP3 See MPEG Audio Layer 3.

MPEG See Moving Picture Experts Group.

MRI See magnetic resonance imaging.

MSI See medium-scale integration.

MTBF See mean time between failures.

MUD See multiuser dungeon.

NAS See network attached storage.

NC See network computer.

NIC See network interface card.

NOS See network operating system.

OCR See optical character recognition.

OLAP See online analytical processing.

OLE See object linking and embedding.

OMR See optical mark reader.

OO See object-oriented.

OOP See object-oriented programming.

OS See operating system.

P3P See Platform for Privacy Preferences.

PBX See private branch exchange.

PC See personal computer.

PCI See Personal Computer Interface.

PCS See Personal Communication Service.

PDA See personal digital assistant.

PDL See page description language.

PDLC See program development life cycle.

PDN See public data network.

PICS See Platform for Internet Content Selection.

PIM See personal information manager.

PNG See Portable Network Graphics.

PnP See Plug and Play.

PoP See point of presence.

POP See Post Office Protocol.

POS See point-of-sale.

POTS See Plain Old Telephone Service.

PSTN See public switched telephone network.

PVC See permanent virtual circuit.

QBE See query by example.

QIC See quarter-inch cartridge.

QoS See quality of service.

RAD See rapid application development.

RAM See random access memory.

RBOCs See Regional Bell Operating Companies.

RFP See request for proposal.

RFQ See request for quotation.

RISC See reduced instruction set computer.

ROI See return on investment.

ROM See read-only memory.

RSI See repetitive strain injury.

SCSI See Small Computer System Interface.

SDLC See systems development life cycle.

SDRAM See synchronous DRAM.

SIMM See single inline memory module.

SMIL See Synchronized Multimedia Integration Language.

SMTP See Simple Mail Transport Protocol.

SOHO See small office/home office.

SONET See Synchronous Optical Network.

SQL See Structured Query Language.

SSI See small-scale integration.

SVGA See Super Video Graphics Array.

TCP See Transmission Control Protocol.

TFT See thin film transistor.

TLD See top-level domain.

TPS See transaction processing system.

UPC See universal product code.

UPS See uninterruptible power supply.

URL See uniform resource locator.

USB See universal serial bus.

VAN See value-added network.

VAR See value-added reseller.

VB See Visual Basic.

VLSI See very-large-scale integration.

VPN See virtual private network.

VR See virtual reality.

W3C See World Wide Web Consortium.

WAN See wide area network.

WLAN See wireless LAN.

WORM See write once, read many.

WWW See World Wide Web.

XML See Extensible Markup Language.

DEFINITIONS

@ In an e-mail address, a symbol used to separate the user name from the name of the computer on which the user's mailbox is stored (for example, frodo@bagend.org). Pronounced "at."

10baseT An Ethernet local area network capable of transmitting 10 megabits of data per second through twisted-pair cabling.

100baseT See Fast Ethernet.

128-bit domestic-level encryption A level of encryption used for secure Web sites and e-mail that uses an encryption bit length of 128. This bit length prevents the message from being intercepted and decoded, but current U.S. export regulations prevent U.S. companies from exporting software that incorporates this strong level of encryption.

1394 port An input-output port that combines high-speed performance (up to 400 Mbps) with the ability to guarantee data delivery at a specified speed, making the port ideal for use with real-time devices such as digital video cameras. Synonymous with FireWire, which is Apple Computer's name for this technology.

3D graphics adapter A video adapter that can display images that provide the illusion of depth as well as height and width.

3-D rendering Transforming graphic images by adding shading and light sources so that they appear to be three-dimensional.

40-bit encryption A minimal level of encryption supplied with most Web browsers. Although this encryption level is insufficient to guarantee confidentiality during Internet information transfers, it is used because it is weak enough to escape U.S. export regulations.

A

abacus A digital computer that originated thousands of years ago. Calculations are performed by using sliding beads to represent figures and by following rules to perform mathematical operations.

absolute cell reference A spreadsheet cell reference that doesn't adjust when you copy or move a formula.

absolute hyperlink In an HTML document, a hyperlink that fully and precisely specifies the file location of the referenced remote document. An absolute link specifies the protocol (such as http:// or ftp://), as well as the name of the computer and the location of the referenced file in the computer's directory structure.

Accelerated Graphics Port (AGP) A port specification developed by Intel Corporation to support high-speed, high-resolution graphics, including 3D graphics.

accelerator A circuit board that speeds up some function of your computer.

acceptable use policy (AUP) An Internet _service provider (ISP) policy that indicates which types of uses are permissible.

acceptance testing In information systems development, the examination of programs by users. See also application testing.

access speed The amount of time that lapses between a request for information from memory and the delivery of the information. Also called access time.

access time See access speed.

accessible software Software that is designed to be easily and conveniently used by people with limited vision, hearing, or dexterity.

account On a multiuser computer system, a user information profile that includes the user's name, password, and home directory location. Unlike a profile on a consumer-oriented operating system, an account provides basic security features that prevent users from accessing or overwriting each others' files.

action A special type of Internet chat group message that describes a behavior.

active cell In a spreadsheet program, the cell in which the cell pointer is located. The contents of the active cell are displayed in the formula bar.

active-matrix LCD A full-color liquid crystal display (LCD) in which each of the screen's pixels is controlled by its own transistor. Active-matrix displays offer a higher resolution, contrast, and vertical refresh rate than less expensive passive-matrix displays. Also called thin film transistor (TFT).

active monitoring In online banking, a security measure in which a security team constantly monitors the system that holds account information for the telltale signs of unauthorized access.

ActiveX control A small program that can be downloaded from a Web page and used to add functionality to a Web browser. ActiveX controls require Microsoft Windows and Microsoft Internet Explorer and are usually written in Visual Basic (VB).

activity light A light-emitting diode (LED) that illuminates when a disk drive is sending or receiving data.

ad network On the World Wide Web, a commercial service that uses cookies to track a user's movements and browsing preferences through all of the network's participating sites. This information is used to present the user with advertisements tailored to the user's interest.

adapter 1. A circuit board that plugs into an expansion slot in a computer, giving the computer additional capabilities. Synonymous with card. Popular adapters for personal computers include video adapters that produce video output, memory expansion boards, internal modems, and sound boards. 2. A transformer that enables a computer or peripheral to work with line voltage that differs from its electrical requirements.

Add or Remove Programs An icon in a computer operating system's control panel that allows for proper installation and uninstallation of programs.

advanced intelligent tape (AIT) An advanced, high-end tape backup standard that is used by organizations to back up the entire contents of a file server or other mission-critical systems.

Advanced Technology Attachment (ATA) See Integrated Drive Electronics (IDE).

adware A type of Internet spyware created by advertising agencies to collect information about computer users' Internet habits.

agent An automatic program that is designed to operate on the user's behalf, performing a specific function in the background. When the agent has achieved its goal, it reports to the user.

alert box In a graphical user interface (GUI), a dialog box that appears on-screen to either warn you that the command you've given may result in lost work or other errors, or that explains why an action can't be completed.

algorithm A mathematical or logical procedure for solving a problem.

algorithmic art In computer art, the use of an unfolding mathematical procedure as a means of artistic expression.

alias A secondary or symbolic name for a computer user or group of users. Group aliases provide a handy way to send e-mail to two or more people simultaneously.

all-in-one computers A system unit that contains all of the computer's components, including input components and the display.

alphabetic check Ensures that only alphabetical data (the letters of the alphabet) are entered into a field.

American Standard Code for Information Interchange (ASCII) A standard computer character set consisting of 96 uppercase and lowercase letters along with 32 nonprinting control characters. Developed in 1963, ASCII was the first computer industry standard.

analog Based on continuously varying values or voltages. Analog techniques are used for the reproduction of music in standard LP records and audio cassettes. See digital.

analog computer A machine that measures an ongoing process using a continuously variable scale. See digital computer.

Analytical Engine A device planned by Charles Babbage in the nineteenth century. Never completed, this device would have been a full modern computer with an IPOS cycle and punched cards for data input.

analytical graphics As opposed to presentation graphics, a type of graphics application in which the user attempts to display all or most of the data so that the underlying patterns become visible.

anchor text In the World Wide Web, the on-screen text of a hyperlink.

animation A method of creating the illusion of movement by saving a series of images that show slight changes in the position of the displayed objects, and then displaying these images in sequence fast enough that the eye perceives smooth movement.

anonymity On the Internet, the ability to post a message or visit Web sites without divulging one's identity. Anonymity is much more difficult to obtain than most Internet users realize.

anonymous FTP An Internet service that enables you to contact a distant computer system to which you have no access rights, log on to its public directories, and transfer files from that computer to your own.

antivirus program A utility that checks for and removes computer viruses from memory and disks.

applet 1. A small- to medium-sized computer program that provides a specific function, such as emulating a calculator. 2. In Java, a mini-program embedded in a Web document that, when downloaded, is executed by the browser. Both leading browsers (Netscape Communicator and Microsoft Internet Explorer) can execute Java applets.

AppleTalk A networking protocol developed by Apple Computer that enables Apple Macintosh computers to connect to LocalTalk, EtherTalk, and token ring networks.

application file See program file.

application software Programs that enable you to do something useful with the computer, such as writing or accounting (as opposed to utilities, which are programs that help you maintain the computer).

application testing In information systems development, the examination of programs individually, and then further examination of the programs as they function together.

application workspace The area within an application window that displays the document.

archival backup A procedure in which a backup utility backs up all files on the hard disk by copying them to floppy disks, tape, or some other backup medium. See incremental backup.

archival storage See offline storage.

archive A file that contains two or more files that have been stored together for convenient archiving or network transmission.

area chart See pie chart.

argument set In spreadsheet programs such as Microsoft Excel, the part of a mathematical function that contains its passable parameters or variables.

arithmetic-logic unit (ALU) The portion of the central processing unit (CPU) that makes all the decisions for the microprocessor, based on the mathematical computations and logic functions that it performs.

arithmetic operations One of the two groups of operations performed by the arithmetic-logic unit (ALU). The arithmetic operations are addition, subtraction, multiplication, and division.

arithmetic operators A set of symbols corresponding to the standard operations of grade-school arithmetic (addition, subtraction, multiplication, and division).

ARPANET An acronym for the Advanced Research Projects Agency Network, from which the Internet developed.

arrow keys See cursor-movement keys.

article In Usenet, a message that begins discussion on a new subject. Compare follow-up article.

artificial intelligence (AI) A computer science field that tries to improve computers by endowing them with some of the characteristics associated with human intelligence, such as the capability to understand natural language and to reason under conditions of uncertainty.

artificial system A collection of components constructed by people and organized into a functioning whole to accomplish a goal.

aspect ratio In computer graphics, the ratio between an image's horizontal and vertical dimensions.

assembler A program that transforms source code in assembly language into machine language readable by a computer.

assembly language A low-level programming language in which each program statement corresponds to an instruction that the microprocessor can carry out.

assistive technology A technology that helps people with limited vision, hearing, or dexterity use the computer comfortably and productively.

Asymmetric Digital Subscriber Line (ADSL) A type of Digital Subscriber Line (DSL) service for Internet access. ADSL enables download speeds of up to 1.5 Mbps.

asynchronous Not kept in time (synchrony) by the pulses of a system clock or some other timing device.

asynchronous communication A method of data communication in which the transmission of bits of data isn't synchronized by a clock signal, but instead is accomplished by sending bits one after another, with a start bit and a stop bit to mark the beginning and end, respectively, of each data unit.

AT form factor A system unit case design that was introduced with IBM's Personal Computer AT (short for Advanced Technology).

ATA (AT attachment) A hard disk interface originally designed by IBM for its 1984 Personal Computer AT. More recent versions, such as ATA/66 and Ultra ATA (also called Ultra DMA) offer performance approaching that of SCSI hard drives.

ATA-2 Current standard IDE/ATA interface for entry-level devices.

ATA-5 Newest version of the IDE/ATA standard.

attachment A binary file, such as a program or a compressed word processing document, that has been attached to an e-mail message.

attribute In HTML, an optional or required setting that controls specific characteristics of an element and enables authors to specify values for these characteristics.

ATX form factor Developed by Intel, the ATX form factor provides better accessibility to system components, better cooling, more full-sized expansion slots, and a more convenient layout for system upgrades.

Audio output A type of computer output that consists of sound, music, or synthesized speech.

authentication In computer security, a method of preventing unauthorized users from accessing a computer system, usually by requesting a password.

authoring tools In multimedia, application programs that enable the user to blend audio files, video, and animation with text and traditional graphics.

autocorrect In a word processing program, a feature that automatically corrects common typographical errors as you type.

automated teller machine (ATM) A computer-based kiosk that provides bank customers with 24-hour access to their funds.

automatic Able to run without human intervention.

automatic guided vehicle (AGV) In computer-integrated manufacturing, a small automated machine that provides supplies where they are needed.

automation The replacement of human workers by machines.

autorepeat A keyboard function that causes a character to repeat if you hold down the key.

autosave A software feature that backs up open documents at a user-specified interval.

auxiliary storage See storage.

avatar In a graphical MUD, a character that represents the person who is controlling the avatar's appearance, movement, and interaction with other characters.

B

back door A secret decoding mechanism that enables investigators to decrypt messages without first having to obtain a private key.

backbone In a wide area network (WAN), such as the Internet, a high-speed, high-capacity medium that transfers data over hundreds or thousands of miles. A variety of physical media are used for backbone services, including microwave relay, satellites, and dedicated telephone lines.

background application In a multitasking operating system, any inactive application. Compare foreground application.

background color In HTML, the color assigned to the background of a Web page.

background graphic In HTML, a graphic displayed as a Web page's background. Most browsers automatically repeat (tile) a background graphic so that the image fills the entire page, even if the browser window is enlarged.

backup A file (or group of files) containing copies of important data. These files may be specially formatted so that, should the need arise, they can be used to restore the contents of the hard disk in the event of a hard disk failure.

backup file A copy of a file created as a precaution in case anything happens to the original.

backup utility A program that copies data from a secondary storage device (most commonly a hard disk) to a backup medium, such as a tape cartridge.

bad sector In magnetic storage media such as hard drives, a sector of the disk's surface that is physically damaged to the point that it can no longer store data safely.

bandwidth The amount of data that can be transmitted through a given communications channel, such as a computer network.

banner ad On the World Wide Web, a paid advertisement—often rectangular in shape, like a banner—that contains a hyperlink to the advertiser's page.

bar chart In presentation graphics, a graph with horizontal or vertical bars (rectangles) commonly used to show the values of the items being compared.

bar code A binary coding system using bars of varying thickness or position that provide information that can be scanned into a computer.

bar code reader An input device that scans bar codes and, with special software, converts the bar code into readable data.

baseline The line on which the base (but not the extender, if any) of each character is positioned. An extender is the portion of certain letters (such as p and y) that extend below the baseline.

BASIC Acronym for Beginner's All-Purpose Symbolic Instruction Code. An easy-to-use high-level programming language developed in 1964 for instruction.

basic input/output system (BIOS) Read-only memory (ROM) built into the computer's memory that contains the instructions needed to start the computer and work with input and output devices.

Basic Rate Interface (BRI) In ISDN, the basic digital telephone and data service that is designed for residences. BRI offers two 56 Kbps or 64 Kbps channels for voice, graphics, and data, plus one 16,000 bps channel for signaling purposes.

batch processing A mode of computer operation in which program instructions are executed one after the other without user intervention. Batch processing uses computer resources efficiently but is less convenient than interactive processing, in which you see the results of your commands on-screen so that you can correct errors and make necessary adjustments before completing the operation.

benchmark A standard measurement used to test the performance of different brands of equipment.

beta version In software testing, a preliminary version of a program that is widely distributed before commercial release to users who test the program by operating it under realistic conditions.

binary digit See bit.

binary file A file containing data or program instructions in a computer-readable format that is unreadable by humans. The opposite of a binary file is an ASCII file.

binary numbers A number system with a base (radix) of 2, unlike the number systems most of us use, which have bases of 10 (decimal numbers), 12 (feet and inches), and 60 (time). Binary numbers are preferred for computers for precision and economy. Building an electronic circuit that can detect the difference between two states (high current and low current, or 0 and 1) is easy and inexpensive; building a circuit that detects the difference among 10 states (0 through 9) is much more difficult and expensive. The word *bit* derives from the phrase *binary digit*.

bioinformatics A field that develops database software for storing genetic information and making it available for widespread use.

biological feedback device A device that translates eye movements, body movements, and brain waves into computer input.

biometric authentication A method of authentication that requires a biological scan of some sort, such as a retinal scan or voice recognition.

BIOS screen The information seen on the computer screen that provides information about the BIOS software encoded in the computer's ROM.

bit Short for binary digit, the basic unit of information in a binary numbering system.

bit depth In a scanner, the length (expressed in bits) of the storage unit used to store information about the scanned image. The greater the bit depth, the better the scanner's resolution.

bit length In encryption, the length (expressed in bits) of the key used to encode and decode plaintext data. The greater the bit length, the stronger (less breakable) the encryption.

bitmapped graphics Images formed by a pattern of tiny dots, each of which corresponds to a pixel on the computer's display. Also called raster graphics.

bits per second (bps) In asynchronous communication, a measurement of data transmission speed. In personal computing, bps rates frequently are used to measure the performance of modems and serial ports.

biz newsgroups In Usenet, a category of newsgroups devoted to commercial concerns.

block element In HTML, one of two basic types of elements (the other is inline element). A block element starts on a new line and comprises a separate paragraph, or block. Block elements include P (text paragraph), BLOCKQUOTE (indented quotation), and UL (bulleted list).

blue screen of death A feared error message with a blue background that appears when Microsoft Windows NT has encountered an error condition; typically resolved only by system rebooting.

body In HTML, one of two elements that make up an HTML document's global structure. The body contains the text and markup that is visible in a browser window.

body type The font (usually 8- to 12-point) used to set paragraphs of text. The body font is different from the font used to set headings, captions, and other typographical elements.

bold In character formatting, a character style in which the letters of a font appear thicker and darker than normal.

bookmark A Web browser navigational tool that allows Internet users to tag or mark favorite sites so they can be easily accessed.

Boolean search A database or Web search that uses the logical operators AND, OR, and NOT to specify the logical relationship between search concepts.

boot To start the computer. See cold boot and warm boot.

boot sector A portion of the computer's hard disk that is reserved for essential programs used when the computer is switched on.

boot sector virus A computer virus that copies itself to the beginning of a hard drive, where it is automatically executed when the computer is turned on.

boot sequence The series of operations that the computer runs through every time the power is switched on or the computer is restarted. See cold boot and warm boot.

bootstrap loader A program stored in the computer's read-only memory (ROM) that enables the computer to begin operating when the power is first switched on.

border Lines that are added to the top, bottom, left, or right side of a paragraph.

bots Miniprograms capable of carrying out a variety of functions on the Internet, such as greeting newcomers to Internet chat groups.

bounce message An e-mail message informing the user that another e-mail message could not be delivered to its intended recipient. The failure may be due to an incorrectly typed e-mail address or to a network problem.

Braille output devices An output device that prints computer output in raised Braille letters, which can be read by people with severely limited or no vision.

branch control structure See selection control structure.

branch prediction A technique used by advanced CPUs to prevent a pipeline stall. The processor tries to predict what is likely to happen.

broadband A type of data communication in which a technique called *multiplexing* is used to enable a single transmission line to carry more than one signal.

broadband ISDN (BISDN) A high-bandwidth digital telephone standard for transmitting up to 1.5 Mbps over fiber-optic cables. See Basic Rate Interface and Integrated Services Digital Network.

broken link On the World Wide Web, a hyperlink that refers to a resource (such as a sound or a Web page) that has been moved or deleted. Synonymous with stale link.

browse view In a database, a way of viewing records one by one.

browser A program that enables the user to navigate the Web. The two leading browsers are Netscape Navigator, part of Netscape Communication's Netscape Communicator package, and Microsoft Internet Explorer. A browser serves as the client for Web and other types of Internet servers.

brute force In programming, a crude technique for solving a difficult problem by repeating a simple procedure many times. Computer spell-checkers use a brute-force technique. They don't really "check spelling"; they merely compare all the words in a document against a dictionary of correctly spelled words.

bubble-jet printer See inkjet printer.

bug A programming error that causes a program or a computer system to perform erratically, produce incorrect results, or crash. The term *bug* was coined when a real insect was discovered to have fouled up one of the circuits of the first electronic digital computer, the ENIAC. A hardware problem is called a glitch.

build In a presentation graphics program, a type of bulleted list in which the bullet items appear one by one. Animation effects enable the new items to slide in from the side.

build-or-buy decision In the development of information systems, the choice of building a new system within the organization or purchasing it from an outside vendor.

built-in function In a spreadsheet program, a complex formula that is automated with a simple command. To add a large column of numbers, for example, you can use the sum function instead of typing each cell address.

bulleted list In Microsoft Word, bulleted lists are useful for listing items or giving instructions.

bus A term that describes the pathways that are used to move computer data, especially between peripherals or over a network.

bus mouse A type of mouse that connects to an expansion board mounted on the computer's expansion bus.

bus topology The physical layout of a local area network that does not use a central or host computer. Instead, each node manages part of the network, and information is transmitted directly from one computer to another.

business process reengineering (BPR) The use of information technology to bring about major changes and cost savings in an organization's structure. Also called reengineering.

business-to-business (B2B) e-commerce A type of e-commerce where one business provides another business with the materials and supplies it needs to conduct its operations.

byte Eight bits grouped to represent a character (a letter, a number, or a symbol).

C

C A high-level programming language developed by Bell Labs in the 1970s. C combines the virtues of high-level programming with the efficiency of assembly language but is somewhat difficult to learn.

C++ A flexible high-level programming language derived from C that supports object-oriented programming but does not require programmers to adhere to the object-oriented model.

cable modem A device that enables a computer to access the Internet by means of a cable TV connection. Some cable modems enable downloading only; you need an analog (POTS) phone line and an analog modem to upload data. The best cable modems enable two-way communications through the cable TV system and do not require a phone line. Cable modems enable Internet access speeds of up to 1.5 Mbps, although most users typically experience slower speeds due to network congestion.

cache memory A small unit of ultra-fast memory used to store recently accessed or frequently accessed data, increasing a computer system's overall performance.

calculated field In a database management program, a query that instructs the program to perform an arithmetic operation on the specified data and display the result.

calculator A device designed to help people solve mathematical problems.

call center A computer-based telephone routing system that automatically connects credit card authorization systems to authorization services.

callback system A method of network control that serves as a deterrent to system sabotage by verifying the user ID, password, and telephone number of the individual trying to access the system.

cancel button In a spreadsheet program, a button positioned near the entry bar that cancels the text inserted in the entry bar area.

Caps Lock A toggle key that switches the keyboard into a mode in which uppercase letters are produced without pressing the Shift key.

car navigation system A computer-based driving accessory that displays digitized maps and tracks the car's location using a satellite-based positioning system.

card reader A device capable of reading information on flash memory cards and transferring it to a computer.

carpal tunnel syndrome (CTS) A painful swelling of the tendons and the sheaths around them in the wrist.

Cascading Style Sheet (CSS) In Web publishing, a way to specify document formats in which specific formatting attributes (such as alignment, text style, font, and font size) are assigned to specific HTML tags, so that all subsequent uses of the tag in the same page take on the same formats. Like a style sheet in a word processing document, CSS enables a Web designer to make a single change that affects all the text marked with the same tag.

case control structure In structured programming, a logical construction of programming commands that contains a set of possible conditions and instructions that are executed if those conditions are true.

CAT (computerized axial tomography) scanner In health care, a computer-controlled imaging device used to diagnose patients.

category 5 (cat-5) A type of twisted-pair cable used for high-performance digital telephone and computer network wiring.

cathode ray tube (CRT) A vacuum tube that uses an electron gun to emit a beam of electrons that illuminates phosphorus on-screen as the beam sweeps across the screen repeatedly.

Cave Automated Virtual Environment (CAVE) A virtual reality environment that replaces headsets with 3D glasses and uses the walls, ceiling, and floor to display projected three-dimensional images.

CD-R discs Compact disc-recordable storage media that cannot be erased or written over once data has been saved; they're relatively inexpensive.

CD-R drives Compact disc-recordable devices that can read standard CD-ROM discs and write data to CD-R discs.

CD-ROM See compact disc read-only memory.

CD-ROM drive A read-only disk drive that reads data encoded on compact discs and transfers this data to a computer.

CD-ROM jukeboxes Devices that contain as many as 256 CD-ROM drives, providing storage for massive amounts of data.

CD-RW drive A compact disc-rewritable drive that provides full read/write capabilities using erasable CD-RW discs.

CD-RW discs Compact disc-rewritable storage media that allows data that has been saved to be erased or written over.

cell 1. In a spreadsheet, a rectangle formed by the intersection of a row and a column in which you enter information in the form of text (a label) or numbers (a value). 2. In telecommunications, a limited geographical area in which a signal can be broadcast.

cell address In a spreadsheet, a unique identifier associated with each cell.

cell pointer The mouse pointer, when moved across the worksheet, becomes a cell pointer and is shaped like a cross. Use the cell pointer to select one or more cells.

cell reference In a spreadsheet, a way of specifying the value of one cell in another one by entering its cell address.

cell site In a cellular telephone network, an area in which a transmitting station repeats the system's broadcast signals so that the signal remains strong even though the user may move from one cell site to another.

cellular telephone A radio-based telephone system that provides widespread coverage through the use of repeating transmitters placed in zones (called cells). The zones are close enough so that signal strength is maintained throughout the calling area.

centered alignment In word processing, a way of formatting a block of text so that it is centered on the page, leaving both ends unaligned.

central processing unit (CPU) The computer's processing and control circuitry, including the arithmetic-logic unit (ALU) and the control unit.

certificate authority (CA) In computer security, a company that verifies the identity of individuals and issues digital certificates attesting to the veracity of this identity.

certification An endorsement of professional competence that is awarded on successful completion of a rigorous test.

channel In Internet Relay Chat (IRC), a chat group in which as many as several dozen people carry on a text-based conversation on a specific topic.

character Any letter, number, punctuation mark, or symbol produced on-screen by the press of a key or a key combination.

character code An algorithm used to translate between the numerical language of the computer and characters readable by humans.

character formatting The appearance of text, including character size, typeface, and emphasis.

character set The collection of characters that a given computer is able to process and display on-screen.

charge-coupled device (CCD) A small matrix of light-sensitive elements used in digital cameras and scanners.

chart A graphical representation of data, such as is created by spreadsheet programs.

chart type In a spreadsheet program, a style of chart, such as column chart, bar chart, line chart, or pie chart.

check-screening system A computer system used in point-of-sale (POS) terminals that reads a check's account number and accesses a database of delinquent accounts.

child directory A directory inside another directory.

chip An integrated circuit (IC) that can emulate thousands or millions of transistors.

chipset A collection of supporting components that are all designed to work together smoothly on a computer motherboard.

chunks Concise hypertext documents that contain many links to other documents.

circuit switching A type of telecommunications network in which high-speed electronic switches create a direct connection between two communicating devices. The telephone system is a circuit-switching network.

citation In a word processing document, a reference to a bibliographic item that is referenced within the text. Citation options include footnotes and endnotes.

citation format A set of guidelines for typing footnote or bibliographic information. When you write a paper for a college class, you will be asked to follow a certain citation format.

citing sources Providing enough information about the source of information you are using so that an interested or critical reader can locate this source without difficulty.

class In object-oriented (OO) programming, a category of objects that performs a certain function. The class defines the properties of an object, including definitions of the object's variables and the procedures that need to be followed to get the object to do something.

click To press and release a mouse button quickly.

click-and-mortar In electronic commerce, a retail strategy in which a Web retail site is paired with a chain of local retail stores. Customers prefer this strategy because they can return or exchange unwanted goods more easily.

clickstream The trail of links left behind to reach a particular Web site.

client 1. In a client/server network, a program that runs on users' computers and enables them to access a certain type of data. 2. On a computer network, a program capable of contacting the server and obtaining needed information.

client program The part of client/server computing that handles interaction with the user and is installed on users' desktop systems. See server program.

client/server A method of organizing software use on a computer network that divides programs into servers (programs that make information available) and clients (programs that enable users to access a certain type of data).

client/server computing A software application design framework for computer networks in which software services are divided into two parts, a client part and a server part.

client/server network A computer network in which some computers are dedicated to function as servers, making information available to client programs running on users' computers.

clip art A collection of graphical images stored on disk and available for use in a page layout or presentation graphics program.

Clip Organizer In Microsoft Office, a repository of clip art and images that can be inserted into a document or presentation.

clipboard A temporary storage location used to hold information after it has been copied or cut. See cut and paste.

clock speed The speed of the internal clock of a microprocessor that sets the pace at which operations proceed in the computer's internal processing circuitry.

clock tick One "beat" of the computer's internal clock.

clone A functional copy of a hardware device, such as a personal computer. Although clones of Apple Macintosh computers exist, this term almost always refers to clones of IBM computers and their microprocessors. Compare IBM compatible.

close To remove a window from the desktop. With some applications, closing the last window terminates the application.

close tag In HTML, a tag that's used to indicate where the heading text stops.

closed architecture See proprietary architecture.

cluster On a magnetic disk, a storage unit that consists of two or more sectors.

coaxial cable A high-bandwidth connecting cable in which an insulated wire runs through the middle of the cable.

COBOL (Common Business-Oriented Language) An early, high-level programming language for business applications.

code of conduct A set of ethical principles developed by a professional association, such as the Association for Computing Machinery (ACM).

code-and-fix In programming, an early method of program development in which the programmer first created a program, and then tried to correct its shortcomings.

codec Short for compression/decompression standard. A standard for compressing and decompressing video information to reduce the size of digitized multimedia files. Popular codecs include MPEG (an acronym for Motion Picture Experts Group), Apple's QuickTime, and Microsoft's AVI.

cold boot A system start that involves powering up the computer. Compare warm boot.

collaboratory A laboratory that is made accessible to distant researchers by means of the Internet.

collision In local area networks (LANs), a garbled transmission that results when two or more workstations transmit to the same network cable at exactly the same time. Networks have means of preventing collisions.

color depth The number of colors that can be displayed on a monitor at one time.

color laser printer A nonimpact high-resolution printer capable of printing in color.

column In a spreadsheet, a block of cells going down the screen.

column chart In presentation graphics, a graph with vertical columns. Column graphs are commonly used to show the values of items as they vary at precise intervals over a period of time.

command A user-initiated instruction that tells a program which task to perform.

command line An area where commands are typed in a command-line user interface.

command-line user interface In an operating system, a variety of user interface that requires users to type commands one line at a time.

commercial software Copyrighted software that must be paid for before it can be used.

common carrier A public telephone or data communications utility.

common carrier immunity A basic principle of telecommunications law that absolves telecommunications carriers of responsibility for any legal or criminal liability resulting from messages transmitted by their networks.

Common Object Request Broker Architecture (CORBA) In object-oriented (OO) programming, a leading standard that defines how objects can communicate with each other across a network.

communication device Any hardware device that is capable of moving data into or out of the computer.

compact disc read-only memory (CD-ROM) A standard for storing read-only computer data on optical compact discs (CDs), which can be read by CD-ROM drives.

compact disc-recordable (CD-R) A "write-once" optical storage technology that uses a CD-R drive to record data on CD-R discs. Once you've recorded on the disc, you can't erase the stored data or write over the disc again. You can play the recorded CD on most CD-ROM drives.

compact disc-rewritable (CD-RW) A read/write optical storage technology that uses a CD-R drive to record data on CD-RW discs. You can erase the recorded data and write new data as you please. Most CD-ROM drives can read the recorded data. CD-RW drives can also write to CD-R discs, but you can write to CD-R discs only once.

CompactFlash A popular flash memory storage device that can store up to 128 MB of digital camera images.

compatible The capability to function with or substitute for a given make and model of computer, device, or program.

compatible computers Computer systems capable of using the same programs and peripherals.

compiler A program that translates source code in a third-generation programming language into machine code readable by a computer.

complementary metal-oxide semiconductor (CMOS) A type of semiconductor often used in computers for battery-powered circuits that store the date, time, and system configuration information.

completeness check Determines whether a required field has been left empty. If so, the database prompts the user to fill in the needed data.

complex instruction set computer (CISC) A type of central processing unit that can recognize as many as 100 or more instructions and carry out most computations directly.

Component Object Model (COM) In object-oriented (OO) programming, a standard developed by Microsoft Corporation that is used to define how objects communicate with each other over networks.

component reusability In programming, the capability to create a program module that can perform a specific task and be used in another program with little or no modification.

computer A machine that can physically represent data, process this data by following a set of instructions, store the results of the processing, and display the results so that people can use them.

computer addiction A psychological disorder characterized by compulsive and prolonged computer usage.

computer crimes Actions that violate state or federal laws.

computer ethics A new branch of philosophy dealing with computing-related moral dilemmas.

computer fluency A high level of computer conceptual knowledge and skills sufficient to enable a user to apply the computer creatively in novel situations.

computer information system (CIS) A computer system in which all components are designed to work together.

computer literacy A standard of knowledge and skills regarding computers that is sufficient to prepare an individual for working and living in a computerized society.

computer literate Used to describe persons who are skilled computer and Internet users.

computer network A collection of computers that have been connected together so they can exchange data.

computer science (CS) A scientific discipline that focuses on the theoretical aspects of improving computers and computer software.

computer security risk Any event, action, or situation—intentional or not—that could lead to the loss or destruction of computer systems or the data they contain.

computer system A collection of related computer components that have all been designed to work smoothly together.

computer virus A program, designed as a prank or as sabotage, that replicates itself by attaching to other programs and carrying out unwanted and sometimes dangerous operations.

computer virus author A programmer who creates computer viruses to vandalize computer systems.

computer vision syndrome (CVS) An eyesight disorder, such as temporary nearsightedness and blurred vision, that results from focusing closely on a computer screen for long periods of time.

computer-aided design (CAD) An application that enables engineers and architects to design parts and structures. The user can rotate the design in three dimensions and zoom in for a more detailed look. Also see computer-aided manufacturing (CAM).

computer-aided manufacturing (CAM) Software used to drive computer-controlled manufacturing equipment. CAM systems often use output from computer-aided design applications (CAD).

computer-aided production engineering (CAPE) See virtual manufacturing.

computer-aided software engineering (CASE) Software that provides tools to help with every phase of systems development and enables developers to create data flow diagrams, data dictionary entries, and structure charts.

computer-assisted instruction (CAI) The use of computers to implement programmed instruction. More broadly, CAI describes any use of computers in education.

computer-based education (CBE) A generic term that describes any use of computers for educational purposes.

computer-based training (CBT) The use of computer-assisted instruction (CAI) programs to educate adults.

computer-integrated manufacturing (CIM) The integration of computer technology with manufacturing processes.

computerized information system (CIS) A computer-based information system, composed of data, hardware, software, trained personnel, and procedures, that provides essential services to organizations; collects mission-critical data, processes this data, stores the data and the results of processing, and disseminates information throughout the organization.

computer-managed instruction (CMI) The use of computers to help instructors manage administrative teaching tasks, such as tracking grades.

computer-supported cooperative work (CSCW) A collection of applications that supports the information needs of workgroups. These applications include e-mail, videoconferencing, and group scheduling systems.

condensed spacing In character formatting, a character style in which characters are squeezed together more tightly than normal.

conditional control structure See selection control structure.

configuration file A file that stores the choices you make when you install a program so that these choices are available each time the program starts.

confirmation A message originated by a program that verifies that a user command has been completed successfully.

congestion In a packet switching network, a performance interruption that occurs when a segment of the network experiences overload.

congestion management system In transportation engineering, a computer-based system that reduces traffic congestion by means of traffic light synchronization and other techniques.

connectionless Not directly connected to another computer on the network. A connectionless network protocol enables two networked computers to exchange data without requiring an active connection to exist between them.

connector A component that enables users or technicians to connect a cable securely to the computer's case. A male connector contains pins or plugs that fit into the corresponding female connector.

consistency check Examines the data entered into two different fields to determine whether an error has been made.

constructivism A school reform movement that places emphasis on students constructing knowledge for themselves rather than learning it by rote.

contact manager A program that helps you keep track of contacts by maintaining a list of addresses, phone numbers, and fax numbers. Information is also maintained through the use of a notepad, automatic telephone dialing with a modem, and search and sort capabilities.

content In HTML, the text of a document.

content model In HTML, a specification of the type of information that can be placed between the start and end tags of an element.

contention In a computer network, a problem that arises when two or more computers try to access the network at the same time. Contention can result in collisions, which can destroy data.

contention management In a computer network, the use of one of several techniques for managing contention and preventing collisions.

context menu See popup menu.

continuous speech recognition The decoding of continuous human speech (without artificial pauses) into transcribed text by means of a computer program.

control method In an information system, a technique used to reduce the flow of information to people who do not need it (such as routing information so that it goes to only those people who really need to see the information).

control structure In structured programming, a logical element that governs program instruction execution.

control unit A component of the central processing unit (CPU) that obtains program instructions and sends signals to carry out those instructions.

conversion utility A special translation program that enables a program to read and create files in formats other than those the program normally creates.

cookie A text file that is deposited on a Web user's computer system, without the user's knowledge or consent, that may contain identifying information. This information is used for a variety of purposes, such as retaining the user's preferences or compiling information about the user's Web browsing behavior.

cooling fan A part of the system unit that prevents components from being damaged by heat.

cooperative multitasking In operating systems, a method of running more than one application at a time. If the active application crashes, however, the whole system must be restarted.

copper wire In telecommunications, a type of network cabling that uses strands of copper coated with insulation.

copy In the editing process, a command that enables the user to duplicate selected text, store this text in a temporary storage location called the clipboard, and insert (paste) the text in a new location.

copy protected Secured against unauthorized copying by some means, such as the inclusion of a necessary piece of hardware.

copyright infringement The act of using material from a copyrighted source without getting permission to do so.

copyright management infrastructure (CMI) Enables vendors of copyrighted digital media to track and control the use and copying of their products after consumers purchase them.

copyright protection scheme A method used by software manufacturers to ensure that users cannot produce unauthorized copies of copyrighted software.

copyrighted Protected legally against copying or modification without permission.

cordless keyboard A type of keyboard that connects to the computer by means of an infrared port.

cordless mice A type of mouse that connects to the computer by means of an infrared port.

corporate espionage The unauthorized access of corporate information, usually to the benefit of one of the corporation's competitors.

cost/benefit analysis An examination of the losses and gains, both tangible and intangible, related to a project.

cracker A computer user obsessed with gaining entry into highly secure computer systems.

crash An abnormal termination of program execution.

credit card authorization A system used in point-of-sale (POS) terminals that connects to an authorization service through a call center each time a credit card purchase is made.

critical thinking The capacity to evaluate the quality of information.

cross-functional team A method of designing products in which people who were formerly separated, such as engineering and finance professionals, work together in a team from the beginning of a project.

cross-platform network A computer network that includes more than one type or brand of hardware and operating system. In many colleges and universities, for example, the campus local area network includes Macintoshes, UNIX computers, and Windows PCs.

cross-platform programming language A programming language that can create programs capable of running on many different types of computers.

cross-platform standard A standard that assures interoperability on two or more brands or types of computers or computer operating systems.

cryptanalysis Code breaking.

cumulative trauma disorder (CTD) An injury involving damage to sensitive nerve tissue due to motions repeated thousands of times daily (such as mouse movements or keystrokes). Also called repetitive stress injury (RSI).

cursor A flashing bar, an underline character, or a box that indicates where keystrokes will appear when typed. Also called insertion point.

cursor-movement keys A set of keys on the keyboard that move the location of the cursor on the screen. The numeric keypad can also move the cursor when in the appropriate mode. Also called arrow keys.

custom software Application software designed for a company by a professional programmer or programming team. Custom software is usually very expensive.

cut and paste An editing operation in which characters or graphics are copied into a temporary storage location (called the clipboard) and then inserted somewhere else.

cybercrime Crime carried out by means of the Internet.

cybergang A group of computer users obsessed with gaining entry into highly secure computer systems.

cyberlaw A new legal field designed to track developments in cybercrime.

cyberphobia An exaggerated fear of computing that leads people to avoid computers and may result in physical symptoms.

cyberstalking A form of harassment in which an individual is repeatedly subjected to unwanted electronic mail or advances in chat rooms.

cylinder A single track location on all the platters of a hard disk. See track and platter.

D

data The raw material of computing: unorganized information represented for computer processing.

Data Access Page In the Microsoft Access database management system, the object used to post data to the Web.

data archiving The process of transferring infrequently used data to backup devices, where the data will be accessible should the need arise.

data backup The process of making copies of data so that it can be restored in the event of a catastrophic system failure, such as the loss of a hard disk drive.

data bus A high-speed freeway of parallel connections that enables the CPU to communicate at high speeds with memory.

data compression The reduction of a file's size so that the file can be stored without taking up as much storage space and can be transferred more quickly over a computer network. Two types of compression are lossless compression (the compressed file can be decompressed without losing any original information) and lossy compression (some of the original information is permanently removed).

data dependency A microprocessor performance problem in which a CPU is slowed in its functioning by the need to wait for the results of instructions before moving on to process the next ones.

data dictionary In information systems development, a collection of definitions of all data types that may be input into the system, including field name, data types, and validation settings.

data diddling A computer crime in which data is modified to conceal theft or embezzlement.

Data Encryption Standard (DES) A commonly used symmetric key encryption developed by U.S. security agencies.

data file A named unit of information storage that contains data rather than program instructions.

data flow diagram A graphical representation of the flow of data through an information system.

data glove A device that translates hand and arm movements into computer input.

data independence In a database, the storage of data in such a way that it is not locked into use by a particular application.

data integrity In a database, the validity of the stored data; specifically, its freedom from error due to improper data entry, hardware malfunctions, or transmission errors.

data mart A large database that contains all the data used by one of the divisions of an organization.

data mining The analysis of data stored in data warehouses to search for previously unknown patterns.

data processing A professional field that focuses on the use of computers to create transaction processing systems for businesses.

data projector An output device that projects a computer's video output onto a large screen so that an audience can see it.

data redundancy In a database, a design error in which the same data appears more than once, creating opportunities for discrepant data entry and increasing the chance that the data will be processed incorrectly.

data storage hierarchy In data processing, a means of conceptualizing storage that envisions a scale ranging from the smallest unit of data (the bit) to the largest (the file).

data transfer rate 1. In secondary storage devices, the maximum number of bits per second that can be sent from the hard disk to the computer. The rate is determined by the drive interface. 2. The speed, expressed in bits per second (bps), at which a modem can transfer, or is transferring, data over a telephone line.

data type In a database or spreadsheet program, a particular type of information, such as a date, a time, or a name.

data validation In a database, a method of increasing the validity of data by defining acceptable input ranges for each field in the record.

data warehouse A very large database, containing as many as a trillion data records, that stores all of a firm's data and makes this data available for exploratory analysis (called data mining).

database A collection of information stored in an organized way.

database file A file containing data that has been stored in the proprietary file format of a database program.

database management system (DBMS) An application that enables users to create databases that contain links from several files. Database management systems are usually more expensive than file management programs.

database object In Microsoft Access, a tool for designing and using database components (including tables, forms, and queries).

database program An application that stores data so that needed information can be quickly located, organized, and displayed.

database server In a client/server computing network, a program that makes the information stored in databases available to two or more authorized users.

database vendor 1. A company that compiles information into large databases. 2. A company that creates and sells database software.

datasheet view In Microsoft Access and Microsoft Excel, a data viewing option that enables the user to view the numerical data underlying a chart or a table.

date field In a database, a space that accepts only date information.

daughterboard An auxiliary circuit board that is designed to mount on the surface of a motherboard.

dead key A keyboard shortcut that adds a diacritical mark to the next letter you type.

debugging In programming, the process of finding and correcting errors, or bugs, in the source code of a computer program.

decision support system (DSS) A program that helps management analyze data to make decisions on semistructured problems.

declarative language A language that can be used to identify the components of a text. Synonymous with markup language.

decode One of four basic operations carried out by the control unit of a microprocessor. The decode operation figures out what a program instruction is telling the computer to do.

decrement (v.) To decrease. (n.) A specified unit by which a quantity should be decreased.

defamation An unfounded attack on the character or reputation of an individual or company.

default In a computer program, a fallback setting or configuration value that is used unless the user specifically chooses a different one.

default folder In e-mail, a folder that appears automatically when you set up your e-mail account and cannot be deleted. The inbox folder, sent mail folder, and deleted mail folder are all default folders.

default start page The Web document that appears when you start your Web browser or click the Home button. Most Web browsers are set up to display the browser company's home page, but you can easily change this setting so that the browser displays a more useful default home page.

default user interface In an operating system, the user interface (the means of interacting with the user) that appears automatically, based on preset options in the program. Some operating systems enable users to choose more than one user interface.

deliverable In the development of an information system, the outcome of a particular phase of the systems development life cycle (SDLC).

Delphi An object-oriented programming compiler based on Pascal. Although Delphi is similar to Microsoft's Visual Basic (VB), it has not been able to match Visual Basic's success.

demodulation In telecommunications, the process of receiving and transforming an analog signal into its digital equivalent so that a computer can use the information.

demote In an outlining utility, to lower the status of a heading (for example, by moving it from II to B).

denial of service (DoS) attack A form of network vandalism that attempts to make a service unavailable to other users, generally by flooding the service with meaningless data. Also called syn flooding.

deregulation A type of legislative reform in which government protections or regulations are removed in an effort to spur competition.

desktop computer A personal computer designed for an individual's use. Desktop computers are increasingly used to gain access to the resources of computer networks.

desktop environment A user interface that simulates a knowledge worker's desktop by depicting computer resources as if they were files and folders.

desktop publishing (DTP) The combination of text, graphics, and advanced formatting to create a visually appealing document.

device driver A program file that contains specific information needed by the operating system so that a specific brand or model of device will function.

diacritical mark A mark added to a character in a language other than English, such as an accent, tilde, or umlaut.

dialog box In a graphical user interface (GUI), an on-screen message box used to request information from the user.

Difference Engine A clockwork calculating machine created by Charles Babbage in the nineteenth century and capable of solving equations and printing tables. Technology at the time had not advanced enough to produce this invention.

digital A form of representation in which distinct objects, or digits, are used to stand for something in the real world, such as temperature or time, so that counting can be performed precisely.

digital audio tape (DAT) A magnetic tape backup medium that offers data backup capabilities at relatively low cost.

digital camera A camera that records an image by means of a digital imaging system, such as a charged-coupled device (CCD), and stores the image in memory or on a disk.

digital certificate A form of digital ID used to obtain access to a computer system or prove one's identity while shopping on the Web. Certificates are issued by independent, third-party organizations called certificate authorities (CA).

digital computer A machine that represents data by means of an easily identified symbol, or digit. See analog computer.

digital data storage (DDS) A digital audio tape (DAT) storage medium that stores up to 40 GB of backup data on a single cartridge.

Digital Display Working Group (DDWG) An industry association working to define digital video output.

digital light processing (DLP) projector A computer projection device that employs millions of microscopic mirrors, embedded in a microchip, to produce a brilliant, sharp image.

digital linear tape (DLT) A tape backup medium that offers faster data transfer rates and more storage capacity than quarter-inch cartridge (QIC) or digital audio tape (DAT) drives, at a significantly higher cost.

Digital Millennium Copyright Act (DMCA) A 1998 law that imposes stiff penalties for anyone convicted of disclosing information about how a copyright management infrastructure (CMI) works.

digital rights A type of intellectual property right that gives the holder the lawful ability to sell digital reproductions of a work.

digital signatures A technique used to guarantee that a message has not been tampered with.

Digital Subscriber Line (DSL) A general term for several technologies that enable high-speed Internet access through twisted-pair telephone lines. Also called xDSL. See Asymmetric Digital Subscriber Line (ADSL).

digital video Digital technologies for capturing and displaying still photography and full-motion images.

digital video camera Camera that uses digital rather than analog technologies to store recorded video images.

digital video disc (DVD) The newest optical disc format, DVD is capable of storing an entire digitized movie. DVD discs are designed to work with DVD video players and televisions.

digital video disc-RAM (DVD-RAM) A digital video disc (DVD) format that enables users to record up to 2.6 GB of data.

digital video disc-ROM (DVD-ROM) A digital optical disc format capable of storing up to 17 GB on a single disc, enough for a feature-length movie. DVD is designed to be used with a video player and a television. DVD discs can be read also by DVD-ROM drives.

Digital Video Interface (DVI) The standard created by the Digital Display Working Group that provides connections for LCD and other flat panel devices.

digitizing tablet In computer-aided graphics, a peripheral device used with a pointing device to convert hand-drawn graphics into data that a computer can process.

direct access file In business data processing, a type of data file in which the computer can gain direct and immediate access to a particular unit of storage, without having to go through a sequence of data.

Direct Broadcast Satellite (DBS) A consumer satellite technology that offers cable channels and one-way Internet access. To use DBS for an Internet connection, a modem and phone line are required to upload data.

direct conversion In the development of an information system, the termination of the current system and the immediate institution of the new system throughout the whole organization.

direct memory access (DMA) channels Set of circuits that enable peripheral devices to access the computer's main memory (RAM) directly, without having to go through the CPU.

directory A logical storage unit, often represented as a folder, that enables computer users to group files in named, hierarchically organized folders and subfolders. In magnetic and optical disks, a file that contains a list of all the files contained on the disk and information about each file.

GLOSSARY

disaster recovery plan A written plan, with detailed instructions, specifying an alternative computing facility to use for emergency processing until a destroyed computer can be replaced.

discrete speech recognition A speech recognition technology that is able to recognize human speech only when the speaker pauses between words.

disgruntled employee A current or former employee who has real or imagined grievances. Most computer crime and sabotage stems from disgruntled employees and embezzlers rather than external intruders.

disintermediation The process of removing an intermediary, such as a car salesperson, by providing a customer with direct access to rich information and warehouse-size selection and stock.

disc A portable storage optical media, such as CD-ROM.

disk A portable storage magnetic media, such as floppy disks, that provides personal computer users with convenient, near-online storage.

disk cache A small amount of memory (up to 512 KB), usually built into the electronics of a disk drive, used to store frequently accessed data. Disk caches can significantly improve the performance of a disk drive.

disk cartridge A removable cartridge containing one or more rigid disks similar to those found in hard disks.

disk cleanup utility A utility program that removes unneeded temporary files.

disk drive A secondary storage mechanism that stores and retrieves information on a disk by using a read/write head. Disk drives are random-access devices.

disk scanner A utility program that can detect and resolve a variety of physical and logical problems related to file storage.

diskette See disk.

display The visual output of a computer, usually portrayed by a monitor or a liquid crystal display (LCD).

display adapter See video adapter.

display type In word processing or desktop publishing, the typeface or font used for titles and heading text. Sans serif fonts are usually chosen for display type.

distance learning The use of telecommunications (and increasingly the Internet) to provide educational outreach programs for students at remote locations.

distributed hypermedia system A network-based content development system in which individuals connected to the network can each make a small contribution by developing content related to their area of expertise. The Web is a distributed hypermedia system.

DMA conflict A common cause of system instability that was caused when users inadvertently configured peripherals so that they competed for the same DMA channel. Occurred before plug-and-play peripherals came into use.

DNS server See domain name server.

document A file created with an application program, such as a word processing or spreadsheet program.

document formatting In a word processing document, options that alter the appearance of the entire document, such as orientation and paper size.

document map In a word processing program, an on-screen window that provides a visual guide to the document's overall organization.

documentation In information systems development, the recording of all information pertinent to the development of an information system, usually in a project notebook.

document-centric In a software suite, a user interface concept in which what counts is the document the user is creating rather than the software being used to create a portion of the document. Menus and toolbars dynamically and automatically change to those relevant to the type of data being edited.

domain In a computer network, a group of computers that are administered as a unit. Network administrators are responsible for all the computers in their domains. On the Internet, this term refers to all the computers that are collectively addressable within one of the four parts of an IP address. For example, the first part of an IP address specifies the number of a computer network. All the computers within this network are part of the same domain.

domain name On the Internet, a readable computer address (such as www.microsoft.com) that identifies the location of a computer on the network.

domain name registration On the Internet, a process by which individuals and companies can obtain a domain name (such as www.c34.org) and link this name to a specific Internet address (IP address).

domain name server An Internet server program that maintains a table showing the current IP addresses assigned to domain names. Also called DNS server or name server.

Domain Name System (DNS) The conceptual system, standards, and names that make up the hierarchical organization of the Internet into named domains.

dongle A small peripheral that must be connected to a user's computer for the particular copy-protected program to function.

dot-com The universe of Internet sites, especially those doing electronic commerce, with the suffix com appended to their names.

dot pitch On a monitor, the space (measured in millimeters) between each physical dot on the screen.

dot-matrix printer An impact printer that forms text and graphic images by hammering the ends of pins against a ribbon in a pattern (matrix) of dots. Dot-matrix printers produce near–letter quality printouts.

double data rate (DDR) SDRAM A type of SDRAM that can both send and receive data within a single clock cycle.

double-click To press and release a mouse button twice quickly.

double-density (DD) A floppy disk format that offers up to 800 KB of storage.

download To transfer a file from another computer to your computer by means of a modem and a telephone line. See upload.

downsizing In corporate management, a cost-reduction strategy involving layoffs to make a firm leaner and more competitive. Downsizing often accompanies technology-driven restructuring that theoretically enables fewer employees to do the same or more work.

downwardly compatible Capable of running without modification when using earlier computer components or files created with earlier software versions.

drag To move the mouse while holding down a mouse button.

drag handle In a graphics program, a small rectangular mark that appears on an image's border that enables the user to drag, scale, or size the graphic image.

drawing program An application program used to create, edit, and display vector graphics.

drill-and-repeat test In programmed instruction, a method of testing students and ensuring that they learn the material. If students miss questions on a drill-and-repeat test, they are guided back to the material that explains the missed questions.

drill-down A technique used by managers to view information in a data warehouse. By drilling down to lower levels of the database, the manager can focus on sales regions, offices, and then individual salespeople, and view summaries at each level.

drive A computer storage device, such as the hard disk drive. The name is derived from the motors that "drive" the movement of the media that store data.

drive bay A receptacle or opening into which you can install a floppy drive, a CD-ROM or DVD-ROM drive, or a removable drive.

drive interface The electrical pathway between a secondary storage device, such as a hard disk, and the computer. The drive interface is a leading factor in determining the speed of a storage device.

drive letters On PCs, the storage device designation, such as Drive A for the floppy disk and Drive C for the hard disk.

driver A utility program that is needed to make a peripheral device function correctly.

dual inline memory module (DIMM) A plug-in memory module that contains RAM chips. DIMMs use a 64-bit bus to transfer data between the memory and the processor, which is required for many new computers.

dual-inline packages (DIP) Chip packages that are affixed to a socket by means of two parallel rows of downward-facing pins.

dual scan LCD See passive matrix LCD.

dumpster diving A technique used to gain unauthorized access to computer systems by retrieving user IDs and passwords from an organization's trash.

DVD players Digital video disc devices for watching movies.

DVD-R discs Digital video disc-recordable optical storage media that, like CD-R discs, cannot be erased or written over once data has been saved.

DVD-RAM See digital video disc-RAM.

DVD-ROM See digital video disc-ROM.

DVD-ROM discs Optical storage media that can hold up to 17 GB of data.

DVD-ROM drive A read-only disk drive that reads the data encoded on DVD-ROM discs and transfers this data to a computer.

DVD+RW discs Digital video disc-read/write optical storage media that allow you to write, erase, and read from the disc many times.

dye sublimation printer A thermal transfer printer that produces results that rival high-quality color photographs. Dye sublimation printers are slow and extremely expensive.

dynamic random access memory (DRAM) A random access memory chip that must be refreshed periodically; otherwise, the data in the memory will be lost.

E

e-book A book that has been digitized and distributed by means of a digital storage medium.

e-book reader A book-sized device that displays an e-book.

e-commerce See electronic commerce.

economically feasible Capable of being accomplished with available fiscal resources. This is usually determined by a cost/benefit analysis.

edit menu In a graphical user interface (GUI), a pull-down menu that contains standard editing commands, such as Cut, Copy, and Paste.

edutainment Software combining education and entertainment that provides educational material in the form of a game so that the education becomes entertainment.

effect In a graphics program, a processing option that changes the appearance of an image. For example, some graphic programs can manipulate a photograph so that it looks like a watercolor painted on textured paper.

electrical engineering (EE) An engineering discipline that is concerned with the design and improvement of electrical and electronic circuits.

electronic commerce The use of the Internet and other wide area networks (WANs) for business-to-business and business-to-consumer transactions. Also called e-commerce.

electronic data interchange (EDI) A communications standard for the electronic exchange of financial information through information services.

electronic mail See e-mail.

Electronic Recording Machine—Accounting (ERMA) A computer system developed in 1959 by General Electric that could read special characters. ERMA had a major effect on the banking business, where it was used to digitize checking account information.

electronic vault In online banking, a mainframe computer that stores account holders' information.

electronic warfare In information warfare, the use of electronic devices to destroy or damage computer systems.

electronics A field within electrical engineering that is concerned with the use of transistors to amplify or switch the direction of electrical current.

element In HTML, a distinctive component of a document's structure, such as a title, heading, or list. HTML divides elements into two categories: head elements (such as the document's title) and body elements (headings, paragraphs, links, and text).

element name In HTML, the code name used to differentiate an element, such as a level-one heading (H1) or a paragraph (P).

e-mail Electronic mail; messages sent and received through the use of a computer network.

e-mail address A series of characters that precisely identifies the location of a person's electronic mailbox. On the Internet, e-mail addresses consist of a mailbox name (such as jsmith) followed by an at sign (@) and the computer's domain name (as in jsmith@hummer.virginia.edu).

e-mail attachment A computer file that is included with an e-mail message.

e-mail client A program or a program module that provides e-mail services for computer users, including receiving mail into a locally stored inbox, sending e-mail to other network users, replying to received messages, and storing received messages. The better programs include address books, mail filters, and the capability to compose and read messages coded in HTML. Also called user agent.

e-mail server An application that sends mail across the Internet and stores incoming mail until it is downloaded by an e-mail client.

embedding See object linking and embedding (OLE).

emergency disk A disk that can be used to start the computer in case the operating system becomes unusable for some reason.

Emergency Position Indicating Radio Beacons (EPIRB) A yachting safety device that emits a radio signal indicating the device's precise position, which the device determines by using signals from geographical positioning system (GPS) satellites.

emoticon See smiley.

empty element In HTML, an element that does not permit the inclusion of any content. The <BR> element is an example of an empty element.

Encapsulated PostScript (EPS) A graphics format used to print images on PostScript printers.

encapsulation In object-oriented programming, the hiding of all internal information of objects from other objects.

encryption The process of converting a message into ciphertext (an encrypted message) by using a key, so that the message appears to be nothing but gibberish. The intended recipient, however, can apply the key to decrypt and read the message. See also public key cryptography and rot-13.

encryption algorithm A step-by-step method for encrypting and decrypting a message.

encryption key A formula that is used to make a plaintext message unreadable.

end tag In HTML, the closing component of an element, such as </A>. All elements begin with a start tag; most require an end tag.

endnote In a word processing program, a feature that automatically positions and prints footnotes at the end of a document, rather than the bottom of the page.

Enhanced IDE (EIDE) An improved version of the IDE drive interface offering faster data transfer rates, access to drives larger than 528 MB, and access to four secondary storage devices instead of two. Also called ATA-2.

enhanced keyboard A keyboard with 101 keys that is typically supplied with desktop computers in the United States.

enhanced parallel port (EPP) A type of parallel port that, unlike the older Centronics parallel port standard, supports bidirectional communication between the computer and printer and offers significantly faster transmission speeds (up to 2 Mbps). EPP is a standard defined by an international standards body. Compare extended capabilities port (ECP).

ENIAC (Electronic Numerical Integrator and Computer) Considered the first large-scale electronic digital computer ever assembled, created in 1946 by Dr. John Mauchly and J. Presper Eckert.

Enter button In a spreadsheet program, a button that confirms the text typed in the entry bar area and inserts this text into the active cell.

enterprise storage system The collection of online, nearline, and offline storage within an organization. The system typically makes use of servers connected to hard disks, massive RAID systems, tape libraries (high-capacity tape systems), optical disc libraries, and tape backup systems.

enterprise-wide system An information system available throughout an organization, including its branch offices.

entity-relationship diagram (ERD) In the design of information systems, a diagram that shows all the entities (organizations, departments, users, programs, and data) that play roles in the system, as well as the relationships between those entities.

entry-level drive A storage device typically found on the least expensive computers marketed at a given time.

ergonomic keyboard A keyboard designed to reduce (but not eliminate) the chance of a cumulative trauma disorder (CTD), an injury involving damage to sensitive nerve tissue caused by motions repeated thousands of times daily.

error message A message originated by a program that warns the user about a problem of some kind. The user's intervention may be required to solve the problem.

Esc A key that is often used to interrupt or cancel an operation.

Ethernet A set of standards that defines local area networks (LANs) capable of operating at data transfer rates of 10 Mbps to 1 Gbps. About 80 percent of all LANs use one of several Ethernet standards.

Ethernet card A network interface card (NIC) designed to work with Ethernet local area networks (LANs).

ethical principle A principle that defines the justification for considering an act or a rule to be morally right or wrong. Ethical principles can help people find their way through moral dilemmas.

ethics The branch of philosophy dealing with the determination of what is right or wrong, usually in the context of moral dilemmas.

e-tickets Tickets for airline flights that are purchased online and can be picked up at small self-serve kiosks in airport terminals.

e-trading site On the Internet, an online brokerage that enables investors to buy and sell stocks without a human broker's intervention.

even parity An error-checking technique that sets an extra bit to 1 if the number of 1 bits in a byte adds up to an odd number.

event-driven In programming, a program design method that structures the program around a continuous loop, which cycles until an event occurs (such as the user clicking the mouse).

exception report In a transaction processing system (TPS), a document that alerts someone of unexpected developments, such as high demand for a product.

exclusion operator In database and Internet searching, a symbol or a word that tells the software to exclude records or documents containing a certain word or phrase.

executable See executable file and executable program.

executable file A file containing a script or program that can execute instructions on the computer. Program files usually use the .exe extension in the filename.

executable program A program that will run on a certain type of computer.

execute One of four basic operations carried out by the control unit of a microprocessor. The execute operation involves performing a requested action, such as adding or comparing two numbers.

execution cycle In a machine cycle, a phase consisting of the execute and write-back operations.

executive information system (EIS) A system that supports management's strategic planning function.

executive support system (ESS) A type of decision support system designed to provide high-level executives with information summarizing the overall performance of their organization on the most general level.

expanded spacing In character formatting, the provision of extra space between each character.

expansion board A circuit board that provides additional capabilities for a computer.

expansion bus An electrical pathway that connects the microprocessor to the expansion slots. Also called I/O bus.

expansion card See expansion board.

expansion slot A receptacle connected to the computer's expansion bus that accepts an expansion board.

expert system In artificial intelligence (AI), a program that relies on a database of if-then rules to draw inferences, in much the same way a human expert does.

Extended Binary Coded Decimal Interchange Code (EBCDIC) A character encoding scheme developed by IBM and used on its mainframe computer systems.

extended capabilities port (ECP) A parallel port standard that is virtually identical to the enhanced parallel port (EPP) standard, except that it was defined by two companies in advance of the issuance of the EPP standard.

extended character set A set of characters that can be accessed only by increasing the number of bits per character from the standard seven bits to eight bits (one byte). The extended character set was never standardized, so the PC and Macintosh versions are not compatible.

extended data out (EDO) DRAM A type of dynamic RAM (DRAM) that provides faster speeds because it can begin fetching the next item to be stored in memory at the same time that it is sending an item to the CPU.

extended keyboard A Macintosh keyboard that closely resembles the enhanced keyboard sold with most desktop PCs.

Extensible Markup Language (XML) A set of rules for creating markup languages that enables Web authors to capture specific types of data by creating their own elements. XML can be used in HTML documents.

extension A three-letter suffix added to a DOS filename. The extension is often supplied by the application and indicates the type of application that created the file.

external drive bay In a computer case, a receptacle designed for mounting storage devices that is accessible from the outside of the case.

external modem A modem with its own case, cables, and power supply that plugs into the serial port of a computer.

extranet A corporate intranet that has been opened to external access by selected outside partners, including customers, research labs, and suppliers.

eye-gaze response system A biological feedback device that enables quadriplegics to control computers by moving their eyes around the screen.

F

facsimile machine A device that transmits scanned images via the telephone system (also known as fax machine).

facsimile transmission (fax) The sending and receiving of printed pages between two locations, using a telephone line and fax devices that digitize the page's image.

fair use An exception to copyright laws made to facilitate education, commentary, analysis, and scholarly research.

fall back In modems, to decrease the data transfer rate to accommodate communications with an older modem or across a dirty line. Some modems also fall forward if line noise conditions improve.

Fast ATA An entry-level hard drive interface standard that offers data transfer rates of up to 16 Mbps. Synonymous with Fast IDE and ATA-2.

Fast Ethernet An Ethernet standard for local area networks (LANs) that enables data transfer rates of 100 Mbps using twisted-pair cable; also called 100baseT.

Fast IDE See Fast ATA.

fast-page mode (FPM) DRAM A type of dynamic RAM (DRAM) that provides faster speeds because it can replace data stored within a row of a data page without having to replace the entire page.

fault-tolerant system A computer system under development by computer scientists that can keep running even if it encounters a glitch in programming.

fax modem A modem that also functions as a fax machine, giving the computer user the capability of sending word processing documents and other files as faxes.

fax software A utility program that transforms a modem-equipped PC into a device capable of sending and receiving faxes.

fax-on-demand An information service in which faxes can be requested by means of a telephone call, and then automatically sent to the caller.

female connectors Connectors with receptacles for external pins.

fetch One of four basic operations carried out by the control unit of a microprocessor. The fetch operation retrieves the next program instruction from the computer's memory.

fiber-optic cable A network cable made from tiny strands of glasslike material that transmit light pulses with very high efficiency and can carry massive amounts of data.

field In a database, an area for storing a certain type of information.

field code In a word processing program, a code that, when inserted in the text, tells the program to perform an operation specified by the code, such as inserting the time and date when the document is printed.

field emission display (FED) A flat-panel display technology that uses tiny CRTs to produce each on-screen pixel.

field name Describes the type of data that should be entered into the field.

file A document or other collection of information stored on a disk and identified as a unit by a unique name.

file allocation table (FAT) A hidden on-disk table that keeps vital records concerning exactly where the various components of a given file are stored. The file allocation table is created at the conclusion of the formatting process.

file compression utility A program to reduce the size of files without harming the data.

file defragmentation utility A program used to read all the files on a disk and rewrite them so that files are all stored in a contiguous manner. This process almost always improves disk performance to some degree.

file finder A utility that enables one to search an entire hard disk for missing file.

file format See format (definition 1).

file infector A computer virus that attaches to a program file and, when that program is executed, spreads to other program files.

file management program An application that enables users to create customized databases and store in and retrieve data from those databases.

file menu In a graphical user interface (GUI), a pull-down menu that contains standard file-management commands, such as Save and Save As.

file server In client/server computing, a computer that has been set aside (dedicated) to make program and data files available to client programs on the network.

file sharing In a local area network (LAN), the modification of a file's properties so that other users may read or even modify the file.

File Transfer Protocol (FTP) An Internet standard for the exchange of files between two computers connected to the Internet. With an FTP client, you can upload or download files from a computer that is running an FTP server. Normally, you need a user name and password to upload or download files from an FTP server, but some FTP servers provide a service called anonymous FTP, which enables anyone to download the files made available for public use.

file viewer A utility program that can display the contents of a certain type of file.

filename A unique name given to a stored file.

fill In a spreadsheet program, a copying operation that copies the contents of the current cell to the specified range.

fill handle In a spreadsheet program, a fill handle is a rectangular box on a cell corner that can be used to specify the size of a fill area. The fill command fills a range of cells with values from selected cells.

filter In e-mail, a rule that specifies the destination folder of messages conforming to certain criteria.

filtering software A program that attempts to prevent minors from accessing adult material on the Internet.

firewall A program that permits an organization's internal computer users to access the Internet but places severe limits on the ability of outsiders to access internal data.

FireWire port Synonymous with 1394 port. FireWire is Apple Computer's name for 1394 port technology.

first sale doctrine A principle of copyright law stipulating that a person who legally obtains a copyrighted work may give or sell the work to another person without the author's permission.

fixed disk A hard disk that uses nonremovable platters.

flame In Usenet and e-mail, a message that contains abusive, threatening, obscene, or inflammatory language.

flash BIOS See flash memory.

flash memory A special type of read-only memory (ROM) that enables users to upgrade information contained in memory chips. Also called flash BIOS.

flash memory card Wafer-thin, highly portable solid state storage system that is capable of storing as much as 1 gigabyte of data. Used with some digital cameras, the card stores digitized photographs without requiring electrical power to maintain the data.

flat file A type of file generated by a file management program. Flat files can be accessed in many different ways but cannot be linked to data in other files.

flatbed scanner A device that copies an image (text or graphics) from one side of a sheet of paper and translates it into a digital image.

flat-panel display A low-power, lightweight display used with notebook computers (and increasingly with desktop computers).

flicker An eye-straining visible distortion that occurs when the refresh rate of a display is below 60 Hz.

flight simulator A program that acts like the aircraft on which a pilot is training.

floating-point notation A method for storing and calculating numbers so that the location of the decimal point isn't fixed but floating. This allows the computer to work with very small and very large numbers.

floating-point unit (FPU) A portion of the microprocessor that handles operations in which the numbers are specified in floating-point notation.

flooding A type of antisocial behavior found on Internet Relay Chat characterized by sending repeated messages so that no one else can engage in the conversation.

floppy disk A removable and widely used data storage medium that uses a magnetically coated flexible disk of Mylar enclosed in a plastic envelope or case. Although 5.25-inch floppy disks were standard, they became obsolete due to the development of the smaller, more durable 3.5-inch disk.

floppy disk drive A mechanism that enables a computer to read and write information on a removable medium that provides a convenient way to move data from one computer to another.

flowchart In structured programming, a diagram that shows the logic of a program.

flush left alignment In word processing, a way of formatting a block of text so that the left side is aligned but the right side is not.

flush right alignment In word processing, a way of formatting a block of text so that the right side is aligned but the left side is not.

fly-by-wire system In an aircraft, a computer-based control system that eliminates the pilot's direct physical control over the aircraft's control surfaces (such as flaps and rudders) in favor of computer-controlled mechanisms.

FM synthesis A method of generating and reproducing music in a sound card. FM synthesis produces sound similar to an inexpensive electronic keyboard.

FMD-ROM Fluorescent multilayer disc-read only memory. FMD-ROM discs contain fluorescent materials embedded in the pits and grooves of the disc's layers. When the laser beam strikes a layer, the light that is bounced back is also fluorescent. This type of light can pass undistributed through the disc's many layers, so that errors are eliminated.

folder A graphical representation of a directory. Most major operating systems display directories as though they were file folders.

folder list In an e-mail program, a panel that shows the default and personal mail folders, including the inbox.

folder structure An organized set of primary and secondary folders within which to save your files.

follow-up article In Usenet, a message posted in reply to another message.

font A set of characters that has a name (such as Times Roman) and a distinctive design that falls into one of two broad categories, serif (characters that have small finishing strokes) and sans serif (characters that lack finishing strokes).

foot mouse A type of mouse that is controlled by motions of the feet rather than the hands.

footer An area at the bottom of the page, but above the bottom margin, that can be used for page numbers or for text that appears on each page of the document.

footnote A type of citation that pairs an in-text (and usually numbered) reference with a source citation that appears at the bottom of the page.

footprint The amount of room taken up by the case on the desk.

foreground application In a multitasking operating system, the active application.

Form In the Microsoft Access database management system, the object used to collect data.

form factor A specification for mounting internal components, such as the motherboard.

form letter A generic message sent to many people that uses database output to create the illusion that the message is individually written and addressed. Business word processing programs can generate form letters using a feature called mail merging.

format 1. A file storage standard used to write a certain type of data to a magnetic disk (also called file format). 2. To prepare a magnetic disk for first use. 3. In word processing, to choose the alignment, emphasis, or other presentation options so that the document will print with an attractive appearance.

format menu In a graphical user interface (GUI), a pull-down menu that allows you to modify such features as font style and paragraph settings.

formatting The process of modifying a document's appearance so that it looks good when printed.

Formatting toolbar In Microsoft Office, a default-loaded toolbar that includes icons for various functions, including choosing document font size and style.

formula In a spreadsheet program, a mathematical expression embedded in a cell that can include cell references. The cell displays the formula's result.

formula bar In a spreadsheet program, an area above the worksheet that displays the contents of the active cell. The formula bar enables the user to work with formulas, which normally do not appear in the cell.

Fortran An early third-generation language that enabled scientists and engineers to write simple programs for solving mathematical equations.

fourth-generation language (4GL) A programming language that does not force the programmer to consider the procedure that must be followed to obtain the desired result.

fractal geometry The study of a certain type of irregular geometric shapes, in which the shape of internal components is similar to the overall shape. Fractal shapes are common in nature.

fragmentation A process in which the various components of a file are separated by normal reading and writing operations so that these components are not stored close together. The result is slower disk operation. A defragmentation utility can improve a disk's performance by placing these file components closer together.

frame 1. In a word processing program, a unit of text or a graphic image that has been formatted so that it will appear and print in a precise location on the page. Material placed within frames does not "float" when text is inserted or deleted above the frame. 2. A capability of Web browsers, frames can show more than one HTML page simultaneously.

frames In a video or animation, the series of still images flashed on-screen at a rapid rate.

frame rate In a video or animation, a measurement of the number of still images shown per second.

frame relay A type of packet-switching network that enables an organization to connect to an external network's point of presence for a lower cost than a permanent leased line.

free e-mail service A Web-based service that provides e-mail accounts free of charge. The service is supported by advertising.

freeware Copyrighted software that can be freely copied but not sold.

frequently asked questions (FAQ) A document that contains topical information organized by the questions that are commonly asked concerning the topic.

front panel An area on the front of most computers containing various indicator lights and controls.

FTP client A program that is able to assist the user to upload or download files from an FTP site. There are many standalone FTP clients, and FTP downloading capabilities are built into Web browsers such as Netscape Navigator. Microsoft Internet Explorer 5.0 can upload files to FTP servers as well as download files.

FTP server On the Internet, a server program that enables external users to download or upload files from a specified directory or group of directories.

FTP site An Internet-accessible computer that is running an FTP server.

full backup The process of copying all files from a secondary storage device (most commonly a hard disk) to a backup medium, such as a tape cartridge.

full-motion video A video presentation that gives the illusion of smooth, continuous action, even though it consists of a series of still pictures. The key to full-motion video is a frame rate fast enough to create the illusion of continuous movement.

function In spreadsheet programs such as Microsoft Excel, one of the two basic types of formulas (along with mathematic expressions). In a function, operations can be performed on multiple inputs.

function keys A row of keys positioned along the top of the keyboard, labeled F1 through F12, to which programs can assign various commands.

fuzzy logic A branch of logic concerned with propositions that have varying degrees of precision or confidence.

G

G or GB Abbreviation for gigabyte, approximately one billion (one thousand million) bytes or characters.

Gantt chart A bar chart that summarizes a project's schedule by showing how various activities proceed over time.

gas plasma display A flat-panel display technology. Although gas plasma displays have excellent image quality, they are very expensive and consume too much power to be used on portable computers.

gate An electronic switch; same as transistor.

Gbps A data transfer rate of approximately one billion bits per second.

genealogy program A special-purpose application program to assist in tracing and compiling family trees.

General Public License (GPL) A freeware software license, devised by the Open Software Foundation (OSF), stipulating that a given program can be obtained, used, and even modified, as long as the user agrees to not sell the software and to make the source code for any modifications available.

general-purpose computer A computer that can run a variety of programs, in contrast to an embedded or dedicated computer, which is locked to a single function or set of functions.

genetic algorithm An automated program development environment in which various alternative approaches to solving a problem are introduced; each is allowed to mutate periodically through the introduction of random changes. The various approaches compete in an effort to solve a specific problem. After a period of time, one approach may prove to be clearly superior to the others.

GIF animation A graphics file that contains more than one image stored using the GIF graphics file format. Also stored in the file is a brief script that indicates the sequence of images, and how long to display each image.

gigabit A unit of measurement approximately equal to one billion bits.

Gigabit Ethernet An Ethernet local area network (LAN) that is capable of achieving data transfer rates of 1 Gbps (one billion bits per second) using fiber-optic cable.

gigabit per second (Gbps) A data transfer measurement equivalent to one billion bits per second.

gigabits per second Points of Presence (gigaPoPs) In Internet II, a high-speed testbed for the development of next-generation Internet protocols, a point of presence (PoP) that provides access to a backbone service capable of data transfer rates in excess of 1 Gbps (one billion bits per second).

gigabyte (G or GB) A unit of measurement commonly used to state the capacity of memory or storage devices; equal to 1,024 megabytes, or approximately one billion bytes or characters.

glass cockpit In aviation, a cockpit characterized by a profusion of data displays.

Global Positioning System (GPS) A satellite-based system that enables portable GPS receivers to determine their location with an accuracy of 100 meters or less.

global structure In an HTML document, the top-level document structure created by using the HEAD and BODY tags.

global unique identifier (GUID) A uniquely identifying serial number assigned to Pentium III processor chips that can be used by Web servers to detect which computer is accessing a Web site.

graphical browser On the World Wide Web, a browser capable of displaying graphic images as well as text. Early browsers could display only text.

Graphical MUD A multiuser dungeon (MUD) that uses graphics instead of text to represent the interaction of characters in a virtual environment.

graphical user interface (GUI) An interface between the operating system and the user. Graphical user interfaces are the most popular of all user interfaces but also require the most system resources.

graphics accelerator A display adapter (video card) that contains its own dedicated processing circuitry and video memory (VRAM), enabling faster display of complex graphics images.

graphics file A file that stores the information needed to display a graphic. Popular graphics file formats include BMP (Windows Bitmap), JPEG, and GIF.

Graphics Interchange Format (GIF) A bitmapped color graphics file format capable of storing images with 256 colors. GIF incorporates a compression technique that reduces file size, making it ideal for use on a network. GIF is best used for images that have areas of solid color.

graphics output A type of output that consists of visual images, including charts and pictures.

graphics tablet A graphics input device used with CAD applications to enter graphic data precisely.

grayscale monitor A monitor that displays black, white, and dozens or hundreds of shades of gray. Grayscale monitors are often used to prepare copy for noncolor printing.

grounding strap A wrist strap worn when repairing or upgrading computer components. The strap can be connected to an electrical ground to prevent the discharge of static electricity, which can ruin computer components that contain semiconductor chips.

group e-mail address An e-mail address that directs an e-mail message to more than one person.

gutter In document formatting, extra space on the side of each page that allows for binding.

H

hacker Traditionally, a computer user who enjoys pushing his or her computer capabilities to the limit, especially by using clever or novel approaches to solving problems. In the press, the term hacker has become synonymous with criminals who attempt unauthorized access to computer systems for criminal purposes, such as sabotage or theft. The computing community considers this usage inaccurate.

hacker ethic A set of moral principles common to the first-generation hacker community (roughly 1965–1982), described by Steven Levy in *Hackers* (1984). According to the hacker ethic, all technical information should, in principle, be freely available to all. Therefore, gaining entry to a system to explore data and increase knowledge is never unethical. Destroying, altering, or moving data in such a way that could cause injury or expense to others, however, is always unethical. In increasingly more states, unauthorized computer access is against the law. See also cracker.

handheld computer See personal digital assistant.

handheld scanner A scanner used to digitize images of small originals, such as photographs or small amounts of text.

handle In a spreadsheet program, a rectangular box on a cell corner that can be used to specify the size of a fill area.

handwriting recognition software A program that accepts handwriting as input and converts it into editable computer text.

hanging indent A type of indentation that does not indent the first line but does indent the following lines.

haptics A field of research in developing output devices that stimulate the sense of touch.

hard copy Printed computer output, differing from the data stored on disk or in memory.

hard disk A secondary storage medium that uses several rigid disks (platters) coated with a magnetically sensitive material and housed in a hermetically sealed mechanism. In almost all modern computers, the hard disk is by far the most important storage medium. Also called hard disk drive.

hard disk controller An electronic circuit that provides an interface between a hard disk and the computer's CPU.

hard disk drive See hard disk.

hardware The physical components, such as circuit boards, disk drives, displays, and printers, that make up a computer system.

hardware MPEG support Circuitry built into a computer to improve MPEG video playback speed and quality.

hashing In data processing, the process in which the position of a record is determined through the use of a mathematical computation to produce an address where the unique key field is stored.

hashing algorithm A mathematical formula used to determine the address of a record in a direct access file.

head In HTML, one of two main portions of the document (the other is the body). The head contains elements that do not appear in a browser's display window.

head actuator Mechanism on a floppy disk drive that moves the read/write head to the area that contains the desired data.

head crash In a hard disk, the collision of a read/write head with the surface of the disk, generally caused by a sharp jolt to the computer's case. Head crashes can damage the read/write head, as well as create bad sectors.

header In e-mail or a Usenet news article, the beginning of a message. The header contains important information about the sender's address, the subject of the message, and other information.

head-mounted display See headset.

headset A wearable output device with twin LCD panels for creating the illusion that an individual is experiencing a three-dimensional, simulated environment.

heat sink A heat-dissipating component that drains heat away from semiconductor devices, which can generate enough heat in the course of their operation to destroy themselves. Heat sinks are often used in combination with fans to cool semiconductor components.

help menu In a graphical user interface (GUI), a pull-down menu that provides access to interactive help utilities.

help screen In commercial software, information that appears on-screen that can provide assistance with using a particular program.

help utilities Programs, such as a table of contents of frequently requested items, offered on most graphical user interface (GUI) applications.

hexadecimal number A number that uses a base 16 number system rather than a decimal (or base 10) number system.

hierarchy In Usenet, a category that includes a variety of newsgroups devoted to a shared, general topic.

hierarchy chart In structured programming, a program planning chart that shows the top-down design of the program and the relationship between program modules. Also called structure chart.

High Definition Television (HDTV) The name given to several standards for digital television displays.

high FD (HiFD) A Sony removable disk storage format that can store up to 200 MB using a drive that is also capable of reading 3.5-inch floppy disks.

high-density (HD) A floppy disk storage format that can store up to 1.44 MB of data.

high-level programming language A programming language that eliminates the need for programmers to understand the intimate details of how the computer processes data.

history list In a Web browser, a window that shows all the Web sites that the browser has accessed during a given period, such as the last 30 days.

home directory In a multiuser computer system, a directory that is set aside for an individual user.

home page 1. In any hypertext system, including the Web, a document intended to serve as an initial point of entry to a Web of related documents. Also called a welcome page, a home page contains general introductory information, as well as hyperlinks to related resources. A well-designed home page contains internal navigation buttons that help users find their way among the various documents that the home page makes available. 2. The start page that is automatically displayed when you start a Web browser or click the program's Home button. 3. A personal page listing an individual's contact information, and favorite links, and (generally) some information—ranging from cryptic to voluminous—about the individual's perspective on life.

horizontal application A general-purpose program widely used across an organization's functional divisions (such as marketing and finance). Horizontal applications are also popular in the consumer market.

horizontal scroll bar A scroll bar that enables the user to bring areas of a document into view that are hidden to the left or right.

host In a computer network, a computer that is fully connected to the network and is able to be addressed by other hosts.

hostile environment In laws concerning sexual harassment in the workplace, a working environment characterized by practices (such as sexually explicit jokes or calendars) that make some workers feel as though the workplace is offensive or oppressive.

Hot swapping Connecting and disconnecting peripherals while the computer is running.

HTML editor A program that provides assistance in preparing documents for the Web using HTML. The simplest HTML editor is a word processing program that enables you to type text and add HTML tags manually. Standalone HTML editors provide automated assistance with HTML coding and display some formats on-screen.

hub In a local area network (LAN), a device that connects several workstations and enables them to exchange data.

Human Genome Project (HGP) A research project seeking to identify the full set of genetic instructions inside human cells and find out what those instructions do.

hyperlink In a hypertext system, an underlined or otherwise emphasized word or phrase that, when clicked, displays another document.

hypermedia A hypertext system that uses various multimedia resources, such as sounds, animations, and videos, as a means of navigation as well as decoration.

hypertext A method of preparing and publishing text, ideally suited to the computer, in which readers can choose their own paths through the material. To prepare hypertext, you first "chunk" the information into small, manageable units, such as single pages of text. These units are called *nodes*. You then embed hyperlinks in the text. When the reader clicks a hyperlink, the hypertext software displays a different node. The process of navigating among the nodes linked in this way is called *browsing*. A collection of nodes interconnected by hyperlinks is called a web. The Web is a hypertext system on a global scale.

Hypertext Markup Language (HTML) A language for marking the portions of a document (called elements) so that, when accessed by a program called a Web browser, each portion appears with a distinctive format. HTML is the markup language behind the appearance of documents on the Web. HTML is standardized by means of a document type definition in the Standard Generalized Markup Language (SGML). HTML includes capabilities that enable authors to insert hyperlinks, which when clicked display another HTML document. The agency responsible for standardizing HTML is the World Wide Web Consortium (W3C).

Hypertext Transfer Protocol (HTTP) The Internet standard that supports the exchange of information on the Web. By defining uniform resource locators (URLs) and how they can be used to retrieve resources anywhere on the Internet, HTTP enables Web authors to embed hyperlinks in Web documents. HTTP defines the process by which a Web client, called a browser, originates a request for information and sends it to a Web server, a program that responds to HTTP requests and provides the desired information.

I

I/O bus See expansion bus.

I/O device Generic term for any input or output device.

IBM compatible personal computer A computer that can use all or almost all software developed for the IBM personal computer and accepts the IBM personal computer's cards, adapters, and peripheral devices. Compare clone.

icon In a graphical user interface (GUI), a small picture that represents a program, a data file, or some other computer entity or function.

IDE/ATA See Integrated Drive Electronics (IDE).

identify theft A form of fraud in which a thief obtains someone's Social Security number and other personal information, and then uses this information to obtain credit cards fraudulently.

image editor A sophisticated paint program for editing and transforming complex bitmapped images, such as photographs.

image processing system A filing system in which incoming documents are scanned and stored digitally.

impact printer A printer that generates output by striking the page with something solid.

inbox In e-mail, a default folder that contains any new mail messages, as well as older messages that have not been moved or deleted.

inclusion operator In database or Web searching, a symbol or keyword that instructs the search software to make sure that any retrieved records or documents contain a certain word or phrase.

increment (v.) To increase. (n.) A specified unit by which a quantity should be increased.

incremental backup The process of copying files that have changed since the last full backup to a backup medium, such as a tape cartridge.

indecency In U.S. law, the use of four-letter words or any other explicit reference to sexual or excretory acts that violates community decency standards.

index page In Web publishing, the page that the Web server displays by default (usually called index.html or default.html).

indexed file See indexed sequential file.

indexed sequential file A file with records that can be accessed either directly (randomly) or sequentially. Also called indexed file.

Industry Standard Architecture (ISA) bus A bus architecture used for expansion slots introduced in the IBM PC/AT. Although they are slower than the PCI bus architecture, ISA expansion slots continue to appear in new computers for compatibility.

information Processed data.

information hiding A modular programming technique in which information inside a module remains hidden with respect to other modules.

information kiosk An automated presentation system used for public information or employee training.

information literacy The capability to gather information, evaluate the information, and make an informed decision.

information overload A condition of confusion, stress, and indecision brought about by being inundated with information of variable value.

information processing cycle A complete sequence of operations involving data input, processing, storage, and output.

information system A purposefully designed system that brings data, computers, procedures, and people together to manage information important to an organization's mission.

Information Superhighway A term coined by former U.S. Vice President Al Gore to describe the phenomenon of media convergence.

information systems (IS) department In a complex organization, the division responsible for designing, installing, and maintaining the organization's information systems.

information terrorism The intimidation of a person, an organization, or a country by means of sabotage directed at information systems.

information warfare A military strategy that targets an opponent's information systems.

information-literate person Someone who knows how to gather information, evaluate the information, and make an informed decision.

infrared A data transmission medium that uses the same signaling technology used in TV remote controls.

inheritance In object-oriented (OO) programming, the capacity of an object to pass its characteristics to subclasses.

inkjet printer A nonimpact printer that forms an image by spraying ink from a matrix of tiny jets.

GLOSSARY

inline element In HTML, an element that can be included in a block element. Some inline elements enable Web authors to choose presentation formats such as bold or italic.

input The information entered into a computer for processing.

input device Any device that is capable of accepting data so that it is properly represented for processing within the computer.

input/output (I/O) port A circuit that enables a peripheral device to channel data into and out of the computer.

insert mode In word processing, a text insertion mode in which the inserted text pushes existing text to the right and down.

insertion point See cursor.

install To set up a program so that it is ready to function on a given computer system. The installation process may involve creating additional directories, making changes to system files, and other technical tasks. For this reason, most programs come with setup programs that handle the installation process automatically.

instant messaging (IM) system Software program that lets you know when a friend or business associate is online. You can then contact this person and exchange messages and attachments.

instruction A unique number assigned to an operation performed by a processor.

instruction cycle In a machine cycle, a phase consisting of the fetch and decode operations.

instruction set A list of specific instructions that a given brand and model of processor can perform.

intangible benefits Gains that have no fixed dollar value, such as access to improved information or increased sales due to improved customer services.

integer A whole number.

integrated circuit (IC) A semiconductor circuit containing more than one transistor and other electronic components; often referred to as a chip.

Integrated Drive Electronics (IDE) A popular secondary storage interface standard commonly found in PCs that offers relatively good performance at a low cost. Although IDE is a commonly used interface, newer computers use either Enhanced IDE (EIDE) or Ultra ATA. Also called Advanced Technology Attachment (ATA).

integrated learning system (ILS) A mainframe-based system used to bring computer-assisted instruction (CAI) to schools.

integrated program A program that combines three or more productivity software functions, including word processing, database management, and a spreadsheet.

Integrated Services Digital Network (ISDN) A worldwide standard for the delivery of digital telephone and data services to homes, schools, and offices using existing twisted-pair wiring. The three categories of ISDN services are Basic Rate Interface (BRI), Primary Rate Interface (PRI), and Broadband ISDN (BISDN).

Intelligent Transportation System (ITS) A system, partly funded by the U.S. government, to develop smart streets and smart cars. Such a system could warn travelers of congestion and suggest alternative routes.

interactive multimedia A presentation involving two or more media, such as text, graphics, or sound, and providing users with the ability to choose their own path through the information.

interactive processing A type of processing in which the various stages of the information processing cycle (input, processing, storage, and output) can be initiated and controlled by the user.

interactive TV Features that enable users to engage in two-way communication with a digital television set. Interactive TV will enable broadcasters and cable TV providers to implement features such as user-selectable movies, weather broadcasts selected by ZIP code, and news on selected topics.

interexchange carrier (IXC) In the public switched telephone network (PSTN), a company that provides long-distance or regional trunk services between local telephone exchanges.

interface A means of connecting two dissimilar computer devices. An interface has two components, a physical component and a communications standard, called a protocol. The physical component provides the physical means for making a connection, while the protocol enables designers to design the devices so that they can exchange data with each other. The computer's standard parallel port is an example of an interface that has both a distinctive physical connector and a defining, standard protocol.

interlaced monitor A monitor that refreshes every other line of pixels with each pass of the cathode gun. This often results in screen flicker, and almost all monitors now are noninterlaced.

internal drive bay In a computer's case, a receptacle for mounting a storage device that is not easily accessible from outside the computer's case. Internal drive bays are typically used to mount nonremovable hard drives.

internal modem A modem that fits into the expansion bus of a personal computer. See also external modem.

International Telecommunications Union (ITU) A branch organization of the United Nations that sets international telecommunications standards.

Internet An enormous and rapidly growing system of linked computer networks, worldwide in scope, that facilitates data communication services such as remote logon, file transfer, electronic mail, the World Wide Web, and newsgroups. Relying on TCP/IP, the Internet assigns every connected computer a unique Internet address (called an IP address) so that any two connected computers can locate each other on the network and exchange data.

Internet 2 The next-generation Internet, still under development.

Internet address The unique, 32-bit address assigned to a computer that is connected to the Internet, represented in dotted decimal notation (for example, 128.117.38.5). Synonymous with IP address.

Internet client A user program for accessing information on the Internet, such as e-mail or a Web site.

Internet hard drive Storage space on a server that is accessible from the Internet.

Internet Inter-Orb Protocol (IIOP) In object-oriented (OO) programming, a standard that allows Web browsers to request information from objects by using the Common Object Request Broker Architecture (CORBA).

Internet Message Access Protocol (IMAP) In Internet e-mail, one of two fundamental protocols (the other is POP3) that governs how and where users store their incoming mail messages. IMAP4, the current version, stores messages on the mail server rather than facilitating downloading to the user's computer, as does the POP3 standard. For many users, this standard may prove more convenient than POP3 because all of one's mail is kept in one central location, where it can be organized, archived, and made available from remote locations. IMAP4 is supported by Netscape Messenger, the mail package in Netscape Communicator; Microsoft Outlook Express; and by other leading e-mail programs.

Internet Protocol (IP) One of the two core Internet standards (the other is the Transmission Control Protocol, TCP). IP defines the standard that describes how an Internet-connected computer should break data down into packets for transmission across the network, and how those packets should be addressed so that they arrive at their destination. IP is the connectionless part of the TCP/IP protocols.

Internet protocols The standards that enable computer users to exchange data through the Internet. Also called TCP/IP.

Internet Relay Chat (IRC) A real-time, Internet-based chat service, in which one can find "live" participants from the world over. IRC requires the use of an IRC client program, which displays a list of the current IRC channels. After joining a channel, you can see what other participants are typing on-screen, and you can type your own repartee.

Internet service A set of communication standards (protocols) and software (clients and servers) that defines how to access and exchange a certain type of information on the Internet. Examples of Internet services are e-mail, FTP, Gopher, IRC, and Web.

Internet Service Provider (ISP) A company that provides Internet accounts and connections to individuals and businesses. Most ISPs offer a range of connection options, ranging from dial-up modem connections to high-speed ISDN and ADSL. Also provided is e-mail, Usenet, and Web hosting.

Internet telephony The use of the Internet (or of nonpublic networks based on Internet technology) for the transmission of real-time voice data.

Internet telephony service providers A long-distance voice messaging service that provides telephone service by means of the Internet or private data networks using Internet technology.

InterNIC A consortium of two organizations that provide networking information services to the Internet community, under contract to the National Science Foundation (NSF). Currently, AT&T provides directory and database services, while Network Solutions, Inc., provides registration services for new domain names and IP addresses.

interoperability The ability to work with computers and operating systems of differing type and brand.

interpreter In programming, a translator that converts each instruction into machine-readable code and executes it one line at a time. Interpreters are often used for learning and debugging, due to their slow speed.

interrupt request (IRQ) Lines that handle the communication between input or output devices and the computer's CPU.

intranet A computer network based on Internet technology (TCP/IP) that meets the internal needs of a single organization or company. Not necessarily open to the external Internet and almost certainly not accessible from the outside, an intranet enables organizations to make internal resources available using familiar Internet tools. See also extranet.

IP address A 32-bit binary number that uniquely and precisely identifies the location of a particular computer on the Internet. Every computer that is directly connected to the Internet must have an IP address. Because binary numbers are so hard to read, IP addresses are given in four-part decimal numbers, each part representing 8 bits of the 32-bit address (for example, 128.143.7.226).

IPOS cycle A sequence of four basic types of computer operations that characterize everything computers do. These operations are input, processing, output, and storage.

IPv6 The Next Generation Internet Protocol, also known as IPng, is an evolutionary extension of the current Internet protocol suite that is under development by the Internet Engineering Task Force (IETF). IPv6 was originally intended to deal with the coming exhaustion of IP addresses, a serious problem caused by the Internet's rapid growth. However, the development effort has broadened to address a number of deficiencies in the current versions of the fundamental Internet protocols, including security, the lack of support for mobile computing, the need for automatic configuration of network devices, the lack of support for allocating bandwidth to high-priority data transfers, and other shortcomings of the current protocols. An unresolved question is whether the working committee will be able to persuade network equipment suppliers to upgrade to the new protocols.

IPX See IPX/SPX.

IPX/SPX In local area networks (LANs), a suite of network and transport layer protocols developed by Novell for use with the NetWare network operating system.

IrDA port A port housed on the exterior of a computer's case that is capable of sending and receiving computer data by means of infrared signals. The standards that define these signals are maintained by the Infrared Data Association (IrDA). IrDA ports are commonly found on notebook computers and personal digital assistants (PDAs).

IRQconflict A serious system failure that results if two devices are configured to use the same IRQ but are not designed to share an IRQ line.

ISDN adapter An internal or external accessory that enables a computer to connect to remote computer networks or the Internet by means of ISDN. (Inaccurately called an ISDN modem.)

italic A character format in which characters are slanted to the right.

iteration control structure See repetition control structure.

J

Java A cross-platform programming language created by Sun Microsystems that enables programmers to write a program that will execute on any computer capable of running a Java interpreter (which is built into today's leading Web browsers). Java is an object-oriented programming (OOP) language similar to C++, except that it eliminates some features of C++ that programmers find tedious and time-consuming. Java programs are compiled into applets (small programs executed by a browser) or applications (larger, standalone programs that require a Java interpreter to be present on the user's computer), but the compiled code contains no machine code. Instead, the output of the compiler is bytecode, an intermediary between source code and machine code that can be transmitted by computer networks, including the Internet.

Java Virtual Machine (VM) A Java interpreter and runtime environment for Java applets and Java applications. This environment is called a virtual machine because, no matter what kind of computer it is running on, it creates a simulated computer that provides the correct platform for executing Java programs. In addition, this approach insulates the computer's file system from rogue applications. Java VMs are available for most computers.

JavaScript A scripting language for Web publishing, developed by Netscape Communications, that enables Web authors to embed simple Java-like programming instructions in the HTML text of their Web pages.

Jaz drive A removable drive from Iomega that can store up to 2 GB.

jewel boxes Plastic protective cases for storing CD-ROM discs.

job instruction training (JIT) A method of on-the-job training where decision-making is eliminated as much as possible.

joint application development (JAD) In information systems development, a method of system design that involves users at all stages of system development. See also prototyping.

Joint Photographic Experts Group (JPEG) A graphics file format, named after the group that designed it. JPEG graphics can display up to 16.7 million colors and use lossy compression to reduce file size. JPEG is best used for complex graphics such as photographs.

joystick An input device commonly used for games.

justification The alignment of text at the beginning and end of lines. Text can either be flush left, flush right, centered, or justified.

justified alignment In word processing, a way of formatting a block of text so that both the left and right sides are aligned.

just-in-time (JIT) manufacturing A method of monitoring inventory that triggers the manufacturing process only when inventory levels are low.

K

K or KB Abbreviation for kilobyte, approximately one thousand bytes or characters.

Kbps A data transfer rate of approximately one thousand bits per second.

kernel The essential, core portion of the operating system that is loaded into random access memory (RAM) when the computer is turned on and stays in RAM for the duration of the operating session. Also called supervisor program.

kerning The process of adjusting the space between wide and narrow characters so that the results are pleasing to the eye.

key In cryptography, the procedure used to encipher the message so that it appears to be just so much nonsense. The key also is required for decryption. Public key cryptography has two keys: a private key and a public key. A user makes the public key known to others, who use it to encrypt messages; these messages can be decrypted only by the intended recipient of a message, who uses the private key to do so.

key escrow The storage of users' encryption keys by an independent agency, which would divulge the keys to law enforcement investigators only on the production of a valid warrant. Key escrow is proposed by law enforcement officials concerned that encryption would prevent surveillance of criminal activities.

key field or primary key This field contains a code, number, name, or some other information that uniquely identifies the record.

key length Term used to describe the length (in bits) of an encryption key.

key recovery A method of unlocking the key used to encrypt messages so that the message could be read by law enforcement officials conducting a lawful investigation. Key recovery is proposed by law enforcement officials concerned that encryption would prevent surveillance of criminal activities.

keyboard An input device providing a set of alphabetic, numeric, punctuation, symbolic, and control keys.

keyboard shortcuts The use of a modifier key as a shortcut to menu commands.

keyword In a command-line interface, words that tell the operating system what to do (such as "format" or "copy").

kilobits per second (Kbps) A data transfer rate of approximately one thousand bits of computer data per second.

kilobyte (K or KB) The basic unit of measurement for computer memory and disk capacity, equal to 1,024 bytes or characters.

kiosk A booth that provides a computer service of some type.

knowledge base A database of represented knowledge.

knowledge management system An information system that captures knowledge created by employees and makes it available to an organization.

knowledge representation The process of eliciting rules from human experts.

L

label In a spreadsheet, a text entry that explains one or more numerical entries.

land Flat reflective areas on an optical disc.

landscape In document formatting, a page layout in which the text runs across the wide orientation of the page.

laptop computer A portable computer larger than a notebook computer but small enough to be transported easily. Few are being made now that notebook computers have become so powerful.

large-scale integration (LSI) A technology used to assemble integrated circuits (IC). LSI was achieved in the early 1970s and could fit up to 5,000 transistors on a single IC.

laser printer A popular nonimpact, high-resolution printer that uses a version of the electrostatic reproduction technology of copying machines.

last mile problem The lack of local network systems for high-bandwidth multimedia communications that can accommodate the Information Superhighway.

latency In a packet-switching network, a signal delay that is introduced by the time network routers consume as they route packets to their destination.

launch To start an application program.

layer In a computer network, a level of network functionality governed by specific network protocols. For example, the physical layer has protocols concerned with the transmission of signals over a specific type of cable.

LCD monitors The thinner monitors used on notebook and some desktop computers.

LCD projector An output device that projects a computer's screen display on a screen similar to those used with slide projectors.

leader In word processing, a character that is automatically inserted before a tab stop.

leading The space between the lines of text. Pronounced "ledding."

leased line A permanently connected and conditioned telephone line that provides wide area network (WAN) connectivity to an organization or a business.

left drag In the My Computer primary file management utility for PCs, an action done on a folder or file to automatically move or copy the folder or file.

left pane In the My Computer primary file management utility for PCs, one of two main default windows. It displays links to system tasks, such as viewing system information. See also right pane.

legacy Obsolete; most often used to describe old mainframe systems.

legacy system A technically obsolete information system that remains in use, often because it performs its job adequately or is too expensive to replace.

legend In a chart, an area that provides a key to the meaning of the symbols or colors used on the chart.

letter-quality printer A dot-matrix printer that can produce characters that appear to be fully formed, like those printed by a laser printer.

level 2 (L2) cache See secondary cache.

libel A form of defamation that occurs in writing.

life cycle In information systems, the birth, development, use, and eventual abandonment of the system.

light pen An input device that uses a light-sensitive stylus to draw on-screen or on a graphics tablet or to select items from a menu.

line chart A graph that uses lines to show the variations of data over time or to show the relationship between two numeric variables.

line printer In business data processing, a high-speed printer that prints an entire line of text at a time.

linker See assembler.

linking See object linking and embedding (OLE).

Linux A freeware operating system closely resembling UNIX developed for IBM-compatible PCs but also available for other platforms, including Macintosh.

Linux distribution A CD-ROM containing the Linux operating system and a collection of drivers, GUI interfaces, and application programs.

liquid crystal display (LCD) A small, flat-screen monitor that uses electrical current to control tiny crystals and form an image.

listserv An automatic mailing list server developed by Eric Thomas for BITNET in 1986.

list server In e-mail, a program that automatically sends a copy of every message submitted to the mailing list to the address of each of the mailing list's subscribers. Also called reflector.

list server address In a mailing list, the e-mail address of the list server rather than the mailing list. To subscribe or unsubscribe to a mailing list, you send requests to the list server address.

list view In a database, a way of viewing database records as a list.

load To transfer program instructions from storage to memory.

loading The process of transferring data from an input or storage device into the computer's memory.

local access and transport area (LATA) In the public switched telephone network (PSTN), the area served by a local exchange carrier (LEC).

local area network (LAN) A computer network that connects computers in a limited geographical area (typically less than one mile) so that users can exchange information and share hardware, software, and data resources.

local exchange carrier (LEC) A telecommunications company that serves a local access and transport area (LATA).

local loop In the public switched telephone network (PSTN), the last segment of service delivery, typically consisting of analog connections from neighborhood distribution points.

local newsgroup In Usenet, a category of newsgroups that are devoted to the concerns of the organization (such as a university or company) running the local server.

LocalTalk A protocol developed by Apple Computer that provides peer-to-peer networking among Apple Macintosh computers and Macintosh-compatible peripherals such as laser printers. LocalTalk is a low-level protocol that works with twisted-pair phone cables.

location toolbar A Web browser feature that provides a text box indicating the URL of the page being viewed; also known as the address toolbar.

log in To authenticate yourself as a user with a valid account and usage privileges on a multiuser computer system or a computer network. To log in, you supply your user name and password. Also called log on.

log on See log in.

logic bomb A flaw concealed in an otherwise usable computer program that can be triggered to destroy or corrupt data.

logic error In programming, a mistake made by the programmer in designing the program. Logic errors will not surface by themselves during program execution because they are not errors in the structure of the statements and commands.

logical data type A data type that allows only a yes or no answer

logical field In a database, a space that accepts only yes and no values.

logical operations One of two groups of operations performed by the arithmetic-logic unit (ALU). The logical operations involve comparing two data items to see which one is larger or smaller.

looping See repetition control structure.

lossless compression In data compression, a method used to reduce the size of a file that enables the file to be restored to its original size without introducing errors. Most lossless compression techniques reduce file size by replacing lengthy but frequently occurring data sequences with short codes; to decompress the file, the compression software reverses this process and restores the lengthy data sequences to their original form.

lossy compression In data compression, a method of reducing the size of multimedia files by eliminating information that is not normally perceived by human beings.

low-level language A language that describes exactly the procedures to be carried out by a computer's central processing unit, such as machine or programming language.

M

M or MB Abbreviation for megabyte, approximately one million bytes or characters of information.

Mac OS Operating system and user interface developed by Apple Computer for Macintosh computers; introduced the first graphical user interface.

machine cycle A four-step process followed by the control unit that involves the fetch, decode, execute, and write-back operations. Also called processing cycle.

machine dependence The dependence of a given computer program or component on a specific brand or type of computer equipment.

machine language The native binary language consisting of 0s and 1s that is recognized and executed by a computer's central processing unit.

machine translation Language translation performed by the computer without human aid.

macro In application software, a user-defined command sequence that can be saved and executed to perform a complex action.

macro virus A computer virus that uses the automatic command execution capabilities of productivity software to spread itself and often to cause harm to computer data.

maglev (magnetic levitation) A railway technology in which magnetic fields are used to raise the train off the railway surface, thus eliminating friction and enabling speeds rivaling those of aircraft.

magnetic disks Random access devices that are one of the two most common magnetic media.

magnetic resonance imaging (MRI) In health care, a computer-controlled imaging device used to diagnose patients.

magnetic storage A storage system that uses magnetically encoded disks or tapes to store data.

magnetic storage media In computer storage systems, any storage device that retains data using a magnetically sensitive material, such as the magnetic coating found on floppy disks or backup tapes.

magnetic tapes Sequential storage devices that are one of the two most common magnetic media.

magnetic-ink character recognition (MICR) system A scanning system developed by the banking industry in the 1950s. Check information is encoded onto each check before it is used to reduce processing time when the check comes back to the bank.

magneto-optic (MO) disc An erasable disk that combines magnetic particles used on tape and disk with new optical technology.

magneto-optical (MO) drive A data storage device that uses laser technology to heat an extremely small spot on a magneto-optical (MO) cartridge so that the magnetic medium used in the MO disk becomes capable of having its magnetic orientation changed by the read/write head.

mailbox name One of the two basic parts of a person's e-mail address: the part to the left of the at sign (@), which specifies the name of the person's mailbox. To the right of the @ sign is the domain name of the computer that houses the mailbox. A person's mailbox name often is the same as his or her login name.

mailing list An e-mail application that enables participants to send a message that will be mailed to all of the lists' participants. Similarly, replies to this message (if not addressed only to the sender of the original message) will be seen by all participants.

mailing list address An e-mail address that identifies the mailbox to which mailing list messages are sent.

mailto URL In HTML, a type of URL that enables Web authors to create a link to a person's e-mail address. When the user clicks the mailto link, the browser displays a window for composing an e-mail message to this address.

main board See motherboard.

mainframe A multiuser computer system that meets the computing needs of a large organization.

male connectors Connectors with external pins.

management information system (MIS) A computer-based system that supports the information needs of management.

managers People in an organization who decide how best to use the organization's resources, including money, equipment, and people, so that the organization achieves its goals.

margin The space around the edge of the paper that is left blank when a document is printed.

margin loan In stock investing, a risky strategy in which investors borrow money to purchase stocks. The strategy pays off when share prices rise. In a bear (declining) market, however, investors who purchased stocks on margin loans may accumulate more debt than their finances can handle.

Mark Sense Character Recognition A data input system that can recognize pencil marks on printed forms.

markup language In text processing, a system of codes for marking the format of a unit of text that indicates only that a particular unit of text is a certain part of the document, such as an abstract, a title, or an author's name and affiliation. The actual formatting of the document part is left to another program, called a viewer, which displays the marked document and gives each document part a distinctive format (fonts, spacing, and so on). HTML is a markup language.

mass storage system A backup storage device used in a mainframe system. Mass storage systems can store hundreds or even thousands of high-capacity tape backup cartridges in a carousel-like system.

master In a graphics program, a template that contains the formatting and graphics that will appear on every page.

master file A file containing all the current data relevant to an application.

master page In desktop publishing (DTP), a page that acts as a template for how all other pages will appear.

master slide In presentation graphics, a template slide that contains a presentation's background and any additional information that will appear on every page of the finished presentation.

master view In a desktop publishing or presentation graphics program, a view that shows the underlying template that is used to display each page.

math coprocessor A separate chip that frees the main processor from performing mathematical operations, usually operations involving floating-point notation.

mathematic formula In spreadsheet programs such as Microsoft Excel, one of the two basic types of formulas (along with functions). In a mathematic formula, or expression, the mathematic order of operation is followed.

maximize To enlarge a window so that it fits the entire screen.

Mbps In networking, a data transfer rate of approximately one million bits per second.

mean time between failures (MTBF) A hard disk manufacturer's estimate of how many drives of the same brand and model would need to be in operation for one of them to fail per hour.

mechanical mice A type of mouse that uses a rotating ball to generate information about the mouse's position.

medium-scale integration (MSI) A technology used to assemble integrated circuits (ICs). MSI was achieved in the late 1960s and could fit between 20 and 200 transistors on a single IC.

megabyte (M or MB) A measurement of storage capacity equal to 1,024 kilobytes, or approximately one million bytes or characters.

megapixel Type of digital camera that has a charge-coupled device with at least one million elements.

memory Circuitry that stores information temporarily so that it is readily available to the central processing unit (CPU).

memory address A code number that specifies a specific location in memory.

memory bus See system bus.

memory resident A program, such as an operating system's kernel, that resides in random access memory whenever the computer is turned on.

menu bar In a graphical user interface (GUI), a rectangular bar (generally positioned near the top of the application window) that provides access to pull-down menus. On the Macintosh, an active application's menu bar is always positioned at the top of the screen.

menu-driven user interface An interface between the operating system and the user in which text-based menus show options, rather than requiring the user to memorize the commands and type them in.

message list In an e-mail program, a list of all current e-mail messages.

message window In an e-mail program, an on-screen panel that displays the contents of the message currently highlighted in the message list.

Metcalfe's Law A prediction formulated by Bob Metcalfe, creator of Ethernet, that the value of a network increases in proportion to the square of the number of people connected to the network.

method In object-oriented programming, a procedure or operation that processes or manipulates data.

metropolitan area network (MAN) A high-speed regional network typically used to connect universities with other research facilities in a large metropolitan area.

microcomputer A computer that uses a microprocessor as its CPU.

micron One thousandth of a millimeter.

microphone An input device that converts sound into electrical signals that can be processed by a computer.

microprocessor An integrated circuit containing the arithmetic-logic unit (ALU) and control unit of a computer's central processing unit (CPU).

Microsoft Windows Generic name for the various operating systems in the Microsoft Windows family, including, but not limited to, Microsoft Windows CE, Microsoft Windows 3.1, Microsoft Windows 95, Microsoft Windows 98, and Microsoft Windows NT.

Microsoft Windows 2000 Professional A high-performance operating system for corporate computer users that combines the features of Windows NT Workstation with the easy-to-use interface of Windows 98.

Microsoft Windows 2000 Server A high-performance operating system designed for use on client/server networks in corporations and other large organizations. Windows 2000 Server is the successor to Windows NT Server.

Microsoft Windows 3.x A family of programs developed by Microsoft Corporation, including Windows 3.1, Windows 3.11, and Windows for Workgroups 3.1. Although they are often treated like operating systems, these programs are actually MS-DOS applications.

Microsoft Windows 95 An operating system developed for IBM-compatible PCs by Microsoft Corporation. Unlike Windows 3.x, Microsoft Windows 95 is a true operating system that introduced numerous improvements over its predecessors. Microsoft Windows 95 is a 32-bit operating system that is downwardly compatible with 16-bit programs developed for Windows 3.x. Also called Win 95.

Microsoft Windows 98 A 32-bit operating system developed for IBM-compatible PCs by Microsoft Corporation as the successor to Windows 95. Windows 98 offers easier Internet connectivity and the availability to work with peripherals that require universal serial bus (USB) or Accelerated Graphics Port (AGP) slots. Like Windows 95, Windows 98 is downwardly compatible with applications developed for Windows 3.x. Also called Win 98.

Microsoft Windows 98 SE SE is short for second edition. According to Microsoft, Windows 98 SE is the best choice for home computing because it offers the best support for multimedia.

Microsoft Windows CE An operating system for palmtop and personal digital assistant computers developed by Microsoft Corporation.

Microsoft Windows ME Like Windows 95 and Windows 98, Microsoft Windows ME combines 16- and 32-bit code. New features include support for home computer networks, in which two or more computers can share a single Internet connection.

Microsoft Windows NT A 32-bit operating system developed by Microsoft Corporation for use in corporate client/server networks. The operating system consists of two components, Microsoft Windows NT Workstation (for users' systems) and Microsoft Windows NT Server (for file servers).

Microsoft Windows NT Server A network operating system for file servers. When used with Microsoft's BackOffice suite of server software, Windows NT Server provides a suite of software for enterprise information systems development, including messaging and database access.

Microsoft Windows NT Workstation A 32-bit operating system for networked client computers, developed by Microsoft Corporation.

Microsoft Windows XP The first Microsoft operating system family that uses the same, underlying 32-bit code for all three versions (consumer, corporate desktop, and server).

Microsoft Windows XP Home Edition An improved version of Windows 2000 Professional designed for home users that replaces all previous versions of Windows designed for home users (including Windows 95, 98, and ME).

Microsoft Windows XP Professional Updated version of Windows 2000 Professional. XP Professional is designed for desktop computer users in networked corporate settings.

Microsoft Windows XP Server Updated version of Windows 2000 Server. XP Server is designed to make information and services available on corporate computer networks.

microwave An electromagnetic radio wave with a very short frequency.

middleware In object-oriented programming, standards that define how programs find objects and determine what kind of information they contain.

millisecond (ms) A unit of measurement, equal to one-thousandth of a second, commonly used to specify the access time of hard disk drives.

minicomputer A multiuser computer that meets the needs of a small organization or a department in a large organization.

minimize To reduce the size of a window so that it appears only as an icon or an item on the taskbar.

mirror site On the Internet, a duplicate version of a popular site that is created to ensure that users will be able to access the site without encountering errors or delays.

mirroring/duplexing The technique used by Level 1 RAID devices to assure that each hard disk is paired with at least one additional disk that contains an exact copy of its data.

mission-critical system An information system that is of decisive importance to an organization's primary mission. In a university, the information systems that handle student registration are mission-critical systems. Compare safety-critical system.

mnemonic In programming, an abbreviation or a word that makes it easier to remember a complex instruction.

modeling A method by which spreadsheet programs are able to predict future outcomes.

modem Short for modulator/demodulator, a device that converts the digital signals generated by the serial port to the modulated analog signals required for transmission over a telephone line and, likewise, transforms incoming analog signals to their digital equivalents. The speed at which a modem transmits data is measured in units called bits per second, or bps. (Although bps is not technically the same as baud, the terms are often and erroneously used interchangeably.)

modifier keys Keys that are pressed to modify the meaning of the next key that's pressed.

modular programming A programming style that breaks down program functions into modules, each of which accomplishes one function and contains all the source code and variables needed to accomplish that function.

modulation The conversion of a digital signal to its analog equivalent, especially for the purposes of transmitting signals using telephone lines.

modulation protocol In modems, the communications standard that governs how the modem translates between the computer's digital signals and the analog tones used to convey computer data over the Internet. Modulation protocols are defined by ITU standards. The V.90 protocol defines communication at 56 Kbps.

module A part of a software program; independently developed modules are combined to compile the final program.

monitor A television-like device that produces an on-screen image.

monochrome monitor A monitor display that shows one color against a black or white background.

monospace font A typeface in which the width of every character is the same; produces output similar to that of a typewriter.

Moore's Law A prediction by Intel Corp. cofounder Gordon Moore that integrated circuit technology advancements would enable the semiconductor industry to double the number of components on a chip every 18 to 24 months.

moral dilemma A situation in which people run into difficulty trying to figure out how existing rules apply to a new situation.

morphing An animated special effect in which one image transforms into a second image.

motherboard A large circuit board containing the computer's central processing unit, support chips, random access memory, and expansion slots. Also called a main board.

motion capture An animation technique that involves filming actors dressed in costumes containing sensors, which record the actors' movements. The resulting action sequences provide a lifelike basis for animation.

mouse A palm-sized input device, with a ball built into the bottom, that is used to move a pointer on-screen to draw, select options from a menu, modify or move text, and issue commands.

mousepad A clean, flat surface for moving a mouse on.

Moving Pictures Experts Group (MPEG) A set of standards for audio and video file formats and lossless compression, named after the group that created it.

MPEG Audio Layer 3 (MP3) A sound compression standard that can store a single song from an audio CD in a 3M file. MP3 files are easily shared over the Internet and are costing recording companies billions of dollars in lost royalties due to piracy.

MS-DOS An operating system for IBM-compatible PCs that uses a command-line user interface.

multidisplay video adapter An adapter that enables users to hook up two monitors without having to purchase a second video adapter.

multifunction devices Machines that combine printing, scanning, faxing, and copying.

multifunction printer An inkjet or laser printer that also functions as a scanner, a fax machine, and a copier.

multimedia The presentation of information using graphics, video, sound, animation, and text.

multimedia CAI A version of computer-assisted instruction that makes use of the personal computer's multimedia capabilities, including high-quality sound, rich graphics, and video.

multiplayer online gaming The use of the Internet to enable two or more users to play against one another in popular computer games.

multiple series In a chart such as a bar chart or line chart, the use of more than one data series to compare two or more items.

multiple undo A feature of many of today's application programs that enables the user to undo more than one editing change. Some programs offer unlimited undo.

multiplexing A technique that enables more than one signal to be conveyed on a physical transmission medium.

multiprocessing The use of two or more processors in the same computer system at the same time.

Multipurpose Internet Mail Extensions (MIME) An Internet standard that specifies how Internet programs, such as e-mail programs and Web browsers, can transfer multimedia files (including sounds, graphics, and video) through the Internet. Before the development of MIME, all data transferred through the Internet had to be coded in ASCII text.

multiscan monitor A monitor that automatically adjusts its refresh rate to the output of the video adapter.

multisession PhotoCD A standard for recording PhotoCD information onto a CD-ROM during several different recording sessions. Unlike standard CD-ROM drives, drives that are Multisession PhotoCD-compatible can read information recorded on a disk during several different pressings.

multitasking In operating systems, the capability to execute more than one application at a time. Multitasking shouldn't be confused with multiple program loading, in which two or more applications are present in random access memory (RAM) but only one executes at a time.

multithreading In multitasking, the capability of a computer to execute more than one task, called a thread, within a single program.

multiuser Designed to be used by more than one person at a time.

multiuser dungeon (MUD) A text-based environment in which multiple players can assume online personas and interact with each other by means of text chatting.

Musical Instrument Digital Interface (MIDI) A standard that specifies how musical sounds can be described in text files so that a MIDI-compatible synthesizer can reproduce the sounds. MIDI files are small, so they're often used to provide music that starts playing automatically when a Web page is accessed. To hear MIDI sounds, your computer needs a sound card. MIDI sounds best with wavetable synthesis sound cards, which include sound samples from real musical instruments.

N

name The first part of a filename. It is separated by a period, or dot, from the second part of the name, called the extension.

name box In a spreadsheet program, an area that displays the name of the active cell.

nanometer A billionth of a meter.

nanorobots Atoms and molecules used to perform certain tasks in nanotechnology.

nanosecond (ns) A unit of time equal to one billionth of a second.

nanotechnology Manipulating materials on an atomic or molecular scale in order to build microscopic devices.

National Television Standards Committee (NTSC) The organization that defines the display standards for broadcast television in the U.S.

native application A program that runs on a particular brand and model of processor or in a particular operating system.

natural language A human language, such as English or Japanese.

near-letter-quality printout Print quality that is almost as good as printed text.

near-online storage A type of storage that is not directly available, but can be made available by a simple action such as inserting a disk.

nest In structured programming, to embed one control structure inside another.

NetBEUI This LAN protocol defines Microsoft Windows NT–based networks.

netiquette Short for network etiquette. A set of rules that reflect long-standing experience about getting along harmoniously in the electronic environment (e-mail and newsgroups).

Netscape extensions Additions to standard HTML added in the mid-1990s by Netscape Communications, Inc., in an effort to provide Web designers with more presentation options.

network access point (NAP) In a wide area network (WAN), a location where local and regional service providers can connect to transcontinental backbone networks.

network architecture The overall design of a computer network that specifies its functionality at every level by means of protocols.

network attached storage (NAS) devices High-performances devices that provide shared data to clients and other servers on a local area network.

network computer (NC) A computer that provides much of a PC's functionality at a lower price. Network computers don't have disk drives because they get their software from the computer network.

network effect An economic term for the rewards consumers get when they purchase a popular product rather than a less popular, even if technologically superior, one.

network interface card (NIC) An adapter that enables a user to connect a network cable to a computer.

network laser printer A nonimpact, high-resolution printer capable of serving the printing needs of an entire department.

network medium A physical condition that links two or more computers.

network operating system (NOS) The software needed to enable data transfer and application usage over a local area network (LAN).

network version A version of an application program for use by more than one person at a time on a local area network (LAN).

network warfare A form of information warfare characterized by attacks on a society's information infrastructure, such as its banking and telecommunications networks.

neural network In artificial intelligence, a computer architecture that attempts to mimic the structure of the human brain. Neural nets "learn" by trial and error and are good at recognizing patterns and dealing with complexity.

newsgroup In Usenet, a discussion group devoted to a single topic. Users post messages to the group, and those reading the discussion send reply messages to the author individually or post replies that can be read by the group as a whole.

NNTP server See Usenet server.

node In a LAN, a connection point that can create, receive, or repeat a message.

nonimpact printer A printer that forms a text or graphics image by spraying or fusing ink to the page.

noninterlaced monitor A monitor that refreshes the entire screen with each pass of the cathode gun. Because this reduces flicker and eye strain, almost all monitors today are noninterlaced.

nonprocedural Not tied down to step-by-step procedures. In programming, a nonprocedural programming language does not force the programmer to consider the procedure that must be followed to obtain the desired result.

nonresident Not present in memory. A nonresident program must be loaded from secondary storage when it is needed.

nonvolatile Not susceptible to loss. If power is lost, the data is preserved.

normal layout In an application program, an on-screen rendition of the document's appearance that does not attempt to show all of the features that will appear in the printout.

normal view A view available in Microsoft PowerPoint that shows the outline view on the left side of the screen and the slide view on the right side of the screen.

normalization In database management, a formal process of database design that assures the elimination of duplicate data entry (data redundancy).

notebook computer A portable computer that is small enough to fit into an average-size briefcase but includes nearly all peripherals commonly found on desktop computers.

notes view In a presentation graphics program, a view of the presentation that enables you to see your speaker's notes.

NTSC converter A device needed to connect a computer to a TV.

NuBus A 32-bit wide expansion bus used by older Macintosh computers. Newer Macintoshes use the Personal Computer Interface (PCI) bus.

nuking A type of antisocial behavior found on Internet Relay Chat characterized by exploiting bugs that cause computer crashes.

Num Lock A toggle key that determines whether the numeric keypad functions in cursor movement mode or number entry mode.

numbered lists In Microsoft word, numbered lists are useful for listing items or giving instructions.

numeric check Ensures that numbers are entered into a field.

numeric field In a database, a space that accepts only numbers.

numeric format In a spreadsheet program, the way values appear in cells. Examples of numeric formats are currency and date.

numeric keypad A set of keys, usually on the right side of the keyboard, for entering numeric data quickly. The numeric keypad can also move the cursor.

O

object 1. In object-oriented programming (OOP), a unit of computer information that contains data and all the procedures or operations that can process or manipulate the data. 2. Nontextual data. Examples of objects include pictures, sounds, or videos.

object code In programming, the machine-readable instructions created by a compiler from source code.

object linking and embedding (OLE) A Microsoft Windows standard that enables applications to exchange data and work with one another dynamically. A linked object, such as a graphic or paragraph, is dependent upon, or linked to, the source file such that if the object changes in the source file it also changes in the destination file. An embedded object is simply copied into a program.

object-oriented database The newest type of database structure, well suited for multimedia applications, in which the result of a retrieval operation is an object of some kind, such as a document. Within this object are miniprograms that enable the object to perform tasks such as displaying graphics. Object-oriented databases can incorporate sound, video, text, and graphics into a single database record.

object-oriented (OO) programming A programming technique that creates generic building blocks of a program (the objects). The user then assembles different sets of objects as needed to solve specific problems. Also called OOP, for object-oriented programming.

obscenity In U.S. law, a literary or artistic work that is obviously designed to produce sexual arousal, violates established community standards, and has no literary, artistic, or scientific value.

odd parity An error-checking protocol in which the parity bit is set to 1 if the number of 1 digits in a byte equals an even number.

office application An application program that is useful for anyone working with words, numbers, graphic images, and databases in a contemporary office setting. This category includes word processing, spreadsheet, and presentation graphics software, as well as database management programs designed for use by untrained users.

Office Clipboard In Microsoft Office, a feature that temporarily stores in memory whatever has been cut or copied from a document, allowing for those items to be used within any Office application.

office suite A collection of separate office applications that have been designed to resemble each other as closely as possible and to exchange data smoothly. The leading office suite package is Microsoft Office. Compare integrated program.

offline storage A type of storage that is not readily available and is used to store infrequently accessed or backup data.

off-the-shelf software See packaged software.

online Directly connected to the network.

online analytical processing (OLAP) In a decision support system (DSS), a method of providing rich, up-to-the-minute data from transaction databases.

online banking The use of a Web browser to access bank accounts, balance checkbooks, transfer funds, and pay bills.

online processing The processing of data immediately after it has been input by a user, as opposed to waiting until a predetermined time, as in batch processing.

online service A for-profit firm that makes current news, stock quotes, and other information available to its subscribers over standard telephone lines. Popular services include supervised chat rooms for text chatting and forums for topical discussion. Online services also provide Internet access.

online stock trading The purchase or sale of stock through the Internet.

online storage A type of storage that is directly available, such as a hard disk, and requires no special action on the user's part to enable.

online travel reservations A rapidly growing area of e-commerce that allows consumers to use the Internet to research, book, and purchase airline flights, hotel rooms, and rental cars.

on-screen keyboard utility An accessibility feature that displays a graphic image of a computer keyboard on-screen so that people with limited dexterity can type conveniently.

open To transfer an existing document from storage to memory.

open architecture A system in which all the system specifications are made public so that other companies may develop add-on products, such as adapters.

open protocol A network standard placed in the public domain and regulated by an independent standards organization.

open source software Software in which the source code is made available to the program's users.

operating platform See operating system.

operating system (OS) A program that integrates and controls the computer's internal functions and provides a user interface.

operationally feasible Capable of being accomplished with an organization's available resources.

optical character recognition (OCR) Software that automatically decodes imaged text into a text file. Most scanners come with OCR software.

optical mark reader (OMR) A reader that senses magnetized marks made by the magnetic particles in lead from a pencil.

optical mice A type of mouse that uses a low-power laser to determine the mouse's position.

optical resolution A measure of the sharpness with which a scanner can digitize an image.

optical storage A storage system in which a storage device retains data using surface patterns that are physically encoded on the surface of plastic discs. The patterns can be detected by a laser beam.

order of evaluation In any program that evaluates formulas, the order in which the various operations are performed. Some programs evaluate formula expressions from left to right, while others perform operations in a given order.

organization A collection of resources (personnel and equipment) arranged so that they can provide some kind of product or service.

orientation In document formatting, the layout of the page (either portrait or landscape).

outline view In a word processing or presentation graphics program, a document display mode that enables you to see an outline of the document or presentation.

output The results of processing information, typically shown on a monitor or a printer.

output devices Monitors, printers, and other machines that enable people to see, hear, and even feel the results of processing operations.

outsourcing The transfer of a project to an external contractor.

overclock To configure a computer system so that it runs a processor faster than it is designed to run; it may make the system unstable.

P

package A collection of programs. A common example of a package is Microsoft Office, which bundles a word processing program and a spreadsheet program with other applications.

packaged software Ready-to-use software that is sold through mass-market channels and contains features useful to the largest possible user base. Synonymous with off-the-shelf software and shrink-wrapped software.

packet In a packet-switching network, a unit of data of a fixed size—not exceeding the network's maximum transmission unit (MTU) size—that has been prepared for network transmission. Each packet contains a header that indicates its origin and its destination. See also packet switching.

packet sniffer In computer security, a device that examines all traffic on a network and retrieves valuable information such as passwords and credit card numbers.

packet switching One of two fundamental architectures for a wide area network (WAN); the other is a circuit-switching network. In a packet-switching network such as the Internet, no effort is made to establish a single electrical circuit between two computing devices; for this reason, packet-switching networks are often called connectionless. Instead, the sending computer divides a message into packets, each of which contains the address of the destination computer, and dumps them onto the network. They are intercepted by devices called routers, which send the packets in the appropriate direction. The receiving computer assembles the packets, puts them in order, and delivers the received message to the appropriate application. Packet-switching networks are highly reliable and efficient, but they are not suited to the delivery of real-time voice and video.

page In virtual memory, a fixed size of program instructions and data that can be stored on the hard disk to free up random access memory.

page description language (PDL) A programming language capable of precisely describing the appearance of a printed page, including fonts and graphics.

page formatting In word processing applications, page formatting allows you to format text, which involves specifying the font, alignment, margins, and other properties.

page layout In an application program, an on-screen rendition of the document's appearance that shows all or almost all of the features that will appear in the printout.

paging An operating system's transference of files from storage to memory and back.

paint program A program that enables the user to paint the screen by specifying the color of the individual pixels that make up the screen display.

paper size The size of the paper that is available for use in the printer. Most programs can work with a variety of paper sizes, but you must configure the program to work with nonstandard sizes.

paragraph In word processing, a unit of text that begins and ends with the Enter keystroke.

paragraph formatting In a word processing document, presentation options that can be applied to a block of text, such as justification and indentation.

parallel conversion In the development of an information system, the operation of both the new and old information systems at the same time to ensure the compatibility and reliability of the new system.

parallel port An interface that uses several side-by-side wires so that one or more bytes of computer data can travel in unison and arrive simultaneously. Parallel ports offer faster performance than serial ports, in which each bit of data must travel in a line, one after the other.

parallel processing The use of more than one processor to run two or more portions of a program simultaneously.

parent directory In the relationship between a directory and a subdirectory, the directory that contains the subdirectory.

parity bit An extra bit added to a data word for parity checking. See even parity and odd parity.

parity checking A technique used to detect memory or data communication errors. The computer adds the number of bits in a one-byte data item, and if the parity bit setting disagrees with the sum of the other bits, the computer reports an error. See even parity and odd parity.

parity error An error that a computer reports when parity checking reveals that one or more parity bits are incorrect, indicating a probable error in data processing or data transmission.

partition A section of a storage device, such as a hard disk, that is prepared so that it can be treated as if it were a completely separate device for data storage and maintenance.

passive matrix LCD An inexpensive liquid crystal display (LCD) that sometimes generates image flaws and is too slow for full-motion video. Also called dual scan LCD.

password A unique word that a user types to log on to a system. Passwords should not be obvious and should be changed frequently.

password guessing In computer security, a method of defeating password authentication by guessing common passwords, such as personal names, obscene words, and the word "password."

paste In the editing process, a command that inserts text stored in the clipboard at the cursor's location.

path The sequence of directories that the computer must follow to locate a file.

pattern recognition In artificial intelligence, the use of a computer system to recognize patterns, such as thumbprints, and associate these patterns with stored data or instructions.

PC 100 SDRAM A type of SDRAM capable of keeping up with motherboards that have bus speeds of 100 MHz.

PC card Synonymous with PCMCIA card. A computer accessory (such as a modem or network interface card) that is designed to fit into a compatible PC card slot mounted on the computer's case. PC cards and slots are commonly used on notebook computers because they offer system expandability while consuming a small fraction of the space required for expansion cards.

peer-to-peer network A computer network design in which all the computers can access the public files located on other computers in a network.

pen Input device that looks like a writing pen except that its tip is equipped with electronics instead of ink.

pen computer A computer operated with a stylus, such as a personal digital assistant (PDA).

Pentium A 64-bit microprocessor manufactured by Intel, introduced in 1993. The Pentium introduced many improvements over the 80486, including a superscalar architecture and clock speeds up to 200 MHz. Also called Pentium Classic.

Pentium II A 64-bit microprocessor manufactured by Intel, introduced in 1998. The Pentium II includes the MMX instruction set, contains 7.5 million transistors, and runs at clock speeds of 233 MHz and higher.

Pentium MMX A 64-bit microprocessor manufactured by Intel and introduced in 1997. The Pentium MMX includes a set of multimedia extensions, 57 processor instructions that run multimedia applications faster. It contains 4.5 million transistors and runs at clock speeds up to 233 MHz.

Pentium Pro A 64-bit microprocessor manufactured by Intel, introduced in 1995. The Pentium Pro introduced many new features, such as enhanced pipelining and a large on-board cache. Because it is optimized to run only 32-bit software, however, the Pentium Pro is found mainly in servers and engineering workstations.

performance animation See motion capture.

peripheral A device connected to and controlled by a computer, but external to the computer's central processing unit.

Peripheral Computer Interface (PCI) bus A bus architecture used for expansion slots and introduced by Intel in 1992. It has displaced the VESA local bus and has almost displaced the ISA bus.

permanent virtual circuit (PVC) A high-speed network connection that enables organizations to connect to external data networks at a cost lower than that of a leased line.

personal certificate A digital certificate attesting that a given individual who is trying to log on to an authenticated server really is the individual he or she claims to be. Personal certificates are issued by certificate authorities (CA).

Personal Communication Service (PCS) A digital cellular phone service that is rapidly replacing analog cellular phones.

personal computer (PC) A computer system that meets the computing needs of an individual. The term PC usually refers to an IBM-compatible personal computer.

personal digital assistant (PDA) A small, handheld computer that accepts input written on-screen with a stylus. Most include built-in software for appointments, scheduling, and e-mail. Also called palmtop.

personal finance program A special-purpose application program that manages financial information. The best personal finance programs manage many types of information, including checking accounts, savings and investment plans, and credit card debt.

personal firewall A program or device that is designed to protect home computer users from unauthorized access.

personal identification number (PIN) A number used by a bank customer to verify identity when using an ATM.

personal information manager (PIM) A program that stores and retrieves a variety of personal information, such as appointments. PIMs have been slow to gain acceptance due to their lack of convenience and portability.

personal laser printer A nonimpact high-resolution printer for use by individuals.

personal productivity program Application software, such as word processing software or a spreadsheet program, that assists individuals in doing their work more effectively and efficiently.

phased conversion In the development of an information system, the implementation of the new system in different time periods, one part at a time.

photo communities Web-based communities that enable users to upload their pictures and make them available to friends and family at no charge.

photo printer See snapshot printer. Specially designed printers with flash memory card readers that enable users to bypass the computer completely.

PhotoCD See Multisession PhotoCD.

photo-editing program A program that enables images to be enhanced, edited, cropped, or sized. The same program can be used to print the images on a color printer.

phrase searching In database and Web searching, a search that retrieves only documents that contain the entire phrase.

physical modeling A technique used to simulate what occurs when a real musical instrument produces a sound, such as a plucked guitar string.

pie chart A graph that displays a data series as a circle to emphasize the relative contribution of each data item to the whole. Also known as area chart.

pilot conversion In the development of an information system, the institution of the new system in only one part of an organization. When that portion of the organization is satisfied with the system, the rest of the organization then starts using it.

pin grid array (PGA) A complex pattern of downward-facing pins designed to fit into a compatible receptacle.

pipelining A design that provides two or more processing pathways that can be used simultaneously.

pit A microscopic indentation in the surface of an optical disc that absorbs the light of the optical drive's laser, corresponding to a 0 in the computer's binary number system.

pixel Short for picture element, the smallest element that a device can display and out of which the displayed image is constructed.

placeholder An area that is set aside to receive data of a certain type when this data becomes available.

plagiarism The presentation of somebody else's work as if it were one's own.

Plain Old Telephone Service (POTS) A term used to describe the standard analog telephone service.

plaintext A readable message before it is encrypted.

Platform for Internet Content Selection (PICS) A voluntary rating system, widely endorsed by companies contributing to the Internet, used to inform users of cyberporn on the Internet.

Platform for Privacy Preference Project (P3P) A set of standards developed by the World Wide Web Consortium (W3C) for informing Web users of a site's use of personal data.

platter In a hard drive, a fixed, rapidly rotating disk that is coated with a magnetically sensitive material. High-capacity hard drives typically have two or more platters.

plotter A printer that produces high-quality output by moving ink pens over the surface of the paper.

Plug and Play (PnP) A set of standards jointly developed by Intel Corporation and Microsoft that enables users of Microsoft Windows–based PCs to configure new hardware devices automatically. Operating systems equipped with plug-and-play capabilities can automatically detect new PnP-compatible peripherals that may have been installed while the power was switched off.

plug-in program Software that directly interfaces with a particular program and gives it additional capabilities.

point A standard unit of measurement in character formatting and computer graphics that is equal to 1/72 inch.

point of presence (PoP) A locality in which it is possible to obtain dialup access to the network by means of a local telephone call. Internet service providers (ISPs) provide PoPs in towns and cities, but many rural areas are without local PoPs.

point-and-shoot digital cameras Digital cameras that typically include automatic focus, automatic exposure, built-in automatic electronic flash with red eye reduction, and optical zoom lenses with digital enhancement.

point-of-sale (POS) terminal A computer-based cash register that enables transaction data to be captured at the checkout stand. Such terminals can automatically adjust inventory databases and enable managers to analyze sales patterns.

pointer An on-screen symbol, usually an arrow, that shows the current position of the mouse.

pointing device Any input device that is capable of moving the on-screen pointer in a graphical user interface (GUI), such as a mouse or trackball.

pointing stick A pointing device introduced by IBM that enables users to move the pointer around the screen by manipulating a small, stubby stick that protrudes slightly from the surface of the keyboard.

POP3 Also spelled POP-3. The current version of the Post Office Protocol (POP), an Internet standard for storing e-mail on a mail server until you can access it and download it to your computer.

popup menu A menu that appears at the mouse pointer's position when you click the right mouse button.

port An interface that controls the flow of data between the central processing unit and external devices such as printers and monitors.

port conflict A serious system instability that occurs when two input/output devices attempt to use the same I/O port.

portable Able to be easily removed or inserted or transferred to a different type of computer system.

portable keyboard A small folding keyboard often used with a handheld computer.

Portable Network Graphics (PNG) A graphics file format closely resembling the GIF format but lacking GIF's proprietary compression technique (which forces publishers of GIF-enabled graphics software to pay a licensing fee).

portal On the Web, a page that attempts to provide an attractive starting point for Web sessions. Typically included are links to breaking news, weather forecasts, stock quotes, free e-mail service, sports scores, and a subject guide to information available on the Web. Leading portals include Netscape's NetCenter (www.netcenter.com), Yahoo (www.yahoo.com), and Snap! (www.snap.com).

portrait mode In document formatting, a page layout in which text runs down the narrow orientation of the page.

positioning performance A measure of how much time elapses from the initiation of drive activity until the hard disk has positioned the read/write head so that it can begin transferring data.

post To submit a message to an online newsgroup; the message itself may be referred to as a post or posting.

Post Office Protocol (POP) An Internet e-mail standard that specifies how an Internet-connected computer can function as a mail-handling agent; the current version is POP3. Messages arrive at a user's electronic mailbox, which is housed on the service provider's computer. You can then download the mail to a workstation or computer and print, store, or reply to it.

post-implementation system review In the development of an information system, the ongoing evaluation of the information system to determine whether it has met its goals.

PostScript A sophisticated page description language (PDL) widely used in desktop publishing.

Power Macintosh A line of Macintosh computers based on the Motorola Power PC processors, which use RISC design principles.

power-on self test (POST) The series of system integrity tests that a computer goes through every time it is started (cold boot) or restarted (warm boot). These tests verify that vital system components, such as the memory, are functioning properly.

power outage A sudden loss of electrical power, causing the loss of all unsaved information on a computer.

Power PC A series of processors developed by Motorola that utilize RISC design principles. Apple Computer's Power Macintosh systems use Power PC processors.

power supply A device that supplies power to a computer system by converting AC current to DC current and lowering the voltage.

power surge A sudden and sometimes destructive increase in the amount of voltage delivered through a power line.

power switch A switch that turns the computer on and off. Often located in the rear of a computer.

precedence The position of a given operation, such as addition or multiplication, within a program's default order of evaluation.

preemptive multitasking In operating systems, a method of running more than one application at a time. Unlike cooperative multitasking, preemptive multitasking allows other applications to continue running if one application crashes.

preferences A list of the user's preferences for an application program's configuration. Preferences are stored so that they remain in place the next time the program is opened.

preformatted A floppy disk that has been formatted before it is packaged and sold.

presentation graphics A software package used to make presentations visually attractive and easy to understand.

Pretty Good Privacy (PGP) The most widely used digital signature and certificate system.

primary cache A small unit (8 KB to 32 KB) of ultra-fast memory included with a microprocessor and used to store frequently accessed data and improve overall system performance.

primary folder A main folder such as is created at the root of a drive to hold further subfolders. Also called top-level folder.

Primary Rate ISDN (PRI) An ISDN connection designed for medium-sized organizations that offers twenty-three 64 Kbps data/voice channels.

print area In a spreadsheet program, a user-defined area that tells the program how much of the spreadsheet to print.

print driver Files placed on a hard drive after a printer install that contain the printer's instruction set.

print layout view In a word processing program, an on-screen view of the document in which all or most printed features are visible. The print layout view is fully editable.

print preview In a word processing program, an on-screen view of the document in which all printed features are visible. The document is not editable in this view.

printed circuit board A flat piece of plastic or fiberglass on which complex patterns of copper pathways have been created by means of etching. These paths link integrated circuits and other electrical components.

printer An output device that prints computer-generated text or graphics onto paper or another physical medium.

privacy The right to live your life without undue intrusions into your personal affairs by government agencies or corporate marketers.

private branch exchange (PBX) An organization's internal telephone system, which is usually digital.

private key A decryption key.

procedural language A programming language that tells the computer what to do and how to do it.

procedure The steps that must be followed to accomplish a specific computer-related task.

processing The execution of arithmetic or comparison operations on data.

processing cycle See machine cycle.

processor socket In contemporary motherboard designs, a socket that enables a knowledgeable user to mount a microprocessor chip without damaging the chip or the motherboard.

productivity software Programs that help people perform general tasks such as word processing.

professional workstation A very powerful computer system for engineers, financial analysts, and other professionals who need exceptionally powerful processing and output capabilities. Professional workstations are very expensive.

profile In a consumer-oriented operating system such as Windows 98, a record of a user's preferences that is associated with a user name and password. If you set up two or more profiles, users see their own preferences. However, profiles do not prevent users from accessing and overwriting each others' files. Compare account.

program A list of instructions telling the computer what to do.

program development life cycle (PDLC) A step-by-step procedure used to develop software for information systems.

program file A file containing instructions written in a programming language to tell the computer what to do; also called an application file.

program listing In programming, a printout of the source code of a program.

program specification In software development, a technical description of the software needed by the information system. The program specification precisely defines input data, the processing that occurs, the output format, and the user interface.

programmable Capable of being controlled through instructions that can be varied to suit the needs of an individual.

programmed instruction A method of introducing new material by means of controlled steps in a workbook.

programmer A person skilled in the use of one or more programming languages. Although most programmers have college degrees in computer science, certification is an increasingly popular way to demonstrate one's programming expertise.

programming language An artificial language composed of a fixed vocabulary and a set of rules used to create instructions for a computer to follow.

project dictionary In the development of information systems, a compilation of all terminology relevant to the project.

project management program Software that tracks individual tasks that make up an entire job.

project notebook In the development of an information system, a place where information regarding system development is stored.

project plan A specification of the goals, scope, and individual activities that make up a project.

promote In an outlining utility, to increase the importance of a heading by moving it up in the hierarchy of outline categories (for example, by moving it from B to II).

proportional font A font in which the shape of each character determines how much space it requires and in which more characters fit on a line than in a monospace font; a proportional font closely resembles printed text.

proprietary architecture A design developed by a company and treated as a trade secret; the design can be copied only on payment of a licensing fee. Also called closed architecture.

proprietary file format A data-storage format used only by the company that makes a specific program.

proprietary protocol In a network, a communications protocol developed by a company and not available for public use without payment of a licensing fee.

protected mode A processing mode, first offered on Intel's 32-bit 80386 microprocessor, the enables users to access virtually unlimited amounts of memory.

protocol In data communications and networking, a standard specifying the format of data and the rules to be followed. Networks could not be easily or efficiently designed or maintained without protocols; a protocol specifies how a program should prepare data so that it can be sent to the next stage in the communication process. For example, e-mail programs prepare messages so that they conform to prevailing Internet mail standards, which are recognized by every program involved in the transmission of mail over the network.

protocol stack In a computer network, a means of conceptualizing network architecture in which the various layers of network functionality are viewed as a vertical stack, like the layers of a layer cake, in computers linked to the network. When one computer sends a message to the network, the message goes down the stack and then traverses the network; on the receiving computer, the message goes up the stack.

protocol suite In a computer network, the collection of network protocols that defines the network's functionality.

prototyping In information systems development, the creation of a working system model that is functional enough to draw feedback from users. Also called joint application development (JAD).

proximity operator In database and Web searching, a symbol or keyword that tells the search software to retrieve records or documents only if two specified search words occur within a certain number of words of each other.

PS/2 mouse A type of mouse that connects to the computer by means of the PS/2 port.

PS/2 port An input/output port that enables users to attach a specially designed mouse (called a PS/2 mouse) without requiring the use of the computer's built-in serial ports.

pseudocode In structured programming, a stylized form of writing used as an alternative to flowcharts to describe the logic of a program.

public data network (PDN) A network that builds its own high-speed data communications network using microwaves, satellites, and optical fiber, and sells network bandwidth to companies and government agencies.

public domain software Noncopyrighted software that anyone may copy and use without charge and without acknowledging the source.

public key In public key cryptography, the encoding key, which you make public so that others can send you encrypted messages. The message can be encoded with the public key, but it cannot be decoded without the private key, which you alone possess.

public key cryptography In cryptography, a revolutionary new method of encryption that does not require the message's receiver to have received the decoding key in a separate transmission. The need to send the key, required to decode the message, is the chief vulnerability of previous encryption techniques. Public key cryptography has two keys: a public one and a private one. The public key is used for encryption, and the private key is used for decryption.

public key infrastructure (PKI) A uniform set of encryption standards that specify how public key encryption, digital signatures, and CA-granted digital certificates should be implemented in computer systems and on the Internet.

public switched telephone network (PSTN) The world telephone system, a massive network used for data communication as well as voice.

pull-down menu In a graphical user interface (GUI), a named item on the menu bar that, when clicked, displays an on-screen menu of commands and options.

pumping and dumping An illegal stock price manipulation tactic that involves purchasing shares of a worthless corporation and then driving the price up by making unsubstantiated claims about the company's value in Internet newsgroups and chat rooms. The perpetrator sells the shares after the stock price goes up but before other investors wise up to the ploy.

Q

quality of service (QoS) In a network, the guaranteed data transfer rate. A major drawback of the Internet for real-time voice and video, as well as for time-sensitive data communication, is that it cannot assure quality of service. Network congestion can delay the arrival of data.

quarter-inch cartridge (QIC) A tape cartridge using quarter-inch wide magnetic tape widely used for backup operations. QICs can hold up to 5 GB on a single cartridge.

Query In the Microsoft Access database management system, the object used to ask questions of the database.

query by example (QBE) In a database, a method of requesting information by using a blank form that corresponds to the record form. You fill out one or more fields in the form, and the search software uses your response to try to match any records in the database that contain the data you supplied.

query language A retrieval and data-editing language for composing simple or complex requests for data.

QuickTime An Apple Computer–developed file and compression format for digital video.

quote In e-mail, text from a previous message that is copied into a reply message.

QWERTY keyboard A keyboard that uses the standard keyboard layout in which the first six letters on the left of the top row spell "QWERTY."

R

RAID (Redundant Array of Inexpensive Disks) A storage device that groups two or more hard disks containing exactly the same data.

radio transmission A signaling technique now being used by some wireless local area networks (WLANs) for greater security.

Rambus DRAM Type of RAM that uses a narrow but very fast bus to connect to the microprocessor.

RAMDAC Abbreviation for Random Access Digital to Analog Converter. This chip converts a video card's digital output to the analog output required by most monitors.

random access An information storage and retrieval technique in which the computer can access information directly, without having to go through a sequence of locations.

random access file See direct access file.

random access memory (RAM) Another name for the computer's main working memory, where program instructions and data are stored to be easily accessed by the central processing unit through the processor's high-speed data bus. When a computer is turned off, all data in RAM is lost.

random access storage device A storage device that can begin reading data directly without having to go through a lengthy sequence of data.

range In a spreadsheet, a rectangular group of cells treated as a unit for a given operation.

range check Verifies that the entered data fall within an acceptable range.

range expression In a spreadsheet program, a statement that indicates a group of cells to be treated as a unit for an operation.

rapid application development (RAD) In object-oriented programming, a method of program development in which programmers work with a library of prebuilt objects, allowing them to build programs more quickly.

raster graphics See bitmapped graphics.

ray tracing A 3D rendering technique in which color intensity on a graphic object is varied to simulate light falling on the object from multiple directions.

read To retrieve data or program instructions from a storage device such as a hard or floppy disk.

read/write The capability of a primary or secondary storage device to record (write) data and to play back (read) data previously recorded or saved.

read/write device A device that can read and write.

read/write head In a hard or floppy disk, the magnetic recording and playback device that travels back and forth across the surface of the disk, storing and retrieving data.

read/write medium A storage medium that enables users to write as well as read data. Compare read-only.

read-only Capable of being displayed or used but not altered or deleted.

read-only memory (ROM) The part of a computer's primary storage that contains essential computer instructions and doesn't lose its contents when the power is turned off. Information in read-only memory cannot be erased by the computer.

real-time processing A type of processing that deals with data as it is generated by an ongoing process, such as a live video feed or text chatting.

record In a database, a group of one or more fields that contains information about something.

redo In the editing process, a command that reverses the effect of the last undo command or repeats the last editing action.

reduced instruction set computer (RISC) A type of central processing unit in which the number of instructions the processor can execute is reduced to a minimum to increase processing speed.

reengineering See business process reengineering (BPR).

reflector See list server.

refresh rate The frequency with which the screen is updated. The refresh rate determines whether the display appears to flicker.

Regional Bell Operating Companies (RBOCs) The local and regional telephone companies created after the divestiture of telephone monopoly AT&T.

register 1. In a microprocessor, a memory location used to store values and external memory addresses while the microprocessor performs logical and arithmetic operations on them. 2. In commercial software and shareware, to contact the software vendor and submit a form that includes personal information such as the user's name and address. Registering allows the software vendor to inform the user of important information and software updates.

registration fee An amount of money that must be paid to the author of a piece of shareware to continue using it beyond the duration of the evaluation period.

registry 1. A database that contains information about installed peripherals and software. 2. In Microsoft Windows, an important system file that contains configuration settings that Windows requires in order to operate.

regular weight In character formatting, a darkness level that is normal for a given font.

relational database A type of database that uses the contents of a particular field as an index to reference particular records.

relative cell reference In a spreadsheet program, a cell reference that is automatically adjusted when it is relocated.

relative file A special type of direct-access file that does not use a mathematical formula (hashing algorithm) to determine the address of records, but bases the address on the key field, which is numbered with an integer.

relative URL In HTML, a URL that refers to a file located in the same directory as the referring file or in a nearby directory.

removable drive A hard disk that uses a data cartridge that can be removed for storage and replaced with another.

removable hard disk A hard disk that uses a removable cartridge instead of a sealed unit with a fixed, nonremovable platter.

repetition control structure In structured programming, a logical construction of commands repeated over and over. Also called looping or iteration control structure.

repetitive strain injury (RSI) See cumulative trauma disorder (CTD).

replication In a spreadsheet program, the duplication of a group of cells into another group of cells. Formulas are automatically adjusted to account for the new cell addresses.

Report In the Microsoft Access database management system, the object used to present data.

report file A file that holds a copy of a report in computer-accessible form until it is convenient to print it.

report generator In programming, a programming language for printing database reports. One of four parts of a database management system (DBMS) that helps the user design and generate reports and graphs in hard copy form.

report language In database management, a computer language that enables the user to specify which information to display or print.

request for proposal (RFP) In the development of information systems, a request to an outside vendor to write a proposal for the design, installation, and configuration of an information system.

request for quotation (RFQ) In the development of information systems, a request to an outside vendor or value-added reseller (VAR) to quote a price for specific information components.

resolution A measurement, usually expressed in linear dots per inch (dpi) both horizontally and vertically, of the sharpness of an image generated by an output device such as a monitor or a printer.

resource In a network, any useful device or program that can be shared by the network's users. An example of a resource is a network-capable printer.

restore To return a window to its size and position before it was maximized.

résumé manager A program that provides expert assistance in the preparation of résumés.

return on investment (ROI) The overall financial yield of a project at the end of its lifetime. ROI is often used by managers to decide whether a project is a good investment.

right pane In the My Computer primary file management utility for PCs, one of two main default windows. It displays the various files and drives you can choose from. See also left pane.

ring topology The physical layout of a local network in which all nodes are attached in a circle, without a central host computer.

rip and tear A confidence scam that involves convincing people that they have won a large sweepstakes prize but they cannot obtain the needed information unless they pay a fee. The prize never materializes, and the perpetrators disappear.

robot A computer-based device that is programmed to perform useful motions.

robotics A division of computer science that is devoted to improving the performance and capabilities of robots.

ROM BIOS (basic input/output system) See basic input/output system (BIOS).

root directory The top-level directory in a secondary storage device.

rot-13 In Usenet newsgroups, a simple encryption technique that offsets each character by 13 places (so that an e becomes an r, for example).

rotational speed In hard disks, the number of revolutions the disks make in one minute (rpm). Rotational speed is the largest single factor in determining drive speed. Currently, hard disks have rotational speeds as high as 10,000 rpm.

router In a packet-switching network such as the Internet, one of two basic devices (the other is a host). A router is an electronic device that examines each packet of data it receives and then decides which way to send it toward its destination.

row In a spreadsheet, a block of cells going across the screen.

RS-232 standard A standard maintained by an international standards organization that defines the operation of the serial ports commonly found on today's computers. Synonymous with RS-232C.

RS-422 standard A standard maintained by an international standards organization that defines the operation of the serial ports found on Apple's Macintosh and some other computers. The RS-422 is a more recent version of the earlier RS-232 standard. It offers higher data transfer rates than its predecessor.

rule A straight line.

ruler A bar that measures the document horizontally or vertically with reference to the printed page's edges or margins. Typically, the ruler shows the cursor's current position, margin settings, indentations, and tab stops.

runtime Able to run without having the original installed application. A runtime version of a PowerPoint presentation, for example, can run on a computer that does not have Microsoft PowerPoint installed.

S

safe mode An operating mode in which Windows loads a minimal set of drivers that are known to function correctly.

safety-critical system Any computer system that could subject human beings to death or injury if it fails to operate correctly. The Federal Aviation Administration's air traffic control (ATC) system is an example of a safety-critical system.

salami shaving A computer crime in which a program is altered so that it transfers a small amount of money from a large number of accounts to make a large profit.

sampling In sound cards, a sound synthesis technique that modifies sound samples of musical instruments.

sans serif font A typeface style for letters that does not include finishing strokes.

SATAN A network security diagnostic tool that exhaustively examines a network and reveals security holes. SATAN is a double-edged sword: In the hands of network administrators, it is a valuable tool for detecting and closing security loopholes. In the hands of intruders, it is an equally valuable tool for exposing remaining loopholes and gaining unauthorized access to a network.

satellite In data communications, a communications reflector placed in a geosynchronous (stationary) orbit.

save To transfer data from the computer's memory to a storage device for safekeeping.

save as A command that enables the user to store a document with a new name.

scale To increase or decrease the size of an image without affecting the image's aspect ratio.

scaling In graphics, to adjust the scale of a chart to make sure that it conveys information effectively.

scanner A device that copies the image (text or graphic) on a sheet of paper and translates it into a digital image. Scanners use charge-coupled devices to digitize the image.

scientific visualization The use of computer systems to discover hidden patterns in large amounts of data.

screenreader An accessibility program that reads text appearing on various parts of the computer screen for people with limited or no vision.

script A short program written in a simple programming language, called a scripting language.

scripting language A simple programming language that enables users to create useful programs (scripts) quickly. VBScript is one example of a scripting language.

scroll To bring hidden parts of a document into view within the application workspace.

scroll arrow An arrow appearing within the scroll bar that enables the user to scroll up or down (or, in a horizontal scroll bar, left and right) by small increments.

scroll bar A vertical or horizontal bar that contains scroll arrows and a scroll box. The scroll bar enables the user to bring hidden portions of a document into view within the application workspace.

scroll box A rectangular control positioned within the scroll bar that enables the user to bring hidden portions of a document into view. Unlike scroll arrows, the scroll box is used to scroll by large increments.

search engine Any program that locates needed information in a database, but especially an Internet-accessible search service (such as AltaVista or HotBot) that enables you to search for information on the Internet.

search operator In a database or a Web search engine, a word or a symbol that enables you to specify your search with precision.

secondary cache A small unit (256 K to 1 MB) of ultra-fast memory used to store frequently accessed data and improve overall system performance. The secondary cache is usually located on a separate circuit board from the microprocessor, although backside cache memory is located on the processor. Also called level 2 (L2) cache.

secondary folder See subfolder.

secondary storage See near-online storage.

section In a word processing document, a portion of a document that is separated from the others so that it can contain unique formats, such as column layout or footnote numbering.

section break A nonprinting symbol that can be placed within a word processing document to create sections within the document.

sector A pie-shaped wedge of the concentric tracks encoded on a disk during formatting. Two or more sectors combine to form a cluster.

secure mode In a Web browser, a mode of operation in which all communication to and from the server is encrypted.

security The protection of valuable assets stored on computer systems or transmitted via computer networks.

seek time In a secondary storage device, the time it takes for the read/write head to reach the correct location on the disk. Seek times are often used with rotational speed to compare the performance of hard drives.

select To highlight something on-screen, usually with the mouse and other times with the keyboard.

selection control structure In structured programming, a method of handling a program branch by using an IF-THEN-ELSE structure. This is more efficient than using a GOTO statement. Also called conditional or branch control structure.

selective availability In the U.S. Geographical Positioning System (GPS), a Defense Department imposed signal degradation intended to make GPS signals useless for enemy missile guidance systems.

semiconductor A material that can selectively conduct or impede the flow of electrical current. By fabricating devices made of differing semiconductor materials arranged in layers, electronics manufacturers can mass-produce highly complex electronic devices at very low cost per unit.

sequence control structure In structured programming, a logical construction of programming commands executed in the order in which they appear.

sequencer A program that enables composers to write, record, edit, and play back musical notation on a computer.

sequential access An information storage and retrieval technique in which the computer must move through a sequence of stored data items to reach the item to be retrieved.

sequential file A file in which the entries are processed in the order in which they were encoded.

sequential storage device A storage device that cannot begin reading data until the device has moved through a sequence of data in order to locate the desired beginning point.

serial mouse A type of mouse that connects to the computer by means of a serial port.

serial port An input/output (I/O) interface that is designed to convey data in a bit-by-bit stream. Compare parallel port.

series In a spreadsheet program, a range of values used to generate a chart.

serif font A typeface style for letters that includes finishing strokes.

server A computer dedicated to providing information in response to external requests.

server address In a mailing list, the e-mail address of the list server, rather than the address of the list itself. For subscribing and unsubscribing to a mailing list, send messages to the server, not the list.

server program The part of client/server computing that runs on a high-powered, centralized minicomputer that everyone on the network can access with the appropriate security clearance. See client program.

set-top appliance A computer-based unit that works with cable TV data and enhances the television viewing experience (in some cases, by enabling Internet access).

setup program A utility program provided by a computer's manufacturer that enables users to specify basic system configuration settings, such as the correct time and date and the type of hard disk that is installed in the system. Setup programs are accessible by pressing a special key (such as Delete) during the computer's power-on self test (POST).

shading A formatting option in which a color or pattern appears in the background of a paragraph, table cell, or some other formatting unit.

shadow A type of character formatting in which characters appear with a simulated shadow.

shareware Copyrighted software that may be tried without expense but requires the payment of a registration fee if you decide to use it after a specified trial period.

sheetfed scanner A device that draws in single sheets of paper, copies an image (text or graphics), and translates the image into a digital image.

sheets In Microsoft Excel workbook files, the 255 sets of columns and rows intersecting at cells.

shell In an operating system, the portion of the program that provides the user interface.

shell access An inexpensive Internet access, through the user interface of a UNIX computer.

shill In an auction, an accomplice of the seller who drives up prices by bidding for an item that the shill has no intention of buying.

shoulder surfing In computer security, a method of defeating password authentication by peeking over a user's shoulder and watching the keyboard as the user inputs his or her password.

shrink-wrapped software See packaged software.

shutter The sliding metal piece on a floppy disk the protects the disk from fingerprints, dust, and dirt.

signature In e-mail and Usenet newsgroups, a brief file (of approximately three or four lines) that contains the message sender's name, organization, address, e-mail address, and (optionally) telephone numbers. You can configure most systems to add this file automatically at the end of each message you send. Netiquette advises against long, complicated signatures, especially when posting to Usenet.

signature capture A computer system that captures a customer's signature digitally, so that the store can prove that a purchase was made.

Simple Mail Transport Protocol (SMTP) An e-mail communication standard specifying how servers should send plaintext messages across the Internet.

simulation A method used to discover something about the real world by creating a working model of it, which can then be explored by varying its characteristics to see what happens.

single-edge contact (SEC) Chip packages that are designed to be pressed into a slot; the connectors are aligned along one of the package's edges.

single inline memory module (SIMM) A plug-in memory module that contains RAM chips. SIMMs use a 32-bit bus to transfer data between the memory and the processor. Many newer computers have 64-bit buses that require DIMMs.

single-lens reflex (SLR) digital camera Expensive digital camera that offers features such as interchangeable lenses, through-the-lens image previewing, and the ability to override the automatic focus and exposure settings.

single-session CD A CD that can accept only one "burn" (recording) session.

single-tasking Capable of running only one application at a time.

site license An agreement with a software publisher that allows multiple copies of the software to be made for use within an organization.

site registration On the World Wide Web, a process used to gain entry to a Web site that requires you to provide your name, e-mail address, and other personal information, which may be disclosed to marketing firms.

size To increase or decrease the size of one of the dimensions of an image. Compare scale.

slack space Space that is wasted when a disk's cluster size is too large.

slide In a presentation graphics program, an on-screen image sized in proportion to a 35mm slide.

sleep See standby.

slide layout In a presentation graphics program, a view of the document that shows each slide individually.

slide show view In a presentation graphics program, a view of the document that displays the slides in a sequence.

slide sorter view In a presentation graphics program, a view of your presentation in which all your slides are represented by small thumbnail graphics. You can restructure your presentation by dragging a slide to a new location.

slide view In a presentation graphics program, a view of your presentation that enables you to see your slides, just as they will appear when displayed for presentation purposes.

small caps In character formatting, a formatting option in which the lowercase letters appear as small capital letters.

Small Computer System Interface (SCSI) A bus standard for connecting peripheral devices to personal computers, including hard disks, CD-ROM discs, and scanners.

small office/home office (SOHO) Small businesses run out of homes or small offices—a rapidly growing market segment.

small-scale integration (SSI) A technology used to assemble integrated circuits (ICs). SSI was the first integration technology used to build ICs and could fit only 10 or 20 transistors to a chip.

Smalltalk An early object-oriented programming language that many OO promoters believe is still the only pure OO language.

smart car A car with microprocessors that provide more control and interaction with the environment. A smart car can diagnose internal problems, operate safely, warn the driver of potential problems, and help with navigation.

smart tags In Microsoft Office, icons attached to items, allowing various choices for how text is treated when pasted within an application or between applications.

smartcard A card that resembles a credit card but has a microprocessor and memory chip, enabling the card to process as well as store information.

SmartMedia A flash memory storage device designed for digital cameras that is capable of storing up to 128 MB of digital image data.

smiley In e-mail and newsgroups, a sideways face made of ASCII characters that puts a message into context and compensates for the lack of verbal inflections and body language that plagues electronic communication. Also called emoticon.

snapshot printer A thermal transfer printer that prints the output of digital cameras at a maximum size of 4 by 6 inches. Snapshot printers are less expensive than other thermal transfer printers.

social engineering A method of defeating password authentication by impersonating a network administrator and asking users for their passwords.

socket In Internet and UNIX, a virtual port that enables client applications to connect to the appropriate server. To achieve a connection, a client needs to specify both the IP address and the port address of the server application.

soft copy A temporary form of output, as in a monitor display.

software One of two basic components of a computer system (the other is hardware). Software includes all the instructions that tell the computer what to do.

software crisis A period of time in the 1960s when programming was extremely inefficient due to poor programming practices.

software engineering A new field that applies the principles of mainstream engineering to software production.

software license An agreement included with most commercial software that stipulates what the user may and may not do with the software.

software piracy Unauthorized duplication of copyrighted software.

software programs Input that gives the computer specific instructions of what to do.

software suite A collection of full-featured, standalone programs that usually share a common command structure and have similar interfaces.

sole proprietorship A business run and owned by only one person.

solid state device An electronic device that relies solely on semiconductors (rather than vacuum tubes) to switch or amplify electrical current.

solid state disk (SDD) A storage device that is composed of high-speed RAM chips.

solid state storage device This device consists of nonvolatile memory chips, which retain the data stored in them even if the chips are disconnected from their current source.

sort In a database, to rearrange records according to a predetermined order, such as alphabetical or chronological order.

sound board See sound card.

sound card An adapter that adds digital sound reproduction capabilities to an IBM-compatible PC. Also called a sound board.

sound file A file containing digitized sound that can be played back it a computer is equipped with multimedia.

sound format A specification of how a sound should be digitally represented. Sound formats usually include some type of data compression to reduce the size of sound files.

source code The typed program instructions that people write. The program is then translated into machine instructions that the computer can execute.

source data automation The process of capturing data at its source, eliminating the need to file paper documents or record data by keying it manually.

spaghetti code In programming, source code that contains numerous GOTO statements and is, in consequence, difficult to understand and prone to error.

spam Unsolicited e-mail or newsgroup advertising.

spammer A person who sends unsolicited e-mail messages containing advertisements.

speaker A device that plays the computer's audio output.

specialized search engines Web location programs that index particular types of information, such as job advertisements.

special-purpose program A program that performs a specific task, usually for a specific profession. Examples include printing greeting cards and calculating stresses in an engineering project.

speculative execution A technique used by advanced CPUs to prevent a pipeline stall. The processor executes and temporarily stores the next instruction in case it proves useful.

speech recognition The use of a computer system to detect the words spoken by a human being into a microphone, and translate these words into text that appears on-screen. Compare speech synthesis.

speech recognition software A computer program that decodes human speech into transcribed text.

speech synthesis The capability of a computer to speak through synthesized computer-generated voices.

spider A small piece of software that crawls around the Web picking up URLs and information on the pages attached to them.

spindle speed The rotational speed of a hard disk, measured in revolutions per minute (rpm).

spinoff technology Devices based on discoveries originally made in military or space research.

spreadsheet A program that processes information in the form of tables. Table cells can hold values or mathematical formulas.

spreadsheet programs The computer equivalent of an accountant's worksheet.

SPX See IPX/SPX.

spyware Internet software that is placed on a computer without the user's awareness, usually during a shareware or freeware download.

SQL Abbreviation for structured query language. SQL is a standardized query language for requesting information from a database.

stale link On the Web, a hyperlink that refers to a document that has been moved or deleted. Synonymous with broken link.

standalone e-mail client A program sold commercially that provides e-mail services for computer users. Most people use e-mail capabilities built into Web browsers rather than buying commercial programs.

standalone program An application sold individually.

standard newsgroups In Usenet, a collection of newsgroups that every Usenet site is expected to carry, if sufficient storage room exists. The standard newsgroup hierarchy includes the following newsgroup categories: comp.*, misc.*, news.*, rec.*, sci.*, soc.*, and talk*. A voting process creates new newsgroups within the standard newsgroup hierarchies.

standard toolbar In Microsoft Office, a default-loaded toolbar that includes icons for various functions, including opening, closing, and printing files.

standby A low-power state that allows an operating system to be restored to full power quickly without going through the lengthy boot process; called sleep in the Mac OS.

star topology The physical layout of a local network in which a host computer manages the network.

start tag In HTML, the first component of an element. The start tag contains the element's name, such as <H1> or <P>.

statistical function In a spreadsheet program, a built-in function that performs a useful task such as determining an average.

status bar An area within a typical application's window that is reserved for the program's messages to the user.

status indicator A small indicator light on a keyboard that shows when a toggle key keyboard function is turned on.

storage A general term for computer components that offer nonvolatile retention of computer data and program instructions.

storage area network (SAN) Links high capacity storage devices to all of an organization's servers, which makes any of the storage devices accessible from any of the servers.

storage device A hardware component that is capable of retaining data even when electrical power is switched off. An example of a storage device is a hard disk. Compare memory.

storage hierarchy A classification scheme that divides storage devices into three categories: online (directly available), near-online (easily available), offline (not easily available).

storage media A collective term used to describe all types of storage devices.

stored-program concept The idea underlying the architecture of all modern computers that the program should be stored in memory with the data.

streaming audio An Internet sound delivery technology that sends audio data as a continuous, compressed stream that is played back on the fly.

streaming video An Internet video delivery technology that sends video data as a continuous, compressed stream that is played back on the fly. Like streaming audio, streaming video begins playing almost immediately. A high-speed modem is required. Quality is marginal; the video appears in a small, on-screen window, and motion is jerky.

striping In RAID drives, a method of duplicating the data in which each disk contains a portion of every disk's data.

strong AI In artificial intelligence, a research focus based on the conviction that computers will achieve the ultimate goal of artificial intelligence, namely, rivaling the intelligence of humans.

strong encryption Methods of encrypting text so that it is very difficult or impossible to break.

structural analysis and design tools Methods of graphical analysis that systems analysts can use to convey a description of an information system to managers, programmers, and users.

structural sabotage In information warfare, attacks on the information systems that support transportation, finance, energy, and telecommunications.

structural unemployment Unemployment caused by advancing technology that makes an entire job obsolete.

structure In HTML, the overall pattern of a document's organization into units containing information of a certain type, such as titles, headings, or an abstract.

structure chart See hierarchy chart.

structured programming A set of quality standards that make programs more verbose but more readable, more reliable, and more easily maintained. A program is broken up into manageable components, each of which contributes to the overall goal of the program. Also called top-down program design.

style In word processing programs, a collection of formatting options that have been grouped and saved under a distinctive name so that they can be easily applied subsequently.

style sheet In word processing, desktop publishing, and Web publishing, a formatting method in which named styles are defined in a separate document. When changes are made to the style sheet, these changes are reflected in all the documents linked to the style sheet for formatting.

stylus A pen-shaped instrument used to draw on a graphics tablet or to input commands and handwriting to a personal digital assistant (PDA).

subdirectory A directory created in another directory. A subdirectory can contain files and additional subdirectories.

subfolder A folder within a folder, usually created to allow for better file organization. Also known as secondary folder.

subject guide On the World Wide Web, an information discovery service that contains hyperlinks classified by subjects in broad categories and multiple levels of subcategories.

subnotebook A portable computer that omits some components (such as a CD-ROM drive) to cut down on weight and size.

subscribe To sign up to receive regular postings, such as from a newsgroup on the Internet.

subscript A character formatting option that places characters below the line.

summary report In a transaction processing system (TPS), a document that provides a quick overview of an organization's performance.

Super Video Graphics Array (SVGA) An enhancement of the VGA display standard that can display as much as 1,280 pixels by 1,024,768 lines with as many as 16.7 million colors.

supercomputer A sophisticated, expensive computer that executes complex calculations at the maximum speed permitted by state-of-the-art technology. Supercomputers are used mostly by the government and for scientific research.

SuperDisk A removable hard disk made by Imaton that can store up to 120 MB of data per disk. The drive can also work with 3.5-inch floppy disks.

superscalar architecture A design that lets the microprocessor take a sequential instruction and send several instructions at a time to separate execution units so that the processor can execute multiple instructions per cycle.

superscript A character formatting option that places text above the line.

superuser status In multiuser operating systems, a classification normally given only to network administrators, enabling them to access and modify virtually any file on the network. If intruders obtain superuser status, they can obtain the passwords of everyone on the network.

supervisor program See kernel.

surge A momentary and sometimes destructive increase in the amount of voltage delivered through a power line.

surge protector An inexpensive electrical device that prevents high-voltage surges from reaching a computer and damaging its circuitry.

swap file In virtual memory, a file on the hard disk used to store pages of virtual memory information.

swapping In virtual memory, the operation of exchanging program instructions and data between the swap file (located on the hard disk) and random access memory (RAM).

symmetric key encryption Encryption techniques that use the same key for encryption and decryption.

syn flooding See denial of service (DoS) attack.

Synchronized Multimedia Integration Language (SMIL) A scripting language that enhances Web browsers with multimedia capabilities without the use of plug-in programs.

synchronous communication In a computer network, the use of a timing device to demarcate units of data.

synchronous DRAM (SDRAM) The fastest available memory chip technology.

Synchronous Optical Network (SONET) A standard for high-performance networks using optical fiber.

syntax The rules governing the structure of commands, statements, or instructions given to a computer.

syntax error In programming, a flaw in the structure of commands, statements, or instructions.

synthesizer An audio component that uses FM (frequency modulation), wavetable, or waveguide technology to create sounds imitative of actual musical instruments.

system A collection of components purposefully organized into a functioning whole to accomplish a goal.

system administrator In a multiuser computer system, the individual who is responsible for keeping the system running smoothly, performing backup and archiving operations, supervising user accounts, and securing the system against unauthorized intrusions.

system bus Also called memory bus.

system clock An electronic circuit in the computer that emits pulses at regular intervals, enabling the computer's internal components to operate in synchrony.

system requirements The stated minimum system performance capabilities required to run an application program, including the minimum amount of disk space, memory, and processor capacity.

system software All the software used to operate and maintain a computer system, including the operating system and utility programs.

system utilities Programs such as speaker volume control and antivirus software that are loaded by the operating sytem.

system utility programs Programs, such as file management and file finder, that provide a necessary addition to an operating system's basic system-management tools.

system unit The case that houses the computer's internal processing circuitry, including the power supply, motherboard, modem, disk drives, expansion cards, and a speaker.

systems analysis A discipline devoted to the rational and organized planning, development, and implementation of artificial systems, including information systems.

systems analyst A computer professional who helps plan, develop, and implement information systems.

systems development life cycle (SDLC) An organized way of planning and building information systems.

systems engineering A field of engineering devoted to the scientific study of artificial systems and the training of systems analysts.

T

T1 A high-bandwidth telephone trunk line capable of transferring 1.544 megabits per second (Mbps) of data.

tab stop In a word processing program, a position within the current paragraph to which the cursor will move when the Tab key is pressed.

table 1. In HTML, a matrix of rows and columns that appears on a Web page, if the user is browsing with a table-capable browser (such as Netscape Navigator). 2. In database terminology, a table stores information in a list of records, each of which has one or more fields.

table In the Microsoft Access database management system, the object used to store data.

tactile display A display that stimulates the sense of touch using vibration, pressure, and temperature changes.

tag In HTML, a code that identifies an element (a certain part of a document, such as a heading or list) so that a Web browser can tell how to display it. Tags are enclosed by beginning and ending delimiters (angle brackets). Most tags begin with a start tag (delimited with <>), followed by the content and an end tag (delimited with </>).

tangible savings Reduced labor, service, and material costs due to the replacement of a system.

tape libraries High-capacity tape systems often found in enterprise storage systems.

task pane In Microsoft Office, a feature that usually appears on the right side of an opened application window and that provides various options, such as for opening or formatting work.

tax software An application capable of preparing tax payments using on-screen simulations of tax forms. Some tax programs include specialized tax forms and content-based advice to assist the user.

TCP/IP The two most important Internet protocols. See Transmission Control Protocol and Internet Protocol.

technically feasible Able to be accomplished with respect to existing, proven technology.

telecommunication The use of the public switched telephone network (PSTN) and public data networks (PDNs) for data communication.

telecommuting Performing work at home while linked to the office by means of a telecommunications-equipped computer system.

telemedicine The use of computers and the Internet to make high-quality health care available to underserved populations.

template A standard format used to create standardized documents.

tendonitis A physical disorder in which tendons and their sheaths become irritated from repeated exertion.

terabyte (T or TB) A unit of measurement commonly used to state the capacity of memory or storage devices; equal to 1,024 gigabytes, or approximately one trillion bytes or characters.

terminal An input/output device consisting of a keyboard and a video display that is commonly used with mainframe and minicomputer systems.

tertiary folder A folder within a subfolder.

tertiary storage See offline storage.

testbed In engineering, a small-scale version of a product that is developed in order to test its capabilities.

text box An area capable of containing text that can be inserted into a graphic image.

text field In a database, a space that accepts only characters (letters, numbers, and punctuation marks).

text file A file containing nothing but standard characters, that is, letters, punctuation marks, and numbers.

text-only browser A Web browser that cannot display graphics.

text output A type of computer output that consists strictly of characters (letters, numbers, and punctuation marks).

text slide In a presentation, a slide that contains nothing but text.

thermal transfer printer A printer that uses a heat process to transfer colored dyes or inks to the paper's surface. Although thermal transfer printers are the best color printers currently available, they are very expensive.

thin film transistor (TFT) See active-matrix LCD.

third-generation language (3GL) A programming language that tells the computer what to do and how to do it but eliminates the need for understanding the intimate details of how the computer works.

thread 1. In multithreading, a single type of task that can be executed simultaneously with other tasks. 2. In Usenet, a series of articles on the same specific subject.

thumbnail A small version of a graphic image that enables you to see what it looks like before you spend time opening the much larger file containing the full version of the image.

tile To size graphics or windows so that they are all the same size and take up all the available screen space.

time bomb A destructive program that sits harmlessly until a certain event or set of circumstances makes the program active.

time-limited trial versions Internet-offered commercial programs capable of being used on a trial basis for a period of time, after which the software is unusable.

time series A type of column chart that shows changes over a period of time.

timesharing A technique for sharing the resources of a multiuser computer in which each user has the illusion that he or she is the only person using the system.

title bar In a graphical user interface (GUI), the top bar of an application window. The title bar typically contains the name of the application, the name of the document, and window controls.

toggle key A key on a keyboard that functions like a switch. When pressed, the function is turned on, and when pressed again, the function is turned off.

token A handheld device used to gain access to a computer system, such as an automated teller machine (ATM).

toolbar In a graphical user interface (GUI), a bar near the top of the window that contains a row of graphical buttons. These buttons provide quick access to the most frequently used program commands.

tools menu In a graphical user interface (GUI), a menu that provides access to special program features and utilities, such as spell-checking.

top-down program design See structured programming.

top-level domain (TLD) name The last part of an Internet computer address. For computers located in the United States, it indicates the type of organization in which the computer is located, such as commercial businesses (com), educational institutions (edu), and government agencies (gov).

top-level folder See primary folder.

topology The physical layout of a local area network.

touch screen A touch-sensitive display that enables users to input choices by touching a region of the screen.

touchpad An input device for portable computers that moves the pointer. The touchpad is a small pad in front of the keyboard that moves the pointer when the user moves a finger on the pad.

track One of several concentric circular bands on computer disks where data is recorded, similar to the grooves on a phonographic record. Tracks are created during formatting and are divided into sectors.

trackball An input device, similar to the mouse, that moves the pointer. The trackball looks something like an inverted mouse and does not require the desk space that a mouse does.

trackpad See touchpad.

trackpoint An input device on some notebook computers that resembles a tiny pencil eraser; you move the cursor by pushing the tip of the trackpoint.

trade show A periodic meeting in which computer product manufacturers, designers, and dealers display their products.

traditional organizational structure In an organization, a method used to distribute the core functions of the organization into divisions such as finance, human resources, and operations.

transaction An exchange of goods, services, or funds.

transaction file A file used to store input data until it can be processed.

transaction processing system (TPS) A system that handles the day-to-day operations of a company; examples include sales, purchases, orders, and returns.

transceiver A device used to regulate the electrical connection between a computer and a local area network (LAN).

transfer performance A drive's ability to transfer data from the drive as quickly as possible.

transistor A device invented in 1947 by Bell Laboratories that controls the flow of electricity. Due to their small size, reduced power consumption, and lower heat output, transistors replaced vacuum tubes in the second generation of computers.

Transmission Control Protocol (TCP) One of two basic Internet protocols (the other is Internet Protocol, IP). TCP is the protocol (standard) that permits two Internet-connected computers to establish a reliable connection. TCP ensures reliable data delivery with a method known as Positive Acknowledgment with Re-transmission (PAR). The computer that sends the data continues to do so until it receives a confirmation from the receiving computer that the data has been received intact.

transparency A clear acetate sheet used with an overhead projector for presentations.

trap door In computer security, a security hole created on purpose that can be exploited at a later time.

Trojan horse An application disguised as a useful program but containing instructions to perform a malicious task.

Turing test A test developed by Alan Turing and used to determine whether a computer could be called intelligent. In a Turing test, judges are asked to determine whether the output they see on computer displays is produced by a computer or a human being. If a computer program succeeds in tricking the judges into believing that only a human could have generated that output, the program is said to have passed the Turing test.

turnover line In an indentation, the second and subsequent lines.

twisted pair An inexpensive copper cable used for telephone and data communications. The term *twisted pair* refers to the braiding of the paired wires, a practice that reduces interference from electrical fields.

two-megapixel Type of digital camera that can produce sharp images at higher enlargements such as 8 by 10 inches.

typeface A complete collection of letters, punctuation marks, numbers, and special characters with a consistent and identifiable style. Also called font.

typeover mode In word processing, a text insertion mode in which new material replaces (types over) existing text.

U

ubiquitous computing A scenario for future computing in which computers are so numerous that they fade into the background, providing intelligence for virtually every aspect of daily life.

Ultra ATA A drive interface that offers data transfer rates twice as fast as its predecessor, Enhanced IDE (EDIE). Also called Ultra DMA (Direct Memory Access).

Ultra DMA (Direct Memory Access) See Ultra ATA.

Ultra DMA/100 The latest version of the Ultra DMA/66 standard enables data transfer rates of up to 100 MHz, but these drives require a special cable.

Ultra DMA/66 An IDE hard disk standard capable of transferring data at speeds of up to 66 Mbps.

Ultra Wide SCSI A SCSI (Small Computer Systems Interface) standard that enables hard disk data transfer rates of up to 40 Mbps.

Ultra160 SCSI See Ultra3 SCSI.

Ultra3 SCSI A SCSI standard that can transfer data at speeds of up to 160 Mbps. Synonymous with Ultra160 SCSI.

unauthorized access In computer security, the entry of an unauthorized intruder into a computer system.

undo In the editing process, a command that reverses the action of the last editing change.

undocumented feature A program capability not mentioned in the program's documentation.

Unicode A 16-bit character set capable of representing almost all of the world's languages, including non-Roman characters such as those in Chinese, Japanese, and Hindi.

uniform resource locator (URL) In the World Wide Web, one of two basic kinds of Universal Resource Identifiers (URI), a string of characters that precisely identifies an Internet resource's type and location. For example, the fictitious URL http://www.wolverine.virginia.edu/ ~toros/winerefs/merlot.html identifies a World Wide Web document (http://), indicates the domain name of the computer on which it is stored (www.wolverine.virginia.edu), fully describes the document's location in the directory structure (~toros/winerefs/), and includes the document's name and extension (merlot.html).

uninstall To remove a program from a computer system by using a special utility.

uninterruptible power supply (UPS) A device that provides power to a computer system for a short period of time if electrical power is lost.

universal product code (UPC) A label with a series of bars that can be either keyed in or read by a scanner to identify an item and determine its cost. UPC scanners are often found in point-of-sale (POS) terminals.

universal serial bus (USB) An external bus architecture that connects peripherals such as keyboards, mice, and digital cameras. USB offers many benefits over older serial architectures, such as support for 127 devices on a single port, Plug and Play, and higher transfer rates.

universal service A basic principle of U.S. telecommunications law, which holds that service providers have an obligation to provide service in areas where it is not economically attractive to do so, such as remote rural regions. Taxes are used to subsidize the extension of service to such areas.

UNIX A 32-bit operating system that features multiuser access, preemptive multitasking, multiprocessing, and other sophisticated features. UNIX is widely used for file servers in client/server networks.

upgrade processor A microprocessor that upgrades older systems.

upgrade socket A receptacle on a motherboard for an upgrade processor.

upload To send a file to another computer by means of a computer network.

Usenet A worldwide computer-based discussion system that uses the Internet and other networks for transmission media. Discussion is channeled into more than 50,000 topically named newsgroups, which contain original contributions called articles, as well as commentaries on these articles called follow-up posts. As follow-up posts continue to appear on a given subject, a thread of discussion emerges; a threaded newsreader collates these articles together so readers can see the flow of the discussion.

Usenet client Software that comes with most browser suites that communicates with a Usenet server.

Usenet server A computer running the software that enables users to read Usenet messages, post new messages, and reply to existing messages. The server software also ensures that new messages are shared with other servers so that all participating servers are able to make the same messages available. Also called an NNTP server.

user A person who uses a computer and its applications to perform tasks and produce results.

user agent See e-mail client.

user ID A word or name that uniquely identifies a computer user. Synonymous with user name.

user interface The part of system software that interacts with the user.

user name A unique name that a system administrator assigns to you that you use as initial identification. You must type this name and also your password to gain access to the system.

user response Input the computer requires from the operator for a process to continue.

utilities See system utility programs.

utility program A program that is designed to assist the user with tasks related to computer system maintenance, such as defragmenting the hard drive.

V

V.34 An ITU modulation protocol for modems transmitting and receiving data at 28,800 bits per second (bps). An addition to the protocol enables transmission rates of up to 33.6 Kbps.

V.90 An ITU modulation protocol for modems transmitting and receiving data at 56 Kbps.

vaccine See antivirus program.

vacuum tube A device that controls the flow of electrons. Vacuum tubes were used extensively in first-generation computers, but they failed often and were replaced shortly thereafter by transistors.

validation In a database, a method of increasing data integrity by ensuring that users enter the correct data type in each field.

value In HTML, most attributes require a value, which is usually surrounded by quotation marks and preceded by an equals sign.

value-added network (VAN) A public data network that provides value-added services for corporate customers, including end-to-end dedicated lines with guaranteed security. VANs, however, also charge an expensive per-byte fee.

value-added reseller (VAR) An independent company that selects system components and assembles them into a functioning system.

VBScript A scripting language used to write short programs (scripts) that can be embedded in Web pages.

vector graphic An image composed of distinct objects, such as lines or shapes, that may be moved or edited independently. Each object is described by a complex mathematical formula.

vendor A company that sells goods or services.

vertical application A program for a particular line of business or for a division in a company.

very-large-scale integration (VLSI) A level of technological sophistication in the manufacturing of semiconductor chips that allows the equivalent of up to 1 million transistors to be placed on one chip.

VGA connector A physical connector that is designed to connect a VGA monitor to a video adapter.

video accelerators Video adapters with fast processors.

video adapter Video circuitry that fits into an expansion bus and determines the quality of the display and resolution of your monitor. Also called display adapter.

video capture card An expansion board that accepts analog or digital video signals, which are then compressed and stored.

video card See video adapter.

video editor A program that enables you to view and edit a digitized video and to select special effects.

Video for Windows A Microsoft video and compression format for digital video.

video graphics adapter (VGA) A video adapter that conforms to the VGA specification, which is capable of displaying data at a resolution of 640 x 480.

Video Graphics Array (VGA) A display standard that can display 16 colors at a maximum resolution of 640 pixels by 480 pixels.

video output A type of computer output that consists of a series of still images that are played back at a fast enough rate to give the illusion of continuous motion.

video RAM (VRAM) A random access memory chip that maximizes the performance of video adapters.

videoconferencing A technology enabling two or more people to have a face-to-face meeting even though they're geographically separated.

view menu In a graphical user interface (GUI), a menu that provides access to document viewing options, including normal layout, print layout, and document magnification (zoom) options.

viewable size The area of a monitor display used to display an image.

virtual manufacturing A design process in which a powerful computer assembles digitally drawn parts to ensure that they fit well and function as planned. Also called computer-aided production engineering (CAPE).

virtual memory A means of increasing the size of a computer's random access memory (RAM) by using part of the hard disk as an extension of RAM.

virtual private network (VPN) A method of connecting two physically separate local area networks (LANs) by using the Internet. Strong encryption is used to ensure privacy.

virtual reality (VR) A computer-generated illusion of three-dimensional space. On the Web, virtual reality sites enable Web users to explore three-dimensional virtual reality worlds by means of VR plug-in programs. These programs enable you to walk or "fly" through the three-dimensional space that these worlds offer.

Virtual Reality Modeling Language (VRML) A scripting language that enables programmers to specify the characteristics of a three-dimensional world that is accessible on the Internet. VRML worlds can contain sounds, hyperlinks, videos, and animations as well as three-dimensional spaces, which can be explored by using a VRML plug-in.

virus Hidden code within a host program that may be destructive to infected files.

vision technology See eye-gaze response system.

visual aids Graphical supplements to a presentation, such as slides or transparencies.

Visual Basic (VB) A programming language developed by Microsoft based on the BASIC programming language. Visual Basic is one of the world's most widely used program development packages.

visual display system The video adapter and monitor that generate a computer's images.

vocabularies In XML, sets of elements and tags designed for use in a particular field.

voice recognition See speech recognition.

volatile Susceptible to loss; a way of saying that all the data disappears forever if the power fails.

W

warm boot To restart a computer that is already operating.

warm start See warm boot.

waterfall model A method in information systems development that returns the focus of the systems development project to a previous phase if an error is discovered in it.

waveform A type of digitized audio format used to record live sounds or music.

waveguide synthesis A method of generating and reproducing musical sounds in a sound card. Waveguide synthesis simulates what happens when a real musical instrument produces a sound; it is superior to wavetable and FM synthesis.

wavetable synthesis A method of generating and reproducing musical sounds in a sound card. Wavetable synthesis uses a prerecorded sample of dozens of orchestral instruments to determine how particular notes should sound. Wavetable synthesis is far superior to FM synthesis.

Web See World Wide Web (WWW).

Web browser A program that runs on an Internet-connected computer and provides access to information on the World Wide Web (WWW).

Web-enabled devices Devices that have the ability to connect to the Internet and e-book readers.

Web layout In Microsoft Word, a document view that approximates the document's appearance if it were saved as a Web page and viewed by a Web browser.

Web integration A variety of techniques used to make information stored in databases available through Internet or intranet connections.

Web page A document you create to share with others on the Web. A Web page can include text, graphics, sound, animation, and video.

Web server On the Web, a program that accepts requests for information framed according to the Hypertext Transfer Protocol (HTTP). The server processes these requests and sends the requested document.

Web site A computer that is accessible to the public Internet and is running a server program that makes Web pages available.

WebCam A low-cost video camera used for low-resolution videoconferencing on the Internet.

Webmaster A person responsible for the visual layout of a Web site, its written content, its links to other locations, and often the techniques to follow up on customers' inquiries.

weight The darkness or thickness of a character.

what-if scenario In business, an experiment using make-believe data to see how it affects an outcome, such as sales volume.

wheel mouse A type of mouse that has a dial that can be used to scroll through data on-screen.

whisper A special type of Internet chat group message that, instead of being seen by everyone on the channel, is seen by only the one person to whom it is sent.

whistleblowing Reporting illegal or unethical actions of a company to a regulatory agency or the press.

whiteboard A separate area of a videoconferencing screen enabling participants to create a shared workspace. Participants can write or draw in this space as if they were using a chalkboard in a meeting.

wide area network (WAN) A commercial data network that provides data communications services for businesses and government agencies. Most WANs use the X.25 protocols, which overcome problems related to noisy analog telephone lines.

wildcard A symbol that stands for any character or any group of characters.

Win 95 See Microsoft Windows 95.

Win 98 See Microsoft Windows 98.

window border The outer edge of a window on a graphical user interface (GUI); in Microsoft Windows it can be dragged to change the size of the window.

window controls In a graphical user interface (GUI), a group of window management controls that enable the user to minimize, maximize, restore, or close the window.

Windows Bitmap (BMP) A bitmapped graphics format developed for Microsoft Windows.

wireless communication A means of linking computers using infrared or radio signals.

wireless keyboard Battery-powered keyboards that use infrared or radio waves to send signals to a computer.

wireless LANs (WLANs) Local area networks that use a radio signal spread over a seemingly random series of frequencies for greater security.

wireless mice See cordless mice.

wizard In a graphical user interface (GUI), a series of dialog boxes that guide the user through a complex process, such as importing data into an application.

word completion prediction program An accessibility feature designed for people with limited dexterity that presents a menu of possible word completions.

word processing program An office application that enables the user to create, edit, format, and print textual documents.

word size The number of bits a computer can work with at one time.

word wrapping A word processing feature that automatically moves words down to the beginning of the next line if they extend beyond the right margin.

workbook In a spreadsheet program, a file that can contain two or more spreadsheets, each of which has its own page in the workbook.

workflow automation An information system in which documents are automatically sent to the people who need to see them.

workgroup A team of two or more people working on the same project.

worksheet The graphical accounting pad that appears in spreadsheet programs. Also called spreadsheet.

worksheet tab In a spreadsheet program, a tab that enables the user to determine which worksheet to display within a workbook.

workstation A powerful desktop computer that meets the computing needs of engineers, architects, and other professionals who require detailed graphic displays. In a LAN, a workstation runs application programs and serves as an access point to the network.

World Wide Web (WWW) A global hypertext system that uses the Internet as its transport mechanism. In a hypertext system, you navigate by clicking hyperlinks, which display another document (which also contains hyperlinks). Most Web documents are created using HTML, a markup language that is easy to learn and that will soon be supplanted by automated tools. Incorporating hypermedia (graphics, sounds, animations, and video), the Web has become the ideal medium for publishing information on the Internet. See also Web browser.

World Wide Web Consortium (W3C) An independent standards body made up of university researchers and industry practitioners devoted to setting effective standards to promote the orderly growth of the World Wide Web. Housed at the Massachusetts Institute of Technology (MIT), W3C sets standards for HTML and many other aspects of Web usage.

worm A program resembling a computer virus that can spread over networks.

write To record data on a computer storage device.

write once, read many (WORM) An optical disc drive with storage capacities of up to 15 G. After data is written, it becomes a read-only storage medium.

write-back One of four basic operations carried out by the control unit of a microprocessor. The write-back operation involves writing the results of previous operations to an internal register.

write-protect notch See write-protect tab.

write-protect tab On a floppy disk, a tab that prevents the computer from overwriting or erasing the disk's contents.

WWW See World Wide Web (WWW).

WYSIWYG A type of on-screen document view in which the user sees the results of formatting choices on-screen. WYSIWYG stands for "what-you-see-is-what-you-get."

X

X.25 A packet-switching network protocol optimized for use on noisy analog telephone lines.

X-10 A standard for computer-controlled home automation devices.

xDSL See Digital Subscriber Line (DSL).

Xeon A 64-bit microprocessor manufactured by Intel. Introduced in 1998, the Xeon uses a wider socket with more contacts to increase communication speed between the processor and components on the motherboard. Due to its high cost, the Xeon is used mostly in servers and high-end workstations.

Z

zero-insertion force (ZIF) socket A receptacle for microprocessors that makes it easy to remove and install them without the risk of bending pins.

Zip disk A removable storage medium that combines the convenience of a floppy disk with the storage capacity of a small hard disk (100 to 200 MB).

Zip drive A popular removable storage medium, created by Iomega Corporation, that provides 100 to 200 MB of storage on relatively inexpensive ($10 each) portable disks.

zoom To increase or decrease the magnification level of a document as displayed in the application workspace.

zoom level The degree of magnification of a document within the application workspace.